Robert E. Henthorn

CHRISTIAN BEGINNINGS

By

MORTON SCOTT ENSLIN
TH.D. (Harvard)
PROFESSOR OF NEW TESTAMENT LITERATURE AND EXEGESIS, THE CROZER THEOLOGICAL SEMINARY

HARPER & BROTHERS PUBLISHERS
NEW YORK AND LONDON

CHRISTIAN BEGINNINGS

Printed in the United States of America

L-Y

T. V. E.

A. S. E.

CONTENTS

INTRODUCTION

There is no dearth of good *Introductions to the New Testament.* Jülicher, Moffatt, and Bacon—to mention but three—have long been standard, and will continue to be studied with profit for many years to come. In recent years there have appeared several more. It is not unnatural that each scholar wishes, if not to embalm, at least to preserve his own views on the New Testament as a whole. I suppose I must plead guilty to the same desire, at least in part. For many years I have felt a distinct need for a work of somewhat different compass, one that should include between one set of covers a reasonably comprehensive survey of many other matters beside an introduction to each of the twenty-seven books which Christians have long considered of especial value. The New Testament did not produce Christianity. Christianity, on the contrary, produced the New Testament. The student who starts his study of the New Testament with Matthew or even with the earliest of the Pauline letters is under a great handicap. He can truly appreciate these writings only as he understands why Christians felt themselves impelled to write. And Christianity itself did not spring into being full grown like Athene from the head of Zeus. She was the child of Judaism, although an unwanted child and soon disowned. But the Judaism that gave birth to a Jesus and a Paul was not that of the Old Testament prophets. This has often been conceded by Christians who have expatiated on the decay of a once noble religion into a barren and formal legalism. This appears to me an almost total misapprehension. The experiences through which the little nation passed during the five or six centuries before the dawn of the Christian era might well have proved her downfall; instead they made a tremendous and lasting contribution. At once pugnaciously conservative and yet always receptive to new ideas, the Jew exacted his toll from Babylon, Persia, Egypt, Greece, and Rome. The doubts and the fears, the glowing confidence and wistful longings of these eventful years—all these were in the blood of Jesus and his early followers. But within little more than a century after his death the new religion which he had unwittingly begotten had become so completely acclimated to the wider Mediterranean world and had drunk so deeply at wells which no Jewish hand had delved that a Justin Martyr, hard put to answer the pagan charge that Christianity had stolen its rites and teachings, could only account for the obvious similarities by the counter charge that evil demons centuries before had seen what was destined to come to pass, and had frantically but vainly concocted counterfeits to discredit the genuine when it should appear. It is only as the student gains some inkling of all this that he can hope to understand these writings, for as some nameless wit has well said: "The simple gospel is not nearly so simple as simple people sometimes think." Then when these writings had been produced, what happened to them? Did they become canonical overnight? Do we have them today precisely as they left their authors' hands? Surely these questions are of consequence not only to the minister but to "Everyman," if he would call himself educated, for the Bible has long since ceased to be simply a book of religion.

For thirteen years I have sought to introduce my students to the New Testament in this fashion. Each year I have found, as every other teacher does, the time seems shorter. One purely selfish purpose in writing this book was to free my conscience when I dallied in pleasant fields and talked "more and more about less and less." At least my class would have the opportunity of reading a reasonably complete and balanced statement. Thus the volume is severely practical in its scope. It is intended really to introduce the New Testament. It makes no claim to be exhaustive despite its size, which is larger than I could wish. Every one of the forty-six chapters could be, and has been, expanded into a sizeable volume. While I have not entirely forgotten the expert and have made occasional suggestions intended principally for his consideration, I have tried never to forget the reader who is not and never will be a professional scholar. Accordingly, I early decided to omit, so far as was practicable, the reference to works other than in English, for, unfortunate though it is, most American students are limited to one tongue. Whenever possible, standard foreign works have been cited in translation, even though later and better German editions are available. Thus I have regularly referred to Schürer's and Jülicher's works in their English dress, although occasionally adding a reference to the latter's seventh edition. I have resolutely kept Greek out of the volume. Only in a very few cases have a few words trickled in, generally in footnotes, and almost always with an interpretation. This has not been easy; to describe the task of the textual critic without use of Greek is a task to try one's ingenuity and add grey to one's hair. I have finally decided not to include a bibliography. This was not done solely to save space. Most teachers, I believe, prefer to suggest their own collateral reading. Furthermore, I am firmly convinced that one of the chief disciplines a student has is to work out his own bibliography. Many of the more important works are referred to in the text and notes. The rest the student can find for himself; the general reader will probably not want them.

It is quite impossible to express adequately my obligation and indebtedness to the countless scholars whose works I have freely used. I have tried to be punctilious in expressing specific indebtedness in the footnotes; it may well be that I am under even greater obligation than I realize. There is little originality, after all, in scholarship. The newest and most spectacular "discovery" oftentimes turns out to have been discovered and then forgotten a century or more ago. I have tried to present a fair picture of the various views on this problem or that, when competent opinions differ. On the other hand, I have not hesitated to express my own opinions; even if, as occasionally is the case, the voice of the majority is contrary and the matter is highly debatable. I think in every such case there is ample indication that no unwary reader may be tempted to follow blindly, thinking he is running with the main herd. Regularly I have quoted from the text of the American Revised Version of the Bible, copyrighted 1919 by the International Council of Religious Education, and wish to express my indebtedness to them for this permission. While many of the translations of the classic authors are my own, I have not hesitated to make use of the many and admirable renderings which have been made available by the industry of many scholars living and dead to whom I would make this grateful, if general, acknowledgment.

I feel it a real obligation—but much more than a mere obligation, a sincere joy—to express my indebtedness to Frederick Lincoln Anderson, for many years professor of New Testament Interpretation at the Newton Theological Institution. For nearly twenty years I can count him a respected teacher and a generous friend. He is not responsible for the views expressed; none the less, it was he who aroused in me the love for this book and the desire to know more about it.

PART I

THE BACKGROUND

Chapter I

UNDER FOREIGN DOMINION

At the death of Solomon (933 B.C.) the united kingdom split, and gradually, to the ire of the Chronicler, the northern kingdom, Israel, gained the ascendancy. Foreign powers were making themselves felt. By location Israel and Judah formed the buffer between Syria on the north and Egypt on the south. Due to complex causes, both within and without, their strength became lessened and in 722 came the so-called fall of the northern kingdom before Sargon of Assyria. Although Judah's time was not for 136 years, this is not to be interpreted as due to her superior strength, but rather to Israel's more exposed location and greater value as plunder.

As the war clouds of the rising Assyria and Babylonia are reflected in the sky the prophets raise their voices anew. And a strange note it seems to us. With our knowledge today we can see how Israel had come to a worship of one God. Apparently each local shrine had originally had its own Baal; gradually, however, Jehovah[1] had increased and had come to stand alone. Still, however, he was the Lord God of Israel. But more was to follow. After the northern kingdom had fallen and the southern could see all too plainly the handwriting on the wall a taking stock was necessary. If Judah fell, did that mean that Jehovah was impotent? that the gods of the other nations were more powerful? The prophets refused such an answer. By no means. Jehovah was all-powerful. He was merely using these foreign foes as whips with which to scourge Israel for her sins. Think of that faith—almost impudence it seems to us—for this little tottering nation to declare that Assyria and Babylonia were but instruments in the hands of her god. While this impending peril was not the only cause, it must not be disregarded in an attempt to account for the elevation of Jehovah.

And then in 586 came the collapse of the southern kingdom, after two unsuccessful attempts to throw off the Babylonian yoke. The lenient treatment of Nebuchadnezzar in putting down the first revolt was not repeated; this year saw the burning of the temple and the breaching of the city walls.

Then followed a period of "captivity," but not of imprisonment. Although Jerusalem was apparently laid waste, only a small fraction of its inhabitants were transported to Babylonia, and many of them soon found life by no

[1] The conventional spelling of the name will be used in these pages, since it has seemed pedantic to print the tetragrammaton and since the present writer has no desire to perpetuate a fresh guess as to the original pronunciation.

means intolerable. None the less, although all did not spend their entire time weeping by the rivers of Babylon, hatred of the conqueror was real. In the sudden rise to power of Persia, following the spectacular conquest by Cyrus of the Medes and Lydians, Israel saw her hopes rise once more. Babylon would fall next, and in 538 the triumphal entry of Cyrus into Babylon fulfilled these hopes.

> Jehovah hath broken the staff of the wicked, the sceptre of the rulers; that smote the peoples in wrath with a continual stroke, that ruled the nations in anger, with a persecution that none restrained.[2]

The next two hundred years saw Persia's sway. In accord with Cyrus' general policy the Jews were free to return home and to rebuild their temple. Later Judaism with its emphasis on the omnipotence of Jehovah in this saw Cyrus as Jehovah's agent.

> Now in the first year of Cyrus king of Persia, that the word of Jehovah by the mouth of Jeremiah might be accomplished, Jehovah stirred up the spirit of Cyrus king of Persia so that he made a proclamation throughout all his kingdom, and put it also in writing, saying, Thus saith Cyrus king of Persia. All the kingdoms of the earth hath Jehovah, the God of heaven, given me; and he hath charged me to build him a house in Jerusalem, which is in Judah. Whosoever there is among you of all his people, his God be with him, and let him go up to Jerusalem, which is in Judah, and build the house of Jehovah, the God of Israel (he is God), which is in Jerusalem. And whosoever is left, in any place where he sojourneth, let the men of his place help him with silver, and with gold, and with goods, and with beasts, besides the freewill-offering for the house of God which is in Jerusalem.[3]

It is to be doubted if Cyrus would have appreciated this description. Some Jews returned, but the universal return as described by the Chronicler in Ezra 2 cannot be accepted. Persia had no intention of restoring Israel. The administration of her vast empire demanded a highly developed organization and clear-cut centralized policy which gave little or no opportunity for even such nominal independence as, as we shall see, Rome granted. On the whole, Persian control was far less irksome than had been slavery to Babylonia; on the other hand, it appears highly probable that many sanguine hopes for restored independence were blasted. The temple was not rebuilt for years, and even when that was finally accomplished at the insistence of Haggai and Zechariah the expected good times failed to appear. National hopes as centred in Zerubbabel met with short shrift. Persia's general attitude toward the administration of her Empire is epitomized in the Behistun inscriptions of Darius: "By the grace of Ahuramazda these lands have conformed to my decree; even as it was commanded unto them by me, so was it done." And the kings kept paid officials, called the King's Ears or King's Eyes, whose duty it was to keep a sharp watch for incipient uprising or rebellion.

[2] Isa. 14:5,6.
[3] Ezra 1:1-4.

Although the Jews soon realized that whatever part Jehovah had had in elevating Cyrus, there was to be no opportunity for a restored monarchy, and that it was easier to obtain permission to erect a temple than to build city walls, there was ample opportunity for religious development. The not unnatural result was an increased emphasis on religion. The high priest became the head of Judaism; now that there was no king to overshadow him he enjoyed far more power than had the priests in the days of the monarchy. It was not, however, a political power. In Breasted's happy phrase: "The Jewish state was . . . a *religious* organization, a church with a priest at its head."[4]

This development was at least partially due to the fact that Persian religion was as favourable to Judaism as her political policies were hostile to local independence. That both Persian and Jew worshipped one supreme God gave a ready bond of sympathy; in addition, a bitter hatred of idolatry and a keen expectation of a glorious age in the future were common to both. Consequently, in these two centuries of Persian control Judaism underwent many changes, and changes which were no less real because they were less the result of conscious borrowing than of stimulation. Ideas were in the air; and Judaism accumulated a good deal which was alien to her early inheritance.

Persian dualism with its notions of the powers of good as personified in the Supreme Being in ceaseless clash with the forces of evil under their prince gives us the New Testament devil, the god of this age,[5] who thus became identified with the totally different Satan of the Old Testament. A belief in future life, with its recompenses and punishments, usurps the older view, that "there is no work, nor device, nor knowledge, nor wisdom, in Sheol, whither thou goest,"[6] which appears to be presupposed by the almost fanatical desire for a son and the resultant institution of levirate marriage. With the increasing confidence that only one place (and that Jerusalem) could serve as a sanctuary for sacrifice there developed the institution of the synagogue as the actual centre of the nation, in practice if not in theory. Discussion of these developments, which can be but listed here, may profitably be postponed to the study of Judaism, as such, in a subsequent chapter. It is important, however, to realize that these long years of exile and captivity, which might easily have become a flood in which they perished, became in reality a bath of regeneration.

It may be wondered how it was that Judaism with its tough-bitted insistence on its own supremacy and its growing confidence that God had revealed his complete and entire will could have acquired these alien strains. Again it is to be emphasized that it was not so much conscious borrowing as almost imperceptible stimulation from forces which did not seem so

[4] J. H. Breasted, *Ancient Times,* p. 216.
[5] II Cor. 4:4.
[6] Eccl. 9:10.

strange. They were living in the world, and simply went further than they knew. There are many more things than vice which we "first endure, then pity, then embrace." And again, Judaism always laid its emphasis on action. God's supreme and complete will had been revealed. Israel was to keep his law; that was as well their joy as their task. It was breaking the law that constituted sin; a generous latitude was always left to individual notions, and it is hardly an exaggeration to say that throughout Israel's history there have been as many opinions as there have been individuals to hold them. Many are our heritages from Judaism; heresy-hunting, however, is not one of them. Many mistaken notions to the contrary notwithstanding, as we shall later see, it was not distinctions of belief which aroused Jewish hostility toward Jesus. Without always realizing it, Judaism has ever been receptive to new ideas and new notions. Because of this she has survived through the centuries, herself the veritable century plant, often dying, but always to blossom anew. And it was during these years, to us years of almost complete silence, that she gained a by no means negligible access of strength.

But now a star appears in the western sky in the person of the young Alexander of Macedon, and two years after the battle of Issus (333 B.C.), which had made him master of all western Syria, he met and signally defeated Darius at Gaugamela, a little town near Arbela (331 B.C.), in what justly merits the name, one of the fifteen decisive battles of the world, and put to an end for ever the Persian supremacy.

The ephemeral rise of the young Macedonian has been so often and ably reviewed that it need not be repeated here. At the age of twenty-two he dealt the western satraps of Darius III a crushing defeat at the Granicus River (334 B.C.) in Asia Minor, near the site of ancient Troy—the first blow in his successful attempt to overthrow the kingdom of Persia, then mistress to the Ægean, and to make good his title, Master of Greece. Two years later (333 B.C.), having followed the track of Xenophon's immortal Ten Thousand, he pushed through southern Asia Minor and met the main Persian army under the personal direction of Darius III. The two armies clashed at Issus, and again Alexander was victor. Darius in terror offers terms of peace. He is even willing to surrender all his territory west of the Euphrates. Alexander refuses; why accept half the loaf when the whole was his for the taking? The vision of world empire is before his eye. Though young in years, his was the genius of the wise tactician. Before pushing east he wished to reduce the seacoast of the Mediterranean, in order to bring about the collapse of the Persian fleet, the unrivalled mistress of the Sea.

In accord with this determination he proceeded at once against Damascus and Tyre. The latter city stood siege, and for seven months held out. When it finally fell, his vengeance was terrible. Next he turned south to Gaza on the coast road to Egypt. After a two-month siege this city too fell, and received the same severe treatment.

Josephus preserves a romantic and edifying tale of Alexander's awe and reverence before the Jewish high priest, whom "God had honoured with the high-priesthood," who stays him on his way to Jerusalem to exact vengeance for the failure of the Jews to obey his peremptory demand to sever their allegiance to Persia and send him aid against Tyre. The story is highly coloured, and reminds us of the picture of Cyrus presented by the Chronicler in Ezra 1. Whether, in fact, Alexander visited Jerusalem at all is a moot question. At any rate, he did not destroy it. Judea was apparently incorporated into the satrapy of Cœle-Syria, with Samaria as the capital city. Later the Samaritans got into trouble with Alexander and were severely punished on his return from Egypt. Judea, however, Josephus tells us, was left in quiet. This treatment of Judea was in keeping with his aim of welding East and West together, rather than of annihilating the East. His aim was frankly a world empire. His teacher, Aristotle, had urged him to treat the Greeks as freemen, the Orientals as slaves. Wisely he sought the better way of uniting all. To achieve this he sought to use Greek civilization, with its language and culture, both so dear to him, as the medium. In him the earlier dreams of Xenophon and Isocrates found their fulfilment.

In 332 he was master of Egypt, which capitulated without struggle, and thus gave the last blow to the once proud Persian fleet, now deprived both of its harbours and of all contact with the army. Now he could turn east for the final conflict with tottering Persia. And the next year saw the end of the Persian power, so long the mistress of the East. At Gaugamela, near Arbela, on the Tigris West and East met (331 B.C.). The Persian force was hopelessly outclassed; even the scythe-wheeled war chariots with which Persia sought in vain desperation to check the Macedonian advances were unavailing. Darius III fled, soon to fall by an assassin's hand. Alexander's dream was realized. Persia was finally his. Although his untimely death—he was but thirty-three—in 323 prevented the realization of his world ambition, he had effectually removed the barrier between East and West, and had brought the magic of Greek civilization into the Oriental world.

Unlike the eastern war lords, his advance was marked by something more lasting than desolation and ruin. An Assyrian monarch might inscribe:

> With battle and slaughter I assailed and took the city. Their possessions I carried away. Many of their soldiers I carried away. Of some I cut off hands and limbs; of others the noses, ears, and arms; of many soldiers I put out the eyes. I devastated the city, dug it up, in fire I burned it; I annihilated it.

Instead, wherever Alexander went, Greek culture took root; in Egypt had been founded the city of Alexandria, destined to receive from Athens the torch of Greek learning and in her stead become the schoolmistress of the world. His empire cracked—there was none able to succeed their impetuous master—but Greek kingdoms appeared throughout Asia, destined to endure for centuries; and far more significant than his battles were the strides in knowledge that resulted from his campaigns. East and West had become united. Writing in the middle of the second century of our era the Greek historian Arrian piously remarked of this prince of generals, he, "who was like no other man, could not have been given to the world without the special design of Providence." Nor do his words seem an entire overstatement.

At the death of Alexander the great empire crumbled overnight. He had left no heir,[7] but there were many claimants. One of his generals, Perdiccas, had received his signet, and sought to maintain the imperial interests until the birth and growth of the expected heir. His rivals combined against him, and in 321 his own soldiers murdered him at Memphis, whither he had proceeded against Ptolemy.

The empire fell into the hands of a group of men known to us as the Diadochi or Successors, among whom were Ptolemy, Antigonus, Seleucus, Lysimachus, and Antipater. Ptolemy had received Egypt, but not content had determined to gain Cœle-Syria, in which lay Palestine, as a buffer against his rivals to the north and east. This with Cyprus he soon secured (320 B.C.). He is said to have entered Jerusalem on a Sabbath, thus meeting with no resistance—on the plea of desiring to sacrifice—and to have carried off many Jews to Egypt as colonists.

This maritime plain became the theatre of war between the armies of Ptolemy and Antigonus, as Palestine, like a veritable shuttlecock, passed back and forth from the one to the other. Antigonus easily regained Syria in 315, but three years later lost at least the southern half as a result of the battle of Gaza, only to regain it the next year. Suffice it to say, this ancient Alsace-Lorraine changed hands at least five times in less than ten years.

Antigonus, who had been confirmed in his possession of the kingdom of Phrygia in the nominal agreement at Triparadeisus in 321, was the ablest and most ambitious of the Diadochi, and accordingly in the most dangerous position. He gradually made his power felt. Eumenes, who had been appointed by Perdiccas to the district south of the Black Sea, had always been hated by the rest, and had been declared a public enemy. By 315 Antigonus had brought about his death and appropriated his domain. It became perfectly patent that his ambitions would stop at nothing short of Alexander's whole domain.

Naturally this ambition resulted in a coalition against him of the rest of the successors. Lysimachus of Thrace, Cassander (who had succeeded his father Antipater in Macedon and Greece), and Seleucus, the able general to whom

[7] Later a posthumous son was born to his widow, but he plays no part in our story. In his thirteenth year he was murdered by Cassander. Than his there have been few more pathetic stories in history.

had fallen Babylon, combined, and finally Ptolemy joined them on the promise that while Seleucus should gain Syria, he would receive Cœle-Syria[8] including Palestine, that is, apparently the territory south of Damascus. The combined force was finally successful against him and his able son Demetrius at the battle of Ipsus in Phrygia (301 B.C.). Seleucus gained all of Syria from the Mediterranean to the Indus. Some twenty years later he wrested almost all of Asia Minor from Lysimachus who had gained the western half as his part of the spoils. Seleucus settled in Syria and built his capital city, Antioch, on the Orontes, with its harbor Seleucia. This was the start of the Seleucidæ[9]—the ruling house of Syria—destined to play such an important part in the affairs of Palestine.

Alexander's empire was now in four parts: Lysimachus had Thrace and a part of Asia Minor; Cassander, Macedon and Greece; Seleucus, Syria and all east to the Indus; Ptolemy, Egypt and the southernmost part of Syria, including Palestine. Because of Ptolemy's but indifferent help in the campaign against Antigonus, the other members of the coalition had assigned Palestine to Seleucus. Ptolemy, however, had proceeded to occupy it, and apparently it remained in the control of his house until the victory of Antiochus the Great at Panium in 198, although some historians, as Schürer, maintain that it was not until some twenty years later that it passed definitely into Egyptian control.

Geographically Palestine should have belonged to Northern Syria since the desert to the south is the real frontier between Egypt and Syria. On the other hand, Ptolemy had at once realized its peculiar importance as a buffer, while in addition the timber of the Lebanons was by no means to be despised by a land as poor as Egypt was in this respect. Accordingly, it is no wonder that this little land should have been the cause of constant trouble between the two rivals. Of the actual history of Palestine during the years of Egyptian control we know very little. The external history of Palestine during the years of Egyptian control appears to have been limited to a passive survey of the

[8] Strictly speaking, Cœle-Syria means the hollow between the Lebanons and Anti-Lebanons. Polybius refers to it as "a cañon called Marsyas, which lies between the skirts of Libanus and Anti-Libanus, and is contracted into a narrow gorge by these two mountains. Just where the valley is narrowest it is divided by marshes and lakes, from which the scented reed is cut" (*Hist.* v,45). The term is, however, popularly employed by Polybius as well as others to indicate all Palestine and Phœnicia to the Egyptian frontier. The Jewish commonwealth itself, to use Schürer's convenient term, was limited to Judea, that is, the district south of Samaria, which was essentially a distinct province. It did not embrace Galilee, the Perea (land east of the Jordan) which was made up both of Hellenistic cities and native communities, nor the seacoast cities. Thus the sway of the high priest was over a decidedly limited district. Cf. Schürer, *History of the Jewish People,* Div. I, Vol. I, pp. 186-192.

[9] Seleucus' return to Babylon in 312 B.C. (following the repulse of Antigonus at Gaza) was later regarded the beginning of the Seleucid empire and the moment from which subsequent dates were to be reckoned. Cf. "Thus the yoke of the heathen was taken away from Israel in the hundred and seventieth year" (I Macc. 13:41). This hundred and seventieth year was 143 B.C. A convenient table for the conversion of dates may be found in Schürer, *op. cit.,* Div. I, Vol. II, pp. 393-398.

struggle between the Ptolemies and Seleucids, and even the details of this struggle in the first decades are very meagre. Of her internal development we know correspondingly little. Apparently her lot was comparatively easy. Aside from the appointment of governors and the imposition of taxes, she appears to have been given practical independence. Josephus[10] preserves a highly coloured story of the difficulties which arose during the high-priesthood of Onias II, when the latter, due either to his inability or perhaps to his pro-Syrian leanings, failed to pay his taxes. The story is not without difficulties with regard to chronology and is also replete with the gossipy details which Josephus was wont to employ when his sources ran dry. It gives a vivid picture of what may well have been the method employed to farm the taxes out. Such a power as we are told this Joseph and his son Hyrcanus as tax farmers enjoyed for more than twenty years could hardly have failed to result in the rise of a wealthy class in Jerusalem vastly more interested in the Hellenistic culture of Alexandria than in the strict Jewish piety. Egypt, so far as we know, never employed coercive measures to hellenize Palestine as did the Seleucids later, notably as we shall see Antiochus IV. None the less, she was in every respect a Greek kingdom, and her century of suzerainty can hardly have failed to leave its impress.

But changes far more drastic were coming. The power of the Ptolemies in the compact and easily protected Egypt had increased during the long reign of Ptolemy II Philadelphus (285-246); while under his successor, Ptolemy III (246-221), real inroads had been made into the territory of the Seleucids, which was so large as to be unwieldy, if not actually inchoate. For a time a large section of North Syria had been under Egyptian control, while Palestine had remained firm in the latter's grasp, although Syria had made at least three definite attempts to wrest it away. During the reign of the dissolute Ptolemy IV (221-204) a decline, however, set in. Two years before the latter's accession to the throne, Antiochus III, popularly and rightly surnamed the Great, had succeeded his brother Seleucus II as sixth in the Syrian line. Within a few years he turned his attention to a systematic attempt at the conquest of Palestine. His chief seaport, Seleucia, now in the hands of Egypt, was regained and he turned south. Following varying fortunes, a wearisome negotiation was entered into by the two kings, which failing of its purpose gave way to further warfare. In 217 came the decisive battle of Raphia, a little south of Gaza. Ptolemy was successful and Antiochus withdrew to Syria. A few years later Ptolemy died, and in the resultant weakness of Egypt—the heir was but five years of age and a series of regents was disastrous—Antiochus saw his chance. With Philip V of Macedon he made a concerted drive against Egypt, this time successful. As a result of his victory at Panium (198 B.C.), near the head waters of the Jordan, later to be the site of Cæsarea Philippi, Cœle-Syria passed into the hands of Syria. Egypt was never

[10] *Antt.* 12,4,1 ff.

to regain it. Many of the Jews hailed Antiochus as their saviour. They had been ill-treated by Scopas, the Egyptian general, and remembered that after Raphia Ptolemy had sought to push his way into the holy of holies.[11] Antiochus appears to have treated the Jews kindly. Thousands were settled in Syria as colonists; taxes were remitted; Antiochus, in contrast to Ptolemy Philopator, is said to have been most scrupulous in his observance of the niceties of the Jewish law. But changes were in store, and the enthusiasm of the hour was destined soon to wane.

Coincident with the transfer of Palestine to Syria we see the rise of a Hellenistic party in Jerusalem. The Seleucids were far more enthusiastic in their attempt to foster Greek culture than had been the Ptolemies. Syria had been eager to accept the latest fashions in civilization, and she was equally eager to impart it. In this respect she was a true child of Alexander the Great. In the days of Egyptian control Greek must have become familiar at least to a measure in the upper classes in Jerusalem, although Palestine as a whole was not then bilingual, nor did she ever become so. Now with Syria in the saddle the Hellenists—Greek apers—increased in number and influence, to the disgust of many Jews. They could see the handwriting on the wall. For many others this new, freer civilization was becoming highly fascinating. This group naturally became coincident with the pro-Syrian element; the anti-Hellenists, on the contrary, became increasingly pro-Egyptian as a natural reaction, although Egypt was Hellenistic to the core. Although Hellenism was thus becoming increasingly fashionable among the gilded youth of Jerusalem, there was no forcible attempt to promote the spread of foreign ways throughout the reign of Antiochus the Great or of his elder son and successor, Seleucus IV. But this was soon to change.

In 175 B.C. Seleucus IV, who had succeeded to the Syrian throne twelve years before on the death of his father, Antiochus the Great, was murdered by his prime minister, Heliodorus, who ostentatiously put the infant crown prince on the throne. This was a gesture which deceived no one. The elder prince, Demetrius, later to ascend the throne, had been sent to Rome as a hostage. He was thus free from Heliodorus' plottings, but was powerless to claim his rightful position. His arrival at Rome as a hostage had freed his father's younger brother, Antiochus, from that position. The latter had left Rome for Athens, where word came of the confusion in Syria. With an armed force he appeared in Antioch; Heliodorus vanishes from history, and the newcomer soon sits on the throne of the Seleucids with the title Antiochus IV (175-164). It is hard to estimate him dispassionately. Hatred of him instantly blazed up. He chose the title Epiphanes ("the illustrious"); some nameless wit in his court parodied it to Epimanes ("the mad man"), which must have seemed to many most apt as they looked askance at his playboy practical jokes and theatrical absurdities. He was greatly enamoured of Hel-

[11] At least this story is dramatically recounted in III Macc. 1 and 2.

lenism, without apparently having any very deep appreciation of the real values of this culture. On the other hand, he was an astute politician and a clever trickster. He was by no means the weak demagogue that has often been pictured. Of all the Syrians he was the most hated by the Jews. Even yet we can sense this fury in the book of Daniel with its mention of the "little horn, before which three of the first horns were plucked up by the roots" and which had "eyes like the eyes of a man, and a mouth speaking great things."[12]

His accession in Syria secured the triumph of the pro-Syrian party in Jerusalem. Previous to his advent there had been no studied attempt at hellenization; now this changed and the initiative was taken in the highest quarters where we might least have expected it. Joshua, the brother of the high priest, Onias IV, was the acknowledged leader of the Hellenist party. This precious Joshua or, to give him the name he preferred, Jason by gifts to Antiochus contrived to get himself appointed high priest with *carte blanche* to turn Jerusalem into a second Antioch. Now Greek customs were openly introduced into Jerusalem. The gymnasium, without which no Greek town could feel itself a city, rose before the citadel. Young bloods of Judea contended with Greeks in the games. Many to avoid ridicule submitted to operations to remove the stigma of circumcision;[13] they affected Greek garb, in particular the petasus, or broad-brimmed hat, and were eager to get themselves enrolled as citizens of Antioch. Jerusalem received a Greek constitution, and afforded Antiochus a cordial welcome with "torch light and much shoutings"[14] on the occasion of his visit to the city, much to the satisfaction of the monarch, who rejoiced in Hellenism not only for its own sake, but also because of its effectiveness as a means of breaking down local peculiarities and aloofness and of making possible the unity in his kingdom which he so desired.

As can be easily imagined, all this aroused deep resentment in the hearts of the more conservative. Their attitude stands revealed in II Macc. 4:11-15:

He (*sc.* Jason) brought up new customs against the law: for he built gladly a place of exercise[15] under the tower itself, and brought the chief young men under his subjection, and made them wear a hat. Now such was the height of Greek fashions and increase of heathenish manners, through the exceeding profaneness of Jason, that ungodly wretch, and no high priest: that the priests had no courage to serve any more at the altar, but despising the temple, and neglecting the sacrifices, hastened to be partaker of the unlawful allowance in the place of exercise, after the game of Discus called them forth; not setting by the honours of their fathers, but liking the glories of the Grecians best of all.

[12] Dan. 7:8.
[13] Josephus, *Antt.* 12,5,1.
[14] II Macc. 4:22.
[15] *I.e.*, gymnasium.

Harsh words these, but there were undoubtedly many saying them. We would err if we drew the contrast too sharply. It is probably true that the particular brand of Hellenism that became popular in Syria was not always of the highest sort. The desire for a strong mind in a strong body was highly commendable; the gymnasiums and the revival of interest in the Greek classics no doubt met real needs. On the other hand, it is undeniably the case that often what was intrinsically wholesome became quite the reverse and tended to fill Syrian cities with arrogant and insolent braggadocios, contemptuous of the earlier simplicity and homely morality. It was not wholly this phase, however, that awakened opposition in Jerusalem. It was not the opposition of outraged godliness to godlessness. Rather it was essentially a deep-seated abhorrence towards new and foreign notions and practices. The Jew was different from other people, and was proud of it. This outward sign which was causing the Jerusalem youth to feel countrified before their city friends was God's own seal, betokening the fact that they were different. Their customs, which they fondly believed were hallowed by centuries of almost universal observance—nay which had been instituted by God himself in the very beginning—their proudest birthright, were being wantonly discarded by these misguided Esaus, hungering for the red pottage of Syria. It is easy to stigmatize such an attitude intolerant conservatism; such a label does not free the student of history from the necessity of understanding it, nor should it blind his eyes to the fact that it was precisely this intolerant conservatism which enabled Judaism to weather the many hurricanes that beset her course.

Soon fresh fuel was heaped on the flames of discontent. In 171 a certain Menelaus (Menahem) was sent to Antioch by Jason. He improved this shining opportunity to offer Antiochus three hundred talents more than Jason was paying, could he become high priest. Such piety could not go unrewarded. Menelaus received the appointment. To raise the promised tribute, he helped himself to some of the temple treasure. A riot of indignation resulted. Jason fled to the other side of Jordan to bide his time, and Menelaus "who had the fury of a cruel tyrant, and the rage of a wild beast"[16] was seated in his holy office.

These efforts by Antiochus and his creatures to hellenize—which meant essentially to heathenize—tended to drive the disgruntled Jews still closer to Egypt. As has been already pointed out, some of them had at first turned to Syria with enthusiasm. Antiochus the Great had seemed their saviour. The results of a hundred years' contact with Egypt, however, were not easily broken, and Syria's now intolerant attitude and rapacity disabused their earlier sanguine hopes. Syria needed money to pay Rome, who had already made herself felt in the days of Antiochus the Great. Accordingly, her greed in the matter of taxes. Taxes on the salt mined at the Dead Sea; taxes amount-

[16] II Macc. 4:25.

ing to a third of the grain harvested, to a half of the all too scanty fruits; poll taxes, crown taxes, temple taxes, to say nothing of the sovereign right to seize cattle and stores in the name of military conscription—all this fomented unrest.

In 170 war broke out again between Syria and Egypt over the vexed question of Palestine. The sympathies of the Jews were with Egypt. A rumour came to Jerusalem that Antiochus had been slain. This was a signal for Jason to attempt an unsuccessful *coup de main* to regain his old position. Antiochus, however, was not dead, as Jerusalem soon realized, and on his return to Syria stopped at Jerusalem, entered the holy of holies, carried off the golden altar of incense, the table of shewbread, and everything else he could lay his hands upon, even stripping the gold plating from the front of the temple.[17] In the spring of 168 he made another attempt on Egypt, ostensibly to regain Pelusium, and Egypt appealed to Rome, who had already interested herself in matters Syrian. In 190 Scipio had checked Antiochus the Great at Magnesia and had wrested all of western Asia Minor to the Halys River from the Seleucidæ. Rome's answer was decisive. Antiochus must withdraw at once. Polybius preserves the incident in all its dramatic setting. Popilius, the Roman legate, handed Antiochus the Senate's decree.

> On the king (*i.e.,* Antiochus), after reading the dispatch, saying that he desired to consult with his friends on the situation, Popilius did a thing which was looked upon as exceedingly overbearing and insolent. Happening to have a vine stick in his hand, he drew a circle round Antiochus with it, and ordered him to give his answer to the letter before he stepped out of that circumference. The king was taken aback by this haughty proceeding. After a brief interval of embarrassed silence, he replied he would do whatever the Romans demanded. Then Popilius and his colleagues shook him by the hand, and one and all greeted him with warmth.[18]

Disappointed in his hope of recouping his waning fortunes—the vast kingdom of Seleucus had now shrunk to little more than Syria itself—Antiochus cast wrathful eyes on Palestine and the strong pro-Egyptian party that his policies had fostered in Jerusalem. Their joy at his recent discomfiture was more real than politic. Those who "kept the Jewish superstition alive" were to be exterminated, for Antiochus now clearly saw that the Jewish opposition was religious. Instead of refusing to allow this to take a political aspect, as was later to be the policy of Rome, he made a systematic effort to crush it. A Syrian officer—II Maccabees calls him Apollonius—came to Jerusalem with a large force and treacherously attacked on the Sabbath after proffering terms of peace. Then followed terrible scenes of carnage. The walls were breached; a citadel on the Acra was built up, to be a menace for nearly thirty years; women and children were sold into slavery, and drastic prohibitions of

[17] I Macc. 1:20-24; II Macc. 5:11-21; Josephus, *Antt.* 12,5,3.

[18] Polybius, *Hist.* xxix,27(11).

Judaism were enacted: Sacrifice to Jehovah was to cease; Sabbath observance was prohibited; circumcision was a capital offence; possession of a copy of the Scripture meant death. The most galling act of all took place a short time later. On Dec. 15, 168, a heathen altar to Zeus was erected on the top of the great altar of sacrifice, and ten days later a hog was sacrificed upon it. The temple sanctuary was smeared with blood; in the general riot soldiers committed the grossest indecencies in the revered courts. The "abomination of desolation" still throbs in the passionate hatred of such contemporary writings as Daniel and Judith. Nor were these measures restricted to Jerusalem. Strict search in all Jewish communities was inaugurated. Many in terror gave allegiance. For others the mask was now torn off; such was the true nature of the vaunted culture. The issue was clear. If Judaism was to live, she must fight.

Chapter II

THE MACCABEAN REVOLT AND THE HOUSE OF HASMON

For the moment the scene of our story shifts from Jerusalem to the little hill town of Modein, twenty miles northwest of Jerusalem. To his farm in this town the old priest, Mattathias, had withdrawn with his five sons during the profanation and the resultant confusion.[1] Mattathias, as a prominent resident, is called upon to set an example of obedience, and is promised immunity. His answer and the consequences of the refusal are best told in the word of I Maccabees:

> Then Mattathias answered and spake with a loud voice. Though all the nations that are under the king's dominion obey him, and fall away every one from the religion of their fathers, and give consent to his commandments: yet will I and my sons and my brethren walk in the covenant of our fathers. God forbid that we should forsake the law and the ordinances. We will not hearken to the king's words, to go from our religion, either on the right hand, or the left. Now when he had left speaking these words, there came one of the Jews in the sight of all to sacrifice on the altar which was at Modin, according to the king's commandment. Which thing when Mattathias saw, he was inflamed with zeal, and his reins trembled, neither could he forbare to shew his anger according to judgment: Wherefore he ran, and slew him upon the altar. Also the king's commissioner, who compelled men to sacrifice, he killed at that time, and the altar he pulled down. Thus dealt he zealously for the law of God, like as Phineas did unto Zambri the son of Salom. And Mattathias cried throughout the city with a loud voice, saying, Whosoever is zealous for the law, and maintaineth the covenant, let him follow me. So he and his sons fled into the mountains and left all that ever they had in the city.[2]

This was the Sarajevo of the Maccabean uprising. Soon joined by others, they lurked in the passes and defiles of northern Judea—a more ideal spot for such activities could hardly be imagined—to sally forth to destroy all signs of heathenism and to kill apostate Jews. A veritable wave of terror set in.

The revolt was supported at the beginning by an influential group of the devotedly religious who called themselves, or were nicknamed, Ḥasidim or Asideans, that is, "the pious." Their interests were not political; they took to arms in desperation solely because they believed their religion was

[1] Gruesome stories of the scenes may be read in II Macc. 6 and 7.
[2] I Macc. 2:19-28.

at stake. When once the revolt was successful, with the altar reconsecrated and worship restored under a high priest of undoubted Aaronic descent, they lost further interest. It was a vastly different thing to use arms to gain political independence; such a course lay outside their interests. Their accession to the Hasmoneans, as the patriots were dubbed since Mattathias was a descendant of Hasmon, brought both strength and prestige.

After a few months, in 167, Mattathias died, and the active leadership fell to the third of his five sons, Judas. These five—John, Simon, Judas, Eleazar, and Jonathan—are popularly known as the Maccabees, from the nickname *Maccabæus* ("hammerer") which Judas received. The story of the dramatic successes of the band under Judas' leadership against far larger and highly trained Syrian armies reads like a fairy tale until one realizes the difficulties these soldiers met, trained as they were to open fighting on the Syrian plains, when they were forced to chase these Judeans back and forth through the unfamiliar defiles of rocky Judea. In addition, political difficulties were constantly arising in Syria which compelled withdrawal of the royal forces at critical moments. All of these difficulties Judas capitalized. At first Apollonius, the governor of Samaria (who had oversight of Judea), sought to check the disturbance. His defeat and the subsequent discomfiture of Seron, military commander of Cœle-Syria, alarmed Antiochus. Three generals with 40,000 foot and 7,000 horse[3] were dispatched post haste to Judea and were defeated near Emmaus (166). The next year Lysias, who had been left in charge of the whole southern domain during the absence of Antiochus in the east, changed the plan of military tactics, which had been so uniformly unsuccessful, and, circling Judea, attacked from the south at Bethsura, near Hebron, but with no better success. "Then said Judas and his brethren, Behold, our enemies are discomfited: let us go up to cleanse and dedicate the sanctuary."[4] Although unable to drive out the garrison in the Acra, he cleansed the sacred area, demolished the hated altar, and constructed a new one. Whether the consecration which the original stones had received at the time of the erection of the altar, centuries before, was powerful enough to overcome the defilement of hog's blood and the resultant heathenish idolatry was quite beyond him. He was a fighter, not a lawyer. With commendable common sense he built his altar of new stone, carefully laying the dubious ones aside "until there should come a prophet to shew what should be done with them." Thus three years to a day after that first hateful sacrifice to Olympian Zeus, the smoke of sacrifice ascended once more and worship was restored. This success has been perpetuated in the annual Feast of Lights or, as it is often called, of Dedication.[5]

[3] I Macc. 3:39.
[4] I Macc. 4:36.
[5] Cf., for example, John 10:22.

Then followed expeditions led by Judas and his brothers against neighbouring tribes, terrified by his success. These were soundly trounced, but the loyal Jews in these remoter districts were finding themselves in a most precarious position. Judas sensibly determined to centralize his supporters. While he proceeded across the Jordan to Gilead, he sent Simon to Galilee. Both were successful, and brought back those Jewish colonists to greater safety in Judea. The significance of this de-judaizing of Galilee and the Perea should not be overlooked. We shall have occasion later to consider its consequences.

Now started a campaign to restore Jewish independence. This was made possible by the timely civil strife in Syria. Antiochus had died (164), not, as the author of Daniel[6] had expected he would, on the coast road between Syria and Egypt, but in the Persian city, Tabæ.[7] At once strife over the succession arose. Philip, a friend of Epiphanes, had been appointed regent during the minority of the young heir, Antiochus V, but Lysias had been left in control in Syria. He at once appointed himself Antiochus' guardian. This is but one of many cases which give us the clue to the surprising advances the Jews made. The Maccabeans were skilful enough to turn these moments of civil unrest in Syria to their own advantage and to play one leader against another.

At once Judas made a determined attack on the thorn in Judea's side, the Acra. This brought Lysias back from Antioch. A crushing defeat for Judas was the result. His brother Eleazar was slain, and his force retreated to Jerusalem. Fortunately for Palestine, Lysias could not make effective use of the opportunity. Philip had returned to Syria and was marching against Antioch. Lysias must return to Syria; accordingly, he offered terms of peace whereby they might "make use of and live according to the laws of their fathers."[8] Although Jerusalem had fallen, although the citadel still remained a menace, the battle for religious liberty had been successful. Menelaus, the high priest who had been so largely responsible for the whole disturbance, was exiled and later executed, and Alcimus, a zealous Hellenist, although of unimpeachable Aaronic descent, was installed in his stead. Enforced Hellenism from the outside was over; its presence from within was by no means dead.

Changes had taken place in Antioch. The young Antiochus V (Eupator) and his general, Lysias, had been successful against Philip, but soon found themselves confronted by Demetrius, the son of Seleucus IV. During his

[6] Dan. 11:40-45. Indeed this sudden error in "prophecy"—Antiochus' career is sketched with the utmost fidelity in 11:21-39; then suddenly an alien note is sounded—provides decisive evidence with regard to the date of the "prophecy." It is, unfortunately, far harder to achieve accuracy when one essays to "prophesy" before an event than afterward!

[7] Polybius, *Hist.* xxxi,11.

[8] Josephus, *Antt.* 12,9,7.

enforced stay in Rome as a hostage he had grown to maturity, and twice had sought to gain the Senate's support in his claim to the Syrian throne. Despairing of success in this direction, he had fled from Rome, and suddenly appeared in Antioch, got into power, and executed both of his rivals (162 B.C.).

To him Alcimus appealed for help against Judas, who was causing him decided difficulties. Bacchides was dispatched by the new king to install Alcimus and to punish the traitors. At this moment a significant change in the temper of the Jews is seen. The Asideans had rallied to the side of Judas when religious liberty was at stake. That, however, had now been secured; Alcimus' promises were fair, his Aaronic descent undoubted. Accordingly, they lost interest in further warfare. Political independence or aggrandizement held no attraction. They turned from Judas and accepted the new régime. According to I Maccabees, Alcimus slew sixty of them. Whether this disillusioning treatment alienated them or not we cannot say, for they disappear from the pages of history. Whether, as has been often maintained, they make their appearance later in the Pharisees or the Essenes or both we can reserve for later consideration.

Alcimus soon found himself in difficulties. Bacchides had enjoined obedience to him and had made gestures against the recalcitrant, but upon his return to Syria, although deprived probably of the support of the Asideans, Judas had at once got the upper hand. In this unequal struggle Alcimus was obliged once more to seek protection from his Syrian master. Demetrius felt he could not afford to disregard Judas, who had become far too powerful, and accordingly sent Nicanor into Palestine to end this difficulty once and for all. To his amazement, however, Nicanor fared no better than had his predecessors: first an unsuccessful manœuvre to get Judas by trickery, then a repulse near Jerusalem, finally a crushing defeat at Adasa (161). Here he lost his life, and his head and hand were hung up as trophies on the temple gates. The anniversary of this happy event—"Nicanor's Day"—was celebrated as an annual festival.

For the moment Judas had a breathing space. However, he knew all too well the inevitable result. Another army would soon appear to avenge Nicanor. He had been remarkably successful: superior knowledge of the Judean hills, complications in Syria's political household, amazing good luck—all these had aided him; but if he was not to be defeated in the end by the sheer force of fresh troops, outside help was imperative. In this crisis, according to I Maccabees he turned to the rising power of the West, which had thwarted Antiochus Epiphanes' dreams for Egypt, and which thirty years before had checked Antiochus the Great at Magnesia—Rome. Judas was no prophet, nor was he enough of a statesman to see that this queen of the West was destined to exercise great power in Palestine, eventually to achieve its destruction. He needed help, and Rome was the archenemy of Syria. His appeal to the Senate for confederacy and peace was successful. The ambassadors were returned with the treaty emblazoned on bronze shields. Each was to help the other in war.

All this, however, took time, and time was precious. No sooner had Demetrius learned of the discomfiture of Nicanor's forces than he sent Bacchides with a fresh army to the south. By the time Rome's peremptory order to Syria reached Antioch, the army had left. With his present force Judas was powerless; of the three thousand (I Macc. 9:5), all but eight hundred deserted. Judas could not be restrained. With this tiny remnant he held his ground at Eleasa—the Jewish Thermopylæ—and there fell (161). For seven years he had fought bravely. He had brought the struggle for religious liberty to a successful conclusion, and had also encouraged a desire for political independence. At his death it appeared that this latter hope could never be realized. His army was routed; many of his erstwhile supporters failed to share his dreams of a restored Israel; Syria had been finally aroused to the seriousness of the situation. Yet these dreams were to be realized—not through force of arms, for his successors must pursue a different course of action—but through the sagacious policy of the later leaders who cleverly turned Syria's extremity into Palestine's opportunity.

Now the ground was clear for Alcimus to be high priest in more than name. Judas, his archenemy, was dead; his forces had been routed. Championing Alcimus, the Hellenists sought to strike while the iron was hot and to root out the rest of the Hasmoneans. Of the five sons of Mattathias three were still alive, John, Simon, and Jonathan. In this crisis Jonathan was appealed to. He was the crafty politician rather than the warrior. During the eighteen years of his leadership (161-143) Israel was to make great seeming advances, not due so much to her own strength but through the clever way that Jonathan and his successors turned the weakness of Syria with its ever-present rival claimants for the throne to the advantage of Palestine.

Wishing to avoid Alcimus, who had returned with Bacchides on the latter's expedition which had accomplished the death of Judas, Jonathan first retreated to the wilderness of Tekoah, and then sent his baggage with his eldest brother, John, across the Jordan to the Nabateans, who had been friendly to Judas. These plans, however, miscarried. The party was attacked by a robber clan, and John was killed. Jonathan went across Jordan to avenge his brother, but found himself confronted by Bacchides. It was a critical moment, but Jonathan rallied to it:

> Then Jonathan said to his company, Let us go up now and fight for our lives; for it standeth not with us today, as in time past: For behold the battle is before us and behind us, and the water of Jordan on this side and on that side, the marsh likewise and wood, neither is there place for us to turn aside. Wherefore cry ye

now unto heaven, that ye may be delivered from the hand of your enemies. With that they joined battle.[9]

The Jordan was crossed, and Bacchides repulsed. But greater dangers faced the new leader. As has already been pointed out, Syria had consistently allowed herself to be outmanœuvred by the rebels. Bacchides appears now to have become convinced of the sheer folly of attempting to chase this band of outlaws from pillar to post. On the contrary, he threw a ring of heavily fortified cities around Judea (Jericho, Emmaus, Bethhoron, Bethel, Timnath, Pharathon, Tephon, Bethsura, and Gazara,[10] and sent as hostages the sons of the leading men to the citadel in Jerusalem.

This common-sense procedure successfully throttled opposition. For the moment the Hellenists were free to move as they pleased. In this Alcimus played a prominent part. It is perhaps not precisely clear what is to be understood by the reproach: "he commanded that the wall of the inner court of the sanctuary should be pulled down; he pulled down also the works of the prophets";[11] at any rate it aroused bitter resentment, and his sudden death in agony appeared heaven sent.[12] More important than the death of Alcimus is the fact that for six years (159-153) the office of high priest remained vacant until the crafty Jonathan himself appeared in his pontifical robes, the appointee of an ambitious pretender to the throne of the Seleucids.

Shortly afterward Bacchides returned to Syria. The girdle of Syrian fortresses had paralysed resistance; there was no longer a high priest to defend: "the land of Judea was in rest two years." Later the opponents of Jonathan, now inclined to be a bit too confident in their supremacy, sought to eliminate him entirely. Word was sent to Syria that the rebel leader could be taken. Bacchides responded to this overture and came south. He soon found his task was greater than he had anticipated, since Jonathan had got wind of the plan. Bacchides quickly tired of the thankless task of pursuing the will-o'-the-wisp natives through their own haunts, concluded some sort of a treaty with Jonathan, and returned to Syria, after wreaking his displeasure on many of the Hellenists who had involved him in the débâcle. The next few years are passed over in silence by I Maccabees. The sword had ceased in Israel. Jonathan appears to have resided in Michmash as a sort of privileged freebooter, like David had before him in Hebron. The one comment that we hear, *viz.*, that Jonathan "began to govern the people" and that "he destroyed the ungodly men of Israel," would indicate that during these years he was gradually gaining more and

[9] I Macc. 9:44-47.

[10] I Macc. 9:50,52.

[11] I Macc. 9:54. Cf. Schürer, *op. cit.*, Div. I, Vol. I, p. 236, n. 5.

[12] It is perhaps not out of place to observe that most of those of whom ancient writers disapproved died "with great torment."

more power at the expense of his rivals in Jerusalem. But more was soon to follow.

As has been already indicated, the clue to the surprising advances of Judea lies in the story of Syria's weakness. It is difficult to find an instant in the later years of the Seleucids when there were not several rival claimants to the throne. In 153 serious difficulties arose. An unknown adventurer, named Alexander Balas, claimed to be a natural son of Antiochus Epiphanes, and established himself in Ptolemaïs as a rival to Demetrius. He received support from the latter's rivals, even from Ptolemy Philometor of Egypt. In the resultant civil war in Syria Demetrius was no longer able to interfere in Palestine. On the contrary, he sorely needed Jewish support, and Jonathan became essential. Overtures were made and accepted. Jonathan entered Jerusalem as chief of the native state; the garrisons in the neighbouring towns fled. Only the office of high priest failed; even that was soon to be his. Balas, too, needed supporters, and proceeded to overbid his rival. He appointed Jonathan high priest, and enrolled him as among the "king's friends." At the Feast of Tabernacles Jonathan made his appearance in the robes of office, high priest, as Wellhausen sardonically remarked, by the grace of Balas.[13] It need hardly be emphasized that his ambition to hold this office was not due to any humble or pious desire to offer sacrifice to Jehovah. From the days when religious toleration had crowned Judas' early efforts the consistent aim of his followers had been to achieve independence and temporal power.

Demetrius sought, but in vain, to bring Jonathan back to himself. Larger offers, even the promise of surrendering the Acra, failed to lure the crafty Jonathan, who was now convinced that Balas would be successful, favoured as he was by Rome. Nor was he disappointed. Soon Balas triumphed; Demetrius fell in battle. During the short usurpation of Balas (150-145) Jonathan was highly honoured as one of his "first friends." A nominal tribute was paid, but save for the Acra in Jerusalem Judea was to all intents free. But Balas was not without rivals. In 147 the young son of Demetrius, Demetrius II, came from Crete "into the land of his fathers," and at once received support from those disgusted with the utterly worthless usurper. Jonathan alone of the erstwhile foreign supporters remained firm. He defeated Apollonius, the governor of Cœle-Syria, who was now championing Demetrius, at Azotus, and burned the city. The routed force of Apollonius fled for refuge into the temple of Dagon, which temple Jonathan without compunction set in flames. For this act of fealty Balas rewarded him with the town of Ekron. Two years later, however, Balas was worsted and murdered. It might have seemed that Jonathan would have been undone by the failure of his patron, especially as he had ventured to besiege the Acra. Demetrius II summoned Jonathan to Ptolemaïs. Jona-

[13] Wellhausen, *Israelitische und Jüdische Geschichte*, p. 253.

than went boldly and apparently convinced the new monarch that it was for his interest to overlook his erstwhile zeal for Balas. At any rate, Jonathan returned to Jerusalem with three frontier districts in Samaria and with the promise of subsequent exemption from tribute. The Hasmoneans were increasing as the Seleucids were tottering.

Soon Jonathan found opportunity to repay his new patron. Trypho, an officer of the murdered Balas, sponsored the latter's young son as claimant for his father's throne under the title Antiochus VI. Demetrius' cruelty and the insolence of his Cretan henchmen had already aroused great opposition to him. Jonathan promised assistance on condition that the Acra be surrendered. Demetrius readily promised, "for he lied in all that ever he spake," and Jonathan with a force of three thousand relieved him in the nick of time. Demetrius rashly failed to keep his promise. In anger Jonathan swung to the side of Trypho, who was soon successful against the quite incompetent Demetrius. The young Antiochus confirmed Jonathan in his governorship of Judea, while Simon was named military governor of the coastal plain from the Ladder of Tyre to the Egyptian frontier.

Jonathan turned this power to his own advantage. He was expected to fortify those outposts which had been won from Demetrius; he took pains, however, to man them with Jewish troops. He also started a new wall in Jerusalem to cut off the hated Acra from the upper market and to starve it into submission. His plan was clever; it was also transparent, and Trypho had no illusions regarding Jonathan's unselfish devotion to himself or to his young master Antiochus. It may be, as I Maccabees represents, that Trypho had personal grounds for fear of Jonathan, namely, that since his sponsoring of the dubious claims of the young Antiochus had been due to his desire to gain the crown for himself, he feared Jonathan might seek to thwart him. However that may be, as soon as he had a breathing space, he turned towards Judea. Jonathan came to meet him with an equal force. Trypho was shocked. Why this armed force? He had come to hand over to his loyal colleague those districts between Judea proper and the seacoast territory of Simon. If Jonathan would accompany him to Ptolemaïs, this should all be accomplished. And, amazing as it may seem, the crafty Jonathan actually was deceived. Yielding to the tempting offer, he followed Trypho, who promptly imprisoned him.

In this crisis (143), Simon, the last of the five sons, steps into the breach. Jerusalem was strengthened; Joppa, already nominally under the command of Simon, was manned by Jewish troops. Trypho attacked, but was repulsed. He persisted in veiling his true purpose, and represented that Jonathan was being held captive simply because he had failed to pay the promised fees for the many concessions he had received. Simon patiently met all these overtures, and paid the sums demanded. Trypho meanwhile sought to outflank Simon and get to Jerusalem before him. Failing in this, he slew Jonathan in rage and retreated to Syria through the region east of the Jordan.

Simon struck while the iron was hot. He flatly demanded from Demetrius absolute independence, with complete freedom from taxation. Syria was in no position to refuse. We can still read the note of exultation, "Thus the yoke of the heathen was taken away from Israel in the hundred and seventieth year (143)."[14]

Gazara, the fortress on the road to Joppa, was taken; Judea's strongholds were increased; and finally in the May of 142 the Acra, which for so many years had been the thorn in Jerusalem's flesh, was starved into submission. In 141, in grateful recognition of his ability, Simon was confirmed by popular vote high priest and governor—Demetrius in the preceding year had bestowed these offices upon him—with the double position to be hereditary until a faithful prophet should arise and direct otherwise. Even more significant than the capture of the Acra was this conquest of popular support. Simon had achieved the goal that Judas had longed for twenty years before. The struggle of the Maccabees had been successful.

Then followed a short time of peace and prosperity for the Jews. Demetrius was too hard pressed by Trypho, who had now appeared in his true colours, as claimant of the throne, after having had his young protégé Antiochus treacherously murdered, to interfere in Judea. The Hellenists were forced to accept the new régime or to vacate the land. Joppa had become a Jewish post; convenient access to it from Jerusalem had been gained through the capture of Gazara. Judea began a lively trade, and for the moment Jerusalem was flourishing.

The treaty which Jonathan had made with Rome soon after his break with Demetrius I was now renewed. Simon felt secure enough to coin his own money, although his own name did not appear upon it. This privilege was later "granted" to Simon by the new claimant of the Seleucid throne; Simon, it may be observed, however, had been busy coining his money for more than a year before this privilege was conferred.

This new figure in Syrian politics is of interest, for he was, as Wellhausen remarked, "hewn of entirely different wood" from his brother Demetrius II.[15] Demetrius had pushed east against the Parthians (140 B.C.), seeking to recover certain provinces which this new and threatening power had seized. After varying fortunes he had been imprisoned, and for ten years (138-128) drops from history. His younger brother, Antiochus VII, surnamed Sidetes, was appealed to in this crisis by Cleopatra, wife of the captured Demetrius. She, hard pressed by Trypho, who had gained control of the army, invited her brother-in-law to wed her and to ascend the throne. Nothing loath, the ambitious young Antiochus had hastily returned from

[14] I Macc. 13:41.

[15] Wellhausen, *Israelitische und Jüdische Geschichte,* p. 258.

Rhodes to Syria. Even before landing he had sent word to Simon confirming him in all his power and specifying his right to coin money with his own stamp.[16] Trypho was routed, and later decisively defeated at Dora, whither he had fled and had stood siege. Though he escaped for the moment, he was overtaken at Apamea, where he lost his life.

Simon had responded to Antiochus' initial friendly overtures, and had even sent a strong force to Dora to assist his new friend against Trypho. In the course of the months following his arrival on the Phœnician coast, the new king's confidence had rapidly increased. Now he considered himself able to dispense with Simon's friendship. The troops were curtly refused, and word was sent to Simon that he was to relinquish his unlawfully acquired extra-Judean territory, including the seaport Joppa, the citadel Gazara, and the Acra in Jerusalem. Should Simon refuse, the Syrian legate was empowered to accept the sum of a thousand talents as a *quid pro quo*. Simon refused the terms as exorbitant, but was willing to pay a hundred talents. Antiochus sought to enforce his demand, but Simon's sons—he himself was too old to lead his forces in person—so signally defeated the enemy that no further attempt was made during Simon's rule.

Then came his tragic end. His position had become a tempting prize for ambitious rivals. His son-in-law, Ptolemy, who held an important military command in the Jericho plain, plotted to murder Simon and his sons and thus to clear the way for his own accession. Simon and his two elder sons Mattathias and Judas, were victims of this treachery. The plan, however, miscarried, since John Hyrcanus, the third son, received word of the plot in time to refuse the dinner invitation and to escape. For thirty years he was destined to rule over Judea.

So ended the family of the Maccabees. In the little more than thirty years that had passed since Mattathias had boldly flung down the gauntlet in Modein, much had been accomplished. Not only had the danger of forced apostasy been averted, but the yoke of thralldom to Syria had been thrust aside, and a Maccabean prince—that is, a prince in all but name—had been made at once hereditary ruler and high priest of an enlarged Judea. But mighty changes were in store in the near future. Like Cæsar, the Hasmoneans were ambitious; like Cæsar, they reaped the inevitable harvest.

Hyrcanus at once claimed his inheritance and hastened to Jerusalem, arriving, fortunately, before Ptolemy. In disappointment the latter retreated to Dagon near Jericho. Here he would undoubtedly have fallen into the hands of his irate brother-in-law save for his threat to murder Hyrcanus' mother, whom he had in his power, unless the siege was abandoned. Hyrcanus' unwillingness to cause his mother's death and the

[16] I Macc. 15:6.

fortunate arrival of a Sabbatic year enabled the disappointed Ptolemy to escape to Philadelphia across the Jordan, where he drops out of sight.

Antiochus Sidetes had neither forgotten nor forgiven Simon's effective resistance to his desire to regain control of Joppa and Gazara, and early in Hyrcanus' reign he came in person against him. Instead of meeting him in the mountains, as Judas had so often done, Hyrcanus stood siege in Jerusalem and was finally forced to make terms, entailing the breaching of the Jerusalem walls, the payment of tribute for such towns as Joppa and Gazara, and the payment of five hundred talents indemnity. These terms, while by no means satisfactory, were far better than had been feared, and are probably to be explained as due to the intervention of Rome, whose aid had been sought in keeping with the existing treaty.

But even this indignity was of short duration. Soon Sidetes was involved in fresh difficulties with Parthia. At first successful, he was later defeated, and to avoid becoming a prisoner committed suicide (128 B.C.). His brother Demetrius, whom the Parthians had freed to embarrass Sidetes, returned to his throne. With him came chaos. Foolishly he sought to meddle in Egypt. Ptolemy VII countered by sponsoring Alexander Zabinas, who speedily worsted Demetrius, compelling him to flee for his life. Although Demetrius was soon murdered (125?), Zabinas found himself opposed by the king's son, Antiochus VIII Grypsos (125-113, 111-96),[17] who soon (123) vanquished Zabinas. After nine or ten years Grypsos was attacked by his cousin Antiochus IX Cyzicenos, who for two years (113-111) was master of Syria. Although Grypsos soon regained the greater part of his domain, and ruled it till his death (96 B.C.), Cyzicenos settled down as ruler of Cœle-Syria (111-95), and, weak and theatrical as he was, served as a buffer between his more ambitious kinsman and Hyrcanus. Thus it was that soon Hyrcanus was able to disregard the Syrian claim, and that he and his successors were free from further overlordship from the north. Syria had received her death blow. It was only a question now of giving her decent burial.

Following the death of Sidetes, Hyrcanus, now freed from the need of following his Syrian master in fruitless campaigns against Parthia, turned his attention to matters in Palestine, in the hope of enlarging his domain. He was the first of the Jewish princes to employ foreign mercenaries, and with them extended the bounds of his state. First he appears to have pushed across Jordan and to have taken, after a lengthy siege, the redoubtable fortress of Medeba; then into Samaria, where Shechem soon fell. The Samaritan temple on Gerizim, always a thorn in the flesh of every pious Jew, was destroyed—a deed highly acceptable to all save the Samaritans. Flushed with this success, he turned south to Idumea, a dis-

[17] His elder brother, Seleucus V, had claimed the throne, but had been assassinated by his own mother, Cleopatra (125?).

trict which had caused Judea much difficulty and was destined to play an important rôle in the later story through her greatest son, Herod. Here in Idumea his success continued, and the inhabitants received the choice of becoming Jews or exiles. They accepted circumcision. This enforced marriage of Jacob and Edom was to be fraught with tremendous results, for thereby the Hasmonean dynasty was to be first dominated and eventually overthrown. What a story could be written of the "If I had only known's" of history! It was from this people, whom the proud Jewish aristocracy contemptuously styled "half Jews," that the most capable and strongest king the Jews ever had was to appear, Herod, son of Antipater, the Richelieu of Jewish politics. Here we have but one more example of history's seemingly eternal jest: The conquered is ever conqueror.

Hyrcanus was the first of Jewish rulers to have his own name stamped on his coins. In all but name he was king. This was reserved for his son and successor, Aristobulus. The last campaign of Hyrcanus revealed the weakness of Syria, now split into two parts, as mentioned in an earlier paragraph. According to Josephus, the inhabitants of the city of Samaria, a Macedonian colony,[18] had aroused Hyrcanus' ire by interfering with a Jewish colony, Marissa. Using this as an excuse, Hyrcanus proceeded against it. Samaria appealed to Antiochus Cyzicenos for aid. This was promptly given, but was unsuccessful. A second time Cyzicenos appeared, this time with some Egyptian troops, which he had gained from Ptolemy Lathurus, co-regent of Egypt. In spite of this help Hyrcanus eventually triumphed, and Samaria after a lengthy siege was annihilated. During the same campaign Scythopolis came into his control. Thus Hyrcanus' territory extended from Carmel to Scythopolis in the north, south through Judea and Idumea. Most of the seacoast of this territory was his; slight gains had been made across the Jordan. It is even possible that a portion of southern Galilee had fallen into his hands,[19] although we have no record of campaigns here. Judea was now a nation among nations. Under his successors, Aristobulus and Jannæus, the boundaries might be still extended, but at the cost of internal strength. Under Hyrcanus the peak of prosperity for Israel was realized.

Troubles, however, were brewing, and their causes are not far to seek. The simple piety and religious fervor that had characterized the brave stand of Mattathias had given way to a desire for conquest. Enthusiastic memories of the palmy days of David and of Solomon—memories which had lost nothing in the lapse of years—had been revived. Once again a Jewish king was perhaps to rule over a reunited Israel. The prophecy was

[18] Samaria the city is to be differentiated from the territory of Samaria, which Hyrcanus had already conquered, and whose capital was Shechem.

[19] The reason for this assumption will appear later.

fulfilled: Jehovah had visited the sheep of his flock and had made them as his goodly horse in the battle.[20] Joel too might have rejoiced: ploughshares had been beaten into swords, and pruninghooks into spears. The weak had said, I am strong.[21]

Nothing succeeds like success. The phenomenal advances of a half-century must have tended to allay the disquietude of many a saint who might well have had qualms of conscience at the sight of the high priest leading armies of mercenaries. Yet after all Hyrcanus was high priest, and he was proud of it. For his successors it was to become a stepping-stone, a political job; all desire to sacrifice humbly before Jehovah had departed. Not so for him. As Wellhausen rightly remarks, the balance between state and church still remained undisturbed. Josephus praises him in most appreciative fashion. In the Talmud he is spoken of with reverence and appreciation. Had he not destroyed the abominable Samaritan temple on Gerizim? Had not circumcision been forced upon the Idumeans? Many of the pious must have found sweet consolation in those thoughts.

Yet although the nation supported its leader enthusiastically, there appeared even during his reign a growing dissatisfaction. Josephus recounts the story replete with the gossipy details he so much enjoyed.[22] The story is certainly legendary; yet it may well be of value to the historian. According to the tale, Hyrcanus gave a dinner party, partly to allay growing opposition on the part of the Pharisees—a group Josephus here mentions for the first time. Hyrcanus graciously expressed the desire that should his conduct be open to reproach they might feel free to point it out. All flattered him until finally a Pharisee named Eleazar remarked that he lacked one thing. He should resign his office of high priest and content himself with the civil government. It is one thing for a ruler to ask for criticisms, another to get them. Pressed for an explanation, Eleazar replied that it was noised about that Hyrcanus' mother had been a captive in the reign of Antiochus Epiphanes, perhaps intimating not too delicately that his paternity was not certain, or at least that he was obviously ineligible to the sacred office. At this gratuitous insult, the Pharisees as well as Hyrcanus were angered. Their rivals, however, the Sadducees, used the occasion for their own ends. The Pharisees, they told him, might outwardly condemn Eleazar; inwardly, however, they approved, as Hyrcanus could see if he demanded that the Pharisees set Eleazar's punishment. Incensed at the mildness of the penalty, "stripes and bonds," Hyrcanus broke with them and joined the Sadducees.

Essentially the same story is preserved by the rabbis,[23] although in this recension Jannai (Alexander Jannæus) replaces Hyrcanus. That the story

[20] Zech. 10:3.
[21] Joel 3:10.
[22] *Antt.* 13,10,5 f.
[23] Kiddushin 66a.

is historical in the sense of explaining the real reason for the break between the Pharisees and Hyrcanus (or Jannæus) is most improbable. That such a story came to be told, however, attests the fact, independently substantiated, that during these years the political aspirations of the high-priest rulers, actually kings in all but name, were arousing fears and discontent. We can reserve a detailed discussion of the Pharisees and Sadducees as such until a later chapter.

John Hyrcanus was succeeded by his eldest son, Aristobulus, of whose short reign we know very little. Josephus, our chief source of information, preserves little beside the lurid story of his cruel treatment of his mother and brothers and of his consequent remorseful death in agony. On the other hand, he concludes this sorry statement with the contradictory remark:

> He was naturally a man of candor, and of great modesty, as Strabo bears witness in the name of Timagenes, who says thus: "This man was a person of candor, and very serviceable to the Jews, for he added a country to them, and obtained a part of the nation of the Itureans for them and bound them to him by the bond of the circumcision of their genitals."[24]

It is, accordingly, not improbable that the distressing story of domestic unhappiness reflects the growing antipathy of the Pharisees to their Hasmonean masters.

Apparently Hyrcanus had intended that Aristobulus should succeed him as high priest; the widow was to administer the government. Aristobulus, however, thought differently and promptly imprisoned his mother and brothers,[25] thus assuming full control over Palestine. Josephus states he assumed the title king; Strabo,[26] on the contrary, asserts this of his successor, Alexander Jannæus. The only other bit of information we have about his short rule is also perplexing, namely, his partial conquest of the Itureans. As has been often pointed out, the Itureans were the Arabians in the Lebanons, a district remote from the apparent northern boundary attained by Hyrcanus. Hence it has often been assumed that the term is inaccurately used for the inhabitants of northern Galilee. The matter is perhaps impossible of solution. At any rate, it would render probable the suggestion in an earlier paragraph that Hyrcanus' northern conquests may well have extended into southern Galilee, since it is highly improbable that his successor attempted the conquest of a district separated from his own domain by territory as yet unsubdued. Whoever the Itureans were,

[24] *Antt.* 13,11,3.

[25] Wellhausen (*Israelitische und Jüdische Geschichte,* p. 262, n. 4) assumes that these were his stepmother and stepbrothers, since he was so much older than Alexander Jannæus and because he was at first so kindly disposed to Antigonus, who would thus be his own brother.

[26] *Geogr.* xvi,2,40.

they were compelled to become Jews, even though their conversion was scarcely more than skin-deep. Thus during his short reign of but a single year (104 B.C.), Aristobulus seems to have contributed his share in extending the boundaries of the Jewish state.

No sooner was Aristobulus dead than his widow Alexandra released from prison his brothers and married the eldest, Alexander Jannæus.[27] Of the marriage Wellhausen[28] tersely comments: "He was twenty-four, she thirty-seven; from this fact the nature of the marriage is evident." Thus in 104 B.C. both civil and religious power were vested in the capable if ruthless young grandnephew of Judas the Maccabee. He was by nature a warrior, and his long reign (104-78 B.C.) was entirely devoted to extending his domain; he was successful in this endeavour, but his was a losing battle. The territory he gained at such terrible cost was to be wrested from his house within a score of years after his death.

Upon his accession to his brother's throne the interior of Palestine from the Lebanons to the desert south of Idumea was nominally his. East of the Jordan the territory was but partially subdued; furthermore, the majority of the seaboard towns were outside his domain. To these latter he first turned his attention. Again came foreign complications which came near to thwarting his designs at the start. During his siege on Ptolemaïs, north of Carmel, the inhabitants in their extremity appealed to Ptolemy Lathurus, who was then in Cyprus awaiting an opportunity to attack his mother, Cleopatra III of Egypt. Ptolemy accepted the invitation and repulsed Jannæus. Thereupon Jannæus played the risky game of pretending allegiance to Ptolemy while at the same time urging Cleopatra to proceed against her unfilial rival. In rage Ptolemy revenged himself by a ruthless campaign in Galilee until checked by his mother's forces. As it was, Cleopatra is said to have considered the suggestion of seeking to reunite Palestine with Egypt, but was fortunately dissuaded by her Judean generals as well as by influential Jews in Alexandria.

This initial disastrous campaign by no means damped Jannæus' ambitions. Better success awaited him in the south, whither he now proceeded after a partially successful campaign east of the Jordan, during which he had subdued Gadara, just south of the Sea of Galilee, and the strongly fortified Amathus. Raphia and Anthedon in the Philistine plain capitulated. Gaza, which had incurred his wrath through its alliance with Ptolemy, was next attacked, but seems to have withstood him nearly a year, confident that it would receive aid from the Nabatean king, Aretas. Finally, however, through treachery the city fell into his hands and received the full brunt of his rage for its long defiance. Apparently these campaigns in the east and south occupied the first nine years of his reign.

[27] Josephus does not refer specifically to this marriage, but it is clearly implied.

[28] *Israelitische und Jüdische Geschichte*, p. 263.

During these years the opposition against him was increasing in violence. The dissatisfaction which had arisen in the days of Hyrcanus against a high priest whose real interest lay in leading mercenaries rather than in humble adoration of the true King had gone on apace. And the fact that Jannæus had not been over-successful in his initial campaigns as a warrior from choice may well have swelled the discontent. Stories are told which, while they are themselves of little import, illustrate the growing antipathy. For example, one year during the celebration of the Feast of Tabernacles, he was pelted with lemons as he was officiating at the altar, and is said by Josephus to have had six thousand of his subjects executed in revenge. To protect himself from further insult he had a wooden screen built about the altar. The time was ripe for rebellion; nor was its coming long delayed.

A year or so after his conquest of Gaza he had crossed the Jordan and in an encounter with Obodas, son of the former Nabatean chieftain Aretas, had lost his army, as a result of pursuing the wily Arabian into a ravine, where, hemmed in on all sides, his soldiers were crushed to death by camels which the enemy drove over them. This débâcle caused many of his erstwhile supporters to join the opposition. His prestige was gone. Jerusalem on his return was the scene of a civil war which raged for six years (94-89 B.C.). We know nothing of the details of the rebellion save that Josephus asserts that though the king slew more than 50,000 of his rebellious subjects, they refused all overtures of peace and even appealed in their extremity to Demetrius III, one of the five sons of Antiochus VIII, who had been in conflict with one another since their father's death. Demetrius, true Syrian incompetent that he was, was only too ready to meddle in Jewish affairs, and dealt Jannæus[29] a crippling blow near Shechem.

It was a critical moment. The rebels had been ready to invoke foreign aid, but now that the Syrian seemed about to become supreme, they weakened. They remembered Antiochus Epiphanes and the bloody years of struggle to free themselves from the Syrian yoke. Better to have a worthless high priest who was a Jew—and Jannæus had been that; circumcision had always followed victory—than to be subject once again to a Syrian king. Six thousand Jews deserted to Jannæus. The tide turned and Demetrius departed. The rebellion was soon over. In revenge and as a warning for the future, Jannæus is said to have had eight hundred of the leaders of the opposition crucified while he dallied openly with his con-

[29] That Josephus' figures cannot always be relied upon is evidenced by the discrepancy between his two statements of Jannæus' force in this encounter. *Wars* 1,4,5 states he had 1,000 horsemen, 8,000 mercenaries on foot, and "that part of the Jews which favored him, to the number of 10,000." *Antt.* 13,14,1 gives the figures 6,200 mercenaries and 20,000 Jews of his party. Josephus' phrase, "his party," has usually been understood to signify the Sadducees, who aided him against the Pharisees, who were the instigators of the civil war. That the Pharisees may properly be regarded in this light is by no means clear.

cubines, and to add to the terror had his soldiers cut the throats of the wives and children before the eyes of the dying wretches on the crosses. Many fled in terror from Jerusalem that dread night, and Jannæus received the nickname *Thracida*, that is, "son of a Thracian," akin to our epithet, "Hun."

Though now free from opposition at home, Jannæus became once more involved in foreign affairs. Antiochus XII of Syria, the youngest of the five sons of Antiochus VIII Grypsos who had been in constant conflict among themselves since 95 B.C., sought to check the rising menace of the Arabian Aretas who was striving for Damascus. Antiochus tried to head him off by a hasty march through Judea. This Jannæus sought to prevent, and even built a wall and trench from Joppa to Antipatris. The Syrians broke through, but were worsted by Aretas, who quickly became master of Cœle-Syria. Soon Jannæus, whose land extended into territory desired by Aretas, felt his power. He was forced to retreat into Judea, and though standing siege in a town on the road between Joppa and Jerusalem was soon defeated. Just what his relations with Aretas were is not clear, for soon he was engaged in another campaign across Jordan, seeking to subdue those communities which still opposed him. In this campaign he was largely successful. Several important towns capitulated, among them Dion, Heshbon, Pella, Gerasa, and Gamala. When he returned to Jerusalem, flushed with victory, his reception was far different from that a dozen years before. Nothing succeeds like success.

The whole district from the Lebanons to the Egyptian frontier and from the Mediterranean to the desert was nominally in his control, although probably several of the seacoast towns were not his. That this domain was thoroughly loyal is not for a moment to be thought. Many of the towns must be conquered again and again. Nor were his subjects all loyal Jews. The rough-and-ready tactics of forcing all the vanquished to become circumcised, which he zealously practised as his father and brother had done before him, could hardly be expected to achieve very lasting results. As a matter of fact, the land across the Jordan, to mention but one example, was and remained gentile territory in spite of Jewish zeal. One of the first reforms that the Roman general Pompey instituted after his conquest of Palestine was to free these east Jordan cities from their irksome bondage to Jerusalem. This is but one example of the artificial and fragile nature of the expanded kingdom of Hyrcanus' two successors. The game had not been worth the candle, and the silly attempt to bring unwilling converts into the Jewish fold was to reap its proper reward.

Jannæus, who had died in the field attempting to bring Ragaba, one of the transjordanian fortresses, into subjection, was succeeded by his widow, Alexandra. She, doughty woman that she was, completed the destruction of the city and then returned to Jerusalem to rule in her husband's stead for nine years (78-69 B.C.). With the aid of the army and the strong outposts established by Jannæus little opposition from outside was to be feared. One crisis occurred, but was weathered successfully. Tigranes of Armenia had made himself master of Syria several years before Jannæus' death and had forced Aretas to withdraw. He apparently had hopes of pushing south into Palestine. Fortunately for Alexandra, however, Lucullus the Roman had become such a menace in his Armenian campaign that Tigranes was compelled to abandon his hopes for further conquest and to turn homeward. Alexandra seems also to have attempted the subjugation of Damascus, but without success.

The most significant aspect of her rule was the change in policy at home. Josephus, with his happy knack of composing appropriate deathbed speeches, recounts that during his fatal illness Jannæus had counselled his wife to seek the favour of the Pharisees who were so hostile to himself. That this was the case is perhaps improbable. Nevertheless, the canny widow, sensing the popular dissatisfaction that had so menaced her husband and had been paralysed but not removed, at once sought to make her position secure through overtures to the opposition. Accordingly, she gave vastly more authority to the local Jerusalem council than it had enjoyed during the previous reigns. In addition to the nobles and priests who had apparently formerly constituted this council, she introduced a new group, the Scribes. Her brother, Simon ben Shetach, a Pharisee, seems to have been her confidant. As a result of these tactful modifications she weathered the storm that must otherwise have broken as soon as the dread figure of Jannæus was removed. Josephus, an ardent Pharisee himself, complacently remarks: "While she governed other peoples . . . the Pharisees governed her,"[30] and again, "So she had indeed the name of the Regent; but the Pharisees had the authority."[31] Schürer[32] and most modern historians accept his statements unqualifiedly. Rather, it would seem to me probable that her policy was not quite so completely passive, but, as suggested above, that she sought to strengthen her precarious position by permitting to a greater degree the voices of her non-imperialistic subjects and by recognizing the scholarly, that is, the scribal, group who had already displaced in the popular eye the less highly educated priests as the real religious leaders of Israel. In consequence of this increased recognition the actual leadership in things religious became confirmed to the Scribes and to their supporters, the Pharisees, so that Josephus might well say, "The Pharisees have the multitude on their side."[33] During these nine years of freedom their leaders achieved the position to which their learning entitled them, and from which they were never displaced. This, however, does

[30] *Wars* 1,5,2.

[31] *Antt.* 13,16,2.

[32] "During these years the Pharisees were the real rulers in the land," *op. cit.,* Div. I, Vol. I, p. 309.

[33] *Antt.* 13,10,6.

not mean that either the Pharisees or the Scribes became the political dictators of Israel, as has often been implied from the statements of Josephus. This period, during which the reins of absolute rule were to a measured degree slackened succeeding the tyrannical Jannæus and preceding the days of the absolute Herod and the later procurators, may well have become idealized in the eyes of later Pharisees. "Under Simon ben Shetach and Queen Salome (*i.e.,* Alexandra)," ran the tradition, "rain fell on the eve of the Sabbath, so that the corns of wheat were as large as kidneys, the barley corns as large as olives, and the lentils like golden denarii; the scribes gathered such corns, and preserved specimens of them in order to show future generations what sin entails."[34]

Since the office of high priest could not be hers, she caused the appointment of her elder son, the weak-minded and thoroughly incompetent Hyrcanus. The younger, Aristobulus, a true son of his father, was occasionally used by the queen as a general, but was kept out of actual power as a dangerous rival. Accordingly, he was obliged to bide his time until he might swing into the saddle. Eventually his time came. All had by no means sympathized with Alexandra's moderation. Prisoners had been released; many who had fled from Jerusalem in terror at the collapse of the rebellion had returned. Customs and traditions had been revived; new educational advances were made. While all this was highly satisfactory to those whose chief delight lay in the law of the Lord, it was highly distasteful to the real supporters of Jannæus and his predecessors. Their lot was made the more unpleasant by the zeal their opponents showed in wreaking whatever vengeance was possible upon their erstwhile war lords. These latter, accordingly, got themselves appointed to the various fortresses through the land.

Alexandra's fatal illness proved her ambitious son's opportunity. The already disgruntled nobles were ready to support him; they were now strategically placed throughout Palestine. Without difficulty he became a most menacing figure overnight. Before the outbreak of actual hostilities Alexandra died and the harmless Hyrcanus II, already high priest, was in nominal command. He was no match for his brother, and was speedily defeated near Jericho and deprived of his twofold position as high priest and king. Quite placidly he retired to the former house of Aristobulus as a private citizen, while his energetic young brother took up his residence in the palace.

At this stage of the story a very important figure comes to prominence, Antipater the Idumean. His father had been military governor of Idumea under Jannæus. To his command the son had succeeded. This man more than any other was responsible for the upset of the Hasmonean dynasty, and by his scheming brought to the Jewish throne its greatest king, his own son, Herod. Antipater was the Richelieu of Palestine. His policy was always to

[34] Ta'anit 23a, quoted by Schürer, *op. cit.,* Div. I, Vol. I, p. 311.

be the directing influence, to hold all the threads in his hand, to be the power behind the throne, but to allow another to sit upon it.

At the victory of Aristobulus he felt the time ripe. Recognizing that Hyrcanus would be far more easily controlled than his impetuous and able brother, he sought to arouse his injured friend to action. Finally he convinced him that his royal brother was plotting his death, flattered his vanity, and prevailed upon him to hasten to Petra, the capital of Aretas the Arabian, from whom he had already received the promise of assistance. Once here, it was easy to persuade Hyrcanus to attempt to regain his position. Aretas promised assistance on condition of the return of twelve cities to the south and east of the Dead Sea which Jannæus had captured. With the strong support of the Arabians Aristobulus was repulsed, many of his followers deserted, and he was forced to retreat to Jerusalem, where he stood siege in the temple, supported loyally by the priestly faction. Eventually the besieged, untrained though their attackers were in besieging a city, must have surrendered had it not been for the intervention of the power before whom Judea was to bow and lose forever her independence—Rome.

Since 88 B.C. Roman legions had been in the East attempting the subjection of Mithradates of Pontus, who had been ever anxious to invade the Roman province of Asia, and of his ofttime ally, Tigranes of Armenia. Although Sulla had defeated Mithradates, the latter had recouped his fortunes, and the struggle had gone on. In 69 B.C. Lucullus had checked the two kings—in the course of this campaign, it will be remembered, he had ended Tigranes' hope of the conquest of Palestine—and had wrested Syria from Tigranes, who had held it since 83 B.C., and had set up Antiochus XIII as nominal king. Shortly after this the direction of eastern affairs was transferred to Pompey, due largely to Cicero's eloquent championing of the bill presented to the Senate by Manilius. To Pompey thus fell the credit of finally crushing the power of Rome's archenemy, Mithradates. This he soon accomplished (66-65 B.C.). He recognized Tigranes' position in Armenia, but refused him Syria, which he organized as a new Roman province. His aim was to extend Roman rule to the Euphrates. In this reorganization he intended to include Palestine as a part of this newly created province, since he considered it virtually a province of the old Seleucid empire which had revolted and had gained temporary freedom. His general, Scaurus, who was in Damascus, saw in the civil war between the two priest-kings, Hyrcanus II and Aristobulus II, his opportunity, and hastened south. Although both sides made overtures to him, he wisely considered it easier to disperse the Arabian rabble than to take Jerusalem by storm. Accordingly, he raised the siege and ordered the Nabateans to leave the territory under the penalty of Rome's wrath. Thus Aristobulus was temporarily reinstated in his position, pending Pompey's arrival and final decision. Apparently Hyrcanus' erstwhile supporters returned their allegiance to Aristobulus, now that Rome had spoken, for Josephus records that after Scaurus' departure Aristobulus "with a great army" dealt the combined forces of his brother and Aretas a crushing defeat at Papyron.[35]

For two years Aristobulus remained undisturbed. Upon Pompey's arrival in Damascus to make definite arrangements for the administration of Palestine both brothers sought him, each to defame the other and to seek his support. Along with them came a third group who did not wish either, but desired the restoration of the hierocracy. This latter protest was the consequence of the growing dissatisfaction with the royal form of government of which the later Hasmoneans with their desire for conquest had given them their fill. The interpretation often put upon their protest that it was due to the fact that the priests had usurped the throne of David and were thus no legitimate kings is quite unfounded.

At the moment Pompey was busy with plans for a campaign against the Nabateans, and accordingly reserved his final decision. Aristobulus now lost whatever chance he may have had of gaining a favourable verdict by leaving Pompey at Dium, whither he had accompanied the Roman legions, and hastening to Alexandrium. This brought matters to a crisis. Pompey at once proceeded against him, and forced him to flee to Jerusalem. Pompey followed. When Aristobulus saw the Roman eagles before his gate his courage failed—so great was the dread of Rome—and coming to Pompey, promised to open the gates. Gabinius, a lieutenant of Pompey's, came to receive the city, but found it ready for resistance. Now only one course was open to Pompey. Summarily arresting Aristobulus, he started the siege of Jerusalem. Through the aid of Hyrcanus' followers the city was gained without bloodshed, but Aristobulus' forces retreated to the temple mount. To gain that meant a three-month siege. Finally, on a Sabbath in the June of 63 B.C. a breach in the temple wall was made, the temple was captured, and in the resulting massacre twelve thousand Jews are said to have lost their lives. Out of curiosity Pompey entered the holy of holies, and to his amazement found it empty.[36] Pompey's act was not one of wanton insult, but nevertheless the Jews never forgave it. The temple treasure remained untouched; next day saw the temple purified and the regular service of worship in full swing. It is an interesting commentary upon the place religion bore in Judaism that during the dreadful days of the siege itself the daily sacrifices had still continued uninterrupted.

Aristobulus and his two sons were sent to Rome to grace Pompey's triumph; Hyrcanus was restored as high priest and as ethnarch of Judea, but the independence of Palestine was forever past. The year 63 B.C. marks the end of

[35] *Wars* 1,6,3; *Antt.* 14,2,3.

[36] This may well account in part for the curious notion which the Romans always seem to have had that the Jews were atheists.

Jewish history. From now on Palestine was a tributary to Rome. Herod the Great and Agrippa might later be styled king; they were simply agents of Rome. Her territory shrank overnight. The important seacoast towns which had been gained at such terrific cost were taken from her and added to the Roman province of Syria. Samaria, the many Hellenistic towns and strongholds in Galilee and especially east of the Jordan, were set free from the hated Jewish yoke of servitude. Only the non-Grecian Idumea was left to the extra-Judean territory. And Judea herself was no longer a kingdom even in name. Hyrcanus now bore the title ethnarch, not king, and was responsible for good order to the Roman governor of the province of Syria

All this was in line with Rome's sensible *laissez faire* policy for the administration of her provinces. With actual local governments she never sought to interfere. Her aim was to have strong and steady control, and she realized this could usually be best accomplished by native princes who knew and understood the peculiarities of their own peoples. Accordingly, Pompey's arrangement was a distinct blessing to the peoples of the East. Jewish pride and desire for domain were offended, but the instability and top-heaviness of such a kingdom as Jannæus' gave way to a solid and common-sense administration. The regions which Jerusalem had lost were not Jewish, but predominantly gentile. There could never be peace so long as these unnatural and decidedly arbitrary conditions remained. The petty princes of Syria who had appeared as a consequence of the crumbling of the Seleucid empire and the ambitious sheiks like Aretas now gave way to a firm administration of the peace.

Chapter III

THE RISE AND RULE OF HEROD

For several years after Pompey's departure peace reigned in Palestine. The conquest had been a blessing, since it had introduced a strong hand to hold all over-ambitious princes in order. Hyrcanus II was now both high priest and ethnarch, under the general oversight of the governor of Syria. The real power, however, lay in the hands of his able and ambitious self-appointed adviser, Antipater, who had emerged from the débâcle with increased strength, and whose policy—later to be followed scrupulously by his son Herod—was: keep in favour with Rome, and in Rome stand always with the victor.

The dashing of the hopes of Aristobulus and his following of swaggering aristocrats was highly satisfactory to the Pharisees and their sympathizers. To be sure, they had lost their freedom, but their political interest was never large and had been more or less thrust upon them. Their general attitude is expressed by the ideal: "Love work, eschew domination, and hold aloof from the civil power."[1] They were well rid of the hated Hasmonean line. No high priest with hands reeking with the unholy blood of conquest would again sacrifice at the altar. The nation had once again been chastened for her sin. This attitude is well seen in a psalm coming from this period:

God laid bare their sins in the sight of the sun; all the earth hath learned the righteous judgments of God. . . . The holy things of God they took for spoil; and there was no inheritor to deliver out of their hand. They went up to the altar of the Lord when they were full of all uncleanness; yea, even in their separation they polluted the sacrifices, eating them like profane meats. They left not a sin undone, wherein they offended not above the heathen. For this cause did God mingle for them a spirit of error, he made them to drink of the cup of unmixed wine until they were drunken. He brought him that is from the utmost part of the earth, whose stroke is mighty; he decreed war against Jerusalem and her land. The princes of the land met him with joy; they said unto him, Blessed is thy path! come ye, enter in with peace. They made the rough paths even before their entering in, they opened the gates that led into Jerusalem; her walls they crowned with garlands. He entered in, as a father entereth into his sons' house, in peace. He established his feet and made them very firm. He occupied her strongholds, yea, and the wall of Jerusalem. For God led him in safety, because of their blindness. He cut off their princes and every wise councillor; he poured out the blood of the dwellers in Jerusalem like the water of uncleanness, he carried away their

[1] Abot 1,10.

sons and their daughters whom they had begotten in their defilement. They had done according to their uncleanness, even as their fathers did, they polluted Jerusalem and the things that had been dedicated unto the name of God.[2]

Although many of the liberated cities in Palestine reckoned their independence from the year of Pompey's conquest, and the Pharisees and their followers rejoiced in the collapse of the Hasmonean line, this sentiment was by no means universal in Judea. Much as they honoured the Scribes, they prized their freedom higher. The fact of being once again a subject nation was galling, although Rome's demands were not excessive. This dissatisfaction was naturally fanned by the war party of Jannæus and Aristobulus. The result was that party strife was forgotten; Rome was seen as the common foe.

For five or six years there seems to have been no overt acts. Scaurus and his two successors in Syria, Marcius Philippus and Lentulus Marcellinus, were involved in intermittent warfare with the Arabians, but Palestine seems to have been comparatively quiet. But following these years of quiet came five years (57-52 B.C.) of rebellion with no less than four distinct revolts. Aristobulus and his family had not been executed by Pompey, but had been sent to Rome to grace the latter's triumph. There they had been settled on the right bank of the Tiber. The elder son, Alexander, however, had escaped and finally made his appearance in Palestine. Getting together a force of some ten thousand of his disgruntled fellow-patriots, he made an ill-omened attempt to regain the throne. Hyrcanus was powerless, but Gabinius, who had been sent to Syria a few months before, quickly put down the insurrection, and to avoid similar outbreaks sought to destroy the spirit of national unity by dividing the Jewish territory into five mutually independent districts, with Jerusalem, Jericho, Gazara, Amathus, and Sepphoris the respective centres, each with its own council. Hyrcanus was deprived of the little civil authority he had formerly had. The land was thus actually a part of Syria. The two succeeding years each saw another fruitless attempt—the first led by Aristobulus and his second son, Antigonus (56 B.C.), the second by Alexander (55 B.C.). Both attempts were but flashes in the pan, but they had one highly significant result, increased prestige for the ambitious Idumean, Antipater.

During the whole period Antipater had been playing his cards well. First of all, he had been of decided help to Scaurus in his campaign against the Nabateans which Pompey had earlier planned. Then in these insurrections he had aided Gabinius so wholeheartedly and efficiently that he became the Roman governor's chief adviser in Judea. Apparently as a reward for loyalty Gabinius at this time reappointed Hyrcanus ethnarch at the request of Antipater, but the real power was in the hands of his minister. Never did the latter make the mistake of trying to thrust himself to the fore. Though in

[2] Psalms of Solomon 8:8-26 (ed. Ryle and James).

complete control, his deference and courtesy to his master were scrupulously maintained.

The fourth of these revolts was the result of Rome's own greed. The famous triumvirate—Pompey, Cæsar, and Crassus—was now in control. To Crassus, following his consulship of 55 B.C., fell Syria, where he hoped to gain military glory by taking Mesopotamia from the Parthians. Such an expedition required money. In shameful violation of his word he stripped the Jerusalem temple of its treasure, a deed which both Pompey and Gabinius had shunned, although the latter had exacted heavy tribute. This act fanned the popular hatred to a fury which Crassus' death in Parthia the next year (53 B.C.) did not abate. On the return of Cassius, his lieutenant and successor, strong measures were necessary to put down the revolt which had broken out. This time the moving figure was neither Aristobulus nor his sons, but one of their henchmen, Pitholaus. This fourth uprising came to a sorry end near Tarichеæ on the Sea of Galilee; Pitholaus was executed at the request of Antipater, and thirty thousand of his followers are said to have been sold into slavery.[3]

Shortly after came the dreadful period of civil war in Rome. It is impossible to overemphasize its significance. As Schürer acutely remarks: "From Cæsar's crossing the Rubicon down to the death of Antony, B.C. 49-30, the whole Roman history was reflected in the history of Syria and also in that of Palestine."[4] The death of Crassus had dissolved the triumvirate; the long series of disagreements between Pompey and Cæsar came finally to a head. Rome was too small a place for them both. The Senate decreed that Cæsar must retire from office on July 1 or be declared a public enemy. Mark Antony, Cæsar's friend then tribune, vetoed the bill. Cicero sought a compromise. It was of no avail. A week later the Senate passed its famous "last decree," throwing the government into the hands of the military power in spite of the tribune's veto. Cæsar no longer delayed, but crossed the Rubicon[5] onto Italian soil and proceeded at once against Rome.

In Palestine Antipater continued on the side of his erstwhile patron, Pompey, as did all the East. At first it looked ominous for him, for one of Cæsar's first acts was to aid Aristobulus to regain Palestine in order to hamper Pompey. This danger was averted since Aristobulus was poisoned before he could leave Rome, and his son Alexander was beheaded in Antioch. Pompey's star was setting. Within sixty days Cæsar had become master of Italy; then following his brief campaign in Spain he hastened into Greece. The two armies finally joined battle on the plains of Thessaly near Pharsalia, Aug. 9, 48. Pompey's army, though twice the size of his rival's, was no match for the veterans who had so often routed hordes vastly greater than their own,

Caesar's Army meets Pompey's

[3] Josephus, *Antt.* 14,7,3; *Wars* 1,8,9.

[4] *Op. cit.*, Div. 1, Vol. 1, p. 376.

[5] For the account of this dramatic incident with the famous words: "The die is cast," see Plutarch, *Cæsar* 32.

and was utterly defeated. Pompey fled to Egypt and soon was murdered by the treacherous Egyptians, who feared that they would be drawn into the conflict.

In this crisis Antipater at once changed sides, and made himself extremely valuable to his next patron. Not only did he give most efficient assistance to Cæsar's ally, Mithradates of Pergamum, at Ascalon, as the latter was hastening to Egypt to aid him, but he actually saved the day for Cæsar in Alexandria, by relieving him in the nick of time from the attack of the Egyptian mob. Furthermore, he was able to win the large Jewish population of Alexandria to Cæsar's side. For all this Cæsar was grateful. The divisions of Gabinius were abolished; the claims of Aristobulus' younger son, Antigonus, were contemptuously dismissed; Hyrcanus was confirmed in his position as hereditary high priest, reëstablished ethnarch of Judea, and elevated to senatorial rank; Antipater became authorized as Hyrcanus' prime minister, was granted Roman citizenship, and freed from tribute. Once more Jerusalem became the capital of the land and Jews were again in control of Jewish affairs. To be sure, the boundaries were not extended to embrace the territory gained by John Hyrcanus and his two sons, for the Greek cities retained their freedom. But the rich Esdraelon plain and, even better, the seaport Joppa were returned; Jerusalem's walls, demolished by Pompey, were now rebuilt. In addition to this, Jews were exempted from military service in the Roman legions and their religious prejudices were respected. Cæsar's assassination three years later (44 B.C.) was a source of genuine sorrow throughout all Jewry.

Shortly after Cæsar's departure from Syria, where he had acted the munificent patron of Antipater, another figure destined to play an important rôle in the history of the Jews makes his appearance. This was Herod, the younger son of the crafty Antipater.

Firmly established in favour with Cæsar, Antipater made it perfectly clear that if the nationalists sought to displace him they would bring upon themselves the wrath of Rome as well as that of himself and Hyrcanus. Further to strengthen his position he appointed his two sons, Phasaël and Herod, governors of Judea and Galilee, respectively. It is upon the latter that our interest is centred. No more ideal spot for the imperious young Idumean—he was but twenty-five at the time of his appointment—could be conceived. Galilee was a turbulent place, seething with discontent. Its past history had made it largely gentile. Centuries before, at the time of the fall of the northern kingdom, it had been colonized from the East. In the early days of the Maccabean uprising the bulk of the remaining Jews had been withdrawn to the south by Simon. Later it had been conquered by Aristobulus and Jannæus, and perhaps also, as we have seen, by John Hyrcanus. Yet distinct from some of the conquered territory it had become distinctly Jewish. As is often the case, the new converts seem to have exhibited an enthusiasm immature but almost fanatic in its intensity. As we shall see, this district was to remain the hotbed of incipient rebellion. At once Herod found himself in conflict with a group headed by Hezekiah. Josephus, with his pro-Roman interests and the desire to minimize all Jewish opposition to the empire, gives a one-sided picture of this group, which he dismisses as a band of robbers. Herod inflicted drastic punishment upon them, and executed the ringleader, Hezekiah, along with many of his followers. Instead of being rejoiced to see the outlaws discomfited, the Sanhedrin in Jerusalem prevailed upon Hyrcanus to summon the young leader to account. Although at first abashed by his appearance—he came as no penitent—the council started proceedings against him. Hyrcanus, however, warned by Sextus Cæsar, the governor of Syria, adjourned the council and urged Herod to flee. On his return to Galilee he was appointed by Sextus military governor of Cœle-Syria. All of this reveals that the group in Galilee was certainly no mere group of mountain brigands, but militant nationalists who saw in Antipater and his sons the actual representatives of the hated Rome. Not only Sextus' championing and later rewarding Herod for crushing them, but also the attitude of the Sanhedrin in seeking to punish Herod for his drastic actions—the claim was that they alone were empowered to pronounce the death sentence—becomes intelligible. The affair nearly had disastrous consequences. Determined to wipe out the disgrace he had suffered at the hand of the Sanhedrin, Herod soon returned with an armed force, and but for the pleas of his father and brother would have ousted Hyrcanus. Thus the only result of the Sanhedrin's action was to seat Antipater and his sons the more securely in the saddle. But fresh difficulties soon arose.

Two years later, on the ides of March (44 B.C.) Cæsar was assassinated. Cassius, one of the conspirators, fled to Syria. Indeed, shortly before his death Cæsar had himself appointed him to be governor of this province which he had defended so successfully against the Parthians a few years before. Soon he made himself master of the province, gained the support of the legions of Cæcilius Bassus, an erstwhile supporter of Pompey, who had wrested Syria from Sextus Cæsar in the spring of 46, and thus had forestalled his rival Dolabella, whom Antony had contrived to have appointed.

For the maintenance of his army money was necessary. From Judea seven hundred talents were demanded, and when Emmaus, Lydda, Gophna, and Thamne failed to contribute their share, the luckless inhabitants were sold as slaves. Seeing the way the wind blew, Herod threw in his lot with Cassius, aided him in collecting the tribute, and for his zeal was confirmed in his office as governor of Cœle-Syria.

A few months later an unhappy circumstance contrived to thrust him even more to the front. Antipater was murdered through the cunning of a certain Malichus, who apparently hoped to supplant him. Herod with the aid of his brother and the connivance of Cassius avenged his father's death.

Now Judea, too, was in the hands of Herod, for while at the departure of Cassius there had been incipient rebellion, incited by Antigonus, the two sons of Antipater had triumphed although apparently at the loss of some territory in Galilee. About this time Herod sought to strengthen his position by becoming betrothed to Mariamne, the daughter of Alexander and thus the granddaughter of both Hyrcanus and Aristobulus. Though the marriage did not take place for five years, the alliance tended to make his position less obnoxious to Jewish sensibilities.

Once more came fresh complications and the need of changing sides. Cassius had joined his fellow conspirator, Brutus, and with him had proceeded to Macedon. In the late autumn of 42 B.C. they had met the combined forces of Antony and Octavian at Philippi and after the hopeless rout had committed suicide. To the victors belonged the spoils. Octavian took the West; Antony became absolute master of the Roman East, and with it, of course, Syria. This might well have spelled disaster for Herod, and so his enemies hoped. No less than three delegations for the purpose of defaming Herod were sent to Antony during his leisurely march to Egypt (41 B.C.). They were quite unsuccessful. Antony had been an intimate friend of Antipater's during his campaigns under Gabinius, and well knew the effective support he could count on from his able son. Furthermore, Hyrcanus had himself championed the claims of Herod and Phasaël. As a consequence, Antony disregarded the attacks, overlooked the fact that Herod had supported Cassius, and appointed him and Phasaël tetrarchs with full political power. Hyrcanus remained high priest; his political power had, however, passed to the sons of his former minister.

The one force in the East which Rome feared was Parthia, and not without reason. During his stay in Syria Cassius had entered into negotiations with them to aid him against the partisans of Cæsar. Now while Antony was disporting himself with Cleopatra in Egypt their menace had become real. Pacorus of Parthia, incited and aided by the fugitive Titus Labienus, had crossed the Euphrates and gained possession of Syria. Antigonus, the arch-enemy of Herod, seized this opportunity for his own advantage. Supported by many disgruntled Jews, he proceeded against Herod and Phasaël, having previously entered into negotiations with Pacorus for the latter's support. Soon the Parthians arrived. By trickery they got possession of Hyrcanus and Phasaël, who too late awoke to the fact that the invaders were but creatures of Antigonus. The only course open to Herod was flight. Leaving his family in the fortress on Masada, he first turned for help to Petra. But the Arabian king, fearing the Parthians, would not receive him. In disappointment Herod hastened to Alexandria to his master, Antony. Here again he was disappointed. Finally alarmed by affairs in Syria, Antony had stopped his love-making and had hastened to Tyre, one of the few cities that had remained loyal. But here word reached him that his presence in Rome was imperative.

His wife Fulvia—according to Plutarch, in order to stir up such a commotion that her wandering spouse must return—had precipitated a crisis between himself and Octavian. With two hundred ships he hastened to Rome. Though a civil war now seemed imminent, mutual friends of Antony and Octavian succeeded in patching up a peace. This was made the easier since Fulvia had opportunely died, thus making a marriage between Antony and Octavian's sister, Octavia, possible. To her credit, it may be remarked in passing, for three years Octavia kept her husband in Athens, where with commendable zeal he attended to his duties without dallying with the siren of the Nile.

Disappointed at not finding his patron in Alexandria, Herod had refused Cleopatra's offer to command an expedition of hers, and had set sail for Rome. He arrived in the nick of time (40 B.C.). Antony and Octavian, once more friends, were parcelling out the Roman world. Herod had little difficulty in enlisting their aid, for both realized his ability. He would be a loyal ally against Antigonus who had not only aided the Parthians but was flouting Roman authority by his royal claims. Within seven days after his arrival in Rome as a fugitive Herod had left it again, having heard himself lauded in the Senate and, best of all, having received the title "King of the Jews." All that he needed now was his kingdom!

Early in the spring of 39 B.C. Herod arrived in Ptolemaïs with the intention of making his new title a reality. He soon found his task was to be a very difficult one. During his months of absence the rebellion had increased. Antigonus was established in Jerusalem with the title high priest and king; Phasaël had committed suicide; Hyrcanus had been deprived of his ears by Antigonus to render him for ever ineligible to the sacred office[6]—one account of this deed was that Antigonus had actually bitten them off with his own teeth!—and had been carried off as a prisoner to Parthia by the departing allies of the newly established king. To be sure, Ventidius, who had been sent by Antony to the East to take the place of Decidius Saxa, who had fallen before Labienus, had driven Labienus and his Parthian troops back to Taurus, and thus had become master of Syria and Palestine (39 B.C.). Antigonus had been forced to pay a heavy tribute, but had not been displaced.

Herod's position was difficult, but hardly desperate. He proceeded at once to Galilee, got together an army, and with nominal help from Silo, the lieutenant of Ventidius, took Joppa, hastened to Masada, where his relations were hard pressed by the enemy, relieved them in the nick of time, and proceeded to Jerusalem. Had he had any real support from the Romans, he would probably have succeeded. This, however, he did not receive. Silo, as a result of bribes from Antigonus, suddenly refused to

[6] Lev. 21:16-24.

continue the campaign, although victory was about in their hands, and insisted upon going into winter quarters. In disgust, Herod, obliged to postpone his plans for the capture of Jerusalem, sent his brother Joseph against the Idumeans, and himself hastened to Galilee. Soon Sepphoris was his. After a lively campaign against the insurrectionists who had retreated to inaccessible caves—the whole dramatic account is vividly told by Josephus[7]—he succeeded in subduing Galilee.

Early in the next year (38 B.C.) Ventidius had been obliged to check a new invasion by the Parthians. In this he was successful. Pacorus, who with Labienus had been the moving spirit, was slain, and Ventidius now felt free to move against Antiochus of Commagene, whom he besieged in Samosata. During this time Herod had received no help from Rome. To be sure, just before leaving for his campaign against Antiochus, Ventidius had sent Herod a force under Macheras. The latter was, if anything, worse than Silo and yielded to Antigonus' bribes. In disgust Herod decided the time had come for action. Antony himself was now at Samosata, directing the siege. To him Herod determined to go. Disregarding the plea of the faithless Macheras, who apparently dreaded Antony's wrath, Herod departed, was cordially welcomed by Antony, and returned with the assurance, this time actually fulfilled, that he should receive real assistance. When Herod reached Syrian Antioch bad news awaited him: his brother Joseph had disregarded his explicit instruction and had been slain near Jericho; in Galilee the insurrectionists had again risen, had regained the territory, and had drowned many of Herod's supporters in the lake. Herod did not delay. With two Roman legions and the promise that Sosius—the successor of Ventidius—would himself speedily follow, he hastened south, regained Galilee, and pushed into Judea. After an indecisive battle near Jericho he destroyed Antigonus' force under Pappus at Isanas, and, had it not now become necessary to postpone further operations on account of the approach of winter, would have marched at once against the demoralized Antigonus in Jerusalem.

With the advent of spring he prepared for the siege, and then, perhaps as a foretaste of his coming victory, left his army to go to Samaria to consummate the marriage with Mariamne, contracted nearly five years before. It was an opportune time, for Sosius, though on the march, had not arrived. On his return to his army, Herod started the siege in earnest with the efficient aid of Sosius and his strong forces. Within two months the first two walls had been taken—the attack, of course, was from the north—but the upper city and temple court were still in the hands of Antigonus. Although there could be but one outcome, the besieged fought with a fury almost fanatic. As Wellhausen well remarked, "It was actually less faith than hate which inspired the Jews and blinded their eyes to the obvious madness of opposition

[7] *Antt.* 14,15,5; *Wars* 1,16,4.

to the superior power."[8] Soon came the end; the temple area was theirs. Infuriated by the mad resistance of the city, both the Romans and Herod's forces started a carnival of blood. Antigonus in terror came out of his hiding-place and threw himself a suppliant at the feet of Sosius. The sneering Roman with the gibe, "Antigone," put him in chains. For a time Herod must have feared the victory would be more costly than defeat. He did not want his capital destroyed, nor did he desire to add unnecessary fuel to the hatred of his subjects. Well did he realize the consequences of the earlier siege when Pompey had entered the holy of holies. This must at all costs be prevented. Finally he prevailed; the temple was saved, and the looting ceased, although to attain the latter, Herod had to promise to indemnify from his own purse the soldiers for the spoils which were rightly theirs. In fact, all through the siege—and, for that matter, through his entire reign—Herod seems always to have sought in a blunderbuss fashion to placate his people who would not be placated. Just before the temple fell he had allowed animals to be taken in to the enemy on the false plea that they were necessary for sacrifice.

Finally the Romans left the city and returned to meet Antony at Antioch. Antigonus went as a captive. Herod took no chances. Remembering the civil strife which Aristobulus and his two sons had fomented after they had been carried to Rome by Pompey, he had no desire to see such history repeated. He prevailed upon Antony to end the danger. In answer to his request the head of Antigonus fell beneath the ax of the Roman executioner.

And thus did the government of the Asmoneans cease, a hundred and twenty-six years after it was first set up. This family was a splendid and an illustrious one, both on account of the nobility of their stock and of the dignity of the high-priesthood, as also for the glorious actions their ancestors had performed for our nation: but these men lost the government by their dissensions one with another, and it came to Herod, the son of Antipater, who was of no more than a vulgar family, and of no eminent extraction, but one that was subject to other kings. And this is what history tells us was the end of the Asmonean family.[9]

Herod, like his father Antipater before him, had ruled in the name of Hyrcanus. This was, however, in the past. Now not only was he actually king, but called himself so. The act of the Senate three years before had become fact. He was one of the *reges socii*, a king who owed his coronet to Rome, and kept it only as long as pleased her. He need pay no tribute, but must provide troops in time of war. He might keep an army, but it must not be so large as to arouse suspicion that he was seeking to cut loose from the empire. He might coin money. Herod, curiously enough, although enjoying Augustus' favour and confidence, seems to have been restricted to copper. The one paramount requirement—and no excuses for failure were ever ac-

[8] *Israelitische und Jüdische Geschichte,* p. 303.
[9] Josephus, *Antt.* 14,16,4.

cepted—was that he administer his territory efficiently and keep the peace. And this Herod did. For more than thirty years Herod administered his district so efficiently that not only did he continue in favour at Rome, but received large accessions of land. In fact, not only did he rule a territory larger than had ever before been subject to Jerusalem, but he was, in spite of the oft-expressed contempt of the disgruntled Jerusalem nobility for this "insolent king who is not of the race of the priests," far and away the most able and competent ruler the Jews ever had. His reign has been compared with that of Solomon. Actually it far surpassed it. His borders were again and again extended, and the newly added districts were put in thorough order. But his was not so much an age of conquest as of building. Though an Idumean by birth, he was in spirit a Hellenist. He did not make the mistake of striving to thrust Hellenism down his people's throat, as had Antiochus Epiphanes. Nevertheless, he introduced it in no less degree. Theatres, amphitheatres, chariot races, gladiatorial shows, games—all these made their appearance. Not only within his borders but as far west as Athens and Rome evidences of his lavish hand and purse were to be found.

To understand Herod it is necessary to observe that his political life was an ellipse: the two foci were Herod and Rome.

Herod made no initial false gesture of conciliation. Forty-five nobles of Antigonus' court were summarily executed and their wealth confiscated. The advent of Herod meant the downfall of the Sadducees, who had become more and more the dominant factor in Jewish politics. They might and did continue to exert an influence, but they had received their deathblow, and their numbers rapidly dwindled. When the new Sanhedrin convened, it soon found itself shorn of most of its power; not until after the deposition of Archelaus did it again become a dominant force in Jewish politics. Nor did the other leading party, the Pharisees, fare much better; although always inclined as they were to "hold aloof from the civil power," they came into less conflict and accordingly suffered less loss than did their rivals. It is unwise to over-emphasize the fact that Pollio the Pharisee and his disciple Sameas advised the besieged to open the gates to Herod. This they probably did, and it is not unlikely that others of their group assented, but not because of any affection for Herod. Rather, they apparently saw in him the scourge of God, the opponent of Antigonus and the Sadducaic aristocracy. Once more it was the old story of bitter opposition to the incestuous marriage of religion and politics. If David might not even build a temple to God since he was a man of war with hands stained by blood, how much less tolerable was it when those who claimed to be his successors and occupied his throne dared to usurp the holy garments and minister in the temple! With the death of Antigonus this outrage was never repeated, for the gentile Herod could not become high priest.

This brings us to the crux of his difficulties. First, last, and all the time

Herod's chief trouble lay with the women of his acquaintance. Three of them ultimately caused his downfall. Of these three one hated him with cold and calculating intensity; one blew now hot, now cold; one passionately loved him. They were respectively his mother-in-law, Alexandra, proud Hasmonean princess and daughter of the exiled Hyrcanus; Cleopatra of Egypt, who stole his choicest lands and sought to entice him into adultery with her; and Salome, his unscrupulous but devoted sister.

When Herod married Mariamne during the siege of Jerusalem, he was brought into a somewhat more friendly relationship with the Hasmonean line. After all, he had always shown the highest respect for Hyrcanus II and had protected him against his younger brother and the latter's son. Now he brought the old man back to Jerusalem—the Parthians had long since freed him from actual bondage and allowed him to live comfortably in Babylon—and showed him the greatest deference. Since, however, the old man had lost his ears, he could not resume his sacerdotal office. In his place Herod appointed an obscure Babylonian priest, Ananel, making the choice apparently to avoid the danger of giving such authority to the none too friendly Jerusalem hierarchy.

Alexandra realized perfectly that, in spite of his deference to her father, Herod had effectively overthrown the dynasty of her house. Her wrath was all the more intense because her seventeen-year-old son, Aristobulus, had not succeeded his grandfather as high priest. At once she sought to enlist the aid of Cleopatra, who had the ear of Antony. Cleopatra, who was trying to oust Herod and gain his territory, was willing. Herod sensed his danger and effectively checked it. Deposing Ananel, he installed his wife's brother. This sealed the youth's doom, for he had now become a real menace to Herod. A strict watch was set on Alexandra. Finding this irksome, she attempted to flee with her son to Cleopatra, but the scheme miscarried. In his first year of office the young high priest was drowned at Jericho, where he had retreated after officiating at the Feast of Tabernacles (35 B.C.). Although Herod expressed the keenest grief at the tragedy, Alexandra was not deceived. Through Cleopatra's help she got Antony to summon Herod to account for the murder.

Herod was in suspense. Well did he know the hatred of Alexandra and her friends; Cleopatra, too, was only too eager to accomplish his downfall and would spare no pains to insure his disgrace with Antony. It was with heavy heart that Herod left for Laodicea. Just prior to his departure he made his uncle Joseph, who chanced also to be Salome's husband, regent and instructed him, should the worst occur, to slay Mariamne lest she fall into the hands of another man.

Contrary to his fears, he was exonerated by Antony. The opposite report, however, came to Jerusalem. Just as Alexandra had persuaded Joseph to let her and Mariamne flee to a near-by Roman garrison, another report, this time favourable, came, and the scheme for flight fell through. On Herod's return his sister Salome informed him of the plan, and further to prejudice him against Mariamne—for the proud Salome hated the beautiful queen because of the latter's thinly veiled contempt for "the Idumean woman"—charged Mariamne with adultery with Joseph. At first, Herod disbelieved it; later, learning that Mariamne knew of his command to Joseph, he refused to believe that it had been told merely to show the queen how her husband loved her, and summarily executed Joseph, but permitted his wife to live.

Though Cleopatra had not succeeded in ousting Herod, she received shortly after nearly all the Palestinian seacoast, a large grant of land in Arabia, and, worst of all, Herod's prize possessions, the district around Jericho rich with palm and balsam, and the salt and pitch rights. Herod thus had to lease back from her his own lands and collect—or pay himself—the corresponding fees from Malichus the Arabian. This lavish series of gifts was but part of Antony's madness. In 37 B.C. the triumvirate—Antony, Octavian, and Lepidus—had been renewed for five years. Shortly after, Lepidus had been ousted by Octavian, and Antony, forgetting his good resolution, left Octavia and returned to Cleopatra. Matters went from bad to worse. He sought to make Alexandria his capital, celebrated a triumph there to the scandal of the Romans, gave his mistress—he now posed as her husband—not only the districts already mentioned but other Roman domains, including Cyprus and Cilicia, on the absurd claim that they had formerly belonged to the Ptolemies, and even bestowed the title "kings" upon the two sons he had had by Cleopatra, settling by secret will certain provinces over which they should reign. Octavian got wind of this; the secret will was opened and the treason came to light.

Since the end of the five-year period was now at hand (32 B.C.), the Senate intervened; Octavian, who had brought the West into peace and quiet, felt the time was ripe, and bitterly denounced his erstwhile associate. The next year, Cleopatra was formally proclaimed a public enemy and war was declared. The decisive battle was at Actium (31 B.C.). Octavian was victor. Cleopatra's ships fled in the midst of the encounter, and Antony, demoralized by this defection, soon followed. During the next few months Cleopatra played her trumps. She sought to ingratiate herself with Octavian, but learning that she was to be exhibited in Rome at his triumph, she committed suicide, as had Antony a short time before. The West had again conquered. Octavian was in the seats of the mighty.

This downfall of Antony might well have spelled doom for Herod. He had not been personally involved, for, though he had wanted to come to Antony's assistance, Cleopatra had prevented it. She had forced him to go against the Nabatean Arabs to collect her taxes. Her desire was twofold: first, to prevent Herod from establishing further claim upon the gratitude of Antony; second, she hoped that by embroiling Herod and the Arabs to wear them both out and to appropriate their domains. To further this scheme she actually aided Malichus. Her plans, however, totally miscarried. Herod was successful. Antony, whom she had confidently expected to triumph, was routed. The one man upon whose fidelity Antony had counted was prevented thus from aiding him. Herod saw the collapse of Antony with horror. He is said to have counselled him to cut himself loose from Cleopatra and to try again. When Antony refused, Herod wisely decided to quit before it was too late. As he had turned from Pompey to Cæsar after Pharsalia (48 B.C.), to Cassius after Cæsar's assassination (44 B.C.), to Antony after Philippi (42 B.C.), so now he switched allegiance to Octavian and gave most efficient aid to Didius, governor of Syria, in preventing a company of Antony's gladiators from sailing from Cyzicus to Egypt to the aid of their now desperate master.

Now Herod wants to go to Octavian at Rhodes. Two preliminary steps were necessary. The aged Hyrcanus was executed. Most historians roundly condemn Herod for this act. To be sure, Hyrcanus was an inoffensive old man whose whole life had been one long tragedy, forced as he had been into the political limelight against his will; yet he could be a very real danger in the hands of the unscrupulous Alexandra at such a critical hour. If we cannot applaud, we can at least appreciate Herod's dilemma. The other task involved his wife Mariamne. The story is told that again he gave secret instruction—this time to Sohemus—to slay the queen should Herod fail with Octavian. This command with its sequel is so similar to the earlier incident that many consider it a doublet.

Now Herod appears before Octavian; he proudly admits his earlier loyalty to Antony. Will Octavian receive him as a supporter? Indeed yes. Octavian confirms him in his rank. A little later, as Octavian proceeded to Egypt to complete the destruction of Antony, Herod showed him the greatest attention. Then a few months later came the glad news. Octavian was supreme; Antony and Cleopatra had both committed suicide (Aug., 30 B.C.). Herod's wise choice had been justified. He hastened to Egypt, proffered his felicitations; they were graciously accepted and rewarded. His rich lands around Jericho were returned, the Phœnician seacoast and the cities of Gadara, Samaria, and Hippos were granted him. Thus the whole overturn of Roman politics had been greatly to Herod's advantage. In the place of Antony, fast coasting to destruction, stood the popular Octavian, hailed as the saviour of the world. And Cleopatra, always a thorn in his side and a real menace, was removed. With hopes high, Herod returned to Jerusalem from Antioch, whither he had gratefully accompanied his munificent patron.

On his arrival home his joy turned to gloom. His beloved Mariamne showed no joy at his success; on the contrary, she openly reproached him for the murder of her grandfather and brother and made it perfectly clear that her love for him was past. This was a bitter disappointment to the proud king. Though at a later date he had nine wives living side by side in his palace and turning it into a perfect Bedlam with their plots and jealousies, during Mariamne's life there was no rival. Even Doris, his first wife, and her son Antipater, had been dismissed. Salome, however, was overjoyed at the rupture and did all in her power to bring it to a crisis to rid the palace of the presence of this coldly disdainful favourite. Soon she succeeded. She bribed Herod's cupbearer to say that Mariamne had prepared a poison drink for her husband; the queen's eunuch confessed under torture that his mistress hated the king because she knew of the secret word to Sohemus. Herod was convinced of his queen's unfaithfulness, and soon both the indiscreet minister and the lovely Hasmonean were executed (29 B.C.).

For several months it seemed as if Herod's star had set. Forgetting his cares of state, he sought to drown his grief in hunting and drinking. Soon he fell sick in Samaria, and word came to Jerusalem that he was dying. Alexandra felt the time had come to rid herself of her detested son-in-law. To achieve this end she sought to get control of the two citadels in Jerusalem. Word came to Herod. Sick though he was, he roused himself; all his grief and remorse changed to wild rage against this detestable woman whose plottings had brought him so often to destruction's door. The pleasure of her execution (28 B.C.) was far more effective than the doctor's physic in restoring Herod's strength and reason.

Two years later the last step in rooting out possible rivals was taken. The incident is worth telling, for it gives a good picture of the plots and counterplots in the Herodian court during these early years. Following the disgrace and execution of Joseph, Herod had appointed Costobarus, an Idumean, as governor of Idumea (34 B.C.). Not only was Costobarus Joseph's political successor; he, too, married Salome. In his first years of office he had sought to weaken his patron's power by negotiations with Cleopatra. Although Herod had learned of it, Salome had persuaded her brother to forgive the treason. Now, however, Salome had tired of her husband and sought to rid herself of him. She told Herod that her husband had hid and protected the two young sons of Babas, distant kin of the Hasmoneans, whom Herod had sought for in vain. Costobarus, she said, had never given up his plan to gain Idumea for himself. These two youths were to be his tools. With the death of the treacherous Costobarus and the two princes whose existence had always been a source of apprehension for Herod, he felt at last free from outside danger.

> There were now none at all left of the kindred of Hyrcanus; and the kingdom was entirely in Herod's own power, and there was nobody remaining of such dignity as could put a stop to what he did against the Jewish laws.[10]

Now with Herod firmly established on his throne we must look for the

[10] *Antt.* 15,7,10 (end).

moment to Rome to see what was happening there, for the history of Herod—save for the sinister family disorder of his last years—is but a miniature of that of Augustus.

Julius Cæsar had been assassinated—Shakespeare to the contrary notwithstanding—for his imperial longings. Octavian had them in a lesser degree, but was wise enough to study the causes of his uncle's downfall. Since the end of the second triumvirate in 32 B.C. his power had rested on no constitutional basis, but rather upon his prestige, his annual consulship, and the readiness of the Senate to grant him whatever he wished.

Finally in 27 B.C. he declared that it was his wish that the republic be restored; laid down voluntarily the extraordinary powers he had received, including command of the armies and control of the provinces; and signified that the Senate was now supreme. At once the Senate voted him proconsular power over all the frontier provinces which required armed support, voted him the name Augustus with the title, *princeps senatus,* and changed the name of the month *Sextilis* to *Augustus* in his honour. Thus his position was secure. He had surrendered all claims to dictatorship, had disabused all fear that he desired to restore the hated kingdom, and had secured in a most regular and legal fashion command of the army.[11] Apparently sincere in his wish that the Senate become the responsible body, he left Rome for the West and it was not until 24 B.C. that he returned. The Senate in the meanwhile had shown itself incapable of independent action—their almost invariable answer to his every request was that his will was law without their action. During his absence his fellow-consul Murenas had plotted to remove him. Accordingly, his return saw drastic changes. Resigning his perennial consulship, he received the *tribunicia potestas* for life. Now he was doubly fortified. The Senate's grant in 27 B.C. assured him control of the standing army through his proconsular authority over the frontier provinces; the people had now invested him with the control of legislation and the veto. The net result was that he held all the reins of authority in his own hand, yet without the onus of having stolen prestige from the Senate. Thus the term "dyarchy" is more apt than "monarchy."

This access of power was especially applauded by the provinces, which rightly preferred a strong ruler like Augustus to the rival cliques in the Senate and the irresponsible magistrates who regularly had retired from their short tenures of office with ill-gotten fortunes. A full discussion of the new arrangements for provincial administration may be reserved for a later chapter. Here it may suffice to say that Augustus had no intention of carrying out Cæsar's and Antony's scheme of an empire extending beyond the Euphrates. That was to be the eastern boundary of an empire not

[11] Cf. Tacitus, *Annal.* i,1 "*. . . et Pompei Crassique potentia cito in Cæsarem; Lepidi atque Antonii arma in Augustum cessere, qui cuncta discordiis civilibus fessa nomine principis sub imperium accepit.*" *Idem* i,9 "*. . . non regno tamen neque dictatura, sed principis nomine, constitutam rem publicam.*"

too large to be efficiently controlled. The key provinces were naturally those along the frontiers. These were now in his own hands, and their governors were responsible solely to him and retained office during his pleasure. While in a province such as Syria an experienced veteran was usually governor, in some of the smaller and more difficult provinces—such, for example, as Palestine—native princes, who knew the temper and peculiarities of their subjects and yet were loyal to Rome, were preferred, so long as they were strong enough to keep the peace and sensible enough not to kick up insurrection.

This explains Herod's favour in the eyes of Augustus. Absolutely loyal to his new master, he sought in every way to advance the Augustan plans. As Augustus planned and built, so planned and built Herod. His favour with Augustus continually rose. During his long reign his territory was practically doubled, so that the little land embraced a territory far larger than that of the palmy days of David and Solomon.

Actually he was an excellent ruler. He was generous to a fault; in times of famine he relieved the resulting distress, at one time buying eight hundred thousand measures of corn which he distributed free. He is said to have clothed whole villages in winter. On at least two occasions he made drastic reductions in the taxes: thirty-three percent in 20 B.C., twenty-five percent in 14 B.C. Following the lead of Augustus, his building activity was carried on with a lavish scale—temples, gymnasiums, cloisters, amphitheatres, and aqueducts. Samaria was rebuilt under the name Sebaste and furnished with a temple in honour of the emperor. Other cities were built and named in honour of his relatives and friends. Among them were Antipatris, Phasaëlis, and Agrippium. New citadels—one at Jericho in honour of his mother, Cypros; two named after himself Herodium and set in strategic places, Geba in Galilee, Heshbon across the Jordan—encircled his domains with efficient garrisons.

Trade flourished. A satisfactory harbour was the need of the day. On his whole inhospitable coast Joppa was the only port south of Tyre. On the site of Strato's Tower a new and magnificent city, Cæsarea Stratonis, arose with a splendid harbour protected by huge moles two hundred feet wide. At its entrance stood twin statues, the one in honour of Rome, the other of Augustus. This city, which took twelve years to build, became the most important in Judea; years later, when Roman procurators had succeeded to Herod's power, this was their capital city, although Jerusalem continued to share the nominal honour.

Nor did he stand as patron of architecture solely in his own domain. Far from Palestine his munificence was reflected. Temples, baths, porticos, and monuments were erected not only in the seacoast cities of Syria, *viz.*, Tyre, Sidon, Berytus, Tripolis, but in Damascus and Antioch. The Pythian temple at Rhodes; a restored portico on the island of Chios, whither he had accompanied Agrippa; numerous public buildings at Nicopolis, a city built by Augustus on the site of his victory over Antony at Actium—these are but examples of his zeal. In his list of benefactions Josephus records: "And are not the Athenians, and Lacedemonians, and Nicopolitans, and that Pergamus which is in Mysia, full of decorations that Herod presented them withal!"[12] Even today fragments of inscriptions provide tangible proof of the accuracy of the stories.

The chief glory was, however, the new temple in Jerusalem. The actual labour on the shrine itself lasted but eighteen months, although eight years were required on the surroundings. The last detail, however, of this gem of all Palestine was not completed until the days of Albinus (62-64 A.D.). And then, less than a decade later, it was fired by the conqueror's torch! Its magnificence—white marble with its overlay of gold and precious stones—gleaming high on the summit of Zion, and bursting into sudden view as pilgrims came over the top of Olivet on the Jericho road, gave rise to the rabbinical saying: "Whoever has not seen the temple of Herod has seen nothing beautiful."[13]

No better illustration of the relation between Herod and his subjects can be found than is afforded in the story of the construction of the temple. Not only would it be a crown for his realm; it would also tend to placate the people, for Herod passionately wanted to be known as a popular sovereign. Suspicion rather than gratitude met his plan. Rumours spread that the religion of Jehovah was to be stamped out; the promise to build a new temple was a mere subterfuge to allow the old one to be torn down. Soon the actual building showed the rumours false; still suspicion persisted, in spite of Herod's scrupulous care not to offend religious sensibilities. Priests were taught the trades of mason and carpenter that no unconsecrated foot need defile holy ground. No attempt was made to blot out the distinction between Jew and gentile.

When you go through these first cloisters, unto the second court of the temple, there was a partition made of stone all round, whose height was three cubits: its construction was very elegant; upon it stood pillars, at equal distances from one another, declaring the law of purity, some in Greek, and some in Roman letters, that no foreigner should go within that sanctuary.[14]

[12] Josephus, *Wars* 1,21,11. This whole chapter should be read.

[13] Cf. also Josephus, *Wars* 5,5,1-8; *Antt.* 15,11,1-7.

[14] Josephus, *Wars* 5,5,2. In 1871 one of these pillars was excavated, bearing the following inscription:

ΜΗΘΕΝΑΑΛΛΟΓΕΝΗΕΙΣΠΟ
ΡΕΥΕΣΘΑΙΕΝΤΟΣΤΟΥΠΕ
ΡΙΤΟΙΕΡΟΝΤΡΥΦΑΚΤΟΥΚΑΙ
ΠΕΡΙΒΟΛΟΥΟΣΔΑΝΛΗ
ΦΘΗΕΑΥΤΩΙΑΙΤΙΟΣΕΣ
ΤΑΙΔΙΑΤΟΕΞΑΚΟΛΟΥ
ΘΕΙΝΘΑΝΑΤΟΝ.

"No foreigner is to enter within the balustrade and embankment around the sacred place; whoever is caught will be responsible for his death which will follow."

Nor did Herod himself ever transgress it, although, says Josephus, he caused a secret passage to be built underground from the Antonia to the inner temple to guard against possible insurrections.

Yet this scrupulous care was at once forgotten when over the great east gate of the temple was placed a golden eagle. This perfectly natural gesture of courtesy to Rome aroused deep resentment. Indeed, one of the last deeds of Herod was to execute some forty pious thugs who tore it down as an insolent gesture to the dying monarch.

Not only building, but other forms of Greek culture were enthusiastically championed by Herod. Both in Cæsarea and Jerusalem games were celebrated every fourth year; his munificence in aiding the restoration of the famed Olympic games resulted in his name being inscribed as one of the perpetual managers of those games. Culture and learning were zealously fostered. He surrounded himself with a group of literati, chief among whom was his faithful adviser and friend, Nicolas of Damascus, to whose prolific writings—Athenæus says Nicolas' history contained 144 books—Josephus was so indebted. It was to this group that Eurykles, the rascally Lacedemonian, joined himself with such baleful results.

Nor was his activity restricted to the purely ornamental. Jerusalem had received a new and adequate water supply; his domain was at peace. Banditry had been put down with a firm hand. The circle of fortresses checked inroads from predatory neighbours. His secret police and a strict curfew legislation may well have been irksome; at least it checked the looting of orderly citizens as well as secured the government. In spite of the fierce resentment that could only see Edom grafted upon Rome, the office of high priest used to the alien's own advantage, and an ancient Sanhedrin stripped of its power, if not its prestige, Herod's moderation seems almost surprising. No replica of himself appeared on his coins. Again and again his influence with Roman dignitaries secured justice for Jews who dwelt outside his domain.

The highest tribute to his ability is the fact that his reputation grew so steadily in the eyes of Augustus that from time to time the latter added troublesome frontier districts to Herod's domain, confident that under his oversight the peace would be secure. One example may suffice. After Antony had mastered Iturea and executed Lysanias, he had given the territory to Cleopatra. She in turn farmed the territory out to Zenodorus. The latter weathered the storm which sank Antony and Cleopatra, and was confirmed by Augustus as tetrarch of the "house of Lysanias." Later, however, he not only failed to check the brigands in the neighbouring Trachonitis, but shared their spoils. This endangered the stability of the eastern frontier and made the caravan route from Damascus to the East insecure. Augustus at once intervened, and to secure the peace handed over the three districts, Trachonitis, Batanea, and Auranitis, to Herod (23 B.C.), much to the wrath of Obodas and his Nabateans. Zenodorus protested, but in vain. Three years later, when Augustus visited the East, Zenodorus renewed his complaints. Augustus not only refused to hear them, but added Zenodorus' own domain, which extended south to the Sea of Galilee and thus included Ulatha and Panias, to Herod's kingdom (20 B.C.). Nor did Augustus stop there. Josephus' statement may be a bit fulsome, but the facts he records are undoubtedly substantially correct:

> He also made him one of the procurators of Syria, and commanded that they should do everything with his approbation; and, in short, he arrived at that pitch of felicity, that whereas there were but two men that governed the vast Roman empire, first Cæsar and then Agrippa, who was his principal favorite, Cæsar preferred no one to Herod besides Agrippa; and Agrippa made no one his greater friend than Herod beside Cæsar: and when he had acquired such freedom, he begged of Cæsar a tetrarchy for his brother Pheroras, while he did himself bestow upon him a revenue of a hundred talents out of his own kingdom, that in case he came to any harm himself, his brother might be in safety, and that his sons might not have dominion over him.[15]

Perhaps the climax of his whole reign was the visit of this Marcus Agrippa, high commissioner of the East, in 15 B.C. Agrippa is said to have been amazed and delighted at what he saw. In Jerusalem Agrippa "offered a hecatomb of sacrifices to God." Such a signal compliment to their king from the illustrious Roman could not fail to impress Herod's subjects, even against their will. This triumph of Herod's was followed by his trip the next year in Agrippa's retinue north. The journey was one triumph after another. Again and again native Jews embraced the opportunity to appeal to Herod to use his influence for redress of wrongs. Nor did Agrippa refuse his requests.

Thus in many ways Herod's reign were halcyon days. Outside of Judea proper, where religious prejudices did not run so high, Herod appears to have been eminently popular. But dark and bloody days were in store for this truly unfortunate monarch, who could hold his realm secure but whose palace was a seething inferno of plotting and murder.

The tragedy of domestic misery which took place during the last years of Herod's reign has been often told. Indeed, since Josephus' account is so full and vivid, it provides, together with the purely legendary and unhistoric story of the Slaughter of the Innocents, the popular picture of the king, and has caused his real ability to be often overlooked. The story can be briefly told.

In his palace dwelt his several wives—he had had ten in all—each with her children; his sons and daughters with their mates and children; his brother Pheroras who for several years contented himself with receiving the

[15] Josephus, *Antt.* 15,10,3. Pheroras became thus tetrarch of Perea.

revenue from his tetrarchy and took up his residence there only towards the end of his life when his brother's palace was closed to him; his jealous and trouble-making sister Salome, now with one husband, now another; numerous eunuchs, courtiers, and other servants. Among them moved Herod, exultant in having his relations with him, but suspicious and wishing to have no secrets kept from him. It has been well said: "He heard everything, but saw nothing. When he entered his palace, his eyes grew dim." In such a setting only tragedy could result.

His marriage to Mariamne has often been acclaimed as a most politic move. Perhaps it was, but its consequences were dire, for he was thus brought into the most intimate and galling relationship with a family which would have none of him. The earlier chapter of the story—his passionate and clumsy love for his beautiful queen; the constant plotting of her completely malignant and vicious mother; the pathetic end of her aged grandfather; and the murder of her younger brother—has been told. It had seemed, when the sons of Babas had been harried out, that the contest between the dying house and its ruthless supplanter was over. But this was far from the case.

By Mariamne he had had five children. Of these a son died at an early date, the two daughters play no part in the story; in the veins of the two sons, Alexander and Aristobulus, flowed true Hasmonean blood—the pride and arrogance of an Antigonus, the stupidity of a Hyrcanus. Their father sent them to Rome immature boys to be educated under the personal direction of Asinius Pollio. They returned some years later (18 or 17 B.C.) stalwart men. Their arrival spelt disaster. Whatever public sentiment had been years before when Antigonus and his forbears had ruled, those years had taken on a roseate hue. The good old days may often have been very bad old days—and in this case they were—but in the light of present difficulties past disasters fade. At once they caught the fancy of the populace. Salome regarded them, as she had her imperious sister-in-law, with bitter hatred, and at once sought to undermine them with their father. This task was made the easier both by the favour they had aroused in the popular eye and by their own unguarded resentment at their mother's fate. The situation was intensified through the marriage of Aristobulus to Salome's own daughter Berenice. His brother married Glaphyra, daughter of the crafty and powerful Archelaus of Cappadocia.

Salome, aided by her brother Pheroras, played her cards well. Injudicious words of the two princes, dutifully reported by Berenice to her mother, were repeated to Herod, together with the charge that the youths were conspiring to enlist Archelaus' aid in accusing Herod before Augustus. To check their ambition Herod reinstated an older son, Antipater, who together with his mother Doris had been repudiated by Herod at the time he had wedded Mariamne. This afforded Antipater, who now takes his place as the archvillain of the piece, his entering wedge. Now he was appointed chief heir, accompanied Agrippa to Rome to be presented to Augustus, and his mother took up her residence in the palace. The next year he contrived to bring matters to a head: Herod takes Alexander and Aristobulus to Rome to accuse them formally before the emperor. Augustus contrived to smooth matters down, and Antipater, hypocritically masking his rage, congratulated his two half-brothers for being appointed co-heirs with himself. Next Pheroras fell into disgrace. Twice he had refused to divorce his beloved wife in order to marry a daughter of the king. To add to this, he was accused of having told Alexander (falsely) that Herod had been intimate with Glaphyra. Alexander, in wrath, appropriated to his own passions Herod's favourite eunuchs, and furthermore spread the most scandalous stories of doings in the royal court, lending an air of probability by involving himself in the story—he had, he said, yielded to Salome's insistent lustful advances. Then all hell broke lose. Eventually, however, Archelaus straightened the matter out by pretending rage at his worthless son-in-law and threatening to take his daughter home. At this, Herod rallied to his son's defence, as Archelaus had hoped, and the wily Cappadocian returned home satisfied.

Soon, as if these heartrending quarrels with his sons and brother were not enough, he became involved in further difficulties in which Salome played an important, if innocent, part and which might well have cost him his favour with Augustus if not his crown. It chanced that the energetic young Sylleus, prime minister of the Arabian king Obodas, visited Herod's court, and chancing to see Salome, at that moment a widow, fell passionately in love with her, although she was old enough to be his mother. Salome, to quote for a moment Josephus, "because she was at this time less in favour with her brother, looked upon Sylleus with some passion and was very earnest to be married to him." If the whole affair had not had such serious consequences, it would have been ludicrous. Herod, learning of the romance through the titterings of the court women, had his brother observe their actions at table. And "by the signals which came from their heads and eyes" he was straightway convinced "that they were both evidently in love." At this interesting juncture the bashful Sylleus hastily departed, but returned a few weeks later to make formal request for Salome's hand. Herod, persuaded by Salome, was willing, provided Sylleus would submit to circumcision and become a Jew. This Sylleus refused, and returning home in anger involved Herod in serious trouble with Augustus. The circumstances were as follows.

In Trachonitis there had been for years considerable restiveness towards Herod. During Herod's absence in Rome a rumour was spread that he was dead; instantly a revolt broke out. This was checked by Herod's officers, but the ringleaders fled to Arabia. On his return Herod took stern measures to punish the trouble-makers. Their relatives were executed, but the culprits themselves, now augmented to about a thousand, were beyond his reach, but were constantly raiding his frontier. Herod appealed to Saturninus, governor of Syria, for permission to force the Arabians to surrender the trouble-makers and to pay the six hundred talents which Sylleus owed him. Upon receiving this permission he proceeded to enforce his rights. In spite of Arabian opposition he was successful, summarily executed the robbers, settled three thousand Idumeans in Trachonitis to keep the peace, and returned to Jerusalem.

News of this affair came to Sylleus, who was now in Rome. At once he proceeded to use it to Herod's disadvantage. He completely garbled the story to Augustus, representing Herod as a reckless disturber of the peace. This touched Augustus on a sore point. It was the one unforgivable sin. In anger he wrote Herod that while heretofore he had considered him a friend, he should now treat him as a subject. The Arabians, egged on by Sylleus, began to invade the Perea, while the inhabitants of Trachonitis rose against the Idumean garrison. Herod, in disgrace with Augustus, was afraid to move. To be sure, Aretas, who had succeeded Obodas as king in Arabia, wrote Augustus that Sylleus was a dishonest and licentious servant, had actually murdered his erstwhile master Obodas, and was plotting to gain the kingdom for himself. Still Augustus refused to believe the stories. In this crisis Nicolas of Damascus set out for Rome. He finally convinced Augustus of Sylleus' duplicity and proved that the latter had completely distorted the facts; that Herod had been guilty of no recklessness, but had been entirely justified in what he had done, had been authorized by Saturninus, and had been most moderate. Augustus was convinced. Sylleus was sent home to repay his debt to Herod and then to be executed. Augustus was on the point of dispossessing Aretas of Arabia—he had incurred his anger for not having waited for Roman confirmation—and transferring it to Herod to make amends for his unjust suspicion, when a letter was received from Herod asking permission to execute his sons, Alexander and Aristobulus. Eurykles, a scoundrelly member of Herod's band of literati, had acted as a continual plotter and had engineered the whole scheme. Herod was convinced, and upon the advice of Salome decided to act. This letter cost Herod Arabia, for, although Augustus granted permission to Herod to act as he saw fit, he felt it unwise "to add another government to him, now he was old, and in an ill state with relation to his sons."[16] Upon Augustus' advice Herod called a council, composed half of Romans, half of Jews. The evidence was heard; the majority of the judges were convinced of the guilt of the accused; the two sons were executed and three hundred supporters were stoned to death (7 B.C.).

So far Antipater had been successful. Now he started to corrupt his

[16] Josephus, *Antt.* 16,10,9.

father's friends; even Pheroras became his tool. The lynx-eyed Salome could not be fooled. Step by step she followed the plot and reported to her brother. Finally becoming suspicious, Antipater sought and received permission to go to Rome. During his absence there Salome convinced her brother of the true character of his favourite son. Finally Herod's eyes were opened. Antipater was summoned home. A little apprehensive, yet not realizing that the game was up, for Herod had not revealed his true feeling in the letter, Antipater returned. At once he sensed his danger, but it was now too late to fly. Putting on a bold face, he entered his father's presence—Varus, the new governor of Syria, sat at Herod's side—and sought to embrace him. The air was electric. Herod rose:

> Even this is an indication of a parricide, to be desirous to get me into his arms, when he is under such heinous accusations. God confound thee, thou vile wretch; do not thou touch me till thou hast cleared thyself of these crimes that are charged upon thee. I appoint thee a court where thou art to be judged: and this Varus, who is very seasonably here, to be thy judge; and get thou thy defence ready against tomorrow, for I give thee so much time to prepare suitable excuses for thyself.[17]

The next day he was convicted. Herod, now an old and broken man, stayed punishment until word should come from Augustus. Word finally came. Augustus had approved the death sentence, although he gave Herod permission instead to banish the villain, should he choose. It is reported that Augustus, always a coiner of *bon mots*, had remarked, "Better is it to be Herod's pig than son."[18] Herod was on his death bed. An insolent demonstration took place. The golden eagle over the temple was torn down. Indomitable Herod, dying though he was, rallied; the forty ringleaders were burnt alive, the rest executed. And Antipater, just as he thought he had escaped death, for word had been brought that Herod was dead, was led out to his well-deserved execution. Five days later in Jericho Herod died in agony (4 B.C.).

The funeral was magnificent. The bier was of gold embroidered with precious stones; the body, dressed in royal purple, wearing both diadem and crown of gold and holding his sceptre, lay on a rich purple bed. His many sons and relations, heavily armed guards, five hundred servants with spices in their hands—all these conveyed the dead monarch to his last resting-place in Herodium. In all the pomp there was not a single trace of sorrow. Like Jehoram before him, he "departed without being desired."

[17] Josephus, *Wars* 1,31,5.
[18] Macrobius, *Saturnal.* ii,4,11. In Greek, of course a neat pun *ὗν – υἱόν*.

Chapter IV

TETRARCHS, PROCURATORS, AND AGRIPPA

THE death of Herod left Palestine without a king. Herod had made three wills in rapid succession. In the first, Antipater, then basking in his father's favour, had been nominated with Herod (Philip), a son of the second Mariamne, as successor. When Antipater's wickedness came to light, the will was promptly altered. Antipas, a son by Malthace, became heir to the whole kingdom. But this will, too, was speedily changed by the bewildered old man. In place of one heir, three sons of Herod were to share the kingdom: Antipas was to receive Galilee and Perea with the title tetrarch; his elder brother Archelaus Judea, Samaria, and Idumea with the title king; Philip, their half-brother and son of Cleopatra of Jerusalem, the heterogeneous district to the northeast of the Sea of Galilee which had been granted Herod piecemeal by Augustus—Gaulanitis, Trachonitis, and Paneas. His title, like Antipas', was to be tetrarch. Salome received the three important cities, Jamnia, Ashdod, and Phasaëlis. Other members of his family received grants of money; to Augustus a princely sum was left. Thus Palestine was dismembered, although a half-century later it was to be once more temporarily reunited.

Even before Archelaus could hasten to Rome for the sanction of Augustus the storm broke. At first Archelaus may have tried conciliatory measures; against his will he deposed the high priest and appointed a new one. During the Passover season, however, fresh disturbances broke out; Archelaus sent out his troops; three thousand of the rioters were killed, and the rest of the pilgrims sent home. At this juncture the new king sailed for Rome. His was a critical situation. The confusion he had left at home speedily turned into anarchy. Philip, who had remained behind, was powerless. The Roman officer, Sabinus, whom Augustus had sent temporarily to administer Herod's domain, was worse than useless. Not only was he unable to quiet the troubles, but actively fomented them by robbing the temple openly at the time of Pentecost. The holiday visitors, always ready for excitement, joined in, and Bedlam was let loose in the city. Quickly the insurrection spread. Leaders arose simultaneously in Idumea, near Jericho and Emmaus, in Galilee, and across the Jordan. Several of these—Judas, the son of that Hezekiah whom Herod had summarily executed, near Sepphoris in Galilee; a former slave of Herod named Simon in the Perea; a shepherd Athronges supported by his four militant brothers—actually sought to gain the kingdom themselves.

In this crisis, which was fast becoming dangerous, Varus, then governor of Syria, found it necessary to intervene. He had already come south at the time of Sabinus' arrival, but thinking the situation in hand had returned to Antioch. Now he hastened south with relief legions. The first blow was struck in Galilee. Sepphoris, the scene of Judas' insurrection, was burned to the ground and its populace sold into slavery. Then by forced marches through Samaria—this alone of Herod's domain had refrained from insurrection—he hastened to Judea. The rebels melted before the dreaded legions. Relentlessly Varus pursued them, thoroughly dispersed them, crucified two thousand of the ringleaders, and returned to Antioch, leaving the land numbed if not quiet. Archelaus and his brother Antipas returned to find their land in a sorry plight, many towns in ruins, the people sullen and hostile.

During this interlude of blood Augustus had considered the disposition of the territory. At least two hearings had been held. Archelaus' claims had been challenged by Antipas, who demanded the whole domain as the second will had specified. He even claimed, and he was supported by many of his other relatives, that Herod had been insane when he issued the third will. Two delegations of Jews had pleaded that Judea be annexed directly by Rome; if this were refused, they preferred Antipas to Archelaus. But the eloquence of Nicolas of Damascus, whom Archelaus had inherited together with his land, saved the day. Augustus was loath to alter Herod's will—another proof of the favour which the dead king had enjoyed in Roman eyes—and the final will was ratified practically as written: The Greek cities, Gaza, Gadara, and Hippos, were taken from Archelaus and added to the province of Syria. Archelaus must content himself with the title ethnarch. He should receive the title king if he should later prove worthy. This was never realized.

Now Palestine—like "all Gaul"—was divided into three mutually independent parts: the ethnarchy of Archelaus, roughly half of the former kingdom, including Samaria, Judea, and Idumea with the exception of the cities above mentioned; the tetrarchy of Antipas, comprising Galilee and Perea with a tribute roughly one-third of what his brother received; and the tetrarchy of Philip, the remaining territory—Batanea, Auranitis, Trachonitis—with a still smaller tribute.

Archelaus, of whom we know little—Josephus' sources obviously ran dry for this period—at once commenced to rebuild his limited domain. We learn, curiously enough, only of the activity in and about Jericho. In this city the palace which had been demolished during the days of the rebellion was restored; twelve miles to the north appeared a new city, Archelaïs; a valuable palm grove near by received a new water supply. In addition to manipulating the office of high priest—during his short reign he appointed two—he completely scandalized Jewish scruples by marrying Glaphyra, the widow of his ill-fated half-brother Alexander. Not only had Glaphyra borne three children to Alexander, but had separated from her second husband, King Juba of Libya.[1] Thus from every angle the union was outrageous in Jewish eyes, although quite innocent from the standpoint of sophisticated Rome. He even alienated the Samaritans who had been staunch supporters of Herod and had remained completely aloof from the hostile demonstration of 4 B.C. Finally in the tenth year of his rule Jews and Samaritans alike appeared in Rome to bring formal accusations of gross mismanagement against him (6 A.D.). This was the one offence Augustus would not condone. Archelaus was summoned peremptorily to Rome, convicted of the charge, and banished without ceremony to Vienna, a city on the Rhone. His territory became a Roman province with a governor, called a procurator, directly responsible to the emperor. This situation continued through the ministry of Jesus. But, before we consider the steps taken to transform Judea into a Roman province, we may turn for the moment to see how the other two brothers fared in their domains.

At the same time that Archelaus had returned to Jerusalem as ethnarch his two brothers, Antipas and Philip, had been confirmed in their rule. Though Archelaus was removed after nine years of incompetence—during the boyhood of Jesus—and his domain was turned into an imperial province under procurators of whom Pontius Pilate was the fifth, both Antipas and Philip were more successful. Philip remained in office till his death in 34 A.D.; Antipas five years longer (39 A.D.), then, as a consequence of the ambition of his wife and the greed of his brother-in-law, to fall into the bad graces of Caligula and to be banished. Both of them were thus ruling throughout Jesus' life and ministry, while it was in Antipas' territory that almost all his life was spent.

Antipas was the shrewdest and ablest of Herod's sons. Of him we know little except for gossipy bits from Josephus and occasional comments in our gospels, as "that fox," which Jesus is said to have employed.[2] He was never a favourite with Augustus, as his father had been, although no charges were ever brought against him. Disappointed at the beginning of his term of office at receiving but a small part of the kingdom when he had expected the whole domain, he may well have hoped to receive the territory of Archelaus at the time of the latter's disgrace. But no such fortune was his. With the accession of Tiberius, however, everything changed. Through the twenty-three years of this emperor's reign Antipas basked in royal favour. Apparently he occupied the position of spy to keep the morbidly suspicious emperor informed of affairs in the East. It has been not improbably conjectured that

[1] Josephus' (*Wars* 2,7,4) statement that Juba was dead is quite in error, as Schürer, *op. cit.*, Div. I, Vol. II, p. 40, n. 7, demonstrates.

[2] Luke 13:32.

it was this function which brought him into Pilate's bad graces;[3] certainly his relations with Vitellius, legate of Syria, were often strained.

He inherited his father's fondness for magnificence and building. Some ten years after his appointment he rebuilt the city of Sepphoris which had been razed by Varus, and made it his capital. Sepphoris was but an hour's walk across the hills from Nazareth. That Jesus was one of the workmen who helped in restoring it to be "the ornament of all Galilee" is surely quite within the reach of probability. Across the Jordan in the Perea he rebuilt the fortress town Betharamphtha and named it Livias, later changed to Julias, both names in honour of the wife of Augustus. A few years later (26-27 A.D.) he built the magnificent city of Tiberias near the hot springs of Emmaus on the heights overlooking the west shore of the Sea of Galilee. The fact that this city was built on the site of an old burying-ground made it unpopular for the stricter Jews. This was not so serious as it would have been in Judea, for the population in both Galilee and Perea was hybrid. Many were compelled to settle there; gifts and largesses were granted others to ease their consciences. Thus with its mixed population it became a definite Hellenistic centre. Its organization was definitely Greek with a council of six hundred headed by an archon and committee of ten. Along with its palace and synagogue was a stadium. Its streets were colonnaded, while the whole was surrounded by a wall. Although not so large as Sepphoris, which it now supplanted as capital of the whole tetrarchy, it is said to have been even more magnificent. Today it remains the only town of the many which then girdled the lovely lake.

Although a pagan at heart, he sought successfully not to affront his Jewish subjects. Like Herod before him, he put no image on his coins. Apparently he joined with the Jews in a successful protest against Pilate's attempt to set up the votive shields in Jerusalem. The fact that he remained in office over forty years speaks well for his tact and ability.

His disastrous downfall was due to the cardinal weakness of all the Herods—entanglements with women. Early in his career he had married the daughter of Aretas, king of the Nabateans. This was a wise political move, for the Nabateans had always been restive as they saw territory they felt their own in Jewish hands. Now some years later while on a trip to Rome he had lodged en route with his half-brother Herod—called Philip, probably through confusion with Philip the tetrarch, by gospel writers[4] but not by Josephus—who had been appointed by Herod to be Antipater's eventual successor in the first will, but who had later incurred his father's suspicions and had lived as a private citizen. During this visit Antipas fell in love with his sister-in-law Herodias. On his return home she soon came to him with her daughter Salome. Antipas' first wife, getting wind of her hus-

[3] Luke 23:12.
[4] Mark 6.17; Matt. 14:3; Luke 3:19 (inferior Mss.).

band's unfaithfulness, contrived to go to her father Aretas. Now the latter's only tie with Antipas was broken, and he became openly hostile, but apparently had to bide his time for revenge. In 36 A.D. actual hostilities broke out. Antipas was signally defeated and appealed to his patron, Tiberius. The latter, incensed at Aretas' high-handed measures, sent Vitellius, still legate of Syria, against the disturbers of the peace, with orders to bring back Aretas dead or alive. Vitellius, as already remarked, had no love for his colleague, but could not disobey the imperial order. While the campaign was under way, word came of Tiberius' death. At once Vitellius left Antipas in the lurch and returned to Syria, ostensibly to await orders from the new emperor.

Antipas' star was setting. Not only was he obliged to see his enemy, Aretas, who was well in his grasp, escape, but he had lost his powerful friend, Tiberius. He soon found that in the new emperor Gaius (Caligula) 37-41 A.D. there had once more arisen a new king who knew not Joseph. The young wastrel brother of Herodias, Agrippa, whom Antipas at his wife's request had once had to aid, had long been a boon companion of the new emperor. Soon he contrived to bring Antipas into disfavour at Rome. He, Agrippa, had received the tetrarchy of Philip, now dead, and with it the title king. This piqued the ambitious Herodias. Finally she prevailed upon her husband to request the same title for himself. Antipas was reluctant, for he rightly feared Gaius. Finally he yielded and started for Rome. Agrippa craftily contrived to have Antipas accused of plotting with Rome's enemy, Sejanus, and of having a large arsenal stored up. The latter charge Antipas could not deny. His disgrace was immediate. Shorn of his power, he was summarily banished and his territory entrusted to the unscrupulous Agrippa. Thus ended the long rule of Antipas. The only bright spot in his sudden downfall was the loyalty of Herodias, who had involved him in the fatal mess. Scorning imperial clemency for herself, she followed her husband into exile with the words:

> Thou, indeed, O emperor! actest after a magnificent manner, and as becomes thyself, in what thou offerest me; but the kindness which I have for my husband hinders me from partaking of the favour of thy gift, for it is not just that I, who have been made a partner in his prosperity, should forsake him in his misfortunes.[5]

We can defer until later the question of John the Baptist's part in Antipas' misfortune. What is now of moment is to remember that during Jesus' ministry Antipas was high in Roman favour at the head of the tetrarchy of Galilee and Perea.

Of the last of Herod's three heirs we know next to nothing. By his father's will he had received the territory to the east and north of the Sea of Galilee. It was far from being a promising inheritance. Naturally turbulent, one of

[5] Josephus, *Antt.* 18,7,2.

the reasons Augustus had given it to Herod was to ensure its peace. Herod had had to employ strong measures to bring it into line. In Batanea he had settled a Jewish colony from Babylon as a garrison; in Trachonitis some three thousand Idumeans to keep the peace. For the most part its inhabitants were Arabs and Syrians. Philip, however, proved an excellent ruler. He appears to have been just, peace-loving, and with his people's interests at heart. Until his death he kept the peace, and, better yet, the goodwill of his turbulent subjects who had hitherto been such a menace to the *pax Romana*. Of him Josephus writes:

He had shown himself a person of moderation and quietness in the conduct of his life and government; he constantly lived in that country which was subject to him; he used to make his progress with a few chosen friends; his tribunal also, on which he sat in judgment, followed him in his progress; and when any one met him who wanted his assistance, he made no delay, but had his tribunal set down immediately, wheresoever he happened to be, and sat down upon it, and heard his complaint: he there ordered the guilty that were convicted to be punished, and absolved those that had been accused unjustly.[6]

Well outside Jewish influence, his was openly a gentile court. Images were used on his coins, but without disturbing his subjects. Like all the Herods, he was fond of building and on the site of Panium, his capital, erected the beautiful city of Cæsarea Philippi which had the rights of asylum. On the northeast shore of the Sea of Galilee, where the Jordan flows in, he transformed the village of Bethsaida—apparently not to be identified with the Bethsaida of the gospels—into a flourishing city which he named Julias, after the profligate daughter of Augustus. Since Julia was banished by her father in 2 B.C., this building took place early in Philip's reign.

The one other item preserved to us is concerned with his family life. A bachelor for many years, he finally married Salome, the daughter of Herodias[7] by her former marriage, and thus allied himself even more closely with his half-brother Antipas, with whom he seems to have been on friendly terms. At his death in 34 A.D. his territory was first annexed to the province of Syria, and then three years later was transferred by the new emperor Gaius (Caligula) to his boon companion, Agrippa, under whom for a short time all Palestine was once more to be united.

In 6 A.D., while Antipas was tetrarch of Galilee and Perea and Philip remained secure in his domain, Archelaus had come to grief. Angered at the evident proof of mismanagement, Augustus had banished him and, ignoring Antipas' wistful hopes, had decided to place the confiscated territory under direct Roman rule as a province. Quirinius, who at this time chanced to be

[6] *Antt.* 18,4,6.

[7] Apparently to be identified with the dancer who asked for John the Baptist's head according to the gospel story (Mark 6:22; Matt. 14:6).

governor of Syria, was entrusted with the preparatory measures. Here we may briefly consider the types of provinces Rome had.

As we have already seen, Octavian—soon to be known as Augustus—following the defeat of his erstwhile ally, Antony, had speedily become the chief figure in Roman politics. Quickly he had gathered the various threads into his own hand and by the senatorial decrees of 27 and 23 B.C. had become the undisputed master of the situation. Control of the military and absolute authority over all frontier provinces which required troops had been achieved in a masterful manner. The remaining provinces, which constituted no especial problem nor danger, he graciously allowed the Senate to control.[8]

Augustus' provinces, known as the "provinces of Cæsar," fell into two classes: (1) the more important and wealthy districts received as governors men of senatorial rank, to be sure, but whose entire responsibility was to the emperor; their title was *legati pro prætore*; (2) minor provinces which required troops to keep order, either because of their frontier location or the restlessness of their inhabitants, on the other hand, received as governors members of the equestrian class—an order which Augustus had shortly restored. These governors, who like their brothers, the proprætors, were responsible solely to the emperor, were known as *procuratores*. Egypt, too, was directly in Augustus' hand, but its administration was different. Nominally Augustus was king of Egypt. His local representative was accordingly a viceroy. This officer was also a knight, for no senator might ever set foot in Egypt. This precaution was taken to prevent any senatorial *coup de main*, for Egypt was of vital importance to Rome, being, as it was, the great granary of the empire.

The remaining provinces were known as the "provinces of the people" and were responsible to the Senate. Annually they each received as governor an officer with the title *proconsul*. The proconsul might or might not have actually held the consulship in Rome; in the case that he had, five years must elapse before his provincial incumbency began. In contrast to the imperial governors (*legati pro prætore* and *procuratores*) whose term of office depended on the pleasure of the emperor, the office of proconsul was limited strictly to one year with no possibility of reappointment. With these general facts in mind we can pick up the threads of the story.

At the same time that Coponius was sent as first procurator to Judea, Quirinius, the new proprætor of Syria, was sent to Jerusalem to enroll the inhabitants as provincials and to assess the taxes. To achieve these ends a census was necessary. To Quirinius' surprise, opposition met him. Together

[8] In this connection it will be well to reread pp. 51-53; Duckworth's essay, "The Roman Provincial System" in Jackson and Lake, *The Beginnings of Christianity*, Vol. I, pp. 171-217, provides a full and authoritative account of the whole matter.

with an age-long reluctance to any "numbering," as intense as it was irrational, was the feeling that since the land belonged to God all taxes therefrom were his peculiar property and that a personal (poll) tax was a fresh badge of servitude. The real opposition, however much the leaders may have stressed a religious note, was surely a patriotic unwillingness to lose the last vestige of the independence which they had fought so hard to achieve. Judas of Galilee (called by Josephus, "a Gaulonite of a city whose name was Gamala")[9] and who probably, although this has been disputed, is to be identified with Judas the son of the Hezekiah whom Herod had many years before executed,[10] sought to raise an insurrection in Galilee. Though Galilee was not included in the census or taxation, the feeling of Jewish solidarity had not been affected by the dismemberment of Herod's kingdom. The revolt of Judas was short-lived; he was soon defeated and killed, and Judea was now definitely under Roman rule.

A word of caution may not be out of place here. It is often said that this revolt of Judas' was the start of the Zealot party which from that time on was constantly fomenting opposition to Rome and which ended by plunging the nation into its final bloody destruction. Far from this being the start of the movement, it would appear to have been but one additional step in the opposition that blazed out first many years before in Galilee as a protest against Rome's hireling Antipater and his son Herod. Josephus, with his desire to minimize Jewish opposition to Rome, had stigmatized Hezekiah as a robber and brigand. It is most probable that Hezekiah and his followers had considered themselves patriots of the first water. Again, the term Zealot for this home-rule party, while almost universally employed, is most uncertain. Josephus contents himself with calling them "the fourth philosophy," *i.e.,* the fourth group or sect in Judaism, whom he thus distinguishes from the other three: Pharisees, Sadducees, and Essenes. His first explicit use of the term "Zealot" is of one group of these disgruntled patriots who many years later (66 A.D.) under the leadership of John of Gischala started a reign of terror. Nor is the revolt of Judas, or for that matter any of the subsequent disturbances of "the fourth philosophy," safely to be dubbed "Messianic." The first leader in the history of Judaism who seems to have called himself definitely a Messiah was Bar Cochba in the days of Hadrian (*ca.* 132 A.D.).[11] No greater danger confronts a student of Christian beginnings than that of using technical phrases in a loose and inexact sense, popular though the practice be.

Although the new province of Judea (comprising the three districts Judea, Samaria, and Idumea) was nominally quite distinct from Syria, in special

[9] *Antt.* 18,1,1.

[10] See p. 42.

[11] For the moment we can reserve the question as to whether Jesus of Nazareth made such a claim. With this possible exception the above statement holds.

emergencies the procurator appears to have been required to consult his northern colleague. The latter apparently had authority to interfere at his own discretion if he feared the situation was becoming unmanageable. At any rate, several such occasions are mentioned by Josephus.[12] That the Syrian legate could himself call a procurator to account is doubtful; that he could relieve him from office, send him to Rome for trial, and assume temporary command is proved by the action of Vitellius, who in 36 A.D. sent Marcellus to relieve Pilate whom he ordered to Rome.

Except for this power of intervention, the procurator, who was directly responsible to none save the emperor, was supreme in his province. In him were vested full military, judicial, and financial authority. In contrast, to an important province such as Syria with a standing army of several legions,[13] Judea had only auxiliary troops, raised from the country itself. Since Jews were exempted from military service from the time of Julius Cæsar, these troops appear to have been largely recruited from the district around Sebaste, and were popularly known as the Sebastians. Garrisons were maintained in strategic points through the province; in Jerusalem a cohort was garrisoned in the Antonia, just to the north of the temple.

The procurator lived in Cæsarea and contented himself with seeing that the machinery of government ran smoothly. He would go up to Jerusalem with an additional guard at the times of the various feasts to make certain that the festival throngs did not become over-boisterous. On other occasions Jerusalem was quite free from his presence. Judea was divided into some eleven toparchies, each with its local Sanhedrin. Before these local courts the great majority of cases were tried. Those of sufficient importance to warrant it were referred to the great Sanhedrin in Jerusalem which had gained a new lease of life and importance with the new system of administration which entrusted it with most matters of government. It has usually been assumed, not alone from the express statement in John 18:31 but from the descriptions of the trial of Jesus as given in the Synoptists, that the sentence of death was forbidden the Sanhedrin; that this sentence the procurator alone might pass. But this, while perhaps not improbable, is by no means sure and has often been flatly denied.[14] Further questions as to its composition and province may be reserved until a later page.

The picture, often painted, of Judea being ground down by harsh governors is hardly historic. Rome was a remarkably cautious and long-suffering mistress. Her governors were always instructed to allow the provinces as much freedom from irksome control as was possible. The Jews were accorded especial privileges. Their religious prejudices were scrupulously guarded. Roman guards aided the temple police in keeping the sacred pre-

[12] *Antt.* 18,8,2-9 (cf. *Wars* 2,10,1-5); *Antt.* 20,1,1; *Wars* 2,14,3; 2,16,1; 2,18,9-11.
[13] Three in the days of Augustus; four in the days of Tiberius.
[14] See Juster, *Les juifs dans l'empire romain*, Vol. II, pp. 132-142.

cincts inviolate. No attempt to force emperor worship upon Judea was ever made, save perhaps by the mad Caligula—and that attempt was speedily given up after its dismal failure. A simple superscription, without the head of the emperor, appeared on the coins. To be sure, the governors had the authority—and exercised it—to appoint and depose high priests. This, though a scandal, was nothing new, for Herod and Archelaus had both done it. Until 36 A.D. the robes of the high priest were kept in the Antonia under the authority of the governor, and were formally handed over to him at such times as he needed them. Later this restriction was removed. The abuses of taxation which are familiar to all readers of Cicero's blistering arraignment, *Against Verres,* were no longer practised. Rome carefully audited the financial sheets of her provinces. The governor received a fixed salary. The taxes, amounting perhaps to six hundred talents, were for the most part spent in bettering the province itself—roads, harbours, and public buildings. The balance went to the imperial treasury. No longer were the taxes farmed out, but were collected by salaried government officers. The procurator was of course the head of the financial organization. He apparently worked in conjunction with the local Sanhedrins in the actual collection.

The most real source of grievance in an otherwise excellent arrangement was the matter of the customs (internal revenue). These, in contrast to the direct taxes, were still farmed out. That is, bids were made for the right to collect the duties in the various districts. To the highest bidder went the privilege. All the money collected by this individual, known as a publican,[15] over the bid was his; should he fail to collect the full amount, he must make it good from his own pocket. It need hardly be said that this latter circumstance rarely occurred. The position of publican and his subordinates was open to abuse of power, especially if the governor winked at excesses. For the most part there seems to have been a fixed tariff for each sort of duty and an attempt to prevent extortion and graft. None the less, since the duties were so numerous—the list is a truly formidable one—and could be collected so often on the same consignment on even a short journey, they constituted a sore point. The collector was naturally cordially hated. Was he not a servant of Rome engaged in a legal theft of what belonged to Jehovah? For a Jew to be engaged in such a nefarious trade—and not a few Jews succumbed to the temptation of a lucrative position—was doubly obnoxious. Both the rabbinical literature and the gospels heap contempt upon them. In the former they are usually designated "robbers"; in the latter they are regularly associated with sinners and harlots.

Thus the actual government was pretty much in the hands of the native aristocracy, of which the high priest was the head. Both at the time of the death of Herod and later at the deposition of Archelaus there had been a

[15] The individuals referred to as "publicans" in the gospels are improperly so styled. They were his underlings.

definite request that the territory be appended to Syria. This request had been prompted by the double hope of getting rid of the house of Herod and of obtaining actual self-government under the Roman ægis. Though this request had been refused and a governor was now in the field, it soon must have become clear to the unprejudiced that affairs had turned out far better than had been feared. Actually the more solid and stable element in Judea appears to have accepted the new order with resignation, if not with alacrity. But the fires of revolt were not out. They were to be kept alive by the fanatic patriots who stubbornly believed that eventually, and that right early, God himself would rally to their defence and would overthrow all opposition, even that of proud Rome herself, should they but make the initial move. In spite of the fears of the politically powerful and the disapprobation of the learned and devout, this band was destined to persist in their mad hopes which ended in a dreadful carnival of blood.

The first four procurators of Judea are hardly more than names to us. Coponius, Marcus Ambivius, Annius Rufus, and Valerius Gratus followed one another in rapid succession. The last of these, Josephus says, was in office eleven years, but of these years he records next to nothing.[16] In 26 A.D. the fifth was appointed, Pontius Pilate. Estimates of Pilate are difficult. Christian prejudice, due to his part in the execution of Jesus, finds confirmation in the story of Josephus of his several clashes with his subjects and in the bitter words which Philo quotes from the letter of Agrippa to Gaius.[17] On the other hand, it is to be observed that Tiberius kept him in office for ten years (26-36 A.D.). This is no light recommendation, for Tiberius, especially in his latter years, kept a lynx-eyed watch on his provinces. And when in 36 A.D. Pilate dispersed a crowd which he well might have thought dangerous to peace and order, he was promptly suspended and sent to Rome by his senior colleague in Syria. Accordingly, when reading the stories of Josephus, one should remember that the latter is at pains to cull out and magnify all the outrages of the later procurators in order to try to prove his contention that a naturally friendly and grateful nation had been driven against its will into the fearful rebellion of the years 66-73 A.D., largely as a result of the reckless and incompetent governors whom Rome had sent. Nevertheless, since Pilate is of especial interest to us because of his minor part in the tragedy on Calvary, we may briefly mention the little that is known.

Hardly had Pilate reached Judea when the first clash came. For reasons which are by no means clear, troops were dispatched from Cæsarea to Jerusalem, ostensibly to go into winter quarters, but actually, according to Josephus, "to abolish the Jewish laws." Under cover of the night the im-

[16] *Antt.* 18,2,2.
[17] *Legatio ad Gaium* 38(§§299 ff.)589M.

perial standards bearing Tiberius' image were taken into the city. In the morning they were discovered and the word spread. Incensed at this deadly insult—no previous governor had attempted this—many flocked to Cæsarea to demand that the offence be removed. For five days Pilate remained obdurate; on the sixth the mob was admitted to the racecourse, only to find itself surrounded by soldiers who threatened them with death if they did not desist and return quietly home. Far from being cowed, the Jews bared their necks to the Roman swords, preferring to die than to yield. Pilate could not afford to take such a step, and ordered the offending banners withdrawn to Cæsarea.

This incident is significant. It reveals the restraint under which a governor worked. He must keep order but without unnecessary violence. Furthermore, it reveals the essentially freer atmosphere in Cæsarea; there the banners were at least tolerated, in Jerusalem they were taboo. Pilate may well have felt such distinctions too subtle for him.

A little later another difficulty occurred. Pilate started the construction of a new aqueduct to bring water to Jerusalem from a distance of some twenty-five miles. A distinct advantage for Jerusalem, and a costly one, he not unnaturally considered that the expense might be borne by the temple treasure. When, in spite of opposition, he persisted, he was confronted by a wrathful, shrieking mob and personally insulted. This he would not brook. Soldiers in civilian dress mingled with the crowd and dispersed it.

A third incident, somewhat resembling that of the banners, is mentioned in the letter of Agrippa to Gaius, already mentioned. Votive shields were set up in the palace of Herod—used by Pilate as his Jerusalem residence. Although these shields bore no images, but were simply inscribed with the name of Tiberius, an uproar resulted. Agrippa and his four sons joined their pleas to those of the Jerusalemites, but in vain. Finally a letter was sent to Tiberius. Peremptory word came to Pilate and the shields were withdrawn.

The statement in Luke 13:1, "Now there were some present at that very season who told him (*i.e.,* Jesus) of the Galileans, whose blood Pilate had mingled with their sacrifices," indicates that Jewish restiveness provoked other disturbances in addition to those described by Josephus.[18] An outburst of fanaticism in Samaria caused his downfall. An imposter claimed to be able to reveal the sacred utensils of the temple which from the time of Moses had lain concealed. His hearers were impressed and followed him with weapons to a little town at the foot of Gerizim. From there they planned to ascend the mountain. The scheme miscarried. In the village they were surprised by Pilate's soldiers; many were slain, others imprisoned and later executed. In indignation the Samaritans complained

[18] Cf. also the reference to those men "who in the insurrection had committed murder," of whom Barabbas was one (Mark 15:7).

to Vitellius, the proprætor of Syria; in spite of the fact that the crowd had been heavily armed—which may well have led Pilate to be skeptical regarding the innocence of their design—Vitellius at once relieved Pilate from office and ordered him to make his defence to Tiberius. Before Pilate arrived in Rome Tiberius had died; here the luckless governor, who seems throughout his ten year service to have sought zealously to maintain order and to better his province, drops from the pages of history but not from those of legend and romance.

Marcellus, whom Vitellius had appointed procurator pro tem. until Pilate should be returned or his successor appointed, appears, if we can believe Josephus, to have been hardly more than a figurehead during his brief incumbency. Josephus does not further mention him, but contents himself with recounting the popularity of Vitellius who remitted all taxes on fruits bought and sold in Jerusalem, and did away with the custody of the vestments of the high priest. It is not improbable that even before his disgrace Pilate had suffered some diminution in authority due to the advent of Vitellius, endowed as that latter was with extraordinary power by Tiberius.[19] With the death of Tiberius Marcellus was replaced by Marullus, who remained in office during the four years of Gaius (37-41 A.D.), but without exciting any comment from Josephus.

The death of Tiberius was not such a blessing as his subjects had enthusiastically believed. Tiberius' prophecy that his young grandnephew, Gaius (Caligula), would prove to be a curse both to himself and everyone else[20] was speedily justified. Tiberius' will, in which Gaius was named only co-heir with the emperor's weakling grandson, was annulled by the Senate, and the son of the beloved Germanicus was invested with the title *imperator* and the full power which Augustus and Tiberius had enjoyed. Hopes ran high at the thought of having exchanged the morbid and dread misanthrope for the gallant young Gaius, who but a few years before—he was now but twenty-five—had been the idol of his father's troops and had received the affectionate nickname *Caligula*, from the little boots his doting mother Agrippina let him wear to please them. Those hopes were destined to cruel disappointment. His opening speech to the Senate was full of the fairest promise. His aim was to be that of Augustus. Like his illustrious predecessor, he would share his responsibilities with the Senate. After a gala six months he fell dangerously ill. Unfortunately, he recovered; the remaining three and a half years of his rule were one long debauch of murder, lust, and theft, brought to an end in his own palace

[19] Cf. Tacitus, *Annal.* vi,32—"*Et cunctis quæ apud Orientem parabantur L. Vitellium præfecit.*"

[20] "*'Exitio suo omniumque Caium vivere' et 'se natricem populo Romano, Phaëthontem orbi terrarum educare'* "—Suetonius, *Caligula* 11.

by the hand of one of his prætorian guards. That the empire continued its course in spite of its madman ruler was due partly to the fact that Augustus had welded together an organization so able that it could run itself, partly to the wise and courageous statesmen, both at home and abroad, who dared to call down the lightning on their own heads by modifying their ruler's mad demands.

One of the first acts of the new emperor, Gaius, had been to give to his boon companion, Agrippa, grandson of Herod the Great, the territory which had formerly been the tetrarchy of Philip, together with the smaller tetrarchy of Lysanias. For several years these districts had been loosely appended to the great province of Syria. With them went the title of king. The story of his whole career, as sketched by Josephus,[21] reads like a romance. With Hasmonean blood in his veins—his grandmother was Herod's favourite, Mariamne—educated in Rome; befriended by the Roman matron Antonia; constantly getting into one financial scrape after another; at one time on the verge of suicide; for a time occupying a minor position in the tetrarchy of Antipas through the good offices of the latter's wife, Herodias, Agrippa's sister; soon leaving this position and taking up with the proprætor of Syria; speedily convicted of taking bribes there and forced to leave that province; barely escaping arrest more than once for his debts, yet always contriving to borrow from some sympathetic friend—he had finally found himself in a Roman prison as a result of an incautious word to his friend Gaius, which had been tattled to Tiberius and construed by the latter as treason against himself. Since Gaius rightly considered this last misfortune of Agrippa's to be the result of the latter's loyalty to himself—how disinterested Agrippa had been is quite another matter—it is not surprising that when he had become emperor

> there did not many days pass ere he sent for him to his house, and had him shaved, and made him change his raiment; after which he put a diadem upon his head, and appointed him to be king of the tetrarchy of Philip. He also gave him the tetrarchy of Lysanias, and changed his iron chain for a golden one of equal weight.[22]

How Agrippa soon contrived to gain for himself through sharp dealing the domain of his brother-in-law Antipas (39 A.D.), although the latter had once proved to be a friend in need, has already been told.[23]

Soon came the assassination of Gaius and the accession to the Roman throne of his fifty-year-old uncle Claudius (41-54 A.D.). Estimates of this new emperor are difficult. Destitute of practical experience in governing, long looked upon with ill-disguised contempt by his intimates for his irresolution of character, dominated by the imperial freedmen—chief among

[21] *Antt.* 18,6,1-11.
[22] Josephus, *Antt.* 18,6,10.
[23] P. 65.

whom was the wretched Callistus who had aided him to the throne—he soon proved as unsatisfactory to the Senate as had his predecessor. The coarseness of life in the imperial court and the outrageous insolence of the freedmen is vividly portrayed in the fragments of the *Satyricon* of Petronius known as "The Banquet of Trimalchio." On the other hand, Claudius had been an eager student of Roman history and gave himself whole-heartedly to the administration of his empire. Due perhaps partially to his desire to follow the precedents of his predecessors, especially Julius and Augustus, he adopted the wise plan of managing Judea as Augustus had done, through a local prince who understood the people and was at the same time loyal to Rome.

King Agrippa was the logical man. Claudius was already under obligation to him for his influence upon the Senate. Furthermore, Agrippa had become a popular hero in Jewish eyes and would be most useful in quieting an outraged Judea. During the anti-Jewish uprising in Alexandria Agrippa had been mobbed and thus had become a martyr; a little later he had presented a petition to Gaius in behalf of the Alexandrian Jews. Most popular of all was his effectual aid to the Palestinian Jews in dissuading Gaius from his mad insistence that a statue of himself be set up in the temple in Jerusalem. To kotow to the emperor, who was now demanding divine honours from his subjects, and to annoy the local Jews, an altar to Gaius had been set up by the heathen citizens of Jamnia. This the infuriated Jews promptly demolished. Wind of this came to Rome. Wrathfully the emperor commanded that a statue of himself be set up in the Jerusalem temple. At the same time word was sent to Petronius, the new proprætor of Syria, to proceed to Jerusalem with a strong force to see that the order was executed. To all this the latter most reluctantly complied. As he expected, deep-seated opposition broke out; in vain he counselled the Jewish leaders not to make a bad matter worse. They replied that though they would not raise arms against Rome, they would die rather than see their laws thus shamefully violated. In desperation Petronius wrote a cautious letter to Gaius requesting a delay "until the harvest was over." This did not aid matters; it simply deferred the evil day and exasperated Gaius. Finally the growing opposition led the perplexed Petronius to take the final step. He withdrew his soldiers to Antioch and wrote the emperor to advise him to rescind the obnoxious edict which he had not dared to enforce.

At this juncture Agrippa, who was in Rome and had not heard of the crisis in Palestine, learned of it. In horror he used his personal influence with Gaius and, contrary to expectation, succeeded where even Petronius had failed. The edict was withdrawn, although Gaius pettishly forbade any interference with altars or temples to himself which might be built outside of Jerusalem and sent word to Petronius to commit suicide for having ventured to disobey his command. Fortunately for Petronius, the message was delayed; four weeks before the belated messenger arrived word had come to Antioch that Gaius was dead.

Accordingly, the whole Roman province of Judea—Judea, Samaria, and Idumea—was added to the kingdom of Agrippa. Once again a Jewish king sat in the seat of David. The Jewish blood might be thin, but through the Hasmonean grandmother it was there. For three years (41-44 A.D.) he ruled over the reassembled Palestine of his grandfather Herod. He seems to have been as popular as Herod had been hated. He had come in on the flood wave of popularity; his first act was to hang up in the temple, as a sign of reverence for its sanctity, the golden chain he had three years before received. Before such piety hatred against Rome, which might well have led to a flash-in-the-pan rebellion, quickly subsided. While probably no more a Jew at heart than his illustrious predecessor, he was always meticulous to avoid shocking the religious scruples of his subjects. How well he succeeded is illustrated by the encomiums pronounced upon him by Josephus and the rabbinical writings. One example may suffice. The story is told that on the Feast of Tabernacles he read the passage Deut. 17:15, "One from among thy brethren shalt thou set king over thee; thou mayest not put a foreigner over thee, who is not thy brother." Remembering his Idumean blood, he burst into tears, thinking himself meant, only to be comforted by the shout: "Be not grieved, Agrippa! Thou art our brother, thou art our brother!"[24] His prospective son-in-law, Epiphanes of Commagene must first promise to be circumcised; an outrage upon a Jewish synagogue on the Phœnician coast was speedily stopped through his influence; Palestinian coins were free from images. Although, like a true Herod, he built lavishly, erected outside of Palestine theatres and baths at his own expense, had the games celebrated in Cæsarea, and apparently erected statues in that latter city to his daughters,—of this activity Josephus tactfully remarks: "But Agrippa's temper was mild and equally liberal to all men. He was humane to foreigners, and made them sensible of his liberality"[25]—"he kept himself entirely pure; nor did any day pass over his head without its appointed sacrifice."[26]

Apparently he flirted with the dream of making his little kingdom independent of Rome. At any rate, Marsus, the new governor of Syria, thought the walls of Jerusalem were becoming suspiciously high and broad. His report to Claudius brought from the latter an order to stay this building.

[24] This tradition is found in the Mishna Soṭah 7,8; Sifrè Deut. §157; Midr. Tannaim *loc. cit.* It is, however, to be observed that all the later rabbis were not so complaisant. According to a Baraita in the name of R. Nathan, "The Israelites made themselves liable to extermination when they flattered Agrippa," *i.e.*, by disregarding Deut. 17:15—G. F. Moore, *Judaism*, Vol. II, p. 190.

[25] *Antt.* 19,7,3.

[26] *Ibid.*

Shortly after, Agrippa invited five of the other vassal princes[27] to a conference at Tiberias. Unfortunately for his scheme Marsus, though uninvited, appeared, too, and promptly interfering sent the others home. Thus the two tentative attempts towards a free Jewry proved worse than useless, for it is not impossible that they were among the reasons that led Claudius' advisers to oppose the latter's plan to send Agrippa's young son to succeed his father. At any rate, when in 44 A.D. a sudden and dramatic illness[28] brought the brief rule of the popular king to a close, Rome reverted to her former policy of sending procurators to the little state. But since in Agrippa Palestine had been reunited, the jurisdiction of these later procurators, of whom Cuspius Fadus was the first, was no longer limited to the former province of Judea—that is, Samaria, Judea, and Idumea—but embraced the whole domain. The appointment of Agrippa had allayed the increasing hatred of the Jews for Rome; now that foreign governors were once more in the land they were to find their task increasingly difficult. The brief interlude had whetted the appetites of the revolutionaries; its close was easily construed a fresh degradation. Small wonder it is that as the years rolled on the air grew tenser and tenser. Each overt act on the part of the populace brought stricter supervision from the governor; this in turn provoked greater opposition. It needed no prophet to see that there could be but one outcome. Disaster was sure; the only question was when would the moment come.

With the fate of the Jewish state trembling in the balance, we can now leave the outward history of the period to review briefly some other aspects of the thought and organization of Judaism, without a knowledge of which a true understanding of early Christianity would be quite impossible.

[27] Herod of Chalcis, Sampsigeram of Emesa, Cotys of Lesser Armenia, Antiochus of Commagene, and Polemon of Pontus.

[28] Josephus, *Antt.* 19,8,2; Acts 12:21-23.

Chapter V

IN THE TIDEWAY OF GREEK THOUGHT

DURING the brief survey of Jewish history we have been chiefly concerned with Palestine; but all the Jews did not live there. In fact, those who lived in Palestine comprised but a fraction, and a small fraction at that, of all Jewry. Furthermore, many Jews who resided in Palestine were actually as much in the dispersion as their brethren in Alexandria or Antioch. The seacoast towns, except Joppa and Jamnia, were prevailingly gentile; the tetrarchy of Philip almost completely so. To be sure, Galilee and part of the Perea were nominally Jewish, but the population was far from pure. When Judas the Maccabee had made his stand against Syria, one of his first moves had been to send Simon into Galilee to round up the Jews there and to settle them near Jerusalem; he himself had performed a similar service across the Jordan. In the very heart of Antipas' domain was a league of ten independent Greek cities. This confederation had taken place when Pompey had freed them from the domination unto which they had been brought by Alexander Jannæus. The largest of them, Scythopolis, was on the west side of the Jordan. The other nine—Hippos, Gadara, Pella, Philadelphia, Gerasa, Dion, Canatha, Raphana, and Damascus[1]—lay in Batanea and the Perea. To speak of the Decapolis as a political unit is surely incorrect. It was simply a league of cities, united by trade bonds, free from Antipas and each apparently loosely under the oversight of the governor of the province of Syria. One needs but recall that even Tiberias, the capital city of Antipas, was built on the site of a graveyard and the great herds of swine who played an important part in the tale of the Gerasene demoniac[2] to find fresh light cast upon the words attributed to Jesus, "Go not into any way of the gentiles, and enter not into any city of the Samaritans: but go rather to the lost sheep of the house of Israel."[3]

Attempts at numbering ancient populations are of necessity largely guesses; consequently the number of Jews at the time of the Christian beginnings has been variously computed. Perhaps four to four and a half million, or roughly seven percent of the total population of the Roman world, is a fair guess. In line with the early and fairly probable statements[4] that there

[1] Pliny, *Hist. Nat.* v,16(18). The exact status of Damascus has been often discussed and is not clear.

[2] Mark 5:1-20.

[3] Matt. 10:5 f.

[4] Cf. Philo, *In Flaccum* 6(§43)523M.

were a million Jews in Egypt alone, rather more in Syria, probably at least ten thousand in Rome at the time of Tiberius, this figure does not seem excessive. Of this total probably not more than seven hundred thousand were to be found in Palestine.

After the northern kingdom had fallen (722 B.C.), about the only part of Palestine of which the inhabitants could claim to be true Israelites were the highlands of Judah and Benjamin. The various conquests of Tiglath-Pileser, Sargon, and Sennacherib and the more systematic deportations of Nebuchadnezzar while not depopulating Palestine, as has sometimes been assumed, removed the flower of Jewry and may be seen as one of the important factors leading to that invisible empire upon which in reality the sun never sets, for, as Agrippa wrote Gaius, Jerusalem was the capital not only of Judea, but of most of the countries of the earth. Subsequent years saw fresh deportations of Jews outside their traditional borders, as those of Artaxerxes Ochus (340 B.C.) on the shores of the Caspian Sea, or of Pompey (63 B.C.) to Rome. These enforced migrations may well be the reasons why Jewish writers regularly regarded the dispersion as a great misfortune—which it distinctly was not, at least for Judaism—a punishment from God for Israel's sins, which would in the golden future be withdrawn when the time of chastening should be over. This familiar view finds expression in one of the Psalms of Solomon:

> They were cast away among every nation, from out of the inheritance which the Lord gave them: that Israel might be dispersed according to the word of God; that thou mightest be justified, O God, in thy righteousness by reason of our transgressions.[5]

Later rabbis, as Eleazar (third century), might make virtue of necessity and see the dispersion of Israel among the nations as God's way of making proselytes.

But deportations were not the only causes of the dispersion. Voluntary migrations to Egypt were also taking place as the overthrow of Jerusalem before Babylonia became imminent. Jeremiah's fulminations,

> Thus saith Jehovah of hosts, the God of Israel, If ye indeed set your faces to enter into Egypt, and go to sojourn there; then it shall come to pass, that the sword, which ye fear, shall overtake you there in the land of Egypt; and the famine, whereof ye are afraid, shall follow hard after you there in Egypt; and there ye shall die,[6]

were disregarded; many turned to the south, and, tragedy of tragedies, forced the prophet to go with them. Colonies of Jews appeared in Migdol,

[5] Psalms of Solomon 9:2 f.

[6] Jer. 42:15 f.

Tahpanhes, Memphis, and Pathros.[7] In Syene and Elephantine were flourishing colonies with a sanctuary and apparently sacrifice to Jehovah. Even after the Persians destroyed the Egyptian sanctuaries this one seems to have remained until finally it was destroyed by Egyptians enraged against Persia. Thus many years before Alexander the road from Palestine to Egypt was open and was trod by many Jews.

Throughout the Persian period Jewish colonization went on apace. By the fourth century there were thousands of Jews in Egypt, Mesopotamia, Persia, and Media, in addition to scattered groups near the Caspian. Due to the religious toleration shown by Persia, the connecting links with the homeland were unbroken. Then came Alexander the Great, and the Jews began to go west. His conquests turned what had been barred and dangerous tracks into safe and open roads for trade, and many Jews hastened to make the most of them.

Of the doings of the emigrant Jews we know little, for they left few permanent memorials. Strabo's remark as quoted by Josephus,[8] "Now these Jews are already gotten into all cities; and it is hard to find a place in the habitable earth that hath not admitted this tribe of men, and is not possessed by them," was anticipated by the Sibyllist who sang in the middle of the second century B.C.,

> All the earth is full of thee,
> Aye, and even all the sea.[9]

While the catalogue of those who were present at Jerusalem for the Feast of Pentecost[10] raises many critical problems which may be reserved for a later page, it evidences the far-flung front of Jewry. Josephus' oft-repeated story[11] of the exploits of the two brothers, Asineus and Anileus, in the city of Nahardea on the Euphrates is not without value to the student as an indication of the numbers of Jews who lived quite content away from Palestine, as well as of their twofold devotion to their ancestral customs and to brigandage and of the not unnatural disfavour with which they were regarded by their neighbours. Another story of Josephus[12]—that of Helena and Izates of Adiabene—which is equally worth the reading, shows their zeal for making proselytes and the not infrequent success—especially among the women—even in the highest circles. Juster[13] refers to a community of Jews in Media at the town of Gazaca so ignorant that they had

[7] Jer. 44:1.
[8] *Antt.* 14,7,2.
[9] *Orac. Sibyll.* iii,271.
[10] Acts 2:9-11.
[11] *Antt.* 18,9,1-9.
[12] *Antt.* 20,2,1-5.
[13] *Les Juifs dans l'empire romain*, Vol. 1, p. 203, n. 2. This very important work, while scarcely adapted for continuous reading, provides an immense amount of information.

never even heard of the Halakah[14] and who found the stories of the Flood and of Job, as recounted to them by Akiba, fascinatingly new.

While actual evidence for Jews in Arabia, as listed by Juster, is scanty and very late, there can be little question that they were there at an early date. Josephus mentions them in his preface to the *Wars*,[15] while "Arabians" were present at Jerusalem according to the catalogue of Acts mentioned above. It will be remembered that Paul went thither immediately after his conversion.[16]

Syria and Asia Minor contained vastly more Jews than did Palestine itself. The intimate, if not always pleasant, connexion between Palestine and the Seleucid empire to the north resulted in large migrations northward. As already mentioned, the title "citizen of Antioch" was one which many Jews had coveted and obtained at an early date. From an early date Ephesus had been a great Jewish centre; in Antioch of Pisidia and in Iconium Paul is said to have frequented the Jewish synagogues, as was also the case when he had crossed over into Europe. In the great mercantile cities of Corinth and Thessalonica and in Athens itself synagogues were to be found. Had we the full story of the uprising of Jews in Cyprus against Trajan, it would probably be as dramatic as the account of the awful struggle a generation earlier in Palestine.

In Alexandria we have the clearest picture of the changes that came into Judaism as a result of residence in an alien but friendly environment. As mentioned in a preceding page, at least a million Jews dwelt complacently in this second Athens and the country to the south. The city itself had been built by Alexander as a step in his program of linking east and west. At his death it had passed into the hands of the Ptolemies. They had proved excellent rulers, and achieved their dreams of making their capital city the chief centre of the intellectual and religious, as well as of the economic, world. The famed museum with its chapels, halls, and libraries has been aptly called the prototype of our college foundations. Such names as Euclid, Apollonius, Eratosthenes, and Ptolemæus give it a fame that can never die. The library was one of the wonders of the world; at the death of Ptolemy Philadelphus numbering 100,000 rolls it was increased by each successive emperor till it reached the stupendous total of 700,000. Then in 47 B.C. during the siege of the city by Julius Cæsar it was burnt—Gibbon says totally. Reëstablished, it once more achieved fame, only to be destroyed by the fanatical caliph Omar in 640 A.D. Incidents such as these turn the historian sick at heart. What a wealth of knowledge of the past would have been ours had it not been for such wanton outrages.

[14] The rules for observing the written law. Readers who share this ignorance may consult p. 106 below.

[15] §2.

[16] Gal. 1:17.

In this truly cosmopolitan city with its temple to Serapis, the cult to Isis replete with imposing and noble ritual, the Jew dwelt an honoured citizen. Not alone in the specifically Jewish quarters to the east of the island Pharos, but throughout the city, his synagogues were to be found. One of them is described in lavish terms in an ancient quotation in one of the tracts of the Talmud as so huge as to be able to contain twice as many as had left Egypt under Moses, and that it was found necessary to indicate to the waiting congregation the proper time for the "Amens" by waving flags.

Here in this oasis to the south, free for the most part from persecution, the Jewish citizens readily assimilated the alien culture and philosophy of the Greeks. Alexandrian Judaism, which made its direct contribution to life and thought through the literature it produced, is of prime importance to us not alone because it throws into clearer relief by contrast the peculiarities of Palestinian or, as it has been called, "normative" Judaism, but because of its influence upon Christianity through the great Alexandrian teachers of the second and third centuries—Pantænus, Clement, and Origen.

Although outside of Alexandria Greek culture never made any very real impress upon the Egyptians, in the city it came to its greatest bloom. From the days of Alexander Greek soon became not only the language of culture, but of business. Inhabitants of the city simply could not live without it. It was in Alexandria that its effect upon Judaism was soonest noticed. Although the Jews of the dispersion retained their religious loyalty and ceremonial observances, and though Jerusalem remained, as Agrippa wrote, "the mother city, not of a single country, but of most of the countries of the world," to which pilgrimages were ever being made, it was impossible for Jews who had spent their lifetime in business in Greek cities to retain Semitic speech. Just as Aramaic had superseded Hebrew, after Alexander Greek became increasingly necessary. In Alexandria it was a sheer necessity, not a luxury. Its adoption was a tribute which the Jews gladly paid to the great gentile community which sheltered them. The Greek was not the scholastic Greek of the museum nor the artificial imitation of it which is seen in those who aped the Attic diction. Rather it was the street patois, a strange conglomerate of many alien elements.

Soon a problem arose. Judaism was primarily a religion of a book. That book was the Torah. And the Torah was written in Hebrew, now an almost unknown tongue to the rank and file in Alexandria. If Judaism was here to survive, a translation was necessary. This need was soon met, and successive years saw the sacred Scriptures appearing in a Greek dress. The so-called *Letter of Aristeas* gives a romantic account of the origin of the translation, known to us today as the Septuagint. Aristeas, a courtier in the service of Ptolemy Philadelphus, in his letter to his brother Philocrates relates a trip he had recently made to Jerusalem. The reason for the trip was as follows: One day the chief librarian in Alexandria had told the king, who was interested in Jewish antiquities, that they needed a translation of the Jewish laws. Philadelphus agreed and sent a deputation to the high priest Eleazar asking for men to perform the task. To this request the high priest gladly acceded, and sent accredited scholars—six from each of the twelve tribes—bearing a copy of the Hebrew Scriptures embossed in gold on fine skins. After the king had tested them with hard questions at a banquet, the work of translation began on the island of Pharos. Each day they compared what they had written and thus produced their text. In seventy-two days the work was finished as if the very period had been prearranged. The work was enthusiastically received by the Jews; when read to the king, he expressed his approval and reverence.

The letter is pseudonymous and legendary, obviously the work of a Jew who, desirous of magnifying the importance of his race, puts this panegyric upon Jewish law and wisdom into the mouth of a gentile noble. Both Philo and Josephus are familiar with it, and the latter points out that it was only the Pentateuch that was thus translated:

> For he [*sc.* Ptolemy Philadelphus] did not obtain all our writings at that time; but those who were sent to Alexandria as interpreters gave him only the books of the law, while there was a vast number of other matters in our sacred books.[17]

Early Christian writers who quoted and added to the letter did not always observe this limitation, and the whole Greek Old Testament came to be known as the Septuagint. Jerome, to be sure, was better informed and remarked, "All Jewish scholars assert that only the five books of Moses were translated by the seventy." Epiphanius, whose claims to sanctity do not rest on either his accuracy or truthfulness, apportions the thirty-six books of Scripture among an equal number of pairs of scholars! Thus stories grow.

Thus the legend casts very little light on the origin of the version. Perhaps the Pentateuch may have been translated early in the third century, but it was almost certainly done, not to enrich the royal library but for the use of Jews whose knowledge of their ancestral tongue had lapsed. The remaining books were apparently translated sporadically as the years went by. The prologue to the Wisdom of Jesus ben Sirach (Ecclesiasticus) indicates that all the Prophets and some of the Hagiographa had been translated by 132 B.C. By the dawn of the Christian era probably almost all of the remaining writings had appeared in Greek dress. The importance of this version can scarcely be exaggerated. Without it it is hard to see how Judaism could have survived among the masses of the dispersion. Nor was its influence limited to Judaism. The early Christians adopted it as their sacred Scripture and exercised such proprietary rights that the second century of our era saw three successive Greek versions—those of Aquila, Symmachus,

[17] Preface to *Antt.* §3.

and Theodotion—produced by an outraged Jewry, nominally to provide more accurate translations; actually because the Septuagint had become essentially a Christian book.

Precisely because Greek had entirely supplanted Hebrew and even Aramaic as the language of thousands of Jews, and because even in Palestine Hellenism had made such advances, a brief excursus here may not be out of place.

That Greek was being spoken in cities such as Cæsarea, Sebaste, Tiberias, Sepphoris, and those of the Decapolis is of course certain. Undoubtedly it was also understood by many Jews in Jerusalem. It should not, however, be taken for granted that it had replaced Aramaic or was even on a parity with it in the smaller towns and villages of Palestine or the East. In spite of many modern loose statements the bilingual nature of Palestine should not be unduly stressed. It is utterly impossible to argue from analogy or to get a cross section of the whole land, since the usage was apparently totally different in different places.

This is made strikingly clear by a detail in the fascinating *Life of Porphyry* by Mark the Deacon. Porphyry was bishop of Gaza (*ca.* 395-420 A.D.), a city which from its very beginning had been non-Jewish. He was very much disturbed by the presence of the heathen temple of Marnas in his diocese. Finally he betook himself to Constantinople and by a series of clever tricks which revealed that at least one son of the light was as wise as those of the world obtained imperial sanction for the demolition of the obnoxious Marneion. On his return to Gaza he still found his task uncompleted, for the devotees of Marnas had fortified their temple. While pondering as to the best means of procedure, a seven-year-old child stepped forward and through divine inspiration gave them instruction in Aramaic. Then to the vast amazement of the listeners he repeated it in Greek. Then Mark says, "And calling his mother the bishop asked her whether she or her son knew the Greek tongue: but she affirmed with oaths that neither she nor her son knew Greek."[18] This incident, occurring about four hundred years after the ministry of Jesus, and in a Greek city, indicates that the Greek tongue was but little known to the lower classes of Palestine at any time.

To cite the presence of Greek inscriptions[19] and the presumption that in the cities Greek was known among the educated classes is as futile as to try to prove that Americans know Latin from the fact that college diplomas are penned in that tongue and that Catholic priests are supposed to be able to converse in it. Occasional Greek words and terms may have worked their

[18] *Vita Porphyris* 68. This very important document is available in English translation and will prove a mine of useful information to the student of Christian beginnings.

[19] The Hasmoneans had coined their money with both Greek and Hebrew inscriptions. From the time of Herod it was limited to Greek.

way into the Aramaic speech, but because a man today uses such words or phrases as *rendez vous, café, restaurant, hors de combat, menu,* and *table d'hôte* does not constitute evidence that he speaks or understands French. When Paul wished to speak to people in Jerusalem he spoke in Aramaic.[20] Similarly, when Titus repeatedly called the Jews to surrender, he "sent Josephus to speak to them in their own language."[21]

Among the better educated classes, on the other hand, it was probably pretty well known. As we have seen, Hellenistic districts surrounded Palestine; even in the interior there were cities like Scythopolis and Sebaste. Before the Maccabean revolt Palestine had been in the hands of rulers whose culture was Greek. Many of the high priests had been on the side of Greek civilization. Some of the Hasmoneans had promoted it. Herod and the Romans had been definite protagonists; the former had surrounded himself with Greek literati; one of them, Nicolas of Damascus, was his chief adviser. Festivals and Greek games, mercenary soldiers, whom Josephus says Herod had employed, the throngs of Greek-speaking Jewish pilgrims who came to the feasts—all these must have made it easy for the Jerusalemites to have picked up a smattering of the language. Galilee was nominally Jewish, though probably largely by the path of conversion, but the cities had large numbers of Greeks, as is indicated by Josephus' remark:

> But Jesus and his party slew all the Greeks that were inhabitants of Tiberias, and as many others as were their enemies before the war began.[22]

Finally, it may be remembered that in the Mishna[23] it is said that at the time of Titus fathers were forbidden to allow their sons to learn Greek. This has usually been interpreted to mean that formerly this had been practised.

We may accordingly conclude that the educated and richer classes in the cities did know Greek—in greater or less degrees—but that the uneducated peasants in the hill countries, among whom were Jesus and his early disciples, did not for many years. And this conclusion is all the securer from the hint in the *Life of Porphyry* that even in the Hellenistic city of Gaza the lower classes had failed to learn the tongue.

The Septuagint may well be called the flower of Alexandrian Judaism; in addition to this were other works which may be briefly mentioned. Any detailed examination would lead us far afield. While Judaism in Palestine was summoning defenders to throw off the galling yoke of enforced hellenization from Syria in the Maccabean revolt, the Jews in Alexandria were concerned with a very different problem. Their attempt was to commend their faith to the gentiles, if not to win converts, at least to create a favourable

[20] Acts 21:40; 22:2.
[21] *Wars* 5,9,2; cf. 6,2,1; 6,6,2.
[22] *Life* 12 (end). This Jesus was the son of Sapphias, one of the rebels in the great war.
[23] M. Sotah 9,14.

and respectful disposition toward Judaism and the law. Accordingly, in contrast to the pugnacious Daniel or gloating Esther the Hellenistic literature is largely apologetic, an attempt to put the best foot forward. Of course in religion apologetics is always combined with polemics. God's herald must always war against the emissaries of Satan. Thus in these writings is regularly contained a bitterly sarcastic attack on the animal worship of Egypt. Of the few monuments of Alexandrian Judaism five may be listed: (1) Wisdom of Solomon; (2) IV Maccabees; (3) Letter of Aristeas; (4) parts of the so-called Sibylline Oracles; (5) Philo.

In all this literature is the attempt to approve Judaism to students of Greek philosophy and to prove that all that is worth while and sound in the latter is contained—was, in fact, anticipated—in the former. Epicureanism was to every Jew an abomination on account of its reputed atheism and emphasis on pleasure as the *summum bonum* of life. His hatred of it was only surpassed by his ignorance of what it actually was. Academic Skepticism as taught by Carneades and Cicero was completely beyond his horizon. Its emphasis upon "suspension of judgment" illustrated by the saying of Sextus Empiricus, "Nothing of itself is either good or ill,"[24] ran counter to everything in his religion. Popular Stoicism, on the other hand, with its theistic turn, its popular monotheism, corresponding hostility to polytheism, and belief in divine retribution, was highly acceptable. Thus in all these writings the classic tetrad of virtues, which from the days of Plato had been the law and the prophets to all Greek ethical thought regardless of school and which Stoicism had appropriated as its own (prudence or wisdom, fortitude, temperance, and justice), plays an important rôle. In the Wisdom of Solomon wisdom is recognized as the root of all the virtues and is practically identified with the "Spirit of God"; her fruits, however, are the classic four.[25] Similarly IV Maccabees evidences Stoic influence:

> For reasoning does not rule over its own affections, but over such as are contrary to justice, and manliness (*i.e.*, courage), and temperance, and prudence; and yet over these, so as to withstand, without destroying them.[26]

> And the forms of wisdom are prudence, and justice, and manliness, and temperance.[27]

Philo finds (allegorically) in the four streams that encompassed Eden an indication of these four cardinal virtues.

The Wisdom of Solomon, written sometime after the Septuagint and before the Christian era, is in regulation manner attributed to Solomon, who is made to prize wisdom above all else. The book is in a way a polemic

[24] xi,140, p. 716.
[25] Wisdom of Solomon 8:7.
[26] IV Macc. 1:6.
[27] *Ibid.* 1:18.

against irreligion in general and against Skeptics and Epicureans in particular. Wisdom is the best thing in the world. Wisdom is religion. True religion is revealed religion as God has given it to the Jews in Scripture. Consequently, the height of folly is irreligion, particularly the denial of divine providence and retributions, and, almost as bad, false religion with its worship of many gods and idols, which finds its culmination in the animal worship of the Egyptians, which every pious Jew, be he ever so irenic, delighted to ridicule. The writing is valuable not alone for itself, but for the light it casts upon its author—probably representative of many of his time. His knowledge of Greek philosophy was but rough-and-ready, acquired, so to speak, "in the air," not as the result of the study of books. That he was of Alexandrian origin is almost certain from his spite toward the worship of animals and his tone in the chapter on the exodus from Egypt and the plagues. Here we have a Jew who thought in Greek; there is no slightest evidence that he knew Hebrew or Aramaic. The Septuagint was his Bible.

Little need here be said of IV Maccabees. Its contrast with the Wisdom of Solomon, however, is instructive. The author, while but a dilettante in Greek philosophy, is very proud of his knowledge and writes in a bombastic and pseudo-literary style, attempting to phrase the most ordinary and commonplace truths with profundity and rhetoric. His thesis is simply: One can live a pious life if he follows the demands of pious reason. This he seeks to prove "with the greatest force from the fortitude of Eleazar, and seven brethren, and their mother, who suffered death in defence of virtue."[28] Then follows a gross and gruesome epitome of those tales of torture from II Maccabees. That the author came from Alexandria is not clear; he is a good illustration, however, of the Hellenistic Jew who sought to ape Greek ways but without the knowledge or ability of a Philo.

Of the Sibylline Oracles only the barest mention is possible. Suffice it to say, from an early time written records of supposed oracles from the Sibyl—later she came to have numerous sisters!—were known and held in the highest reverence. Apparently it was in Alexandria in the second pre-Christian century that Jewish ingenuity turned this effective type of writing to its own advantage. Just as some nameless Jew adopted the clever device of making the courtier Aristeas speak in reverential terms of Judaism and its law, so now the ancient Sibyl is cast in that rôle. Few works of antiquity bristle with more literary and historical problems, for these writings were edited and rearranged not alone by many Jews, but also by later Christians again and again.

In Philo we meet the greatest mind Hellenistic Judaism produced. To what extent he influenced his fellow religionists is uncertain; the influence he exerted upon Christian theology through the famous Alexandrian school

[28] IV Macc. 1:7,8.

cannot be over-emphasized.[29] In contrast to the layman author of the Wisdom of Solomon and the superficial producer of IV Maccabees, in Philo we meet a man thoroughly trained in Greek philosophy but at the same time a fervent Jew whose chief interest is religion. In this latter respect he is head and shoulders above Josephus, who lost what little interest he may originally have had in religion for its own sake as a result of the disaster which his nation had suffered at the hands of those who had a zeal, but not according to knowledge.

For Philo, Greek philosophy and biblical revelation were identical in scope and content. He thus, perhaps in a unique degree, stood as the bridge between Judaism and Hellenism over which Christian theology was to cross. His contributions were many and important. Two may be selected for brief comment. The first of these is his conception of the Logos. God, as pure Being, was transcendent, yet he exercised effective oversight over the phenomenal world. This was effected through the Logos, that is, active divine intelligence, the creative word and revealer of the absolute God. This conception of the Logos—actually almost a secondary god—was a veritable amalgam of the Platonic-Stoic Reason and the Jewish Wisdom and creative word of God. Christianity came later to see in Jesus the embodiment of this divine preëxistent Logos. For Philo, in addition to the Logos were subordinate and partial manifestations of divine reason or logoi. Over this dizzy and swaying bridge between pure Being and the world of phenomena the thinking of millions of his spiritual descendants has sought to pass.

Though his teaching of the Logos has often been hailed as his greatest contribution, his use of allegory as the philosopher's stone which would turn biblical stories into sound philosophical principles has had perhaps even greater effect upon subsequent generations. From the days of Anaxagoras (460 B.C.) the antics of the gods on Olympus had been interpreted in an allegorical sense, for a growing sense of ethical responsibility, quickened by the gibes of the philosophers, had forced the issue. If Homer—the Bible of the Greeks—was not thus to be interpreted, either he was impious or the gods were grossly immoral. Thus the robust story of the loves of Ares and Aphrodite, with the outraged husband Hephæstus standing in the background, was to be seen as a picture of iron subdued by fire and restored to its original hardness by water. When Odysseus filled his ears with wax to drown the songs of the Sirens, we have an allegory of the righteous filling their senses and powers of mind with divine actions and words, so that passions and pleasures which tempt all men on the sea of life might knock at their doors in vain. Of course, according to Homer, Odysseus did no such thing at all. Cornutus, to whom we are indebted for this gem of interpretation, evidences the two requirements for the successful allegorist: *viz.,* (1) indifference to

[29] W. Fairweather, *Jesus and the Greeks,* pp. 161-216, is well worth reading at this juncture.

historical details, with a readiness to suppress or alter them whenever necessary; (2) a complete lack of even a rudimentary sense of humour.

Orthodox Judaism had long seen the values in this type of interpretation. In the Old Testament lay hidden senses and teachings, implicit but not explicit. These were to be recovered at all costs. Sentences, individual words (especially when spelled in an unusual manner), and at a later time even vowel points were of the profoundest value in making the text teach something entirely different from its real meaning.[30] Trivial points thus bore great weight. Rabbi Akiba claimed to have saved the Song of Songs by this means of interpretation. Certainly later Christians did so. Solomon in these exquisite but erotic poems typified Christ; the Shunamite maiden, the Christian church. Thus Christ could sing of the charms of the Church without the somewhat minute anatomical descriptions of the poems offending.

In Philo allegorical interpretation was reduced to a system. Although professing—and believing—to retain the literal sense of the narratives as carrying in themselves historical facts as well as moral insights, he nevertheless made the allegorical more prominent, and never scrupled to turn the story upside down to gain the allegorical significance. Jacob, for example, took a stone for his pillow at Bethel. What this lover of virtue actually did was to select one of the incorporeal intelligences of which the sacred region was full and to apply it to his own mind as to the head of a united body, and, using the pretext as if he were going to sleep, placed the whole of his life as the lightest possible burden upon it.[31]

At times Philo willingly altered the text if he felt that it represented God in an unworthy or impossible sense. How, for example, could Adam actually *hide* from God? Nor did he hesitate to say flatly that some of the statements of the Pentateuch—curiously he rarely quoted either the Prophets or the Writings—could have nothing but an allegorical meaning. How then were we to understand references to "talking serpents" and "trees of life"? In fact, in his writing, especially in the *Allegories of the Sacred Laws*, the modern reader is surprised to see how frankly, if prolixly, Philo recognizes some of the narratives, as the six-day creation of the world or the forming of Eve from Adam's rib, as purely mythical.

I have given more space to this type of pseudo-exposition than it deserves, because of the use made of it by early Christian writers. For Paul the precept, "Thou shalt not muzzle the ox when he treadeth out the corn," was written to allow Christian missionaries to be supported by the people to whom they ministered.

> Is it for the oxen that God careth, or saith he it assuredly for our sake? Yea, for our sake it was written: because he that ploweth ought to plow in hope, and he

[30] See further pp. 104-106.

[31] *de Somniis* 21(§§127 ff.)640M.

that thresheth, to thresh in hope of partaking. If we sowed unto you spiritual things, is it a great matter if we shall reap your carnal things?[32]

When the children of Israel drank from the rock, they "drank of a spiritual rock that followed them: and the rock was Christ."[33] Of the story of Hagar and Sarah he explicitly says:

Which things contain an allegory: for these women are two covenants; one from Mount Sinai, bearing children unto bondage, which is Hagar.[34]

Early Christians found it very valuable as a means of discovering traces of Christ in the Old Testament. The author of the so-called Epistle of Barnabas was peculiarly expert in this sort of thing. When Moses spoke to Joshua—since Barnabas wrote in Greek the latter, of course, was Jesus—and told him that the people should listen to him alone, he did so because the Father was revealing everything concerning his Son Jesus.[35] The classic instance, however, occurs a few pages earlier in the same writing. It is worthy of being quoted in full:

Learn fully then, children of love, concerning all things, for Abraham, who first circumcised, did so looking forward in the spirit to Jesus, and had received the doctrine of the three letters. For it says, "And Abraham circumcised from his household eighteen men and three hundred."[36] What then was the knowledge given to him? Notice that he first mentions the eighteen, and after a pause the three hundred. The eighteen is I and H—you have Jesus[37]—and because the cross was destined to have grace in the T[38] he says "and three hundred." So he indicates Jesus in the two letters and the cross in the other. He knows this who placed the gift of his teaching in our hearts. No one has heard a more excellent lesson from me, but I know that you are worthy.[39]

Similarly Justin Martyr interprets "The government shall be upon his shoulders" to mean "Christ will be hung on the cross." This type of interpretation is, of course, a relic of an earlier, pre-scientific day. No serious student pays any heed to it today, although its exponents still exist. They are usually far less clever than their earlier forbears, for English is not nearly so productive of these subtleties as were Hebrew and Greek.

No survey of the dispersion of Israel would be complete without a brief

[32] I Cor. 9:9-11.

[33] I Cor. 10:4.

[34] Gal. 4:24.

[35] Barn. 12:8.

[36] Greek expresses numerals by the letters of the alphabet. I (ιota) is 10; H (eta) 8; T (tau) 300. Thus 318 would normally be expressed TIH. Barnabas' ingenuity is piqued because instead he read IHT, *i.e.,* 18 and 300.

[37] IH are the first two letters of Jesus when spelled in Greek characters (ΙΗΣΟΥΣ).

[38] From the resemblance of the Greek letter tau (T) to the cross.

[39] Barn. 9:7-9.

mention of Rome, even though the story has often been told. Before the capture of Jerusalem by Pompey it is improbable that there was any Jewish colony on the Tiber. At least that may be inferred from the oft-quoted remark of the later Roman historian, Valerius Maximus:

> He [he is speaking of the prætor Hispalus] compelled the Jews, who had endeavored to corrupt Roman morals by the worship of Jupiter Sabazius, *to return to their homes.*[40]

This took place in the year 139 B.C. The italicized words suggest the transient nature of their visit, and (so Schürer) may refer to the embassy which Simon is said to have sent. If this hypothesis is correct, the reference to "Jupiter Sabazius" would seem to be a confusion between the Phrygian deity so called and Jehovah Sabaoth, and would suggest that some of the members of the embassy were rash enough to try a little missionary work.

On his triumphal return to Rome in 62 B.C. Pompey carried many Jews and settled them on the left bank of the Tiber. There they seemed to have enjoyed many privileges and exemptions. The Roman poets—notably Juvenal—allude to their presence with no great enthusiasm. Suetonius comments on their sincere and noisy grief at the death of Cæsar, whom, as we have already noticed, they had come to feel their benefactor. Augustus did not alter his predecessor's policy, but in 19 A.D. an event occurred which showed that after all they were only tolerated. Fulvia, a Roman matron who had become proselyte, made a donation to four Jews who had pretended it was to be sent to Jerusalem. Her husband, getting wind of it, protested to Tiberius, who ordered four thousand to Sardinia to aid in ridding that island of outlaws; the remainder appear to have been banished.[41] According to Philo, Tiberius allowed them to return, while Josephus asserts that Claudius began his reign with two edicts of toleration for the Jews. A few years later the Roman Jews were expelled as brawlers, or at least suffered a drastic curtailment of their privileges. The brief word of Suetonius, *Judæos impulsore Chresto assidue tumultuantes Roma expulit,* while far from clear, may imply that the "tumult" was between Jews and Christians, and that the historian, writing nearly a century later, thought that the "Chrestus" was himself personally present as ringleader. If so, this would indicate Christians in Rome by 49-50 A.D., as is inherently probable.

Enough has been said to justify the statements of both Strabo and the Sibyl as to the ubiquity of the sons of Abraham in the days of the Christian beginnings.

A subsequent chapter on the nature and emphases of Judaism will indicate how it was that this religion contained in itself the means of cementing into

[40] *Idem Judæos, qui sabazi Jovis cultu Romanos inficere mores conati erant, repetere domos suas coegit*—i,3,2.

[41] Tacitus and Suetonius as well as Josephus attest this edict.

one unit its sons and daughters wherever they might chance to reside. One or two other points may be noticed here in concluding this rapid survey of the far-flung front of Jewry.

At first sight, the student might be inclined to feel that the reforms of Josiah with the centralizing of worship and the prohibition of sacrifice outside of Jerusalem might have proved the doom of Israel when the city fell, and its inhabitants went to the four corners of the earth. That this was not the case is but another proof of Jewish ingenuity in constantly changing and adapting, yet with the calm conviction that it was continuing to stand where the patriarchs had stood.

In theory Judaism was a religion of sacrifice; the temple in Jerusalem was the sole place where sacrifices could be offered. Accordingly a surrogate for the temple became imperative if Judaism were to survive. This was found in the synagogue. In the days of the New Testament synagogues were to be found not alone in Palestine and Egypt, but in all the lands of the dispersion. They had become the rallying-points of Judaism. Here twice each week in addition to the Sabbath services Jews met for study of the Scripture and for prayer. The temple remained the symbol of Judaism; the synagogue exerted the real power. Whatever its actual origin had been, by the Christian era it had become hoary with age and dignity and was popularly believed to go back to Moses; its prayers to the "men of the Great Synagogue."[42]

In the synagogue service selections from the law, that is, the Pentateuch, were read. Ultimately the Pentateuch was divided systematically into lections that it might be read through in a stated period—three years, or later, following the Babylonian practice, in one year. In Palestine and Babylonia the sections would be read in Hebrew, the reading stopping frequently to allow the now unintelligible Hebrew to be translated into Aramaic. For centuries these translations continued to be rough-and-ready paraphrases; later they were reduced to writing and are known as Targums. The skill of the translator must have been taxed if the standard set by Rabbi Judah was often followed:

> He who translates a verse with strict literalness is a falsifier, and he who makes addition to it is a blasphemer.[43]

Outside Palestine and Babylonia the sections were read from the Greek Bible.

Following the section from the law came one from the prophets and historical books. Eventually a cycle of lections, parallel to those from the Pentateuch, was adopted; apparently this was comparatively late. Then followed the sermon which was based on the daily lesson, or used it as a convenient point of departure. There was no fixed ministry. Any qualified man might

[42] For further discussion of this tendency to read back, see below, pp. 105 ff.
[43] See G. F. Moore, *Judaism,* Vol. I, p. 304.

be invited to read, translate, or speak. Scholars who were either members of the particular congregation or present as visitors might be invited; they had no especial rights. This is illustrated frequently in the New Testament. On one occasion Jesus is represented as being invited to read; after reading the lesson which chanced (appropriately) to be from the scroll of Isaiah he handed it back to the attendant, sat down, and expounded it.[44] Similarly in the synagogue in Pisidian Antioch it was said to Paul and Barnabas by the rulers of the synagogue, after the law and the prophets had been read: "Brethren, if ye have any word of exhortation for the people, say on."[45] Of the ancient liturgy two parts are still in use: the Shema and the Shemoneh Esreh. The former, consisting of three short paragraphs from the Pentateuch[46] beginning with the words, "Hear, O Israel, the Lord our God is one Lord," was apparently taken over by the synagogue from the temple service, and thus at least antedates 70 A.D. The latter, while somewhat more recent, is still very ancient (70-100 A.D.). The title means *eighteen* (benedictions); at an early date an additional prayer against apostates—in the modern texts the word "slanderers" has been substituted—was inserted as the twelfth, thus bringing the total to nineteen.

Yet, while the synagogues, which were to be found in every Jewish community at home and abroad, provided the means of worship in lieu of the distant temple, their chief function, as all the early Jewish writers reveal, was instruction. They were, as Philo calls them, houses of instruction. Judaism was, as we shall see, a religion where knowledge was imperative. God had revealed his will to men; they in turn must know it to do it. Thus Josephus remarks:

> Our legislator . . . demonstrated the law to be the best and the most necessary instruction of all others, permitting the people to leave off their other employments, and to assemble together for the hearing of the law, and learning it exactly, and this not once or twice, or oftener, but every week.[47]

Thus study of the law, even though many of its requirements could not be carried out away from Jerusalem, was not only at once the duty and privilege of every Jew wherever he might find himself; it was also one of the most powerful factors in keeping ever before his eye the fact that he was one of the children of Zion. It was the sacred responsibility of parents to teach their children God's law. The very fact of dwelling in an alien land amid surroundings that tended to make law observance difficult must often have tended to make this responsibility the more keenly felt.

Regarding the existence of schools, apart from the synagogue, the evidence

[44] Luke 4:16-21.
[45] Acts 13:15.
[46] Deut. 6:4-9; 11:13-21; Numb. 15:37-41.
[47] *c. Apion*, ii,18.

is not clear. In the Talmud is an interesting tradition, although it is palpably late:

> Verily, let it be remembered to that man for good, R. Joshua ben Gamaliel[48] is his name, for had he not been, the law would have been forgotten in Israel. At first every one that had a father received from him instruction in the law, but he that had no father learned not the law. . . . Thereafter teachers for the children were appointed in Jerusalem. . . . But even this measure sufficed not, for he that had a father was brought by him to school, and was taught there, but he that had no father was not brought there. In consequence of this it was ordained that teachers should be appointed in every district. To them the children were sent when they were sixteen or seventeen years of age. When a teacher became angry with a scholar, the latter stamped his feet and ran away. In this condition education remained until the time of Joshua ben Gamaliel, who acclaimed that in every province and every town there should be teachers appointed, to whom children should be brought at the age of six or seven years.

On the other hand, in praise of the merits of Simon ben Shetach, the brother of Queen Alexandra under whom the Pharisees had had halcyon days, it is recounted in the Palestinian Talmud that he made statutes, of which the second was: The children shall attend the elementary school.

Thus exact statement regarding the prevalence of schools, even in Palestine, during the days of Jesus would be rash. They were probably to be found in Jerusalem and in the larger cities, at home and abroad; that they existed in the remoter country villages, while possible, is by no means certain. When they did exist, they appear to have been of two grades: elementary and more advanced. In the former, the children learned to read the Hebrew Bible and received elementary instruction in its meaning. In the latter, the law was systematically studied following the weekly cycle of the synagogue lections and the unwritten law[49] was memorized. But even where these schools were not available the Scribes sought whole-heartedly to acquaint the masses with the content and implications of the law. Occasional sporadic esoteric sects, like the Essenes, there may have been who jealously guarded their secrets; such, however, was not the temper of Judaism. "Seek and ye shall find" was a lesson Jesus had learned in the synagogue.

Furthermore, there seem to have been very few attempts on the part of the local governments—at least during the days of Roman control—to destroy the sense of solidarity among the Jewish colonists; and those few attempts signally failed. Contributions to the temple in Jerusalem were constantly being sent. A Flaccus in Asia might confiscate such money,[50] but this was exceptional. Augustus had permitted this remitting of gifts and treated the appropriation of such sums by the local authorities as sacrilege. In addition

[48] High priest *ca.* 63-65 A.D.

[49] See below pp. 106 ff.

[50] See Cicero, *pro Flacco* 28.

to these occasional gifts every Jewish male over eighteen years of age contributed annually his half-shekel (two drachma) tax for the support of the temple.[51] This appears to have been one of the few taxes in the history of the world that was cheerfully paid.

Considerable latitude was allowed the local Jewish congregations in the Roman world in the exercise of jurisdiction over their own members, at least in civil matters; that this jurisdiction was extended to criminal matters *outside of Palestine*, while often maintained, especially in the light of the book of Acts,[52] is by no means certain. On the other hand, Paul's own words, "Of the Jews five times received I forty stripes save one . . . once was I stoned,"[53] indicate that such authority was at times exercised, whether lawfully or not. Exemption from military service, because of its demands for Sabbath service, was the order of the day. To use the later phrase coined by Tertullian, Judaism was a *religio licita*.[54] Emperor worship at first might have seemed to endanger the status of the Jew, for he alone remained aloof and refused to subscribe to their claims of divinity. Most of the emperors recognized that this was not constructive disloyalty or treason and winked at it as but another of the silly and barbarian prejudices of this curious people. Josephus painstakingly makes the exact reason for the refusal clear:

> But then our legislator hath forbidden us to make images, not by way of denunciation beforehand, that the Roman authority was not to be honoured, but as despising a thing that was neither necessary nor useful for either God or man; and he forbade them, as we shall prove hereafter, to make their images for any part of the animal creation. Yet hath our legislator nowhere forbidden us to pay honour to worthy men, provided they be of another kind, and inferior to those we pay to God: with which honours we willingly testify our respect to our emperors and to the people of Rome; we also offer perpetual sacrifices for them; nor do we only offer them every day at the common expense of all the Jews, but although we offer no other such sacrifices out of our common expenses, no, not for our own children, yet do we this as a peculiar honour to the emperors, and to them alone, while we do the same to no other person whomsoever.[55]

This refusal to be as other men of necessity drew the bonds of union between Jew and Jew the more tight, and tended to insulate him from outside influence, although at the expense of gaining the title, later borne by Christians as well, "haters of the human race."[56] Philo laments that Jews alone were exempted from the universal religious toleration of the empire.[57] To an

[51] Cf. Matt. 17:24-27.
[52] Acts 9:2; 22:19; 26:11 f. For the critical difficulties underlying this account see pp. 409 f., 414.
[53] II Cor. 11:24,25.
[54] *Apologet.* 21.
[55] *c. Apion.* ii,26 (end).
[56] Cf. Tacitus, *Hist.* v, 5—*Apud ipsos fides obstinata, misericordia in promptu, sed adversus omnes alios hostile odium.*
[57] *Legatio ad Gaium* 16(§117)562M.

extent his words were true, but simply because the Jew himself alone was intolerant.

Yet, none the less, there was a steady stream of gentile converts—proselytes—to Judaism. The very fact that the Jew claimed loudly that he and only he was right threw a glamour then—as such similar claims do today. Many were inclined to take him at his own valuation. In spite of the somewhat jaundiced word, attributed to Jesus,

> Woe unto you Scribes and Pharisees, hypocrites! for ye compass sea and land to make one proselyte; and when he is become so, ye make him twofold more a son of hell than yourselves,[58]

Judaism does not appear to me to have ever been a religion actively engaged in making converts—today we call such an attitude evangelistic—in the sense that early Christianity was. With a feeling of complacency, as it thought of its own long history and especial favour in the eyes of God, there never was a manifest tendency to cheapen all this or try to swell its numbers. Hillel might say, "Love the creatures, and bring them nigh to the Torah," but the emphasis seems to have been one of passive readiness—whosoever would might come; the door stood open—rather than of any general attempt to go into the highways and hedges to constrain men to come in. In the third century R. Eleazar could declare that the reason Israel was scattered among the nations was to make proselytes; that Abraham himself was the type of proselyte and a great maker of them. But the temper of Judaism is seen in the word:

> A man may wish to become a priest or a Levite, but he cannot, because his father was not one; but if he wishes to become righteous he can do so, even if he be a heathen, for righteousness is not a matter of descent.

That is, teachers were willing and glad to make proselytes of those who were willing to pay the price. They must in every case follow the ceremonial laws, including the Sabbath, festival, and food legislation and, above all, must submit to the painful rite of circumcision and the ceremonial bath. The gentile who met these demands became a Jew, entitled to all the privileges and subject to all the requirements of the born Jew. He and he alone may be spoken of as a proselyte. The terms, "half proselyte" and "proselyte of the gate," are unknown to early Judaism and have no place in any serious discussion. To be sure, there were many gentiles who were not ready to burn all their bridges behind them and to become Jews, but who were ready to renounce idolatrous practices and who frequented the synagogue. They were welcomed—or at least tolerated—but had no status whatsoever in Judaism. They were regularly expected to observe the so-called Noachian laws prohibiting: (1) idolatry; (2) blasphemy; (3) cursing judges, *i.e.,* enjoining

[58] Matt. 23:15.

obedience to the Jewish courts; (4) murder; (5) *araiyot, i.e.,* prohibition of various sexual offences; (6) theft; (7) eating flesh cut from the living animal, *i.e.,* the prohibition of flesh with the life blood in it. These were believed to have been binding upon all decent men from the earliest beginning. It was incredible that there could have been a time when they were not in force. Thus, said Judaism, the first six of these laws had been communicated to Adam; they had been repeated to Noah and the seventh added when he was permitted to eat the flesh of animals.

The lofty, if uncompromising, monotheism of Judaism in contrast to the down-at-the-heel polytheism of the Græco-Roman world which had to a measure been discredited through the preceding centuries; the central place that ethics played in the Jewish law; a sort of grudging admiration for the race which seemed to flourish the more it was persecuted; the fact that religions from the East were becoming popular—one might almost say, the fad—in the Roman world—all this justified Josephus' boast,

> Many of [the Grecians] have come over to our laws, and some of them have continued in their observation, although others of them had not courage enough to persevere, and so departed from them again.[59]

If we can believe him, nearly all the women of Damascus were "addicted to the Jewish religion."[60] Nero's empress Poppæa is said to have been distinctly friendly to Judaism. All sorts of legends have gathered around the head of the emperor Antoninus Pius, who, it is claimed, will lead the procession of proselytes in the Age to Come because he had become circumcised. The oft-repeated story of Queen Helena and her son Izates, king of Adiabene,[61] while replete with all the gossipy details so dear to Josephus—especially when his historic sources for a period were running low—reveals that occasionally even reigning princes took the full step to Judaism. The biting words of Juvenal pictures the younger generation in Rome going beyond their fathers and becoming proselytes:

> Some, who have had a father who reveres the Sabbath, worship nothing but the clouds and divinity of the heaven, and can detect no difference between eating swine's flesh, from which their fathers abstained, and that of man. Finally they take to circumcision. Although accustomed to flout the laws of Rome, they learn to practise and revere the Jewish law and all that Moses committed to his secret tome: not to show the way to any not worshipping by the same rite nor to conduct any save the circumcised to the desired fountain. For all this was the father to blame for whom every seventh day was one of idleness and kept apart from all the concerns of life.[62]

Before the eye of every Jew, wherever he might reside, hovered the hope

[59] *c. Apion.* ii,11.
[60] *Wars* 2,20,2.
[61] *Antt.* 20,2,1-4,3.
[62] *Sat.* 14,96-106.

of seeing the holy city at least once before he died. All that was tangible in his religion was embodied in Zion, "whither the tribes go up." Each festival season saw thousands on the roads to and from. Returning, they brought tales of the glories of the temple, of the actual sacrifices there conducted—to the foreign Jew simply rules to be memorized and idealized—of the chanting priests and the fragrant smoke of incense. All this tended to wipe away the intervening miles. This too was his city, his temple. In the future—when he did not know—God would sound his call. The time of punishment and absence would be over. Until then he would wait in hope.

Chapter VI

THE GENIUS OF JUDAISM

MUCH has already been said in the preceding pages of Jewish beliefs and practices. A more detailed and exact statement is here in order. Although, as we shall see in the following chapters, by no means all Jews saw eye to eye, there were certain fundamental concepts held in common by all. These we must now examine.

With the religious life in Israel before the exile we need not concern ourselves. It was not till the promulgation of the Deuteronomic code (*ca.* 621 B.C.) that we can speak of Judaism as such. It was then that the Jew, as we know him, came into existence, with his feeling of uniqueness and corresponding separateness from the non-Jew, to result in the great chasm between Jew and gentile. This feeling of separateness increased until he believed that it had always been in force. Even before the legislation from Mt. Sinai which had given it definite expression, recognition of it had been vouchsafed to Abraham, who had received in his own body a visible sign of his immediate relationship to Jehovah and consequent separation from all not similarly privileged. Since as a people he stood apart from the rest of the world, he must of necessity be more closely joined to his fellows. The result of this was unity and strength, but bought at the expense of popularity, since gentiles in every age have not unnaturally looked askance at this quintessence of clannishness.

Judaism was a revealed religion and took itself seriously as such. Failure to grasp this central fact has led to all sorts of misconceptions about the Jewish law and its fancied burden to Israel. God was the centre of the Jew's life and thought. He it was who had revealed a religion through the fathers and Moses which was destined to become the universal religion of mankind. God had revealed his whole will; everything that men were to do he had revealed to them. Moral conduct, the way men were to worship him and regard him, even their attitudes of mind and will—all these things had been revealed and were man's for the learning. The law—the Jew called it Torah—was thus God's great gift to his children.

Accordingly, the Jew strove with all his might to learn God's will and to do it. Keeping the law was synonymous with morality and religion. And he sought to keep it with no ulterior motive: He did it because he loved God and wished to do his will. Had he been asked why he did it, he might have answered that God's long-deferred promise of a future golden age was dependent upon the conformity of his people to his will as he had revealed it and as they knew it; that if Israel would keep the law but a single day the golden age would dawn. But such an answer, which would simply have reflected the central place the law occupied in his thinking, would have been to a large extent an explanation, not a reason. He sought to do what was right because it was right—and because he desired to do it. God's will had become his.

Say not, I will study the Torah with the purpose of being called Sage or Rabbi, to acquire fortune or to be rewarded for it in the world to come; but do it for the sake of thy love to God, though the glory will come in the end.[1]

Accordingly, keeping of Torah was no hardship. Much nonsense has been written about the burden of the law. We are apt to approach the matter from our own experience with legislatures and Congress which grind out endless absurd and contradictory enactments, which if they were kept would indeed be a burden. Thus for us law is too apt to be regarded as the result of the ingenuity of interested politicians. Such a notion would have been incomprehensible to ancient Judaism. God, not venial men, was its author; his motives were entirely pure and beneficent. Such a difference of attitude makes all the difference in the world. Thus the pious Jew sought to know and to keep the law, not because he *ought* or *must*, but because he *wanted to*. Many were the Jews at the beginning of our era who could have echoed the words of the Psalmist with the fullest sincerity; "Oh, how I love thy law,"[2] or have agreed that for the righteous man "His delight is in the law of the Lord, and on his law doth he meditate day and night";[3] while for him, "The law of thy mouth is better unto me than thousands of gold and silver."[4] To hear that law-keeping was a wearisome burden, a noose around his neck, would have amazed him. The answer was ready to hand: "And I shall walk at liberty; for I have sought thy precepts."[5] Far from being burdened "whosoever receiveth upon him the yoke of Torah, they remove from him the yoke of royalty and the yoke of worldly care."[6] It was rather the gentile who was hedged about with dreads and fears:

The son who serves his father serves him with joy, saying, "Even if I do not entirely succeed (in carrying out his commandments), yet, as a loving father, he will not be angry with me: while the gentile slave is always afraid lest he may commit some fault, and therefore serves God in a condition of anxiety and confusion.[7]

[1] Sifrè 79 b—quoted by Schechter, *Some Aspects of Rabbinic Theology,* p. 68.
[2] Psalm 119:97.
[3] Psalm 1:2; cf. Psalms 19:7; 40:8.
[4] Psalm 119:72.
[5] Psalm 119:45.
[6] Abot 3,6.
[7] Tanḥuma Noah 19.

God had revealed the law; but conversely the law also revealed God, and the true Jew sought as the *summum bonum* of life to be as near like God as possible. This Philo states expressly:

My good man, the best of all prayers, and the end, and proper object of happiness, is to attain to a likeness of God.[8]

This was possible since every man was created in the image of God. Thus the adage, "Ye shall be holy; for I Jehovah your God am Holy,"[9] was the heart of the law. He was to walk in God's ways. As God was kind to the widow, and orphans, and strangers, so must he be.

The notion that for the Jew at the beginning of the Christian era God had become remote, that as the King of the universe he was likened to an Eastern despot, completely inaccessible, to be feared, not worshipped, while still widely held, is entirely mistaken. An examination of the titles with which God was addressed and of the petitions of early Jewish prayers would be sufficient to destroy this misunderstanding.

O our Father, merciful Father, ever compassionate, have mercy upon us. . . . Thou hast chosen us from all peoples and tongues, and hast brought us near unto thy great name forever in faithfulness, to thank thee and proclaim thy unity in love; blessed art thou, O God, who hast chosen thy people Israel, in love. . . . Forgive us our Father, for we have sinned; pardon us our King, for we have transgressed . . . blessed art thou, our God, who art gracious and dost abundantly forgive.[10]

God might be supramundane; he was not extramundane. R. Johanan phrased it aptly: "Wherever you find the almighty power of God, you will find in the context his lowly deeds."[11]

In the later apocalypses angels came to play a prominent part, but they did not lessen the confidence that no intermediary was necessary between man and God. The priest might offer the sacrifice, angels might serve as God's messengers to men, but every Israelite had direct access to him. An occasional reference to the pleading of an intercessor—as Abraham for Sodom[12] or the angel of Jehovah for Jerusalem in ruins[13]—occurs. None the less the confidence of orthodox Judaism is found in the word of R. Judan:

If a man has a patron, when a time of trouble comes upon him, he does not at once enter into his patron's presence, but comes and stands at the door of his house and calls one of the servants or a member of his family, who brings word

[8] *de Decalogo* 15(§73)193M.

[9] Lev. 19:2.

[10] For this catena of passages I am indebted to S. Schechter, *Some Aspects of Rabbinic Theology,* p. 22.

[11] See Moore, *Judaism,* Vol. I, pp. 440 ff.

[12] Gen. 18:22-33.

[13] Zech. 1:12.

to him, "So-and-so is standing at the entrance in your court." Perhaps the patron will let him in, perhaps he will make him wait. Not so is God. If trouble comes upon a man, let him not cry to Michael or to Gabriel; but let him cry unto me, and I will answer him forthwith, as the Scripture says, "Whosoever shall call on the name of the Lord shall be delivered."[14]

Not only was the "humility of God" clearly expressed in Psalm 18:35(36)—though rendered in our English versions by such mistranslations as "gentleness" or "condescension" through the mistaken feeling of reluctance of the Christian translators to posit such a virtue for God[15]—but the rabbis had no hesitation in heaping human qualities and acts upon God. Thus he was best man at the wedding of Adam and Eve; he teaches Torah to Israel and keeps school now in heaven for those who died in their infancy; he prays himself and thus teaches Israel how to pray; he visited Abraham when the latter was sick and mourned with Isaac at his father's death. Not the ascription of the humbler qualities to God, but the exaltation and deification of man aroused the ire of the rabbis. So God could say to Moses:

Though I made thee a God to Pharaoh, thou must not become overbearing (and think thyself God); *I* am the Lord.[16]

In this connection it may be said that all this does not reveal merely a later phase of Judaism. After the second century of the present era conditions were by no means of a nature to make any great advances in Judaism probable; nor is there any evidence that such a change took place. Continuity, and that with very little change, is the most striking impression. It is often said that Rabbinical Judaism took its stand in the great schools, as in that of Hillel. It is far more probable that the phenomenon was much older, going back to the days of the restoration, and that the real revival took place, due to the efforts of those men who were styled the "Men of the Great Synagogue." They laid the tracks on which later Judaism continued to run.

Accordingly, it is reasonably certain that the phrase, "Our Father who art in heaven," which occurs in the Gospel of Matthew was not, as has often been popularly supposed, an indication of a radical about face from the conception of God held by orthodox Judaism, but was one of the many legacies of the Synagogue to the Church. Nor is it to be argued that while for Judaism God may have been the Father of the nation, it remained for Christianity to personalize the relationship, to make him the Father of the individual. There seems to be absolutely no warrant for such a notion, however deeply entrenched it may be in popular belief. It may not be out of place to observe that while the Christian gospels represent Judaism as

[14] Quoted by Moore, *Judaism*, Vol. I, p. 439.
[15] Enslin, *The Ethics of Paul*, p. 257.
[16] *Idem*, p. 258.

often scandalized by Jesus' actions—especially his laxness with regard to the laws of the Sabbath—the prayer he is said to have taught his disciple, "Our Father who art in heaven," did not appear to arouse a ripple of protest. Had not even Solomon remarked: "Thou hast chosen me to be a king of thy people, and a judge of thy sons and daughters;"[17] had he not condemned the wicked for their protest against the just man for making his boast that God was his father?[18]

Since the Jew believed that in the law God had revealed his entire will for man, sin was not a matter of error of judgment or of missing the mark. It was an unfilial act of defiance to a loving, gracious father; in short, rebellion against God. The father said, "Son, go work today in the vineyard"; the son replied, "I will not."[19] In such a situation only one course of action was possible: The son must repent and go into the vineyard; the prodigal must come back from the far country and seek the father's forgiveness. This Isaiah phrases explicitly in his famous word, "Cease to do evil; learn to do well."[20] Repentance was a cardinal point in Jewish thinking. He knew he could never hope to achieve perfect law observance, though he sought to hitch his wagon to the star. God was not unreasonable. "He knoweth our frame; he remembereth that we are dust."[21] Before the earth was created, while the law was still only in the mind of God, there abode coëval with it the possibility of repentance. This vivid phrasing of the later rabbis simply gave expression to the confidence Israel long had had.[22]

God was preëminently a God of justice. "The first question a man is asked at the Last Judgment is whether he has dealt fairly with his neighbour." God never shows partiality or favouritism, never accepts bribes; neither must his people. The ideal man is

He that walketh righteously, and speaketh uprightly; he that despiseth the gain of oppressions, that shaketh his hands from taking a bribe, that stoppeth his ears from hearing of blood, and shutteth his eyes from looking upon evil.[23]

Nor is regret at past misdeeds sufficient. Like Zacchæus, he must make restitution before he can hope to gain divine forgiveness.

Another emphasis of Judaism was upon moral purity with a corresponding emphasis upon a sane and wholesome family life. God was a God of purity. None of the amours or other scandalous action of the gods of the Babylonian and Greek pantheons were ascribed to him. Sexual purity was thus a fundamental requirement for Israel. Adultery was forbidden in the

[17] Wisdom of Solomon 9:7.

[18] *Idem* 2:16. The student who is still skeptical will do well to read Moore, *Judaism,* Vol. II, pp. 201-211.

[19] Matt. 21:28-32.

[20] Isa. 1:16 f.

[21] Psalm 103:14.

[22] For further discussion of sin and repentance, see below, p. 159.

[23] Isa. 33:15.

decalogue; incest and the other perversions were forbidden in Leviticus 18. Marriage was ordained and blessed by God. Had he not chosen precisely this figure to illustrate his bond to Israel? The average Jewish boy was married by his eighteenth year; celibacy was both abnormal and rare. The lament of the Psalmist, "Behold I was brought forth in iniquity; and in sin did my mother conceive me,"[24] was never intended or understood as implying anything reprehensible or defiling in the marriage relation. It was simply the prayer of the contrite sinner, aware that from his very beginning he had erred from the Father's path.

Nor was asceticism ever a characteristic of Judaism. Occasional ascetics and groups of ascetics there may have been; but they were exceptional and exerted very little, if any, influence. The tone of Jewish thinking in this regard is well illustrated by the sayings:

> He who subjects himself to needless self-castigation and fastings or even denies himself the enjoyment of wine is a sinner.

> Are not the things prohibited you in the law enough for you, that you want to prohibit yourself other things?

These were lofty and noble conceptions. Naturally all did not reach the standard set for them then any more than all do now. None the less these were ideals toward which the pious reached. Such was the heritage of the Church from the Synagogue; such the environs that helped to produce a Jesus and a Paul.

Its Literature

A lasting memorial to the central place occupied by the law and its significance as the perfect and complete revelation of God's will for the world is found in the huge literature of interpretation which the law produced. It is only as one understands this phenomenon, commonly dubbed "the rabbinic literature,"—and unfortunately for most students Jew and gentile alike, this knowledge is at second hand and accordingly imperfect and inexact—that he can hope to look through the eyes of the Jew at the time when Christianity made its appearance and gained its growth.

Normative Judaism is a straight line development from the Old Testament and is due, as has already been pointed out, to the fact that the religion took itself seriously as a revealed religion. All the peculiarities of the rabbinic literature—and they are many!—are due to this. God had revealed his whole will for the whole life of man; this revelation, however, was not explicit, but implicit. The Scripture is not at all points clearly intelligible: parts *seem* to be conflicting, but really are not. In short, there was no such thing as a development in God's revelation. All had come

[24] Psalm 51:5.

from Sinai; it could not and did not contradict itself. Since all was implicit—written, so to speak, in invisible ink—a premium was laid on ingenuity. No slightest detail could be overlooked. For example: In Lev. 25:36 it is said, "That thy brother may live with thee." On the significance of these words Akiba and Ben Paturi are said to have had a heated discussion, as to how these words applied to two men thirsting in the desert and with water sufficient for only one. Said the one: "They are to share the limited supply, for the Scripture says 'that *thy brother may live* with thee.'" Said the other, "No, there would not be enough for both; the man is to keep the limited supply for himself, for the Scripture directs that the man himself is to live: 'that thy brother may live *with thee.*'"

Or again, every variant in spelling, every case of unusual word order, might be pregnant with meaning. Thus the school of Akiba found an explanation of the prohibition of the use of the tetragrammaton in the so-called defective spelling of the Hebrew word לעלם in Exod. 3:15. The ordinary way to spell it was לעולם. Now God knew how to spell. Hence there must be a reason for the difference here. It was not to be pronounced לְעֹלָם (l^{e}ōlam) "for ever," but לְעַלֵּם (l^{e}allēm) "to conceal." Akiba was so proficient in this atomistic interpretation and so skilled in finding meat in the most unlikely places that, according to the later rabbis, Moses is said to have been amazed as he sat in a back seat in Akiba's classroom to have heard the learned exegete find matter in his law that he himself had never dreamed of.

All this was no mere casuistic exercise, as has sometimes been said; it was the natural consequence of Judaism's confidence that from the very beginning God had foreseen all the circumstances of life that would ever arise and had been at pains to anticipate them. Whatever was now under his blessing had always been dear to him. God had told all to Moses—all that even later writers as in Esther should say. Many of the prescriptions and proscriptions in the later developed law—even the Passover meal!—were practised in Abraham's household. The law had been created before the creation of the world and was privately communicated to occasional especially eminent figures, but it was not promulgated. It had been revealed to Moses at Sinai, but had been in part forgotten and needed to be recovered exegetically. The custodians of this "unwritten law" were the learned; in it their learning consisted.

Failure to grasp this fundamental thread, namely, that for Judaism there was not—could not be—such a conception as the modern "progressive revelation," not only renders the rabbinic writings totally unintelligible, but throws much of the Old Testament into hopeless confusion. A few illustrations will suffice. From the days of Solomon the temple stood as the outward symbol of the presence of Jehovah. Here was his house. As the years went by it became inconceivable that there could ever have been a time when he had not dwelt with his people. But the time of the building of the first temple was too firmly etched in the memory of man to make possible an error here; there had been no earlier temple. Hence apparently arose the notion of the tabernacle—a movable temple, so to speak—which the children of Israel could bear about with them through the wilderness wandering.

Similarly the office of high priest, as we have seen, apparently emerged during the exile, when a king no longer overshadowed. But there could be nothing new for Judaism; hence we find Aaron in the robes of the high priest many centuries before. Or again, the synagogue, peculiarly an institution of the exile, was read back to the time of Moses. The Noachian laws were known in part to Adam; were completed for Noah.

Perhaps the most striking example is found in the matter of the eighth-century prophets. To us, they seem to have heralded a right-about-face. This should not obscure the fact that not only for later Judaism but for the prophets themselves theirs was no such rôle. They were simply calling Israel back to the paths of true religion which God had long before revealed, in which they had at first walked, but from which they had strayed away.

As has been well said, all rabbinic literature is but an expansion of the Shema. It was the reduction to writing of the unwritten law which had previously been passed on from teacher to pupil, and which—in spite of the frequently quoted ideal that a student should be like a plastered cistern which never lost a drop but which never itself added to its content—had grown so mightily that eventually a rescript of it became a sheer necessity. This reduction took two forms: Midrash and Mishna.

The former were running commentaries on the Scripture. The material—and this applies not only to the Midrash but also to the Mishna and its later interpretations, the Talmuds—was of two kinds: Halakah and Haggadah. The former was the legal matter—the term means literally "rule to go by"—and consisted of a minute discussion of the law, often in hypercritical fashion; it was usually stated very succinctly and without quoting the actual words under discussion. Haggadah, on the contrary, was the exposition of those portions of Scripture not primarily connected with the law itself; it was largely concerned with the practical—didactic and sermonic—values to be found in the Scriptures, and expounded and developed the sacred history and literature in an edifying and often entertaining vein. Nor was the importance of this material lightly viewed. The Halakah might be the substance, the "kidney-fat of wheat," but the Haggadah was the "blood of the grape," which attracted a man's heart like wine. And in the Sifrè it is explicitly said:

If you would learn to know Him at whose word the world came into being, learn Haggadah, for by this means you will come to know the Holy One and cleave to his ways.[25]

The oldest three Midrashim were those on the Pentateuch: the Mekilta on Exodus; the Sifra on Leviticus; and the Sifrè on Numbers and Deuteronomy. While occasional bits of Haggadah were contained in these, they were primarily halakic. In addition to these halakic Midrashim—often called "Tannaite"[26]—were other later Midrashim in which Haggadah largely predominated. The chief of these were the Rabboth, that is, haggadic Midrashim on the Pentateuch and Megilloth.[27] Of these homiletic Midrashim the one on Genesis,[28] called Bereshit Rabbah (from the Hebrew name for Genesis), is the most revered because of both age and subject material. It is a running verse-by-verse commentary on Genesis, omitting only such non-edifying material as the genealogies or repetitions. A book like Leviticus obviously did not yield itself readily to such treatment; accordingly, the haggadic Midrash on this book (known as the Wayyikra Rabbah) is a series of sermons on selected passages, and abounds in popular proverbs and sayings, usually in Aramaic.

The other form in which the oral law was codified was known as Mishna. Here the material was not arranged in the form of running commentaries, but was classified systematically on the basis of an ordered list of subjects called "orders," which in turn were subdivided into treatises and chapters. Tradition ascribes this method of classification to Akiba. These orders, six in number, are:

(1) Seeds (Zeraim). Here are found the laws about agriculture, sabbatical years, and the like. To this order is prefixed the Berakot, a book of prayers and blessings.

(2) Festivals (Moed). Here was included, as the name suggests, the legislation for the Sabbath and the various festivals and fasts.

(3) Women (Nashim) with the rules for betrothal, marriage, divorce; status of widows; the levirate, adultery, and the like.

(4) Injuries (Nezikim) or, as it would be called today, torts and delicts, *i.e.*, civil and criminal law. To this is appended the famous Pirke Abot, sayings of the Fathers, which is purely haggadic and is contained in the Jewish Prayer Book.

(5) Holy Things (Kodashim): laws about sacrifice, excommunication, the furniture and equipment of the temple, and the like.

(6) Uncleannesses (Toharot). Here, as the name suggests, was systemized the legislation regarding the ritual and purificatory baths for women after

[25] Quoted by Moore, *Judaism*, Vol. I, p. 161, to whom I am here, as elsewhere, deeply indebted.
[26] For the meaning and reason for this word, see p. 109.
[27] The "five rolls"—Song of Songs, Ruth, Ecclesiastes, Esther, and Lamentations.
[28] There is no halakic Midrash on Genesis.

menstruation, childbirth; after intercourse or after contact with a corpse; leprosy, and the like.

During the second Christian century this type of codification was cultivated, and several such collections were made. But, when early in the third century one of these, that of Judah the Patriarch, gained preëminence, the designation Mishna gradually became restricted to this particular collection. Individual sayings from the parallel works are preserved in the Talmuds and are known as Baraitas, that is, traditions extraneous to the official Mishna, which latter, gaining almost canonical rank, served for further development of the law. The Mishna, written, of course, in Hebrew, is not to be conceived as coming from the pen of Judah. It is perhaps fair to call him the editor. Some 150 authorities are cited and quoted.

One somewhat similar work may be briefly mentioned, the Tosefta. Its arrangement in six orders is the same as the Mishna, while much of the material is the same. Although the name Tosefta ("Supplement") indicates the views of later Judaism about the relationship of the two works, it is actually not so much a supplement as an amplification. The most conspicuous difference between the otherwise largely parallel works is that the Tosefta frequently cites the biblical passages which serve as the authority for the detailed legislation; this the Mishna almost never does. Furthermore, it contains rather more Haggadah than does the Mishna.

The Mishna was the result of the effort to explain and interpret the law. Now that it had become canonical, it soon became necessary to explain and interpret the Mishna. Since the Mishna cited 150 scholars, there were many contradictions; these must be explained away, and other obscurities or ambiguities clarified. The result was the two Talmuds, one proceeding from Palestine, and properly known as the Palestinian Talmud—although it is often incorrectly called the Jerusalem Talmud—and dating from the middle of the fifth century; the other, the Babylonian Talmud, or in practice *the* Talmud, about half a century later and nearly four times as large. Owing to the closing of the rabbinical school in Tiberias the Palestinian Talmud was never finished, nor did it receive the thorough editing of its fellow from the east.

The Talmuds might be roughly called "Mishnas on the Mishna." Paragraph by paragraph—often sentence by sentence—the Mishna is quoted verbatim, the quotation being followed by the discussion and interpretation, in which especial emphasis was laid on clearing up difficulties and seeming contradictions. Thus the Talmuds consist of alternate sections—Mishna and interpretations. These interpretations, that is, the *new* material, are known as Gemara. It consists largely of the comments of later scholars—the Amoraim—but in addition has occasional Baraitas from the other Mishnas, as well as material from the Tosefta[29] and from the earlier

[29] The Tosefta never had a Talmud.

Midrashim. Together the two Talmuds cover nearly all the Mishna, although the Pirke Abot has no Talmud (Gemara). The bulk of the Gemara is in Aramaic, although the Baraitas are in Hebrew, as of course are the cited blocks of Mishna. Although of necessity Halakah bulks large in the Talmud, it is by no means the only kind of material. On the contrary, the (Babylonian) Talmud contains much edifying and entertaining matter, romantic literature having to do with Alexander the Great, such stories as how Hadrian—always a favourite character in Jewish legend—went down to the bottom of the sea in a diving-bell.

In the preceding pages mention of Tannaim and Amoraim has been made. A brief word of explanation may be useful. According to the traditional view, the canon of the Old Testament closed with the work of Ezra. He was followed by the *Sopherim* (literally, "men of the book") or "Men of the Great Synagogue"; they continued to the Maccabean times and were followed by the famous *Pairs*, that is, two colleagues, more or less friendly rivals, who carried on the tradition in successive generations until the end of the Herodian age, culminating in Hillel and Shammai, the founders of the two great rival schools. The Pairs were in turn followed by the *Tannaim* (teachers) (10-220 A.D.), *i.e.,* to the end of the codification of the Mishna; they by the *Amoraim* (speakers or interpreters) in the years 220-500 A.D., *i.e.,* in the period of the growth and development of the Gemara. Judaism is very careful to preserve these distinctions. Accordingly, such Halakic Midrashim as the Mekilta, Sifra, and Sifrè are called Tannaite Midrashim, since they were produced by the Tannaim, as were also the Mishnas and Tosefta. The Gemara, aside from earlier quotations from the Tannaim, was, of course, the work of the Amoraim.

The nature of these sources explain why they are so difficult to operate with. In the first place stand the technical difficulties. They contain a chaotic mass of material in which legal matter, theology, philosophy, science, anecdotes, and legend hobnob together. Written partly in Hebrew, partly in Aramaic, in an unpointed text, innocent of punctuation save at the end of paragraphs, they are, to quote one who knows them well, "concise to a degree that Thucydides might have envied, and Tacitus striven in vain to imitate."[30] They are not equipped with indices nor other apparatus—nor can they be. One must know where the desired material is or hunt for it. Furthermore, if ever the words of warning, "A little knowledge is a dangerous thing," have point, it is here. The compend of hundreds of scholars, some as early as the second century, others as late as the sixth century, it is necessary to pick and choose, if they are to be of value in revealing the nature of Judaism in the days of the rise of Christianity.

Not alone are they not calculated to answer many of the questions put to them—outlook and interests change through the centuries—but they have

[30] Herford, *Christianity in Talmud and Midrash*, p. 21.

been altered through the years as a result both of copying and of censorship. The first Christian act was to burn them; when this extreme was not resorted to they were rigidly censored to remove all objectional references to Christianity. During the days of the Inquisition this censorship was particularly rife. Perverted Jews—since they turned against their nation to save their own skins, this term is justifiable—enrolled as Dominicans, ferreted out all objectional references. Sometimes they would delete whole blocks, leaving blank spaces; at other times the wording was changed. One device was to print "Sadducee" in place of "heretic" when the latter term might reasonably be supposed to mean Christian. Were one to seek to discover from an uncritical text the tenets of the Sadducees, a curious picture would thus emerge.

When critically used by experts they reveal a Judaism totally different from that pictured by either the ardent apologist or the unsympathetic enemy. The main streams of Judaism flowing down from the earliest sources are here to be seen, but, muddied by the waters from lesser tributaries, only when an expert is at the wheel can they be navigated in safety.

Chapter VII

THE MAKE-UP OF JUDAISM

THE glibness with which we speak of Pharisees, Sadducees, and Zealots, not to mention Scribes, Boëthusians, Herodians, and Therapeutæ, tends to give the impression that we know a great deal more about the make-up of Judaism in the first century than is actually the fact, and that we are so exactly informed as to the peculiarities of each group that, were we to be transported back miraculously to Jerusalem and have the population pass in slow review before us, we could unerringly tag each one, at least after getting into casual conversation with him. Many modern writers have uncanny ability in this direction. From half a line—and that not always of certain text—they can tell whether its author was a Pharisee or Sadducee or Zealot.

All this tends to obscure the fact that actually we know amazingly little about the various sects. In fact, we do not have sufficient information to justify us in calling them sects. Were there different associations to which men belonged? Did a man *become* a Pharisee or Sadducee? Contemporary sources provide no answer to these questions. As we have seen, the rabbinic writings are totally silent;[1] all attempts at identification of sects fail. The fourth century Christian writer Epiphanius in his *Panarion* (*Refutation of All Heresies*) lists seven sects, and for good measure classes the Samaritans as standing halfway between Jew and gentile and containing four different varieties, of whom the Essenes were the first! Epiphanias' reputation for complete untrustworthiness, and for dependence upon personal likes and dislikes instead of facts as a basis for his statements, has led most historians to discount what he here has to say.[2]

Philo has left us a short eulogistic account of an otherwise unknown group of ascetics, and made passing reference to the Essenes; Josephus provides us with most of our all too scanty information regarding the four "sects" into which he divided Jewry—Pharisees, Sadducees, Essenes, and

[1] Here, as in other phases of what we are pleased to call a "dispassionate and scientific investigation of the past," there is an obvious fallacy. We say: "We will let the ancient writers speak for themselves; they shall answer our questions as they themselves will." But we naïvely forget that most of the questions upon which we wish light never occurred to them at all, and that by this inquisitorial device we effectively distort our sources and prevent them from emphasizing the things that seem to *them* significant. A particularly vivid illustration of this attitude is seen in such a work as *In His Steps—What Would Jesus Do?* but there are many others which do not wish to remain in the field of homiletics.

[2] See Jackson and Lake, *The Beginnings of Christianity*, Vol. I, pp. 84 f.

Fourth Philosophy. A manuscript discovered in Egypt at the end of the last century reveals another movement, apparently within the ranks of Judaism, although this has been occasionally challenged, while other names appear in passing reference in the pages of the gospels and elsewhere.

The Pharisees and Sadducees

Of the Jews in the days of Jesus the Pharisees were by all odds the most important. Much labor has been expended upon the derivation of the name. What its origin was we do not know. That it was originally applied by opponents as a nickname is perhaps probable, though by no means certain. Furthermore, the name apparently came to be understood in the sense of "Separatist," although the exact significance is not clear. Some have seen in it those who separated themselves from Judas the Maccabee at the advent of Alcimus.[3] For those who hold this view the later Pharisees were the successors of the Asideans (Ḥasidim). For others the separation was from sin, and referred to their ceremonial purity and diligence in striving to keep the law. Others understand it in the sense of exegetes: those who separated or distinguished the meaning of the law. In the last analysis we could only guess; even if we knew the derivation and significance of the name, we would know no more of the group itself.

Furthermore, their origin is unknown. Perhaps it is to be seen in the Haberim or "associates" who pledged themselves in the time of Hyrcanus to the scrupulous keeping of the laws, especially those having to do with matters of uncleanness, and to the setting apart of the tithes.[4] Such groups are mentioned in the Mishna and may have had their roots here. Under John Hyrcanus the Pharisees make their first definite appearance, although mention is made of them, along with the Sadducees and Essenes, by Josephus in the days of Jonathan.[5] The story of their gradual dissatisfaction with the political aspirations of the ruling house, of the break with Hyrcanus and his successors, and of their rise to the position of unquestioned leadership in things religious during the days of toleration under Alexandra has already been told and need not be repeated.[6] Although (with rare exceptions) they had no hankering for civil power but held aloof, they had become the spiritual mentors for Israel with an influence over the people that their rivals, the Sadducees, could not hope to equal, even though the latter had far greater wealth and political power. So Josephus can say of them:

> Whatsoever they do about divine worship, prayers, and sacrifices, they (*i.e.,* the people) perform them according to their direction.[7]

[3] See pp. 16 f., 19.
[4] So Herford, *The Pharisees,* pp. 30-35.
[5] *Antt.* 13,5,9.
[6] Pp. 28 f., 33 f.
[7] *Antt.* 18,1,3.

An anecdote, in itself of no consequence, illustrates the truth of Josephus' words. According to the teaching of the Sadducees the incense was to be lighted outside the holy place and carried burning within; according to the Pharisees, on the contrary, it must be lighted inside. Once a young priest—a Sadducee—performed this function in the manner approved by the Sadducees. Later his father admonished him: "Though we are Sadducees, we must do as the Pharisees teach, for they have the people behind them."

Suffice it to say that in the days of Jesus and during the rise of the early church they constituted the backbone of Judaism. Firmly entrenched in their religious leadership, revered by the masses, with the synagogues virtually in their control, they alone of the groups known to us survived the dreadful years of revolt against Rome. With the fall of the temple in 70 A.D. the Sadducees leave the field of history; the collapse of the rebellion of Bar Cochba saw the utter downfall of the Home Rule Party. But the Pharisees remained. Herford is well within the facts when he writes:

> The Pharisees were the only guides and teachers who had a word for the people; and they, and none others, saved from the ruins of the Jewish nation all that could be saved, and spoke to the stricken hearts of their countrymen the words of comfort and hope. The Judaism which has come down through the centuries is essentially Pharisaism.[8]

Josephus' description of the views of the Pharisees is in the form of a favourable comparison with those of the Sadducees and Essenes. The Essenes were complete fatalists: "All things are best ascribed to God."[9] The Sadducees, on the contrary, insisted "that to act what is good, or what is evil, is at men's own choice."[10] Between these extremes stood the Pharisees: "It hath pleased God to make a temperament, whereby what he wills is done, but so that the will of men can act virtuously or viciously."[11]

Another characteristic of the Pharisees was their beliefs about life after death.

> They also believe that souls have an immortal vigor in them, and that under the earth there will be rewards or punishments, according as they have lived virtuously or viciously in this life; and the latter are to be detained in an everlasting prison, but that the former shall have power to revive and live again.[12]

These words are obscure and have been interpreted in different ways. It seems quite unnecessary to understand them as implying the transmigration of souls or any other non-Jewish notion. Apparently what Josephus means is that the Pharisees believed in the resurrection of the dead. His obscurity of

[8] Herford, *The Pharisees,* p. 52.
[9] *Antt.* 18,1,5.
[10] *Wars,* 2,8,14.
[11] *Antt.* 18,1,3.
[12] *Ibid.*

utterance is due to his attempt to couch this belief in language which should be intelligible to his Greek readers, to whom resurrection of the body seemed as absurd as immortality of the soul certain.

Belief in the resurrection of the body had been a fundamental part of Jewish thinking at least from the second pre-Christian century. Once the view had become orthodox, Judaism quite forgot that it was new and soon was easily convinced that it had been taught in the Scriptures from the beginning. The Sadducees denied this, not on theological grounds, but because it was an innovation: What was good enough for Moses was good enough for them. Against them the Pharisees quoted Scripture to support their views. Although the notion was of course not a part of these passages, the Scribes were able to read it in. Thus from the words, "Ye shall give Jehovah's heave-offering to Aaron the priest,"[13] R. Johanan deduced that Aaron was still living and hence concluded: "Here is also the resurrection of the dead signified." Many other equally unlikely passages were cited in proof. For example, R. Simai, after referring to Exod. 6:4, cites with approval Gamaliel's dictum that the Pentateuch, Prophets, and Hagiographa all contain proof that the Blessed One will raise the dead. To this the Mishna agrees:

> He has no part in the world to come who denies that the resurrection can be proved from the Pentateuch.

In the Synoptic gospels we find Jesus arguing in precisely this fashion with the Sadducees, while the Pharisees listen in approval.[14] To ridicule the notion of resurrection, the Sadducees propound the hypothetical case of a woman who in turn buried seven less lusty husbands. Who would be entitled to claim her as spouse in the resurrection? Jesus answers in regulation manner. Does not the Scripture say that God said to Moses, I *am* [not, I *was*] the God of Abraham, Isaac, and Jacob? It is inconceivable that God is the God of dead people; hence they are living and the resurrection proved. Furthermore, the other stricture of Jesus, "For when they shall rise from the dead, they neither marry, nor are given in marriage; but are as angels in heaven,"[15] is paralleled by the saying of Rab (a third-century teacher):

> Rab used to say, "In the world to come there is no eating or drinking or marrying or envy or hate; but the pious rest with crowns upon their heads, and are satisfied with the glory of God."[16]

Although the Talmud passage is late, there seems no good reason to question the antiquity of the view expressed, or to assume that it was borrowed

[13] Numb. 18:28.
[14] Mark 12:18-28; Matt. 22:23-34; Luke 20:27-40.
[15] Mark 12:25 and parallels.
[16] Berakot 17a.

from Christianity. Again, the book of Acts asserts that the Pharisees and Sadducees were also divided on the question of angels.[17]

But the distinguishing characteristic of the Pharisee was his acceptance of and reverence for tradition as supplementing the written law. This Josephus phrases explicitly:

> What I would now explain is this, that the Pharisees have delivered to the people a great many observances by succession from their fathers, which are not written in the law of Moses; and for that reason it is that the Sadducees reject them, and say that we are to esteem those observances to be obligatory which are in the written word, but are not to observe what are derived from the traditions of our forefathers. And concerning these things it is that great disputes and differences have arisen among them, while the Sadducees are able to persuade none but the rich, and have not the populace obsequious to them, but the Pharisees have the multitude on their side.[18]

In a word, they were, as he writes in another place, "a certain sect of the Jews that appear more religious than others, and seem to interpret the laws more accurately."[19] Not differences of belief regarding the resurrection or angels, but acceptance or denial of the validity of the oral tradition as a supplement and authoritative interpretation of the law—this was the point of dispute between the Pharisees and Sadducees. The Sadducees maintained that the law (by this was meant the whole written Scripture, not the Pentateuch alone, as is often erroneously stated through confusing them on this point with the Samaritans) was binding, but did not "regard the observation of anything besides what the law enjoins them."[20] It is absurd to see in them, as they are often pictured, simply a political group, bloated millionaires indifferent to things religious. They were Jews, and from their point most loyal Jews. Actually the point of cleavage between Pharisee, Sadducee, and Essene appears to me to lie in their capacity for change. The bulk of the law came from the past when life was simple and uncomplicated. The years had brought their changes; the old law just would not fit. This the Sadducee simply denied; by closing his eyes to the changes he saw no need for alteration. The Essenes, on the contrary, recognized the changes, and sought to turn life back to the simpler days. By retiring from civilization they cut the Gordian knot. The Pharisees sought by their interpretations to make the law fit the new environs, believing as they did that God had provided for every circumstance that could arise. In this they had no idea that they were introducing new notes, although of course they were; they were simply rediscovering old truth. Stand-patters, as the Sadducees were, they none the less had, willy-nilly, to interpret the law, and regularly their interpretations

[17] Acts 23:8.
[18] *Antt.* 13,10,6
[19] *Wars* 1,5,2.
[20] *Antt.* 18,1,4.

were more austere than those of their rivals, but they never considered these interpretations sacred in the same sense that the Pharisees did theirs.

Failure to observe this difference in point of view not only has resulted in a distorted view of the differences between the groups, but in a total misunderstanding of the aim of the Pharisees. The law might say: "Remember the Sabbath day to keep it holy." This, however, was not enough. It was necessary to amplify and explain just what was work and what was not. Many and wonderful were the interpretations which were made. Here lies the origin of the popular notion that the chief joy of the Pharisee was devising new and difficult twists to put in the law. He is thus often pictured as singing:

> Count that day lost, whose low descending sun
> Finds no new "must" that simply can't be done.

All this is simply not historic. These fine-spun distinctions were not dictated by the desire to make the law burdensome, but to facilitate its fulfilment under changed conditions. One example will suffice. Food might not be carried outside of your house on the Sabbath. At once it became necessary to know what "outside of your house" meant. Commonly, houses were built in blocks about a common court. Provided no Sadducee lived in such a unit, all the houses could be considered one. Hence "outside the house" would signify "into the street," but not "into the courtyard." Thus food might be carried from one house to the other without transgressing the law.

Furthermore, the Sabbath legislation was calculated to make the Sabbath a peculiarly delightful day—our "blue Sundays" are no bequest from the Synagogue. To be sure, food might not be cooked on the Sabbath, but the Jews did not relish cold victuals on the Sabbath any more than we do. Accordingly, a clever anticipation of the fireless cooker was devised whereby the stomachs of men might rejoice and the law of God be unflouted. On the Sabbath a peculiarly good dinner was demanded. If necessary, a family should go light for several days to have the wherewithal for a proper meal.

Nor was fasting a requirement as is often supposed. The canting hypocrite portrayed in the gospel[21] with his smug, "I fast twice in the week; I give tithes of all that I get," has tended to give a quite erroneous view here. Fasting on Monday and Thursday was often practised, but was entirely voluntary and an act of uncommon piety. How many people practised it is not clear. Certain classes of people—students, for example—were flatly forbidden to fast. The general assertion that the fast was imposed upon all by the Pharisee or was considered a *sine qua non* of piety appears quite unjustified by the evidence. In the matter of setting apart the tithes the situation appears much the same. Those who banded themselves into associations to separate their tithes (the Haberim) had done it of their own will and accord.

[21] Luke 18:9-14.

Again, it should be pointed out that much of the discussion that seems to us casuistry and hair-splitting was to facilitate the keeping of the law by making it next to impossible to commit what we might call "the deadly sins."[22] Terrible penalties were imposed, but the legislation was so hedged about that in many cases the crime was almost impossible; in others, the conviction. The penalty for blasphemy was death, but blasphemy was not committed by uttering the sacred name or even by using it as an oath. It consisted in "cursing God by the name of God"—"God damn God!"—which it will be admitted would not often occur. Adultery, to be sure, was punishable by stoning to death, but to gain a conviction two eye-witnesses were required. Here, too, convictions were probably infrequent. These instances might be multiplied. Their opponents might charge them with transgressing the commandment of God because of their traditions, or with "teaching as their doctrines the precepts of men."[23] Such criticisms are easy; perhaps they were deserved. None the less, we should not blind ourselves to the fact that the story of the centuries has been a repeated demonstration that it is only through the precepts of men that the laws of God become effective.

Of the Sadducees little more need be said. In the time of Jesus they were a power to be reckoned with, although they were not numerous and were probably rarely to be met with outside Jerusalem. They are rarely mentioned in the gospels, nor is this surprising, since by the time of the composition of the gospels they had passed out of existence. The same obscurity veils the name Sadducee that does Pharisee. It may have been derived from Zadok, who succeeded Abiathar as priest in the days of Solomon. In the time we are concerned with, the Sadducees—whatever their actual origin—were roughly the priestly party in contrast to the popular party of the Pharisees. While the evidence at our disposal would scarcely justify the assumption that all the priests were Sadducees, it is to be observed that in two passages in the book of Acts[24] the chief priests and Sadducees are linked together. In the latter passage it is expressly said: "But the high priest rose up, and all they that were with him (which is the sect of the Sadducees)." The Boëthusians, from whom several high priests were appointed, appear to have been a Sadducaic family, taking their name from Boëthus, who in 26 B.C. had been appointed high priest by Herod, whose anxiety to marry the beautiful daughter Mariamne, was matched by his insistence that she be of distinguished lineage.

Although the synagogue, thanks to the efforts of the Pharisees, had supplanted the temple as the real centre of Judaism, the temple continued to exert tremendous influence, and the priestly ring was wealthy and powerful.

[22] A concept unknown to Judaism.
[23] Cf. Matt. 15:3,9.
[24] Acts 4:1 ff; 5:17.

Apparently the Sadducees were also in the majority in the Sanhedrin, and may safely be said to have controlled what political power Rome had left the little nation.

Reference has already been made to their denial of resurrection, not on the grounds of theology, but because it was an innovation. Similarly their disbelief in angels is hardly to be adduced as evidence that they were rationalists. Rather, the exuberant angelology and demonology which had been inherited from Persia along with resurrection apparently appeared a newfangled innovation—and a vulgar one at that.

The contrast between the rigid conservatism of the Sadducees and the greater adaptability to change on the part of the Pharisees has given rise to a theory that appears to me worthy of more attention than has hitherto been paid to it. This difference of attitude, in the judgment of Finkelstein,[25] arose from their different environs. Originally the Sadducees were the country group. Here they were removed from contact with new ideas. Some of them eventually became wealthy, in short, became the great landholders. Although in later years—as in the days we are considering—they may have come to live in Jerusalem, they continued in their track; wealth, responsibility, and traditions all conspired to make them view with suspicion all innovations. The Pharisees, on the contrary, were originally an urban group. Thus exposed to new ideas and influences, they developed along lines quite impossible for the others. Gradually by their newly acquired eschatological teachings and more democratic ideas they won to themselves the mass of the Judean farmers, leaving for the Sadducees only the comparatively few wealthy families in the nation. Whether this thesis will eventually prove itself or not, it tends to emphasize the difference of attitude between the two groups and gives a not impossible explanation of it. The one caution to be borne in mind, not alone with regard to this particular explanation, but in all attempts to understand the Sadducees, is that however much their wealth and political power may have tended to make them a veritable aristocracy, which sought to entrench itself against popular attack, yet in their own eyes, as well in those of Josephus and the rest of Judaism, they were a religious party characterized by beliefs which were to be rigidly and austerely held.

The Scribes

In the New Testament is occasionally found the phrase "Scribes and Pharisees." Were these, then, two separate classes: a sect of Pharisees, and distinct from them a group of Scribes who were not Pharisees?

The origin of the Scribes was in the far past. Back in the days of Ezra the emphasis upon the law and its interpretation had called into existence

[25] "The Pharisees: their Origin and their Philosophy"—*Harvard Theological Review,* Vol. XXII, No. 3 (July, 1929), pp. 185-261.

a group of men called *Sopherim*. These men, as has been pointed out in a previous page, came to occupy an exalted place in later thinking. They were the Great Synagogue. The very title *Sopherim* was not used of their later successors, who were called *Hakamim*. They may well have made copies of the Scripture and may have counted its letters, but they were first and foremost "Men of the Book." Theirs was the duty to teach and expound it. In a word, they were scholars, not stenographers. Whereas the priests had formerly been the ones to whom Israel had gone for advice, now the scholars had gradually come to occupy this position. What the law *said* was not enough; What did it *mean*? How did it apply in this case, how in that? Such, as we have already seen, was the start of the oral traditional law. Since it was not written down for nearly five hundred years, it had to be passed on from one generation of scholars to the next. Naturally such a responsibility brought respect and distinction.

In the New Testament the Scribes, also called "lawyers" and "teachers of the law,"[26] were the professional teachers and learned men. Although not regarded with the same awe as their shadowy predecessors, their unique knowledge of the will and dictates of God made them men of great importance and well adapted for the positions of judges. Their verdict on the law, when ratified by the Sanhedrin—to which body some of the Scribes apparently belonged—itself became law.

Now as to party. That there was no party of Scribes appears certain, although undoubtedly a sort of informal freemasonry among colleagues existed, parallel to that found today among professional theologians. By the time we are considering the majority of the Scribes were probably of the Pharisaic persuasion—once Mark calls them "scribes of the Pharisees"[27]—but by no means all of the Pharisees were scholars. The majority of the Pharisees were not technically learned men; any of the ame ha-ares[28] might become members of the "brotherhood" by taking the pledges in the presence of three. The Scribes, on the contrary, were the learned—the Ph.D.'s of their time.[29]

In the time we are considering, Judea was the centre of their activity and

[26] In the Synoptic gospels Rabbi is frequently used of Jesus. This is not to be understood as a title, as later was the case. If used at all during these years, it was simply a complimentary term of respect. Neither Hillel nor Shammai has the title in Jewish sources. Later in the school of Jamnia (see below, p. 131) it was applied to Johanan ben Zakkai and those after him as a title "for what we might call a diplomaed Doctor of the Law" (Moore).

[27] Mark 2:16; cf. "Some of the scribes of the Pharisees' part" (Acts 23:9).

[28] For the significance of this term see below, pp. 126-128.

[29] "The Scribes . . . were a learned class whose vocation was the study and exposition of the law. In the first instance biblical scholars, as the name suggests, they became authorities also in the unwritten branch of the law, in the development of which they had the leading part. The Pharisees were a party whose endeavor it was to live in strict accordance with the law thus interpreted and amplified, and to bring the people to a similar conformity. Most of the Scribes were of this party, but the bulk of the Pharisees were not scholars."—Moore, *Judaism*, Vol. I, p. 66.

remained so even after the destruction of Jerusalem. Years later, after the war against Hadrian (134 A.D.), the schools of Galilee gained the ascendancy, but at the time of the ministry of Jesus there was no notable teacher or school there. Consequently the Scribes (and probably the Pharisees as well) had less influence there than we have often been led to suppose. The bulk of the Galilean population was made up of the descendants of converts; now, nearly two centuries after the Maccabean revolt, the populace was strongly Jewish, but fanatically and unlearnedly so. It was not until well along in the second century A.D. that there was there an educated Judaism. On the other hand, outside of Palestine, as at Nisibis, occasional learned schools were to be found a century earlier, which remained great centres of Jewish learning, as the Babylonian Talmud proves. Thus when we speak of Palestinian Judaism—in contrast to the Alexandrian or Hellenistic Judaism—it must not be thought to mean that Palestine had a monopoly; it is simply that Palestine was prominent in the field and that we know most about it.

Three scholars who exerted great influence a little before and during the advent of Christianity were Hillel, Shammai, and Johanan ben Zakkai. The first two have already been mentioned as constituting the last great "Pair," and establishing the two famous rival schools of interpretation. Hillel, to whom is ascribed the Golden Rule—"What is hateful to thee, do not to another"—represented the less conservative and kinder aspect of Judaism. This is perhaps to be attributed to his earlier environs—he came from Babylonia. His chief emphasis was that discussion of the law must ever take cognizance of actual conditions, instead of concerning itself with pure theory. Shammai, his great rival, reflects the more unbending rigorous side of Judaism. Johanan ben Zakkai, who founded the great school at Jamnia which served to preserve Judaism in the days of reconstruction after the fall of Jerusalem and to lay the track on which later rabbinical practice was to run, is probably responsible for the ultimate triumph of the views of the school of Hillel. In typically Jewish fashion the controversy was healed: A voice from heaven was heard at Jamnia saying, "The teachings of both schools are words of the living God, but in practice the Halakah of the school of Hillel is to be followed."[30]

The Ascetic Groups

No survey, however brief, of the make-up of Judaism would be complete without mention of the ascetic groups occasionally there to be found. Three of these sects or orders are known to us, although far less is actually known of them than the voluminous discussions would imply. Of these three the Essenes are described by Josephus as comprising one of the four "philosophical" sects of Judaism (the others being Pharisees, Sadducees, and "Fourth Philosophy"). From Philo also we have received brief mention of them. For

[30] Moore, *Judaism,* Vol. I, p. 85.

knowledge of the second order, the Therapeutæ, we are dependent upon Philo alone. A manuscript discovered at the end of the last century in Cairo describes the third, usually known as the "Covenanters of Damascus." All three of these groups—at least it is true of the first two—were radical departures from orthodox Judaism and apparently exerted very little influence. They were not numerous; the Essenes comprised but four thousand; the number of the other two is not known. The disproportionate space which Josephus gives to his description is not to be explained as due to their importance; rather it evidences his fondness for discussing the bizarre and for revealing his own familiarity with the unusual. Philo's detailed and not unfriendly mention of the Therapeutæ may well have been due, at least in part, to the occasional weariness that comes to every man enmeshed in a complicated economic order and the consequent wistful longing for the simple life.

Asceticism was alien to the genius of Judaism, and not unnaturally so, since asceticism is peculiarly individualistic and dualistic: the longing to rid one's soul of the defiling corruption of the body. To be sure, we meet Rechabites and Nazarites in the pages of the Old Testament. These, however, were not ascetic sects, but were simply reactionaries, men out of step with the times, who were not content, like Nestor, to extol the good old times, but insisted on reënacting them. Thus the Rechabites forbade the drinking of wine, but not on ascetic grounds. It was simply that they believed that the ideal life was the kind the Israelites had spent prior to the occupation of Canaan. This they sought to perpetuate. Vineyards were a sign of civilization and settled life—there were none for the nomads—hence the prohibition of wine.[31] Occasional figures like Elijah and Tishbite there were, but this type was not natural to Israel and its representatives few and far between. Marriage, a sane home life, thankful acceptance of the blessings with which a loving Father had endowed his children—these characterized Israel.

1. The Essenes. From all this the Essene differed radically. According to Josephus[32] the Essenes rejected pleasure as an evil, and praised continence and conquest over pleasure as a virtue. Apparently they were divided on the question of marriage. One group—Josephus would seem to mean that this was the main body—flatly rejected marriage and the procreation of children; another group, however, permitted marriage, but solely for the procreation of children. They were all woman-haters who "guard against the lascivious behavior of women, and are persuaded that none of them preserve their fidelity to one man."[33]

[31] Cf. Jer. 35:1-19.

[32] *Wars* 2,8,2-13; *Antt.* 18,1,5. Cf. also Philo, *On the Virtuous being also free* 12(§§75-87) 457 f.M.; Fragments preserved in Eusebius, *Præparatio* viii,8 and 13. These two passages from Philo are available in Yonge's English translation, Vol. III, pp. 523 ff. and Vol. IV, pp. 219-222.

[33] *Wars* 2,8,2.

They constituted an order to which members were admitted only after passing through various degrees and tests. Vows of secrecy were demanded. Numerous lustrations were practised; women were excluded from their fellowship. According to Pliny[34] they lived apart in communities on the west shore of the Dead Sea; Josephus, however, remarks: "They have no certain city, but many of them dwell in every city."[35] With regard to legal purity they far out-Phariseed the Pharisee. Their life was organized on a communistic basis; private property was unknown. Despising riches, they lived simply, worked hard, wore the simplest of white garments, abstained from the use of oil, ate together, often in silence, had secret teachings in which the names of angels appear to have played a part.

Those who desired admission to their number must live for a year as did they, but outside the fellowship. Full membership could not be achieved until after a three-year probation, and then only after tremendous vows not to communicate their doctrines to any save in the way and manner in which they had received them. The strictest of discipline was practised. Those convicted of sin were expelled from the fellowship. This, in theory at least, meant starvation, for by his oaths the guilty man could not eat food prepared by unclean hands. So Josephus tersely: "He was forced to eat grass, and famish his body with hunger till he perish."

In contrast to the Pharisees and Sadducees they were absolute determinists, were such scrupulous Sabbath observers that they refrained from the most intimate bodily functions on that day, and, as good ascetics should, held that the body was corruptible and perishable, but that the soul was immortal and would live for ever. In this respect they appear to have been in complete discord with orthodox Judaism. It might be conceivable that Josephus has over-emphasized this aspect to make it intelligible to Greek readers. Since, however, he compares this opinion to that held by the Greeks, he apparently is distinguishing them here from other Jews. Furthermore, his description of them "putting up certain prayers, which they have received from their forefathers, as if they made supplication for its [the sun's] rising" and of their extraordinary care that in performing the intimate details of their toilet "they may not affront the divine rays of light" has led many students to see in this group sun-worshippers. Accordingly the most contradictory views of the origin and affiliations of this strange group have been given.[36] Was it a movement emanating entirely from Judaism, was it coloured or influenced from without Jewry, or was it an essentially heathen movement masquerading in Jewish garb? Characteristics now Greek, now Buddhist, now Persian have all been pointed out by scholars to prove the hypothesis approving it-

[34] See passage quoted p. 123.

[35] *Wars* 2,8,4.

[36] For the *hic jacet* see Schürer, *op. cit.*, Div. II, Vol. II, pp. 205-218. See also "The Essenes" printed at the end of J. B. Lightfoot's *Saint Paul's Epistles to the Colossians and Philemon*, pp. 347-417.

self to the particular investigator. Since the group was essentially a secret society, guarding its secrets so vigorously, and since our knowledge is entirely at second hand, all such speculation appears to me at best uncertain. Were I to venture a guess, it would be that the movement was the consequence of an attempt to push back the years and to regain those days when the law was workable without interpretation; but that while thus essentially a movement from Judaism it had acquired certain new elements—partially borrowed from without, partially the development from within. Perhaps, however, it was but the reflection of the wave of weariness and disillusionment which was sweeping over the ancient world, and which, then as now, found expression in occasional praise of the simpler secluded life in contrast to the effete and cloying world of society. That this little movement attracted some notice in the Roman world and had become the nucleus about which legend was growing is revealed by Pliny's somewhat fulsome, if ill-informed, description:

Lying west of Asphaltites [the Dead Sea], and sufficiently distant to escape its noxious exhalations, are the Esseni, a people that live apart from the world, and marvellous beyond all others throughout the whole earth, for they have no women among them; to sexual desire they are strangers; of money they have none; the palm trees are their only companions. Day after day their numbers are fully recruited by multitudes of strangers that resort to them, driven thither to adopt their usages by the tempests of fortune and wearied by the miseries of life. Thus it is, through thousands of ages—incredible to relate—this people eternally prolongs its existence, without a single birth taking place there; so fruitful a source of population to them is that weariness of life which is felt by others.[37]

2. The Therapeutæ. Somewhat similar to the Essenes were the Therapeutæ, if the writing, *Concerning the Contemplative Life,* is actually from the pen of Philo.[38] Although their centre was near Alexandria, this was not the only place they were to be found. In contrast to the Essenes who spent their days in toil, the Therapeutæ devoted their time to contemplation, "studying . . . the laws and sacred oracles of God enunciated by the holy prophets, and hymns, and psalms, and all kinds of other things by reason of which knowledge and piety are increased and brought to perfection."[39] The interval between morning and evening prayers was given over to meditation and the theoretic practice of virtue. The Scriptures were interpreted allegorically; hymns and melodies were composed.

Furthermore, while the Essenes constituted a cœnobite order, the Therapeutæ lived in separate huts or cells, assembling only on the Sabbath and on each fiftieth day, which constituted their special festival, and was called

[37] *Nat. Hist.* v,15(17).
[38] Formerly this was denied; see Schürer, *op. cit.,* Div. II, Vol. III, pp. 357 f.
[39] *de Vit. Contempl.* 3(§25)475M.

the *Pannuchis* ("all night festival"). Unlike the Essenes, women were admitted to the order, apparently on equal terms, but, as is said to be true in heaven, there was no marrying nor giving in marriage. In the common sanctuary was a wall extending part way to the roof. On one side sat the men, on the other the women. Here the law was expounded. On the *Pannuchis* a common meal was held. To it they came "joyful, but with exceeding gravity" and dressed in white. After this meal—it was of the simplest sort: bread and salt mixed with hyssop—they sang and danced, first in two choirs, then gradually uniting in a "spiritual Bacchanal" in which the free love of God was the only drink. Apparently desiring to emphasize the decorum that prevailed, Philo was at pains to remark:

> And the women also share in this feast, the greater part of whom, although old, are virgins in respect of their purity (not indeed through necessity, as some of the priestesses among the Greeks are, who have been compelled to preserve their chastity more than they would have done of their own accord), but out of an admiration for and love of wisdom.

The fate of this strange order, like its origin, is unknown to us. Indeed, were it not for this little essay, perhaps written by Philo as a quiet object lesson to the smart set of Egypt's capital, we would never have heard of these pre-Christian monks of Lake Mareotis.

3. The Covenanters of Damascus. The chance discovery of eight leaves of an ancient Hebrew manuscript among those found in 1896 by Schechter in the Genizah of an old synagogue at Fostat (near Cairo) reveals the existence of another—apparently Jewish—group hitherto unknown. Its origin is best set forth in the words of the manuscript:

> At the end of the devastation of the land arose men who removed the boundary and led Israel astray; and the land was laid waste because they spoke rebelliously against the commandments of God by Moses and also against his holy Anointed, and prophesied falsehood to turn Israel back from following God. But God remembered the covenant with the forefathers, and he raised up from Aaron discerning men and from Israel wise men, and he heard them, and they dug the well. "The well, princes dug it, nobles of the people delved it, with the legislator" (Numb. 21:18). The well is the law, and they who dug it are the captivity of Israel who went forth from the land of Judah and sojourned in the land of Damascus, all of whom God called princes because they sought him. . . . The legislator is the interpreter of the law, as Isaiah said, "bringing forth a tool from his work" (Isa. 54:16), and the nobles of the people are those who came to delve the well with the statutes which the legislator decreed that men should walk in them in the complete end of wickedness; and besides these they shall not obtain any (statutes) until the teacher of righteousness shall arise in the last times.[40]

From this it would seem that a number of Jews, including some priests and

[40] *Fragments of a Zadokite Work* 8:1-10.

Levites, had withdrawn from Judea and had settled in the neighbourhood of Damascus, binding themselves by a new covenant to live in strict accord with the law as enunciated by their legislator.

Although they were not ascetics—in the sense that the Essenes or Therapeutæ were—they had broken loose from society, disgusted by its laxities, and were ultrastrict in their habits. They have been aptly styled "come-outers from Judaism." They styled themselves "Israelites from the land of Judah"; their expected future Teacher was to come from Aaron and Israel, that is, from the tribe of Levi, not Judah. The Essenes sent offerings to the temple, although that these included sacrifices is not clear. Not so these "Covenanters"; the temple in Jerusalem was by them utterly rejected. In its stead they had their own sanctuary with sacrificial worship.

Polygamy, by no means unknown in Palestine, and marriage between uncle and niece were inveighed against; far more stringent Sabbath observance than in Palestinian orthodoxy was required. Particularly severe was the dietary legislation. For example: fish must be split and blooded while alive; grasshoppers and locusts must be boiled or cooked alive; honey in the honeycomb was forbidden. Failure to meet these requirements was severely punished. In addition to the penalties of Mosaic legislation was the dread "Separation from the Purity," that is, expulsion from their "camps."

This group appears to me to have attempted to solve the problems confronting all Jewry: an immovable law in a changing society. The Pharisee sought to adapt and modify the law to make it workable. It was precisely this that these Covenanters refused to do. Rather, leaving the more complicated society behind, they sought once more to reproduce in their "camps" the wilderness experiences of Israel. If the cause of their departure from "the land of Judah" was the activity of those men who were thus "removing the boundary" and "leading Israel astray"—that is, the Scribes—what wonder that the disgruntled in their protest reached extremes which would make the most rigid Pharisee appear a gross latitudinarian?[41] If this hypothesis be sound, the origin of all three of these groups—Essenes, Therapeutæ, Covenanters—would be seen to be due to the same cause, the attempt to go back to the good old days and to live in such a manner that the law unamended would once more exactly fit. The Pharisees, as we have seen, adapted the opposite method of modifying the law to fit the new environs, although they would have been scandalized if they had realized it. Theoretically either course of action was possible; practically, of course, there could be no question. "The moving finger writes, and having writ moves on." Between these two extremes stood the Sadducee. He stubbornly refused to see the problem; by shutting his eyes it conveniently vanished. When his temple crashed about

[41] In this last paragraph I do not mean that the Covenanters and the Pharisees were necessarily contemporaries. Although this appears to me highly probable, we know far too little about the date of the "exodus" of the one and the origin of the other to speak with confidence.

him in 70 A.D., he never emerged from the wreckage. Nor were these three outlooks on life unique to Judaism. Every age has seen them, and in every age the answer has been the same.

The Fourth Philosophy

To his brief survey of the "three sects of philosophy peculiar to Judaism"—Pharisees, Sadducees, and Essenes—Josephus appends a paragraph about "the fourth sect of Jewish philosophy" of which "Judas the Galilean was the author." Little need here be said of this group. I have already sought to show that this group—it would be less confusing to call them the Home Rule Party—was no new emergence in the days of Judas of Galilee, but was simply a movement of Jewish patriots irked by outside control.[42] Starting at least as far back as Hezekiah's[43] opposition to Roman control in the person of Herod and his father Antipater, this movement had continued through the years, seeking to foment rebellion. Its motto, "The sword and not sparingly; no king but Jehovah," well illustrates its temper. How much influence it exerted until shortly before the final outbreak against Rome in 66 A.D. is hard to say. It is probably fair to say that during such troublous months as those in which Gaius sought to set up his statue in the temple it gained new leases of life. But on the whole it apparently was regarded by the Pharisees as a dangerous and absurd evidence of fanaticism. When God saw fit to intervene, he would do it directly without the need of human aid. To the Sadducees and others in positions of wealth and leadership, realizing as they did how easy it would be to upset the ship of state, it was an unmitigated outrage and danger. To what extent it had leavened the thinking of the masses it is impossible to say.

The Ame Ha-ares

This phrase, literally the "people of the land," is often used to designate the common people, or, as they are euphemistically referred to today, the "masses." The singular, am ha-ares, was sometimes employed with various significance to mean "layman," much as the Greek used ἰδιώτης; commonly, however, it was used to distinguish the uneducated from the learned.

Judaism was primarily a religion in which knowledge was required, for, as has been shown in a previous chapter, to fulfil the law required a very exact and comprehensive knowledge of what the law contained and implied. Such a knowledge was naturally beyond the reach of the average man who had neither time nor inclination for the necessary detailed study. The result was that while the rich and politically powerful may be spoken of as constituting the aristocracy, in a larger sense the true aristocracy was that of knowledge, not of wealth or birth. Akiba had been an am ha-ares, but by

[42] At this time it would be well to reread pp. 41 f., 68, 71-77.

[43] Its roots may well have gone back to the days of the captivity.

his steadfast devotion to learning had become a prominent scholar; Aquila, the translator of the Old Testament into Greek for Jewish orthodoxy, was a proselyte. On the other hand, even the high priest himself, if he were not a learned man—and priests then as now usually were not—might be excluded from the society of the learned and regarded by them with contempt. Just as an am ha-ares might become a member of the Haberim by binding himself by oath to abstain from ceremonial defilement and to strive to conform thus to the law's demands—if he had formerly been a flagrant violator of the proprieties and decencies of life, a period of probation was usually insisted upon—and by years of study might become a student, eventually even a teacher as had Akiba; so, on the other hand, a member of the Haberim could forfeit his standing by engaging in certain occupations, or a student by abandoning his studies could sink to the level of the am ha-ares.

Thus between these groups—educated and ignorant—stood a deep gulf. Many statements are preserved expressing the hostility felt by each for the other, and reminding the student of mediæval history of the clashes between "town and gown." "Cursed is the man who lies with any beast" was not too delicately applied to the marriage of a scholar with a woman from the rank of the uneducated, for "they are loathsome and their women are unclean."

Rabbi Eleazar said, "It is lawful to stab an am ha-ares on a Day of Atonement that falls on a Sabbath" [that is, a day of superlative holiness]. Said his disciples, "You mean to slaughter him?" "No," said Eleazar, "slaughtering requires a benediction; stabbing does not."[44]

A similar hatred expressing itself often in picturesque exaggeration was felt by the uneducated.

Rabbi Akiba said, "When I was an am ha-ares, I used to say, 'I wish I had one of those scholars, and I would bite him like an ass.'" His disciples said, "You mean like a dog." He replied, "An ass's bite breaks the bone; a dog's does not."

Just as the word Pharisee has become synonymous with self-righteous hypocrite, so a romantic aura of piety has been cast about the masses. They were the truly godly of the land, the last vestige of genuine religion in a Judaism which had become sterile and arid. They were the righteous remnant of which the prophets had spoken. While the arrogant scholar and hypocritical Pharisee turned a deaf ear to Jesus, "the common people heard him gladly." This view, while widely held, is unfortunately destitute of evidence. That many a godly man or woman was styled am ha-ares in a designation so sweeping that both high priest and outcast received it is likely. Many of those designated "sinners" may have been far from bad men; so styled sim-

[44] For this quotation and the following one, as well as for other material in this section, I am indebted to the note of the late Professor Moore in Jackson and Lake's *Beginnings of Christianity*, Vol. I, p. 443.

ply because they did not or could not practise all the minutiæ of the law. Jesus and his disciples were undoubtedly regarded as ame ha-ares for their latitudinarianism touching the laws of ceremonial cleanness and the Sabbath. Indeed, the attitude of Jesus, an unlettered commoner, in venturing to declare what was the will of God and to criticize those who had made the Divine Will and Revelation a lifetime's study undoubtedly aroused the most intense and not unnatural antipathy from the outraged recipients of his attack. None the less, after all exceptions have been made, to argue that it was in this group that the real piety of Israel was preserved is as silly as maintaining today that the only true devotion to God is to be found among the great unchurched.

Chapter VIII

THE ORGANIZATION OF JUDAISM

IN CONTRADISTINCTION to the make-up of Judaism, a convenient designation of the various groups or sects differing among themselves both as to thought and practice, we may speak of the organization of Judaism. Three institutions may be mentioned: the Sanhedrin, the temple with its priestly hierarchy, and the synagogue. The last of these has already been described; a brief word about the other two will not be out of place.

The Sanhedrin

Although in the days of the Christian beginnings Judea, Samaria, and Idumea no longer enjoyed independence but comprised the Roman province of Judea, governed by a Roman procurator in whom all authority was centred, a very considerable authority, both legislative and judicial, was delegated to the supreme court of Jerusalem, known as the Sanhedrin. It remained not alone the symbol of the days of lost independence, but also a very real power in Jewish life until the destruction of the temple in 70 A.D.

Of its early history we know very little. Later rabbinical exegesis sought to connect it genetically with the council of seventy elders who were said to have aided Moses in his deliberations.[1] This is of course pure fiction, and simply reveals again the rabbinic view that, as in heaven, so on earth, "as it was in the beginning, is now, and ever shall be." Romantic identification of the later body with this traditional group may well account for the number of members. Elders of Israel are mentioned frequently in the Old Testament; nothing, however, indicates that they formed any such autonomous body as the later Sanhedrin. The earliest reference to such a body is in the letter from Antiochus the Great to Ptolemy which Josephus quotes in full.[2] In this letter direction is given that the Senate (γερουσία), priests, scribes of the temple, and sacred singers are to be freed from all taxes. The presumption is that this Senate—apparently an aristocratic council headed by the high priest—does not antedate the Greek period and is a direct result of the influence of the hellenizing policy of Egypt and Syria. With the break between the later Hasmoneans and the Pharisees, the latters' rivals, the Sadducees, who now comprised the priestly aristocracy, became the supporters of the throne and apparently formed the majority of the Senate, although

[1] Numb. 11:16.

[2] *Antt.* 12,3,3.

some recognition seems to have been given to the older priestly dynasty which had now been superseded by the Hasmonean. Alexandra, as has been already indicated,[3] wisely granted this body more independent authority than it had exercised during the previous reigns and in addition to the nobles and priests who had formerly constituted its membership gave some recognition to the Scribes, who had gained great strength through the support not alone of the Pharisees, but of the people as a whole. Hyrcanus had annulled their ordinances at the time of his break with them; now they seem to have been able to force Alexandra to turn the tables. From now on they exerted no little power in the council, although (probably) holding but a minority of seats.

The earliest reference by Josephus to this Senate (*gerousia*) by the title Sanhedrin (*συνέδριον*, literally "court"), which it was later to enjoy, is in the account of the difficulty in which Herod, as governor of Galilee, was involved because of his zeal in chastising Hezekiah and his band.[4] In this circumstance the nature of the body, strongly conservative and opposed to the growing power of Antipater, the pro-Roman, is clearly to be seen. The casual way in which the Sanhedrin is here mentioned does not suggest that it was any new designation for the council. Perhaps Schürer is correct in his suggestion that Josephus used the word here because of the judicial authority it was seeking to exert over Herod, "for it is in this sense that *συνέδριον* is specially used in later Greek."[5]

One of Herod's first acts, after he had become king, was to wreak his displeasure upon this body. Josephus says explicitly, "He slew all the members of the Sanhedrin,"[6] although in a later page he says, "He . . . slew forty-five of the principal men of Antigonus' party."[7] Apparently these two statements are to be reconciled by not pressing the "all" of the former, but limiting it to designate those members of the body who were hostile to him. During his long reign the actual power of the Sanhedrin suffered eclipse; with his death and the dismemberment of his kingdom its authority became limited to Judea proper, thus resembling the Senate (*βουλή*) of the Greek cities, which controlled not alone the city proper, but also the nearby villages and countryside which belonged loosely to such a city. Thus Josephus can say:

> The city Jerusalem is situated in the very middle; on which account some have, with sagacity enough, called that city the Navel of the country. . . . Judea . . .

[3] Pp. 33 f.

[4] *Antt.* 14,9,4. In a preceding chapter (14,5,4) he mentions the five councils (*συνέδρια*) which Gabinius had created when he divided Palestine into five toparchies in the endeavour to destroy the unity of the rebellious little land. In the *Wars* (1,8,5) he had referred to them as "conventions" (*σύνοδοι*).

[5] Schürer, *op. cit.*, Div. II, Vol. I, p. 169.

[6] *Antt.* 14,9,4.

[7] *Antt.* 15,1,2.

was parted into eleven portions, of which the royal city Jerusalem was supreme, and presided over all the neighbouring country, as the head does over the body.[8]

In each of these eleven toparchies into which Judea was divided when it was taken from Archelaus and turned into a province was a local court of twenty-three members before whom the less important cases were heard; the Sanhedrin in Jerusalem, however, was the supreme body and, as the frequent references in the New Testament reveal, remained the dominating force in Jewish life until its overthrow in the débâcle of 66-73 A.D. At that time it was stripped of its power. In Jamnia, to be sure, the doctors of the law formed a so-called Court of Justice (*Bet Din*), which they fondly believed to be a continuation of the Sanhedrin which had existed in unbroken continuity from the time of Moses. This new body, while modelled after the earlier body, was totally different in that it was simply a court—the legislative power enjoyed by the Jerusalem Sanhedrin had been abolished—and at least at first even its judicial power was purely theoretical. Later it apparently regained some real jurisdiction over things Jewish, but even this was actually usurped, never formally granted by the now supreme Rome.

All this makes it very difficult for the student to gain any real information about the earlier body, for the Mishna tract *Sanhedrin*—our chief source of information—describes it in the light of the later *Bet Din*. Thus in this tract the Sanhedrin was a body of Scribes, headed by the supreme teachers of Israel. "The high priest might be a member of the court, but was subject to its jurisdiction." All this is surely not historical, but is simply an ingenious reading back into the past the institution then in effect.

The Sanhedrin would seem to have been made up of two factions: the priestly group with Sadducean sympathies, who held the majority of the seats, and the doctors and scholars from the Pharisees. How the vacancies were filled and for what term the members held office we are completely ignorant. Apparently it consisted of seventy-one members: seventy plus the high priest, who, in spite of the flat denial by the later Jewish tradition, was undoubtedly the president of the body.

As has been indicated, its authority was limited to the eleven toparchies of Judea proper; accordingly, Jesus, for example, was outside its jurisdiction as long as he remained in Galilee or the Perea. Nevertheless, it may well have exerted an *influence* on Jews everywhere, but only as they were willing to yield to its prestige. In Judea, however, it was the supreme native court with almost full power—both legislative and judicial—allowed it by the Roman governors. The sole limit to its power was in the matter of the death sentence. This apparently could be pronounced by the governor alone. Not all cases would come before it; but when the lower courts could not

[8] *Wars* 3,3,5.

agree or when the matter was of sufficient importance it was referred to this body. When once invoked, the decision of the supreme body was final and beyond the realm of appeal. It possessed independent authority, could order the arrest to be made by its own police, and could move against any one within its jurisdiction save Roman citizens. In the case of one of these trespassing beyond the barrier of the temple, even he might be arrested and convicted. Apparently it assembled on Tuesdays and Fridays, as did the lower courts.

Detailed information as to its procedure is given in the Mishna tract *Sanhedrin*. Here it said that the members sat in a semicircle "like half a round threshing floor that all the judges might see the others' faces." Before them stood two clerks to record the votes; in front of them sat three rows of disciples of the learned men to learn the methods of the court. Then follows a detailed account of the treatment of witnesses, the length of the trial, the lapse of time—thirty days—that was afforded the condemned to adduce new evidence before the pronouncement of the sentence, the majority required for a vote of acquittal and of condemnation.

How much of this actually reflects the proceedings of the Sanhedrin when it functioned with real authority, how much it reflects simply the theoretical procedure of the later body which, shorn of its power, could afford to draw up the most intricate rules of procedure since they could never be put into practice, is far from clear. Accordingly, it is perhaps not without value to warn that the not infrequent analyses by modern lawyers, quite destitute of any historical perspective or knowledge, of the trial of Jesus in the light of what they fondly call "the legal proceedings of the Sanhedrin" are utterly worthless in spite of their pseudo-scientific ponderousness and display.

The Temple and the Priestly Hierarchy

The priesthood of the temple had long constituted the aristocracy of the nation. Surely by the days of Ezra and Nehemiah, and probably earlier, none but those of unquestioned descent from Aaron had been allowed to officiate in the temple. Since the fourth century, perhaps even earlier, the high priest had been the recognized head of Israel. Just when the office of high priest arose is difficult to say, although this constituted no problem for traditional Judaism, confident that Aaron had graced that august office.[9] Actually the question is fictitious, since the office never arose suddenly. Rather it was a dignity which grew in the days of the second temple, due to the fact that there was now no king to overshadow. In Haggai and Zechariah (but not in Ezekiel) is clear reference to a chief priest who occupies an office distinctly different from his fellows. In the "Holiness Code" men-

[9] Josephus, *c. Apion.* i,7, mentions the list of "names of our high priests, from father to son, set down in our records, for the interval of two thousand years."

tion is made of the "high priest among his brethren, upon whose head the anointing oil is poured."[10]

The high-priesthood became an hereditary office, and continued as such to the days of Antiochus Epiphanes. Then the Syrian court claimed the right to appoint whom they pleased, and, banishing the rightful Onias, gave the office to the highest bidder. With the estabishment of the Hasmonean line Simon was consecrated high priest "forever until a faithful prophet should arise." From then on until Alexandra the office of high priest and king was held by the same man. This situation, unique in the history of Israel, made the incumbent absolute dictator in things both secular and religious. With the fall of the Hasmoneans and the rise of Herod the office was stripped of much of its power. Herod used it for his own advantage, appointing and deposing at his own pleasure. In this policy he was followed by the Roman authorities. The hundred years between the advent of Herod and the outbreak of the great rebellion saw no less than twenty-eight high priests,[11] of whom Herod himself made seven. Since now the office was not hereditary, it was transferred from one family to another. These families through intermarriage formed an elite inner circle. Since the tremendous wealth of the temple and unceasing revenue came into their hands, they became a very powerful group, veritably a "closed corporation." Thus the term ἀρχιερεῖς ("chief priests") came to be applied not only to the actual incumbent and the past high priests still alive, but to these allied families from which as a general rule the high priest was chosen. As has already been pointed out, they generally tended to sympathize with the Sadducees, although not all the priests were from this group. In the days with which we are chiefly concerned they were at the head of the Sanhedrin—the high priest who chanced to be in office was president—and thus of the local national government.

The priesthood was a distinct order, and was fenced about with restrictions to keep it of pure blood. The priest might marry only an undefiled virgin or a widow. She must be of Israelitish stock, for "he who is a partaker of the priesthood must propagate of a wife of the same nation."[12] The high priest was forbidden to marry a widow. He must be totally free from all bodily defects. In addition to the bodily disqualifications listed in Lev. 21:16-23 the later rabbis went into the matter with painful specificness, listing 142 different bodily defects which debarred. Apparently he must be at least twenty years of age before he could serve.[13] The consecration of a priest was attended with three distinct rites: the washing of his body with

[10] Lev. 21:10.

[11] The succession of high priests was almost kaleidoscopic, but it had not turned into an annual office, as might be implied by the words, "for he [Annas] was father-in-law to Caiaphas, who was high priest that year" (John 18:13; cf. 11:49 and 51).

[12] Josephus, *c. Apion.* i,7.

[13] At least the later rabbinical tradition so relates. See Schürer, *op. cit.,* Div. II, Vol. I, p. 215.

water; the investment with the sacred garments; a series of sacrifices and ceremonies. The

> . . . precious oil upon the head,
> That ran down upon the beard,
> Even Aaron's beard;
> That came down upon the skirt of his garments;
> Like the dew of Hermon,
> That cometh down upon the mountains of Zion[14]

was restricted to the high priest, who was specifically the "anointed high priest." The actual use of oil even for the high priest was apparently discontinued at least by the time of Herod's temple; none the less, he continued to be thus designated.

The receipts of the temple—and incidentally of the priests—were very great,[15] although, if Josephus and the later rabbis are correct, it fell largely into the hands of a select few who thus became very rich at the expense of their lesser colleagues, whom they accordingly despised. This income came from three principal sources: the sacrifices, the taxes, the gifts and offerings. Of the sacrifices the priests always obtained part, for even in the case of the whole burnt offering they received the hides, a source of revenue by no means to be despised. Of the other victims the priests obtained more, ranging from the sin and trespass offerings, of which they received practically all the meat, to the peace and thank offerings, in which they got only a share. Far more important were the taxes which were independent of the sacrifices and which included the first fruits, the *terumah* or payment in kind upon all produce, the tithes, the first born of all clean animals, the equivalent redemptive value in the case of unclean animals, the five-shekel redemption of every male child who openeth the womb, as well as a portion of the proceeds from the sheep-shearing. In addition to these regular contributions, which every pious Jew felt obligated to pay, were irregular gifts and offerings incident to especial vows and the like, and finally fines collected on stolen property which could not be returned to the owner.

All of the above described income went to the priests as their personal property. The support of the temple itself was met by entirely distinct taxes and gifts, prominent among which were the half-shekel tax,[16] the gift of wood for the sacrificial fires, and all sorts of free-will offerings. Since not only the Jews actually residing in Palestine, but all Jewry, wherever dispersed, were included in these benefactions, the toll collected by the temple and its hierarchy was a huge amount.

The duties of the priests were many and varied, but since their number was so great—probably between five and six thousand—the individual priest

[14] Psalm 133:2 f.
[15] For a complete list see Schürer, *op. cit.*, Div. II, Vol. I, pp. 230-254.
[16] See p. 95.

served only a few hours during the year. In the days of Herod's temple the priests were divided into twenty-four courses, each course serving in rotation a week at a time, changing each Sabbath. On the Passover, Pentecost, and Tabernacles all twenty-four courses served simultaneously. These twenty-four courses were further divided into subdivisions, the number of which varied from five to nine. Each course and subdivision was presided over by an official. Some of the duties were performed by stated priests; others were performed by the priests of the particular course on duty, who were chosen by lot.[17] A task such as the offering of the holy incense, according to the Mishna,[18] could be performed by a priest but once in a lifetime. Since a priest was on duty but four or five weeks at most during the year, the majority of them apparently dwelt outside the city throughout Judea. It will be remembered, for example, that Mattathias, the father of the Maccabean revolt, lived in Modein. According to the evidence presented by Strack and Billerbeck[19] a very large proportion of the priests lived in Jericho. This would give point to the story of the Good Samaritan.

The high priest rarely officiated except at the times of the great feasts. Actually he was not obliged to take active part except on the Day of Atonement, although it was usual for him to do so during the preceding week, and according to Josephus on the Sabbaths and times of the new moon.[20] On the Day of Atonement he went alone behind the "veil of the temple" into the holy of holies.

The duties of the priests fell into four classes: (1) the care and custody of the temple, its furnishings, and treasure; (2) the policing of the temple, responsibility for order and decorum, keeping watch in the inner courts, the opening and closing of the great gates; (3) incidental duties such as the oversight and conduct of the music, and of the more menial duties of cleansing and repair of the building itself and its courts; (4) the conduct of the daily sacrifices.

The lesser duties, including the music, were performed by the Levites. In Deuteronomy no distinction between priests and Levites is made; by the time of Ezekiel, however, the line of demarcation was drawn. From then on they are the priests' assistants, and all distinction between the Levites and the "singers and doorkeepers" has disappeared. Like the priests they were divided into twenty-four courses and were carefuly supervised.

One further official may be mentioned briefly—the *Sagan*. Although the rabbinical authorities differ as to his precise status, some making him a sort of substitute high priest, he appears to have been the prefect of the priest-

[17] Cf. Luke 1:8 ff.

[18] M. Yoma 2.

[19] Strack und Billerbeck, *Kommentar zum Neuen Testament aus Talmud und Midrasch,* Vol. II, pp. 180 f. This work is of the utmost importance to the student of the New Testament.

[20] *Wars* 5,5,7.

hood, that is, the στρατηγὸς τοῦ ἱεροῦ or captain of the temple.[21] To use a modern phrase, he was the chief of the temple police. His responsibilities and power were great. It is interesting to observe that no less a personage than Rabbi Hanina ben Teradion, a contemporary of Johanan ben Zakkai and a prominent teacher in Israel, once held this office.[22]

The daily sacrifices fell into two classes. Of the first were the public sacrifices, offered in the name of the people. The cost of these sacrifices was defrayed by the peoples' own offering—especially the half-shekel tax. Some of them occurred every day, others at the time of especial feasts and celebrations. The second class comprised the private sacrifices. They were offered in the name of the individual who sponsored and paid for them. Both of these classes were of three types: (1) the whole burnt offering; (2) the sin and trespass offerings (with all save the fat, which was burned, going to the priests); (3) the peace or thank offering (in which the sacrificer, since no sin was to be atoned for, received the bulk of the meat "as material for a jocund sacrificial feast").

Of the *regular* daily sacrifice in the name of the people (that is, of the first class) there were two. Every morning and every evening a male lamb, one year old and without blemish, was burnt on the great altar which stood in the inner court and in front of the temple proper, separated from it by the brazen laver in which the priests washed their hands and feet preparatory to entering the house.[23] With this burnt offering was a meat and drink offering of flour mixed with oil and baked into a cake and a quarter hin of wine. Immediately preceding the morning sacrifice and following the evening sacrifice (that is, at dawn and 3 P.M.), an offering of incense was burnt, not on the great altar, but on the golden altar of incense, which with the seven-branched candlestick and table of shewbread stood in the front chamber of the temple (ναός). This room, sixty feet long and high and thirty feet wide, was called the *hekal*. Behind the *hekal* and separated from it by a curtain—the veil of the temple—stood the other and smaller room, the *debir*, or holy of holies. This was entirely empty, and was entered but once a year by the high priest, who for that purpose exchanged his elaborate vestments for the simple but costly white robe of fine linen.

Together with the worship went vocal and instrumental music; at intervals two priests sounded a fanfare on their silver trumpets as a signal for the congregation to fall in prayer. Seven psalms formed a sort of sacred series, one for each day in the week, beginning with Sunday. They were the twenty-fourth, forty-eighth, eighty-second, ninety-fourth, eighty-first,

[21] Cf. Acts 4:1; 5:24,26.

[22] Moore, *Judaism*, Vol. II, pp. 114 ff., 482. This should warn that while the (Sadducaic) priests and (Pharisaic) Scribes were usually distinct exceptions occurred.

[23] The whole structure, consisting of the temple itself, its courts, walls, and porticoes, was called τὸ ἱερόν; the temple proper ὁ ναός.

ninety-third, and ninety-second. On the Passover, Feast of Tabernacles, and on each of the eight days of the Feast of Dedication the Hallel (Psalms 113-118) were recited.

But the regular daily sacrifices and those offered in the name of the nation on the feast days constituted but a tiny fraction of the total number of sacrificial victims. The jostling, sweating hosts of pilgrims who surged through the temple courts not alone on the days of especial holiness, but throughout the year, each wanting his part in the ancient custom; the many priests in attendance; the lowing and bellowing of terrified cattle in the pens and on the marble slabs; the billowing clouds of smoke and nauseous stench from burning fat and meat; the cries of the hawkers and money-changers—all this might well have seemed to an even less sensitive observer than Jesus of Nazareth a strange answer to the query of an Isaiah or a Micah.

Though the temple service continued to the fall of the city and was flocked to by thousands of pilgrims anxious to assemble to "Zion whither the tribes go up," actually it had long ceased to be the real centre of Jewish life. It remained a glamorous symbol, a visual proof of the nearness of Jehovah. Once in his lifetime a Galilean peasant might make the trip, but week in week out he attended the simple unpretentious service in his local synagogue. These were the real answer to the prophets' cry.

Chapter IX

HOPES FOR THE FUTURE

As a little state constantly endangered by her more powerful neighbours, Israel's fate was hardly commensurate with her confidence that the supreme God of the whole world was actually King in a peculiar sense of Israel alone. For Israel alone had recognized his sovereignty. At Sinai the people, when informed by Moses of Jehovah's will and laws, had with one voice cried: "All the words which Jehovah hath spoken will we do."[1] The years had told a sad story of internal discord, the rending asunder of the kingdom, the successive collapse of north and south before the powerful invader. Could this be the fate which the supreme God had decreed for his own peculiar people? There could be but one answer. Eventually the scales of the balance would right themselves. A good time was coming; it might be long delayed. God had promised; he could not forswear himself. The days of David and Solomon, when seen through the mists of the years and in contrast to the present abject state of the little land, had taken on a romantic and wholly unhistorical color. Those were the day of gold, but they gave a pattern for the future. Once more, in God's own good time, the golden age would return: freed from the oppression of ruthless and uncircumcised intruders, purged of her sins which had been the actual cause of her downfall, she would experience an era of peace and blessing which would not be transient and fleeting as the earlier good times had been. This in essence was Israel's hope for the future. During the lapse of the years it was destined to be developed, first in one direction and then another. It came to be identified with a restored kingdom with a second David on its throne. The notion of life after death, of a cataclysmic dissolution of the present earth and the birth of a new one, the garish display and eschatological nightmares of the apocalypses peopled by angels and hideous beasts, these came into the picture in the course of the years. None the less these were but developments—one might almost say excrescences. In popular speech—and too often in learned writing—all of these notions have been lumped together under the very misleading and unfortunate title, The Messianic Hope.

The first point to be observed in seeking to disentangle this curiously complex cord is that in the Old Testament the term Messiah—anointed—is not a noun. That is, it is not the title limited to one specific figure destined to appear in the future for a certain and definite purpose. Rather, it is actually

[1] Exod. 24:3,7.

more like an adjective, and as such regularly qualifies some noun expressed or implied. The normal phrase is "anointed of the Lord" and is applied to several figures. Kings, high priests, patriarchs, the nation as a whole, even Cyrus, are so designated. In the days of Herod's temple the actual practice of anointing the high priest had lapsed; none the less, he continued to bear the title "anointed high priest" just the same.

In both the canonical books of the Old Testament and in the Apocrypha the noteworthy thing is that there is no mention at all of what we are wont to speak of as "the Messiah." The earliest reference to the Messiah as a standing title is in the Synoptic gospels. The later literature contains allusions to the coming "King Messiah"; here also the phrases "days of the Messiah," and "woes of the Messiah" are to be found. But this is apparently after the dawn of the Christian era.

Accordingly, to use the term, "the Messianic hope," to describe the expectation of future blessedness to which pious Jews were looking forward in the days of Jesus is to approach the problem from the wrong end, and is open to two serious objections. First, it causes the student to assume that there was *one* expectation that every pious Jew held—a sort of carefully arranged future program or time-table. Judaism was a religion of doing rather than of believing. Obedience to the law, not orthodoxy of belief or opinion, was the requirement. In no sphere of thought is this characteristic more discernible than in the hopes for the future. Many and divergent shades of opinion are to be found. It is quite misleading to speak of *the* hope. A second objection to the usual term is that it tends to throw undue emphasis on the figure of the coming one, the Messiah. The "Messianic Age" should connote the age when the Messiah is to appear. Actually the expectation was for the *era* or *age* itself, not for the party who was to bring it in or to mark its advent. In fact, in large blocks of Jewish thinking there was no such figure. In the great prophecy of the exile[2] such is the case. Here God alone is to be King.[3] So long as Isaiah was considered one book, these later chapters were interpreted in the light of the earlier. Accordingly, the Targum interprets Isa. 42:1, "Behold, my servant whom I uphold; my chosen, in whom my soul delighteth," with the words, "Behold, my servant the Anointed (Messiah), my Chosen in whom my word (i.e., I myself) delights."[4] But we know today that that was not the meaning of the author himself nor of his contemporaries.

Accordingly, such a term as golden age is a far better designation for the hopes of Israel. It was the good time coming when all men everywhere would know and reverence God, when no man need say to his brother, "Know thou the Lord," for all would know him.

[2] Isa. 40 ff.

[3] "For this the unhappy phrase 'messianic age without a Messiah' has been invented."—Moore, *Judaism*, Vol. II, p. 327.

[4] Moore, *op. et loc. cit.*

This hope arose, or gained a fresh lease of life, after the sack of Jerusalem and destruction of the temple (586 B.C.) The temple must be rebuilt. When the temple was restored and sacrifice again was offered, all would be well. Spurred by this word from Haggai and Zechariah the temple was rebuilt, but, unfortunately, all was not well. The expected restoration, Israel's independence, did not materialize. But though many were now identifying the good time, the future golden age, with the restoration of the monarchy under the "scion of David" or David himself, this longing in its definitely national form was not universal. Even in those days many were tolerably well off under Persian rule. The memory of some of the successors of David was still too vivid to evoke unqualified enthusiasm. This attitude is highly significant. From that time on many Jews never had a very violent longing for the day to dawn. Those in comfortable circumstances—political or financial—would have little to gain and much to lose. It smacked too much of revolution. In the days of Jesus the Sadducees and their supporters illustrate well this attitude. And many of the religious leaders seem completely deaf to their warlike brothers. The experiences of the past century under the Hasmoneans were still fresh. Jannæus had occupied the throne of David. Aside from breaking the heads of the heathen—to be sure, this was one of the tasks of the coming ideal ruler (Psalm 110)—his reign had done much to cause the "scion of David" to fade into comparative inconspicuousness. When the day dawned it would probably see a completely theocratic kingdom with God, not man, enthroned. But at best this was a beautiful dream for the future, an added spur to the study of God's laws. It was best to leave the details to God. It was he that was guiding the universe. Years later, when the temple was again in ruins, when Rome's heel was galling the neck of prostrate Israel, when it was noised about that the worst blow yet was soon to fall—Jerusalem was to become a pagan city!—this indifference changed, and a whole-hearted, if utterly mad, nationalism was for the moment revealed. The Messiah would make an end of the Roman empire. But this latter outbreak was many years after Jesus' death.

But in the days of the restoration there were others who were far from satisfied, but who longed for political power—if not for themselves, at least for their nation. Nor did this hope ever die out. A popular and noisy minority constantly harped on the string of restored political supremacy. In the time of Jesus they—the Home Rule Party—were still alive, as the malicious question proposed to Jesus by his opponents makes clear.[5] None the less, although they constituted a problem to be reckoned with, by no means all the nation held those quixotic views. Later the awful fate which came upon the nation popularized the movement and swelled its numbers. But to read this later experience back to the earlier times and to assume that in Jesus' day this was the common and universally held expectation is totally unjusti-

[5] Mark 12:14 f.

fied by the evidence. There was no one view accepted by all. Many men, many minds.

The general features, however, of this peculiarly Jewish hope for the coming golden age are fairly clear. It was to be in the future, but in the present age. It would be upon this earth. It would be brought about by or be coincident with the recognition of the universal sovereignty of God. Would the heathen be converted gradually and would the golden age as a result dawn bright and fair? Would God by special fiat destroy the unbelievers? Opinions differed.[6] But all were agreed that when it dawned God would be recognized and worshipped by all. In a word, it was the good time coming, the universally recognized reign of Israel's God, on this earth but in the future. For some it would be in terms of a political restoration, perhaps with the restored Davidic king;[7] for others it would be purely theocratic; for others, pleasurably vague.

Over against this purely Jewish view is to be discerned an entirely different train of ideas, not Jewish in essence but apparently Persian, yet which none the less came to be adopted by many Jews and regarded as genuinely their own. In contrast to the golden age this other may be called the Age to Come.

The Persian concept in brief was this: There would be in the future a great cataclysm which would bring the present age to a dramatic close. The world would literally come to an end, would be consumed by fire to purify it from evil. The righteous would rise to take their places in a new and glorious world. Judgment would be held and men's fates would be settled by the great supernatural judge, Shaoshyant, God's representative.

These ideas were gradually absorbed, although they were never really thought through by Judaism. As we have seen, the notion of resurrection, which provided a convenient answer to the obvious moral injustices of life, was early taken over by Judaism and made to fit in with the older views. It became popular and came to be considered an original part of God's revelation to Israel. None the less, in spite of scribal ingenuity it remained more or less a patch on an older garment.

The book of Daniel plays an important part in the popularizing of these notions. In the apocalyptic imagery of this writing the heathen nations are represented pictorially by awesome beasts; in contrast to them stands "one like unto a son of man,"[8] who, as the author explicitly says, represents the kingdom of the holy people of the Most High.[9] In the Semitic idiom son

[6] This uncertainty is reflected by the later alternative: The Messiah, son of David, will come only in a generation that is wholly worthy or in one that is wholly guilty.

[7] By some, not David, but Hezekiah, was expected. Cf. Moore, *Judaism*, Vol. II, pp. 347 f.

[8] Dan. 7:13.

[9] Dan. 7:27.

of man (Aramaic *bar nasha*; Hebrew *ben adam*) simply means man in the sense of the Latin *homo* or Greek ἄνθρωπος.[10]
Gradually this purely colourless phrase tended to become a technical title for this supernatural figure who was destined to come to judgment, and who accordingly was totally distinct from the anointed king of the other cycle of ideas who would be of human origin and whose function was to rule over God's people.

Popular thinking is never very successful in preserving parallel notions in water-tight compartments, however much the later historian might desire it. There is a constant tendency for the two to become more or less reconciled, or for ideas of the one to become introduced into the other. Thus on the surface it would seem not improbable that eventually the (Jewish) view of the good time coming would be made to coincide with that of the Age to Come, and that in the latter the still unfulfilled prophecies would be believed to have their realization. Or if the coming Davidic king chanced to be a part of the picture—as we have seen, this was not always the case—he could be transplanted, so to speak, into the new age and, losing his function of destroying Israel's enemies in war, could gradually assume a more universal responsibility for destroying evil and acting as final judge. In a word, *son of David* and *son of man* might eventually become identified.

All this is intrinsically possible. It would be most rash to say that the equation of these two originally utterly distinct figures had never been made by Judaism before the Christian era. We know that it was done by early Christians, who came to see in Jesus the realization of both these figures and so by good mathematics—two things equal to the same thing are equal to each other—identified the anointed king with the supernatural judge to the confusion of all subsequent historians.

But because a thing is possible is not sufficient reason to assume that it was done. And we have in my judgment no clear evidence to warrant the assumption that this identification had taken place—of course, an individual here or there may have toyed with the idea—until after the Christian beginnings. From then on the two threads seem more and more intertwined and titles of the one are bestowed upon the other.

To see how in later days these two views were actually reconciled or accommodated, the one to the other, the apocalypse known as IV Ezra is instructive. Here we have a thoroughgoing attempt at harmonization: The time was near approaching when the Anointed, that is, the Davidic king of Israel, would appear, destroy all opposition, and reign for four hundred years. Then he and all mankind would die—"My son, the anointed one, will die." That marks the end of "this age." Then would come the Resur-

[10] Cf. the parallelism of Psalm 8:4:

> What is *man*, that thou art mindful of him?
> And the *son of man*, that thou visitest him?

rection and Final Judgment, the dawn of the New Age, that is, the "Age to Come."

Here it is to be observed that the original notion that the golden age was to be unending has been modified. It has become a period of interim, a prelude to the Last Judgment, and of limited duration, four hundred years. In the Christian apocalypse—the canonical book of Revelation—the same note is struck, but the period is a thousand years. It should also be observed that in IV Ezra it is God himself who acts as final judge.[11] In other writings his representative performs that function.

One final phrase may be mentioned, "the woes (or travail) of the Messiah." This refers to the period of anguish and horror that in the later popular belief would immediately precede his coming. It has been often interpreted of the sufferings which the Messiah himself would have to undergo. This is totally in error, for it refers explicitly to the agony of mother Zion, in travail to bring forth the Messiah. Just how early this view arose is not clear. The earliest occurrence of the exact phrase is in the generation after the destruction of Jerusalem. The notion itself may well be earlier and be a reflection of the prophetic warning of the "great and terrible day of the Lord." Paul may refer to some such belief in his warning against the dangers of marriage.[12] Apparent references to this in the Synoptic gospels (especially Mark 13:7-27 and parallels) are complicated by the fact that the gospels as we have them do not antedate 70 A.D. Omens of all kinds would herald the approach. Sun and moon would be darkened, swords and armies would be seen in the sky, blood would trickle from stones, fresh water would become salt, nations would rise against nations, families would be split asunder, elders would be insulted, babes would be torn from the arms of agonized mothers. But these dire woes—and the list I have given is not a unit, but a potpourri from several apocalypses—are for the most part late. Just when they became a definite part of the picture is not clear.

In conclusion, it appears to me most unwise to try to give a fictitious appearance of simplicity to a singularly complicated and obscure matter. It is quite rash to try to formulate *the* program and to give to it several well-defined steps—Schürer gives it eleven[13]—for in the same writings different views appear. That in the future God would take care of Israel and that his beneficent rule would be recognized by all was probably a part of every pious Jew's *confessio fidei*; but the various shades of interpretation, incident to the two distinctly different sources—Jewish and Persian—and to the development of each, with the resultant vagueness of detail, prevented any systematic or universally accepted teaching.

[11] Cf. Psalm 50, especially v. 6—"For God is judge himself."

[12] I Cor. 7:28 ff. See my *Ethics of Paul*, pp. 177 f.

[13] *Op. cit.*, Div. II, Vol. II, pp. 154-187.

PART II

THE BEGINNINGS OF THE GOSPEL STORY

PREFACE

The claim for Christianity is often made that it is the "faith once for all delivered to the saints." To the student of history such a claim is not only false; it is positively absurd. Nor is this by any means an admission of weakness or of inadequacy. Rather it is one of the most conspicuous signs of the life and strength of this religion that to none of its tenets could the phrase *semper, ubique, et ab omnibus* be justly subscribed. Many of those in the early and formative years whom men today regard as the pillars of orthodoxy must have seemed far from the light to many of their fellow saints. What a debt every religion—and Christianity perhaps most of all—owes to its heretics, for notions dubbed heresy at bedtime often arise the next morning with a halo of orthodoxy firm upon their brows. Nor was the growth and development due alone to pioneers who dared to be different, who were ever seeking a more adequate and complete expression of their faith. As has already been emphasized, Christianity was the child of Judaism. The joys and the sorrows, the defeats and the longings, of the mother were inherited by the child. Only so can the younger religion be understood. But this, while of tremendous significance, is by no means the whole story. The new religion—even before it had come to know itself as a new religion—had been pushed out of the parent's nest. The world into which it was forced was a new and strange one. Whether it be true of individuals or not, it was certainly true of Christianity that its environment exerted a tremendous influence. Within a score of years it had become a gentile cult. It adopted new conceptions, took on a totally different character, borrowed from all with whom it came into contact, and through its extraordinary eclectic character was able to rival the older and more firmly established cults so successfully that within three hundred years the emperor Constantine, who lacked no quality more conspicuously than piety, saw emblazoned in the sky a cross and heard the congenial word that his campaign would be successful.

In a word, Christianity has never been a stagnant pool; rather it has been a rapidly flowing stream, fed, as it rushes to the sea, by many brooks and rivulets, and partaking of their qualities. As such we shall try to see it in the subsequent pages, and attempt to follow its banks back to its mountain source.

Many difficulties confront us. One is especially real. The chief source of our knowledge of the earliest beginnings is not one book, but a library by many authors, produced not at one time, but which grew many years after the start of the new religion. Contrary to many popular notions, the new religion produced its book; the book did not produce the religion. Again, these writings, which eventually came to be called the New Testament, were written for purely practical purposes: to meet specific needs felt in those days. They were not prepared to edify or to instruct subsequent generations which might desire historical insights into the past. Hence many points about which we would appreciate information are glossed over or omitted entirely. And finally, the gospels, which purport to tell us of the earliest period, were not the first, but among the last of the documents to be produced. Accordingly, we must give due regard to this lapse of time—at the very least forty years—and recognize the probability that again and again the later outlook and ideas have been reflected, at times perhaps unwittingly, yet none the less surely, in the chronicle of the earlier years.

Today we recognize that we cannot hope to reconstruct the early days of the Christian beginnings by an uncritical reading of the four gospels and book of Acts. The authors, no one of whom was himself an eyewitness of the events he recorded, had to depend upon earlier sources, written or oral, and not upon telepathy for their information. When we have reached the period in the developing history of the church in which these writings came to be produced, we shall have occasion to try to see the way the authors used the sources of knowledge at their command. Until then we must satisfy ourselves with a tentative reconstruction of the history, using the results of a century and a half's critical study without retesting or re-proving each point. Later when we consider the various books, the reasons for the assumptions will perhaps be apparent.

Chapter X

JOHN THE BAPTIST AND HIS FOLLOWERS

All four of our gospels begin with reference to the work of John the Baptist, who is depicted as the forerunner of Jesus, his greater successor. Of his early life we know little or nothing. According to Luke he was born of priestly stock, and, as was the case of many of the Old Testament worthies, in the extreme old age of his parents. In this same account he is represented as a relation of Jesus since his mother and Mary were related. That the story rests upon any historical foundation is most improbable. Apparently it is a consequence of the early re-writing of the story of John to bring him into conscious subordination to Jesus. In the Synoptic gospels John appears spectacularly in the wilderness of Judea and in dramatic fashion sounds a note of doom worthy of Jeremiah or Amos: "Repent of your sins; be baptized for the remission of them. If you don't, it will be the worse for you; a catastrophe is coming. Even now the axe is laid at the root of the tree. Those not bearing good fruit will be hewn down." Here is an ascetic figure, living apart from men, awing those who flocked to hear him and convicting them of guilt. In Mark, the eldest of the three accounts, Jesus is represented as being one of the group which listens, and as being baptized. There is no hint of any recognition of him by John, or that it is he who is to be the "greater one" John is so eloquently proclaiming. In Matthew, however, a new and distinctly Christian note is introduced. When Jesus comes to be baptized, John at once recognizes him, and demurs at Jesus' request. "Nay," says he in substance, "it would be far more fitting for you to baptize me." "You are quite right," says Jesus, "but suffer it to be done." In the light of this obvious recognition by Jesus of his dignity the heavenly voice can no longer say—as Mark recorded it—"Thou art my beloved Son, in whom I am well pleased." Rather it proclaims to those who need the information, "This is my beloved Son." In Luke's account this process of subordinating John to Jesus is carried a step farther. Even before their births they had met. When Mary, in whom was the divinely begotten Lord, came into the presence of the pregnant Elisabeth, the latter's babe leaped in her womb, prompting words from Elisabeth which made Mary's *Magnificat* possible. In the Fourth Gospel the climax is reached. John is of a truth only the voice which proclaims Jesus. The author is familiar with the story of the baptism, but recasts it. How unfitting that the divine Word should have been baptized! Rather the Baptist sees him approaching and heralds him: "Behold the

Lamb of God, that taketh away the sin of the world! This is he of whom I said, After me cometh a man who is become before me: for he was before me." The dove is present, but not for Jesus. Well does the Lord, the incarnate Word of God, know his own identity. Rather the appearance is for John, the herald. "And John bare witness saying, I have beheld the Spirit descending as a dove out of heaven; and it abode upon him. And I knew him not: but he that sent me to baptize in water, he said unto me, Upon whomsoever thou shalt see the Spirit descending, and abiding upon him, the same is he that baptizeth in the Holy Spirit. And I have seen, and have borne witness that this is the Son of God."

A careful study of these four accounts leaves but little room for doubt that John the Baptist was thus transformed by Christianity from an independent preacher into the forerunner of Jesus. Nor is it improbable that his message has been similarly edited. It is to be observed that Matthew (altering the phraseology of his source, Mark) makes him utter precisely the same clarion call as did Jesus: "Repent ye; for the kingdom of heaven is at hand."[1] The special teaching of John which Luke alone records[2] is surprisingly like that later found in the mouth of Jesus (cf. especially, "He that hath two coats, let him impart to him that hath none; and he that hath food, let him do likewise"). The question arises whether, after all, the picture of John heralding the advent of the greater one who will baptize the nations in fire is not actually that of Jesus heralding the advent of the son of man, the final Judge, who, as we have already seen, was expected by many Jews to perform this function.

This explanation would appear to me supported by the one passage in Josephus in which John is mentioned.

Now, some of the Jews thought that the destruction of Herod's [*i.e.,* Antipas'] army came from God, and that very justly, as a punishment of what he did against John, who was called the Baptist; for Herod slew him, who was a good man, and commanded the Jews to exercise virtue, both as to righteousness toward one another, and piety toward God, and so to come to baptism; for that the washing [with water] would be acceptable to him, if they made use of it, not in order to the putting away of some sins, but for the purification of the body; supposing still that the soul was thoroughly purified beforehand by righteousness. Now, when many others came in crowds about him, for they were greatly moved by hearing his words, Herod, who feared lest the great influence John had over the people might put it into his power and inclination to raise a rebellion (for they seemed ready to do anything he should advise), thought it best, by putting him to death, to prevent any mischief he might cause, and not bring himself into difficulties by sparing a man who might make him repent of it when it should be too

[1] Matt. 3:2; 4:17.

[2] Luke 3:10-14.

late. Accordingly he was sent a prisoner, out of Herod's suspicious temper, to Macherus, the castle I before mentioned, and was there put to death.[3]

In this brief and intelligible account two points are striking: (1) the reason given for John's execution; (2) the entire absence of any mention of what in the gospels is a highly significant note, the advent of his greater successor. There is no need of an elaborate chain of reasoning as to why Josephus, although he mentioned John, was reluctant to mention Jesus or a mysterious "greater one" whom Christians were now confident was Jesus. The simplest and most likely explanation is that this was not an actual part of John's message. Josephus is not exercising editorial privileges; he is simply recording facts.

On the basis, then, of this critical sifting of the gospel account and of the testimony of Josephus there would seem to be little support for the modern conjecture that Jesus was started on his career through contact with the Baptist, and that he repeated the latter's message even after John's tragic death had sundered the bond of teacher and pupil. It would, accordingly, appear more probable that the paths of Jesus and John did not cross at all and that our gospel accounts preserve little or nothing of the actual history of this enigmatic man. As the years rolled by, John, although originally quite distinct from Jesus, was gradually brought into the Christian picture, if not into the Christian fold.

Nor is the reason for this transformation of the powerful wilderness prophet into the self-abasing voice far to seek. That John the Baptist had been in the early days a distinct hindrance to the rise of Christianity and that traces of this are still to be found in the early Christian records has seemed to many New Testament critics probable. In fact, the Fourth Gospel shows a clear animus against the disciples of the Baptist, and has for one of its purposes the complete and voluntary subjugation of John to Jesus, to be able to say to his followers: "Since your leader clearly recognized that our leader was the true Lamb of God, and gladly reckoned himself as but a voice to proclaim him, so you should cease your independent existence, and with us recognize and follow our common Lord." The occasional references to the disciples of John[4] suggest that his movement had by no means come to an end at the appearance of Jesus; nor is there any sign of a defection from his camp to that of his "greater successor." It is by no means improbable that the twelve individuals, whom Paul is said to have met in Ephesus,[5] who knew only the baptism of John and had never even heard of the Holy Spirit and who were accordingly rebaptized to remedy this lack, belonged to this group still in existence. The great influence that John exerted—

[3] *Antt.* 18,5,2.

[4] Cf. Mark 2.18; Luke 11:1; John 3:23; 4:1.

[5] Acts 19:1-7.

attested alike by Josephus[6] and the gospels[7]—suggests not only that the work of this preacher was no mere flash-in-the-pan, but that it might very well have tended to divert attention from the disciples of the other martyred leader. Furthermore, the famous testimony to John which Matthew and Luke attribute to Jesus—"Among them that are born of women there hath not arisen a greater than John the Baptist: *yet he that is but little in the kingdom of heaven is greater than he*"[8]—and which has never been satisfactorily explained on the basis of the traditional relationship between the two would seem to reveal a rivalry or at least a cleavage between the two groups.

Accordingly, it appears not unlikely that the incorporation of John into the Christian picture was a deliberate and studied attempt by early Christians to vanquish an embarrassing rival. The religions of antiquity provide numerous examples of a new god gradually supplanting an old and eventually being regarded as his son. The most effective way of getting rid of a rival is to align him with one's own cause. Accordingly, it would not be difficult to explain the rise of these stories, even though the tangents of Jesus and John never crossed. The story of the imprisoned Baptist sending his disciples to ask Jesus if he were the Christ[9] would not appear to indicate a cooling of John's ardour shown in such passages as Matt. 3:14 f. and John 1:15-42 but rather to reflect an earlier, less advanced, stage in their rapprochement.

Once John was in the Christian picture it is not difficult to see how the legend of Herodias' wrath might have arisen as an explanation of his untimely end. As has already been pointed out, Josephus gives a quite different and more plausible explanation. That a Herod should have been very much disturbed by an uncouth wilderness preacher's displeasure at his nuptials is perhaps less likely than that he should have trembled with dread at the thought of an increasingly popular movement, the burden of which was the collapse of established society. Rulers are not wont to take kindly such proclamations, even though the agent of the collapse be God himself. Antipas was probably keen sighted enough to realize John's aim was not political; none the less, he was canny enough to realize that such a message might well serve as the spark in the powder-chest of unrest toward Rome and all her hirelings. Naturally, such an explanation of John's demise would not prove acceptable to Christians, especially to those concerned with establishing the innocency of their movement in the eyes of Rome. How much more probable that this second Elijah, staunch advocate of pure morals that he was, had perished at the hands of this more formidable modern Jezebel!

Discussion of the significance of the baptism practised not alone by John,

[6] *Loc. cit.*

[7] Mark 11:27-33.

[8] Matt. 11:11; Luke 7:28.

[9] Matt. 11:2-6; Luke 7:18-23.

but by other sects in Palestine, and of their possible influence upon the externally similar rite which soon made its appearance in the Christian group, may profitably be reserved for a later page. The point of present importance is that the stories about him, regardless of their value for an understanding of later Christianity, would seem to throw far less light than is usually assumed upon the one who is popularly supposed to have designated and to have quickened his greater successor.

Chapter XI

JESUS AND THE GALILEE MISSION

For the beginning of Christianity we must look to Galilee, for it was there that Jesus "began both to do and to teach," for he must be seen as the point of departure for the movement which came eventually to regard itself as a new religion and to be called by his name. Regardless of the differences between his point of view and that of his early followers; regardless of the fact that many of the words attributed to him in the gospels were coloured if not actually produced by the outlook of the age in which they were written; regardless of the practical difficulties encountered in striving to apply these words literally in this twentieth century—none the less, Jesus is to be seen as the centre of the movement, and however he may be portrayed, however much we seek to prove that he was a first-century Jew in outlook and belief, this must not obscure the fact that it was his tremendous personality that gripped those first disciples, that wrested a man like Saul of Tarsus from the things formerly dear to him, and that has continued to the present day in unabated power. The emphasis of the Fourth Gospel is right: The living, deathless person of Christ is the ultimate force in Christianity.

This is not the place for a detailed study of Jesus' life or teaching. It is more than doubtful if either is possible of reconstruction, as is abundantly evidenced by the many attempts; certainly not without a thorough and exact knowledge of the literary relationship and problems of the gospels which must be reserved in this present volume for a later page. Accordingly, this chapter must be rigidly limited to a consideration of his direct influence, in so far as we may with reasonable confidence discover it, in the movement later to be called by his name.

Jesus was born and brought up in the hills of Galilee, in the quiet town of Nazareth, the very name of which is unknown to us in that period outside the gospels and Acts. The Bethlehem stories, regardless of their homiletic beauty, apparently rest upon no historical foundation, but must be regarded as pure legend. A critical examination of the two accounts—the one assuming the fixed residence of the parents in Bethlehem, the homage of Magi guided from the East by a miraculous star, the edict of a cruel king (strangely akin to that told of the infant Moses), the flight into Egypt, and subsequent return to Palestine, but to Nazareth, not Bethlehem; the other telling of a most unusual journey from Nazareth to Bethlehem, undertaken by the expectant mother in compliance with the requirement of a supposed census,[1] the inability to find lodgings, the resultant birth in a stable, the vision of angels granted to shepherds, and their visit to the manger—reveals that they are mutually exclusive, contradicting each other at every point. Their value is real; none the less, this value does not lie in the realm of history.

Nor do we know more of his boyhood or young manhood. At a very early date Christians were struck by these "hidden years" and sought to remedy the lack. The so-called Apocryphal Gospels, of which the Protevangelium of James, the Gospel of Thomas, and the various Infancy gospels are conspicuous examples, plainly evidence the utter lack of information that made the resultant grotesque and repellent stories possible. They simply depict a wonder child, endowed with limitless magical power but destitute of any ethical sense. In this connexion the one story which occurs in the accepted gospels[2] is significant. Due in part to the fact that it occurs in a *canonical* gospel, in part to the chasteness and restraint of the account in contrast to the tales of the malicious and malignant little boy of the other narratives, this story of the visit of the twelve-year-old Jesus to the temple has been often accepted, but usually with the entire evacuation of its meaning. Attempts to understand it as the normal attitude of the respectful little boy, awed by his elders, and thrilled at the thought that he is now a "son of the Law," quite miss the point. In essence the story is of precisely the same character as those in the Apocryphal Gospels. It portrays a unique child, wise beyond his years, aware of his vocation in life, asking his questions quite as a full-grown Socrates might have done, or as Jesus himself later did.

Attempts to probe back into the years before the ministry are utterly fruitless. The utmost that can be said has already been said by Luke, and said magnificently:

> And the child grew, and waxed strong, filled with wisdom: and the grace of God was upon him.
>
> And Jesus advanced in wisdom and stature, and in favor with God and men.[3]

More than this we can never know.

The gospel accounts begin with the story of the baptism of Jesus by John the Baptist. This story has been widely considered, even by critical historians, as resting upon an essentially trustworthy tradition of an actual occurrence, and many fanciful conclusions have been drawn from it: Jesus was started on his mission as a prophet by the Baptist—an explanation which

[1] Attempts to establish the accuracy of the Lucan account by postulating this earlier census, also conducted by Quirinius, as was the other one, definitely known to us (see above, pp. 67 f.) as one in a regular fourteen-year cycle, have been made, notably by Ramsay, *Was Christ Born in Bethlehem?* but have little probability and have not commended themselves to scholars generally.

[2] Luke 2:41-51.

[3] Luke 2:40,52.

would have scandalized the older conservative scholars, hard put to explain the inappropriateness of the sinless Christ deigning to accept baptism[4]—whose disciple he became. It was not until John's imprisonment that he started a really independent mission. He returned to Galilee to avoid encroaching upon the Master's territory. Thus the similarity of the teaching of the two was explained: Jesus' early message was essentially a repetition of the Baptist's. Such an explanation might account for the entrance of Jesus in the rôle of a prophet; however, it simply pushes the difficulty one stage further back by failing to provide a similar impetus for John.

Reasons have already been given in a previous chapter for viewing the whole story of the contact of Jesus and John as the creation of later Christian thinking. It is surely no less arbitrary to assume this relationship of master and pupil and to explain the similarity of teaching as due to the borrowing by Jesus of the message of John than it is to reverse the procedure and to consider the possibility that all the words found in the mouth of the Baptist in the gospel narrative are the result of Christian tradition and actually have as much right to be regarded as words, not of John, but of Jesus, as do the words actually attributed to the latter in the gospel pages. In addition to the reasons already suggested for hesitating to consider the account of the baptism of Jesus by John historical is the utter disregard of baptism, both in practice and in injunction, during the ministry and not improbably in the months—perhaps years—which followed.[5] As the account stands in Mark it was a critical experience for Jesus, a turning point in his career. Then it was that God's Holy Spirit descended upon him, transforming him into God's own prophet, commissioned from on high to sound the clarion call to repentance in preparation for the new age soon to dawn. It is astonishing that an experience of such moment to himself should not have commended itself to him as valuable for others as well. Finally, there is the problem of the source of knowledge of the event—and this applies equally to the subsequent narrative of the Temptation. According to the narratives of the Synoptic gospels—and probability bears them out—Jesus' first contact with followers was in Galilee; the notion of a ministry in Judea with disciples recruited there who followed him into Galilee is sheer assumption. Accordingly the information, if authentic, must have come from Jesus himself. That such information was given by him is also sheer assumption, and, as Origen early pointed out,[6] out of keeping with the character of the one who "on all occasions avoided unnecessary talk about himself." The presumption is that no information prior to the ministry in Galilee was available when the first traditions began to take form. Nor

[4] Ignatius (*ad Eph.* 18:2) remarks that his baptism was "to cleanse the water."

[5] For a discussion of such passages as Matt. 28:19; Mark 16:16; John 3.22; 4:1-2; Acts 2:38-41 which are in apparent contradiction to this statement, see below, pp. 194 ff.

[6] *c. Celsum* i,48 (end).

is it surprising that there was an occasional early attempt to push the prehistory farther back into a period before the time the central figure had come into the public eye. Flat and arbitrary denial of the possibility of the narrative being historic would of course be rash. But in history, as in engineering, one can never be too critical towards bricks destined for the growing edifice. Traditions which we can safely consider reliable do not appear to antedate the preaching in Galilee.

That something occurred in the course of the years before his appearance by the lake that led him to assume the rôle of prophet, confident that he had insights into the heart and purposes of God that the rest of Jewry did not have; confident that when he revealed the coming of the Kingdom—God's most precious boon for men—they, like him, would lay their tasks aside and prepare themselves for the blessed day—all this is perhaps intrinsically possible. But what led to that conviction—sudden or the result of years of reflection—we shall never know. That following this conviction, like the prophet of old, "As Jehovah liveth, what Jehovah saith unto me, that will I speak," he passed through a reaction of doubt and questioning from which he emerged to speak with a confidence which could not be daunted is also not unlikely. This we can assume from the common experience of mankind, not because of the conventional narratives of this period of initial temptation through which the heroes of both legend and history were supposed to have passed. Not only does the balanced structure of the triad of trials found in Matthew and Luke with their apposite quotation of Scripture appear the product of Christian meditation, but the simpler narrative of Mark appears designed for a distinct and practical end. The wild beasts with whom he spent forty days apparently would signify to the Jewish reader evil demons. These Jesus had conquered at the very beginning. Their power was broken; they alone, of all whom Jesus later approached, knew who he was, and feared but must obey him.

With his public appearance in the towns of Galilee on the shore of the lake our information about him begins, although it is far less definite than could be desired. In a curiously obscure phrase,[7] which has caused difficulty from the earliest days, Luke apparently says he was about thirty at the start of his ministry. Whether that rests upon a definite tradition or is a conjecture that when he started his work he was already a mature man is uncertain. Furthermore, although most scholars are agreed that his ministry was limited to Galilee until he "stedfastly set his face to go to Jerusalem," it is impossible to say how long this ministry was. The traditional view that it occupied three years rests upon the Fourth Gospel, which arbitrarily transforms this ministry into a series of visits to attend feasts. The Fourth Gospel is invaluable for an understanding of later Christian thought; it is valueless to the historian seeking information regarding the nature or the

[7] Luke 3:23.

length of the ministry. The other three gospels set no time. Their failure to mention any going to Jerusalem prior to the one ending in his crucifixion would perhaps heighten the probability that the ministry was limited to a few months, scarcely more than a single year. It is to be observed that many of the early writers, including Clement of Alexandria and Origen, reached the same conclusion, although on other grounds.[8] Jesus' words were such that opposition soon flared up against him. All the data preserved by our first three gospels could easily fall within a twelvemonth period. The elaborate synchronism of dates (Luke 3:1,2) apparently suggests 28 A.D. as the time of his public appearance; the spring of 29 A.D. is perhaps the most probable date for the crucifixion.

His message was simple. Mark summarizes it: "The time is fulfilled, and the kingdom of God is at hand: repent ye, and believe in the gospel;" that is, believe that this good news that the Father's greatest gift to men is at hand is true. It can scarcely be doubted that he sounded his message with full confidence that the nation would hearken and rejoice. It was all so clear to him; nothing else in life mattered. The Father had spoken. Of course God's children would obey as soon as they heard his voice. As the weeks went by and as he saw the initial enthusiasm giving way first to apathy, then to bitter opposition, he became quickly disillusioned; soon it was borne home to him that so strait was the gate and narrow the way that few would enter in. By the kingdom of God—Matthew alone prefers kingdom of heaven—he did not apparently mean the gradual amelioration of society, as is often imagined today. His message was pitched in terms of the first century, not the twentieth. The kingdom of God, soon to appear, was the Age to Come, the new age which would suddenly and spectacularly follow the cataclysmic end of the present age. Attempts to soften or alter his message to make it more acceptable to our way of thinking and to make it conform to the verdict of history are utterly superfluous. Much confusion has been caused by the endless debate as to whether the kingdom is present or future. The evidence of the gospels as well as the outlook of early Christianity, as revealed not alone by the opening chapters of Acts but by the letters of Paul, would appear unmistakably to indicate that in his thinking the kingdom was still in the future, but that it would appear at any moment. It was present only in the sense that the coming clouds in the heavens cast their shadow upon the earth. Israel was incessantly talking about God, deluding itself that it was obeying his commands. They must cease this playing at life; must turn back to the Father and recognize his sovereignty at once. Life must be made to conform to the pattern that soon would be introduced. Men must start now to live the kind of lives they would live in the coming kingdom—if they were fortunate enough to have

[8] They understood the phrase, "the acceptable year of the Lord" of Luke 4:19 (Isa. 61:1 f.) literally.

a share in it. "The kingdom of God is among you"[9] does not signify an "inward and invisible power in the hearts of men" wooing them to a growth in righteousness. It is a vivid announcement of the immediacy of the approach of this kingdom and its attendant judgment. It is so near at hand, that for added vividness it may be spoken of as actually here. The purposes of God are inevitable; he has spoken and will fulfil. The shadow of the approaching cloud is even now upon the land. The parable of the Seed Growing Secretly,[10] which has often been interpreted in the sense of the present kingdom, appears to yield exactly the opposite meaning. The seed has been sown; nothing that man can do to thwart it will avail; the harvest must come.

By the word "repent," Jesus meant, as did every other Jew, change of conduct as well as of heart. Everything incompatible with the kingdom—this new age soon to be set up—must be laid aside resolutely. As the merchant gladly sells all his other pearls to purchase the one of great price, or the man who has discovered a treasure hidden in a field sells all his possessions to gain that treasure; so the wise man will consider everything in life, not alone his immediate comfort, but his actual physical well-being, of secondary importance. What is an eye or a hand—parts of a perishable body—worth in comparison with acceptance or rejection by Almighty God at the Judgment soon to be set up! Words which must be watered down when the teaching of Jesus is forced into terms of modern thought are perfectly intelligible without appeal to "oriental hyperbole" when he who lived in the first century is allowed to think and speak as such. Thus there are few matters connected with the gospels clearer or more certain than that Jesus believed in the near approach[11] of this universal sovereignty of God, that is, the near approach of the apocalyptic Age to Come. This was the good news which he and his helpers were to proclaim.

As he proclaimed his message like one of the prophets of old, crowds flocked at first to hear him. Reputed miraculous cures attracted attention. His insistence on the purity of family life, his hatred of sham and pretence, his sympathy for the downtrodden and his depth of understanding, above all, his practical common sense and unflinching bravery, won him a hearing. Apparently some of the listeners stayed with him; soon there came to be a fringe of followers about him as he went from village to village proclaiming God's will and purpose as he believed God had revealed them to him. With some of these followers tradition says he became more intimate, that soon there was an inner circle of disciples with him whom we know as the Twelve. That he formally called twelve men and then conferred upon them especial powers is perhaps doubtful, but that in the course of

[9] *ἐντὸς ὑμῶν* —Luke 17:21.
[10] Mark 4:26 ff.
[11] See also pp. 165 f. below,

time some of his hearers came into more intimate fellowship is most probable. Not only were they to multiply his usefulness, they satisfied the desire for comradeship and for friends of this man who would gladly have taken the whole nation to his heart, but it would not. Then the opposition increased. As he failed to satisfy the turbulent and rebellious Home Rule Party, hundred-per-cent Jews with their strong anti-Roman attitude and their eagerness for rebellion, who must have appeared to him conspicuous examples of the folly of centring one's gaze upon any object save God's kingdom soon to appear; as he came into open clash with the Pharisees because of his complete disregard of their prized interpretations and his cavalier treatment of them personally: it is but natural that he should have been closer drawn to the group which followed him, and should have come to see in them the only hope for the nation. Truly, the way was hard; few seemed able to walk in it. But when this truth was forced upon him and the waves of temptation beat upon him, he refused to yield an inch but accepted the issue and reaffirmed his challenge. Like Seneca's seaman, he could say: "O Neptune, thou canst sink me; thou canst save me if thou wilt. Whatever comes, I will keep my rudder true."

In the gospels there is a very distinct opposition to wealth. Not only the more primitive form of the beatitudes in Luke,[12] but the story of Dives and Lazarus,[13] or the story of the Rich Young Ruler[14] are unmistakable in their teaching, and most naturally reflect the attitude of Jesus himself. It is not that Jesus approached his mission with clear-cut views in this regard, as modern socialists fondly but absurdly maintain. Rather his attitude appears to have come as the fruit of his experience. Those who were wealthy and in seats of power not unnaturally looked askance at the teaching of an impending cataclysm, even though it was to be brought about by an act of God. Those, on the other hand, who had nothing to lose and everything to gain by such an overturn naturally found the teaching more acceptable. Accordingly, it appears probable that this is the reason for Jesus' reported strictures upon wealth. This, he felt, and not unnaturally, was the stumbling-block for those who would otherwise have hearkened to the Father's voice. Riches, his experience led him to feel, were an insuperable bar to an attempt to gain the boon of life—entrance into the kingdom. Since all things were possible for God, it was possible that there might be an exception, but it would require as great a miracle to drag a rich man into the kingdom as to drag a camel through a needle's eye. Attempts have been made to tone down this clear word and to make it a special diagnosis for this particular man, but the evangelists give no support to this attempt to side-step an unpleasant teaching. Matthew recognizes the severity of the word and tones

[12] Luke 6:20-23; cf. Luke 6:20b and 21a with Matt. 5:3 and 6.

[13] Luke 16:19-31.

[14] Mark 10:17-31 and parallels (Matt. 19:16-30; Luke 18:18-30).

down the uncompromising "One thing thou lackest"[15] into "If thou wouldest be perfect."[16] This is perfectly obviously an early attempt to adapt the earlier uncompromising teaching, which was not intended as a social panacea in a society long to continue, but was a means of gaining admittance into the fast-approaching kingdom, into a workable dictum of morality in the early church which was now numbering wealthy men among its members. Precisely the same sort of attempt by Matthew to make uncompromising teachings more workable is seen in his treatment of Jesus' words regarding divorce. In direct clash with the tradition preserved by Paul, Mark, and Luke[17] that there is no ground for divorce, Matthew twice inserts the qualifying clause, "saving for the cause of fornication."[18] Yet he is not to be regarded as an ascetic, as John the Baptist is pictured. On the contrary, his opponents called him "a gluttonous man and a hard drinker."[19] Far from holding himself aloof he appears to have mingled with men and women and to have shown such sympathy with their problems and sorrows—especially in the case of the downtrodden—that he received the nickname "friend of publicans and sinners."

Did Jesus feel that he was the Messiah, the son of David destined for Israel's throne? In recent years this question has been hotly debated. The answer to it is by no means as simple as has often been supposed. The conventional answer has been, Yes; but it rested in no small measure upon the mistaken notion that all popular Jewish thinking in the first century centred about the person of the Messiah. Accordingly, it was argued: Any one to gain a popular hearing must pitch his message in these terms. Thus, although Jesus was by no means satisfied with the conventional thinking on the subject, he must for want of a better designation make such claims for himself. But if, as has been argued in a preceding chapter, the figure of the Davidic King Messiah did not bulk so large in popular thinking, there seems little reason to assume that Jesus felt compelled to accept the rôle unless it was perfectly congenial. As soon as this cardinal point is observed, it becomes highly significant that Jesus appears to have laid his emphasis upon the coming kingdom, not upon the one who was to be king in it. It is the Fourth Gospel which represents Jesus as habitually discoursing at length about himself, the king. That the representation in the Synoptic gospels is more primitive and more probably historic is almost universally conceded. That Matthew and Luke felt that Jesus was the Davidic Messiah is clear. However such a passage as Matt. 11:25-30 was originally intended, it now stands as embodying distinct and unique claims in the mouth of Jesus. Luke is very particular

[15] Mark 10:21.
[16] Matt. 19:21.
[17] I Cor. 7:10-11; Mark 10:11-12; Luke 16:18.
[18] Matt. 5:31 f.; 19:9.
[19] Matt. 11:19; Luke 7:34.

to make clear that Jesus' death was due to this claim alone. On the contrary, Mark 12:35-37 (|| Matt. 22:41-46; Luke 20:41-44) can only be understood as denying that Jesus, although anointed, was the scion of David. Such a denial must have been primitive; it clashes too directly with early Christian thinking. The most natural interpretation of it is that it reflects Jesus' own attitude. Although he conceived himself anointed by God for his service, he rejected the notion that this meant that he was the anointed Davidic king.

Nor is it by any means certain that he claimed to be the supernatural figure, destined to be the Final Judge of men, namely the son of man, although his followers soon after his death were confident that he was that figure and had claimed to be. Indeed, the evangelists are so confident that he had made this claim for himself that they use the phrase as a substitute for "I." A striking example of this editorial revision is afforded by Matthew's alteration of Mark 8:27. In Mark the query reads, "Who do men say that I am?" Matthew (16:13) has "Who do men say that the son of man is?" Again, such passages as Mark 2:10 f.; 27 f. can scarcely be understood save as mistranslations into Greek, where the original Aramaic *bar nasha*, that is, human being,[20] has been mistakenly rendered "son of man," thus giving a specific application to Jesus not originally intended. The second of these passages is particularly clear. Jesus says, "The Sabbath was made for man, and not man for the Sabbath: therefore *man* is lord even of the Sabbath." This is balanced and intelligible; substitution of *son of man*, making a specific reference to Jesus, makes the "therefore" unintelligible. A third type of passage is illustrated by Mark 8:38—

> For whosoever shall be ashamed of *me* and of *my* words in this adulterous and sinful generation, the *Son of man* also shall be ashamed of him, when *he* cometh in the glory of *his* Father with the holy angels.

There would seem to be no compelling reason to identify here the "me" and "my" with the "son of man," "he," and "his." Indeed, it is not failure to believe in or to adopt a correct attitude toward him (Jesus) that Jesus is here condemning, but the rejection of the message which he is sounding. This rejection can only result in condemnation when the son of man appears in the very near future to sit upon his judgment throne.

That the phrase "son of man" was constantly upon Jesus' lips is highly probable. That he meant himself by the phrase is far less certain. That his disciples eventually came to the conclusion that by the enigmatic phrase he had meant himself is certain; that they made this identification after his death rather than during his ministry would appear not unlikely. Thus primitive tradition which revealed too clearly for the growing theological estimates of Jesus' person that he, as God's prophet, had heralded the coming of the

[20] See above pp. 141 f.

supernatural son of man, his successor, soon to appear to set up the Final Judgment and inaugurate the Age to Come, gradually came to be put into the mouth of John the Baptist. The whole imagery of final judgments, of supernatural figures coming on the clouds of heaven, was as natural to the first century as it is unnatural to ours. A man in those days could hold such views without raising the suspicion of mental disturbance. None the less, it is one thing for a first-century Jew to have expected such a figure soon to appear; a totally different thing for him to believe that he himself would be miraculously transformed from a flesh-and-blood man into this figure. With all allowances made, it is hard to conceive how such a view could have been held save at the expense of mental sanity. There seems no reason from the accounts to postulate this last conclusion. But views, which if held by himself before his death can scarcely be understood of a sane and balanced man, are easily understood for the disciples after his death. Then the obstacle was removed. He was now, they were confident, in heaven. There was now no reason why he might not come from heaven on the clouds.

But although it is thus by no means certain that the "Messianic authority," popularly supposed to have been claimed by Jesus, rests on any firm historical basis, the fact that he spoke with authority is constantly stressed in the gospels: ". . . the multitudes were astonished at his teaching, for he taught them as one having authority, and not as their scribes."[21] Although he had the most profound respect for the law, as did every true Jew, and never opposed it or hinted that it would ever pass away, he seems always to have sought to get at the spirit of it, to stress what true obedience to it entailed. He apparently was not concerned with making it either easier or harder. Reference has already been made to his words regarding divorce and the Sabbath. In the former, the law, he maintained, was far more stringent and uncompromising than the contemporary practice: "Moses for your hardness of heart suffered you to put away your wives; but from the beginning it hath not been so." On the contrary, a common-sense interpretation of the purpose of the Sabbath led him to a far more lenient position. In a word, his was essentially a layman's approach, which led him to a disparagement of the traditions of the elders which, he complained, had made void the word of God. This sort of teaching may well have been as popular with the unlearned as it was distasteful to the Scribes and their supporters who looked with contempt at this preacher, destitute in their eyes of any real knowledge of God's law and will, who yet assailed them for precisely those qualities and interests which they believed God had commended to them.

There was a freshness and force to his teaching. The short cut appeal to reason, not precedent, could not fail to attract attention. When charged with doing his healings by the power of evil,[22] he retorted: If the healing of

[21] Matt. 7:28,29 and frequently.
[22] Mark 3:22 ff. and parallels.

men's bodies is a worthy deed, how can the devil sponsor it? He would then be fighting himself. When asked as to the practice of paying taxes to Rome,[23] his answer was equally direct. There was no appeal to precedent. You are enjoying Roman protection, using Roman money; you are under obligation to be loyal to the government whose blessings you enjoy. To the charge that he spent too much time with publicans and sinners, his answer was apposite: "They that are well have no need of a physician, but they that are sick."

The novelty of such a method is revealed by an anecdote told of Hillel. In a remote village the elders were perplexed as to the proper procedure when the fourteenth of Nisan fell on a Sabbath. Was the obligation to slaughter and prepare the victims for the Passover superior to that which forbade labour on the Sabbath? Hillel, who had been a pupil of Shemaiah and Abtalion, was recommended to them as one able to give them the tradition on this point. By three lines of argument he sought to prove that the Passover requirement was the greater. In contempt for his opinion they exclaimed: "How could we expect anything of a Babylonian?" But when after fruitlessly arguing all day he fell back on tradition, "Thus I heard it from Shemaiah and Abtalion," their opposition ceased and they elected him their president.[24]

Such independence of tradition on the part of Jesus must have seemed the height of impudence to the outraged Scribes; to others, favourably inclined toward him, it may well have increased their interest. Surely one who would dare to speak so confidently and without respect for the opinions of the great must be very sure of himself; otherwise how would he venture on so reckless a course!

What then was the authority which he claimed for himself? The most obvious answer is not improbably the correct one, namely, the one preserved in the gospels themselves, that he was a prophet of God. This was apparently the impression he made upon his hearers. It is highly probable that this impression was due to his own belief. If this is the case, he must have believed himself to be inspired by the Holy Spirit, for in the thinking of Judaism the Holy Spirit is specifically the spirit of prophecy. "All the prophets spoke by the holy spirit. The holy spirit is so specifically prophetic inspiration that when Haggai, Zechariah, and Malachi, the last prophets, died, the holy spirit departed from Israel."[25]

Once more God was speaking to his people in the old and accredited way. The prophet like unto Moses long expected had now appeared. As the mouthpiece of God he uttered his clarion call, confident that it was not he but

[23] Mark 12:13-17 and parallels.

[24] Jer. Pesaḥim 33a; Pesaḥim 66a. For this old Baraita I am indebted to G. F. Moore, *Harvard Theological Review*, Vol. XVII, No. 4 (Oct., 1924) p. 366.

[25] G. F. Moore, *Judaism*, Vol. I, p. 237.

God who was calling men to repent and to watch for the appearance of the Final Judge who would baptize the nation with a baptism of fire. This passionate confidence may well have caused him to appear "beside himself."[26] To his opponents it was the frenzy of a man possessed by an evil spirit; to his followers the mark of that divine madness that proclaimed the power of God. To folk accustomed to explain everything out of the ordinary as the result of the presence of a *daimon*, good or bad, Jesus with his scathing denunciations and his impossible demands, his power to quiet the insane, his genial attitude toward children and those in distress, his absolute self-confidence, may well have seemed a most unusual and amazing character, one from the past sent by God to herald a new age.

And this catastrophic end was near at hand. It might come at any moment; when, he did not know. It could not, however, be long delayed. It would come before the present generation had died.[27] It is useless to try to smooth this difficulty away. To attempt to explain this as a misunderstanding of his meaning by his hearers or as a view later developed and attributed to him is most unfortunate. On the one hand, this would demand such an amazing lack of intelligence on the part of his hearers or inability on his own part to express himself clearly on a point of vital importance that we would be justified in doubting whether any reputed recollection from such sources could approach historical probability; on the other, each succeeding year made the difficulty of the expectation more acute, for the generation was dying. Why should his earliest followers have come to such an expectation and have believed he had taught them so, had their leader not so taught?

More impressive, however, than an appeal to any specific passage, which after all may be open to legitimate critical doubt, is the consistent tone and undercurrent of his reported teaching. Were men to follow implicitly the instruction not alone to the rich ruler but as recorded in the Sermon on the Mount—"And if any man would go to law with thee, and take away thy coat, let him have thy cloak also. . . . Give to him that asketh thee, and from him that would borrow of thee turn not thou away. . . . Resist not him that is evil: but whosoever smiteth thee on thy right cheek, turn to him the other also"—it would mean the collapse of society. It is possible to water these words—and there are many more like them—down into more or less innocuous admonition to be generous and even-tempered, but the result of this popular means of justifying present-day ideals by the appeal to the fancied support of Jesus are, to say the least, not impressive nor particularly convincing. The demands *are* impossible if life is to continue as it is. But in the thinking of Jesus this is precisely the point. Life was not to continue. The end was at hand. This might well be an ideal preparation for the Age to Come. Thus it would seem wiser not to call these teachings an "interim

[26] Mark 3:21.

[27] Mark 9:1 and parallels (Matt. 16:28; Luke 9:27).

ethic." Rather they are a "kingdom ethic." This is to be the kind of life lived in the new age soon to appear. To achieve entrance men must begin to live as though the change had actually taken place. In the short time of waiting matters which have seemed of so great concern pale into insignificance. Why concern oneself about wealth, clothing, position, bodily comfort, dignity, national pride which is affronted by subjection to a foreign power? The time is too short for indulging in such idle trivialities. Certainly his earliest followers in Jerusalem, who pooled their property in confidence that before it was expended the kingdom would dawn, appear to have understood him in this sense.

All this should make clear that the view, which still persists in some circles that Jesus' aim was to found a Church, distinct from the Synagogue, is quite improbable. The gospels themselves bear little trace of such a view. The word church (ἐκκλησία) occurs but twice in the whole gospel tradition, and both times in passages which are generally regarded as comparatively late and most improbable as genuine words of Jesus.[28] His message was not for a group of men who were to carry on in an unending world; on the contrary, his followers were to go out and to proclaim the same message that he, as God's prophet, was heralding. Prepare yourselves for the coming day. Live in such a manner toward God that regardless of the time of the coming of the kingdom you will not be caught off your guard. It will come as a thief in the night. Thus attempts to picture Jesus as breaking away from Judaism, of conceiving a new religion in which the Jew and gentile stood alike, equal in the sight of God, would appear to be in flagrant contradiction to probability. To be sure, there are frequent traces in the gospel of this new view, the most conspicuous of which is the so-called Great Commission;[29] but without exception they appear to reflect the later views, and to come from a time when his followers had been forced from the Jewish nest and had gone out into the highways and byways of the gentile world. Once this vision of the wider field had been glimpsed, the early Christians, confident that their movement was being blessed by God, were of course convinced that their Master, fully aware of the purposes of God, had intended it and had blessed it. Accordingly, such rites as baptism and the Lord's supper appear to have arisen when it became evident that the end was not so near as they had expected but that an interim of waiting was to be experienced.

After a time of itinerant preaching in Galilee, he turns south to the nation's capital. In Luke's fine phrase, "he stedfastly set his face to go to Jerusalem." Why did he go? The answer is by no means easy. It may well be that the

[28] Matt. 16:18; 18:17.

[29] Matt. 28:19,20.

increasing opposition had convinced him that his earlier dreams for the nation were not to be realized, that, like the prophets before him, he must fall before the blind prejudice of those to whom he had been sent. But if he were to die, he must first stand in Jerusalem and herald God's word in Zion. A prophet might not die save in Jerusalem. So he turned to the south. But this is easily over-emphasized. From the time of his transfiguration near Cæsarea Philippi the gospels represent him as speaking openly of his death, but invariably appending the mention of his resurrection three days later. This view obviously reflects the thinking of Christians at the time the gospels were written. That it accurately portrays the actual fact is far less certain. The stubborn fact of the dismay of his disciples, their flight back to Galilee, their feeling that the last word had been spoken and that that word was failure make very difficult the view that he had foreseen and openly predicted an event which was to vindicate in so startling a manner his mission, and which could scarcely fail to arouse joyful anticipation, not abject terror. As suggested on a previous page, such a view can scarcely fail to reduce the intelligence of his closest followers to the vanishing-point or to necessitate seeing him speaking in riddles, intelligible only to a later age. It is far wiser not to endeavour to give a fictitious clarity to those days known to us at best at a far remove, but to allow them to remain hidden. Whatever the motives which led him to leave the Galilean hills for the nation's capital, he apparently turned to the south with the confidence that, though he could not see the end from the beginning, God was directing his steps; God's will could not be thwarted; so long as it was day, he would do the will of him who had sent him.

He enters the city of Jerusalem. The gospels represent the pilgrim throngs hailing him joyfully. But any such enthusiasm was at best short-lived. His preaching soon disillusioned them. The opposition in the nation's capital was far more intense than in Galilee. Those in control saw in him a most dangerous figure, the potential source of all sorts of difficulties, a disturber of the *status quo*, a troubler of Israel. With his eye fixed on the coming kingdom, impatient toward any such makeshift remedies as the Home Rule Party were crying for, he dashed any hopes they might have had for him to the ground. His outspoken attitude, which made possible the story told of the cleansing of the temple, sealed his doom. His life was forfeit. A short time—how long we do not know, for there seem to be hints in the gospels of a longer stay in Jerusalem than the traditional week—and he died on a Roman cross. His friends who had accompanied him scattered in dismay and fled back to their old homes. They had hoped in vain that it was he who should restore Israel. But the comradeship of the months with him could not be so quickly broken. He had built himself too vitally into their lives for that. Their first grief gave way; they experienced him again, became convinced that he had not been defeated, and returned to Jerusalem in joy and confidence. The true triumphal entry into Jerusalem was not on the ninth of Nisan but sometime later when these men, in whose hearts had dawned a new confidence, without display reëntered the city that a little earlier had seen the downfall of the prophet of Galilee.

Chapter XII

THE DAWNING CHURCH

THE first period of Christianity[1] was over; the second now under way, and for a time Jerusalem holds our attention. The story is a veritable snarled skein, at best but very imperfectly known to us. The temptation is to look first at one locality, then another, in systematic order, as evidencing the progressive stages reached by this new movement: first, Galilee—there it was that Jesus had proclaimed his message; then, Jerusalem—here the earliest work by his first followers had been accomplished; then, Antioch and the other places mentioned in the account in Acts—in short, to feel that these were, so to speak, successive acts in a drama; that when the curtain rings up each time the preceding scene is completely swept away.

This is all quite mistaken. The account in Acts begins with the Twelve in Jerusalem, and it is with their activities that the first half of the writing is concerned. From then on the account is limited rigidly to the activity of Paul. Other groups and their activities are mentioned only as their paths cross those of the author's chosen heroes. That the author was justified in selecting those incidents that appeared to him of chief importance in the unfolding story of the new movement, which in scarcely more than a single generation had spread from the remote shores of the Galilean lake to the capital of the Roman empire, and in limiting himself rigidly to them, is not to be denied. None the less, the student must not forget that there were other Agamemnons who never found a Homer. For example, there must have been many in Galilee who had felt the force and power of the strange prophet from Nazareth. That all who were affected by his ministry had accompanied him on his fateful journey to Jerusalem or had shared the newborn confidence of a Peter a little later that they were to leave their homes and remove to the nation's capital is most unlikely. None the less, that they had acted, quite unofficially, as informal witnesses to the power of the one who had strangely moved them, and that as they came in contact with other people they had told the story of the prophet who had made his appearance only to fall before the leaders' ire can scarcely be denied. Some such explanation is required to account for the appearance of little groups that we suddenly find existing in districts far from Jerusalem. It would be rash to point

[1] Of course, the term Christianity is not strictly appropriate at this period nor for many years. Usage and the avoidance of roundabout phrases as "the movement later to be known as Christianity" perhaps justify its use here.

to any particular group, for example, those in Damascus against whom, it is claimed, Paul had early proceeded[2] or those in Ephesus whom Paul there discovered, whose knowledge was restricted to the "baptism of John,"[3] as evidence of the activity of those in Galilee. None the less, this group should not be utterly overlooked, even though they may have left few marks in the early tradition.

That at the time of Jesus' arrest his followers fled back to Galilee in dismay would appear reasonably certain in spite of the silence of Luke-Acts which passes over this incident or, perhaps better said, rewrites the account in such a way as to preclude it. Mark, to be sure, has no mention of this experience in Galilee, but clearly indicates familiarity with the tradition of resurrection appearances there: "But go, tell his disciples and Peter, He goeth before you into Galilee: there shall ye see him, as he said unto you."[4] The traditional final parting of the risen Jesus from his disciples[5] and the moving story of the restoration of Peter[6] evidence the fact that the Lucan view was not universally held, but was apparently later and more conventional. Similarly Justin Martyr bears witness to the tradition of the flight of the disciples "who repented of their flight from him when he was crucified, after he rose from the dead."[7]

That behind these few obscure references lies a most significant incident for the history of early Christianity can scarcely be doubted. Would they go back to their earlier tasks with the feeling that the dreams had all been shattered by the hard facts of reality: "We hoped that it was he who should redeem Israel,"[8] or would their confidence in him be strong enough to face the problem of his apparent defeat and to transform it into a new ground for confidence in his eventual victory? Many attempts have been made to explain how the latter conviction was achieved. One thing would appear probable. Before the band of erstwhile followers returned to the nation's capital they had achieved a confidence that their leader had not been defeated by death which did not need to be bolstered up by the discovery of an empty tomb. Underlying the later conventional explanation of a series of supernatural appearances of the risen Lord which nerved them to their new task is the persistent reference to an appearance to Simon or Cephas or Peter.[9] That the most primitive element in the resurrection stories is the enigmatic "The Lord is risen indeed, and hath appeared unto Simon" has commended

[2] Acts 9:1 ff.

[3] Acts 19:1-7.

[4] Mark 16:7; cf. Mark 14:28. Luke alters Mark 16:7 to adapt it to his view (Luke 24:6) and omits Mark 14:28.

[5] Matt. 28:16-20.

[6] John 21:1-23.

[7] Justin Martyr, *Dial.* 106; cf. *Apol.* i,50,12.

[8] Luke 24:21.

[9] Luke 24:34; I Cor. 15:5. Apparently all three are names of the same individual, although this has occasionally been doubted.

itself to many scholars as highly probable. In line with this the words "Simon, Simon, behold, Satan asked to have *you*, that he might sift you as wheat: but I made supplication for *thee*, that thy faith fail not: *and do thou, when once thou hast turned again, strengthen thy brethren*"[10] are highly significant. It is well worth considering whether the revived hopes of the early group are not to be accounted for by the initiative of this one disciple who in Acts appears at first as the leading figure in the Jerusalem circle, and about whom many traditions soon gathered, both as to his prominence during the days of Jesus' ministry and also of his denial and restoration. Coincident with this new confidence, however it had been first achieved, would appear, as has already been argued, the belief that the "son of man" of whom Jesus had so often spoken was none other than Jesus himself, now in heaven whither he had been translated by God, and that he would soon come to establish the kingdom and to take his seat upon the judgment throne.[11]

In this confidence they returned to Jerusalem. How long the stay in Galilee had been is not known, nor is it by any means clear what led them to feel that their work was henceforth to be in Jerusalem. In Jerusalem they appear to have settled down as a separate synagogue with no thought of cutting themselves off from Judaism or of going to the gentile world as crusaders for a world mission. According to the fragmentary evidence given in Acts they visited the temple as did their fellow Jews. That the opposition to them which eventually came was due to any laxity regarding the Sabbath or to any attempt of theirs to disregard the prized interpretation of the Pharisees and Scribes is not hinted. Apparently they soon came to be looked upon as disturbers of the peace because of their preaching of the speedy end of the age and of the excitement which accompanied some of the early meetings. The speeches in the early chapters of Acts, which, while they may not be verbatim reports of the speakers, yet probably give a fair picture of the tone of the early Christian preaching, suggest that these men were decidedly free-spoken with regard to the guilt of their opponents in executing their leader.

But though attempts to see these earliest followers as considering themselves members of a new religion are most improbable, there were differences between them and their fellow Jews. They had become convinced that not only was the end of the world at hand but that the agent of this impending change was their former leader, Jesus of Nazareth, whose return from heaven they were now awaiting. For many years this confidence seems to have remained alive and to have been the distinctive note of their preaching. But the months and years went by and the expected event failed to materialize. While the confidence remained sure that the time must come, it was

[10] Luke 22:31,32.

[11] See further "The Date of Peter's Confession" in *Quantulacumque—Studies Presented to Kirsopp Lake by Pupils, Colleagues, and Friends* (London: Christophers, 1937), pp. 117-122.

necessary to push the time farther and farther into the future. Not alone the pathetic word at the close of Revelation, "Come, Lord Jesus,"[12] but the note that the "bridegroom tarried,"[13] not to mention the petition, "Thy kingdom come,"[14] still evidence the wistful longing. Gradually this expectation, which had been the mainspring of the early disciples, drops from the forefront of the Christian preaching, although a sporadic trace of it now and then appears, as, for example, in the very late writing, II Peter. If, as seems probable, one of the purposes of the Fourth Gospel was to salvage this hope, so sadly tried, and to avoid the danger which menaced, namely, that the promise had been a delusion, by maintaining that the expected coming had already taken place,[15] this would be but one more witness to the central place this expectation had and to the impossibility of trying to understand the early history without understanding it.

But even more distinctive of the early group than this expectation of the coming of the son of man—for, after all, other Jews probably shared this belief—was the fact that they had identified their leader with this supernatural figure. This identification was the centre of the preaching. And its consequences were far reaching. From this simple beginning was to arise the whole complicated and imposing Christology of later Christianity. This can here be only sketched, for the story would carry us far beyond the early Jerusalem days. An interest in the person of Jesus, a desire to explain who he was and to interpret everything in terms of him, came gradually to obscure the fact that he had never made such claims for himself, but had been content to proclaim God's purpose for the nation and to call it to repentance. Thus Jesus became more and more one whose person was to be understood and explained rather than one whose teaching was to be believed and obeyed. And the fact that Jesus had never apparently considered himself a teacher but a prophet may very well have aided this development of thought.

But be that as it may, there can be no question that as the years went by title after title was added. Although the gospels reveal the result of this process, they provide but few clues as to the steps in the process. Although Jesus may well have considered himself anointed of God to proclaim his will, it is far from likely that he thereby conceived himself as the scion of David who was expected by at least some of Jewry to reëstablish national independence. As a matter of fact, the adjective translated by the Greek *χριστός*, although regularly used in the later Jewish writings to designate this expected king, does not appear to have been so limited in the earlier period.[16] Eventually this identification was made as is evidenced by the refusal of the Christians to rally to the banner of Bar Cochba whose Messianic

[12] Rev. 22:20.
[13] Matt. 25:5.
[14] Matt. 6:10.
[15] See below, pp. 242 ff.
[16] See above, pp. 138 f.

claim was sponsored by no less a figure than Akiba. The Christians could not support him, however much they might have so desired, for to do so would have been to deny their Christ. Whether the identification of Jesus with this expected figure was due to a revived hope in Judaism for an expected deliverer as the heel of Rome grew heavier, or whether it was, so to speak, spontaneous, is difficult to say. That the identification took place on Jewish soil is probable, for coincident with the gentile mission the title *χριστός*, "anointed"—intelligible only to the Jew, for he alone used oil for honorific purposes—became simply part of the proper name Christ Jesus or Jesus Christ and a new descriptive title or designation was necessary.[17]

By the author of Luke-Acts, but not by either Mark or Matthew, Jesus was identified furthermore as the "suffering servant" of Isaiah. That this identification was made before his death is utterly improbable. It comes from a time when men were searching the Old Testament for predictions and prophecies of the coming movement, confident that everything that had happened had been prophesied, and conversely that everything that had been prophesied had happened. The fact that Matthew, who was particularly expert in this procedure, failed to adduce Isaiah 53 as a prediction of Jesus' Passion can scarcely be explained save on the ground that this interpretation was unknown to him.[18] Accordingly, it is probable that the view was of comparatively late origin and by no means universally adopted when he wrote. Nor is this surprising. Isa. 53 is not to be considered "Messianic" in the sense that it was understood as a prediction for the future, most certainly not of the Messiah or son of man. Rather it was a statement of Israel's suffering in the past; at least it was so understood by first-century Judaism. Probably, although this is not absolutely certain, no historical figure, aside from the nation itself, was intended by the author or understood by his later readers. Israel was not only the prophet of true religion, but the martyr as well. Eventually, however, Christians were struck by certain superficial resemblances to the traditional story of Jesus' death in this noble description, and, by ignoring other phases of the description which were not so congenial, found in the suffering servant a picture of their crucified Lord. That this was done by Luke is certain. Just before the betrayal Jesus had expressly quoted from the passage and applied it to himself:

> For I say unto you, that this which is written must be fulfilled in me, And he was reckoned with transgressors: for that which concerneth me hath fulfilment.[19]

Even clearer is the identification in the story of Philip and the Ethiopian

[17] See below, pp. 192 f.

[18] In Matt. 12:17 Jesus is identified, to be sure, with the servant (Isa. 42:1 ff.) but with no intimation of suffering. "Atomistic" interpretation of Scripture by Jew and early Christian alike was such that a particular word or verse might be quoted without any regard for its original meaning, context, or related passages.

[19] Luke 22:37.

eunuch.[20] The latter is represented as reading from the book of Isaiah with his book open at the words:

> He was led as a sheep to the slaughter;
> And as a lamb before his shearers is dumb,
> So he openeth not his mouth:
> In his humiliation his judgment was taken away:
> His generation, who shall declare?
> For his life is taken from the earth.

And in answer to the query, "Of whom speaketh the prophet this? of himself, or of some other?" Philip, "beginning from this scripture, preached unto him Jesus."

So this interest in Christological speculation went on apace. We shall have occasion later to see other identifications, some apparently later, others perhaps earlier. Thus in Mark we seem to have the view expressed that Jesus had become the son of God at the time of his baptism, a view later to be espoused by the so-called Adoptionists. For others he was born the son of God, his very birth being a miracle, since God, not any man, was his father. For Paul he was preëxistent, the last man, in contrast to Adam, the first man. He was human born, to be sure, but one who originally had existed in the form of God, but had not grasped at equality with God, but had humbled himself and had gone willingly to his death.[21] In the prologue to the Fourth Gospel—here the influence of the Stoic concept of the Logos, as interpreted by Philo is conspicuous—he is the Logos, the embodiment of the divine creative wisdom, the one through whom all things were made.[22] Of this only-begotten Son it is thus quite proper for Thomas to say, "My Lord and my God."[23]

Although this apotheosis of their leader, son of man though they now believed him to be, was far from the thoughts of the early disciples as they began their lives in Jerusalem, it was the direct consequence of this first characteristic which distinguished them from their fellow Jews—their conviction regarding the prophet who had not been holden by death, but who was momentarily to come to baptize the world with his baptism of fire, and to take his place on the judgment throne.

Then again they believed they were from time to time especially endowed with the Holy Spirit and thus enabled to do wonderful deeds. Jesus had publicly claimed this endowment for himself. His followers had believed his claim: this was what had turned him into God's prophet. Now this endowment was theirs. As Elijah's spirit had passed to Elisha, so the Master's spirit had come upon them. It was their Magna Carta.

[20] Acts 8:26-39.
[21] Phil. 2:6-11.
[22] John 1:1-18.
[23] John 20:28.

There are at least two different stories in the New Testament by which later Christians sought to explain this confidence that from the very first the early church had been so endowed. In Luke 24:49 and Acts 1:4 f., 8 ff., Jesus bids his disciples to wait in Jerusalem until they have received the Spirit. Just as John had baptized with water, they would be baptized with the Holy Spirit. Then follows the Pentecost experience in which in vivid fashion the descent of the Spirit upon the waiting disciples is painted. In John 20:22, on the contrary, a different version is given. On the resurrection evening Jesus fulfils his earlier promise[24] that they would not be left alone. He breathes upon them, and says, "Receive ye the Holy Spirit." The belief that the Spirit had come to them directly from Jesus and that it was to be their authority, as it had been his, would appear central in the early confidence of the church, although opinions differed, at least in a later time, as to the precise manner in which it had made its appearance.[25]

The history of the belief in spirit-possession is a story in itself. The underlying concept was that a spirit, possessing individual existence—thus by no means an attitude of mind—entered a man and dominated him for good or for ill. Thus what the "inspired" or "possessed" man did or said was actually the work of the spirit sojourning in him. Originally God had been regarded as the source of all acts out of the ordinary, good and bad alike. Later the evil manifestations had been attributed to the work of evil spirits, in whom the exuberant angelology and demonology of first-century Judaism saw the ghosts of the wicked people who had perished in the flood. The story of the Gerasene demoniac,[26] in which Jesus converses not with the possessed man, but rather with the many demons in him, provides a vivid picture of the attitude of first-century Judaism. Just as it was a terrible affliction to be possessed by an evil or malevolent spirit, it was a great blessing to be inspired by a good spirit, preëminently by the Spirit of God.

One of the most striking examples of possession is to be found in the so-called glossolalia or ecstatic speaking with tongues. Paul provides a clear picture of this phenomenon in the early group at Corinth.[27] It was an ecstatic utterance or gibberish due to the religious frenzy of the one possessed. Words became unintelligible. Many of the Corinthians were boasting of this ability which they concluded was the sign that God had communicated to them his Spirit. Those of their number not so gifted they were inclined to despise. Paul's attitude toward this phenomenon gives a clear insight into its nature. Although he did not question its validity—he was able to surpass them all

[24] John 14:16; 16:7,13.

[25] That this view actually was that of the early Christians and not a later view, that in the early days the heroes had been so endowed, would appear established by the Pauline epistles. He evidences this confidence for himself and his fellow Christians.

[26] Mark 5:1-20 and parallels.

[27] I Cor. 14.

in this ability![28]—it was of but little value to the other Christians unless interpreted. It tended to breed disorder and confusion and could easily bring the early group into disrepute and contempt. Nor was this merely a local phenomenon in early Christianity. The roving bands of religious enthusiasts who worked themselves into a frenzy by music and bodily contortions,[29] the whirling dervishes, the extreme emotionalists of the present day, as the Holy Rollers or the folk in the more backward communities "getting religion" under the spell of a revivalist—all these provide the background of the story of Pentecost, ancient explanation as it is of the first coming of the Spirit to the early followers of Jesus.

For the author of Acts, Pentecost was of the greatest significance for the early group. It was the moment when the promised spirit had descended in power and had made the first great advance possible. From that moment on the movement was to spread in ever-widening circles. Although the account is highly embellished and rewritten—probably deliberately—to make clear its significance, there does not seem any just reason for considering it pure fiction. On the contrary, it is highly probable that an initial period of high emotional excitement had characterized the group and had convinced them that the outpouring of the Spirit by the prophets long foretold had actually come. The primitive character of the day has been obscured in the Acts account. Speaking with tongues has arbitrarily been interpreted in the sense of miraculous proficiency in foreign languages. None the less, traces of the more primitive tradition are preserved. Some of the skeptical bystanders gibe, "They are filled with new wine,"[30] to which Peter is made to retort: "Since it is only the third hour (9 A.M.), it is far too early for them to be drunk." Why proficiency in foreign languages should have aroused such a charge is not clear; in the case of the inarticulate glossolalia, however, it would have been most apt. Editors may rewrite narratives; fortunately for the later historian they usually leave some clues behind them.

Nor was this rewriting due to misunderstanding his source through failure to interpret what speaking with other tongues meant. Not improbably the old legend of the Tower of Babel (Gen. 11) is in his mind, and its explanation of the multiplicity of languages that had arisen as the consequence of sin. This sign of God's displeasure was not destined to last forever. The view, if not universal, was certainly known at this time that in the future this confusion of tongues would cease. Thus it is expressly said: "And ye shall be for a people of the Lord *and one tongue* and there shall not be a spirit of deceit of Belial."[31] It is probable that this view is in the mind of the author: Pentecost gives a quick glimpse of this future blessed state.

[28] I Cor. 14:18.
[29] Cf. I Sam. 10:5-13.
[30] Acts 2:13.
[31] *Test, XII Patr., Jud.* 25:3.

Hence the host of men from "every nation under heaven"—the reading "Jews" in 2:5 is improbable both on the grounds of text and for internal reasons (cf. its clash with v. 10b)—is most appropriate. At this moment when the veil is for the instant torn aside and the future success of the movement is revealed, gentiles are (proleptically) introduced, although the gentile mission as such does not start, in his judgment, until the time of Stephen's death.

With all due allowance for later embellishments and revision of the story, it would still appear probable that not only did the early Christians believe themselves possessed of the Spirit, but in the early days of the movement they began to attract attention and win followers. That three thousand converts flocked to their banners is improbable. That the police authorities would have permitted such an activity on the part of men whose leader had been recently executed is unlikely. Even in modern times exaggerations in the report of the numbers of converts occur. The question as to whether baptism made its appearance as early as the Acts' account maintains is best reserved for a later page.

A third distinguishing characteristic of the group may be mentioned. It would appear from the early narrative of Acts that for a time the early Christians adopted a kind of communism. This has been heatedly denied, but apparently with little reason, for even the most conservative political economists can scarcely fail to be satisfied with its disastrous failure. Two parallel accounts of the experiment are given.[32] In keeping with their view of a speedy termination of the age and in strict compliance with the teaching of Jesus they pooled all their resources and lived on the resulting capital. However admirable such a policy might have been as a brief interim practice, it could have but one result if life were to continue. They spent their capital and got into difficulties. Their number was growing; needs always grow with income. Soon the time came when there was not enough to go around. The last chapter in this little story would appear to be the feeling of responsibility which some of the neighbouring churches felt for sending aid to the now pauperized, or at least embarrassed, Jerusalem group. Other consideration may have influenced Paul at a later time in his well-known desire to bring a peace offering from his gentile churches. It is tempting to wonder if this early page of apparently authentic church history may not have led him to feel that the gift would be most appropriate.

Although the authorities are pictured as being suspicious of these Galileans and to have attempted from time to time to restrain them—or at least their leaders—the community as a whole regarded them with no unfriendly air. They were pious Jews and showed no trace of breaking away from the Judaism that had mothered them. Eventually, however, came a change. Jeru-

[32] Acts 2:44-47; 4:32-5:11.

salem no longer remained the scene of their preaching, but they begin to push outside the city into adjacent territory, and soon, as the book of Acts continues its story, a distinctly gentile mission makes its appearance. Too often it has been overlooked that the account in Acts is but an epitome of the story; the incidents preserved serve as stepping-stones between the earliest days and the time in which the author himself was living. Whatever sources the author had at his disposal, it can scarcely be doubted that he used them, excerpted them, arranged them, and probably often rewrote them to portray vividly the truly momentous changes that had taken place. It is perhaps fair to say of the incidents selected—and this is particularly true of the early chapters—that they are evaluations of the changes that were taking place rather than actual photographs of specific historical events. It may be, as in the case of Pentecost, that an actual event served as the basis of the story; it should not be neglected that the narrative as we have it is vastly more an interpretation of the significance of that event than a mere chronicle of it.

Precisely the same is to be said of the story of the death of Stephen. This for the author is a highly significant moment. As a result of Stephen's death the whole policy of Christianity was shifted. "They therefore that were scattered abroad went about preaching the word."[33] This was the start of the gentile mission. Many attempts have been made to explain the precise cause of the outbreak of wrath against Stephen. The conventional explanation is that Judaism, while tolerant of these men so long as they remained orthodox in their attitude toward the law and contented themselves with peculiar views about their dead leader, felt outraged when Hellenists came to be of their number. Recently it has been convincingly argued that the word "Hellenists" did not signify "Grecian Jews," but simply gentiles.[34] The difficulty with this explanation is not the incidental, almost casual way, these Hellenists are introduced into the story,[35] but that according to the story the opposition broke out in the synagogue (or synagogues) of the Libertines, Cyrenians, Alexandrians, and of them of Cilicia and Asia;[36] that is, in the synagogue to which the Hellenists most plausibly belonged. Accordingly, it could be argued that, far from orthodox Palestinian Judaism taking offence at this contact with less orthodox foreign Jews, it was the Hellenists themselves who were enraged to find their own numbers being infected. And emphasis could be laid on the fact that a more stiff and suspicious orthodoxy could be assumed for many Jews who had had to fight to preserve their religious heritage in a hostile gentile world, and who had returned to Jerusalem to spend their remaining years under the shadow of Zion.

[33] Acts 8:4 and again 11:19.

[34] Jackson and Lake, *Beginnings of Christianity,* Vol. V, pp. 59-74. In Vols. IV and V, H. J. Cadbury replaced Jackson as co-editor.

[35] Acts 6:1.

[36] Acts 6:9.

The most cautious conclusion is that the problem is not to be solved, since, to use the language of mathematics, we have fewer equations than unknown quantities. In the form in which we have it the story has been so conventionalized and revamped that reconstruction is hopeless. Stephen's speech has long been recognized as casting no light upon the problem. The burden of it is simply: "Ye stiff necked and uncircumcised in heart and ears, ye do always resist the Holy Spirit; as your fathers did, so do ye."[37] That this was the theme of many a Christian sermon of this period and in a measure accounts for the fact that a wider sphere of usefulness came more and more to appeal to the preachers is likely; that it is an actual page of Stephen's speech is as unlikely as that Pericles himself pronounced the magnificent funeral oration which Thucydides records of him. It is tempting to wonder if the seven "deacons" who were selected by the twelve apostles to serve tables, but who, surprisingly enough, soon forsake this particular service to become preachers themselves, do not correspond to the Seventy, whom Luke alone records Jesus had sent out.[38] That the Seventy actually were sent out is most unlikely. The story would appear to come from a later day, when the church was largely gentile. It was unthinkable that Jesus could have neglected these other sheep. As the twelve apostles had been sent to the twelve tribes of the house of Israel, so the seventy had gone out to the gentile nations, regularly represented as seventy in number. Is there, underlying this story of the seven deacons, an earlier account in which the Seven were not so completely subordinated to the Twelve?

The net result, therefore, of a critical appraisal of the story of the Seven, of whom Stephen was the most conspicuous, would appear to be that it is an explanation of the change of policy that gradually but eventually came to some of the group in Jerusalem. It is by no means unimportant that soon the position of leadership passed from Peter to James the brother of Jesus, who appears to have been of a distinctly conservative type. Opposition had taken the place of passive indifference or even mild interest which had at first apparently characterized the community towards the Christian group. In Acts 12 a vivid picture of this changed attitude is given without any explanation as to its causes. It can hardly be coincidence that Jerusalem tended more and more as the years went by to become the stronghold of the distinctly conservative and Jewish wing of Christianity; that other communities, notably Antioch, sprang up and gained in importance as the centres of more progressive and liberal thought, to which those who felt themselves unduly restrained in Jerusalem naturally gravitated.

In Antioch a distinct change of policy is to be seen. Although some in Jerusalem may have come to believe that it was as legitimate for them to

[37] Acts 7:51.
[38] Luke 10:1-20.

make proselytes to their form of Judaism as it was for their fellow Jews; in Antioch affairs took a different turn. A thriving Christian centre soon grew up with gentile converts apparently predominating. Soon a new figure makes his appearance, Saul of Tarsus, later to be known as Paul, the Apostle to the gentiles.

The early years of Saul's life are unknown. That he was a Jew of orthodox parents, though possessing Roman citizenship; that he was born in Tarsus; that he followed the teachings of the Pharisees in his interpretation of the law, as did most Jews; that he was strict to the point of fanaticism in his reverence for the Jewish law and traditions; and that he joined heartily in persecuting the early Christians—this is the sum of our knowledge of his pre-Christian days. Then came his right about face; he became convinced —how we do not know—that Jesus, far from being accursed of God, had but done the Father's will; that he had risen from the dead and was now sitting at the right hand of God, and would soon come to judgment. From persecutor he turned to become the ardent champion of the faith he had once sought to destroy. Following a period of work in Arabia[39] he spent many years in Syria and Cilicia, not improbably about Tarsus, and eventually becomes prominent among the Christians of Antioch. From this city as a base of supplies, so to speak, he spent a decade or more in the hitherto untouched districts of Asia Minor and eastern Europe (Macedonia and Greece), in the course of which he wrote many letters to the churches he had founded, some of which being preserved came later to be regarded as sacred writings. Although Paul may well have been the most influential of all the missionaries to the gentiles, he was surely neither the first nor the only one. The presumption is that others were working in about the same general way as was he. That is, from now on Christianity had come to take its place definitely in the stream of world religions. Eventually— when, it is impossible to say—its adherents came to realize that it was impossible to be at once Jew and Christian. Some tried it, and continued to demand that converts to Christ come by way of Judaism with its law and requirement of circumcision. But this group—usually called judaizers —soon became an almost negligible quantity except in the neighbourhood of Jerusalem, although it is popularly believed that they carried on an active campaign in Galatia. Save for their possible mention in Paul's stinging letter to the Galatians, they do not appear in his correspondence, and a century later Justin Martyr finds it necessary to apologize for his broad-mindedness in conceding that "those who have been persuaded to observe the legal dispensation along with their confession of God in Christ shall probably be saved."[40]

Almost coincident with the rise of the gentile mission it became increas-

[39] So apparently Gal. 1:17 is to be interpreted.
[40] *Dial.* 47.

ingly apparent that Judaism was destined to turn a deaf ear to the gospel. The bitter disappointment of early Christianity can still be read in the words of Paul and also in the gospels as well. In fact, it was the opposition of Jews themselves to Paul, whom they quite properly regarded as a renegade, which forced him to the position, undreamed of by him when he had turned from persecutor to advocate, namely, that Christianity and Judaism were two hostile camps, and that the gospel and the law could not both remain objects of a man's allegiance. Nor was Paul's a unique case. The gulf between Synagogue and Church was constantly growing wider. The flight of the Jewish Christians from Jerusalem to Pella in obedience to what they believed to be a divine revelation during the awful war against Rome, which was the consequence of the growing Jewish unrest under the later procurators, was simply the last blow which separated mother from child. Within fifty years after the Crucifixion, Christianity had become to all intents a gentile religion. The churches still had members of Jewish stock, but they were of the past generation. New recruits must come from the gentile world.

This had not been achieved without a bitter struggle. Even in the book of Acts, which seeks to minimize the disputes between early Christians, the intensity of feeling between two such rival centres as Jerusalem and Antioch is plainly visible. In Paul's writings it is even less restrained. Each group had been suspicious of the other, but eventually the one which had come to see the world as its field, and had been willing to adapt its message to the needs of those whom it wished to gain as converts, won. Then it was but a matter of time until the church should become convinced that this was all a part of the unfolding purpose of God. Was not the gentile mission being visibly blessed by God? Were not nearly all who honoured the name of Christ of gentile stock? Surely this was no accident. God had so ordained it. Furthermore, since Jesus had had all knowledge and knew the end from the beginning, he had foreseen and intended that the religion which was to bear his name should go in these paths. Thus while his words, "Go not into any way of the gentiles, and enter not into any city of the Samaritans," might still be preserved, they naturally came to be interpreted as binding only in the days of his earthly ministry. When he had left the earth to take his seat on the throne on high, he had set for his church its solemn task:

> Go ye therefore, and make disciples of all the nations, baptizing them into the name of the Father and of the Son and of the Holy Spirit: teaching them to observe all things whatsoever I have commanded you: and lo, I am with you always, even unto the end of the world.[41]

And for another nameless Christian, equally convinced that the church's

[41] Matt. 28:19,20.

history had run in the intended path, Jesus' hour for leaving the earth could not have come until gentiles turned to him.[42]

The results of these early years of preaching with an ever increasing field opening up before the Christian preachers were truly momentous. To choose but two examples. It is today perfectly obvious that there is a vast difference between the nature of the messages of Jesus and Paul. At times this has led to unsparing condemnation of Paul and his associates who perverted the simple gospel stream. The slogan, "Back to Jesus," has simply meant "Away from Paul." But although many of the early judaizers may well have shared this feeling, their opposition was as futile as Canute's attempt to hold back the waves. To make it concrete: Had Jesus been able to attend a church service in Corinth in the year 54 A.D., he would have been astounded, and might well have asked himself in amazement: Is this the result of my work in Galilee? But it is none the less certain, that had there been no change, there would have been no Christianity. Regardless of the intrinsic values of teachings, unless men know them they can exert no influence. The revolutionary call of Jesus had been especially adapted to the Palestine of his day. But it was not a message, in the form in which he gave it, to exert any considerable influence on the outside world. Judaism had been known for centuries. There had been a constant flow of proselytes to its synagogues. None the less, because of its very nature it was not a gospel for the Mediterranean world. It was the natural outgrowth of the hopes and longings of a distinct and different race. And because Judaism was an old and firmly established religion, it could invite —it would not seek nor change. Thus the challenge of Jesus with its insistence on repentance, with its content the impending change, pitched in terms intelligible to Judaism, would have fallen on deaf ears in any portion of the Mediterranean basin except Palestine. The Greek and the Roman, like Gallio, "cared for none of these things." Salvation, a feeling of security, hope amid the crumbling ruins of the older religions which had been hamstrung by the merciless criticism of the philosophers—after all these did the gentiles seek. And it was because this new movement was able to break away from—or be thrust outside of—Judaism that Christianity triumphed as it did. Unhampered by a traditional past, it was far-sighted enough under the guidance of such men as Paul to see that the aims and longings of every human heart were legitimate; that it was not necessary for gentiles to banish their hopes and longings or to express them in the terms of Judaism, but that the gospel of Christ was broad enough and deep enough to meet and satisfy the longing of every human heart. This was the profoundest lesson the early church could have learned. And then as now the pew moulded the pulpit fully as much as did the pulpit the pew. As the years went by, the nature of the message necessarily changed. The most

[42] John 12:20 ff.

convincing proof that Christianity did adapt itself to its new environment and came to provide in acceptable and intelligible form the assurance and security that men were questing for is that Constantine saw emblazoned in the sky a cross and heard the congenial word that his campaign would be successful. Had Christianity not finally won out over her neck-and-neck rival, Mithraism, it is not improbable that instead of a cross he would have seen a torch, or perhaps even a helmet.

Accordingly, any attempt to understand the development of early Christianity must recognize the fact that it is largely the story of the transformation and modification of the heritage from Judaism under the influence of the thought and practice of the Græco-Oriental world. To neglect the influence of either heredity or environment cannot fail to give a one-sided and essentially inaccurate picture.

Because of the fact that at the time when all the books of the New Testament except the Pauline epistles received their final form Christianity had become essentially a religion of gentiles, it is easy to neglect the basal Jewish elements in it. A moment's reflection should be sufficient to correct this misconception. The earliest Christian teachers and missionaries were Jewish to their finger tips. Even a man like Paul, who in later years could term as refuse and loss those things which he had previously considered of the greatest value, never lost his essentially Jewish attitude, however much he might seem to inveigh against the law. The Old Testament—Jewish Scripture—was his Bible; its ideals were his ideals. Judaism, he felt, had been false to its heritage; yet precisely the ideals which Paul had come to believe were to be realized only in the Christian and were demanded by the union of the believer with Christ, rather than through the command of the law, had been held as standards for centuries by the orthodox Jew.

What was true of Paul was true of his fellow missionaries. The Old Testament became the Bible of Christians, and remained such even when in the second century specifically Christian writings came gradually to be added to it. The significance of this Christian adoption of the Old Testament cannot be overemphasized. Actually the Septuagint came soon to be regarded as essentially the property of Christians, not Jews. Not only was it believed to be full of prophecies of Jesus, the coming Messiah, but that it had been actually written for Christians. It is highly instructive to remember that the second century saw no less than three successive new translations of the Hebrew Scripture into Greek for Greek-speaking Jews—those of Aquila, Symmachus, and Theodotion. It was not unnatural that after the Septuagint had been taken over by the Christians and was being used as one of the most telling weapons against Jewish antagonists, Judaism came to doubt the accuracy of this version and to crave others which should be truly its own. Gentile Christians found it perfectly natural to consider and refer to themselves as "sons of Abraham." In fact, it was not only natural but distinctly valuable for Christianity to assert that it was the true Judaism, for Judaism was one of the *religiones licitæ* of the Roman empire, recognized and protected by Rome. However aware Christianity might be of the real gulf between herself and her now bitter rival, it was natural for her to endeavour to come in on the wave of toleration.

Again, it is from the early Jewish followers of Jesus that Christianity received the tradition and stories of Jesus and his ministry. That the traditions were conventionalized and revamped, perhaps more drastically than is commonly realized, as early Christian preachers used them in their efforts to make new converts and to edify those already in the church is not to be denied. For the historic materials which are preserved we are indebted to early Jewish followers. But more important than this was the note that was stressed in the early preaching, namely, that the Christian gospel made ethical demands of the greatest severity; in short, that morality and true religion were indissoluble, if not identical. This was the sinew of the early Christian message and was directly due to the heritage from Judaism. The picture of the moral bankruptcy of the gentile world has been grossly overdrawn by Christian apologists. The teaching of Stoicism and the lives and examples of men like Socrates, Epictetus, and Marcus Aurelius can never be overlooked. None the less, the notion that religion and morality were essentially one; that the religious professions and practices of men of unclean lives were abhorrent to God—this notion was not native to the Græco-Oriental world, as is abundantly evidenced by the difficulty Paul found in teaching his gentile churches this lesson to him so obvious. Christianity learned many lessons from the outside world, but this was not one of them. For this outlook, destined to be one of her greatest assets in enabling her to triumph eventually over her rivals, she stood indebted to the synagogue.

But, as has already been remarked, the transfer of this essentially Jewish message to the outside world involved startling and tremendous changes undreamt of by the earliest preachers. When the earliest disciples began to push out and to make proselytes they had no notion of the consequences of their action. To think that at some specific time they deliberately altered their practice—hitherto they had been unconcerned for the gentile world; now they would treat gentiles precisely as they had formerly treated Jews —is absurd. The proselytes they made were proselytes to Judaism. Gentiles might be fit objects to preach to; they were not fit table companions. The bars were by no means let down overnight. This important distinction is not always clear to the reader of the highly compressed account in the early chapters of Acts. A Peter might preach to a Cornelius; none the less, his qualms of conscience at eating with gentiles in Antioch might cause him to stand guilty of hypocrisy in the eyes of a Paul. In the course of long years of work in the gentile world, hampered and opposed by orthodox Jews,

Paul might come eventually to an open break: "There can be neither Jew nor Greek . . . ye are all one man in Christ Jesus;"[43] "circumcision is nothing, and uncircumcision is nothing;"[44] yet it is most improbable that had we a letter from his pen shortly after he had turned from persecutor to friend we would read these words. Eventually even the Christians who most vehemently opposed such latitudinarianism swung into line or else retreated into the shell of an ultra-Jewish gospel—more Jewish, if possible, than orthodox Judaism itself—and exerted no further influence in the movement as a whole. To write the story in detail of the gradual transformation of the early group awaiting the return of the son of man and proclaiming the message they had inherited from the prophet of Nazareth into an independent religion promising to the world salvation through the death and resurrection of the Lord Jesus Christ and made possible by baptism and a sacred meal is impossible. None the less, the general trend of the development is reasonably clear. We can still see evidences of the gradual fusion of such original contradictory views as those of the resurrection of the body and immortality of the soul, of a great final judgment at the end of this age and the immediate rewards and punishments to each individual at the end of his life, of the Galilean prophet anointed by God to proclaim his coming kingdom and the Saviour of the world.

[43] Gal. 3:28 f.
[44] I Cor. 7:19.

Chapter XIII

THE DEVELOPING CHURCH

THE Græco-Roman world in which the early church soon found itself was by no means as religiously bankrupt as has often been alleged. That many of the landmarks of the earlier forms of popular religion had crumbled before the criticism of the philosophers is true; that many men found themselves adrift in an unknown sea without chart or compass, anchors dragging and the familiar stars obscured by fog, is also certain. But that this means a confirmed and morally vicious atheism had taken the place of an exploded polytheism is no truer than would be a similar diagnosis of modern society. To cull salacious passages from Persius or Martial, or to fail to recognize that a Juvenal or Lucian was satirizing and hence deliberately choosing the most reprehensible elements available, results in a completely distorted picture. Furthermore, it is equally easy to point to Epicureanism and to emphasize that the removal of the gods from any intimate concern with the world must have resulted in an easy-going atheism, while the Stoic identification of the divine with nature could not escape a barren godless rationalism. Mature reading of Epicurus or of Epictetus and Marcus Aurelius by no means justifies such a priori conclusions. The readiness with which the provinces introduced a new goddess, Roma, into their pantheon in grateful appreciation for the coming of peace and security into their troubled world, and found it most natural to deify her emperors, first the dead and then the living, is by no means to be overlooked. Furthermore, the older hero cults of the Greeks, notably that of Æsculapius, which had been of such significance in the previous centuries, continued to exert an undiminished influence. And finally, to mention but a few, the so-called mystery cults, both Greek and Oriental, were providing the means of escape from present perils to a joyous and certain confidence, and were making converts at a rate which alarmed many a staid Roman. In short, the Mediterranean world, far from being immersed in indifference or hostility to religion, was showing itself most responsive. As has been acutely remarked, "Not because Gentiles were irreligious, but because they were so incurably and tenaciously religious, Christian propagandists actually made little headway with them at first."[1] Convinced as the early Christians were that their religion alone was true—again a heritage from Judaism—they bitterly opposed these other cults and practices as the stupid productions of wicked demons who were fruit-

[1] Willoughby, *Pagan Regeneration*, p. 2.

lessly striving against the one true God and his Son. Thus Paul reminds his Galatian converts that they had been in subjection to evil demons,[2] not that they had been religiously indifferent. The gentiles had "lords many" but were "without God" (ἄθεοι)[3] not because they were destitute of divinities, but because these divinities were demons or idols; this age had a god, but he was Satan![4] Accordingly the word attributed to Paul as he addressed his gentile hearers on the Areopagus, "Ye men of Athens, in all things I perceive that ye are very religious,"[5] is most apt whether the word, translated by some "religious," by others "superstitious," be considered a compliment or reproach.

As has already been emphasized, distinct changes had taken place between the message of Jesus in Galilee and that of his earliest followers in Jerusalem, even though the latter were quite unaware of the fact themselves. The *post*crucifixion experiences had convinced them that Jesus was more than the prophet of the impending kingdom. Actually he was the one who would momentarily return to earth on the clouds of heaven, himself to establish it. Thus was born the Christological speculations, destined to play such a large part in the triumph of Christianity. So even in the earliest days, while his followers were still on Jewish soil and without any thought of going into the ways of the gentiles, far-reaching changes had come. But the transfer from Jewish to gentile soil brought even more radical changes. Not only did the movement speedily become a separate religion, distinct from Judaism, but, as its message was translated into terms intelligible and appropriate to gentile hearers, it became gradually more and more like the other cults with which it found itself in conflict. By the middle of the second century—and probably much earlier—it had become one of the Græco-Oriental cults, and like the others offered salvation to its converts through its divine Lord. To understand and to appreciate this development a brief consideration of this type of religion is necessary.[6]

There were many kinds of mystery cults in the world at the time of the emergence of Christianity. Nothing is more misleading than to consider them all alike and to deduce from the characteristics of one the nature of them all. None the less, all of these cults appear to have had three characteristics in common: (1) All have some purificatory rite of initiation through which the initiate must pass. (2) All are essentially mysteries of communion with some deity who through this rite comes into union with his votaries.

[2] Gal. 4:3. The obscure στοιχεῖα, usually rendered "rudiments" or "elements," is apparently so to be understood.

[3] Eph. 2:12.

[4] II Cor. 4:4.

[5] Acts 17:22.

[6] In the following pages free use is made of an earlier study in my *The Ethics of Paul*, pp. 45-59.

(3) All look to the future life and secure for the initiate a happy reception in the world beyond the grave. This goal, the gospel of all the mysteries, is clearly expressed in the distich of Firmicus Maternus,

> Be of good courage, ye initiates; because the God has been saved;
> To us also shall be salvation from woes.[7]

Thus Cicero can say, "In the mysteries we learn not only to live happily but to die with fairer hope."[8] For the initiate the statement wrongly attributed to the Epicurean would be amended to, "Eat, drink, and be merry, for tomorrow you do not die at all—for you have been saved." This is strikingly illustrated by the word:

> As truly as Osiris lives, he shall live also; as truly as Osiris is not dead, shall he not die; as truly as Osiris is not annihilated, shall he not be annihilated.[9]

This goal was realized solely through the efficacy of the rites of initiation. It was through them that the secret of salvation became communicated. Much unnecessary confusion has arisen about the nature of these cults through the unfortunate title, "mystery religions." Actually the Greek word translated *mystery* (μυστήριον) does not signify anything either mysterious or vague. Rather it was perfectly well known and clearly defined to the initiate to whom it had been revealed. It was thus a *secret*, known only to the members of that particular cult. This all-important secret had been communicated to him in the ritual of initiation by means of "the things done and the things said."

> Thrice blessed are they who have seen these rites and then go to the house of Hades, for they alone have life there; but all others have only woe.[10]

The cleft between religion and morality is evident. The two need not be antagonistic; none the less, salvation depended upon the efficacy of the vows, not upon purity of life. This gave point to the sneer of Diogenes:

> Pataicion the thief will have a better fate when he comes to die than will Epaminondas, because he has been initiated.[11]

But that this indifference to morality fostered immorality does not seem to have been the case. The cults were *un*moral rather than *im*moral. It is easy to stress the orgiastic excesses that apparently not infrequently followed the initiation rites, as, for example, the *Hilaria* in the cult of Attis, where feasting, masquerade, and often unrestrained ribaldry followed the frenzied mourning, flagellation, and even self-mutilation of over-enthusiastic aspirants for the priesthood. In some of the cults temple prostitutes were to be

[7] *de Errore* 22.
[8] *de Legibus* 2,14.
[9] Cumont, *The Oriental Religions in Roman Paganism*, p. 100.
[10] Sophocles, *Fgm.* 753.
[11] Plutarch, *Quomodo adulescens* 4, p. 21F.

found; not infrequently women were called upon to sacrifice their virginity to the god. Since many of the cults were based upon the perennial miracle of nature's fertility, the awakening of new life in the spring, it is quite possible that not infrequently "the things done and the things said" may well have been calculated to incite emotional extravagances in emulation of nature herself. None the less, it is very easy to exaggerate this phase; against the black picture it is to be remembered that the beautiful *Odes* of Pindar were penned by a devotee to the Orphic rites; that the one passage which we have that describes the initiatory rites of Isis[12] would seem to indicate that far from being degrading they were of a quite different nature; that much of our knowledge of these cults has come to us at second and third hand from those bitterly opposed to them, who, not themselves members of the cults, may accordingly be suspected of failing to differentiate between the nature of the rites themselves and the objectionable abuses of individual priests, adherents, or even outsiders. In the *Bacchæ* of Euripides we gain a real insight. Here the prophet with lofty unconcern retorts to Pentheus, "Dionysus does not constrain women to be chaste"; yet two lines farther on it is said, "Even in the Bacchic orgy the virtuous woman will not be corrupted."[13] That is, the cults were unconcerned with questions of morals. If a person were already virtuous, the cults would not corrupt him; if he were not virtuous, they would not tend to make him so. Crude and often repulsive legends were connected with all the cults and could only be explained away for the more cultivated devotee by some rationalistic effort or by a violent exercise of faith. Often the rites may, as has been already suggested, have been orgiastic in their nature and have incited the more easily excited spectators to acts of emotional extravagances and breaches of the mores (especially since in all the cults save Mithraism men and women were thus thrown together in these most intimate experiences), but that this was not the rule and that it was highly distaseful to the better type of adherent appears probable.

After all, the members of these cults were living in the world. Membership in this cult or that did not cut them off from their fellowmen. They heard the Stoic preachers in the marketplaces. The result is that while the cults themselves had nothing to induce either morality or the reverse, they gradually began to reflect the secular morality of their environment. The coarseness of the older myths and the obscene debauches that occasionally followed the ceremonies may well have appeared highly objectionable to many of the adherents. Nor is there any reason to suppose that every man or woman who joined the cults lost his desire for personal probity and uprightness of life. Thus gradually the cults began to reflect contemporary standards, and during the second, third, and fourth Chris-

[12] Apuleius, *Met.* xi.

[13] *Bacchæ* 314,316.

tian centuries came to contribute in no small degree to the higher moral and spiritual standards of the empire. In the Greek cults this had been to a measure true centuries early.

Each of these cults, as has been already remarked, had its own divine lord with whom the initiate came into union. The evidence is perhaps not absolutely certain, but it appears probable that while some of these lords may have been regarded as divine by nature, the majority were believed to have lived their lives upon earth as men (or women) and to have discovered through their own labours and suffering the way to victory. As a consequence, they had achieved immortality and had been rendered divine. Thus Cicero writes of Hercules: "Hercules has gone to the gods. Never would he have gone thither, had he not, while still among men, made for himself that road."[14] Later in the same writing he remarks that it was by his death that Hercules achieved immortality.[15] Nor was this true only of Hercules; it was believed of many others as well—Dionysus, Isis, or Mithras. It is also of importance to observe that those earthly heroes who gained the secret and power to become immortal while yet on earth were often regarded as children of heavenly parents. Thus the mother of Hercules was Alcmene, his father Zeus. Dionysus, too, was a son of Zeus who had cast loving eyes on Cadmus' daughter Semele. Though the hero had gone on high from the earth, he had left behind the secret; through the initiation rites other mortals became thus possessed of it. Like the god he dies (symbolically) and is made alive again or raised from the dead. Then finally when at the end of life the man actually dies, his spirit remains immortal. This is very clear in the story of Apuleius, already referred to.

By the second century Christianity had become one of these cults. Jesus was the divine Lord. He too had found the road to heaven by his suffering and resurrection. He too had God for his father. He had left behind the secret whereby men could achieve the goal with him. The convert was buried with Christ in baptism, was born again. That Christianity was so regarded is perfectly clear from the pains Justin Martyr takes to prove that these resemblances between Christianity and the other religions were all due to the malignity of the demons. These wretched demons had read the Scriptures and had realized, although imperfectly, what was destined to be. They trembled as they saw their coming overthrow and realized their helplessness to prevent it. To salvage as much as possible and to delude men they hastily concocted rites and ceremonies as near as possible to those they foresaw were to be instituted. Thus they hoped that when Christ appeared and instituted his worship men might be deluded into believing that the Christians were borrowing from older pagan ceremonies and beliefs. To the modern student this explanation of Justin may seem most

[14] *Tusc.* i,14,32.
[15] *Ibid.* ii,8,20.

naïve; none the less, it is highly important as incontrovertible evidence of the growing likeness of Christianity to the other cults which made such an explanation essential.

But though Christianity came to have many characteristics in common with these other older cults, due to the activities of her early missionaries one great difference is apparent. In Christianity morals and religion were one. Purity of life, stedfastness of character—these were never to be disregarded. This note Paul had sounded with all his might. The Christian was in immediate fellowship with his Lord. He had been baptized into his death, had died to the flesh, was a new man in Christ Jesus. But for Paul it did not end here. The Christian's life must conform to his new and exalted status of being "in Christ." He was assured of a place in the eternal destiny of the world. Death had lost its power over him. But this destiny was only for those who actually lived "in Christ." If he failed to live in a fitting way, to bear evidence in his life of this new relationship to God, this failure was proof positive that he was actually not "in Christ" at all. Every Christian would stand before the judgment bar. For those who were really "in Christ" and whose loves and characters proved it this experience would be the time of reward. It would mark for them not the day of wrath, but the day of salvation. To many of Paul's gentile converts this insistence upon ethical conduct sounded an alien note. Was not the efficacy of the rite of admission sufficient? What had matters of conduct to do with religion? For the gentile this was a perfectly natural attitude. It was Paul's lifelong task to try to show his gentile converts that morals and religion were one and the same.

This emphasis upon purity of life and uprightness of character so much emphasized by Paul and the other early missionaries—it was their heritage from Judaism—is almost certainly one of the principal reasons for the steady growth and eventual triumph of Christianity. Its Lord was no unmoral or immoral deity, as were so many of the "lords" of the other cults. No impure stories of his amours and activities needed to be explained or allegorized away. There was nothing in the ritual to cause men of moral refinement to hesitate to take the step. In the lapse of the years this ethical insistence of Christianity proved one of her greatest assets; it may have deterred some of licentious life who might otherwise have been attracted, but it drew to herself many others and welded them into a solid front.

That Christianity soon came to be regarded as one of the many mystery religions of salvation does not appear to be open to legitimate question. The problem lies in a different direction, *viz.,* What caused Christianity to pass from the absolutely non-sacramental type of religion as revealed in the primitive tradition underlying the gospels and early chapters of Acts to a definitely sacramental religion? While many influences are to be seen in this transformation, one factor appears to have been of especial significance—the title which Jesus came to bear. As soon as the followers of Jesus began to strive for converts among non-Jews the question arose as to how he should be referred to. To speak of him as being the "Anointed of the Lord" (χριστὸς κυρίου) was quite impossible, for this phrase was intelligible only to the Jew. To the Greek, who used oil solely for medicinal purposes—the relief of pain, not for purposes of consecration—anointed or *Christ* would signify only "the one smeared with medicated oil." Accordingly, we find *Christ* fast becoming a part of the proper name in the letters of Paul (Jesus Christ or Christ Jesus). As has already been remarked, the disciples of Jesus soon after his death came to regard him as the son of man. But such a title, while perfectly natural to Jews familiar with the apocalyptic speculations, would have been entirely unintelligible in Greek ears. It is not surprising that the phrase never occurs in the Pauline letters. The beliefs which these titles embodied must accordingly find expression in some other title.

As a matter of fact, the title Lord (κύριος) soon became the common appellation for Jesus, as is abundantly evidenced by the Pauline epistles. Although the title is also freely used for Jesus in the gospels, a critical examination of the passages would seem to indicate it the Greek editors' own usage rather than their faithful translation of some Aramaic equivalent. Accordingly, it is highly probable that Jesus was not so addressed by his disciples during his lifetime. It is not improbable that after his death he may have been referred to in some Aramaic circles (apparently this was not the case in Jerusalem) as *Maran* or Lord. Some such assumption is apparently necessary to explain the puzzling *Maranatha* of I Cor. 16:22. Whatever the meaning of the phrase is, it certainly contains the word *Maran*, "Our Lord," and must reflect earlier usage, just as does the preservation of such Aramaic touches as *Talitha cumi, Eloi, Eloi, lama sabachthani* and perhaps *Abba*. But while this apparent (if limited) usage of *Maran* in some Aramaic-speaking circles may perhaps partially explain the employment of the Greek equivalent for Lord (κύριος), the word in Greek had a vastly different connotation. This word was not only used in the general sense of master, lord, sir, but it was used specifically of the Roman emperors in the cult of the Cæsars, and was regularly employed for the divine heads of the different Græco-Oriental salvation cults. Whatever Paul and his fellow Christian missionaries may have meant by the phrase, "Jesus is Lord," it would signify just one thing to their hearers, namely, that Jesus was a divine redeemer-god, even as were the "lords" of the other cults. Whether this was what Paul meant them to believe is one question; that they did so believe seems clear. Accordingly, by this one fact alone, the Christianity which Paul was proclaiming was made to seem like the cults even though these cults may well have seemed to him hateful and creations of the devil.

Furthermore, the fact that this same word was used regularly to translate the divine name in the Septuagint may well have aided in securing for Jesus divine honours. The title Lord was now his. Christians were becoming convinced more and more that the Septuagint was their book, that it was full of prophecies of their Lord. Hence it was by no means unnatural for them to feel that many passages where the divine rights and prerogatives of the Lord, Jehovah, were mentioned were actually references to their Lord Jesus Christ.

Here another point is to be observed. Judaism was never unmindful of its painfully achieved monotheism. Jehovah alone was God. He could never stand one among many. This Jewish heritage at once makes its appearance in Christianity. Jesus and Jesus alone is Lord. In the other cults all the Lords were divine; to be sure, the devotee of a particular cult owed allegiance to his lord alone, yet he had no quarrel with his neighbour who was joined to another. As a matter of fact, it was by no means uncommon for a man to be a devotee of several cults at the same time.

For the Christian this was impossible. All the other cults were the creation of demons. His Lord, and his alone, was divine. All men must recognize him, "for he had a name which is above every name; to him every knee must bow, every tongue confess that Jesus Christ is Lord."[16] Such an intolerance could not fail to awaken a bitter opposition which otherwise the other cults would not have expressed. None the less, it was a distinct source of strength and of ultimate victory. Christian was drawn closer to Christian as they faced the common foe. Not only did it breed a genuine camaraderie, but the very audacity of such a claim could not fail to have a strange and compelling fascination for many who listened to these startling claims, and who would have turned a deaf ear to one content to be but one of many.

Thus the selection of this title Lord for the crucified Jesus was fraught with tremendous consequences. Not only did it contribute, probably unwittingly, to the entire transformation of the nature of the Christian message, but in addition it rendered it at once intelligible and highly acceptable to those who were longing for divine protection in a changing and terrifying world.

With this transformation of Christianity into a religion, which came more and more to appear like the other cults, promising salvation to its converts, baptism came to occupy a very important place as the initiatory rite, the way the convert became consecrated, set apart to God or Christ. In all these cults was a purificatory rite through which the initiate passed.[17] The candidate was

[16] Phil. 2:9 ff.

[17] It is never called baptism. In fact, *βαπτίζω* is never used in Greek writers for a ceremonial or religious purification, although it is used frequently in other senses: *e.g.*, it is used of ships being *sunk*; of men being *plunged* into debt, *soused* in wine, *overwhelmed* in difficulties. Even among Greek-speaking Jews it was but very rarely used of a religious washing. None the less, Josephus' use of the noun *βαπτιστής* (baptizer) for John shows that while rare it was not

cleansed from guilt in water—or in blood, as in the taurobolium—and was thus born anew to communion and fellowship with the Lord whose he now was. The bitterness with which Justin Martyr and Tertullian—to mention but two of the early protagonists—inveighed against the demons for having counterfeited the Christian rite makes argument unnecessary that baptism had at a very early date come to be regarded as parallel to the initiatory rite of the other cults. Thus Tertullian writes:

> We recognize here also the zeal of the devil rivalling the things of God, while we find him, too, practicing baptism in his subjects. What similarity is there? The unclean cleanses! the ruiner sets free! the damned absolves! He will, forsooth, destroy his own work, by washing away the sins which he himself inspires![18]

It has accordingly not infrequently been argued that Christian baptism was thus taken over bodily from the practices of the Græco-Oriental world, and was from the very first distinctly sacramental in its character. Against this suggestion the story of the baptism of Jesus, the baptismal command in the Great Commission, and the mention of the three thousand who were baptized at Pentecost have been urged as proof positive that far from this being the case baptism was practised from the very first by Jesus' followers. Between these two extremes a middle position appears probable. The antithesis, "I baptized you in water, but he shall baptize you in the Holy Spirit,"[19] is most naturally understood to mean that Jesus did not baptize with water, and accords with the entire absence of any mention of such an activity. In the Fourth Gospel, to be sure, it is said that Jesus and his disciples were making and baptizing more disciples than John,[20] yet at once the qualification is given, "Although Jesus himself baptized not, but his disciples." The most natural interpretation of these verses would not seem to be the contrast which the author draws, that although the disciples baptized Jesus himself did not, but rather that baptism was not a phase of the Master's ministry at all, for in all probability as Jesus preached and worked, so did his disciples. The author, convinced, as were all his fellow Christians, that baptism had been in vogue from the very beginning, but familiar with a tradition that Jesus had not baptized, simply drew a contrast where none was implied or legitimate. That even the story of Jesus' baptism at the hands of John is open to legitimate historical question has already been suggested.

About the Great Commission little need be said. As has been already shown, its whole tone reflects the later practice of the church, already involved on a world mission and is in decided contrast to the attitude of the first Jerusalem

---

unknown nor of Christian coinage. It is simply another indication of the wide gaps in our knowledge—linguistic as well as historical—of the early centuries.

[18] Tertullian, *de Baptismo* 5; cf. also *de Præscriptione Hæreticorum* 40, and Justin M., *Apol.* i,62.

[19] Mark 1:8.

[20] John 4:1; cf. 3:22.

followers who apparently shared Jesus' own view of the nature and purpose of his ministry. Furthermore, the command to baptize "into the name of the Father and of the Son and of the Holy Spirit" (the later orthodox formula of the Church as attested by second century writings and the only valid one according to Catholic law) runs directly counter to the early Christian practice, attested by both Acts and Paul, that Christians were baptized "in the name of the Lord Jesus" or some simple variant, as "into Christ Jesus."[21]

Accordingly there is no evidence of baptism before the return of the disciples to Jerusalem. This makes the mention of it in the Pentecost narrative the more difficult. Here it is introduced without explanation as the natural answer to the query of those who had been impressed by Peter's preaching. Had it been a feature of the work of Jesus and his disciples, one might have expected Peter to urge it and the people to receive it. But for an entirely new institution thus to make its sudden appearance is most difficult. Furthermore, it strikes an anticlimactic note. The Pentecost story is the fulfilment of Jesus' prophecy: "For John indeed baptized with water, but ye shall be baptized in the Holy Spirit not many days hence."[22] Baptism in the Spirit is not thus a consequence of baptism in water, but a substitute for it. The promise has been fulfilled, the Spirit has come. Accordingly the mention of the water baptism which followed seems a forced anticlimax and to reflect the latter view that possession of the Spirit and entrance into the Church were dependent upon water baptism. It is not impossible that the narrative of Paul's experience in Ephesus[23] may reveal this later view: Paul discovers twelve men who, though baptized "into John's baptism," had not received the Holy Spirit when they believed, nor had even heard of it. Paul considers their baptism defective, rebaptizes them "into the name of the Lord Jesus," and confers the Spirit. It is thus highly probable that the reference to baptism at the time of Pentecost rests upon nothing more solid than the author's conviction that from the very first it had been a universal custom.[24]

A far more probable clue to the actual rise of this practice is found in a later chapter of Acts; namely, in the work of Philip the Evangelist.[25] In this story we are in the third stage of Christianity, to continue the use of that convenient anachronism—first Galilee, then Jerusalem, now a gradual spreading out to Samaria and other territory not strictly Jewish. Here the situation is reversed. Philip baptizes various folk, Samaritans and the Ethiopian eunuch; later the apostles come down to Samaria—there is no further mention of the eunuch—and confer the Holy Spirit upon those already baptized. This representation of the apostles as a college of high officials who feel constrained to supervise and pass judgment on the work done outside Jerusalem should

[21] Cf. Acts 2:38; 8:16; 10:48; 19:5; Gal. 3:27; Rom. 6:3, etc.
[22] Acts 1:5.
[23] Acts 19:1-7.
[24] A similar situation is implied in Acts 10:44-48.
[25] Acts 8.

not obscure the probability that in this story is to be found the origin of the Christian rite, for here for the first time is found a plausible reason for it. As we have seen, the disciples in Jerusalem remained good orthodox Jews for years after the crucifixion. They had unique views about Jesus and the speedy culmination of the world's history. They had sensational ideas regarding Spirit-possession, may very probably have practised for a time a most unfortunate financial experiment, but in all matters of practice they remained zealous sons of Abraham. No record of any clash with the Pharisees over points of belief nor of any rash words about the validity of the Sabbath are found in the pages of Acts. The difficulties that came were of a different kind. The group became stigmatized as a nuisance and menace to law and order. If the speeches of Acts reflect at all, as apparently they do, the temper and content of early Christian preaching, one wonders not at the clashes when they did come, but at the long-temperedness of those who from their high seats heard reports of what must have seemed to them dangerous millennial nonsense.

Although at first they considered their task to consist in preaching their message to their fellow Jews, they found themselves gradually, as the years went by, forced to seek a wider field; but only gradually, and always with trepidation. It may well be that this account of the work of Philip reflects with accuracy this gradual start.

When these Jews began to preach in heathen territory, they naturally made the customary demands of those who would be their proselytes. That baptism along with circumcision was required regularly of Jewish proselytes at this time is scarcely open to question, although the origin of the rite is quite unknown. Many speculations are possible, but are fruitless. In contrast to the other superficially similar Jewish baths and purifications this one was valid only when official witnesses were present.[26] These early disciples may well have used some such formula as "in the name of Jesus Christ" to show that it was to a form of Judaism where the claims of Jesus were recognized that converts were being bidden.

This would appear an adequate explanation of the start of the practice, and would account for its early presence in the Jewish wing of Christianity, as no explanation which would see it as an outright adoption from the gentile cults of the empire could do. As the movement spread definitely into gentile territory and thus came into the tideway of Græco-Oriental thought and practice, drastic changes resulted. From a truly Jewish proselyte bath it became a life-giving sacrament. That by the end of the first century this stage had been reached is revealed—to mention but one case—by the reference to

[26] The candidate immersed himself. It is not improbable that this was true not only in the case of the baptism by (in the presence of) John but also of early Christian baptism. On this point see C. R. Bowen, "Prolegomena to a New Study of John the Baptist" in S. J. Case (editor), *Studies in Early Christianity,* pp. 129-147.

the eight souls who were "saved through water: which also after a true likeness doth now save you, even baptism."[27] That Paul believed, as the author of I Peter manifestly did, in baptismal regeneration is perhaps improbable; none the less, that even in his eyes it was vastly more than an act of obedience in testimony of an inward change of life cannot seriously be questioned. By it, on the contrary, the initiate was plunged into mystic union with the risen Lord, by the impartation of whose spirit a new life began.

The development in Christianity from its contacts with the gentile world is even clearer in the case of the Lord's supper or sacred meal. Whatever doubts may be felt with regard to Paul's view of the nature of baptism, it is scarcely open to question that in his eyes the Lord's supper was totally distinct from any ordinary meal. He believed that it had been instituted by Jesus who had commanded its repetition.[28] It already had its liturgy, and it possessed magical powers—at least for the misfortune of those who profaned it. The cup and the bread brought the partaker into a real relationship with the blood and body of Christ. By drinking the cup they shared his death. That Paul meant by the words, "This is my body . . . this cup is the new covenant in my blood,"[29] that the Christian actually ate the body and drank the blood of Christ as the heathen ate the body of their lords cannot be proved and is perhaps improbable, although the charge of cannibalism came soon to be made against Christians. None the less, that Paul believed that a direct and intimate union with Christ was achieved by the eating of this consecrated food is undeniable. And herein lay its danger. To eat the bread or drink the cup in an unworthy manner meant to be guilty of the body and blood of the Lord. That this is no mere figure of speech is evidenced by his word: "For this cause many among you are weak and sickly, and not a few sleep.[30] It is impossible to free these words of their obvious meaning.

Furthermore, his comparison of the Christian meal with those in honour of pagan divinities is pointless unless it be conceded that both were capable of bringing about a distinct mystic union—in the one case with Christ, in the other with the demon: "Ye cannot partake of the cup of the Lord, and the cup of demons; ye cannot partake of the table of the Lord and the table of demons."[31] Sacred meals in honour of some divinity were very common in the Græco-Oriental world. They played a distinct part in the initiation rites of the cults. In the Mithraic rites the initiate ate the honey, at Eleusis drank the

[27] I Pet. 3:20,21. Cf. also John 3:5. For the place baptism had come to occupy by the end of the second century see Tertullian, *de Baptismo*, especially 1 and 12.

[28] I Cor. 11:23-26

[29] I Cor. 11:24 f.

[30] I Cor. 11:30.

[31] I Cor. 10:21. See my *The Ethics of Paul*, pp. 142 f.

sacred potion of meal and water and ate the food from the chest. From the cult of *Magna Mater* comes the oft-quoted:

> I have eaten out of the drum,
> I have drunk from the cymbal.

In the Dionysiac orgy the devotees had torn the living animal apart and eaten the bloody flesh. This scene was reënacted in the Orphic cult with the participants eating the sacrificial animal which represented the god himself. Papyri preserve invitations to dine with the Lord Serapis in his temple.[32] The unhappy experience of Paulina[33] in the temple of Isis suggests meals with the lord Anubis were also common. Thus it is not surprising to find Justin Martyr, in his description of the Eucharist, once more inveighing at the demons for their destestable copying:

> Which the wicked demons have imitated in the mysteries of Mithra, commanding the same things to be done. For, that bread and a cup of water are placed with certain incantations in the mystic rites of one who is being initiated, you either know or can learn.[34]

That the Christian meal soon took on a distinctly sacramental character is clear, but that this was the development of a more primitive meal totally free from such notions is highly probable. In the account in Acts of the life of the followers of Jesus in Jerusalem it is said:

> And day by day, continuing stedfastly with one accord in the temple, and breaking bread at home, they took their food with gladness and singleness of heart.[35]

There seems little reason to question this reference to a common meal. The intimate ties of fellowship of these early disciples are sufficient to account for such an act without reference to the common meals of the Essenes or Therapeutæ. Nor need we assume that these meals were intended to commemorate Jesus' death. None the less, they could not fail to arouse afresh memories of the days when he had been with them at table in Galilee; especially of that last time when he had sat with them in Jerusalem on the eve of his arrest and death. That as they had eaten they had spoken of his coming death, that the broken bread and poured out wine had been a natural description of it on the lips of one who had seen parables in all the homely facts of life, is far from impossible. To see in that sacred moment of friendship more than such a spontaneous act seems to deprive it of its real meaning. In the evening meals that followed the disciples could scarcely have failed to have spoken of him, to have felt themselves reliving those days with him. Thus without any

[32] Cf. *P. Oxy.* 110 and 523.
[33] Josephus, *Antt.* 18,3,4.
[34] Justin Martyr, *Apol.* i,66,4.
[35] Acts 2:46.

attempt to give them a formal or ceremonial nature they came gradually and spontaneously to be a continuous memorial to him. Confident that he was soon to come again, it is surely not impossible that the blessing at table was accompanied with a petition for his speedy return. Although, as the months and years went by, the number of the early followers increased and the original intimate fellowship with common meals became impracticable, an occasional meal in common in memory of him appears to have been held. How frequently they were held and whether at regularly recurring times is not clear.[36] That soon some sort of simple litany came to be employed and that by the sheer force of repetition the tradition soon arose that actually Jesus himself had ordained the repetition is perfectly clear from I Corinthians. Paul prefaces his rebuke of those who are profaning the meal with the words: "For I received of the Lord that which also I delivered unto you, that the Lord Jesus in the night in which he was betrayed took bread, etc."[37] The natural explanation of these words is that Paul meant he had gained through natural, not supernatural, means a primitive tradition of the institution of the ceremony by the Lord himself. It is highly instructive to observe that although this belief arose within the first twenty-five years—probably considerably earlier—it is not reflected in the accounts in Mark or Matthew, and that it is very probable that it did not stand originally in Luke. The omissions of the words

which is given for you: this do in remembrance of me. And the cup in like manner after the supper, saying, This cup is the new covenant in my blood, even that which is poured out for you[38]

from manuscripts whose tendency is to add not to subtract from the tradition, the obvious similarity with the Pauline word, and the double giving of the cup (if these verses are retained) have inclined many textual critics to regard these words as an early interpolation into Luke from I Corinthians.

Thus from a simple meal—at first no different from any other—in which the companions of Jesus found their thoughts going back to the one who had been taken from them but who would soon return in glory gradually arose a rite which was destined to occupy a very important place in the new religion. That the Lord's supper, as it soon came to be known, and baptism were deliberately transformed by the early missionaries—for example, Paul—into sacramental rites in order to rival the similar rites in the other cults is totally improbable. It is far more likely that the gentiles, to whom these men were preaching, saw resemblances where none were originally intended and that the process of transformation, while none the less steady, was from the bottom rather than from the top. Whatever the steps in the process be believed to be,

[36] *Didache* 14 and Justin Martyr, *Apol.* i,67,3 ff. would appear to indicate that in the second century it was weekly.

[37] I Cor. 11:23.

[38] Luke 22:19b-20.

it is hard to doubt that well before the end of the first century a new religion which promised salvation to its converts through union with its crucified and risen Lord and which had its sacred rites of initiation and communion had come to rival the claims of other cults promising precisely the same boon. Its claims were contemptuously dismissed. Its refusal to stand one among many, to live and let live; its insistence that it and it alone could bring the true and only salvation—this was to result in a baptism not of water but of blood for many of its adherents. None the less, within three hundred years from the death of its crucified Lord it, like him, had overcome the world.

PART III

THE LITERATURE OF THE CHRISTIAN MOVEMENT

SECTION I

Its Origin

Chapter XIV

PRELIMINARY CONCERNS

DURING these years of development and change, of which the general trend is clear although the details are now unfortunately beyond our reach, a specifically Christian literature was developing.[1] Christianity, like Judaism, was from the very first a religion of a book, but that book for many years did not include the writings we know as the New Testament. On the contrary, throughout the first century and well into the second, the Old Testament, Jewish Scripture, remained the sacred book of the new religion. Christians had adopted it naturally and had come to see in it not alone the prophecy but the complete justification of their religion. Predictive of Christ and of his work in every page, it had been written especially for them—"For whatsoever things were written aforetime were written for our learning, that through patience and through comfort of the Scriptures we might have hope."[2] They were the true sons of Abraham to whom the divine promise had been given. They had no thought of adding to it any distinctively Christian writings, for it was all Christian. Due to Jewish opposition the breach between synagogue and church became increasingly wide, and with this breach came the conviction to one like Paul that the law had lost its binding force—had in fact never possessed this. But this did not mean the rejection of the Scripture; it simply was a protest against what seemed to the Christians an unwarranted use of it. The spontaneous way in which Paul buttressed his arguments with quotations reveals its place of importance; nor is there the slightest reason for feeling that such an attitude was limited to Paul. It is perfectly clear that the earliest form of worship of the Christians was simply a continuance of the synagogue service, in which the reading of passages from both law and Prophets occupied the central place. Eventually additions to the service were made, but this element, even in later years, was never abandoned. Possession of sacred Scriptures, in comparison with which the revered writings of the Greek philosophers were but young, lent a dignity to the struggling churches of which they were both aware and proud. Early Christians, not brought up in Jewish homes, were yet familiar with the Bible, at least with certain limited parts of it. That this familiarity had come largely from the public reading in the service of worship is highly probable. The

[1] At this point pp. 147 f., 183 should be reread.

[2] Rom. 15:4.

Ethiopian eunuch might have had a copy of Isaiah,[3] but it is not likely that there were many Christians who could have afforded the luxury of personal copies. Eventually courses of instruction for candidates were instituted. Apparently, however, this was a development well beyond the time of the first century. During these formative years the average Christian gained his knowledge and reverence for the Scripture from his attendance at the service in which he heard it read and explained. Although during the early years there had never arisen the thought that there would come a time when other writings would be placed alongside the Bible and would even gain greater respect, eventually precisely that happened. In his description of the weekly worship of Christians Justin Martyr writes (*ca.* 150 A.D.):

> And on the day called Sunday, all who live in cities or in the country gather together to one place, *and the memoirs of the apostles* or the writings of the prophets are read, as long as time permits; then, when the reader has ceased, the president verbally instructs, and exhorts to the imitation of these good things.[4]

And in II Peter—written apparently at about the same time—it is said:

> And account that the longsuffering of our Lord is salvation; even as our beloved brother Paul also, according to the wisdom given to him, wrote unto you; as also in all his epistles, speaking in them of these things; wherein are some things hard to be understood, which the ignorant and unstedfast wrest, *as they do also the other scriptures,* unto their own destruction.[5]

That is, by the middle of the second century there existed writings which had been produced by Christians and which had come to be considered a part of the Scripture. Just what writings had achieved this dignity cannot be said, for there was diversity of opinion among Christians. It was not until two centuries later that a list exactly coinciding with our twenty-seven appeared as canonical. Although by the middle of the second century all of these and numerous others had been produced and were coming to occupy an increasingly important place in Christian affection, one cannot speak of them as canonical, in the sense that they had been formally adopted by vote. None the less, there was coming to be a general feeling that some of these writings had a distinct place in the service of worship and the instruction of inexperienced Christians and candidates for admission. There were differences of opinion about some of the writings, but so far as the letters of Paul, the four gospels, and the book of Acts were concerned there can be no question that by the end of the second century they had come to occupy an unquestioned place among Christians everywhere. Individual churches and groups of churches had become convinced of their value. All the later councils did was to approve and sanction formally this spontaneous and intelligent

[3] Acts 8:28.
[4] *Apol.* i,67,3 f.
[5] II Pet. 3:15 f.

choice and to end the discussion regarding the place of others which had hitherto remained on the fringes, *viz.*, Hebrews, Revelation, and several of the Catholic epistles.

Enough has already been said to make it clear that these writings were not penned by their authors to rival or even to supplement the Old Testament, did not become canonical overnight, and showed the greatest divergencies of form and outlook. The fact that they are now regularly and conveniently bound between one set of covers—as, of course, was not the case for centuries after their production—sometimes gives rise to the notion that they are chapters of a book, that the several authors contributed monographs as do modern authors to some *Festschrift.* Such, of course, is far from the case. Instead of being one book, the New Testament is a library composed of writings produced to meet the practical needs of the Christians for whom they were intended.

As they stand in our English Bibles they fall into six different groups:

1. Four gospels,
2. Acts,
3. Thirteen epistles ascribed to Paul,
4. Hebrews,
5. Seven Catholic, *i.e.*, "general" epistles,
6. Revelation.

The first two sections comprise the so-called historical books, that is, those purporting to give the history of Jesus' ministry and its results to the time of the advent of his great apostle Paul in Rome. Then follow twenty-one writings in the form of letters. Thirteen of these have regularly been attributed to Paul, as they all purport to be, although about several of them legitimate questions have often been raised. Of these thirteen nine are addressed to a particular church or group of churches, four to individuals. The so-called Epistle to the Hebrews while having some similarity in outward appearance to these letters is actually quite different in nature and is more of a tract than a letter. The other seven are grouped together as Catholic epistles, and rightly, for in spite of some superficial appearance of being addressed to an individual they are all intended for Christians wherever found. The last of the twenty-seven, the Revelation or, as it is often called, the Apocalypse, stands quite alone in our collection, the sole representative of a type of literature which, though common at the time of its production, soon disappeared although some traces of this kind of writing are to be found in the Synoptic gospels.

Again, the order of the books in our Bible is not chronological. Ancient tradition is almost unanimous in placing the epistles of Paul first, and modern scholarship agrees. Because of the superior authority of those books embodying the teaching of Jesus and because they give a picture of the earlier events, they have always been placed first in the list from the time when the books began to circulate under one cover, although, as will later appear, the relative order of the four gospels themselves was by no means always the same as ours.

In attempting a critical introduction to these various writings there is a distinct advantage in following the natural grouping:

1. The Pauline epistles and Hebrews,
2. The Catholic epistles,
3. The Apocalypse,
4. The gospels and Acts.

This method is not strictly chronological, for some of the Catholic epistles (notably II Peter) are very late, and furthermore it separates the Gospel of John from I John, with which it is closely joined; on the other hand, it is of distinct advantage to examine each writing in line with others of the same general type, and there can be no doubt but that Paul's letters to his various churches resulted in later Christians adopting the epistolary form.

As a matter of fact, at an early date the various books circulated in much these four groups. Before the invention of printing copies of the whole New Testament, while not unknown, were comparatively rare. Instead were to be found (1) "the Gospel," by which were designated our four gospels; (2) "the Apostle" or *Corpus Paulinarum* and including, of course, Hebrews; (3) Acts and Catholic epistles, which eight regularly were copied together; (4) Revelation which generally circulated alone. While this grouping will be followed in general, it has seemed wise to treat Acts with the gospels rather than with the Catholics because of its literary connection with the Gospel of Luke.

But before turning to the Pauline epistles several terms need definition and brief discussion. In contrast to "general introduction," which deals with the New Testament as a whole, is "special introduction," or, as it more commonly is called today, "higher criticism," which deals separately with the problems of each particular book. There has been much unnecessary prejudice aroused by the use of the term "higher criticism." It is called "higher," not, as is often popularly imagined, in arrogant and fancied superiority to the humble writings under discussion, but in contrast to the other type of criticism, *viz.,* textual or "lower." This latter has for its sole object the reconstruction of the exact text of each book as it left the pen of the particular author. If we had the original copy (technically called the autograph) of each of these books, there would be no reason for textual criticism. But since these have long since disappeared and in their place we have thousands of copies, both in Greek and in the various dialects into which the Greek was early translated, and since no two of these copies exactly agree, the textual or lower critic sets for his task the reconstruction, as near as possible, of the *ipsissima verba.* In distinction from this the higher critic deals not with the text—for this he is dependent upon the lower critic—but with the sources and methods employed by the particular author in question. All questions dealing with authorship, date, and general character of the writing are his concern. Who was the author? Why did he write? When did he write? To whom? What were his sources of information? Is the writing as we now have it all from one pen or are two or three writings from the same author telescoped together, or, on the contrary, have two or more different authors all had a hand? In a word, higher criticism is simply historical and literary research helping to evaluate the biblical writings in such a way that they may speak for themselves. Thus it should be evident that the terms "higher" and "lower," as here applied, are the result of the New Testament being considered a river. The lower or textual critic stands downstream at the river's mouth; the higher critic approaches it at a point higher up near its sources. Hence, the notion, first, that "higher" means a self-constituted and absurd arrogance on the part of egotistical scholars, and, second, that criticism means fault-finding adverse criticism, eager in its quest for flaws, is seen to be the sheerest nonsense. Higher criticism is essentially positive; to be sure, it may often destroy unfounded tradition and perverse opinions, but its purpose in this is solely to prepare the ground for constructive building. One of the greatest advances in the appreciation of the Bible which has been made possible by higher criticism is the total discrediting of the old proof-text method of interpretation. According to this perverse practice every biblical passage was considered of equal weight for truth and doctrine. A quotation from Esther or Matthew, from Ecclesiastes or Romans—all stood on the same platform. Higher criticism has revealed that this was based on the unfounded assumption that the Bible was one book equally and completely inspired, that there was no such thing as a progressive revelation. Today we know far better. We recognize the Bible as a collection of books written under varied circumstances by men who were vastly more than the fingers of God, men who lived in some cases centuries apart and whose purposes in writing were often very different. Yet one object they all had, namely, to answer the problems of life as they saw them and not to provide a textbook for life in the twentieth century. Thus higher criticism has not only totally discredited the proof-text method, but it has revealed what the true sphere of the Bible is. Foolish men who try to make the Bible do what its authors never intended it to do have gone far toward discrediting it in the eyes of many men. When we realize this, it takes on a new character. We see it as a progressive revelation of God's power at work in human history; not something superimposed on man from above as a textbook of life, but as a portrayal of the experiences of men in the past at grips with life, with their successes and failures. When it is realized that more than a thousand years intervened between some of the writings in the Old Testament and in the New and that these years had resulted in vast differences in life and thought, contradictions in thought and expression cause no surprise. In a word, higher criticism enables the Bible to speak for itself in intelligible language and to be judged by its own standards.

But before an ancient writing can speak for itself, can tell of its author's outlook on life, and the situation that confronted him, we must have that writing in the form in which it was originally written. As has already been said, during the centuries that elapsed between the time of composition and the appearance of our earliest manuscripts the writings had been frequently copied. As a result numerous changes had been made, both intentional and accidental. But not alone minute changes such as alteration in spelling or word order, but more drastic alterations occur. Additions and interpolations are occasionally to be found. Two or more writings, originally distinct, have been copied together as one. Obviously it is necessary to take matters of this sort into consideration before attempting to interpret the writing. Hence the question of *integrity* is of great importance. By this is meant simply: Is the book as we possess it exactly the same as it was when it left the author's hand? For the sake of clearness a few examples may be not out of place. Many scholars are of the opinion that II Corinthians is not in the form in which Paul composed it, but that two—some would say even three or four—letters have been telescoped. Not that this material is not Pauline, but that he did not write it in its present order. On a subsequent page the reasons will be given for believing that the last four chapters are actually part of a quite different letter which he sent to Corinth before writing chapters 1-9. It is universally recognized that Mark 16:9-20 is not a part of the original gospel, but was added by a later hand many years after the evangelist had finished. The famous section of the Woman taken in Adultery (John 7:53-8:11) was not an original part of this gospel. Several manuscripts have it after Luke 21:38. In the King James Version I John 5:7-8 reads:

> For there are three that bear record *in heaven, the Father, the Word, and the Holy Ghost: and these three are one. And there are three that bear witness on earth,* the spirit, and the water, and the blood: and these three agree in one.

But the italicized words do not occur in any Greek manuscript older than the fifteenth century, nor in the Greek Fathers, nor in any ancient version except Latin. Their earliest appearance, except in Latin dress, is in the fourteenth century. Any use of them, accordingly, to evidence the views of the original author would lead to absurdity. Other famous passages which must be considered more or less doubtful are Luke 22:19b-20, 43-44; 23:34a. In Westcott and Hort's *The New Testament*, pp. 583-600, is given a list of those readings suspected or definitely rejected by those conservative editors.

Under the caption *language and style* many important questions are included. How good is the Greek in the particular book under discussion? How does it compare with that in other books of the New Testament? With other writings purporting to come from the same pen? Is it translation Greek?

(This question is once more to the fore with regard to the gospels.) How do the vocabulary and style of the Pastoral Epistles (I Timothy, II Timothy, and Titus) compare with others from the pen of Paul? Are the differences too great to allow the belief that Paul wrote them? Are the difference of style and phraseology of the Gospel of John and the Revelation explainable on the hypothesis of common authorship?

What were the *occasion and purpose* of the book? Why was it written? To meet what need? Often this is directly stated in the book (cf. John 20:31); at other times only inferences can be drawn.

Who were the *readers* for whom it was intended? (1) Often it is clearly stated as in I Corinthians, II Corinthians, Philippians, Colossians, Philemon; but then arises the query: What was the condition or situation in the church? Was it gentile or Jewish? (2) Sometimes the statement is not clear. For example, who were the "Galatians"? What is meant by "the twelve tribes of the dispersion" (James)? Who is "the elect lady" (II John)? "Gaius" (III John)? (3) Frequently it is not stated at all, as is the case with Matthew, Mark, John, and probably Luke and Acts. (4) Occasionally when it is stated there are legitimate grounds for doubt, as, for example, Ephesians, I Timothy, II Timothy, Titus.

The question of *authorship* is often very important. Often it is not stated and can only be inferred, if at all, from hints, deductions, and tradition. This is true, for example, of the gospels, Acts, Hebrews, I John. Often when it is stated there appear to be grounds for question, as, for example, in the case of the Pastoral Epistles, James, Jude, I Peter, II Peter, Ephesians, II Thessalonians. Here the term *authenticity* (to be sharply differentiated from the quite different *integrity*) is common and signifies: Is the writing what it purports to be? Two kinds of evidence are available: (1) External evidence, *i.e.,* quotations and other comments from early Christian writers evidencing the traditions current at that time. Naturally the line between tradition and sheer guesswork is often only imaginary. (2) Internal evidence. Does the knowledge shown in the book of the history of the times under discussion, of the geography and customs, justify the belief that that individual could have written it? Are the style and outlook on life as shown in the Pastorals consistent with that shown in Romans or I Corinthians? Does the portrait of Paul in Acts allow the traditional view that it was written by a companion and friend of the great apostle? Are there anachronisms? In II Peter 3:16 Paul's epistles are referred to as Scripture in the same sense as the Old Testament. Is it conceivable that such a view prevailed during the lifetime of Peter?

The *date* and *place of origin* are often highly important. (1) None of the writings are plainly dated, although inferences can occasionally be made with fair probability through references or allusion to events of which the dates are known. Dates are not unimportant in spite of much loose popular talk to the contrary. Oftentimes the way in which a passage is to be interpreted is directly consequent upon its date. For example, in the parable of the Marriage Feast reference is made to the anger of the king, the sending forth of his armies, and the resultant burning of the city.[6] If, as is not improbable, this reflects the destruction of Jerusalem in 70 A.D. by the Romans under Titus, it is obviously not a word of Jesus and evidences that this parable at least has been edited and altered in the light of later events. (2) Nor do any of the writings state the place in which it was produced. The citations at the close of the Pauline epistles as printed in the King James Version (but omitted in the American Revised Version) are not originally parts of the letter, but are due simply to the voice of tradition. Sometimes the place of composition may be determined with fair probability from a knowledge of the history of the period, as, for example, in the case of I Thessalonians and the correspondence with Corinth; or from a clue in the book itself, as in the case of James.

It is with questions of this sort—and this list is not exhaustive; each book has particular problems connected with it—that the higher critic must concern himself. It is largely from his careful and unprejudiced investigation of them, from his ability to allow his findings to determine his feelings rather than his feelings his findings, that any real solid basis of knowledge of early Christianity is made possible.

[6] Matt. 22:7.

Chapter XV

THE LETTERS OF PAUL

As HAS been remarked on a preceding page,[1] we know very little of Paul's life previous to his conversion, and, for that matter, of the years immediately following. The obscurity is not lessened by the fact that our two sources of information (Acts and Galatians) are not easily reconciled—in fact, probably stand in distinct disagreement at least in so far as details are concerned. In matters of fact Paul's own account is naturally to be preferred to that of the later writer; even this, however, is so condensed that it is far from clear. Suffice it to say that following his conversion—apparently in or near Damascus—he spent some time in "Arabia," then returned to Damascus. "Then after three years"—apparently this is to be dated from the time of his conversion, although grammatically it might mean after his return from Arabia—he went to Jerusalem, and after fifteen days there went "into the regions of Syria and Cilicia." That these years were spent in zealous preaching for the new cause is implied by the words "And I was still unknown by face unto the churches of Judea which were in Christ: but they only heard say, He that once persecuted us now preacheth the faith of which he once made havoc; and they glorified God in me."[2] But the details of the story are unfortunately not known. Fourteen years later he went to Jerusalem once more, this time with Barnabas.[3] This has usually been interpreted as meaning fourteen years after the previously mentioned visit, that is, seventeen years after the conversion. On the other hand, it may mean fourteen years after the conversion, and has been so understood by several competent historians. Furthermore, we cannot be certain how the years were reckoned. Conceivably "seventeen years" could mean as little as fifteen full years plus a small fraction of the preceding and following years; similarly, "fourteen" need not be more than a few months over twelve. Thus it is impossible to be confident about the chronology of these years. One thing, however, is certain. Paul had been a Christian missionary for several years—at least twelve, not impossibly seventeen[4]—before writing any of the letters known to us.

[1] See p. 180.

[2] Gal. 1:22,23.

[3] Gal. 2:1.

[4] It has occasionally been suggested that instead of "fourteen" "four" should be read in Gal. 2:1. The emendation would be trifling (Δ instead of IΔ, that is, ΔΙΑΔΕΤΩΝ instead of ΔΙΑΙΔΕΤΩΝ) and would simplify the Pauline chronology in two regards: (1) It would not make Paul's conversion so early; (2) it would reduce the period of these years of silence. Both

The importance of this fact is twofold. (1) The account in Acts also passes by this time spent in the regions of Syria and Arabia in silence: "And when the brethren [*sc.* in Jerusalem] knew it, they brought him down to Cæsarea, and sent him forth to Tarsus" (9:30). . . . "And [Barnabas] went forth to Tarsus to seek for Saul; and when he had found him, he brought him unto Antioch" (11:25, 26). From then on the Acts account of Paul's labours is much fuller, sketching out his activities in precisely those districts (and in no others!) from which we have Paul's letters. Most modern scholars have assumed as axiomatic that the author of Acts is unacquainted with the Pauline letters. Such an assumption does make certain disagreements between Acts and the Pauline letters perhaps less surprising. None the less, it is remarkable that the author of Acts passes by in silence the one period of Paul's ministry for which he could get no information from the letters and summarizes it with a word[5] which sounds surprisingly like a paraphrase of the similar word in Galatians.[6]

(2) But even more important than this indication that it might be rewarding to reconsider the relationship of Acts and the Pauline letters is the significance of this period of years for Paul's own thought. All of these letters come from the pen of Paul the mature Christian and experienced Christian teacher. There is no reason to assume that his later career was essentially different from that of the years spent in "Syria and Cilicia." As he went later from place to place making converts and founding churches, so presumably he did in this region. That his career as a Christian missionary began when Barnabas brought him from Tarsus to Antioch is sheer assumption. Even on the assumption that this detail of the story (Acts 11:25) is strictly historical, it is scarcely to be imagined that Paul had been content to do nothing but make tents during the interim or that Barnabas would have turned to him so many years later had he not made a reputation in the meanwhile. Furthermore, the famous list of hardships which Paul boasts of having undergone as a minister of Christ[7] implies many experiences unrelated in the conventional three journeys of Acts.[8] That during these years his thought ripened and matured is scarcely open to doubt. Had we a letter from his pen shortly after he had left Damascus, how different must it have read from even the earliest of those which we now possess, and what a light it would have cast upon pages now dim beyond recall.

His extant letters date from the next ten or a dozen years. During these

---

of these considerations are significant. None the less, there is absolutely no manuscript support for this reading. Hence the conjecture is probably unjustified and has never won any considerable support.

[5] Acts 9:30 f.

[6] Gal. 1:22-24.

[7] II Cor. 11.16-33.

[8] *I.e.*, before departing from Ephesus (Acts 20:1), since this portion of II Cor. apparently is to be dated from Ephesus during this period. See below, pp. 257-260.

years he was travelling back and forth across Asia Minor and Greece, until after an outbreak of hostility against him in Jerusalem and a period of imprisonment in Cæsarea he was sent as a prisoner to Nero's court in Rome. Finally, after many delays and an enforced stay on the island of Malta he reached Rome, where he presumably met his death after another two years of imprisonment.

That Paul wrote his letters to provide a nucleus for a new Christian literature or to enable later Christians to familiarize themselves with his achievements or his beliefs we have already seen is far from the case. Rather, he wrote his letters because he could not at the moment pay personal visits. They all have specific purposes, are all *ultra*practical in their nature. Some of them are in answer to questions which his perplexed churches had raised; some are to check difficulties which he had learned about in some way or another. One is intended to disabuse the minds of a church which he had not yet visited but hoped to visit in the near future of hearsay prejudice against him. One is to urge a fellow Christian to forgive his runaway slave who is returning in penitence; another is to recommend a Christian woman who is removing from one city to another. Had Paul possessed the magic carpet enabling him to be in any place at any time he chose, he would not have written his letters.

They are all *letters* in the truest sense of the word. It is unfortunate that they have been regularly referred to as "epistles," for an epistle is quite distinct from a letter. For while a letter is a purely personal writing, intended for the ones addressed—in Deissmann's happy phrase, the writing of an "I" to a "you"—and hence not intended for general reading or circulation, an epistle is a distinct literary device, a letter only in form, intended for general reading and designed to influence whomsoever it chances to reach. Some of Cicero's letters have come down to us; even the casual reader can scarcely fail to feel the difference between their personal and intimate tone, the casual reference to some incident so well known to the intended recipient as not to need amplification, and the rhetorical and carefully studied *Epistolae Morales* of Seneca. Epistles in the true sense of the word are not lacking in the New Testament. Certainly James, probably Hebrews, are to be so regarded. The writings of Paul are not of that type. Even Ephesians, at least if it be actually Paul's own, can scarcely qualify as an epistle, although it has something of its quality; the writings to "Timothy" and "Titus" are epistles, but they are not from the pen of Paul.

The nature of Paul's letters should warn us that, since they are letters, the writer assumes much as known and accepted by his readers, and can accordingly make a casual reference to an event to them well known. As time goes on, that knowledge is gradually lost and things once clear become involved in doubt and have to be rediscovered or guessed at by later readers who try to make belated use of writings never intended for them.

Thus, to choose but one example, was Titus circumcised or not?[9] No one today knows, in spite of vigorously expressed opinions pro and con. Paul's words admit of either interpretation. The Galatians did know, and hence could understand the allusion.

As a corollary to this, it is to be observed that, since these are letters, the points argued and stressed are often not those of the greatest importance. They are usually points about which differences of opinion existed. To most of the churches addressed, Paul was no stranger. He had spent weeks, in some cases months, with them. They knew his views on the great central facts; these he can take for granted. It is to show them their mistakes in the application of these central facts to their daily life, to help their doubts, that he writes. For example, in I Cor. 15 Paul discusses the resurrection. He does not argue about the resurrection of Jesus. His readers accepted that fact. His emphasis is to convince them that their bodies too will be raised. Regarding that point there was skepticism in Corinth. Furthermore, many of the questions he discusses are those propounded by the perplexed church. He answers the question because it has been raised. Obviously these are often questions which he considered of second-rate importance; else he would have discussed them when present. Failure to observe these characteristics of the true letter distorts them, and has often contributed to the curious notions which have arisen about the thinking of the apostle. It need hardly be said that he was writing for those of his own age, specifically for his own churches, not for us. That again and again his words apply to us is due not to any dual purpose of the apostle to the gentiles, but to the fact that the real problems of life are often much the same even in widely different areas. On the other hand, that many problems which convulsed these early churches have long since ceased to be problems is as clear, from the reading of an epistle like I Corinthians, as is the opposite fact that many new problems have arisen of which he never dreamed, and upon which his writings, accordingly, cast no light at all.

Four of Paul's letters stand together because of the circumstances under which they were composed. When Paul wrote them he was not engaged in missionary activity, but was in prison. These four—Philippians, Philemon, Colossians, and Ephesians—are properly styled "the letters of the captivity." This imprisonment has generally been identified as the period in Rome with which Acts closes. The other six—Galatians, I and II Thessalonians, I and II Corinthians, and Romans—in contradistinction have often been designated "the earlier epistles." But recently it has been urged that the letters of the captivity were written not from Rome, but from Ephesus. If this be admitted, and there is much to be said for the view, the term *earlier* for the other group is unfortunate, since then at least one, probably two, perhaps three, of them in their present form would be not earlier but

[9] Gal. 2:1-5.

later. Nor is the term "missionary epistles," adopted by Bacon, much better. The only letter which we have from Paul's pen that is not distinctly missionary in character is one of that very group, Romans, for this letter, at least in its present form, was the only letter sent by Paul to a church for which he felt no direct responsibility. It is perhaps then unwise to attempt to label the groups; rather, it is better to consider the individual letters in only a roughly chronological order. About two of them, II Thessalonians and Ephesians, legitimate doubts as to authorship can be raised; none the less, each of these depends so completely upon another companion letter, I Thessalonians and Colossians, respectively, that it is advantageous to consider them in these connexions without regard for absolute chronology.

Chapter XVI

THE EPISTLE TO THE GALATIANS

THERE are few more baffling problems for the student of the Christian beginnings than those involved in the letter to the Galatian Christians. That it is a genuine letter of Paul and that we have it essentially as it was first written have rarely been questioned, and never by unprejudiced critics. Forgery is out of the question. The obvious excitement under which it was written; the passionate form of expression; the sudden changes of front—all these are quite unlike the work of a later Christian essaying to write in Paul's manner. Furthermore, although the Greek is at times very difficult with sentences beginning in one sequence and ending in another[1] and although there are many "audacities and flaws in the argument," there is little reason for questioning the integrity of the writing. This is no cool or studied essay. Paul is so excited that his thinking is constantly outdistancing his power of expression.

When we turn to the other questions: What called forth this passionate rebuke and defense? To whom was it directed? When and from where did Paul write? we find ourselves involved in difficulties. Although these latter three questions have always been recognized as most obscure, the occasion and purpose of the writing have usually been considered self-evident. Recently this has been called into question with what appears to me good reason.[2] Before considering the question of purpose it will be well to state simply Paul's apparent argument.

The temper of the writing is evident in the opening words: "Paul, an apostle, not from men, neither through man, but through Jesus Christ and God the Father. . . ." Although Paul generally styled himself an apostle in the opening words of a letter, this emphasis that his apostleship was *not from men* but *from God*, strikes a different note, and reveals that Paul is on the defensive. Furthermore, the complimentary paragraph which regularly stands after the salutation in the other letters—"I thank God for you

[1] "But *from those who were reputed* to be somewhat (whatsoever they were, it maketh no matter to me: God accepteth not man's person)—*they*, I say, who were of repute *imparted nothing to me. . . .*" The normal conclusion to "From those who were reputed" would have been "I received nothing," not "they imparted nothing to me." This break in construction is technically called anacolouthon.

[2] W. Lütgert, *Gesetz und Geist* (1919); J. H. Ropes, *The Singular Problem of the Epistle to the Galatians* (1929). Both of these essays—the latter is based upon the former—deserve more attention than they seem to have received. I find myself in substantial agreement with their main contention, and have made free use of their arguments in the following pages.

. . ."—in which the virtues of the particular group are extolled, probably to make the resultant criticism or suggestions the more palatable, is wanting here. Instead he at once plunges into the attack:

> I marvel that ye are so quickly removing from him that called you in the grace of Christ unto a different gospel.[3]

Then he continues: Actually it is not another gospel at all; it is simply the work of men nullifying Christ's death and making it of no avail.

He has already sounded his challenge that his apostleship is from God and his message likewise from God, not from men. Thus he can say, Let all who preach a different, pretended gospel be accursed! Then he justifies this tone of authority and attack by recounting his life experience, obviously to show how unfounded were the charges against him. God had taken him and had made him his apostle. It was God, not men, who had given him his message. He had not received it from the Jerusalem group; in fact, his contacts with them had been of the slightest, and years after his call. He had never learned anything from them. Even the pillars had had to admit that he had been entrusted by God with the gospel of the gentiles. Later, when Peter had come to Antioch he not only had maintained his independence, but had publicly rebuked Peter, though to do so had meant to stand alone. Since his gospel is from God, he can speak as he does. He has been crucified with Christ—his life is in Christ—when he speaks, Christ speaks through him. This whole section of autobiography (1:10-2:14) which concludes with the almost lyric personal confession (2:15-21) appears intended to justify his thesis that his gospel came not from men but from God, hence no gospel which clashes with his can be from heaven regardless of who it may be that preaches it.

Then with 3:1 he swings into attack against his opponents' contentions:

> O foolish Galatians, who did bewitch you, before whose eyes Christ was openly set forth crucified? This only would I learn from you, Received ye the Spirit by the works of the law, or by the hearing of faith? Are ye so foolish? having begun in the Spirit, are ye now perfected in the flesh? Did ye suffer so many things in vain? if it be indeed in vain. He therefore that supplieth to you the Spirit, and worketh miracles among you, doeth he it by the works of the law, or by the hearing of faith?[4]

The period of bondage to the law is over. You are free in Christ. Faith—the new freedom in Christ—is absolutely opposed to bondage to the law. The just shall live by faith. Men were in subjection to a harsh and cruel taskmaster. Christ has come and has set us free. How can you slip back into such a bondage? Actually for you gentile Christians such a step means reversal to your former pagan idolatry.

[3] Gal. 1:6.
[4] Gal. 3:1-5.

Then for the moment he loses his tone of severity and with moving tenderness appeals to their former love for him[5]—they were formerly ready to give him their own eyes!—to tear themselves away from these false friends:

> My little children, of whom I am again in travail until Christ be formed in you—but I could wish to be present with you now, and to change my tone; for I am perplexed about you.[6]

Then with a change of tone he seeks to turn the tables upon his opponents by a clumsy allegory about Isaac and Ishmael: The Christian is typified by Isaac, the son of the freewoman, the law-keeper by Ishmael, the son of the slave, put out of the house when the true son was born.

Most analyses of the epistle consider that with 5:2 a new main section begins. It appears to me more probable that 5:1-10 serves as a summary to the whole preceding section (3:1-5:10) and that with 5:11 the last (hortatory) division of the letter begins with an indignant and blistering rebuke to his accusers. Then follows the impassioned insistence that liberty is not licence, but that the strictest purity of moral conduct is requisite. Such conduct is not due to the demands of the Mosaic law, but to the demands of the Spirit. It is, in short, the only kind of life open to a man who is in the Christ. "Thou shalt love thy neighbor as thyself." This fulfils the whole requirement in one word. None the less, in 6:1-10 is given a brief but detailed application of this demand to daily life. With 6:10 his task is done. No personal greetings or requests close this letter. Paul is in no mood for such as he dashes off this denunciation. A final sharp warning, a brief appeal, a benediction—that is all.

The purpose and occasion of this spirited defence have been considered crystal clear. From beginning to end the letter is devoted to a bitter denial of the contention that gentile Christians must be circumcised and must keep the Jewish law. The trouble-makers who call forth this attack are neither Jews nor local members of the Galatian churches, but rabid judaizers (Jewish Christians) from Jerusalem who insisted in Antioch[7] that circumcision and keeping of the law were of permanent importance for every Christian, be he of Jewish or gentile stock. Not content with this opposition, they had continued their campaign by following Paul into Galatia, where they had made the same demands. In their endeavour they had sought to discredit Paul's authority: He was not an apostle as were the Twelve; he had proved false to the gospel he had recived from them, even though he sought occasionally to curry favour with (Jewish) men by insisting on circumcision when he felt it safe so to do; his vaunted em-

[5] Gal. 4:12-20.
[6] Gal. 4:19-20.
[7] Acts 15:1 ff.

phasis on freedom from the Jewish law could not fail to be fraught with the most serious moral consequences; in short, Paul was a dangerous leader who was actually preventing his converts from obtaining a complete and unemasculated gospel. Against this attempt to discredit him and his gospel, Paul directs his broadside. This and this alone was the purpose of the letter.

While there can be no question but that a group of men who may be called judaizers is heatedly opposed by Paul, it is not so certain, as has usually been assumed, that they are the only ones in Galatia who had given Paul concern and that the whole letter is directed against them. The retort, "But I, brethren, if I still preach circumcision, why am I still persecuted?"[8] has long been recognized as one of the major difficulties for the interpreter. It is only by a distinct *tour de force* or bold ellipsis of thought that this word can be understood as a retort to judaizers. Preaching circumcision was precisely their aim. Why should they charge Paul with doing it? But here obviously it sounds like a charge which has been brought against him by those who regard preaching circumcision as opposed to freedom in Christ. If, as Paul elsewhere wrote, "And to the Jews I became as a Jew, that I might gain Jews,"[9] if he had been "all things to all men," such a charge is easily understood from *gentile* Christians to whom Paul must have seemed far more the Jew than he believed himself to be, but not from judaizers.

Another difficulty for the view that the whole letter is directed against the judaizers is the ethical exhortation with which the letter ends, the substance of which is: liberty must not be allowed to degenerate into licence. That Paul knew well from his years of experience in gentile lands that insistence upon purity of conduct could never be superfluous does not seem quite to meet the difficulty. In a letter so completely devoted to one theme, such a digression would still remain peculiar. Hence it has been explained that he is anticipating the judaizers' contention: Such an emasculated gospel as Paul preaches, with its boast, "free from the law," must involve licence of the worst sort. Paul would then be striving to meet this opposition and would be demonstrating that their contention was false. But, as Ropes has succinctly remarked:

> But of any such purpose the passage gives no sign. It sounds like a straightforward warning against lax tendencies, addressed to persons who really needed it; it does not sound like an exhibition, for the purpose of argument, of the way in which Paul *would be* capable of treating the matter if he were actually writing to readers who did need the warning.[10]

A third point of difficulty is the exact force of the so-called biographical

[8] Gal. 5:11.
[9] I Cor. 9:20.
[10] *Op. cit.*, p. 23.

section. Here the burden of his argument is: My contacts with Jerusalem were of the slightest; I received nothing from the pillars at all. This heated denial obviously demands that such charges had been made. But to suppose the judaizers charging Paul with having been influenced by their own group is absurd. Accordingly, the traditional theory is forced to assume that the charge depends not upon the source of his gospel, but upon his later departure from what he had learned, that is, "You have proved false to what you learned." But it is not against this charge, but against the former, that he appears to be defending himself. Thus the only way to salvage the current view is to maintain that to undercut the charge that he had proved false to what he learned he took the bull by the horns and denied the latter by implication through denying the former explicitly: "You claim I have proved false to the gospel which I learned. This is absurd. I could not have 'proved false' to it, for I never learned it from men at all. My gospel comes from God." That this line of argument is impossible is not to be maintained. None the less, few will deny that 1:10-2:21 would serve as a natural and pointed argument against non-Jewish critics who were asserting that Paul's boasted gospel of freedom was neutralized by the distinctly Jewish elements which he insisted upon and which were but natural to one who, himself a Jew, had been deeply influenced by the glamour of the Jerusalem leaders and was ever ready to try to ingratiate himself with men.

Thus from the argument of the letter there are indications of others beside judaizers against whom Paul is writing. But in addition to what are plausibly *inferences* of a double front of opposition to Paul are apparently direct references to these two factions. "Tell me, *ye that desire to be under the law . . .*"[11] and "Ye are severed from Christ, *ye who would be justified by the law*"[12] are rightly referred to the judaizing group. But such a verse as "Brethren, even if a man be overtaken in any trespass, *ye who are spiritual,* restore such a one in a spirit of gentleness; looking to thyself, lest thou also be tempted"[13] evidences the presence of another group, for the word "ye who are spiritual" scarcely suggests all the Galatian Christians, nor even that portion which had remained faithful to Paul's teaching. It is not a complimentary phrase, but bears an ironic sting. You who arrogate to yourselves the title "spiritual" should realize that you are under distinct obligations. That such a group existed in Corinth is today regarded as almost certain. Most of the difficulties in Galatians which have tried the ingenuity of all the commentators and writers of introductions, hard put to explain the curiously round-about way Paul met his opponents' charges, would disappear if, as Lütgert and Ropes have argued, we were to rec-

[11] Gal. 4:21.
[12] Gal. 5:4.
[13] Gal. 6:1.

ognize that the hostile personal attacks against which Paul is defending himself did not come from the judaizers whose tendencies he was reproving, but from a quite distinct "radical" party "which stood in opposition both to the judaizers and to Paul."

One further weakness of the traditional view may be added. Although it is usually stated that the judaizing faction came into Galatia from the outside, this is pure assumption. Gal. 2:11 ff. states that *in Antioch* "certain came from James" and caused Paul concern. But that even there they carried on any organized campaign is certainly not asserted and very probably is not implied. This passage has usually been understood in the light of Acts 15:1 ff.;[14] then by an entirely unwarranted generalization "these men from James" were assumed to have dogged Paul's steps into Galatia. Baur and his followers stressed this point. Wherever Paul went he was followed by judaizers who hounded his steps relentlessly. Not only in Galatia but in Thessalonica, Philippi, Corinth, and Rome they were believed to have opposed him. In recent years this view has steadily declined in favour. It has been seen that it was an unwarranted surmise which did not square with the facts. Galatia alone was left to them, and even here, as has been already remarked, there is no definite and positive indication of their activity.[15]

In view of these distinct difficulties in the current theory, the distinctly different solution first suggested by Lütgert in 1919 and ten years later adopted by Ropes appears to me to merit more attention than has been hitherto afforded it. Confessedly it is only a hypothesis; no more, however, can be said for the interpretation it seeks to replace, although this latter has been repeated so often that it has acquired the dignity of an established fact.

In the Galatian churches some of the converts, although of gentile origin, had become enamoured of certain Jewish practices. In this they may well have felt that they were proving faithful to Paul, who not improbably appeared to their uncritical eyes far closer to Judaism than he himself would have admitted. Their Scripture was now Jewish Scripture; the emphasis Paul had laid on moral requirements was essentially that of the synagogue, although Paul had striven to make clear that it was not due to the dictates of the Mosaic law, but to the constraint which came from being new creatures in Christ which entailed this kind of life. They were truly "sons of Abraham." It is not inconceivable that some of these new "sons of Abraham" yielded to the advances of the local Jewish synagogues and made

[14] This is but one more passage which suggests that the author of Acts was familiar with Galatians and has based this incident on Gal. 2:11 ff. If this were the case, the tangle in chronology might be understandable.

[15] Ropes (*op. cit.*, p. 45, n. 14) remarks: "In the ordinary theory the difficulty is generally overlooked that a missionary enterprise at such a distance [that is, from Jerusalem] would in itself have been hard to handle, and especially hard for Christians so poor that Paul had to collect money for their relief." This point appears to me well taken, particularly if by Galatia the remote and inaccessible region of the old kingdom of Galatia is to be understood.

the attempt to introduce circumcision and other Jewish practices among the Christian converts. At the end of the fourth century no less a preacher than Chrysostom of Antioch inveighs against this very practice in his own day. Thus there is no need to assume that these judaizers were of Jewish birth; certainly none to assume they were intruders from without Galatia.

Their new-born missionary zeal among their fellows provoked a crisis. To others in the Galatian churches these proposed innovations were most distasteful. They, too, had accepted Paul's teaching, but far from overemphasizing the Jewish aspect or basis of his gospel had stressed his note of freedom. Not only was the proffered salvation open to gentiles without the necessity of circumcision, but this mystic experience with Christ had made them free from all restraints. They were in Christ, had received the Spirit, had become spiritual. To them the demands of their judaizing fellow Christians were not only absurd, but a negation of their new confidence. They had already gone beyond Paul. Without his heritage in a religion that had insisted upon the identity of religion and morals, his insistence that, though freed from the requirements of the Mosaic law, they were yet subject to the same restraint, although couched in different terms, seemed casuistic hair-splitting. Thus with the natural and logical application of this dangerous doctrine of freedom they reached precisely the position many gentile Christians in Corinth reached. To use a convenient modern phrase, they were "perfectionists," freed from all restraints, moral as well as ceremonial. Any attempt to crib or confine them was a form of hateful bondage, unworthy of one who was free in Christ.

In this local dispute the absent Paul was involved. The growing dissatisfaction of the "spirituals" with Paul's halfway message may well have been increased by the ill-advised and tactless attempts of their opponents to claim Paul's support. Paul was a time-server, a man who was all things to all people. What could one expect from a man who not only had been a most orthodox Jew until a mature man, but who had toadied to the Jewish leaders in Jerusalem many years after his conversion! If, as is certainly possible, perhaps probable, Gal. 2:1-5 means that Paul had circumcised Titus, although, as he ingeniously tries to explain, not under compulsion, this would be but one more cause for their growing exasperation and hostility.

Word comes to the absent Paul of the difficulties convulsing his churches. Unable to come in person, he does the next best thing, writes a letter. Although the judaizing element apparently had not attacked him nor denied his authority, but had claimed his support for their opinions, he saw in their hankering after the new fleshpots of Egypt a most deadly attack on the gospel he had for years been preaching. For his own converts to be blindly and ignorantly attempting to open holes in the dike he had with such difficulty built touched him on a sore spot. And furthermore, they had actually precipitated a crisis, the consequences of which no one could foresee.

On the other hand, the spirituals were charging him with the very qualities he was convinced were not his. For years he had suffered ostracism and hostility from his own race for having disavowed precisely these things which these ignorant and immature gentile Christians were blatantly ascribing to him. They were denying the validity of the one great joy which he had in life, his direct commission from God as an apostle. And yet at the same time that they sat in judgment upon him they were so distorting the teaching of freedom as to endanger the good name of all Christians and to make Christ a reproach. It is small wonder that the angered and perplexed apostle, unable to see at first hand the exact situation, caught between these two fires and fearing lest the rest of the Galatians should be hopelessly led astray, should have written in this heated and—at times—unguarded manner, on the one hand, ascribing to those who were looking with longing to Jewish practices insincerity and the base desire to enhance their own prestige, on the other, indulging in the bitter, almost savage, thrust at the spirituals who were endangering the very structure of the gospel by their misuse of liberty: "I would that they that unsettle you would get themselves castrated!"[16]

Thus the letter would not be the unbroken attack upon one group; rather two groups whose mutually antagonistic notions had precipitated the conflict are attacked. 3:1-5:10 is directed primarily against those who are dallying with things Jewish; yet even in this section the other group is in his mind. His reference to sonship of Abraham is not a *concession*, which (as Ropes insists) would clog his argument if it is conceived of as solely against judaizers, but a positive insistence upon the abiding values of the Hebrew tradition, and is directed against the radical group who, like the later Marcion, see nothing of value in Christianity's heritage from Judaism. With 1:11 he directs himself specifically against these spirituals. The autobiographical section 1:13-2:14 is against their claims of his subordination to Jerusalem and his but quasi apostleship. In 5:11 once more he turns to them, and now that he has shown that a proper appreciation of the abiding value of the Hebrew tradition does not imply bondage to the Jewish law he can insist upon the necessity of purity of life. "I agree with you completely that those who are in the Spirit are not under the law; but to disregard these fundamental virtues through the notion that it is the Jewish law alone which inculcates them is vicious stupidity and will prevent reception into the

[16] Gal. 5:12. In this wish, which, if the hypothesis outlined above be accepted, is directed against the spirituals, not the judaizers, Lütgert (*op. cit.*, pp. 31-34) sees a reference to this practice in the cult of Cybele, strongly entrenched in Galatia. These radicals have gone so far that Paul can wish they would proceed to castration, thus making perfectly clear what they really were—followers of a heathen cult.

kingdom of God. 'If we live by the Spirit (as you claim, and as I agree) by the Spirit let us also walk.' "

The letter is directed "unto the churches of Galatia."[17] Once his readers are addressed "O foolish Galatians."[18] Where was Galatia? Who were the Galatians?

The reason for this traditional problem is easily stated: During the fourth and third centuries B.C. Gauls from the west were invading the Italian and Grecian peninsulas. About 279 B.C. they made their way into the interior of Asia Minor and set up a small kingdom or, better, a robber state, where for fifty years they proved a scourge to the neighbouring tribes and controlled the great northern road from Ephesus to the Euphrates. In 189 B.C. Rome dealt them a severe blow; their independence was over, and for nearly seventy years the little kingdom was apparently dominated by Cappadocia and Pontus. Following the death of Mithradates Pompey completely reorganized Asia Minor. Galatia became a little buffer dependent kingdom made up of three parts. Deiotarus, the most capable of the three rulers, soon got all three parts into his power. His energetic secretary, Amyntas, who shortly after Deiotarus' death had been made king of Pisidia by Mark Antony (29 B.C.), contrived three years later to gain Galatia as well. To connect these two districts a large slice of Lycaonia was given to him. Upon his death (25 B.C.) his kingdom became the imperial Roman province of Galatia. During the years that followed, other districts were added to this province, notably Paphlagonia and Pontus Galaticus. Thus the Roman province of Galatia in the time of Paul was vastly larger than the original kingdom of Galatia; many of the provincials, especially those to the south, were not Gauls (Celts) at all, but Phrygians and Lycaonians.

Had we no information save that in the letter itself, probably no one would have doubted but what the old kingdom to the north, centring about Ancyra, was indicated. "Churches of Galatia" might conceivably, indeed, be the designation of those in any part of the entire Roman province, even those in such cities to the south as Pisidian Antioch, Iconium, Lystra, and Derbe, but the appelation "Galatians" would most certainly have suggested those who were such by race, not Phrygians or Lycaonians who chanced to be included in a purely artificial political unit.[19]

The problem is complicated by the accounts in Acts of Paul's journeys. On the so-called first missionary journey[20] he is described as working in these southern cities—Pisidian Antioch, Iconium, Lystra, and Derbe—and passing through Derbe, Lystra, and Iconium on the second journey strength-

[17] Gal. 1:2; cf. I Cor. 16:1.

[18] Gal. 3:1.

[19] The Roman province of Judea comprised Judea. Samaria, Idumea, and after the death of Agrippa I Galilee and the Perea. Would a writer to natives of Galilee or Samaria have been likely to address them as "O foolish Judeans?"

[20] Acts 13:1-14:28.

ening the churches in the faith.[21] On the other hand, there is no mention that he established any churches in, or, in the judgment of several scholars, that he even visited, that portion of the province which constituted the old kingdom. Hence these scholars concluded, partially from the silence of Acts, partially from the fancied improbability that Paul had pushed so far into the hinterland, that the churches addressed were those in these four cities. This is the South Galatian hypothesis.

Two passages in Acts bring further difficulties—16:6 ff. and 18:23. The natural interpretation of the former is that after they had been prevented from preaching in Asia they went through Phrygia and the Galatian region;[22] from here they emerged "over against Mysia," were prevented from entering into Bithynia, passed by Mysia, and finally reached Troas. These verses have been the object of frequent and heated debate, and are still far from clear. It is perhaps slightly more probable that they imply that Derbe, Lystra, Iconium, (and by implication Pisidian Antioch) were not in "Galatia," and that this latter region was not reached until Paul had been turned back from entering Asia—was it his original intention to go at this time to Ephesus and the other large cities of the Asian coast? On the basis of this hypothesis, he turned northeast somewhere between Pisidian Antioch and the Asian frontier, passed through Asian Phrygia into North Galatia (that is, the old kingdom). That Galatia was his objective is by no means certain. He may well have intended to push through to East Bithynia. If this reconstruction is correct and the churches to which our epistle was written were founded at this time and were accordingly not in those cities which he had previously visited in the south, his statement in the letter that it was due to sickness that he had preached to them first[23] may well indicate that he had intended simply to pass through this district on the way to other fields, but having been delayed by illness had utilized his enforced halt.

Acts 18:23 may be interpreted in either of two ways. For those who understand the southern part of the province of Galatia to be indicated by "the Galatic region," Paul repeated the course of his second journey and pushed on straight to Ephesus. On the other hand, although the order Phrygia-Galatia is here inverted and one difficulty removed, it appears more probable, since precisely the same odd phrase (in inverted form) "the Galatic region and Phrygia" is employed, that the author means that Paul traversed precisely the same districts (northern Galatia and Asian Phrygia) on this journey, too; that is, that instead of keeping south through Cilicia he pushed into Galatia via Cappadocia. On the basis of this interpretation

[21] Acts 16:1-5.

[22] *τὴν Φρύγιαν καὶ Γαλατικὴν χώραν*—lit. "the Phrygia(n) and Galatic region." Unless the word translated "Phrygia" be construed as an adjective "Phrygian" and the whole district be considered a single unit, the order Phrygia-Galatia is fatal to the South Galatian hypothesis.

[23] Gal. 4:13.

the reversal of the order Phrygia-Galatia in Acts 16:6 and 18:23 would correspond to the order in which these two districts were traversed on the respective journeys. The chief objection to the North Galatian view, which is here tentatively advocated, is neither the remoteness of the region, which is usually exaggerated—there is no need of assuming (with Lightfoot and the older scholars) that Paul traversed the whole region, but simply the western part of it, and founded a few churches, none of them far apart, during his enforced stay—nor the cumbersome "Galatic region" for "Galatia," which advocates of the South Galatian view loudly insist indicates territory added at a later date and thus quite distinct from Galatia proper; but the fact that Acts passes by in silence the founding of these churches, although stressing the foundation of other churches to the south to which we would then have no extant letters. This objection, although perhaps serious, is by no means fatal. Few will argue that Acts gives a complete account even of that portion of the story outlined. Several incidents, by no means unimportant, mentioned or implied in Paul's letters, are passed by in silence in the Acts account. Nor is it more surprising that we have no letter from Paul's pen to these churches in the south of Galatia than that we have none to Berœa or Laodicea or to churches in the "regions of Syria and Cilicia" where he laboured for fourteen years. Yet while none of the arguments against the view appears fatal, like its younger rival, it is confessedly only a hypothesis, but one which frees the interpreter from the necessity of performing several feats of linguistic legerdemain.[24]

There are few more completely baffling problems connected with the New Testament than the question of the date and place of composition of Galatians. The two are parts of but one problem and must be discussed together. The most widely divergent answers have been given. It has been considered the latest of Paul's letters, written from Rome;[25] in recent times it has been considered the earliest of Paul's letters, written shortly after the first missionary journey, either from Antioch or en route to Jerusalem. Others have dated it variously between these two extremes. Probably the question is insoluble; none the less, some light is cast on the letter itself and the probable chronology of Paul from certain considerations growing from the discussion.

It has often been maintained that prior to writing this letter Paul had once revisited the churches he had founded. This contention, which, while possible, is by no means as certain as has been frequently asserted, depends

[24] The whole problem may be studied in Schmiedel's excellent article "Galatia" in the *Encyclopedia Biblica*, cols. 1596-1618; Burton, *ICC Galatians*, pp. xvii-liii; Jackson and Lake, *Beginnings of Christianity*, Vol. V, pp. 224-240; and the several books by Ramsay, esp. *The Church in the Roman Empire, St. Paul the Traveler and the Roman Citizen, A Historical Commentary on St. Paul's Epistle to the Galatians.*

[25] Probably through misunderstanding of the words "I bear branded on my body the marks of Jesus" (Gal. 6:17).

upon two lines of evidence. (1) "But ye know that because of an infirmity of the flesh I preached the gospel unto you *the first time*."[26] It has been argued that the italicized words must be so rendered or by their equivalent, "the former time," and thus refer to the former of two visits. This is by no means certain. The exact phrase occurs in three other passages in the New Testament,[27] in each of which it certainly means simply "formerly," that is, at a time previous to that suggested by the context. If Paul had paid them two visits, his readers would have understood the allusion to be to the former of the two; on the other hand, if he had been there but once, the phrase would have been equally correct. His readers knew what he meant; we can only surmise. (2) There are several statements in the course of the letter which may be understood of a second visit[28] in the course of which Paul discovered traces of the difficulty which later took so alarming a turn as to necessitate the present letter. The most important of these passages are 1:9; 4:16,20; 5:3. They admit the possibility, perhaps even the probability, of a second visit, although they do not constitute absolute proof.[29]

Thus the possibilities for dating the letter are seen to be many. For those who hold the North Galatian view it must be subsequent to Acts 16:6, and accordingly hardly before the stay in Corinth,[30] for some time must be allowed for the rise of the schism and for Paul to have received word of it. If two visits are required—and most advocates of the North Galatian view so argue—the earliest date would be during the stay in Ephesus on the third journey.[31] For those who consider the churches of Galatia to have been the cities of Southern Galatia, a still wider latitude is possible,—if but one visit, any time after regaining Antioch at the end of the first journey; if two, then during the stay in Corinth on the second journey or at some subsequent time. But before considering these various possibilities in greater detail another point must be considered.

Acts mentions three visits of Paul to Jerusalem prior to the final tragic one that ended in his arrest and imprisonment;[32] Galatians but two.[33] Does the second visit mentioned in Galatians correspond to the one described in Acts as intended to relieve the famine in Jerusalem (*i.e.*, Acts 11:27-30 and 12:25) or to the one to attend the council (*i.e.*, Acts 15)? It has usually been identified with the latter. This makes Paul's silence regarding the

[26] Gal. 4:13.

[27] John 6:62; 9:8; I Tim. 1:13. Here the phrase τὸ πρότερον is not to be distinguished from the anarthrous πρότερον (John 7:50; II Cor. 1:15; Hebr. 4:6; 7:27).

[28] Burton (*op. cit.*) suggests the possibility of an earlier letter no longer in existence.

[29] A convenient discussion of their bearing on this point will be found in Burton's *Commentary, in loc. cit.*

[30] Acts 18:1-17.

[31] Acts 19:1-20:1.

[32] Acts 9:26-30; 11:27-30 (cf. 12:25); 15:1-35.

[33] Gal. 1:18 f.; 2:1-10.

Apostolic decree[34] surprising, since it would have been a most effective answer to those who considered circumcision essential. For those who understand judaizers from Jerusalem as the source of Paul's difficulty in Galatia, this silence is entirely incomprehensible. Again, the two accounts differ in almost every detail. Peter's conduct in Antioch is at least surprising if such a decree had been already passed; the silence of Paul even more so. Finally, Paul would thus entirely neglect his second visit to Jerusalem, and would lay himself open to the charge of having suppressed evidence regarding his contact with the Jerusalem leaders. This is particularly surprising in view of his heated statement (Gal. 1:20).

Accordingly, some have sought to escape these difficulties by identifying the second visit mentioned in Galatians with the second in Acts. Thus, they maintain, the letter was written before the visit described in Acts 15 took place. The arguments adduced are by no means convincing in the face of the fact that the one element in this visit which Acts mentions, namely, the famine relief, is unnoticed by Paul, while, on the other hand, the discussion with the leaders which Paul makes central is reserved in Acts for the later visit.

A third possibility is worthy of consideration. Between Jerusalem and Antioch there was a distinct rivalry still to be seen in Acts, however much the author has attempted to soften it down. In the traditions of each centre was the story of a visit of Paul from Antioch to Jerusalem. In its Jerusalem form it recorded the desire of the Antiochians to receive the approval of the one group, Jerusalem, which could settle points of practice. Paul had come from Antioch; the leaders from Jerusalem had listened to his statement and had given their verdict. In the Antiochian version the emphasis was quite different. Jerusalem was in financial distress because of an impending famine. The Antiochian Christians had graciously relieved their brethren to the south. Paul had gone not for advice but to bring relief. Confronted with these two distinctly different accounts, the author of Acts failed to recognize them as two accounts of the same story, but preserved them both, making of them different visits. To some this will appear a radical solution. That it relieves a distinct impasse is obvious. Nor would it be a unique assumption. Few will deny that similar situations are to be found not alone in the Old Testament, but in the New. That the stories of the Feeding of the Four Thousand and of the Five Thousand are doublets, and that accordingly such a passage as Mark 8:14-21 is primarily editorial, in order to articulate these two (to Mark) separate incidents, is scarcely open to question. Comparison of Acts 2:1-13 with 4:31, of 2:14-36 with 3:12-26, of 2:37-41 with 4:4, and of 2:42-47 with 4:34-37 will probably convince many that in the early chapters of Acts is evidence that the author

[34] Acts 15:28-29.

had at least two sources which duplicated one another, and that he employed both.

But this cutting of the Gordian knot which has commended itself to such scholars as Weizsäcker, McGiffert, Schwartz, and Lake entails certain consequences, as Schwartz pointed out.[35] Each of these visits of Paul to Jerusalem is followed by a missionary journey to which is prefixed a statement of the preaching of Paul and Barnabas.[36] In both journeys Paul and Barnabas start (or plan to start) together.[37] In both John Mark plays a rôle, and goes to Cyprus (once with Paul and Barnabas, once with Barnabas alone).[38] According to Acts 15:36 the second journey is to be a repetition of the first, and to a measure is until 16:6. Furthermore, no careful reader of Acts can fail to note the condensed ending of the first journey and the equally condensed beginning of the second. The narrative had been full and specific until the travellers reached Lystra and Derbe.[39] Then follows the bare mention of the return to Antioch. The statement, "And he went through Syria and Cilicia, confirming the churches. And he came also to Derbe and to Lystra,"[40] is equally abbreviated. Thus these would appear ground for the assumption that the first and second missionary journeys are in reality but one, and that they have been divided by the author of Acts into two with a return to Antioch intervening, because of his incorrect notion that Paul had twice visited Jerusalem. But that the actual history is to be recovered by simply removing these two editorial patches (Acts 14:21-28 and 15:36-16:1) and by assuming that while Barnabas returned after the quarrel to Antioch Paul continued on to Troas appears to me doubtful. That Luke rewrote his sources is certain, as is abundantly proved by his use of Mark. Had we not Mark, it is improbable that we would ever have realized it and certain that we would not have been able to have recovered the various sources, for Luke's method of composition was distinctly not restricted to the use of scissors and pastepot. But there are three points in the narrative that appear to be of prime importance: the quarrel with Barnabas, the selection of Silas as a travelling companion, the fact that upon their arrival at Troas the narrative becomes fuller and more convincing. That Paul quarrelled with Barnabas in Antioch is attested by Galatians.[41] It is far from impossible that this quarrel was the real source for the Acts story, and that on the basis of this incident and of his knowledge (or conjecture) that Barnabas and Mark had travelled to

[35] *Nachrichten von der königl. Gesellschaft der Wissenschaften zu Göttingen (Phil-historische Klasse)* 1907, "Zur Chronologie des Paulus," especially pp. 269-287. The whole brilliant essay is worthy of the most careful study.

[36] Acts 11:25,26 (cf. 13:1 f.) and 15:35.

[37] Acts 13:2 ff.; 15:36.

[38] Acts 13:5,13 and 15:37-39.

[39] Acts 14:21 ff.

[40] Acts 15:41-16:1a.

[41] Gal. 2:13.

Cyprus[42] while Paul and Silas had travelled through Asia Minor into Europe he revamped the story into two journeys, on the first of which Paul and Barnabas journey together in Cyprus and later in Asia Minor, at the outset of the second, quarrel over John Mark[43] and part. That Silas was with Paul in Europe is attested by allusions in Paul's letters.[44] Upon Paul's arrival at Troas the Acts account becomes dependent upon a source—the famous "We source"[45]—the primitive nature of which most critics have rated high. On the basis of these three points may it not be conjectured that from an earlier account of the parted ways of Paul and Barnabas, following their quarrel in Antioch—the former going with Silas into Asia Minor, the latter going with John Mark into Cyprus—the author has made a single journey of the two leaders to both places? Then because he mistakenly believed that Paul had again visited Jerusalem he follows the return to Antioch with a colorless epitome of the previous journeys of Barnabas and Paul, sending Barnabas with Mark back to Cyprus and Paul with Silas through the district he had already traversed. Paul must be brought to Troas where the "We source" starts. Luke has no especial incidents to recount about this journey of Paul and Silas through Asia Minor, for he has already described it, mistakenly substituting Barnabas for Silas.

That this is a radical reconstruction of the Acts narrative and by its nature can never be proved correct is obvious. That it will be regarded with favour by those critics who consider Acts in its present form the work of a companion of Paul and hence an essentially accurate account is improbable. To others, convinced by Luke's use of Mark in his gospel—the Gospel of Luke and Acts, it is to be repeated, are but parts of one narrative—that he exercised freedom in editing, revamping, and often rewriting his sources, this reconstruction may appear less arbitrary and to indicate in a general manner the source of the very obvious clash between the statement of Paul himself of his contact with Jerusalem and the stories of the visits which Acts was convinced Paul must have made.

Turning back to the question of the date of Galatians, it becomes evident that if this reconstruction be valid any date before the arrival in Corinth even for advocates of the South Galatian hypothesis is most improbable. Attempts to date the letter between the so-called first journey and the second are excluded, since there was no interval; the two journeys are built from elements of but one journey. That Paul reached Corinth in the spring of 50 A.D. and left in the fall of the following year appears highly probable.[46] For those who see the letter written to North Galatia after but one visit

[42] Cf. Acts 4:36.

[43] It is certainly interesting that Mark's defection which was the later cause of the quarrel took place hard by Pisidian *Antioch*. Is this due to confusion?

[44] Cf. I Thes. 1:1; II Cor. 1:19.

[45] See below, pp. 416 f.

[46] See below, pp. 246 f.

to the field this eighteen-month stay in Corinth is a not impossible time of composition.

On the other hand, the lengthy stay in Ephesus during the traditional "third" journey has seemed to most critics the most probable time of composition, and has much to commend it aside from the fact—in itself perhaps of doubtful value—that two visits to North Galatia are thus rendered possible. Evidence that Paul passed through trying days in Ephesus is not restricted to the cryptic word, "I fought with beasts at Ephesus."[47] It was while in Ephesus that he learned of the difficulties in Corinth, and from Ephesus that he wrote that severe letter "out of much anguish and affliction of heart."[48] He left Ephesus for Corinth with the deepest forebodings, for the issue was still undecided. Every critic has commented on the similarities between II Corinthians and Galatians. If one is inclined to conjecture an appropriate time for the composition, these months of anxiety just before leaving Ephesus could scarcely be improved upon. With Corinth ablaze with insurrection, word reaches him[49] that Galatia too is embroiled. Under such circumstances the tone of severity and anger is not surprising from the harassed and despondent man.

Again, there is a marked similarity between Galatians and Romans—not in temper, but in subjects treated. It would almost seem as if Romans were a cooler and more dispassionate restatement of many of the matters in Galatians. Especially is this true regarding the sections on the value of the Jewish Law. As will be shown in a later section, it is beyond dispute that Romans circulated at least in the second century in a different form from that of the present letter—without chapters 15 and 16 and without the specific allusion to Rome. That Romans as we have it was written from Corinth during Paul's final visit to that city in 55 A.D. is certain. It is tempting to conjecture if the first draft of that epistle—the shorter form without specific allusion to Rome—was not written shortly after Galatians, as a corrective to this passionate letter, in the course of which he had gone further than he normally would have done and had laid himself open to legitimate criticism. In the interim he had cooled down; word from Corinth had brought relief from his dread; perhaps a similar word had come from Galatia. This led him to a cooler, more dispassionate statement of his views—it is really his *confessio fidei*—intended to be sent throughout his churches, but especially to those in Galatia. At the same time, or perhaps a little later, he uses this as the nucleus for his epistle to Rome to prepare for his reception in a church for which he felt no personal responsibility—he had not founded it—but which he wished to visit on his trip to the west. That some such relation as this between Romans and Galatians is possible even

[47] I Cor. 15:32.
[48] II Cor. 2:4.
[49] That the distance was not too great to make communication easy is not to be disregarded.

if Galatians were written not from Ephesus, but from Corinth three years before, is not to be denied; yet the longer the interval between Galatians (and its subsequent cooler "second edition") and the Romans which we know, the longer Paul must be assumed to have carried this *confessio fidei* about with him.

Nor is there anything in Galatians itself which appears to indicate an earlier date.[50] All attempts to arrange the undisputed Pauline letters chronologically on the internal evidence of developing thought appear to me arbitrary and fruitless. For every such indication of either "early" or "late" date that one critic has discovered in Galatians, another investigator has found the reverse. Accordingly, perhaps as probable a date as any for Galatians is the summer of 54 A.D., just before his departure from Ephesus for Macedonia and Corinth.[51]

[50] That the words, "I marvel that you are *so quickly* removing from him that called you" (Gal. 1:6), imply that there was no great interval between the founding of the churches and the letter is far from certain. The words in question may be equally plausibly translated "so suddenly."

[51] It is not utterly impossible that there is confirmation of this date in the letter itself. Several scholars, notably Barton (*Journal of Biblical Literature,* 1914, pp. 118-126), understand the words "Ye observe days, and months, and seasons, *and years*" (Gal. 4:10) to refer to the sabbatical year. If 164 and 38 B.C. were both such years of rest, then 54 A.D. would apparently have been such also. (Barton reaches 53 A.D. through failure to observe that from 3 B.C. to 4 A.D. is not seven but six years.)

Chapter XVII

THE FIRST EPISTLE TO THE THESSALONIANS

THE circumstances under which this letter was written may be reconstructed with little difficulty. On the so-called second missionary journey Paul had arrived in Thessalonica from Philippi, where, as he wrote his Thessalonian converts, he had been "shamefully treated."[1] How long he remained in Thessalonica is perhaps not entirely clear. "For three Sabbaths" he is said to have argued with the Jews in their synagogue; then an uproar resulted and Paul and his companions were sent by night to Berœa.[2] That his stay in Thessalonica was limited to three weeks or even less as the Acts account suggests is most unlikely. Not only do the reference to having worked in the city—presumably at his trade—"that we might not burden any of you"[3] and the mention of his conduct while there[4] suggest a considerably longer period of residence, but the fact that during his stay in Thessalonica his friends in Philippi had at least twice sent him help[5] would seem unquestionably to demand a longer stay. That during his stay he had been successful in gaining converts is evidenced by his enthusiastic mention of their growing reputation "not only in Macedonia and Achaia, but in every place."[6] That these converts, as in Galatia, were largely, if not entirely, gentiles is clear from the word:

> For they themselves report concerning us what manner of entering in we had unto you; and how ye turned unto God from idols, to serve a living and true God, and to wait for his Son from heaven, whom he raised from the dead, even Jesus, who delivereth us from the wrath to come.[7]

Leaving Silas and Timothy in Berœa, Paul soon went south to Athens. Here he was rejoined by Silas and Timothy. From Athens he sent Timothy back to Thessalonica, having learned either from his companions or from some other source that difficulties had arisen for his new converts. After a short stay in Athens he proceeded—apparently with Silas—to Corinth, where he was later joined by Timothy. Our knowledge of this trip made by Timothy

[1] I Thes. 2:2; cf. Acts 16:12-40.
[2] Acts 17:1-10.
[3] I Thes. 2:7 ff.
[4] I Thes. 2:10 ff.
[5] Phil. 4:16.
[6] I Thes. 1:8.
[7] I Thes. 1:9-10.

back from Athens to Thessalonica comes from I Thessalonians. The Acts account entirely omits it. According to Acts, from Athens Paul sends word to his companions in Berœa to come "with all speed";[8] this they do, and meet him in Corinth.[9] I Thessalonians, however, enables us to correct the Acts account. Here we have the explicit statement that Timothy was sent from Athens.[10] Timothy has now returned to Paul;[11] his report leads Paul to write the letter. That Paul is writing from Corinth (not Athens) is made probable by his reference to "all that believe . . . in Achaia."[12] Not only has he made converts here, but has information about them. This would appear to exclude Athens.[13] Apparently Paul reached Corinth in the spring of 50 A.D.[14] Three months would appear ample time for Timothy's trip from Athens to Thessalonica, a brief stay in the latter city, and a return to Corinth. Our letter was written immediately upon his arrival in Corinth—"but when Timothy came even now unto us from you"[15]—hence most probably in the summer of the same year (50 A.D.).

Thus the occasion of our letter is the return of Timothy with his report. Perhaps Timothy brought a letter from the Thessalonian church. At least Paul's word that they had no need of being written to[16] suggests that they have written for information; while the word, "we *also* thank God without ceasing,"[17] implies that they have expressed thanks even as he is doing now. The nature of Timothy's report is clear from Paul's letter. The defence which Paul makes evidences the charges he has incurred. When he writes "For our exhortation is not of error, nor of uncleanness, nor in guile,"[18] it is not to anticipate the possibility of such charges, but to refute these actual calumnies. His enemies have made use of his months of absence to try to undermine his influence. His failure to return, they were saying, revealed that his pretended interest in his new gentile converts was simple guile. This he refutes by

[8] Acts 17:15.

[9] Acts 18:5.

[10] I Thes. 3:1-5.

[11] I Thes. 3:6.

[12] I Thes. 1:7.

[13] It would appear unwise to try to explain the divergence between the accounts in Acts and I Thes. by assuming that the author of Acts intentionally omits the arrival of Timothy and Silas in Athens, the expedition of the former to Thessalonica, and of the latter to some other place in Macedonia. Rather the author thought that Silas and Timothy did not rejoin Paul until in Corinth. I Thes. reveals that in this he was in error. The point should not be overlooked when considering the relationship of the author of Acts to Paul. Furthermore, if it be admitted that Acts has not simply dropped out one (to him unimportant) incident here, it does not appear necessary to assume that Silas was sent along with Timothy (but not to Thessalonica), simply because in Acts 18:5 *Silas and* Timothy are represented as coming to Corinth from Macedonia. Mention of Silas is due to the author's error on this point. Timothy was sent from Athens to Thessalonica; Silas presumably travelled with Paul to Corinth.

[14] See below, pp. 246 f.

[15] I Thes. 3:6.

[16] I Thes. 4:9; 5:1.

[17] I Thes. 2:13.

[18] I Thes. 2:3.

explaining that his absence had pained him as much as it had disappointed them. When he found he could not return as he had at first hoped, he had done the next best thing, had sent Timothy to them. The kind of life he had lived in Thessalonica was enough to enable them to distinguish between him and the occasional religious impostors who for impure purposes sought to make converts to this group or that. The actual results of his work were sufficient to prove absurd the contention that the gospel was a vain delusion. His gospel, on the contrary, had come unto them, as they very well knew, not in word only, but also in power.

The nature of these charges and the sharp outbreak in 2:15,16 suggest that while the actual opposition was from their fellow gentiles[19] the instigators of the charges were Jews. Not only were these opponents trying to undermine Paul's influence; they were indulging in active persecution of the little group of Christians. The enthusiastic tone in these first three chapters suggests that they had had no great success as yet; none the less, the fact that rather more than half the letter is devoted to refuting these charges indicates that Paul felt the danger acute.

The remainder of the letter—a reëmphasis of his instruction while with them—is directed to the rebuke of those tendencies which indicated the immaturity of their faith. The word, "And we exhort you, brethren, admonish the disorderly, encourage the faint-hearted, support the weak, be long-suffering toward all,"[20] suggests that there were three groups of Christians in the little community causing trouble: the disorderly, the faint-hearted, and the weak. The nature of each of these three is indicated in 4:11-12; 4:13-5:11; and 4:3-8, respectively.

The disorderly or idlers (ἄτακτοι), perhaps more adequately translated "loafers," would appear to be those who accepted Paul's word that the end was near and, accordingly, had lost what little inclination to work they had formerly had. They were to stop demanding that they be supported in idleness by the rest of the church and were to get to work. Their idleness laid an unnecessary burden on their brethren and furthermore exposed the group to reproach from non-Christians. To them Paul's word was curt and to the point. They were to calm down, that is, rid themselves of their feverish and unwholesome excitement about the speedy end of the age; were to mind their own business; and were to earn their own bread, and thus prove an example of what Christians should be.[21]

The faint-hearted (ὀλιγόψυχοι) were disturbed about their friends who had died since Paul had left Thessalonica. Would they not be deprived of their part in the coming glory when the Lord returned? Paul seeks to relieve this

[19] I Thes. 2:14. The mention of "Jews" makes this certain.
[20] I Thes. 5:14.
[21] I Thes. 4:11,12.

concern,[22] and at the same time strengthens their own confidence and uses this occasion to sound again the note which gentile Christians so sorely needed: the necessity of scrupulous purity of life.[23]

A problem peculiarly trying to a man like Paul with his Jewish heritage of horror at sexual impurity was the bland indifference with which many of his gentile converts regarded this matter. It is no coincidence that his strictures on faulty conduct regularly begin with a stinging attack on this point. It is accordingly highly probable that the weak (ἀσθενεῖς) are to be regarded not as those weak in faith, but those of vicious life.[24] They are to realize that their consecration to Christ entails scrupulous purity of life, "for God called us not for uncleanness, but in sanctification."[25]

Thus I Thessalonians is a typical letter. It is not intended for all Christians everywhere nor even for all of Paul's converts. It is directed solely to the Christians in the important capital city of Macedonia, and its contents are limited to those matters which will tend to make perfect what is still lacking in their faith. After the simple and unostentatious salutation[26] comes the customary complimentary paragraph of thanksgiving, omitted in the heat of Galatians. Then he meets the charges which his enemies, who are not themselves in the church, have circulated, and shows how unfounded they were. Then, turning to the weakness of some of the Thessalonian Christians, he urges purity of life, a quiet and helpful spirit of love, and an understanding faith in God's blessing soon to be revealed, which will relieve the apprehension of the folk for whom the death of their friends had raised theological doubts. With a few general admonitions to harmony and good order and a brief benediction the letter closes.

No serious challenge to the authenticity of the letter has ever been raised save by Baur and his followers, who reached their conclusion not so much from the nature of the letter as from their own a priori views of the kind of letter Paul must have written. No letter could be Pauline which did not represent him fighting tooth and nail against his judaizing opponents. There is no trace of this in the present letter, no impassioned defence of justification by faith, no marshalling of biblical quotations against the claims of his opponents. But the argument that the letter is insignificant and without aim refutes itself. The very fact that it has no ax to grind is the strongest proof of its genuineness, that it was not produced by one masquerading under the name of Paul and striving to gain the prestige of his name for views which he thus hoped to establish. The absence of argument in the letter is

[22] I Thes. 4:13-18.
[23] I Thes. 5:1-11.
[24] So Frame (*ICC I Thes.* 5:14), who quotes Theodore of Mopsuestia's apt comment: *de illis qui fornicatione deturpabantur.*
[25] I Thes. 4:7.
[26] Contrast that of Gal. 1:1-5.

due simply to the fact that Paul is not here assailing a false gospel, as, for example, in Galatians, but a rabid hatred of any gospel at all. A stronger argument might seem at first to lie in the surprising progress the gospel had achieved in Thessalonica during the comparatively brief interval between Paul's arrival in the city and the composition of the letter. But, as Frame rightly remarks,

> The fact that the fame of the little group has spread far and wide, that they have been hospitable to their fellow Macedonians, or that Paul has repeatedly desired to see them is proof not of the long existence of the community, but of the intensity and enthusiasm of their faith.[27]

To these words it might be added that in these complimentary references Paul may be very well applying the literary device advocated by members of the Roman bar of the previous century: Make your introduction of such a character that it will render your hearer favourably disposed to you, willing to be informed, and attentive.[28] Nor is the objection, occasionally advanced, valid that the juxtaposition of faith, love, and hope in the opening paragraph[29] evidences dependence upon the famous lyric I Corinthians 13. Similar occurrences of these three qualities in other letters[30] simply reveal his esteem for these virtues which constituted his nearest approach to a Christian register of virtues akin to the Platonic and Stoic tetrad, temperance, bravery, justice, and wisdom.

Nor is there legitimate ground to question the integrity of the letter. The view has occasionally been expressed that the denunciation of the Jews in 2:14-16 must be regarded in whole or in part a later interpolation; that its unqualified tone is in too great contrast to such a passage as Romans 9-11; and that the concluding words, "but the wrath is come upon them at last" [or, "to the uttermost"], imply the destruction of Jerusalem in 70 A.D. Such a conclusion is quite unwarranted. If every word in the Pauline letters which exhibited a different attitude of mind from every other word on the same general subject were to be considered suspect, we would have a distinctly shorter *Corpus Paulinarum*! Consistency may be a bright gem, but it is not to be found in the Pauline crown. Furthermore, the reference to the wrath by no means implies the destruction of Jerusalem. Rather, during his fifteen years or more of ministry he had experienced so often the opposition and hatred of his fellow countrymen that he had come to see them hastening on their way to certain destruction. It was their own rabid hatred of Christ and his gospel—God's plan for salvation—not Rome's battering-rams or legions,

[27] *Op. cit.*, p. 38. The student will find this balanced and judicious commentary of the greatest value. It is one of the truly excellent volumes in the *ICC*.

[28] Cicero, *de Oratore* ii,19,80—*Jubent enim exordiri ita, ut eum, qui audiat, benivolum nobis faciamus, et docilem, et attentum.*

[29] I Thes. 1:3; cf. also 5:8.

[30] Gal. 5:5 f.; Col. 1:4.

that spelled their doom. Nor is the other asterisked verse, "I adjure you by the Lord that this epistle be read to all the brethren,"[31] open to legitimate doubt. No more natural concluding word could be imagined. The loafers have intimated to the church that they will not hearken? Let them have this read to them!

[31] I Thes. 5:27.

Chapter XVIII

THE SECOND EPISTLE TO THE THESSALONIANS

IN CONTRAST to such letters as Galatians and I Thessalonians, which must be regarded as genuine if any letters at all are from the pen of Paul, for II Thessalonians the situation is distinctly different. Substantial grounds for considering it the production of a later Christian, writing in the name of Paul, exist and must be considered in some detail. Since, however, many competent critics still incline to regard it as Pauline, although they are aware of the difficulties, it is wise to sketch briefly the circumstances under which it must be assumed to have been written, if genuine, before considering the validity of the objections to the traditional view.

The occasion for the letter would be a second report from Thessalonica, shortly after the receipt of the former letter. This letter (I Thessalonians) had not accomplished precisely what Paul had intended. True, the charges against him of lack of interest had been refuted since no further word on that point is given. No mention of the morally "weak" would imply that Paul's word to them had been effective. On the other hand, the rebuke of "those that walk among you disorderly" would imply that the "loafers" had not heeded the former letter, perhaps had seen in Paul's reference to the nearness of the Parousia further justification for their own view of the folly of work in the interim. At any rate, the rebuke is very sharp:

> Now we command you, brethren, in the name of our Lord Jesus Christ, that ye withdraw yourselves from every brother that walketh disorderly, and not after the tradition which you [or, perhaps *they*] received of us. For yourselves know how ye ought to imitate us: for we behaved not ourselves disorderly among you; neither did we eat bread for nought at any man's hand, but in labor and travail, working night and day, that we might not burden any of you: not because we have not the right, but to make ourselves an ensample unto you, that ye should imitate us. For even when we were with you, this we commanded you, If any will not work, neither let him eat. For we hear of some that walk among you disorderly, that work not at all, but are busybodies. Now them that are such we command and exhort in the Lord Jesus Christ, that with quietness they work, and eat their own bread. But ye, brethren, be not weary in well-doing. And if any man obeyeth not our word by this epistle, note that man, that ye have no company with him, to the end that he may be ashamed. And yet count him not as an enemy, but admonish him as a brother.[1]

[1] II Thes. 3:6-15.

Thus the *occasion* for the letter would be the report from Thessalonica and the *purpose* of it the rebuke of these trouble makers who had not only not been chastened by their earlier reproof but had apparently distorted the letter to such a degree that others in Thessalonica—perhaps the faint-hearted—now had an additional worry: Had not Paul written them that the day had already dawned and they were thus unprepared for it![2] This led him to write the central section of the letter (2:1-12) in which he sought to make clear that his earlier statement had been entirely distorted and caricatured. Thus he would be saying in substance: Calm yourselves. The end is not here. You totally misunderstood me if that is what you think I meant. Before it comes several things must transpire. None of them has as yet taken place.

A brief description of the content of the letter will suffice. Following the salutation and greeting comes a paragraph of thanksgiving and prayer for the faithfulness of the community in their affliction, which affliction is to be regarded not as a sign of God's displeasure, but as a proof of God's acceptance of them as worthy of his kingdom. Not only is the tone cooler and less affectionate, but in the concluding words regarding the certainty of God's vengeance upon their enemies[3] is an intensity and vividness very near to gloating. Then follows, as the kernel of the letter, the section dealing with the Parousia.[4] It cannot have come already as some of you believe, for the man of sin (*i.e.,* Antichrist, who must first be revealed in opposition to "all that is called God") has as yet not been revealed. He is still being "restrained" by some one or something with which the Thessalonians are acquainted. Unfortunately, however, we do not share their knowledge; much has been written about this restraining agency—in the same breath Paul refers to it as both neuter and masculine[5]—but little known. Then after a repeated prayer for the steadfastness of his converts and the personal longing to be delivered from "unreasonable and evil men" he turns to the severe criticism of the loafers quoted in a preceding page. The letter closes with a twofold benediction, between which stands the final greeting, obviously intended as a ratification or seal of genuineness—"The salutation of me Paul with mine own hand, which is the token in every epistle: so I write."

If genuine, the date and place of composition would be the same as for I Thessalonians. He is still in Corinth; Silas and Timothy are still with him. In Thessalonica conditions are essentially unchanged. Persecution is still going on; the Jews are still the instigators of it. Yet it can scarcely be assumed that the second letter is written before he hears of the lack of success of the first. The section II 2:1-12 can scarcely be other than an explanation of the misunderstanding caused by the earlier letter, which latter would appear definitely referred to by the admonition that they "be not quickly shaken by

[2] II Thes. 2:1 ff. For the exact meaning of verse 2 see below.
[3] II Thes. 1:6-10. These words have been regarded by some critics as an interpolation.
[4] II Thes. 2:1-12.
[5] II Thes. 2:6 *τὸ κατέχον*; 2:7 *ὁ κατέχων*.

[an] epistle as from us." On the other hand, as will appear presently, the identity of structure and phraseology of the two letters would appear to preclude an interval of more than two months. After even so short an interval it is amazing *how* Paul could have so nearly paraphrased the earlier letter or *why* he should have desired to have done so had he possessed the ability. If I Thessalonians is to be dated from Corinth in the early summer of 50 A.D., II Thessalonians, if genuine, would appear most plausibly to have been written in the late summer or early autumn of the same year.

As was remarked at the beginning of this chapter, many competent critics have found themselves unable to consider the letter Pauline. The question turns on two points: (1) the nature of 2:1-12, and (2) the amazing similarity of this letter to I Thessalonians, of which it is at times scarcely more than a paraphrase. In 2:1-12 is found a view not only not otherwise found in Paul's letters, but in distinct clash with what he frequently implied and at least once explicitly stated: the near approach of the Parousia. About one point there can be no doubt: this section is not only an integral part of the letter—to remove it as an interpolation is to leave the rest of the letter purposeless—but the real reason for writing at all. If Pauline, it was to correct the misunderstanding engendered by the other letter; if by a later hand, to gain the support of Paul's authority for the view expressed.

There are obvious differences between I Thes. 4:13-5:11 and II Thes. 2:1-12, but the real difficulty is sometimes obscured. Some of the differences are patent: according to I Thes. 5:1-11 the day of the Lord will come unexpectedly as a thief in the night; according to II Thes. 2:3 ff. certain signs will precede the coming. This mention of these warning signs gives to the section the appearance of a regulation apocalypse. But this must not be unduly exaggerated. After all, there is no explicit statement that the interval before these signs appear will be a lengthy one, and in the realm of the apocalyptic the suddenness of the end and the appearance of portents and signs often go side by side. Thus the rendering in the American Revised Version, "Now we beseech you . . . that ye be not quickly shaken from your mind . . . *as that the day of the Lord is just at hand*,[6] is quite misleading. The words thus rendered in italics should read *"to wit, that the day of the Lord is (now) present*, or *has already set in*."[7] Thus, although it might be argued that II Thessalonians does not emphasize the long delay, as has sometimes been suggested, an even greater difficulty is introduced. Certainly there is no indication in any of Paul's writings that he had ever spoken in such a way as to suggest to his hearers that he thought that the day had already set in. How the passage in I Thessalonians which this section is apparently intended to correct could have given rise to such a misconception is by no means clear.

[6] II Thes. 2:1 f.

[7] That is, ἐνέστηκεν, which is quite different from "the day of the Lord *cometh*" (ἔρχεται I Thes. 5:2), or "the Lord *is at hand*" (ἐγγύς Phil. 4:5).

There is but one solution of this puzzle which appears to me at all probable. As will be argued in a later chapter, the necessity of shoving the expected return of the Lord further and further into the future might well have proved disastrous to Christian faith. Assuredly it did cause many a heartburn. What could be the reason for the tarrying of the bridegroom? It appears to me highly probable that one of the objects of the author of the Fourth Gospel was to provide a satisfactory answer to this question. And his solution was by no means an orthodox one. It was simply: You have been in error in your expectation that the Lord would return, or rather that he has not yet returned. The coming of the Comforter was the fulfilment of his promise. The Lord is here, has been here for nearly three-quarters of a century. Against this background the otherwise baffling II Thes. 2:1-12 is intelligible. The novel solution proposed by John did not win any general favour. The author of II Thessalonians, like many of his fellow Christians, has come to see that the end was not as close as had at first been expected, and in the mouth of Paul seeks to quiet perplexing doubt. You were wrong in expecting it to come too soon. On the other hand, he by no means agrees with the solution suggested by the Fourth Gospel. No, indeed, the day has not yet dawned. God still has it in store. This explanation is by no means free from difficulties, and perhaps will appear to some as fanciful in the extreme. It has at least the merit of recognizing the meaning of the words of the passage and of suggesting an explanation that really explains.

The point stressed by earlier scholars that the passage contains the so-called Nero Saga and is thus to be seen as later than Paul, coming from a time when it was believed that the then dead Nero would in the future appear in another man of fearful wickedness, has been shown to be without weight. The "man of sin" is not Nero *redivivus*, but the Antichrist. And it has been shown conclusively that the Antichrist legend was not only completely distinct from the Nero Saga, but actually antedated the Christian era.

In conclusion, probably few critics today would be inclined to challenge the authenticity of the letter solely on the basis of the views seemingly expressed in this puzzling section, although some might well feel that in this passage Paul has incorporated a pre-Christian apocalypse essentially as he found it. On the other hand, this section is not to be considered a zero factor. It does arouse suspicions, although alone it is not sufficient to raise the suspicions to reasonable certainty.

A far stronger argument is found in the matter of style and language. At first blush it might appear that the evidence favoured authenticity, for, save for the central passage 2:1-12, the vocabulary and phraseology are thoroughly Pauline. But this is vitiated by the obvious fact, admitted by all critics, that II Thessalonians, save for this one passage, is largely—slavishly is perhaps not too strong a word—a reproduction of I Thessalonians. Frequently the dependence is verbal. Yet though the phraseology is so similar, there is one remarkable change. The warmth and affection are absent; a far cooler tone and lack of feeling is felt. The impression is given that some other writer is striving so hard to imitate I Thessalonians that in the desire to reproduce the letter he has lost the spirit. To meet this situation it has been occasionally assumed by some critics that Paul had directed one of his companions, perhaps Timothy, to write the letter and had himself dictated the central portion. This view is superficially attractive. It is conceivable that Timothy might well have sought to make his composition sound Pauline by the use of earlier phrases, which he as a zealous follower remembered perhaps better than did the master himself. But the theory collapses from its own weight, for not only would Paul have then dictated the one passage that sounds so distinctly un-Pauline, but it is scarcely likely that he would have entrusted the composition of a letter intended to stay a threatened rebellion to any one else. Hence the obvious similarity in style and language is a very strong objection to the traditional view. As has already been remarked, it is amazing *how* Paul could have so nearly paraphrased the earlier letter or *why* he should have done so had he possessed the ability, since the earlier letter had manifestly failed in its purpose.

To Harnack these arguments have appeared compelling, but, convinced as he was that the letter was genuinely Pauline, he offered a different solution. The two letters were written at the same time to two different churches in Thessalonica, one gentile, the other Jewish. This, he argued, would account for the difference in tone and in content. The morally weak were among the gentile Christians; hence no such warning is given in II Thessalonians, which was intended for the smaller Jewish group. I Thes. 5:27—"I adjure you by the Lord that this epistle be read unto all the brethren"—to him demanded two groups which did not regularly meet together. Similarly in II Thes. 2:13 he discovered a reference to this Jewish group in the variant reading "as first-fruits" (ἀπαρχήν) which he preferred to "from the beginning" (ἀπ' ἀρχῆς). To the objection that the salutations are identical he countered that they had become stereotyped and that originally the latter had read "to the church of the Thessalonians of the circumcision," the last four words of which[8] had dropped out of the text early in the tradition of the epistle.

The suggestion is superficially attractive, but open to weighty objections. Perhaps the most serious of these is that there is absolutely no evidence for these two churches which he is thus forced to assume. Nor in the face of such a passage as Gal. 2:11-21 is it easy to conceive Paul's quiet and unprotesting acceptance of these two groups which daily set at naught his fundamental notion that in Christ there was neither circumcision nor uncircumcision. Furthermore, I find it very difficult to understand II Thes. 2:1-12 save as an answer and correction of the corresponding section in I Thessalonians. And

[8] τῶν ἐκ τῆς περιτομῆς.

again, why the formal authentication of the one letter[9] but not of the other? Thus instead of solving the riddle Harnack's solution has, in Jülicher's happy phrase, simply introduced new riddles in place of the old ones.

Thus an impartial examination of the evidence would appear to me to weigh heavily against the tradition of Pauline authorship. The later views of the Parousia are given Pauline support through a letter purporting to come from him. It can hardly be considered a coincidence that the letter which the later writer chose as his model was the one in which Paul treated the subject in a way which to the later writer might well appear to set the apostle forth in a wrong light. Certainly the references in II Thes. 2:2 and 15 to epistles of Paul, in the former of which a warning is given against being deluded by such, are not unnatural in the mouth of a later Paulinist. And finally, the verse already referred to, "The salutation of me Paul with mine own hand, which is the token in every epistle: so I write,"[10] appears to be a conscious attempt at authentication, in which the later writer, although influenced by Paul's occasional autograph greetings at the end of his dictated letters, failed to realize that for Paul these appended words were regularly the expression of his cordial relationship and due to his wish to give a final direct word with his own hand, but instead made of it a transparent effort to gain for his letter the authority of the dead master. Thus the letter would appear to be intended not for Thessalonians alone but for all Christians into whose hands it should fall. Who the author was and from where he wrote we shall probably never know. That it was written after Paul's death, perhaps in the early years of the second century, appears to me very probable.

[9] II Thes. 3:17.
[10] II Thes. 3:17.

Chapter XIX

THE FIRST EPISTLE TO THE CORINTHIANS

Of all the letters of Paul which have come down through the centuries the one we know as I Corinthians stands first as revealing not only the problems which confronted the first gentile Christians but the way in which the great apostle met them. Perhaps Romans yields a more orderly and detailed picture of his views—it is his *confessio fidei*—but it is I Corinthians which reveals him in the midst of what modern psychologists with their love for hyphenated words and notions delight to call "life-situations." Unlike Galatians, for which such questions as when, where, to whom are baffling, I Corinthians yields a ready answer to these queries. Furthermore the argument of the writer is reasonably clear as he seeks to bring the recalcitrant and rebellious church back into line. Nevertheless, when we seek to go below the surface and to discover the nature of the controversy which was fast alienating the church from the one who "had begotten them through the gospel," the matter proves amazingly obscure.

The city of Corinth was a rich and important seaport. The old city had been destroyed by Mummius in 146 B.C. A century later, Julius Cæsar brought out of its ruins the new *Laus Iulia Corinthus.* In 27 A.D., a quarter of a century before Paul arrived from Athens, it had become the capital of the province of Achaia. Its situation—it lay on the narrow isthmus between Greece proper and the Peloponnesus—brought much trade and shipping to its doors. By crossing the isthmus and reëmbarking on the other side the hazardous circumnavigation of the southern peninsula was avoided, no mean advantage in the days of sail. Thus it was the natural stopping-place for vessels from Asia Minor with cargoes for Italy and the west. As a result sailors from all lands were to be found in its streets. Its population was largely immigrant, and its name had become synonymous with luxury and vice. Alciphron remarked in his memoirs: "Never yet have I been to Corinth, for I know pretty well the beastly kind of life the rich enjoy there and the wretchedness of the poor." Temples to Magna Mater, Melkart, Serapis, Isis, and Aphrodite—this last is said to have housed a thousand sacred prostitutes—both attest the cosmopolitan nature of the city and suggest the reasonableness of the byword, "Not every man should go to Corinth."

From Athens, where, if the account in Acts can be trusted, he had not had any real success, Paul reached Corinth apparently in the spring of 50 A.D. That he had intended to make a lengthy stay in this city is by no means certain. I Thes. 3:11 would seem to indicate he had at first hoped to return soon to Thessalonica. Soon, however, he decided to remain in this strategic centre, and it was not until more than eighteen months after his arrival from the north that he left for Cæsarea via Ephesus. That all this time was spent in the city proper is improbable. The reference to "all that call upon the name of our Lord Jesus Christ, in every place"[1] and the more explicit "with all the saints that are in the whole of Achaia"[2] suggest that part of the time was spent in some of the other near-by communities. The brief account of his work in Corinth which is given in Acts states that he became friendly with Aquila and Priscilla, who had recently arrived in Corinth from Rome, but whether they owed their conversion to Paul is not indicated. Opposition on the part of the Jews broke out against Paul; eventually he was haled by them before the Roman proconsul, Gallio, brother of the famous Seneca. This move, however, according to Acts brought upon them only ridicule, for Gallio refused to interfere in what appeared to him a religious squabble between Jews. Not only is the Acts account very brief, but there are several puzzling obscurities. Following the statement that Gallio "drove them from the judgment-seat"[3] is the cryptic remark, "And they all laid hold on Sosthenes, the ruler of the synagogue, and beat him before the judgment-seat. And Gallio cared for none of these things." Who are indicated by "they all"? If, as appears probable, they were the disgusted Jews, what was the cause of their act toward the ruler of the synagogue? Did they think he had been a poor prosecutor? Had he become a Christian? What was his relationship with Crispus who was also "the [not *a*] ruler of the synagogue"?[4] Is he to be identified with "Sosthenes our brother" who joins Paul in saluting the Corinthians?[5]

This reference to Gallio is highly important as giving one reasonably sure fixed point for the Pauline chronology. An inscription at Delphi, in four fragments to be sure, but in the judgment of experts tolerably certain as to meaning, refers to Gallio as proconsul of Achaia and bears reference to the twenty-sixth acclamation of the emperor Claudius. An *acclamatio* was a complimentary decree passed at irregular intervals by the Senate in honour of the emperor. There might be several such in a single year. Since the twenty-second, twenty-third, and twenty-fourth acclamations all fell in the eleventh year of Claudius' reign—*i.e.,* between Jan. 25, 51 and Jan. 24, 52—most archæologists are inclined to reconstruct this Delphic inscription to read "in the twelfth year of his tribunican power"—unfortunately these particular words are not preserved—for we know that his twenty-seventh acclamation

[1] I Cor. 1:2.

[2] II Cor. 1:1.

[3] Acts 18:16.

[4] Acts 18:8.

[5] I Cor. 1:1. Is this another case where the assumption that the author of Acts knew the Pauline letters would tend to explain a puzzle?

was in the twelfth year and before Aug. 1, 52. The governors (proconsuls) of senatorial provinces regularly assumed office in the summer and were appointed for but a single year. Hence it would appear highly probable that it was in the July of 51 that Gallio appeared in Corinth. Although the Acts account does not explicitly state that Paul's trial was coincident with the arrival of Gallio—the Greek is colourless, "Gallio being proconsul"—nor at what part of the eighteen months it occurred, yet the natural run of the narrative is that it was toward the end of his stay in Corinth that Paul was haled before the newly arrived governor. If this is the case, his (Paul's) arrival in Corinth is to be dated in the spring of 50 A.D. He left Corinth some time after the trial (fall of 51) and returned to Antioch via Ephesus and Cæsarea. Aquila and Priscilla accompanied him as far as Ephesus. From Antioch he returned via Galatia to Ephesus and remained there three years,[6] *i.e.,* from the summer of 52 to the autumn of 54. During this stay he wrote the letter we know as I Corinthians a few months before he left Ephesus to revisit his churches in Macedonia and Corinth.[7]

That the letter was written from Ephesus is virtually certain, although it, like every other conclusion of New Testament scholarship, has been denied by some. Several allusions in the letter itself would seem to establish the matter. The words, "the churches of Asia salute you,"[8] imply that he was in Asia. Ephesus was apparently his Asian headquarters. The rest of the verse with its allusion to Aquila and Priscilla and "the church that is in their house" not only makes clear that he is in a place where Christians were to be found, but definitely implies Ephesus.[9] Again, the nature of the letter, as well as these definite references, would seem to require a certain amount of leisure; that is, it is hardly to be seen as produced en route. Thus the debated verse 16:5 is surely to be understood, "But I will come unto you when I shall have passed through Macedonia, for my journey must lead me overland by that route. Hence I will not arrive as soon as if I were to come direct to Corinth by sea." To understand the words to mean "I am *now* passing through Macedonia" appears pedantic and quite unnecessary. Surely the words, "But I will tarry at Ephesus until Pentecost,"[10] leave no room for doubt. Accordingly, the other word, "If after the manner of men I fought with beasts at Ephesus, what did it profit me?"[11] is not to be forced to mean that Paul has left Ephesus at the time of writing. Even the most accurate writers occasionally omit a "here" in such a statement. At any rate, the other

[6] The term "three years" (Acts 20:31) is not to be understood literally three full years. Actually Acts 19:8-10 suggests that it was two years and three months.

[7] The exact point in his Ephesian stay at which he wrote this letter is disputed. I am inclined to the latter part of the three years. I see no reason for assuming a long interval between I Cor. and II Cor. See further on this point pp. 258-260.

[8] I Cor. 16:19.

[9] Acts 18:18,19,26.

[10] I Cor. 16:8.

[11] I Cor. 15:32.

allusions are so clear that unless we resort to the hypothesis that the letter is not a unit but a combination of at least two letters written at different times—which hypothesis, though occasionally championed, appears to me quite unnecessary[12]—it would appear highly probable that the letter is to be seen as written from Ephesus during the last spring—before Pentecost[13]—which he spends in that city, that is, 54 A.D.

While much underlying our letter is obscure and debatable, one point stands out crystal-clear: it is but one of a series of letters between Paul and the Corinthian church which letters give in brief, to use Lake's phrase, "the history of a quarrel."[14] Furthermore, although tradition calls it *First* Corinthians, it is perfectly clear that it was not the first letter Paul wrote to the Corinthians, for he refers to this "previous letter" explicitly and intimates its contents—"I wrote unto you in my epistle to have no company with fornicators; not at all meaning with the fornicators of this world . . . but not to keep company, if any man that is named a brother be a fornicator, etc."[15] Unfortunately this letter is no longer extant, but there is considerable plausibility to the contention that a page of it is to be found in the midst of II Corinthians. The suspect verses—II Cor. 6:14-7:1—not only contain precisely this warning but seem completely out of place in their present location. One need but read II Cor. 6:11-13 + 7:2-4 to see how the intervening passage disrupts the thought.

Some time after he had sent this letter from Ephesus to Corinth he obtains further information about the church which seriously disturbs him. This information comes through persons referred to as "they that are of the household of Chloë."[16] That Chloë was a Christian matron of substance who resided in Corinth and who had sent word to Paul of the difficulty is usually assumed, but, while probable, is by no means certain. Her servants may of course have been in Corinth on business and have brought back home (that is, to Ephesus) word of the difficulty across the Ægean. Just what their report was constitutes the main problem of the letter. At all events, it indicated that the harmony of the Corinthian Christians was imperilled. Perhaps about the same time that "those of Chloë" brought their disquieting news three Corinthians—they are mentioned later in the epistle by name: Stephanas, Fortunatus, and Achaicus[17]—arrive with a letter in which Paul's advice on various matters is asked. The letter we know as I Corinthians is the result. The first part deals with the information received from "those of Chloë"

[12] See below, pp. 252 f.

[13] I Cor. 16:8. That is, he expected to get away shortly after Pentecost. Actually, he later found himself obliged to remain several months longer.

[14] *The Earlier Epistles of St. Paul,* p. 117. The whole chapter (pp. 102-252) should be read.

[15] I Cor. 5:9-13.

[16] I Cor. 1:11.

[17] I Cor. 16:17.

and rebukes the rebellious trouble-makers; the second part answers in order the questions raised by the Corinthians in their letter, but in such a manner as to continue the rebuke of the trouble-makers. Just before writing the letter, although he himself hoped soon to return to Corinth after his long absence,[18] he had sent Timothy overland, perhaps to the churches of Macedonia, and expected that he would eventually arrive at Corinth.[19]

As has been said, the nature of the trouble, that is, the identity of the trouble-makers, in Corinth is obscure. From I Cor. 1:10-17 it has often been argued that there were at least three, perhaps four, separate cliques or parties in Corinth, and that it is against them and the wrangling thus engendered that Paul is writing. Much has been written about the nature of the "party of Paul," "of Apollos," "of Cephas," and "of Christ." Since there is no scintilla of evidence, one's imagination could and did run riot. Since Apollos hailed from Alexandria, his "party" was comprised of the intelligentsia and those addicted to the vain "wisdom of the world." Those of Cephas were obviously the judaizers, and the changes were rung that it was by the name of Cephas, not Peter, that the leader was referred to. My own impression is that not only is this type of reconstruction sheer nonsense, but that these parties are far less important than has often been assumed. Rather, Paul is purposely exaggerating their importance in order not to attack too directly and explicitly the real cause of the trouble, *viz.,* the *pneumatikoi* or "spirituals." Only so can the nature of the questions discussed in chapters 1-4—chapter 2 is particularly to be studied—be accounted for. Does not 4:6 bear this out?

> Now these things, brethren, I have in a figure transferred to myself and Apollos for your sakes; that in us ye might learn not to go beyond the things which are written; that no one of you be puffed up for the one against the other.

Furthermore, the fact that in the later letters which we now call II Corinthians there is no mention of these parties by name would seem to substantiate this hypothesis. The difficulty long brewing has become so serious a menace that Paul quite forgets his earlier innocent subterfuge.

Thus the real trouble-makers were these Christians who had arrogated to themselves the title "spiritual" because of the superior spiritual gifts which they claimed. They could speak with tongues. They were free from the law, all law; and this vaunted freedom, precisely as we saw was the case with their brethren in Galatia, meant the right to do as they pleased. Thus with no regard—simply a feeling of contempt—for their weaker brethren or for what was in Paul's eyes fitting for one in Christ to do, they were doing as they pleased. Some were even leading flagrantly immoral lives. They had the Spirit. Paul was preaching foolishness. "Yes," retorted Paul in substance, "it is foolishness to immature babes, but it is wisdom to mature men who have

[18] I Cor. 4:18-21.

[19] I Cor. 4:17; 16:10. Is this trip the one referred to in Acts 19:22?

gained the true insight into the Christian mystery. You boast that you are spiritual! Actually you are nothing but men of flesh!" Then he continues in his attack upon their unfounded and absurd claims:

> Let no man deceive himself. If any man thinketh that he is wise among you in this world, let him become a fool, that he may become wise. For the wisdom of this world is foolishness with God. For it is written, "He that taketh the wise in their craftiness:" and again, "The Lord knoweth the reasonings of the wise, that they are vain." Wherefore let not one glory in men. For all things are yours; whether Paul, or Apollos, or Cephas, or the world, or life, or death, or things present, or things to come; all are yours; and ye are Christ's; and Christ is God's.[20]

This fancied superiority to all less gifted Christians and the resultant contempt for all restraints, in consequence of which Paul's preaching had seemed to them "in weakness, and in fear, and in much trembling," had shown itself in a sorry collapse in morals. In no uncertain tone Paul utters his rebuke. Actually a man—a Christian—is living in incest with his stepmother, a thing which even the heathen loathe, and you deluded folk actually glory in it, feeling yourselves superior to custom and decency, with your silly prating, "Free from the law." As I wrote you in my previous letter which you misunderstood, purge yourselves from evil and dissolute Christians. You cannot expect to have no contact with vicious folk in the outside world, but you can and must keep your own group clean. Put away the wicked man from among yourselves.

So dreadful in Paul's eyes is this type of conduct that after deprecating their lawsuits with one another—what a picture you are giving to the outside world!—he reverts to it again. Liberty does not mean licence. Fornication and its other beastly practices defile the body of Christ. When you are joined to a harlot, Christ is thus brought into this unspeakable infamy. Flee fornication; glorify God in your body.

Then in chapter 7 he turns to the questions which the Corinthians have propounded in their letter—"Now concerning the things whereof you wrote"[21]—but as he answers them he uses his answers to illustrate the lesson he is trying to drive home to his arrogant and blinded opponents. His insistence upon separateness and scrupulous purity of life had raised doubts in the minds of some of his converts about marriage, celibacy, and divorce. Might it not be better to have nothing to do with so dangerous a thing as marriage? At least, would it not be wise to dissolve such unions when a Christian found himself linked to an unbeliever? How about "virgins," that is, those men and women who had apparently taken certain vows of chastity and yet, while really "virgins," lived together in a sort of spiritual marriage? How about the remarriage of widows? To these queries his answer is clear.

[20] I Cor. 3:18-23.

[21] I Cor. 7:1; cf. the recurrent phrase in 7:25; 8:1; 12:1; 16:1,12. These would seem to indicate the scope of the questions propounded.

The end of the age is near. Stay as you are, if possible. But if unmarried and you find yourselves unable to control your passions, marry rather than lead lives of dissoluteness.

Another perplexing problem to the Corinthians, as it might well have been to all Paul's gentile converts, was involved in the matter of the "things sacrificed to idols," which meant, in a word, the use of any meat on a Christian table. As has already been remarked, practically all meat to be found in the butcher shops of a gentile city had been "consecrated" to some divinity or other. This might involve simply the burning of a few hairs from the animal's tail. But the question was no less acute. Many of the Corinthians, probably the large majority, were gentiles and had been heathen. Paul, like any other Jew, had insisted upon a complete break with heathendom. How could this be done if meat were still to be eaten? Naturally this was no problem for the spirituals. They were eating it with gusto, not only because it tasted good, but because it shocked the "weak." In his answer Paul develops his cardinal principle of forbearance. Though a thing in itself is innocent—as eating meat, save in the house of an idol, a heathen temple, which, of course, might never be done—it may cause a weak brother to stumble. Conduct, however innocent in itself it might be, which would encourage a fellow Christian to go against the dictates of his conscience was scrupulously to be avoided. Thus the arrogant cry of the spirituals, "All things are lawful," is only half the truth. Paul retorts, "All things are lawful *for me*, but not all things are expedient." To illustrate what he means, he calls attention to his own refusal to take advantage of his apostolic prerogatives.[22] Thus in the chapters that follow, where he is at pains to deal with questions incident to conduct in public meetings, this cardinal principle is the basis of the argument. "Knowledge puffeth up, but love edifieth"[23] is the key to the whole epistle. These innovations with regard to the conduct of women and the abuses in connexion with the Lord's supper are to be corrected. In all situations propriety is to be guarded. Thus spiritual gifts are to be judged solely on the basis of whether or not they edify other Christians. Wild speaking with tongues may be good for the man himself—and Paul bluntly tells his opponents who were priding themselves on their ability in this respect that in this he can far outdistance them[24]—but no one else gains value from it, and it may well bring the group into disrepute. Accordingly, the famed chapter in praise of love is not to be considered as an interpolation by a later writer, nor as a bit of poetry flung in here by Paul because of its beauty. Rather it forms an integral part of his argument. Precisely these "gifts of the spirit" which Paul is here subordinating, although they are good in themselves, as, for example, the ability to "speak with the tongues

[22] Cf. I Cor. 9:1-27.
[23] I Cor. 8:1.
[24] I Cor. 14:18.

of men and of angels," are those which the *pneumatikoi* are claiming arrogantly as their unique possession, while the qualities which make for love or evidence its presence, that is, the "fruits of the spirit," are precisely those qualities which his opponents lack so conspicuously.

Probably chapter 15 is to be understood as an answer to some query about the resurrection of the bodies of the individual Christians, although the customary formula, "Now concerning . . ." is absent. The doubt on this point expressed or implied by his gentile converts leads him to an elaboration of his view on this, to him, essential part of Christian faith. In the final chapter he gives directions—in answer to their query—for the making of the collection for the relief of the poor in Jerusalem, and then, after a few remarks regarding his plans, the mention of the hoped-for arrival of Timothy, and an answer to their question as to whether Apollos was coming from Ephesus or not, he concludes with brief greetings from his fellow Christians and a word of benediction.

Any detailed discussion of the authenticity of I Corinthians is here unnecessary. Its attestation is early and strong. Its use by Clement of Rome, Ignatius, and Polycarp is not open to question. Among other second century writers who quote and refer to it are Justin Martyr and Irenæus. Tertullian refers to it as written one hundred and sixty years ago.[25] To be sure, there is not any other Pauline writing by which we may test it, for there is no other letter which has a better claim to genuineness. Those who would deny Pauline authorship for this letter would be forced to deny that any authentic writing of Paul has been preserved. Yet the criteria for judgment are not simply negative. It is what it appears, a genuine and spontaneous attempt on the part of the absent apostle to deal with questions convulsing his church. Thus to see it as a mere collection of disjointed utterances or to deny its authenticity because it is not a systematic exposition of Pauline theology would be absurd. All scholars, regardless of their particular slants, save a few who deny that any of the New Testament writings antedate the second century, agree with the Tübingen scholars' axiom that I Corinthians is a genuine letter of the apostle Paul. And it may be remarked that this is one of the very few axioms about the New Testament which can be safely accepted.

With regard to the integrity of the letter the verdict of scholarship is much the same. Occasional fantastic analyses have been made in the effort to prove that it is a compound of various letters or that it has been violently rearranged. None of these efforts have shown even plausible reasons why such dislocations occurred. J. Weiss' attempt in his immensely valuable commentary, while not so wildly improbable as those of Hagge and Völter, has

[25] The full evidence is conveniently assembled by Moffatt, *Introduction to the Literature of the New Testament*, pp. 114-116.

failed to find much support from other scholars. It is not impossible that occasional passages from the "previous letter" have been included, but attempts to exhibit them have conspicuously failed. It has also been suggested that the letter, as we have it, may be a sort of second edition of Paul's correspondence, edited by himself; that is, that he has assembled it from earlier letters. But this, too, appears to me destitute of proof. It would be well nigh a miracle if the letter were entirely free from later scribal glosses, and reasonable grounds for doubt of an occasional verse or fraction of a verse have been shown, but they are by no means calculated to shake one's confidence in the state of preservation of the text as a whole. That when the various letters were later assembled for more general use some modifications were made is of course possible; that any considerable evidence, however, of such alterations occurs I have not been able to discover.

Chapter XX

THE SECOND EPISTLE TO THE CORINTHIANS

As HAS already been pointed out, I Corinthians was but one letter in a somewhat extended correspondence between Paul and the isthmus city. Between the sending of that letter and the composition of the one traditionally known as II Corinthians a great deal had taken place. Although these events are entirely ignored in the Acts account—this is but another indication of how fragmentary that narrative is, even during the period it essays to chronicle—there are clues in the correspondence itself which would seem to allow a reasonably sure reconstruction. It is necessary to indicate briefly the main points in these later developments, for without this setting the letter, at once the most personal and perplexing of all the Pauline epistles, would be quite baffling.

Already two letters have been sent to Corinth by Paul from Ephesus: the so-called "previous letter," referred to in I Cor. 5:9 and of which a page is probably preserved in II Cor. 6:14-7:1; and our I Corinthians. Paul himself had been the recipient of at least one letter from the Corinthian Church. Some time before sending off I Corinthians he had sent Timothy on a mission, and expected him to reach Corinth eventually, but not before the letter, which would be sent direct.[1] The curious fact is that there is no reference whatever in the later letters to Corinth of this visit; yet Timothy has returned in the interim, for he is joined with Paul in the salutation of II Corinthians.[2] The explanation, that this silence suggests that Timothy was prevented from reaching Corinth, is scarcely probable. Some word of apology or regret would have been expected in that case. Rather the silence seems studied and intentional. The natural explanation is that Timothy's visit had been unsuccessful, and that those who had been "puffed up as though [Paul] were not coming"[3] had not been overawed by even his "beloved and faithful child in the Lord." At any rate, when Paul next sent a messenger to them it was not Timothy, but Titus.[4] It is of interest to observe that Titus and "the brother" who accompanied him are highly and tactfully recommended.

Another of these interim details is important. At least two passages in the last chapters of II Corinthians apparently indicate that Paul had visited

[1] I Cor. 4:17; 16:10.
[2] II Cor. 1:1.
[3] I Cor. 4:18.
[4] II Cor. 8:16 ff.; 12:17 f.

Corinth between his first arrival in that city from Athens and his final visit after having left Ephesus. The two passages read:

> Behold, this is the third time I am ready to come to you.[5]

> This is the third time I am coming to you.[6]

The meaning is clear; Paul has already visited Corinth twice. The only problem is the date of this otherwise unrecorded visit. Was it before I Corinthians or after it? Most interpreters incline to the latter hypothesis. Two passages in I Corinthians apparently look forward to a visit which he anticipates will be painful for him and them:

> Now some of you are puffed up, as though I were not coming to you. But I will come to you shortly, if the Lord will; and I will know, not the word of them that are puffed up, but the power. . . . What will ye? shall I come unto you with a rod, or in love and a spirit of gentleness?[7]

> And the rest will I set in order whensoever I come.[8]

Furthermore, II Cor. 2:1 implies that this visit has taken place and that, as expected, it had been a stormy one:

> But I determined this for myself, that I would not come *again* to you *with sorrow*.[9]

A final detail of this reconstructed interim history is even more significant. II Corinthians mentions a very severe letter which Paul had written "out of much affliction and anguish of heart . . . with many tears; not that ye should be made sorry, but that ye might know the love which I have more abundantly unto you."[10] After he had written this letter, obviously in a temper—whether godly or otherwise—he had feared he had been too severe and had destroyed the possibility of reconciling his church. He had left Ephesus in anxiety: "I had no relief for my spirit, because I found not Titus my brother."[11] Surely this description excludes both our I Corinthians and the "previous letter." Furthermore, II Cor. 2:5 ff. indicates that in this letter he had levelled his attacks at one of the Corinthians, apparently the ringleader of the opposition. This too excludes I Corinthians, for there is no such individual held up to attack. As will be indicated in a later page, he cannot be identified with the man guilty of incest. Accordingly, it is usually felt that another letter, usually dubbed the "severe letter," was

[5] II Cor. 12:14.
[6] II Cor. 13:1; cf. also 13:2.
[7] I Cor. 4:18-21.
[8] I Cor. 11:34.
[9] II Cor. 2:1. The order of the Greek makes clear that he had come once "with sorrow."
[10] II Cor. 2:4; cf. 7:8 ff.
[11] II Cor. 2:13.

written from Ephesus between I and II Corinthians, and was sent by Titus.[12] The real question is not whether there was such a letter—it is obvious that there was—but whether it has been preserved.

There are several weighty reasons for feeling that the last four chapters of II Corinthians (*i.e.,* chaps 10-13) are a part of this intermediate "severe letter." The identification rests on two lines of argument.

First, there is a complete change of tone between chapters 1-9 and 10-13. Each section is a coherent and orderly unit. There is an absolute hiatus, however, between them. This fact is universally admitted, although the explanations of the phenomenon differ. From the opening words to the end of chapter 7 no reader can fail to feel the tone of joyful relief. The dreaded catastrophe had been averted.

> Great is my boldness of speech toward you, great is my glorying on your behalf: I am filled with comfort, I overflow with joy in all our affliction.[13]

> Therefore we have been comforted: and in our comfort we joyed the more exceedingly for the joy of Titus, because his spirit hath been refreshed by you all.[14]

In this relief now that the crisis is past he is like a father talking to his child who has been required to take extremely unpleasant medicine. The pain is gone; therefore the father can reëmphasize that he had "done it for their good," that it "hurt him more than it did them":

> For though I made you sorry with my epistle, I do not regret it: though I did regret it (for I see that the epistle made you sorry, though but for a season), I now rejoice, not that ye were made sorry, but that ye were made sorry unto repentance; for ye were made sorry after a godly sort, that ye might suffer loss by us in nothing. For godly sorrow worketh repentance unto salvation, a repentance which bringeth no regret. . . .[15]

The air is now clear; the storm is passed. In his relief at Titus' favourable news he forgets the difficulties he has passed through—anxiety for his church in Corinth and perhaps in Galatia;[16] actual physical violence, at least danger in Ephesus,[17]—and reaches almost lyric heights in 4:7-18. Now he can

[12] That Titus was the bearer seems evident from a comparison of II Cor. 2:13 with 7:6 ff.

[13] II Cor. 7:4.

[14] II Cor. 7:13.

[15] II Cor. 7:8 ff.

[16] See below, p. 259.

[17] Cf. II Cor. 1:8 ff. What was this "sentence of death"? Is it to be identified with the experience underlying the cryptic word, "If after the manner of men I fought with beasts at Ephesus, what doth it profit me?" This can hardly refer to an actual fight in the arena, for even doughty Paul could scarcely have escaped. Could a Roman citizen have received that sentence? Certainly not without subsequent loss of citizenship. If he had escaped, would it not have been a natural item to have been included in the famous catalogue of sufferings (II Cor. 11:23-29)? Is it to be understood (as the Greek allows) as a condition contrary to fact? Is it (like II Cor. 4:7-18; Rom. 7; Gal. 3:4) to be understood of the condition a Christian must expect to encounter in his glorious but desperately hard struggle in this world, a world which lies under the overlordship of Satan; that is, as a sort of paradigm of life? It is easier to ask the questions than to answer them.

see behind the present difficulties and perplexities of life the glorious evidence of God's plans and purposes. The Corinthians, at least a majority of them, have swung to his side and have become eager to champion him against his opponent. In this state Paul can afford to be magnanimous to his discomfited rival, and at the same time strengthen his own position with the others by implying that the man's action actually had been against *them*, not against Paul.[18] It need hardly be remarked again that such an attitude toward a man guilty of incest is quite improbable, especially in view of his earlier judgment.[19] Then in the last two chapters (8 and 9) he reverts to the matter of the collection which he has long been planning as a gift to Jerusalem on his return to that city. This matter bulked large in Paul's eyes. It is perfectly natural, now that the rebellion is over, that he reverts to it. The awkwardness and repetitious nature of this section is not to be explained on the basis that we have here fragments of other letters, but simply as due to the fact that Paul always felt self-conscious when called upon to raise money, and especially so to the Corinthians who, he apparently felt, might easily misunderstand his motives.

Then suddenly without warning, after this friendly and in sections exalted state of joy, in chapters 10-13 the whole tone changes. The clouds gather, and from his opening words to the close the tone is that of severity and biting sarcasm. The section is scarcely more than an impassioned defence of himself and a bitter attack upon his unruly and disobedient church.

To conceive of this as a conclusion to chapters 1-9 after the battle is won is to me preposterous. If this is actually a part of his letter of forgiving happiness, what sort of jeremiad must the "severe letter" have been which had led him to fear he had written too sharply? To try to explain this change of tone on the basis that our II Corinthians is too long to have been dictated at a sitting and that in the interim his feelings had changed—perhaps he had had a sleepless night or was suffering from bad news from some other church or from indigestion—appears to me conspicuously ill-advised, if not actually puerile.

In the second place, not only is there clear evidence of a distinct break between chapters 1-9 and 10-13, but real reason for feeling that the latter section was written before the former and, in short, is part of the letter referred to in the former. Three passages in each of these sections appear to be intimately connected; but in each case the one from chapters 10-13 is in the present tense, while the corresponding one in chapters 1-9 is in the past tense and appears to be reminiscent of it. Although these passages have often been referred to in earlier discussions, it may be well to print them again in parallel columns. Only so can the impressive nature of the evidence be felt.

[18] II Cor. 2:5-11.

[19] I Cor. 5:3 ff. For a fuller discussion of the probable meaning of these verses see my *Ethics of Paul*, pp. 149-154.

10:6—And being in readiness to avenge all disobedience, when your obedience shall be made full.	2:9—For to this end also did I write, that I might know the proof of you, whether ye are obedient in all things.
13:2— . . . if I come again I will not spare.	1:23— . . . to spare you I forbare to come [*lit.* came not again] unto Corinth.
13:10—For this cause I write these things while absent, that I may not when present deal sharply . . .	2:3—And I wrote this very thing, lest, when I came, I should have sorrow . . .

In addition to these passages there is constant reference in chapters 1-9 to the "severe letter," each mention of which appears most apt as a description of 10-13. A few examples will suffice. The words, "Are we beginning again to commend ourselves?"[20] and "We are not again commending ourselves to you,"[21] certainly imply that he had previously done precisely that. Few will deny that from beginning to end chapters 10-13 fulfil that description, with their emphasis upon his ability, his position as one "not a whit behind the very chiefest apostles," and the list of his heroic sufferings. Furthermore, the visit to Corinth which he was contemplating when he wrote these blistering pages (cf. 12:20 f.; 13:1 f.,10) but which he did not make is adequately explained by the reference to his later change of mind (1:15, 23 ff.). Thus a very strong case may be made for identifying chapters 10-13 as a part of this earlier "severe letter," that is, the hypothetical *III Corinthians*.[22] That it comprised the whole letter, as was argued by some of the older scholars, is improbable. Not only does it appear but a fragment, but the letter must have contained an attack on the "one who hath caused sorrow." This section, in view of his later repentance, along with probably other especially caustic paragraphs, may well have dropped out of sight (as did almost all the "previous letter") in the interval of more than half a century before they came into more general circulation.

These incidents or details connect to form a perfectly intelligible story. Shortly before writing I Corinthians Paul sends Timothy to Corinth. He returns with gloomy news. Paul's letter has not accomplished its purpose. The divisive spirit has increased; distinct hostility to Paul is being felt. In this crisis Paul at once embarks for Corinth. The distance was only 250 miles. With the prevailing north and northwest trades the voyage in either direction need not have taken more than four or five days. The brief stay

[20] II Cor. 3:1.

[21] II Cor. 5:12.

[22] For convenience they may be so designated: I Cor. (the "previous letter"); II Cor. (our I Cor.), III Cor. (the "severe letter," partially preserved in II Cor. 10-13), and IV Cor. (II Cor. 1-9).

in the city was highly unsatisfactory. His presence simply added fuel to the flames already blazing. His personal authority seems to have been openly questioned, his ability sneered at. One of the Corinthians seems to have led the opposition, and have been backed up by many of the others. He could not remain long, even if it had been wise. In Ephesus, too, things were reaching a crisis. In pain and chagrin he returns to the Asian capital. Hardly has he disembarked before he determines to make one more effort. He dictates an impassioned and blistering letter to the recalcitrant Corinthians. That the real trouble-makers in Corinth were not judaizers nor addicts of "Alexandrian philosophy"—whatever that popular phrase may be understood to mean—but the pneumatikoi, as we saw was probable in I Corinthians, is confirmed by II Corinthians. There is no mention of the necessity of circumcision or keeping of the Mosaic law. Rather he defends himself in scandalized indignation against such taunts as the inability to perform miracles or that he was not blessed with the ecstatic gifts. This letter he sends post-haste by Titus. If, as was suggested in a previous chapter, it was about this time that he wrote Galatians, it is tempting to wonder if Paul's mental unrest was not perhaps heightened by learning on his return from Corinth of the defection in Galatia. With Ephesus enflamed against him, beset to the east and west by churches determined to involve themselves in folly, one could well understand the state of mind that prompted the resultant two letters—the "severe letter" to Corinth, the equally excited letter to the foolish Galatians. That Galatia and Corinth were ablaze at the same time is, of course, simply a hypothesis—better said, a guess—although one which appears to the present writer by no means improbable. At least it is to be remembered that many scholars have commented on the similarity of tone—although not of content—in II Corinthians and Galatians. Apparently he dallied with the idea of returning by sea to Corinth, from there to make a flying trip to Macedonia and back to Corinth, thence by sea to Jerusalem. At least it is difficult to interpret II Cor. 1:15 ff. in any other way. But this plan he gives up. Instead he decides to go by the land route through Macedonia and so to Corinth. This will allow time to hear from Corinth;[23] it will also relieve him of the necessity of making the round trip from Corinth to the north. At any rate, with opposition against him blazing in Ephesus he left that city with heavy heart.

While still in Macedonia[24] Titus rejoins him with the good news. The trouble is over. The Corinthians have swung back to Paul, although there is not unanimity of opinion as to the punishment of his antagonist. This unexpected good news—apparently he had come to despair of the Corinthians—prompts him to write them again, this time in a very different vein.

[23] It is by no means impossible that he was still uncertain as to whether he would go to Corinth or not.

[24] II Cor. 7:5 indicates he had arrived; 9:4 suggests he had not yet left; else he would have known whether or not "any of Macedonia" would accompany him.

Titus, who had proved strong where Timothy was weak, is sent back to Corinth with this letter. Paul himself followed after concluding his work in the northern churches, for apparently he did not expect at that time to return to them, but to go from Corinth direct to Jerusalem and then to Rome and the far west.

On the basis of this reconstruction which appears to satisfy all the data at our disposal, if I Corinthians was written in the spring of 54 A.D., there appears to be no reason against dating the "severe letter" from Ephesus on his return from Corinth a few months later, that is, in July of the same year. To be sure, that would require Paul to remain in Ephesus longer than Pentecost. But all that I Cor. 16:8 states is that in the early spring he did not see how he could get away before that time. Later he finds himself still more delayed. Leaving Ephesus in the late summer he proceeds via Troas to Macedonia, there to be met by Titus. That this meeting and the writing of II Cor. 1-9 (from Macedonia) was in November 54 A.D. appears probable if we can rely on the account in Acts. In the highly condensed account in Acts 20:1-6 we learn that Paul spent three months in Greece—that is, of course, Corinth—and then returned to sail from Philippi to Troas "after the days of unleavened bread." Thus if he was back at Philippi in time to leave after the Passover and had spent three months in Corinth, the time of arrival in Corinth would appear to be in December or January, the writing of II Cor. 1-9 some six weeks or two months earlier, hence November. The Acts account further indicates an additional change of plan. Because "a plot was laid against him by the Jews as he was about to set sail for Syria" from Corinth, he changed his plans and took the longer overland trip via Macedonia and Asia Minor. It has been often assumed that this plot was engineered by the Jews in Corinth. Just how such hostility would have led him to abandon the comparatively safe method of sea travel for the dangerous overland journey during which he might easily have been ambushed is difficult to see. It is tempting to wonder if the plot was not laid by Jews in Thessalonica or Philippi, not against Paul personally, but against the welfare of those local churches, and that the reason for Paul's shift of plan was to enable him to go to the seat of the trouble to strengthen his converts against them, not to flee to save his own skin.

Such seems to be the main outline of these letters and the general progress of the quarrel and its happy outcome. Thus II Corinthians would appear to be a composite letter made up of fragments of at least three letters. Some scholars have argued that chapters 8 and 9 formed originally a separate letter or perhaps two letters, and that thus parts of four or even five letters are to be seen in our composite; but, as has already been remarked, this latter conclusion appears to the present writer unwarranted.

But while there are weighty reasons for questioning the integrity of II Corinthians, the authenticity of all the parts is almost universally accepted, although, contrary to I Corinthians, evidence of its use by writers prior to Marcion is not impressive. Nevertheless, the style, language, tone, and type of thought cannot reasonably be questioned. In fact, while a perfectly natural outburst from Paul while on the firing-line, it would be very difficult to suggest any reason which a later writer might have felt for putting such a word in the mouth of the departed hero. It should be remarked that the able critic Jülicher, who is skeptical towards all partition theories for II Corinthians, is inclined to question the authenticity of the fragment 6:14-7:1 and to view it as a later interpolation.[25]

A final word may not be out of place. The question may arise: How could these several letters have been incorporated as one? It must be remembered that when written most of Paul's letters were directed to and intended for local groups only. It was not until long after his death that an effort was made to gather them and to make them available for a wider audience. In the interim some—perhaps many—of his letters had disappeared; some of those that had remained were no longer complete. They probably had been written on papyrus. Even if the sheets had originally been glued to join short rolls, it is certainly not incredible that in the course of the years they might have occasionally been torn, separated, or misplaced. Thus a letter like the "previous letter" appears to have disappeared, all save a fragment which was misplaced among the sheets of other letters. (It is to be observed that II Cor. 6:14-7:1 would just about fill a separate papyrus sheet.) While a long letter like I Corinthians would make a complete roll when copied on papyrus or vellum (parchment), such a letter as II Cor. 1-9, being shorter, would scarcely fill up such a roll. What more natural than that the few pages of the "severe letter" which had been preserved—it is surely easily conceivable now that the quarrel had long since been healed that the more personal sections had disappeared—should have been copied on to fill up the roll? Chronological order was not the important thing. Anything from the pen of the departed hero would be prized. In the process of this copying the sheet from the "previous letter" (II Cor. 6:14-7:1) had become misplaced and was thus embalmed in the wrong place. This is not simply theory. We have definite evidence that such combinations and displacements not infrequently occurred, for example, in the correspondence of Cicero. That it occurred at an early date is evident from the fact that all the extant manuscripts attest the union.

[25] Jülicher-Fascher, *Einleitung in das Neue Testament,* 7th ed., pp. 87 f. This suggestion was not made in the earlier edition which was translated into English.

Chapter XXI

THE EPISTLE TO THE ROMANS

AT FIRST blush the historical questions about this epistle—to whom, when, and from where written—seem relatively simple. If the letter left the pen of Paul, or his scribe Tertius,[1] as we now have it, they are simple. The letter is addressed distinctly "to all that are in Rome, beloved of God, called to be saints."[2] A few verses further, in the paragraph of compliments, he continues: "So, as much as in me is, I am ready to preach the gospel to you also that are in Rome."[3] The recipients of the letter would appear thus definitely and clearly defined.

In 16:1 he refers to "Phœbe our sister, who is a servant of the church that is at Cenchreæ," that is, the eastern port city of Corinth. And since Phœbe is being recommended to the hospitality of the readers—

> that ye receive her in the Lord, worthily of the saints, and that ye assist her in whatsoever matters she may have need of you: for she herself also hath been a helper of many, and of mine own self[4]—

it is scarcely to be doubted that he is writing this commendation from Corinth as she starts her voyage. Furthermore, this is confirmed and dated by his full statement about the collection which is now ready for delivery to the Jerusalem poor:

> But now, I say, I go unto Jerusalem, ministering unto the saints. For it hath been the good pleasure of Macedonia and Achaia to make a certain contribution for the poor among the saints that are at Jerusalem. Yea, it hath been their good pleasure; and their debtors they are. For if the gentiles have been made partakers of their spiritual things, they owe it to them also to minister unto them in carnal things. When therefore I have accomplished this, and have sealed to them this fruit, I will go on by you unto Spain.[5]

The collection is ready; Paul is about to deliver it. From the Corinthian correspondence we know that this was not accomplished until his final visit to Corinth, that is, after II Cor. 1-9. That such a letter as Romans was written en route to Jerusalem is scarcely to be considered seriously. Thus

[1] Rom. 16:22.
[2] Rom. 1:7.
[3] Rom. 1:15.
[4] Rom. 16:2.
[5] Rom. 15:25-28.

it would appear clear that the letter was written from Corinth during his three-month visit, that is, early in 55 A.D.

But the matter is not so simple, after all. For more than a century—David Schulz first raised the objection in 1829—many critics have felt unable to accept chapter 16 as an original part of the letter, although all extant manuscripts carry it. The chapter, it is said, is most unsuitable for Rome. Arguments for and against the hypothesis have been many and voluminous. It will be sufficient to consider the two chief difficulties. (a) The chapter comprises a long list of greetings to Paul's personal friends. Is it probable that at Rome, a city he had never visited, he should have had so many friends, with several of whom at least he is manifestly on intimate terms? Again, among them are several whom we should scarcely expect to meet in Rome. For example, Epænetus is "the first fruits of Asia unto Christ."[6] Priscilla and Aquila are greeted. To be sure, they had originally lived in Rome, but had left that city at the time of Claudius' edict and after a stay in Corinth had removed to Ephesus.[7] Nor are we dependent alone upon Acts. They are referred to, together with "the church that is in their house," in I Corinthians,[8] which we saw was written almost certainly from Ephesus. In II Tim. 4:19 greetings are sent to them. It is improbable that II Timothy is a letter by Paul. None the less, it apparently reflects a belief that at the time when it purports to be written this couple was still in Ephesus, for the letter purports to be written from Rome to Ephesus.

(b) The other difficulty is perhaps even greater. Between the long list of personal friends to be "saluted" and the salutations from eight of Paul's companions[9] stands a most surprising section.

> Now I beseech you, brethren, mark them that are causing the divisions and occasions of stumbling, contrary to the doctrine which ye learned: and turn away from them. For they that are such serve not our Lord Jesus Christ, but their own belly; and by their smooth and fair speech they beguile the hearts of the innocent. For your obedience is come abroad unto all men. I rejoice therefore over you: but I would have you wise unto that which is good, and simple unto that which is evil. And the God of peace shall bruise Satan under your feet shortly.[10]

This reference to the teaching they had learned naturally suggests the teaching they had learned from Paul, while the polemic seems far more fitting if directed to a group of his own churches for whom he is responsible than to a group of strangers, to whom he is writing to allay suspicions and to reveal himself in his true colours, not to interfere nor to exercise lordship "in other men's labors."

[6] Rom. 16:5.
[7] Acts 18:2 f., 18 f., 26.
[8] I Cor. 16:19.
[9] Rom. 16:21-23.
[10] Rom. 16:17-20.

Suffice it to say that if this chapter were not attached to Romans, it is safe to say that in spite of the lack of any specific salutation and the fact that of course Phœbe could have been recommended to one church as well as to another, no one would have dreamed of questioning that we have here a letter of introduction of the Cenchrean Phœbe to the Christians in Ephesus. There is, however, no manuscript evidence that this letter ever existed apart from Romans. Furthermore, the real difficulty is the absence of any plausible explanation of how such a letter to Ephesus was eventually attached to one to Rome. Again, it may be said that although Aquila and Priscilla had settled in Ephesus it is to be remembered that their real reason for leaving Rome was to escape Claudius' displeasure. Claudius was now dead—the date of his death was Oct. 13, 54—and the edict was hence no longer in effect. They may well have returned to their former home. Perhaps some of those whom Paul salutes may have belonged in their household and thus have returned with them. Thus the evidence is hard to evaluate. If the problem stood alone, it would probably be wise, although with some misgivings, to accept the chapter as a real part of the letter to Rome, rather than to attempt to invent explanations of the later curious marriage.

But this problem is intertwined with another and more important one. This problem can be stated without difficulty: the difficulty is to solve it. There is clear evidence that our epistle once existed in a shorter form which omitted chaps. 15 and 16 (with the possible exception of the final doxology, 16:25-27) and with no mention of Rome in 1:7 and 1:15. The evidence for this latter point may be indicated first. The bilingual manuscript Gg substitutes "in love" for "in Rome" in 1:7 and omits the words in 1:15. Furthermore, the very valuable minuscule 1739, in which the text of Romans was copied not from the exemplar of the manuscript but from the *Commentary* of Origen—now unfortunately extant only in the Latin translation of Rufinus—has a scribal note to the effect that the words "in Rome" were not in his original.

Although no manuscript of this shorter recension (without chapters 15 and 16) exists, the fact that such a form was in existence at a very early date and was widely used is indubitable. (a) In his *Commentary*, referred to in the preceding paragraph, Origen states that Marcion cut away everything after 14:23.[11] As the text of his comment shows, it is not clear precisely what he meant by "cut away," since it apparently is to be differentiated from "completely removed" (*penitus abstulit*).[12] Apparently, however, the

[11] *Caput hoc* [*i.e.*, Rom. 16:25-27, the passage Origen is annotating] *Marcion, a quo scripturæ evangelicæ atque apostolicæ interpolatæ sunt, de hac epistula penitus abstulit: et non solum hoc, sed et ab eo loco ubi scriptum est "omne autem, quod non est ex fide, peccatum est"* (that is, 14:23) *usque ad finem cuncta dissecuit*—Migne, *Patr. Græca* xiv,1290A(687).

[12] For further discussion of this point and the other textual problems see Lake, *The Earlier Epistles of St. Paul*, pp. 335-350, and Moffatt, *Introduction to the Literature of the New Testament*, pp. 139-144.

text of Romans which Marcion used ended with 14:23, but that he was responsible for the abbreviated form is not so certain. (b) Of even greater significance is the witness of the so-called "capitulations" or chapter headings found in many manuscripts of the Vulgate.[13] These chapter headings, which give a sort of table of contents or brief epitome of the epistle, divide the letter into fifty-one sections. The fiftieth reads as follows:

> Concerning the danger of injuring one's brother by one's meat, and that the kingdom of God is not meat and drink but righteousness and peace and joy in the Holy Spirit.

That this is an epitome of Rom. 14:15-23 is, of course, obvious. Equally clear is it that the next capitulation, the fifty-first,

> Concerning the mystery of God kept in silence before the passion but manifested after his passion,

can refer only to 16:25-27. Hence the text from which these capitulations were made—that it is far older than the Vulgate is evidenced by the wording—did not contain 15:1-16:23 (24). (c) Furthermore, it is probable that such was essentially the text of Irenæus, Tertullian, and Cyprian, who, although they quote the rest of Romans constantly, do not quote from these chapters. In fact, Clement of Alexandria and Origen are the only ante-Nicene fathers to quote from Rom. 15-16. Nor can it be said that 16:1-16,21-23, would not have offered natural material for quotations. In Cyprian's catalogue of Scripture enjoining holding aloof from heretics surely 16:17-20 would have been a natural addition had he known it. It is also to be remarked that not only do we fail to find any quotation from these chapters in Tertullian, but that the letter once refers to Rom. 14:10 as *in clausula*, which can only mean "at the end," that is, in the last section of the letter.[14] (d) And finally the uncertainty of location of the doxology, 16:25-27. Some manuscripts have it after 16:23,[15] others after 14:23, others in both places, still others in neither, while finally the recently discovered Chester Beatty papyrus containing the Pauline letters (𝔓[46]) places it at the end of chapter 15, that is, after 15:33.

The evidence, which I have barely listed, is quite sufficient to establish the fact that at an early date two versions of Romans existed, one essentially[16]

[13] Berger, *Histoire de la Vulgate,* refers to forty-eight.

[14] For this evidence I have made free use of the volume by Lake, already referred to, which not only conveniently summarizes but evaluates the evidence.

[15] 16:24 is certainly to be omitted. Its proper place is 16:20, although one type of text, which did not contain 16:25-27, transposed it to stand after 16:23 to end the epistle. In some other Mss. it occurs after 16:20 and also *after* the doxology; in a few inferior and late Mss. after 16:20 and also *between* 16:23 and the doxology. This latter very poorly attested and utterly improbable reading was adopted by Erasmus and preserved in the *Textus Receptus* and hence in the King James Version.

[16] The reason for the qualification "essentially" is that there are weighty reasons which have made several competent critics (including Jülicher and Moffatt) suspicious of the Pauline

as we have it today, the other with no reference to Rome and without chapters 15 and 16. So much is reasonably clear; the problem consists in explaining the rise of these two rival forms. Four possibilities exist in theory at least.

(a) Paul wrote it essentially as we have it, and it was later shortened by some one else for doctrinal or liturgical reasons;
(b) Paul wrote it essentially as we have it, and later shortened it himself to give it a more general character;
(c) Paul wrote the short recension, and it was later added to by some one else;
(d) Paul wrote the short recension, and later added the other material and inserted the specific references to Rome.

Of these four possibilities both (b) and (c) seem most unlikely. The former would necessitate the view, occasionally expressed even today, that Paul later edited his earlier correspondence to adapt it for general circulation. This notion is destitute of evidence, and runs counter not only to Paul's clearly expressed view of the nature of his mission, but also to the chronological facts of his life. Nor is the other view, that chapter 15 is by another hand, at all probable. There is no break in thought between chapters 14 and 15; rare indeed would be the skill of the later falsarius. Furthermore, it appears to me most improbable that a writer after Paul's death should either put into his hero's mouth the expectation to visit the west at a time when history had shown that such was not realized, or reëmphasize the ministration at Jerusalem which had had such a sorry result. On the other hand, the first alternative is by no means impossible, and is maintained in some form or other by the majority of writers. Marcion's name is often suggested as the one who shortened the text. That he edited drastically the canon of Christian writings he accepted is well known. Due to his anti-Semitic attitude he sought to divorce Christianity not only from Judaism but from the Old Testament. His hero Paul's writings were purged here and there to remove those sections wherein Paul spoke too enthusiastically regarding Israel as the people of God. Hebrews and the Pastoral Epistles he omitted probably on critical grounds. An expurgated form of the other ten Pauline letters, together with the Gospel of Luke, comprised his Scripture. A plausible case can be presented for the view that Origen's famous

nature of the doxology. The insecurity of position, the formal and liturgical ring of the words, the reference to "my gospel" all incline me to see this as a later (but comparatively early) addition to the text, perhaps when the various Pauline letters were first assembled for more general use. On the other hand, the fact that 𝔓[46] places it after 15:33 is not to be disregarded. Does this suggest that it was added to both versions (*i.e.*, with and without chapter 15) and that when chapter 16 came later to be copied in the same roll it was transferred to the end of this addition? I must confess that this reading of 𝔓[46] to a measure lessens my own suspicions with regard to the genuineness of the doxology.

remark meant, not that Marcion had explained away or whittled away by one means or other the substance of these verses—had that been the case surely Tertullian would have pounced upon it—but that he had definitely shortened the text. But the difficulties raised by this hypothesis are many. This version was widely circulated and in the most orthodox circles. Would the work of the archheretic Marcion have been so received? Just why this section should have displeased Marcion is hard to see. An occasional verse—"For I say that Christ hath been minister of the circumcision for the truth of God, etc."—might have disturbed him, but there is more pro-Jewish material earlier in the letter. And what was his objection to "in Rome"? Again, any explanation of the short recension must include the problem of chapter 16. The two problems, I am convinced, are intertwined. If it was actually written by Paul to recommend Phœbe *to Rome*, and was thus a part of the letter, it is hard to see the ground for Marcion's objection to it. On the other hand, if not an original part of the letter, we are still confronted by the difficulty already referred to—how did this letter to Ephesus get attached to a letter to Rome? In the face of these difficulties, I could accept this solution only as a last hope, that is, if no other solution offered itself. And such is not the case.

The fourth alternative, that the short recension was the earlier, has much to commend itself. That it is far from impossible that it was intended as a sort of follow-up letter, written after his first concern and chagrin at the bad news from Galatia had been relieved, and to tone down the rash and exaggerated statements in the earlier letter (Galatians), has already been suggested in the chapter devoted to Galatians.[17] Now in Corinth which had swung into line—perhaps word of a similar change of heart from Galatia had arrived—he penned this cool and balanced statement of his views. Not only would it be valuable in Galatia; it was almost equally appropriate for any of his churches. It would be particularly valuable in Ephesus, as a stay and support to the Christians there, harried as they were by their opponents. Whether Paul had several copies made for Asia Minor—one for the churches of Galatia, others for Ephesus and its neighbouring cities—or whether the messenger to Galatia stopped in Ephesus to allow for the letter being read is debatable. I am inclined to the former guess, that is, that to chapters 1-14—the original letter, intended for all his churches in Asia Minor—he appended the introduction of Phœbe and the salutation of his Ephesian friends (chapter 16) *in the draft intended for Ephesus.* At about the same time he feels it wise to communicate with Rome. Although he is not responsible for that church, he nevertheless hopes to visit it soon on his way to evangelize the west. It will be of distinct value to correct any mistaken notions those Christians may have received from rumour or malicious misstatement. What more appropriate word could he write than this matured

[17] Pp. 231 f.

and carefully phrased *confessio fidei*? Thus he directs Tertius to make another copy—this time with a distinct mention of Rome—and himself adds a few more paragraphs amplifying his views regarding the mutual responsibilities of Christians, and making clear his purpose in coming to Rome (chapter 15). This is simply a hypothesis—the same is to be said for every other explanation of the complicated problem—but it appears to me a by no means impossible or even improbable one.[18]

But whether the letter was written fresh for Rome or was a partially revised copy of a letter intended primarily for other Christians it fitted the situation admirably. It is not to be interpreted so much as a polemic against those who had poisoned the Roman Christians' minds as a prophylactic against such propaganda. It is not to be considered a tract; it is a genuine letter, although of a quite different character from the intensely personal Galatians or letters to Corinth. It is far more carefully wrought out. To be sure, Paul did not think of it as becoming Scripture, but it may be hazarded that he did not expect it to be read casually and then thrown in the waste-basket.

Following the salutation, words of greeting, and thanksgiving (1:1-15), comes the body of the letter. This latter falls into two main divisions 1:16-11:36 and 12:1-15:33. The former of these is argumentative and expository, expressing in full and precise form his mature belief regarding the Christian mystery of salvation; the latter is hortative—since this is so, it behooves us to live in a fitting way.

In 1:14 f. he has declared his obligation to God to preach the gospel and in keeping with this his desire to preach it to them in Rome. Then in verses 16 and 17 he defines the gospel in precise terms and states his thesis—the rest of the letter is simply an orderly expansion of these words—

> For I am not ashamed of the gospel: for it is the power of God unto salvation to every one that believeth; to the Jew first, and also to the Greek. For therein is revealed a righteousness of God from faith unto faith: as it is written, But the righteous shall live by faith.

This righteousness is not something imparted (or imputed) to the Christian—that is, that he is not made to *merit* salvation—but rather through certain great redemptive acts God has made it possible for man to enter into right relation with him (God), that at the final assize he may stand acquitted. All this, however, is made possible through the Christian's union with Christ. In a word, his faith in Christ is actually a new life which he has apprehended.

Following this thesis, he argues that this proffered salvation is a salvation offered to all, and that more than that it is the only way. (The old-

[18] This is very similar to the somewhat more complicated solution advocated by Renan.

fashioned hymn, "There is no other way but his way," catches Paul's exact emphasis.) All men everywhere are under the wrath of God, and rightly, because of their wickedness. This applies alike to gentile (1:18-32) and to Jew (2:1-3:20). The former did not have the Mosaic law to guide him—better said, to warn him. None the less he is without excuse, for in his conscience was the unwritten law—the capacity, that is, to recognize at least partially the essential obligation of moral law—as surely engraved as was for the Jew the Mosaic law on the tables of stone.[19] But though all have failed, God has made this redemption possible through the death of his Son, through union with whom all may be acquitted. The one condition is faith, that is, newness of life in Christ; but this does not do away with the Law. Actually it establishes it. The Scripture teaches unmistakably that Abraham was justified by faith and that circumcision was given not as a means, but later in the sealing of the covenant that had already been made on the basis of his faith.

Then in chapter 5 he shows the Christians' ground for rejoicing:

> Being therefore justified by faith, we have peace with God through our Lord Jesus Christ; through whom also we have had our access [by faith] into this grace, wherein we stand.[20]

That is, the Christian's own experience of new peace, with the age-long antagonism and warring in his conscience now at an end, reveals and attests the truth of the teaching. Next, he raises and answers the all-important question: What is this "faith in Christ" which I mean? His answer to this query extends through 8:17. Then in the concluding words of chapter 8 is the almost lyrical expression of the sense of safety and joy that such assurance inspires, ending in the magnificent thanksgiving:

> Nay, in all these things we are more than conquerors through him that loved us. For I am persuaded that neither death, nor life, nor angels, nor principalities, nor things present, nor things to come, nor powers, nor height, nor depth, nor any other creature, shall be able to separate us from the love of God, which is in Christ Jesus our Lord.[21]

Then follows the problem of Israel's unbelief and rejection (9:1-11:36). This certainty of salvation which God vouchsafes to all men is by no means contradicted by the fate of Israel. God *has* rejected them—here he meets squarely the national objection of the Jew that this salvation should have come to the Jews: they were God's chosen people—but it was because of their unbelief, and after all was but temporary. Every potter has the right to make from his clay the sort of vessels he chooses, be they for honour

[19] For a fuller discussion of the place the unwritten law occupied in Paul's thinking see my *Ethics of Paul*, pp. 102 ff.

[20] Rom. 5:1 f. The reading, "let us have peace," although it has high manuscript support, is surely wrong.

[21] Rom. 8:37-39.

or dishonour. Thus this rejection is not to be construed as a sign of God's lack of justice; its cause was Israel's attempt at justification through works rather than through faith. To lack of understanding was added wilful disobedience. Yet not all Israel has gone astray; a faithful remnant has been chosen out. And again, the rejection was but temporary. God has made use of Israel's failure, and has thus been enabled to bring in the gentiles; yet it is still possible for Israel—or rather for those who remain—again to be grafted in, "and so all Israel shall be saved."[22] This figure of the wild olive grafted into the old stump is not wholly a matter of history for Israel. It contains a very pertinent warning for gentile Christians. Eternal vigilance is the price of success. "If God spared not the natural branches, neither will he spare thee!"

In many ways the argument in this whole section is laboured and unsatisfactory to modern thought. The figure of grafting wild olive branches into the stump of the cultivated tree is hardly such as to commend itself to horticulturists—Paul is never happy in his use of figures;—while the figure of the potter and the clay, although hallowed by usage, is equally unsatisfactory, since in the modern emphasis upon the rights and dignity of men—which heady draft has been copiously drunk today—many are unwilling to be treated as clay in any one's hands, even God's. Thus to the query, "Thou wilt say then unto me, Why doth he still find fault? For who withstandeth his will?" the answer, "O man, who art thou that repliest against God?" appears a complete begging of the question. Logic has broken down. The proper answer appears to us, "He should not." But it should be remembered that Paul had not been emancipated. Notions of a finite God, the pleasing speculation of twentieth-century humanism, had not been born. For him God was still God. If we allow him his postulates, his conclusions do not appear so completely forced or painfully perverse.

Thus through the whole first section of the letter the emphasis continues: There is no other way than his way, that is, faith. There is no security except through a constant abiding life in Christ. Otherwise, even those who feel themselves so secure will be cast out.

With 12:1 begins the hortatory and so-called "practical" section. To regard it as a sort of appendix of loose, disjointed admonitions after the main work of the epistle is over is to miss the point utterly. Far from being an appendage, it is the capstone to the whole argument. Since God has provided this way, at infinite cost to himself, it behooves men to live in a fitting and proper manner both within the community and to the world at large; that is, in his own words:

I beseech you *therefore*, brethren, by the mercies of God, to present your bodies a living sacrifice, holy, acceptable to God, which is your spiritual service.[23]

[22] Rom. 11:26.

[23] Rom. 12:1.

Thus his challenge finds its fulfilment in this series of crisp, short admonitions which evidence the kind of life that the man who is in Christ must of necessity live. The imminence of the final great day was an added spur to righteous living. Then follows the matter of the "strong and the weak." Here the matter is most obscure. It does not appear to reflect the same situation as that evidenced in the letters to Corinth, that is, the question of whether or not one should eat meat which has been offered to idols. Rather, it has apparently to do with the kind of food appropriate to Christians. As in the epistle to Corinth, Paul limits his advice to the moral side of the matter. Forbearance is the quality demanded. One must not let his acts keep a brother away from Christ. Meat is not worth that. But in addition to the danger of those who had faith to eat meat despising those whom they dubbed "weak," was the equal danger that those who were scrupulous in these matters should exercise unchristian and censorious judgment over the more liberal group. The whole section with the fitting conclusion (15:1-13) is one of the choicest and most beautiful pleas for tolerance and lack of censorious judgment. Then with a brief and more personal word, to which is appended a statement of his plans and his reasons for writing to the Romans (15:14-33), he brings the letter to a close. To this letter, as he apparently framed it for Rome, stands now chapter 16 with its lists of salutations (16:1-16) and greetings (16:21-23) interrupted by the sharp word of warning against sowers of strife (16:17-20), and the formal (probably sub-Pauline) liturgical doxology (16:25-27).

The epistle, then, is not to be seen as an attack upon judaizers or even Jews; rather, it is a calm and deliberate statement, made possible in part by his years of opposition from the ranks of Judaism. It is, if one may use a modern phrase which would have been entirely unintelligible to Paul, as near an approach to the philosophy of Christianity as the doughty and unphilosophical apostle to the gentiles could frame.

How far it was called into being by the exigencies of the church at Rome will depend upon the view taken as to the origin of the epistle. At any rate, the tone is cool and unprejudiced. The law is spoken of in a quite different fashion from the heated epistle to Galatia; yet although he admits that the advantage of the Jew is great—as he could do only with careful qualifications in the former letter—he never compromises. The impotence and need of *all* men, Jew and gentile alike, is remedied solely through faith in Christ.

Since I am inclined against the view that the letter was planned with Rome in mind (but rather was later adapted to the need of the moment there), it appears to me most unwise to search the epistle for clues as to the nature of that church. It may perhaps be said that since some passages (as 1:5, 13-15; 11:13 f.; chapters 7-11) strongly suggest that the readers were primarily, if not almost entirely, gentile, it might be construed that had the Roman church been otherwise Paul might have felt such a letter not particularly appropriate. Further guesses, however, appear to me unprofitable. The style of the epistle is often that of the diatribe, that is, in the then popular form of public address, replete with crisp, staccato phrases in which the writer to make his argument the clearer represents himself in a dialogue with an imaginary interlocutor. Thus it is surely not the Roman (or the Galatian) Jew whom he addresses: "But if thou bearest the name of a Jew, and restest upon the Lord . . ."[24] He is simply answering the objections which opponents might logically raise to his Christian readers as they had so often done to him personally in the past. Although the letter provides far less sure material for the reconstruction of the history and make-up of the church at Rome than used to be argued, it remains an invaluable source of knowledge for the thought of the one who penned it.

[24] Rom. 2:17.

Chapter XXII

THE LETTERS OF THE CAPTIVITY AND THE HYPOTHETICAL EPHESIAN IMPRISONMENT

In contrast to the six letters already discussed stand four other letters which for many years have been grouped together and considered coming from a later stage in Paul's life, at a time when he was no longer free to move about as he chose. These four—Philippians, Colossians, Ephesians, and Philemon—are commonly styled "the letters of the captivity." Colossians and Ephesians are very intimately connected in many ways, and must be regarded as penned at the same time if both are genuine. Nevertheless, Philemon and Colossians are also inseparably joined. The word of quiet dignity with which Colossians ends, to refer to but one passage—

> The salutation of me Paul with mine own hand. Remember my bonds. Grace be with you[1]—

is sufficient evidence that in these three letters Paul is now, in a literal sense, a "prisoner for Jesus Christ." But it is no less clear that a similar condition must be assumed for Philippians. Not alone the general tone of the letter, but the words,

> Now I would have you know, brethren, that the things which happened unto me have fallen out rather unto the progress of the gospel; so that my bonds become manifest in Christ throughout the whole prætorian guard,[2]

leave little room for doubt.

But that this demands that these four letters must therefore be later than the other six is by no means certain, although this is ofen assumed. The reason for the assumption, however, is clear. But two captivities or lengthy imprisonments of Paul are referred to in Acts, the two years in Cæsarea and the two years in Rome. Hence, it is usually argued, these letters must not only be later, but several years later, since most critics have felt that certain indications in the letters themselves definitely exclude Cæsarea. Then much has been made of the so-called more developed thought, particularly in the case of the Christology, in these letters. Many of these findings are probably exaggerated and secondary. It is probably fair to say that the strongest argument for Rome was the weakness of the argu-

[1] Col. 4:18.
[2] Phil. 1:12 f.

ment for Cæsarea. But for most scholars this argument, although essentially negative, was convincing. It is to be observed, however, that this line of reasoning is rendered valid only by the assumption that the narrative in Acts is essentially complete and accurate. If there should be reason to feel that Paul had suffered more imprisonments than the two therein related, the whole question would be reopened, and the purely negative argument favouring Rome as the place of composition would appear far less convincing.

There appear to be very real reasons for believing that the account in Acts omits mention of an imprisonment—possibly more than one—prior to those at Cæsarea and Rome which occurred in Ephesus during the three years spent in that city. Only the main reasons for this hypothesis which has attracted several scholars can be mentioned here.[3] The reference to several imprisonments—"in prisons more abundantly"[4]—can scarcely be based solely on the Philippian experience[5] or the trial before Gallio in Corinth.[6] While the words, "If after the manner of men I fought with beasts at Ephesus," as already remarked,[7] can scarcely be understood of an actual appearance in the arena, they may very well be understood as a reference to an imprisonment in which he had feared that that was to be the outcome, and which not only is still vivid as he writes, "even unto this present hour we both hunger, and thirst, and are naked, and buffeted, and have no certain dwelling place,"[8] but remains a terrible memory—"yea, we ourselves have had the sentence of death within ourselves."[9] Furthermore, the mention of the brave act of Aquila and Priscilla, "who for my life laid down their own necks,"[10] must not be disregarded. Quite independent of the nature of Romans 16, this can only refer to some previous experience, and it is more natural to understand it, not as a reference to the difficulty in Corinth, but to that "affliction which befell us in Asia."[11] Similarly, the reference to his "fellow prisoners" Andronicus and Junias[12] is most naturally explained on the basis of a recent imprisonment, in which other Christians as well had been in jeopardy. Probably no weight at all should be given to the early legends occasionally found of Paul's experiences with the lion in the

[3] It is elaborately argued by G. S. Duncan, *St. Paul's Ephesian Ministry,* who gives a convenient résumé of the history of the view (pp. 59-65). The penetrating essay by C. R. Bowen, "Are Paul's Prison Letters from Ephesus?" in the *American Journal of Theology,* Vol. XXIV (Jan. and April, 1920), pp. 112-135, 277-287, is worthy of study.

[4] II Cor. 11:23; cf. 6:5.

[5] Acts 16:19-40.

[6] Acts 18:12-17.

[7] P. 256, n. 17.

[8] I Cor. 4:11.

[9] II Cor. 1:9; cf. also its penumbra in II Cor. 6:9 ("as dying, and behold we live") and perhaps 4:8 ff.

[10] Rom. 16:3.

[11] II Cor. 1:8.

[12] Rom. 16:7.

Ephesian arena.[13] They are palpably mere expansions of I Cor. 15:32. On the other hand, the statement in the prologue to Colossians in the so-called "Marcionite Prologue," *apostolus iam ligatus scribit eis ab Epheso,* attests that in the second century the view that Paul had suffered imprisonment in Ephesus and had written the Colossian epistle during that imprisonment was not unknown. Apparently this was based upon the judgment of Marcion, who may well have been a heretic, but apparently stood head and shoulders over all his contemporaries not only in respect for Paul, but in real critical ability.

The reason for the silence of Acts in regard to this highly probable imprisonment will probably remain one of the many unsolved problems incident to that perplexing book. Conjectures are possible but fruitless. That the whole narrative is, to say the least, highly compressed for those years in Ephesus few will deny. Furthermore, the story of the uproar caused by the silversmiths and their ringleader Demetrius, and the rescue of Paul from the crowd, "the more part [of which] knew not wherefore they were come together," by the gallant Ephesian official, although singularly good material for proving the essential innocence of early Christianity in general and of its leader Paul in particular, can scarcely fail to arouse historical qualms. It is perhaps not utterly improbable that the writer saw fit to substitute this incident for an account whose "witnessing power" was less evident.

At any rate, few readers of the Pauline epistles—and, for that matter, of Acts—will deny the inherent possibility that Paul could not spend twelve months—not to mention three years—in any city without spending a part of it in prison. Thus the evidence would seem to point, in spite of the silence of Acts, to an Ephesian imprisonment. Whether the so-called "letters of the captivity," any or all, are to be ascribed to this period instead of to Rome—for that question is thus reopened—is a separate question and must be reserved for the subsequent chapters in which the letters in question are examined.

[13] These are mentioned by Duncan, *op. cit.,* pp. 69 f.

Chapter XXIII

THE EPISTLE TO THE PHILIPPIANS

PHILIPPI, the first city in Europe in which Paul laboured, was at that time a highly strategic spot for a Christian centre. Originally a small and unimportant village called Krenides, it had been taken by Philip of Macedon in the middle of the fourth century and made an important outpost on the Thracian frontier. Here the conspirators Brutus and Cassius had suffered defeat at the hands of Antony and Octavian. The city had afterward grown by leaps and bounds until finally, probably shortly after his victory at Actium, Augustus made it a Roman colony, Colonia Julia Augusta Philippensis, and bestowed upon it the prized "Italic right," whereby its inhabitants shared the same rights and privileges enjoyed by citizens of Italy itself. Its rich silver and gold mines, which had been prized by the Phœnicians and developed by Philip, continued to make its importance secure. Its situation—"the almost continuous mountain barrier between the East and West is here depressed so as to form a gateway for the thoroughfare of the two continents"[1]—assured it of constant travel and commerce. The Egnatian way linked it with Rome.

Here in this city Paul founded a church on the so-called second missionary journey. Although imprisoned and subjected to other indignities at that time, and later made uncomfortable by his Jewish enemies, he appears to have had real affection for this church. This letter is the most personal and spontaneous of all that we have from his pen. It evidences an affectionate relationship undisturbed by the clashes and disputes so common in his other letters. Contrary to his usual custom of independence he had allowed them to aid him financially, convinced, apparently, that his readiness to accept their gifts would not be misinterpreted. At least twice they had aided him in the near-by city of Thessalonica;[2] apparently this aid had also reached him in Corinth.[3] Now after several years he is in prison, but his friends have not forgotten him. Through their fellow member Epaphroditus a token of their continued love has shortly come:

> But I rejoice in the Lord greatly, that now at length ye have revived your thought for me; wherein ye did indeed take thought, but ye lacked opportunity.[4]

During his stay Epaphroditus had fallen ill, but had now recovered. He was

[1] J. B. Lightfoot, *Saint Paul's Epistle to the Philippians,* 8th ed., p. 48.
[2] Phil. 4:15 f.
[3] II Cor. 11:9.
[4] Phil. 4:10.

anxious, however, to return, for his friends at home had learned of his sickness[5] and were worrying about him. Paul sends him home, and with him this letter. No theological questions are discussed; no difficulties settled. It is simply an expression of his love to the church, made possible by the return of a messenger. There are but few quotations from the Old Testament—they are unnecessary, for there are no moot points to be buttressed—no subtle reasonings or involved arguments. He thanks them for their gift, not because of its value alone, but because of their love which had prompted it; then he relieves their anxiety about him. He is in bonds; the situation is depressing. A weary desire to be free from the hindrances which his enemies are so tireless in putting in his path is his; yet this expression of love and confidence from his friends in Macedonia so touches him that as he writes them his joy appears in every line. Here at least is one place where his labour has borne fruit. The old commentator Bengel has truly said: *Summa epistolae: gaudeo, gaudete*—"the sum and substance of the letter is expressed by the words, I rejoice; rejoicc ye!"

Following the salutation and peculiarly intimate greeting (1:1-11) he tells them of his situation and of his hope soon to be with them, though, if he were to have a free choice between life and death, he would prefer to be with Christ (1:12-26). With a skilful turn he exhorts them to humility, undismayed by the opposition of their enemies whose very plottings give them the chance to suffer in behalf of Christ (1:17-30). Remember him. Though he had everything in his power, willingly he had relinquished them; unlike Adam, in that he did not put forth his hand to seize equality with God, he had humbled himself and in consequence had been highly exalted (2:1-11). With such an example they in Philippi will "do all things without murmurings and questionings" (2:12-18). Then he announces the coming of Timothy whom he hopes soon to send, the hope of his own visit, and the return of Epaphroditus (2:19-30). Here he might have ended with the word, "Finally, my brethren, rejoice in the Lord" (3:1), but instead resumes his word of exhortation. It is in the form of a sharp warning against their Jewish enemies whom he stigmatizes the "concision," that is, those whose circumcision is simply of the flesh, not of the heart, since they are opposing God by hindering his plans for gentile salvation. Certainly these folk are not to be seen as judaizers, but as Jews whom Paul fears may succeed in seducing his converts into practices which will nullify their new freedom. The Philippians are not to be deluded; to their untutored gentile eyes the proffered gifts may seem attractive. They are to remember Paul's own experience. He had all these things—and had them as no gentile could ever hope to—he knew them at first hand; yet though in the eyes of men he might well have boasted, he appraised them at their real value, and counted them as less than nothing,

[5] Phil. 2:25-28.

as a distinct loss, and had gladly relinquished them. His converts are to follow his example, and to be on their guard lest their prize be filched:

> For our citizenship is in heaven; whence also we wait for a Saviour, the Lord Jesus Christ: who shall fashion anew the body of our humiliation, that it may be conformed to the body of his glory, according to the working whereby he is able even to subject all things unto himself.

With such a citizenship before them, they will not be foolish enough to prize entrance to the Jewish race; with such a refashioning of their bodies promised, they will not get themselves mutilated at the hands of men:

> Wherefore, my brethren, beloved and longed for, my joy and crown, so stand fast in the Lord, my beloved.[6]

Then he refers to a squabble between Euodia and Syntyche, about which we have no other information, and urges the other Christians, including the enigmatic "true yokefellow,"[7] to aid them to reconciliation (4:2 f.). Then with a word of encouragement he again appears about to end the letter (4:4-7), only to break off again to thank them for their gift. Then with an appropriate benediction and brief mention of greetings he closes (4:10-23).

The intimate and unstudied touch is seen in the difficulty he finds in actually ending the letter. Again and again he tries, but always another word must be said, another postscript added. The letter presents Paul in a quite different aspect from that in such letters as Galatians or II Corinthians. It is the same Paul, but he is in a different temper. The trouble in Corinth provokes his bitterest sarcasm and scalding rebukes. In his excitement at the inroad in Galatia words dripping with gall flow from his pen (especially Gal. 5:12). The attitude of the Philippians evokes a different Paul. Of his enemies "some indeed preach Christ even of envy and strife. . . . What then? only that in every way, whether in pretence or in truth, Christ is proclaimed; and therein I rejoice, yea, and will rejoice."[8] We would be the poorer if these words had been lost.

Most interpreters of the letter are convinced that Rome is the place from which Paul is writing. The only problem, they feel, is in what part of this term of imprisonment it is to be dated. That he was a prisoner is clear. In addition to the explicit mention of his bonds[9] the whole tone of the letter makes this certain. The greeting—"All the saints salute you, especially they that are of Cæsar's household"[10]—and the debatable reference to the "whole prætorian guard[11] are appropriate in a letter from Rome, but they are not so

[6] Phil. 3:2-4:1.
[7] Perhaps this is not an epithet, but a proper name—Synzygus.
[8] Phil 1:15-18.
[9] Phil. 1:7,12 ff.
[10] Phil. 4:22.
[11] Phil. 1:13.

conclusive as has often been argued. Certainly "Cæsar's household" does not mean Nero's Roman palace. It has often been argued that such a term is easily understandable for Cæsarea, the capital city of an imperial province, where the retinue of Cæsar's procurator engaged in managing the *res familiaris* would without violence be so designated. Furthermore, if the words are rightly translated "prætorian guard" there is no reason to deny that a detachment of soldiery in Cæsarea might be so referred to. Yet it is quite possible that "prætorium" is the correct translation and that it refers to the residence of the governor.[12] On the other hand, the reference to Paul's hope for speedy release and his plan to visit them[13] can only with violence be seen as coming from Cæsarea, for at that time his eyes were fixed on the west; he had finished his work in Philippi; and, if the Acts account can be trusted, he had probably already "appealed to Cæsar" which would automatically have ensured his voyage to Rome. Nor do the words imply that his visit will be delayed for many years. Thus it has been assumed that the letter was written in Rome, and that in the interim he had decided to give up his contemplated trip to Spain and to return to the scene of his earlier labours.

But if, as has been argued in Chapter 22, we accept the probability of an imprisonment in Ephesus, the question arises as to whether or not the epistle might emanate from that city. To be sure, Asia was a senatorial, not an imperial, province; yet the evidence would seem to justify the view that even in such a province, governed as it was by a proconsul who was responsible to the Senate, there was regularly an officer of the emperor in charge of those properties and incomes which were vested in the emperor. Thus it is not impossible that the references to the "household of Cæsar" and to the "whole prætorian guard (?)" are to be understood as applying to this Ephesian officer and his retinue.

At any rate, there are three definite reasons for favouring Ephesus beyond Rome as the place of the writing. First, reference to his anticipated visit to Philippi is at once intelligible, and without the assumption of a change of plans or the subterfuge that it is only a remote possibility perhaps to be realized in after-years. In the second place, the distance between Rome and Philippi was far greater and more difficult to traverse than that between Ephesus and Philippi. Two long trips by foot, each of nearly four hundred miles with a two-day crossing from Brundisium certainly involved a deal more than one from Ephesus via Troas, easily made in less than two weeks, and with the greater part accomplished by boat. Nor is this point to be minimized, for before the writing of the letter two round trips have been made: word has gone (directly or indirectly) from Paul to Philippi; Epaphroditus has been sent. Word of his illness has reached Philippi, and Paul

[12] Cf. Matt. 27:27; Mark 15:16; John 18:28,33; 19:9; Acts 23:35. In these references all save the last refer clearly to Pilate's Jerusalem residence; the last to that in Cæsarea.

[13] Phil. 2:24 and (more doubtfully) 1:27.

has learned that they have been disquieted by the news. Not only that, but Paul expects soon to send Timothy on the same journey and after his return to go himself. Of course, such a wholesale order is not impossible, but it appears to me that the difficulty of this stupendous amount of travel has often been overlooked. And finally, the mention of the gifts the Philippians had sent previously appears more natural if the interval had been comparatively short and not from seven to ten years, as would be the case if the letter is to be dated from Rome. Perhaps Timothy's intended visit should also be mentioned. It is tempting, in view of these other reasons favouring Ephesus, to wonder if this prospective visit of Timothy's is not the same as that referred to in I Cor. 4:17; 16:10 f. and Acts 19:22. If this be admitted, we would naturally date the letter as earlier than I Corinthians, for in this latter writing Timothy has already started. Thus a date late in 53 or early in 54 A.D. would appear to me probable. Nor is there anything in the letter which demands a later date. Attempts to view all of the letters of the imprisonment as late because of a more advanced type of thought appears to me to have been distinctly overstressed. Certainly in the case of Philippians to try to see such development is to follow an *ignis fatuus*, while to argue that its tone—smiling through tears—is explainable only on the basis that Paul is now looking backward over his long career and with folded hands is contemplating the end and hence is at Rome is quite unwarrantable. In Asia, too—that is, in Ephesus—he has despaired of life. A Roman prison was not the only place that might have produced in Paul a feeling of uncertainty and solemnity. But even this can be exaggerated, for after all in this very epistle he says he hopes soon to be with them again! Thus, while these various points by no means amount to a mathematical demonstration, they do appear to me distinctly to favour Ephesus, and to suggest the likelihood that, far from being the last of the (genuine) Pauline letters, written just before he met his death in Rome, it is to be classed as one of the earlier epistles that have been preserved and antedated only by I Thessalonians and the "previous letter" to Corinth.

In former years arguments against the authenticity of Philippians were occasionally raised, principally by the Tübingen scholars and their disciples. Their chief objection was the absence of that distinctly Pauline polemic without which no letter could be genuine. That criterion has long since been seen to be faulty. So far as style and language are concerned, no letter can make a stronger claim to be from Paul. Furthermore, the view was occasionally expressed that there were distinct anachronisms in the letter. Most of these objections were trivial and perverse; for example, that in 4:3 the Clement referred to was the shadowy Clement of Rome or that by the word, "true yokefellow," Peter is meant, and hence that this letter, like II Peter, evidences the later attempt to bring these two erstwhile opponents into harmony. The mention of "bishops and deacons" (1:1) is somewhat different

Neither of these terms is otherwise used as a title for an official in any of the Pauline letters (although the latter term occurs occasionally in the sense of servant), nor is this reference to officials paralleled in the address of any of the other letters. If the words are to be understood in the later ecclesiastical sense, they can scarcely be genuine. Perhaps, however, they are to be understood loosely, much in the sense of I Thes. 5:12—"those who are over you." Interpreters of the epistle have often referred to the possibility that this unparalleled reference to such is due to the fact that they had been instrumental in collecting the gift for Paul. But even if this explanation be unsatisfactory—and at best the words are suspicious—it is surely wiser to consider them an early gloss than by retaining them to throw doubt on the letter as a whole. Nor is there any reason to doubt the genuineness of 2:6-11, although Paul might conceivably have been somewhat perplexed about his "doctrine of kenosis," of which modern scholars speak so confidently. The claim that this passage gives a different conception of preëxistence than do I Cor. 15:45-49 and Rom. 8:3 appears to me at best insecure. It is to be observed that the "heavenly man" spoken of in I Cor. 15 is not the preëxistent Christ but the risen and glorified Christ. Furthermore, it appears to me that the passage in Philippians is contained in essence in II Cor. 8:9. Nor does the recent speculation about the original *Urmensch* in the so-called syncretistic religions cast any real light. Underlying our passage is rather to be seen the genuinely Pauline contrast between the first man, Adam, and the last man, Christ. Adam had sought for equality and stretched out his hand for the fruit. Jesus, far from striving to grasp this equality (cf. verse 6), had voluntarily humbled himself. Thus there would appear to be nothing un-Pauline in the passage, and it is quite unnecessary to assume (with Porter)[14] that Paul is here making use of an earlier conception with little or no adaptation.

Nor are the arguments against the integrity of the epistle any more impressive. It has occasionally been claimed that we have two letters, 1:1-3:1 and 3:2-4:23. Holtzmann remarks poetically that "the rush of all the tides of criticism upon this passage raises the suspicion of a hidden rock." The "finally, my brethren" might suggest that he was drawing to a close, but throughout the letter the style is distinctly conversational and unstudied. The words, "to write the same things to you, to me indeed is not irksome, but for you it is safe,"[15] probably do indicate that he had written them previously. But the assumption that the reference in Polycarp's epistle to the Philippians[16] to the letters which Paul had written to them evidences the fact that in his day two letters circulated and were later combined to form our canonical epistle is quite unwarranted. There is little reason to doubt that several letters of Paul have disappeared. What more natural than that

[14] F. C. Porter, *The Mind of Christ in Paul*, pp. 204-228.
[15] Phil. 3:2.
[16] *ad Phil.* 3:2.

one or more to Philippi are among that number? Nor is the contrast in tone between Paul's treatment of those who "preach Christ even of envy and strife" (1:15-18) and those whom he stigmatizes "dogs, evil workers, and concision" (3:2 ff.) such as to suggest that they originally stood in different letters. The two groups are certainly different, and if the interpretation of the latter which has been adopted in the earlier part of this chapter is correct, the constant dread which Paul had that his gentile converts might yield to the proffered fleshpots of Judaism may well have led him to the sharper (certainly not un-Pauline) attack.

All in all, this little letter to his friends whose conversion marked the "beginning of the gospel"—at least in Europe—appears not only fully entitled to be considered genuine and in the form in which it left the hands of the apostle's scribe, but as one of the finest possessions preserved from antiquity.

Chapter XXIV

A PRELIMINARY SURVEY OF COLOSSIANS, EPHESIANS, AND PHILEMON

THE place and date of composition of these three letters can best be discussed together. No careful reading and comparison of Colossians and Ephesians can fail to reveal their remarkable similarity. Outline, structure, phraseology—all are practically identical. If both are considered from the pen of Paul, there can be no reasonable doubt that they were written at the same time. In both Paul appears as a prisoner.[1] Both letters are to be delivered by the same messenger, Tychicus, the description of whom is couched in identical terms:

Col. 4:7,8—All my affairs shall Tychicus make known to you, the beloved brother and faithful minister and fellow-servant in the Lord: whom I have sent unto you for this very purpose, that ye may know our state, and that he may comfort your hearts.	Eph. 6:21,22—But that ye also may know my affairs, how I do, Tychicus, the beloved brother and faithful minister in the Lord, shall make known to you all things: whom I have sent unto you for this very purpose, that ye may know our state, and that he may comfort your hearts.

To be sure, in Colossians Onesimus, the returning slave of Philemon, is mentioned as co-bearer with Tychicus of the letter. He is not mentioned in Ephesians. This is of no consequence, however, since Onesimus would naturally leave Tychicus at Colosse, the home of Philemon, while Tychicus would continue with the letter we call Ephesians, which latter writing, if actually from Paul's pen, must be regarded not as a letter to Ephesus but as a circular letter intended for several churches in different communities. This would further account for the presence of the personal greetings in Colossians (4:10-17) and their absence in Ephesians.

No less certainly must Philemon be seen as intimately connected with Colossians. The little note is to be carried with Onesimus, who in turn, as has been already remarked, is associated with Tychicus as the bearer of Colossians.[2] In Philemon, as in Colossians, "Timothy our brother" is associated with Paul as writer, while in both of the letters the same friends

[1] Cf. Col. 4:3,18; Eph. 3:1; 6:19 f.
[2] Col. 4:9.

send their greetings—Aristarchus, Mark, Epaphras, Luke, and Demas.[3] Archippus is saluted in both the letters.[4] Other similarities between Colossians and Ephesians will appear later in the discussion of the authenticity of the latter; these, however, are quite sufficient to establish the fact that all three, if genuine, were not only written at the same time, but sent by the same messengers.

To the questions, when? and from where? the usual answer is from Rome, during the two years' imprisonment mentioned in the closing words in Acts. Occasional voices have been raised in favour of Cæsarea, but the points which were formerly stressed in favour of the Palestinian port are discounted today. The explanation that since Colosse lay on the road *between* Cæsarea and Ephesus naturally Onesimus would not be mentioned in the letter to Ephesus is completely quashed by the fact that Ephesians cannot be regarded as addressed to Ephesus. Nor is the argument valid that they cannot come from Rome, since in 60 A.D., according to Tacitus,[5] an earthquake demolished the near-by city of Laodicea, and yet no mention of this catastrophe is made in Colossians.[6] Even if this date for the earthquake be accepted (Eusebius[7] dates it four years later and includes Colosse and Hierapolis), this would not preclude Rome, since according to the more probable chronology Paul arrived in that city in 58 A.D. On the one hand, the request that Philemon prepare the guest chamber for Paul[8] has seemed to most critics—precisely as did the hope of soon visiting Philippi—definitely to exclude Cæsarea from consideration as the place of writing for any of these letters. But is this request much more natural if Paul is in Rome? Not only was he then planning to go to the west—and there is no reason to assume that his imprisonment (no new thing that!) had caused him to weaken—but the request for the guest chamber in far-away Colosse does seem a bit unnatural and premature. Furthermore, while little can be said with confidence about the probable place of refuge of the runaway Onesimus, it is perhaps unlikely that he had accomplished the twelve-hundred-mile flight to Rome, and even if he had, that he would have ventured to come to Paul, under official surveillance as the latter was. The argument that the theology of Colossians-Ephesians evidences an advance beyond the other letters so great as to be intelligible only if coming from a distinctly later date—hence from Rome—appears to me far less impressive than the usual statements would suggest, and may be reserved for examination until a later page. Furthermore, the similar conclusion from the fact that Paul

[3] Col. 4:10-14; Philm. 29. The only difference is that Jesus Justus sends greetings in Col. but not in Philm.

[4] Col. 4:17; Philm. 2.

[5] *Annal.* xiv,27.

[6] Cf. also Col. 4:13.

[7] *Chronicon* Olymp. ccx (*Griech. Christl. Schrift.*, Vol. 24, p. 183—*In Asia tres urbes terræ motu conciderunt, Laodicia Hierapolis Colossæ.*

[8] Philm. 22.

refers to himself by a word[9] usually translated "the aged" is quite unwarranted. Not only do we know far too little of Paul's chronology to decide at precisely what period Paul could refer to himself as an old man, but there is a very real probability that the word should, as the Greek allows, instead be translated "ambassador." Not only does this meaning fit the context better, but it would appear to be a conception of himself which he elsewhere had expressed.[10] In short, the evidence for Rome is distinctly weak. For Ephesus, however, the matter is quite different. What more natural than that Paul should have hoped to visit the near-by city of Colosse before he left Ephesus for his final visit to Macedonia and Corinth? The request for lodging would from there—it was not a tenth of the distance—be as natural as from Rome artificial. And for Onesimus the trip to Ephesus would surely have been easier to accomplish than to Rome.

If one is inclined to hazard a guess as to what brought Paul and Onesimus together, that of Deissmann lies near at hand. It was not that the still free Onesimus had ventured to approach Paul, but that he had himself been arrested in Ephesus and had thus met Paul as a fellow prisoner, who not only converted him but perhaps became a surety for him to the prison authorities to enable him to return home.[11] Finally, the presence of the six companions who send greetings to Colosse would also appear as evidence, slight though it is, for Ephesus rather than for Rome, for there is no direct evidence that any one of them—not to mention them all—accompanied Paul on his voyage to Rome. After all, he was going as a prisoner at Roman expense. His entourage was presumably not large! Thus, as in the case of Philippians, while the evidence can scarcely be said to be conclusive, it would appear to me to favour Ephesus as the place from which these three letters (assuming for the moment that Ephesians is genuine) were written, and perhaps during the latter part of the stay in that city, some months later than Philippians and I Corinthians, that is, in the summer of 54 A.D.

[9] πρεσβύτης—Philm. 9.
[10] II Cor. 5:20; cf. also Eph. 6:20.
[11] Deissmann, *St. Paul*, p. 18.

Chapter XXV

THE EPISTLE TO PHILEMON

THIS delightful little note is addressed to Philemon and is the only letter addressed to an individual which we have preserved from Paul's pen. With Philemon Apphia and Archippus are also greeted. As early as Theodore of Mopsuestia these latter were identified as Philemon's wife and son. While this is, of course, not improbable, it is sheer surmise. The occasion of the letter is perfectly plain. Onesimus, Philemon's slave, had run away, probably with money from his master:

> But if he hath wronged thee at all, or oweth thee aught, put that to mine account; I Paul write it with mine own hand, I will repay it.[1]

He has come into contact with Paul and has become a Christian. A mutual affection has sprung up; none the less, Paul insists that he return to his master. He is sending Tychicus with a letter to Colosse. He sends Onesimus with him, joins his name with that of Tychicus, perhaps as a tactful expression of his newborn confidence in the slave, and at the same time writes the personal letter to Philemon to urge the latter to forgive his runaway slave and to restore him to his confidence, now that he has become a new man. The delightful little pun—even Jove occasionally smiles—on the meaning of Onesimus' name[2] should not be overlooked. Formerly in spite of his name—"the useful or profitable one"—he had been quite the reverse; "now [he] is profitable to thee and to me." The playful little thrust that Philemon is to treat Onesimus "no longer as a slave, but more than a slave, a brother beloved," is surely not to be pushed to mean a bid for his emancipation. Neither here nor elsewhere does Paul argue for or against slavery. On the contrary, he assumes it as a matter of course.[3]

That Philemon was an inhabitant of Colosse is evident from Col. 4:9, where his slave, Onesimus, is referred to as "one of you," that is, a Colossian. Although Paul had never been in Colosse,[4] Philemon owed his conversion to him personally (v. 19). The natural assumption is that Philemon had met Paul in Ephesus, during the latter's stay in that city. As we have

[1] Philm. 17,18.

[2] Philm. 11; cf. the similar pun in verse 20.

[3] Cf. especially I Cor. 7:21-24. For a fuller statement of Paul's attitude, see my *Ethics of Paul*, pp. 205-210.

[4] See p. 289.

seen, Paul is on intimate enough terms with him to bid him get the guest-chamber ready.

Rarely has the authenticity of this beautiful little letter been challenged save by the Tübingen school and the Dutch Radicals. Few unbiased critics will disagree with that master of style, Renan:

> Few pages have an accent of sincerity so pronounced. Paul alone could have written this little masterpiece.

To view it as an attempt by a later writer to settle the question of slavery or to consider it modelled after the famous letter of the younger Pliny to Sabinianus is quite absurd. If any letter of those we possess is Pauline, surely Philemon is one of them.

Appended notes: 1. Although there is no reason to assume any literary dependence by either writer, the letter of Pliny, already referred to, is not without interest to the reader of Philemon, not only as offering a distinct parallel, but as tending to correct the view that slave-baiting was the universal practice of Greeks and Romans.

> Your freedman, with whom you had told me you were vexed, came to me and throwing himself down before me clung to my feet, as if they had been yours. He was profuse in his tears and his entreaties; he was profuse also in his silence. In short, he convinced me of his penitence. I believe that he is indeed a reformed character, because he feels that he has done wrong. You are angry, I know; and you have reason to be angry, this also I know; but mercy wins the highest praise just when there is the most righteous cause for anger. You loved the man, and, I hope, will continue to love him. Meanwhile it is enough, that you should allow yourself to yield to his prayers. You may be angry again, if he deserves it; and in this you will be the more readily pardoned if you yield now. Concede something to his youth, something to his tears, something to your own indulgent disposition. Do not torture him, lest you torture yourself at the same time. For it *is* torture to you, when one of your gentle temper is angry. I am afraid lest I should appear not to ask but to compel, if I should add my prayers to his. Yet I will add them the more fully and unreservedly, because I scolded the man himself with sharpness and severity; for I threatened him straitly that I would never ask you again. This I said to him, for it was necessary to alarm him; but I do not use the same language to you. For perchance, I shall ask again, and shall be successful again; only let my request be such, as it becomes me to prefer and you to grant. Farewell.—*Ep.* ix,21.

2. A new and distinctly different view of the letter is maintained by John Knox, *Philemon among the Letters of Paul*, 1935. The letter is far more than a note asking the owner of Onesimus to treat kindly the returned runaway slave. Paul's purpose is to urge the owner to give him (Paul) this slave in whom he has seen much promise. Actually it is not Philemon, but Archippus of Colosse who is the master. Philemon is overseer of the Chris-

tian churches of the Lycus valley and resides in Laodicea. He is to exert his influence upon Archippus. Thus this little letter which is delivered first to Philemon for his perusal is the much debated "letter from Laodicea" (Col. 4:16). Apparently Paul's request was granted. Onesimus fulfils Paul's hopes and becomes a Christian leader. He is in later years the bishop of Ephesus to whom Ignatius, while en route to Rome to martyrdom, devotes a large part of his letter to the Ephesians. It was Onesimus, furthermore, who, after gathering those letters of Paul known to him, penned Ephesians to provide an adequate introductory epistle (see below, p. 298). He included this little letter which, despite the fact that it was to seem so insignificant to later Christians, had had so great a significance for him personally.

Chapter XXVI

THE EPISTLE TO THE COLOSSIANS

COLOSSE was a little second-rate town in Phrygia on the south bank of the Lycus River, a tributary of the Meander near the mouth of which latter lay Miletus. The great city of Ephesus was a little more than a hundred miles to the west. Ten miles west of Colosse on the Lycus was Laodicea, founded by Antiochus the Great and named by him in honour of his wife Laodice; three miles due north of Laodicea lay Hierapolis, whose famed healing baths were frequented by hosts of pilgrims. These three neighbouring cities—Colosse had declined in importance and was now overshadowed by the others—were closely associated by the bonds of trade. Wines, dyestuffs, and wool were the chief exports.

Paul was not the founder of the church; nor, apparently, had he ever visited it.[1] The founder of the church was Epaphras,[2] a resident of Colosse, who had also worked in Laodicea and Hierapolis. Apparently he had not been as successful in the latter city; at least it is not mentioned in 2:1, nor is a letter to that city referred to, as is probably the case for Laodicea.[3] Although there were Jews in all three cities, the population was of course predominantly gentile. The unqualified reference to the former days of the Colossian Christians—"and you, being dead through your trespasses, *and the uncircumcision of your flesh*"—would indicate that this church at least was exclusively gentile.[4]

Apparently Epaphras has visited Paul, a prisoner in Ephesus, to report the condition of his work. On the whole the report is favourable:

> For though I am absent in the flesh, yet am I with you in the spirit, joying and beholding your order, and the stedfastness of your faith in Christ;[5]

but a part of the report leads Paul to wish to write the community at once, before Epaphras himself returns. Furthermore, he desires to send Onesimus back to Philemon. Accordingly, Tychicus is dispatched on this double errand.

But to thank the Christians in Colosse for their interest, to reciprocate their prayers, and to counsel them to stand firm in righteousness is not by

[1] Cf. Col. 1:4,7,9,23; 2:1.
[2] Col. 1:7; 4:12 f.
[3] Col. 4:16; but cf. pp. 295 f.
[4] Col. 2:13, cf. also 1:21,27.
[5] Col. 2:5.

any manner of means the sole object of the letter. A group—for want of better name they are usually styled "errorists"—have been assailing the church at Colosse. Thus the main purpose of the letter is to unmask these false teachers and to warn the Christians against them. It is extraordinarily difficult to get a clear picture of who these errorists were and what their antecedents. All sorts of speculations have been advanced, but none are particularly convincing. Certainly they were not simply orthodox Jews, although the reminder that they (his readers) "were also circumcised with a circumcision not made with hands"[6] and the disparaging remark about feast days, new moons, and Sabbaths[7] suggest some connexion. On the other hand, the warning against the one who "maketh spoil of you through his philosophy and vain deceit, after the tradition of man, after the rudiments of the world, and not after Christ, for in him dwelleth all the fulness of the Godhead bodily";[8] the warning against such useless and perishable ordinances as "Handle not, nor taste, nor touch";[9] the insistence upon purity and the obscure warning against some sort of false humility, a worship of angels, and a new entanglement with "the rudiments of the world,"[10] that is, some sort of cosmic demons—all this suggests that it was some variety of queer theosophical speculation having also an ascetic tendency and hence, not unnaturally, a consequent laxness of morals. These errorists do not seem to have attacked Paul nor to have attempted directly to overthrow his teaching. Rather their contention appears to have been that his was an incomplete gospel which they could bring to completion. Against this contention Paul insists upon the absolute supremacy of Christ and his complete adequacy. When this is kept in mind, many of the problems of the so-called "higher Christology" of the letter solve themselves. No external philosophy, no spirit worship, no ascetic practices are needed to complete the gospel. Christ is the all in all; the first-born of all creation, the one in whom not alone all things consist but in whom dwelleth all the fulness of the Godhead bodily, the one who has brought a complete and unqualified salvation through despoiling openly and triumphantly all the principalities and powers, and the one with whom all Christians are inextricably joined in the death to the old and birth to the new.

The analysis of the letter is simple. First, the salutation and thanksgiving for their progress and the prayer for their steadfastness in the service of God who has redeemed them through Jesus Christ. This latter prayer, which becomes a full and elaborate statement of his exalted place, is perfectly natural as soon as we observe that it is in essence an answer to the claims of inadequacy set forth by the errorists (1:1-2:7). Then follows a

[6] Col. 2:11.
[7] Col. 2:16.
[8] Col. 2:8,9.
[9] Col. 2:21.
[10] Col. 2:20-23.

more explicit attack (but now continued as a direct assault) upon these errorists and their contentions (2:8-3:4). A brief statement of the true Christian ethic, as opposed to the unnecessary man-made ascetic restrictions of their would-be teachers, follows. One might call this third section (3:5-4:1) the beginning of a handbook of Christian morals, starting as it does with general injunctions and principles, and then continuing in the form of specific precepts for family life: wives, husbands, parents, children, slaves, and masters. With a brief word of advice, a reference to the visit of Tychicus and Onesimus, greetings from Paul's friends, including Epaphras, a word to Archippus, and the briefest sort of benediction (4:2-18), the letter closes.

The letter has been viewed with suspicion by many critics who did not and would not subscribe to the views of the Tübingen school nor to the wholesale objection of the Dutch Radicals. The two chief arguments raised against its authenticity are (1) the type of errorist attacked, (2) the lofty Christology. The first objection, although stressed by the older scholars, has today lost much of its cogency. There is little to connect the errorists with Gnosticism, that second century heresy about which Irenæus wrote with such painful fulness. As has already been remarked, attempts to classify and identify the errorists have not been particularly convincing. Similarities with Neopythagoreanism, with Persian, Babylonian, even Indian speculations have been asserted, but nothing which closely resembles the teaching of the great Gnostic figures of the second century is to me apparent. Jülicher is apparently well within the facts when he speaks of this particular "Gnosticism" as being "actually older than Christianity."

The other objection, the lofty Christology, especially evident in the opening prayer (1:9-23), but by no means restricted to that section, is, at least at first glance, more weighty. Such designations of Christ as "the first-born of all creation" (1:15), the one "through whom and unto whom all things have been created" (1:16), "the *head* of the body, the church (1:18)—in the so-called "earlier epistles" Christ is the sum total of Christians: they make up his body—the statement that "in him dwelleth all the fulness of the Godhead bodily" (2:9); the striking and unparalleled mention of him as having made "peace through the blood of his cross" (1:20)—these are not found in the other letters, and may frankly be admitted to constitute a distinct advance. But it must be remembered that Paul is striving to meet the errorists on their own ground. It is Christ, not God, who is being threatened. Thus it is perfectly natural to find Paul stressing so elaborately—even extravagantly—Christ's complete adequacy and supremacy. There is no need of worshipping angels or other spirits. Such an act is not only absurd but outrageous: Christ is Lord of all. Furthermore, Paul's custom of repeating the accusation of his opponents, of couching his own replies in the phraseology of their queries or attacks, is not to be forgotten. It is extremely probable that this tendency is to be seen here, and that many of the predicates of Christ which appear to us un-Pauline are simply the claims of the errorists which Paul has coolly appropriated and predicated for Christ. Paul was a past master of that gentle art. Nor is the objection fatal that the form in which the ethical admonitions are grouped evidences a later date, that, in place of the spontaneous word of advice or rebuke as the occasion arose, we have here a later development, the start of systematic charts for conduct with specific do's and don't's. Two points are to be borne in mind: (1) the specific precepts of the errorists may not unnaturally have led Paul to an equally explicit statement; (2) and more important, Paul is writing to a church which he had not personally founded nor instructed, but for whom he feels full responsibility. We have no other such letter to serve as a criterion of how he acted under such circumstances. That the style is different from that of Galatians or Romans is obvious. The crisp, salty phrasing is gone; long clauses, sentences running on indefinitely and with obscurities in meaning, are frequent; at times the Greek is corrupt, occasionally completely unintelligible (cf. 2:18,19). On the other hand, the amount of agreement with the other letters is large; the fact that the text of the letter is in a very bad state of preservation and the possibility that in writing to a group which he did not know personally he found himself cramped and sought (vainly) a more literary style are not to be overlooked.

These various considerations appear to me to outweigh the arguments against its authenticity and to render unnecessary the hypothesis that in its present form long interpolations, especially in the first two chapters, are to be seen. The most thoroughgoing of such attempts was that by H. J. Holtzmann, who regarded Colossians of distinctly composite nature: at its core lay a genuine Pauline epistle which had served as the model for the non-Pauline Ephesians, and then had been revamped and increased by large interpolations from that later letter. But this and the other hypotheses appear more complicated and improbable than the one they seek to replace.

Unlike Ephesians, there is no sure reference to Colossians in the Apostolic Fathers. Marcion made use of it. Earlier than him we have no mention of it. Probably Justin Martyr refers to it; Irenæus surely made use of it. It is found in the so-called Muratorian canon. That is, from the middle of the second century it regularly appears as one of the "Pauline body." Its probable date and place of composition have been considered in an earlier chapter.

Chapter XXVII

THE EPISTLE TO THE EPHESIANS

As THIS letter stands it is addressed to Ephesus. This was the city in which Paul had spent between two and three years on the so-called third missionary journey, that is, 52-54 A.D. Here he had worked with vigour and result, although exposed to opposition and danger. Finally, in the late summer or early fall of 54—Acts makes his departure shortly after the riot of the silversmiths—he left the city for Macedonia and Corinth. As was observed on an earlier page, Romans 16 with its long list of greetings, evidencing a wide acquaintance in that city, is probably to be regarded as a letter to Ephesus. At the end of the century it was still a flourishing Christian centre, as is seen by the favourable reference to it in Rev. 2:1-7. We can be very certain that Paul was not only well informed about the city and its problems, but stood on intimate terms with the Christian group which he had established and with which he had worked. Certainly if the story told in Acts of his touching farewell with the Ephesian elders who had come to Miletus to bid him Godspeed on his journey to Rome be accepted, ties of genuine affection bound him to his Ephesian converts, or at least to their leaders.

With this picture of Paul's relationship to Ephesus in mind "Ephesians" can scarcely be read without astonishment. In no sense—save perhaps in barest form—is it a letter. A brief and colourless salutation, no personal paragraph of thanksgiving for these particular readers—in its place a long and impassioned pæan of praise to God for his choice of his people—no personal greetings at the end: there is scarcely a personal touch in the whole letter. Paul had never visited Colosse, yet that letter is comparatively warm, with personal touches and greetings; yet this other purely impersonal epistle —for it is more that than a letter—purports to be addressed to a city in which he had laboured long. Nor can it be said that perhaps the letter antedates the Ephesian ministry. Its relationship with Colossians and Philemon definitely forbids. Certainly the writing strikes one as being appropriate for any group of Christians, particularly for those whom Paul had never known personally. Jülicher's description of it is well within the facts:

> It is more of a sermon than of a letter—a sermon on the greatness of that Gospel which is able to bridge over all the old contradictions in humanity, and on the

grandeur of that one Church of Christ by which salvation is made sure, and on the precepts by which the members of this church ought to regulate their lives.[1]

Perhaps it is not misleading to call it a comprehensive outline of the Christian gospel.

Following the briefest sort of salutation, "Paul" gives an impassioned praise to God who has graciously chosen his people "before the foundation of the world," has revealed to them the mystery of his will, and sealed them with his spirit. Among these fortunates stand his readers (1:1-23). Then he contrasts their former state—"dead through . . . trespasses and sins"—with the present—"alive together with Christ," saved by grace (2:1-10). All bonds of separation are now broken down; no longer are the gentiles excluded—"ye that once were far off are made nigh in the blood of Christ." They are built into the household of God, "being built upon the foundation of the apostles and prophets, Christ Jesus himself being the chief corner stone" (2:11-22). To proclaim this glad news of reconciliation and union—the unsearchable riches of Christ—has been his glorious task. His present tribulation, far from discouraging them, should cause them to increase in the knowledge of the love of Christ (3:1-20). Then follows the practical section. They are to walk worthily of the divine call which they have received, which demands a perfect harmony and unity of spirit—one Lord, one faith, one baptism, one God and Father of all, who is over all, and through all, and in all—that they may truly be that building of perfect structure, the head of which is Christ (4:1-16). Thus no longer can they walk in darkness and vice, but in a genuine purity of life and speech (4:17-32). Then, as in Colossians, follows a demand for personal holiness, couched in more general terms (5:1-21) and concluding with the enumeration of the duties of each member of the Christian household—wives, husbands, children, fathers, slaves, and masters (5:22-6:9). To this section the entreaty to put on the complete Christian armour for battle against the wiles of the devil stands as a conclusion (6:10-20). Then with a reference to Tychicus and a petition for peace "for the brethren" and grace for "all them that love our Lord Jesus Christ with a love incorruptible" the epistle closes (6:21-24).

Many problems raised by the epistle are baffling; one thing, however, is indisputable. If the epistle is actually from the pen of Paul, it was not addressed to Ephesus. The whole tone of the writing forbids, while several passages afford certain proof:

For this cause I also, *having heard* of the faith in the Lord Jesus which is among you, and the love which ye show toward all the saints, cease not to give thanks for you . . . (1:15,16);

For this cause I Paul, the prisoner of Christ Jesus in behalf of you gentiles,—*if so be that ye have heard of the dispensation of that grace of God which was given*

[1] *Encyl. Bibl.*, Vol. I, col. 866.

me to you-ward; how that by revelation was made known unto me the mystery, as I wrote before in few words, *whereby, when ye read, ye can perceive my understanding* in the mystery of Christ . . . (3:1-4);

But ye did not so learn Christ; *if so be* that ye heard him, and were taught in him, even as truth is in Jesus . . . (4:20,21).

Thus if the words *at Ephesus* in 1:1 are an original part of the writing, we have a document not from Paul but from a later writer who failed utterly in impersonating Paul to a familiar group of friends.

But these words cannot be defended on critical grounds. The two oldest manuscripts of the New Testament, the Chester Beatty papyrus, and the most trustworthy of the later minuscules[2] omit them, while several of the Fathers—Origen, Basil, and Jerome—testify to their absence. Marcion cannot have known them, for in his canon he calls it the "epistle to the Laodiceans," and is severely taken to task for it by Tertullian. No convincing reason for the deletion of these words has ever been given, although many half-hearted suggestions have been made.

Archbishop Ussher, adopting the earlier suggestion of Beza, sought to get around the critical difficulties by assuming that it was a circular letter, addressed not to Ephesus (at least not exclusively) but to several churches. Thus in place of the words *at Ephesus* he conjectured that a space was left, and that the bearer of the letter in reading it to the various churches supplied *extempore* the appropriate designation. "At Ephesus" was a later conjecture to fill in the intolerable gap. This hypothesis has been widely adopted although with occasional modifications. Yet it fairly bristles with difficulties. There is no evidence that circular letters were ever written with gaps; all the examples we have are couched in quite different terms. As previously remarked, Marcion referred to the letter as "to Laodicea." In connexion with this Col. 4:16 has been considered significant:

And when this epistle hath been read among you, cause that it be read also in the church of the Laodiceans; *and that ye also read the epistle from Laodicea.*

Was Marcion correct? Was the letter originally written to Laodicea, but later, perhaps because of the unfortunate collapse of that church (Rev. 3:14-22), the emendation was made, both to remove the mention of Laodicea and to provide Ephesus with a letter from its great apostle? But if it was addressed to Laodicea, its impersonal tone (in contrast with Colossians which was addressed to another church which stood in precisely the same relation to Paul)[3] and the absence of a greeting from Epaphras who had laboured there[4] are to say the least surprising. If, on the contrary, it was not addressed specifically to Laodicea, but was a circular letter for the whole district, and

[2] B ℵ 1739 424 (=67**) 𝔓[46]. For their significance see Chapter 46.
[3] Cf. Col. 2:1.
[4] Col. 4:13.

Paul is here telling his Colossian readers that they can obtain (a copy of?) it "*from* (ἐκ) Laodicea," the query is surely pertinent: why would it be necessary to send to Laodicea for it? Would not Tychicus have brought both letters to Colosse when he himself came? That at the same time Paul wrote Colossians he wrote another letter to Laodicea which has not been preserved would seem far more probable than that our "Ephesians" is a letter either *to* Laodicea or *from* Laodicea. The reason for Marcion's identification of the letter may be reserved for the moment.

One thing is clear, if Ephesians is considered genuine, it must be regarded as an epistle written not for one church, but for several and at the same time as Colossians. As has been pointed out, the situation presented in both is precisely the same. Tychicus is the bearer. The outlines of the two letters are identical; the verbal coincidences are striking, even in passages where the exact wording is immaterial. The manual of Christian ethics is essentially the same. In short, Ephesians appears to be essentially a replica of Colossians, omitting the personal and controversial matter applicable to a particular church and with certain additions, such as the exhortation to coöperation (4:1-16) and the reference to the spiritual panoply (6:10-20).[5] But for whom was the general circular epistle intended? Colosse would receive its own letter; so apparently would its neighbouring Laodicea. But this circular letter was so essentially a replica of Colossians and not improbably of the hypothetical "Laodiceans" that it seems unlikely that Paul would have felt a general letter (but containing largely the same material) to *all* of these churches necessary, since each was to receive its own and to exchange them with the others. On the other hand, this circular letter can scarcely have been intended for a locality other than the Lycus River valley, since Tychicus was to carry it. Accordingly, the theory of Ephesians as a circular letter appears by no means free from difficulty. On the other hand, no rival hypothesis appears tenable if the letter be considered from the pen of Paul.

But aside from these difficulties there are other weighty reasons for doubting that the epistle is actually from Paul. The external evidence is excellent. Ignatius, Polycarp, and Hermas almost surely, Barnabas very possibly, used it. It is extremely possible that it was employed by I Peter. Thus a date much below 100 A.D. is highly unlikely.

The vocabulary of the letter, however, exhibits striking differences from that of the other letters. There are thirty-eight words in the epistle which do not occur elsewhere in the New Testament, forty-two more which, while occurring elsewhere, do not occur in any letter of Paul's. This, although of some weight, would not be definitive; yet it must be observed that other

[5] For a careful analysis and comparison of the two letters see Moffatt, *An Introduction to the Literature of the New Testament*, pp. 375-381; Abbott, *ICC Eph.-Col.*, pp. xxiii f.; Bacon, *An Introduction to the New Testament*, pp. 109 f.

words, although found in Paul's letters, are used here in a different sense. Again the appearance of synonyms—for example, "devil" occurs twice in the epistle (and in the Pastorals) but not in Paul's (other) letters instead of Satan which he uses seven times—is not to be overlooked. The style is distinctly different from all the letters save perhaps Colossians. Long turgid sentences, cumbrous phrases, "an unparalleled number of genitival formations" (Moffatt), such curious redundancies as "counsel of his will," "strength of his might," while not sufficient in themselves to compel an adverse judgment, have a cumulative effect when added to other evidence. Three specific verses have long been singled out as providing especial difficulty to the traditional view: (1) In 2:20 the church is spoken of as being "built upon the *foundation of the apostles and prophets*, Christ Jesus being the chief corner stone." Although Paul was never unduly reticent about his authority, such a phrase from one who was himself an apostle is strange. (2) A few verses further on the mystery of Christ is referred to as having been at length revealed "unto his holy apostles and prophets."[6] To be sure, "holy" to Paul signified something quite different from what it does to us. None the less, it appears either as a curious redundancy—of course the apostles and prophets were holy, for all Christians were—or else, if the epithet does have the later complimentary sense, it would appear bad taste in the mouth of one who was one of those so termed.[7] (3) In 4:11 the list of church officials is given: "And he gave some to be apostles; and some, prophets; and some, evangelists; and some, pastors and teachers." Opinions differ as to whether this ecclesiastical situation can be reconciled with that described in I Cor. 12:28. It certainly is a quite different characterization, and would appear to evidence a growing tendency to a more definite ecclesiastical system. Evangelists are otherwise mentioned in the New Testament only in Acts 21:8 and II Tim. 4:5, although the term is not infrequently used in the late ecclesiastical writers.

It is by no means easy to evaluate the evidence and to decide whether the epistle is to be accepted as coming from the pen of Paul or from a later disciple, who to a measure has caught the master's spirit, but who also—especially in his interpretation of the relation of Christ to the universe—shows a definite advance towards the Johannine conception. The obvious similarity with Colossians, far from being a guaranty of the genuineness of Ephesians, is precisely the reverse. Not only is it difficult to see why Paul should have indulged in such laborious copying and for whom it was intended but the subtle differences between the two are all the more apparent. One example will suffice. The figure of Christ as the "head" of the "body" appears in both writings (cf. especially Col. 2:10,19 with Eph.

[6] Eph. 3:5.

[7] Nor should the similarity between this conception of the recent revelation of what had long been kept a secret and that expressed in the (probably un-Pauline) Rom. 16:25 f. be disregarded.

4:16), but with an amazing difference of meaning underlying the phraseology. According to Colossians Christ is the head of the cosmic forces; the "world"—the cosmos—is the body. In Ephesians he is the head, and the church is the body.[8] Such literary dependence, but with subtle changes in meaning, is precisely what is to be expected from a later copyist, striving to gain for his work the authority of a great name. On the other hand—and this is the chief argument for its genuineness—it is difficult to see just what the purpose of the *falsarius* is. Recently Goodspeed[9] has sought to meet this difficulty. His thesis is that Ephesians was written by a man who, following the clues in Acts which had but recently appeared, retraced Paul's journeys to collect the writings of the hero of that book. For this collection he needed an introductory writing which should be of a character to enable the reader to appreciate the various letters. Ephesians was the result. It is a mosaic of all the genuine letters. Since the author lived in Colosse and was thus most familiar with Colossians, he naturally modelled his writing after that letter. The hypothesis is of interest; nor is it easy to think of a more plausible one. Perhaps this would best account for the appearance of the words "at Ephesus" in the opening words. Presumably the author simply wrote "to the saints who are also faithful." Marcion, who accepted the epistle as Paul's, apparently conjectured that it was the one referred to in Col. 4:16. If Goodspeed is correct that it was written from Colosse, it may be that in the neighbouring city of Ephesus eventually one copy received the specific designation "at Ephesus," both to harmonize the letter with all the others and to provide the Christians there with a specific word from their great apostle. The early evidence for the use of the letter by the writers already referred to renders any date far below 100 A.D. distinctly improbable. It is only fair to say that in our present state of knowledge "Ephesians" still remains one of the great enigmas, nor is there much reason to hope that it will ever be otherwise.

[8] So Dibelius, *Die Briefe an die Kolosser, Epheser, Philemon*, p. 113.

[9] E. J. Goodspeed, *The Meaning of Ephesians.*

Chapter XXVIII

THE PASTORAL EPISTLES

THESE three treatises, purporting to be letters from Paul to his two friends Timothy and Titus, are so intimately joined, each with the other two, and evidence such a marked degree of similarity, not only in structure and phraseology, but in purpose, that they cannot be treated separately. In these short writings 175 words occur which are not found in any of the other twenty-four writings, and of these there are 96 in I Timothy (over 15 to the page), 60 in II Timothy (nearly 13 to the page), and 43 in Titus (over 16 to the page). While there is a considerable body of words which appear in the ten letters commonly ascribed to Paul, but not in any other writing in the New Testament, their frequency of occurrence is markedly less and ranges from but 4 to the page in Romans to 6.2 to the page in Philippians.[1] Word-counting can, and often does, lead to plausible but fictitious results when blindly employed. But evidence such as this, buttressed as it is by such recurrent phrases as "faithful is the saying," which occurs five times in these letters[2] but nowhere else in the New Testament, can scarcely lead to any other conclusion than that these writings are very intimately joined. Nor is the identity of purpose less clearly marked. In the phraseology of the writings themselves, their aim is to teach "how men ought to behave themselves in the house of God" (I Tim. 3:15), that as a result they may "live soberly and righteously and godly in this present world" (Tit. 2:12). That is, the purpose of the author is primarily ethical. This desired goal is to be accomplished by the rejection of all false doctrine which can lead only to shipwreck, as it has in the past in the case of Hymenæus and Alexander; by strict discipline which shall stop the mouths of vain talkers and deceivers; by clear-cut rules of moral conduct which shall ensure the proper kind of life and speech among all Christians; and by the careful selection and oversight of those men and women who are to be entrusted with the direction of the Christian communities. In short, they are "little treatises on elementary church-law, or primitive church-manuals."[3]

For nearly a century and a half the three writings have been generally

[1] For these figures I am indebted to P. N. Harrison, *The Problem of the Pastoral Epistles*, p. 20. The whole section dealing with the linguistic evidence is worthy of careful study.

[2] I Tim. 1:15; 3:1; 4:9; II Tim. 2:11; Tit. 3:8.

[3] J. H. Ropes, *The Apostolic Age*, p. 120.

called the Pastoral Epistles,[4] because they purport to contain instructions for Timothy and Titus in their pastoral function. These men are now responsible for the welfare of certain districts. They are to guard the true deposit with which they have been entrusted; are to rebuke and unmask the wicked and foolish teachers who are causing a moral and spiritual pestilence in the church; are to see to it that the officers who are to assist them be of pure life and of sound doctrine; and, finally, are to set the proper example by their own temperance, sobriety, and orthodoxy. That this is simple literary subterfuge is perfectly obvious. They are not letters in any sense of the word. "Timothy" and "Titus" are simply lay figures, who are made to receive the type of instruction which the author feels the churches require. Thus "Paul" finds it necessary to emphasize his apostleship and to dwell on his past career. It is highly probable that Timothy would have known that Paul had been "appointed a preacher and an apostle, a teacher of the gentiles in faith and truth";[5] but not only must Paul proclaim this fact and clinch it (as he did another declaration to the rebellious Galatians) with the words: "I speak the truth, I lie not," but he finds it necessary to rehearse the fact that he had been a blasphemer, and a persecutor, and injurious, but that since he had done all this ignorantly in unbelief he had obtained mercy. Nor is it to be expected that Timothy, who had been associated for many years with Paul, stood in desperate need of receiving instruction that he might know "how men ought to behave themselves in the house of God" or that he needed to be told that the "house of God" was actually the "church of the living God, the pillar and ground of the truth" (I Tim. 3:15). None the less, this fellow apostle not only is admonished, "Let no man despise thy youth; but be thou an ensample to them that believe, in word, in manner of life, in love, in faith, in purity" (I Tim. 4:12), but is warned to flee youthful lusts and to live decently (II Tim. 2:22). It would be easy to multiply almost indefinitely these incongruities, but, as has been said in a different connexion, "It is not necessary to use battering-rams on gates that stand open." The whole situation is impossible, not to say absurd and grotesque, if we assume the historic Paul writing personal letters to the historic Timothy and Titus in real situations. But if we admit that we have here the work of a later writer seeking to meet the circumstances of his own day and wishing to gain for his instruction the authority of the now long-dead Paul, the absurdity is removed. In a word, the situation, Paul to Timothy and Paul to Titus, is simply stage-setting. Not only has the author made constant use of the letters of Paul to quarry from them Pauline phrases—usually they are as flat in their new setting as they were pointed in the original—but in addition he has simply transferred to his

[4] For a convenient summary of the history of this usage, the roots of which go back to Thomas Aquinas, see Harrison, *op. cit.*, pp. 13-16.

[5] I Tim. 2:7; cf. II Tim. 1:11.

writing the fact that years before, during Paul's ministry, he had felt it wise to urge the Corinthians not to "despise" Timothy who was his "beloved and faithful child in the Lord."[6]

A brief summary of the contents of these tracts (or epistles) will reveal their nature. I Timothy—After a brief and formal salutation comes an attack upon the false teachers who are sowing strife and perverting morals contrary to the sound doctrine which had been entrusted to Paul, who by God's grace had been changed from a persecutor to one faithful for that service. This task is now Timothy's (1:1-20). Then problems in the life and administration of the churches are considered. Prayer is to be offered by Christians for all men, including "kings and all that are in high places" (2:1-7). Men, however, are the ones to offer such prayer (2:8), while women, in accord with their subordinate position, are to perform their own proper duties (2:9-15). Then follows an enumeration of the qualities to be required of bishops, deacons, and deaconesses (?) (3:1-13), which is necessary since Paul may be delayed in coming to give the instruction in person (3:14-16). The attack on the false teachers is then once more resumed. Timothy is to stand firm in his opposition to the seducing spirits and doctrines of demons which in a later day are to seduce the church (4:1-16). His attitude toward the young and old of both sexes, especially toward "widows," elders (presbyters), slaves, and masters is prescribed (5:1-6:2). Then once more a bitter attack on all who teach a different doctrine, especially on those who are commercializing their preaching (6:3-10), and the earnest admonition to the "man of God" to flee from such practices and to "keep the commandment without spot, without reproach" (6:11-16). After a charge to warn the rich against the pitfalls of wealth and the final injunctions to "Timothy" to guard the deposit and to stand firm against the profane babbling of his Gnostic opponents, the writing closes with the simple benediction, "Grace be with you" (6:17-21).

II Timothy—After the greeting (very similar to that of I Timothy) follows a complimentary paragraph, much as in the genuine Pauline letters. Timothy is commended for his unfeigned faith, and is urged to stand firm in the midst of all difficulties and to show the same endurance as Paul himself (1:1-2:13). This section is interrupted by a reference to the former kindness of Onesiphorus, and the defection of Phygelus and Hermogenes (1:15-18). Then follows a confused section in which Timothy apparently receives instruction for the kind of life he himself should live and for his warning against the errorists; yet from the context it would appear to be intended to guide him in his choice of those who shall be "able to teach others also" (2:14-26). Chapter 3 continues the description of these imposters who in the last days shall come (3:1-9); against them Timothy is

[6] I Cor. 16:11; 4:17.

to stand fast, strengthened as he is by his experience with and instruction from Paul himself (3:10-17). With a final solemn charge to stand firm against these wicked workers, now that Paul is at the end of his earthly course (4:1-8), and with personal instructions to Timothy to come to Paul, forsaken as he is by all save Luke (4:9-18), the writing closes with greetings and a brief benediction (4:19-22).

Titus—Although this epistle is by far the shortest of the three, the salutation is the longest and with a decidedly theological tone (1:1-4). Titus then receives instructions for his work in Crete, similar to Timothy's in Ephesus. The various qualifications for elders and (or?) bishops are enumerated with especial reference to the errors and vices incident to Crete, where it has been rightly said, "Cretans are always liars, evil beasts, idle gluttons" (1:5-16). Titus is to "speak the things which befit the sound doctrine" for the guidance of the aged men, aged women (the aged to instruct the younger), the younger men, and slaves, and at the same time to watch his own conduct and to guard his authority (2:1-15). He is to inculcate obedience to their rulers and a desire for good works in place of the kind of vicious life practised before the kindness of God had been manifested. This is concluded with specific instructions for the treatment of the disobedient (3:1-11). Then with a brief personal word about his own (Paul's) plans, directions for Titus, a final admonition to encourage his Cretans to fruitfulness, the epistle ends with a salutation and the same benediction "Grace be with you all" (3:12-15).

Thus if we disregard the setting—Paul to Timothy or to Titus—and the occasional personal touches which, especially in II Timothy, are pasted on, the nature of the little writings is clear—primitive church-manuals with particular reference to church officers. Bishops, elders, deacons, widows—all receive words of instruction. The personal qualities essential for candidates for their offices are listed. No longer is the church recruited from the spiritually gifted. A more settled order has now been achieved. Whether bishops and elders (presbyters) are the same or are the titles for different officers is obscure. Nevertheless, we have reached the definite beginning of the monarchical episcopate which occupies so important a position in the letters of Ignatius. Furthermore, the detailed regulations for the appointment of widows and the care to prevent any save those who are "widows indeed" from being so enrolled evidence unmistakably the fact that these precautions have been found necessary, and reveal the lapse of years. The second stage in Christian life and thought is now in view. The passionate belief in the speedy approach of the Parousia, which bulked so large in the thinking of Paul, has passed. There is no trace of it in these writings. Rather their emphasis upon a secure and orderly organization reveals the belief that life far from ending on the morrow is to continue for some time.

A similar distinct difference from Paul is found in the author's attitude toward the false teachers he reproves. That these latter do not correspond perfectly to such second-century heresiarchs as Basilides or Marcion may be admitted freely, although the mention of the "fables and endless genealogies" (I Tim. 1:4), of the ascetic prohibition of marriage and the eating of meat (I Tim. 4:3), of the prohibition of wine—that in the "medicinal advice" to Timothy (I Tim. 5:23) a polemic against the formal ascetic practice of substituting water for wine in the Lord's supper is to be seen is highly probable—the warning against the "knowledge (*gnosis*) which is falsely so called" (I Tim. 6:20) all accord with what we learn from writers like Irenæus and Tertullian of the views and practices of Gnosticism in the second century. At any rate, the way in which the author opposes them is surely non-Pauline. Instead of the careful—to us often hypercritical—definition and elaboration of the differences between himself and his opponents which ever characterized Paul, in these writings the false teachings are lumped together with little or no discrimination and denounced *en bloc*. After a catalogue of evildoers the author can even conclude, "and if there be any other thing contrary to the sound doctrine."[7] In this we have an unmistakable sign of the hardening of the church system between the orthodox and all those who are not.

The evidence of a date quite beyond Paul and of an essential difference of point of view is further seen in the author's attitude toward Christianity itself. Paul's fundamental emphasis, the believer's death to the flesh and new life in the spirit, that is, the new man "putting on Christ," is entirely absent, although it would have been most apposite in these attacks on the false teachers. Nor is faith stressed as the way a man becomes identified with Christ. In its place stand *piety* (εὐσέβεια), a word never employed by Paul but which occurs in these three writings no less than eleven times, and *good works*. Upon these a man's salvation depends. Thus he can write:

> But if any provideth not for his own, and specially his own household, *he hath denied the faith* and is worse than an unbeliever.[8]

Again, the author can make Paul say—in the midst of the encomium which at all events sounds distinctly self-complacent if not arrogant in the mouth of the one praised—"I have kept the faith."[9] Obviously faith is no longer a way of life; it is loyalty or adherence to certain religious beliefs, such as the unity of God[10] or the fulfilment of the divine mercy.[11] Christianity is now an objective system which men can accept or reject:

[7] I Tim. 1:10.
[8] I Tim. 5:8.
[9] II Tim. 4:7.
[10] Cf. I Tim. 2:5.
[11] Cf. I Tim. 3:16.

But the spirit sayeth expressly, that in later times *some shall fall away from the faith*, giving heed to seducing spirits and doctrines of demons. . . .[12]

Between the repeated command to Timothy to "guard that which is committed unto thee"[13] and the exhortation of Jude to "contend earnestly for the faith which was once for all delivered unto the saints"[14] there would not appear to be any appreciable difference of point of view. A comparison of the two passages:

For whom he foreknew, he also foreordained to be conformed to the image of his Son, that he might be the firstborn among many brethren: and whom he foreordained, them he also called: and whom he called, them he also justified: and whom he justified, them he also glorified.[15]

Fight the good faith of the faith, lay hold on the life eternal, whereunto thou wast called, and didst confess the good confession in the sight of many witnesses.[16]

confirms this shift of emphasis and hardening of Christianity into a system of beliefs. Surely for Paul the *believer* is foreordained to salvation; equally clear is it that for this author *salvation* is foreordained to the believer. The importance of this shift of emphasis, which is far from an accidental variation by the same man, should not be overlooked.

Mention has already been made of the total failure in these epistles of words employed by Paul on every page of his letters and the corresponding use in these epistles of words never employed by him. An exhaustive survey of this evidence is outside the province of this book, nor is it necessary, for it has been often made. Suffice it to say that the difference of vocabulary is not due to the treatment of different subjects where such variance would be natural. The situation is here quite different. It is the little words—conjunctions, particles, and adverbs—which so clearly portray a writer's style. For the Greek stylist there is an impassable gulf between the Pauline letters and these epistles in this respect. Again, whole families of new words make their appearance in these brief writings. Particularly striking in this respect is the almost totally different vocabulary for virtues and vices. Again, as remarked in the case of "faith," words used by Paul are frequently employed in these writings in a totally changed sense. Then again, the style is very different from Paul's. There are no anacoloutha; all is regular and colourless, smooth, and commonplace. As is to be seen in the analyses of the epistles, there is little order or arrangement; rather they are compendia of more or less loosely attached passages. All this is very different from the compact and closely knit arguments in the other letters.

[12] I Tim. 4:1.
[13] I Tim. 6:30; II Tim. 1:14.
[14] Jude 3.
[15] Rom. 8:29,30.
[16] I Tim. 6:12.

Naturally the force of these arguments will be greatly reduced for those restricted to the use of the text in translation. It is, however, no overstatement that in the eyes of nearly every critic the strongest argument against the Pauline authorship of these writings lies in these amazing differences of vocabulary and style.

A final argument against the genuineness of the epistles is found in the impossibility of finding a place for them in the lifetime of Paul. It is easy to demonstrate[17] that the required situations will not fit into the outline of his life as we know it. For example, in I Timothy Paul is a free man and has shortly before gone to Macedonia, leaving Timothy in Ephesus (1:3). This might suggest the departure from Ephesus at the end of the three-year visit. Unfortunately, however, Timothy accompanied Paul, as is clear from the salutation of II Corinthians. In Titus it is clear that Paul has been with Titus in Crete (1:5) and has left him behind to organize churches there. Where is such a visit to be placed? Surely Acts 27 gives no intimation that the voyage to Rome gave Paul opportunity to familiarize himself with things Cretan. In II Timothy he is a prisoner at Rome at the end of his life, forsaken by all save Luke. Now he suddenly wants the cloak which he had left at Troas, and the books and parchments. If this is the Roman imprisonment at the end of Acts, these articles have been in Troas for a good number of years. Now Timothy is to fetch them. And Trophimus? He was left at Miletus sick (II Tim. 4:20, *pace* Acts 21:29). Certainly the reference does not imply that he had been on his sick bed for several years. To avoid these (and they are but a few of the rough spots) a second captivity has been often hypothesized. That is, following Paul's two-year stay in Rome, he was freed, and then went to Crete, Macedonia, and Ephesus; finally was rearrested, and after a close confinement died in Rome. The difficulty with this hypothesis is that there is absolutely no evidence for it—the early tradition of his labour in Spain[18] is scarcely more than a deduction from his hope expressed in Rom. 15:28. As Bernhard Weiss many years ago remarked, "The hypothesis of a second imprisonment is confirmed only by the Pastoral Epistles, if they are genuine, and the genuineness of the Pastoral Epistles can only be proved by adopting this hypothesis." And with the solid reasons, already enumerated, for viewing these writings as not only non-Pauline but as coming from a distinctly later date, there would appear little profit in chasing this circle.

It would appear, then, that we can hardly err in calling these epistles *Paul-like* rather then Pauline, that is, pseudonymous productions of a Paulinist, written at a time well removed from Paul, as is evidenced not only by the solidification of his thought but by the absence of any mention of

[17] Cf. Jülicher, *Introduction to the New Testament,* pp. 189-193; latest German edition, pp. 176-179.

[18] I Clem. 5:6,7.

the Parousia and by the state of church organization. There is now a definite catholic faith to be fought for and defended, which Paul has held to the end. Not only are the qualifications of church officers now catalogued, but some form of ordination is now in use—"with the laying on of the hands of the presbytery" (I Tim. 4:14). Paul is the author's especial hero. Many phrases which would be distinctly bad taste in the mouth of Paul are thus explicable; for example:

> I have fought the good fight, I have finished the course, I have kept the faith: Henceforth there is laid up for me the crown of righteousness, which the Lord, the righteous judge, shall give me at that day, and not to me only, but also to all them that have loved his appearing.[19]

In Paul's name the author is striving to safeguard Christianity. Perhaps those critics are right who hazard the guess that this subterfuge was adopted because the opponents were either flouting Paul's authority or claiming it. Why he wrote three epistles instead of one he has not intimated. Guesses are fruitless. Is it to give an increased effectiveness both by repetition and by the address to widely scattered groups of churches?

There is no evidence which indicates from where the letters were written. Rome has been suggested on the basis of Latinisms, but this argument is of little weight. It is best not to hazard a guess. Nor can the date be fixed with any certainty. That it is well below the Apostolic Age is obvious. The first sure reference to the letters is in Polycarp's epistle to the Philippians, which is usually dated *ca.* 115 A.D., although so early a date is far from certain. Marcion did not include them in his canon. Had he believed them from Paul's pen he would scarcely have refrained, although naturally he would have deleted certain sections, as he did from the other letters of Paul. Aside from the letter of Polycarp, the date of which appears to me far from certain, there is no reference to these epistles before the middle of the second century. Perhaps the most probable date for all three would be 100-125 A.D., although personally I do not consider a date fifty years later impossible.[20]

Although there is a pretty general agreement among critics that the epistles are not Pauline, some scholars have inclined to the view that they are built up from genuine Pauline fragments. II Timothy and (less certainly) Titus exhibit this; in I Timothy they feel it more doubtful. Elaborate reconstructions have been attempted by various scholars, notably Harnack, McGiffert, Bacon, and Harrison; and various conclusions have been drawn as to the order in which the three were composed. Personally,

[19] II Tim. 4:7,8.

[20] Recently D. W. Riddle, *Early Christian Life,* pp. 195-216, has argued that they are *anti-* and hence *post-*Marcion. There is more to be said for this contention than is generally conceded. Cf. especially the warning against the "oppositions [literally *antitheses*] of the knowledge which is falsely so called" (I Tim. 6:20) and the sweeping commendation of "every scripture inspired of God" (II Tim. 3:16).

their arguments appear to me to carry little or no weight. Several references might seem personal—for example, the request to bring the cloak and the books,[21] the reference to Hymenæus and Alexander,[22] the mention of the evil done by Alexander the coppersmith[23]—but with the Pauline letters before him as models, it is scarcely to be doubted that the author would desire to give a verisimilitude to his own work. That he has incorporated fragments of the extant letters again and again is certain; that occasionally he has achieved a fair similarity to Paul's style is not to be denied, but that he had access to genuine fragments outside of the canonical letters is by no means sure; and any attempt to isolate such appears a waste of effort. The argument that the personal touches in II Timothy "sound natural" proves nothing at all. It is a poor writer who cannot achieve some degree of success in such a direction. Unless we assume that every pseudepigrapher was totally devoid of skill and that, therefore, every touch that "sounds natural" must of necessity be the result of preservation, not invention, there would appear little in these epistles not completely and satisfactorily explained by the hypothesis that the writer had made careful use of the extant letters of Paul and whatever other tradition was available, and, without any disquieting thought that a later age, with different standards of literary honesty, would accuse him of dishonest motives, sought not only to write to the Christians of his own age as he assumed Paul would have done, but to make his writing as Paul-like as possible.

[21] II Tim. 4:13.
[22] I Tim. 1:20.
[23] II Tim. 4:14 f.

Chapter XXIX

THE EPISTLE TO THE HEBREWS

THE purpose of the unknown writer "to the Hebrews" is distinctly practical. Only so can the writing be understood. But the word "practical" must not be understood in the sense in which the letters of Paul are practical. The interest of the writer is theological—perhaps dogmatic is the proper word—rather than ethical. His purpose is to confirm and strengthen Christians who are in danger of lapsing into indifference, of yielding to pressure, of falling away from the living faith. The traditional interpretation has been that this relapse was a slipping back into Judaism, that Jewish Christians were in danger of backsliding. It is far wiser to view the writing as a burning warning against slipping away, not *to* Judaism, but *from* the living God, that is, into a worldly life and religious indifference. His great thesis—and almost every sentence directly impinges upon this—is that Christianity is the final and absolute religion. It is the Platonic *idea* of religion, of which all other religions are simply shadows or copies. Christianity is the true reality. Thus his abundant reference to Judaism and its inferiority to Christianity are not for the purpose of minimizing Judaism, but of exalting Christianity. It is not to warn men from falling back into Judaism which is inferior, but to warn them from falling away from Christianity, which is infinitely superior to even a splendid religion like Judaism. Such a fall, which even now threatens, would be tragic. "Therefore we ought to give the more earnest heed to the things that were heard, lest haply we drift away from them. For . . . how shall we escape, if we neglect so great a salvation?"[1]

Precisely because Christianity alone can offer salvation or, as he elsewhere phrases it, "forgiveness" lies the peril. The Jewish ritual with successive high priests entering the holy of holies time and again to offer the sacrifice implies that such service was not efficacious, else it would not—could not—be repeated. On the contrary, Christ, the true high priest, went in but once and offered his own blood. This wrought forgiveness, but it was once and for all. It can never be repeated. Consequently there can never be a second forgiveness. Sin after baptism cannot be removed. Hence the fearful peril entailed in falling away. This emphasis, so central to his thought, and which explains the essential fusing of the practical and the theological in his message, appears again and again.

[1] Hebr. 2:1-3.

For as touching those who were once enlightened and tasted of the heavenly gift, and were made partakers of the Holy Spirit, and tasted the good word of God, and the powers of the age to come, and then fell away, it is impossible to renew them again unto repentance; seeing they crucify to themselves the Son of God afresh, and put him to an open shame. For the land which hath drunk the rain that cometh oft upon it, and bringeth forth herbs meet for them for whose sake it is also tilled, receiveth blessing from God: but if it beareth thorns and thistles, it is rejected and nigh unto a curse; whose end is to be burned.[2]

For if we sin wilfully after that we have received the knowledge of the truth, there remaineth no more a sacrifice for sins; but a certain fearful expectation of judgment, and a fierceness of fire which shall devour the adversaries. A man that hath set at nought Moses' law dieth without compassion on the word of two or three witnesses: of how much sorer punishment, think ye, shall he be judged worthy, who hath trodden under foot the Son of God, and hath counted the blood of the covenant wherewith he was sanctified an unholy thing, and hath done despite unto the Spirit of grace? For we know him that said, Vengeance belongeth unto me, I will recompense. And again, The Lord shall judge his people. It is a fearful thing to fall into the hands of the living God.[3]

For ye know that even when he afterward desired to inherit the blessing, he was rejected; for he found no peace for a change of mind in his father, though he sought it diligently with tears.[4]

This emphasis was to convulse Christian thought for centuries after the writer had gone to his unknown grave. A few years later the author of the *Shepherd*, while recognizing its validity, sought as a temporary expedient to give a sort of second chance through the special *fiat* of the angel of repentance.[5] I John attempts a somewhat different solution: There is a distinction between sins. This later led to the Catholic doctrine of deadly and venial sins. During the early days of persecution, when some "lapsed" under pressure and the church was convulsed over their status, this uncompromising teaching of "to the Hebrews" played an important part. In subsequent years it was directly responsible for the natural but dangerous expedient of putting off baptism until the end of life to avoid the bitter consequences of a subsequent fall.

The author's argument is clear and logical. God has now sent his final and supreme utterance through his Son, who is associated with him in the creation and control of the world. He came to earth to join himself to flesh and blood that he might have many brethren. Since he was tempted "in all points like as we are," he can appreciate our temptations as the angels cannot; since

[2] Hebr. 6:4-8.
[3] Hebr. 10:26-31.
[4] Hebr. 12:17.
[5] Hermas, *Mand.* iv, 3,1-7.

he remained without sin, he can help them that are tempted. As the mediator of our forgiveness he is the great high priest; and, as such, is a merciful and trustworthy high priest (1:1-5:10). Then comes a section (5:11-6:12) which has often appeared as a sort of interlude of rebuke: you are ignorant; you who should be teachers need again to be taught your A B C's. But that it is intended as such and evidences that the writing is a letter to a distinct group is improbable. As such, it would be a curious method of teaching. Even though you have shown yourselves unfitted for the solid food appropriate for full-grown men and instead have need of milk, yet I will give you the meat, and later, if God permits, will then give you your diet of milk! Rather, this little interlude appears for the purpose of arousing the readers' interest and of making them properly aware of the majesty and import of the thesis which he has just stressed—Christ, the author of eternal salvation, has been named of God a high priest after the order of Melchizedek (Hebr. 5:10)—and which he now turns to expand and justify as the chief glory of Christianity.

The chief glory of Christianity is that its institutions are real and abiding. They are no mere copies, as were the provisional, though noble, institutions of Judaism, which could not effect forgiveness. Christianity can effect forgiveness, for, instead of a high priest offering daily a sacrifice of the blood of sheep and goats, Christ, the great high priest without successor, offered his own blood once and for all. That was effective, as is evidenced by the fact that it is never to be repeated (6:13-10:39). Let your loyalty be firm, remembering that faith—always implying something unseen through its nature as the power of apprehension of that which lies beyond the senses—is the distinguishing characteristic of Christians, even as it has been the characteristic of all the leaders of religious history since the world began. With such a heritage and with such a host of witnesses let us run with steadfast endurance the race that is set before us, realizing that the terrors of Sinai are as nothing in comparison with the terrors of the living God who has given now his final and therefore his *only* offer of grace to those who persist in faith (11:1-12:29). With a few disjointed exhortations and personal references (chapter 13), which stand in amazing contrast to the rest of the writing, the "epistle" ends.

Thus the thesis is developed that Christianity is the final and absolute religion. The substance of Christianity is the supreme and abiding nature of Jesus Christ. In his cosmic relation he is exalted above the angels; in the history of redemption he far surpasses Moses and Joshua; as distinct from the Aaronic priesthood, where member follows member—nothing ultimate and final there—he is the high priest forever after the order of Melchizedek. Nor is this a descending scale or an anticlimax. The real climax to the argument comes on this last note:

Now in the things which we are saying the chief point is this: We have such a high priest, who sat down on the right hand of the throne of the Majesty in the heavens, a minister of the sanctuary, and of the true tabernacle, which the Lord pitched, not man.[6]

This writing, today almost unknown—it has been well said that for the average Christian, clerical as well as lay, Hebrews is simply "the book which mentions Melchizedek"—is a real literary achievement. Written in by far the best Greek in the New Testament, it is obviously the production of a man of culture and letters. Not only is he a thoroughgoing Platonist, but he is familiar with and tacitly accepts that later development in the Stoic-Platonic synthesis, conspicuously evidenced by Philo and his successors in Alexandria, the notion of the *Logos*. As certainly as does the author of the Fourth Gospel, he opens his writing with the identification of Christ as the *Logos*. To be sure, he does not use the term; but his description of him as "the effulgence of his glory, and the very image of his substance . . . upholding all things by the word of his power"[7] is unmistakable. Furthermore, his phraseology here and even more conspicuously in 6:5—"tasted the good *word* of God"—evidences his familiarity with this teaching and his unwillingness to confuse his argument by the introduction of the word *logos*, which might be interpreted in its philosophical and technical sense which he did not at that moment wish.[8] In passing it may be noted that this feel for language and unwillingness to use a technical term in a different sense stamps the writer as a scholar. He is, as has been aptly said, the schoolman of the New Testament."

Two questions naturally rise: "Who wrote it? and, For whom was it written? Probably neither will ever be answered although gallons of ink have been spilt in what Wrede aptly designated "a labour of Sisyphus."

One thing is clear. Paul did not write it. Today none save a few Catholic theologians unhappily fettered by the Council of Trent would dream of disagreeing with the judgment of Calvin: "Who then composed it is not to be discovered, however hard one labours, but that the nature of the thought and that the style are quite unlike Paul's is abundantly evidenced."[9] All the lines of evidence converge here. (1) The absence of his name, of the greeting to the readers, and of the complimentary paragraph would be not only unparalleled but unthinkable. (2) The author's reference to the way he had learned the gospel—"which having at first been spoken through the Lord, *was confirmed unto us by them that heard*"[10]—definitely excludes Paul. Never could he so speak. This point was sufficient for both Calvin and Mar-

[6] Hebr. 8:1,2.

[7] Hebr. 1:3.

[8] In both cases he substitutes ῥῆμα for the possibly ambiguous λόγος.

[9] *Quis porro eam composuerit non magnopere curandum est, sed ipsa dicendi ratio et stylus alium quam Paulum satis testantur.*

[10] Hebr. 2:3.

tin Luther, and has been for most critics. (3) The style and theology, as Calvin remarked, are quite different from Paul's. As opposed to the latter's Greek tinged with Hebraisms, full of anacoloutha and daring liberties, the language of this writing is, as has been already said, the purest Greek in the New Testament. The diction is faultless; the sentences beautifully rounded and polished. There may well be occasional overtones from some of the Pauline letters, but they evidence a writer who approaches his problem from a totally different angle.

It is not until the end of the second century that we find any voice raised to ascribe it to Paul.[11] From then on the Alexandrian school inclined to class it as Pauline, although they keenly felt the differences of style and thought, and sought to account for them. Pantænus—for that is apparently the "blessed presbyter" referred to by Clement—considered it from Paul, and explained the absence of his name at the beginning of the letter as due to his humility, for the Lord, not Paul, was the apostle to the Hebrews.[12] Clement himself thought that Paul had written the letter in Hebrew (Aramaic?) and that Luke had translated it. Occasionally this translation theory has been revived, but it is utterly improbable. Origen considered that Paul was the author of the material, but that another—who he was "God only knows"—had put it in written form.[13] In the western church, on the contrary, it was not until the middle of the fourth century that it was classed as Pauline and considered canonical. Tertullian and Novatian had ascribed it to Barnabas. Both Jerome and Augustine were familiar with traditions which denied Pauline authorship, and Augustine himself in his later years regularly referred to it as anonymous, but by this time (beginning of the fifth century) it was universally considered canonical.

It would be completely profitless to consider the host of other candidates who from time to time have been suggested—Barnabas, Silas, Timothy, Aquila, Priscilla, Clement of Rome, Luke. It would be sheer guesswork, and based upon the dubious assumption that the name of the author of any writing destined to become a part of Holy Scripture must of necessity have been mentioned somewhere else in the New Testament. Most students will admit that it is very probable that not all the Christians of ability and influence of the first century chance to be mentioned in the casual letters of Paul or the fragmentary and partial account in Acts. All that we can say of him is that he was a man of literary training, perhaps a Jew, although this is far less certain than has often been assumed,[14] steeped in Platonic thought and acquainted with views which flourished in Alexandria, and with some fa-

[11] For a partial qualification to this statement see below, pp. 314 ff.

[12] This he deduced from Hebr. 3:1.

[13] Even this secondary Pauline form is utterly improbable. For a possible explanation of how Paul's name came to be attached to it in tradition see pp. 314 ff.

[14] This assumption is based on his familiarity with the Old Testament. But against this is his total silence about the cardinal emphasis of Judaism—keeping of the law.

miliarity with the teachings of Paul; in short, that he was a man who lived in an "intellectual and almost dogmatic atmosphere."[15]

The exact date of this writing is also hard to fix. The *terminus ad quem* (latest possible date) is the time of the composition of I Clement, since this latter writing clearly uses it, especially in chapter 36. I Clement is usually dated about 96 A.D. on the assumption that its opening words refer to the "Domitianic persecution." Personally, I consider this "persecution" largely a figment of Christian imagination and see no reason for understanding Clement's apology for not having written earlier as more than the conventional excuse for procrastination of which every letter-writer in his and each subsequent century has made use. There would appear to be no other reason which would compel a date earlier than 120 A.D. for Clement. Hence, a few years earlier, say 110 A.D., would appear to be the *terminus ad quem* for Hebrews. The *terminus a quo* is more difficult. Although it is clearly *post*-Pauline, some have urged a date prior to 70 A.D. This view is based upon the assumption that the writing is to avert an apostasy to Judaism. Therefore, it is argued, had the temple in Jerusalem been already destroyed, that would have been the author's trump card. But the temple service is actually represented as still going on (10:1 ff.). This assumption, however, is totally in error. In the first place, as has been earlier suggested, the purpose of the writing is not to avert an apostasy to Judaism, but a falling away from Christianity into irreligion. In the second place, the writer is not concerning himself with the temple in Jerusalem at all; it is the imaginary Mosaic tabernacle which he constantly depicts as the shadow of the true (Christian) tabernacle.[16] In a word, he is drawing his comparisons and knowledge not from contemporary Jewish thought and practice but from the Pentateuch. Accordingly, there is no force to the argument for an early (*ante* 70 A.D.) date. The whole tone and outlook of the writing favour a later date; the primitive days are now far behind (cf. 2:3). The reference to the "former days" when they had stood firm, the rebuke of their weakness, the almost total disregard of the Parousia, the separation of the "leaders" from the rest of the saints—all this implies a lapse of time. Furthermore, if, as seems to me highly probable, the writing is a treatise, not a letter, and is intended for all Christians, it would appear then to be appreciably later than the Pauline letters which had set the fashion for Christian writing, but had been intended for specific groups, confronting equally specific problems. This gradually led to the writing of general, that is, catholic, epistles and treatises intended for all Christians everywhere. Accordingly, *mutatis mutandis* I would incline to date it between 85-110 A.D., perhaps rather nearer the latter than the former limit.

[15] Ropes, *Apostolic Age*, p. 272.

[16] In place of the words ἱερόν and ναός which he never uses, he habitually refers to the σκηνή—the Septuagint rendering of the Mosaic tabernacle.

Before considering the final question: To whom was it addressed? or better, For whom was it intended? it is necessary to consider the preliminary question, What sort of a composition is it? Although it is customary to refer to it as an "epistle," in the preceding pages it has been scrupulously referred to simply as a "writing." The reason for this reserve is as follows: Except for the final chapter there is nothing in the writing which resembles either a personal "letter" or more formal "epistle." There is no salutation, no mention of the writer's name—which latter was as essential to an early letter or epistle as the signature is for us today—no paragraph of compliment or congratulation, no statement of the reason why he writes, such as the importance of the subject or errors which have arisen to make it necessary. The rebuke in 5:11 ff. is not so to be construed. Rather it implies: Such immaturity is a quality which may well lead the reader to shrink away from the teaching which the author wishes to give. Actually it is not until 3:1 that even a casual reference to any readers is made. On the other hand, chapter 13 is obviously the conclusion of a letter. In the last verses especially, the personal note, the mention of the writer's intended visit, the visit of Timothy, the assumption that the readers will be interested in the condition of the writer—all this stands in striking contrast to the body of the writing. Nor can it be assumed on the basis of the last chapter and the occasional superficial references to readers (5:11-6:12; 10:32-34) that originally a salutation stood at the beginning and that it was later lost, intentionally or accidentally. No writer who could pen so magnificent an opening paragraph could ever have marred it by any preceding salutation. Furthermore, save for the final chapter, the references to readers—even 5:11 ff. and 6:9-12—do not imply any local or specific group, any more than do such passages as I Peter 4:12 or 5:9. They are perfectly natural as the praise and blame of Christians is general. That occasionally the author may have had some particular case in mind and that that led him to phrase himself as he did is not to be denied and is quite probable; none the less, there appears to me no reason for assuming anything more. What then is the relationship of chapter 13 to the preceding twelve chapters? It appears to be a late addition by some other writer who desired to give to the writing the appearance of a Pauline letter. Regularly Paul's letters close with a series of practical exhortations. So this writing is made to close. No one can fail to feel the abrupt shift in 13:1. Certainly the connection is at best very tenuous. Furthermore, and this is the important point, 13:19 and 13:23 contain a most amazing contradiction. In 13:19 the author begs his readers to pray for him that he may be the more speedily restored to them. Certainly the natural meaning of the word underlying "restore" is that the author is now restrained, apparently in prison. Yet in 13:23 there is no hint that he is thus hindered. He will see them soon; if Timothy, who has been set at liberty, arrives in time, the two will see them together. As Wrede pointed out in his penetrating essay, *Das literarische Rätsel des Hebräer-*

briefs,[17] this contradiction would be completely explained if we assume that the author sought to give a Pauline flavour here and borrowed from two of the Pauline letters, but that he was not completely at home in the rôle which he assumed and accordingly involved himself in a contradiction. The following passages should be pondered.

Hebr. 13:18 f.—Pray for us. . . . And I exhort you the more exceedingly to do this, that I may be restored to you the sooner.	Philm. 22—But withal prepare me also a lodging; for I hope that through your prayers I shall be granted unto you.
Hebr. 13:23—Know ye that our own brother Timothy hath been set at liberty; with whom, if he come shortly, I will see you.	Phil. 2:19,23,24—But I hope in the Lord Jesus to send Timothy shortly unto you. . . . Him therefore I hope to send forthwith, so soon as I shall see how it will go with me: but I trust in the Lord that I myself also shall come shortly.

There are other distinct parallelisms between Hebr. 13 and Philippians—for example 13:16 || 4:18; 13:21 || 4:20; 13:24 || 4:21 f. Similarities with other Pauline writings are perhaps also to be seen (cf. 13:18 with II Cor. 1:11,12). It is to be observed, however, that these resemblances are restricted to chapter 13. Is not the curiously indefinite phrase, "*They of Italy* salute you," naturally explained on the basis of "All the saints salute you, especially *they that are of Cæsar's household*"[18] if the author is seeking to impersonate the imprisoned Paul who he believes had written Philippians from his Roman bondage? A full demonstration of the argument is here impossible. Suffice it to say that to me it appears highly probable that our writing ended originally with 12:29, was anonymous, was a treatise (or homily) intended for no especial church or group of churches, but for all Christians to whom it might come, and that later—perhaps at the time that the title "To the Hebrews" was affixed, although this is less certain—this final chapter was added with the distinct purpose of giving to the writing the stamp of Pauline authority. The question may be asked: Why, if this were the case, did this later writer not prefix a Pauline salutation to make the attempt the clearer? The most probable answer is that he was unwilling to risk marring so perfect a writing by so palpable an attempt. That he was the master of the contents of chapters 1-12 is obvious, not alone from such touches as 13:3,7 (cf. 10:32-34),

[17] For this discussion of chapter 13 I am deeply indebted to this essay which warrants far more attention than it seems to have received. The principal point of difference between Wrede's view and my own is his assumption that the author of chapters 1-12 later changed his plan and *himself* wrote chap. 13 to give to the whole a Pauline appearance. This appears to me improbable.

[18] Phil. 4:22.

but from the neat reference to the main argument of the treatise in the words, "Jesus Christ is the same yesterday, today, yea and for ever" (13:8).

Thus the later title, "To the Hebrews," does not help us in our quest for the recipients. This was probably added to make it parallel with the other "Pauline" epistles "To the Romans," "To the Galatians," etc. Actually the choice of the title, "To the Hebrews," was a most unhappy one. It apparently resulted from the view that it was to warn Jewish Christians from a relapse into Judaism. As we have seen, the probability that this was not the purpose, the failure of any warning against circumcision or anything else distinctly Jewish, the lateness of date—all this makes it far more likely that it was intended for all Christians into whose hands it might fall, and that, since at the end of the first century Jewish Christians were now few and far between, the majority of these readers would be gentiles. The frequent quotations from the Old Testament and the reference to the "seed of Abraham" need provide no difficulty. All Christians, gentiles and Jews alike, accepted the Old Testament as Christian Scripture. Paul makes it perfectly clear that gentile Christians found no difficulty in considering themselves the true seed of Abraham.[19]

Thus the customary designation of the writing, "The Epistle to the Hebrews," is doubly wrong. It is not an "epistle"; it was not written to "Hebrews." Rather, it is to be seen as an anonymous treatise or homily by an unknown for all Christians everywhere. Its purpose was to arouse Christians to their old-time faith and to warn them from backsliding. To this end he explains Christianity as the one true and final religion, gloriously effective to salvation through the superlative glory of the person and work of Jesus Christ. At a later time another unknown Christian sought to give to the writing a Pauline touch by adding an "epistolary conclusion." Did he go a step farther and by the addition of the personal pronoun "of me" in 10:34 seek to give an additional Pauline touch in the reference to "my bonds"? That some one did this at an early date is clear. Perhaps it was the author of the final chapter.

[19] *E.g.*, Rom. 4:1,12.

Chapter XXX

THE CATHOLIC EPISTLES

IN CONTRAST to the *Corpus Paulinarum*, the term used at an early date to designate the thirteen letters which bear his name and the Epistle to the Hebrews, stand seven other writings—James, I and II Peter, I, II, and III John, and Jude—which surely as early as the first of the fourth century, and probably considerably before that time, were not infrequently referred to as the Catholic Epistles. For centuries the significance of the word *catholic* in this connexion has been debated. Clement of Alexandria employed it to designate the letter of the Jerusalem church mentioned in Acts 15—"in the catholic epistle of all the apostles"[1]—while Origen referred not only to the separate writings, I Peter, I John, and Jude, but also to the so-called Epistle of Barnabas by this term. In his famous *Church History*, written about 325 A.D., Eusebius not only uses the term for the separate epistles,[2] but for all seven:

> These accounts are given respecting James, whose is said to be the first of the epistles called catholic; but it is to be observed that it is considered spurious, since not many of the ancients have mentioned it, and not even that called the epistle of Jude, which is also one of the seven called catholic. Nevertheless we know that these, with the rest, are publicly used in most of the churches.[3]

> In the work called *Hypotyposes* . . . he [Clement of Alexandria] has given abridged accounts of all the canonical Scripture, not even omitting those that are disputed, I mean the epistle of Jude, and the other catholic epistles, and the epistle of Barnabas, and the so-called apocalypse of Peter.[4]

These passages make it clear that for these writers the term catholic did not mean "recognized," that is, "canonical," for Eusebius not only expressly states that the majority of them were "disputed" but also quotes Apollonius' attack upon the heretic Themison:

> Moreover, Themison, who was completely clad in a most plausible covetousness . . . dared to imitate the apostles by drawing up *a certain catholic epistle*, to instruct those who had a better faith than himself, to contend with words of empty

[1] *Strom.* iv,15.

[2] *Cf. Hist. Eccl.* vii,25,7 and 10. Here he is quoting Dionysius of Alexandria, who wrote about 260 A.D.

[3] *Hist. Eccl.* ii,23,24 f.

[4] *Hist. Eccl.* vi,14,1.

sound, and to blaspheme against the Lord and the apostles and the holy church.[5] Thus it would seem scarcely open to question but that for him and the eastern wing of Christendom (including Alexandria) the word signified "encyclical," that is, intended for all Christians everywhere, or at least for large groups of Christians in various places. Both Œcumenius, bishop of Tricca in the tenth century, and the twelfth-century lexicographer Suidas so understood it, while the scholastic Leontius of Byzantium (*ca.* 600) explained: "They were called 'catholic' since they were not written to one group as the epistles of Paul." Two passages in Eusebius, however, are confessedly difficult. Having referred to I Peter as "acknowledged," that is, enjoying both apostolic authorship and general acceptance, in contrast to II Peter, which "we have not, indeed, received to be canonical, yet as it appeared useful to many it was studiously read with the other Scriptures," he spoke of other writings ascribed to Peter—*Acts*, a gospel bearing his name, *Preaching,* and *Apocalypse* and concludes: "we know nothing of their being handed down *as catholic writings* (ἐν καθολικαῖς)."[6] In describing the work of Dionysius of Corinth, after remarking that he "was most useful to all in the *catholic epistles that he addressed to the churches,*" he mentions some of these "catholic epistles." One was to the Lacedæmonians, others to the Athenians, to the Nicomedians, to the church at Gortyna with the other churches of Crete, to the church at Amastris together with those in Pontus, to the Cnossians, to the Romans and addressed to Bishop Soter, and a final one to his own sister, Chrysophora.[7] In neither of these passages does the word catholic appear to equal general: in the former it can scarcely be other than "accepted" or canonical; in the latter passage the letters are clearly intended for specific groups, however appropriate they may have been for Christendom at large. Perhaps, however, the difficulty may be partially explained: Is the usage in the former of the two passages caused by Eusebius' view that all the real "catholic epistles" were from the pens of apostles, and that thus, by a not too exact use of language, he employs "catholic" in the sense, "apostolic"?

One reason for the debate over the meaning of the word is the curious difference in usage between the East and West. The East continued to use the term catholic for these seven letters, but never for those of Paul—in itself, this suggests its connotation—in the West, however, although Jerome occasionally used the term, the regular title for these letters was not "catholic," but "canonical." Thus Jerome can write of the "seven letters which are styled canonical"; by the sixth century apparently this was the almost unvaried habit, although the term "canonical" was not rigidly restricted to these seven as was the parallel term "catholic" in the East. It

[5] *Hist. Eccl.* v,18,5; cf. also the "catholic epistles" of Dionysius of Corinth referred to below.
[6] *Hist. Eccl.* iii, 3,1 f. Lake reads ἐν καθολικοῖς ("in catholic tradition").
[7] *Hist. Eccl.* iv,23.

is conceivable that this usage arose through a misunderstanding of what "catholic" meant, understanding it mistakenly to mean "universally accepted" instead of "universally destined," but this like many other questions is far from sure.

As a matter of fact, the designation of these writings as catholic, that is, general, was most apt. Superficially it might not seem appropriate for II and III John, the former of which is addressed to "the elect lady," the latter to "Gaius, the beloved." But not improbably these designations are but figurative—much as in the case of the letters to Timothy and Titus. Short though the letters are, they are apparently intended for all Christians. Nor, as will be seen in the next chapter, is I Peter to be considered any exception. That letter, too, is intended for all Christians everywhere. Perhaps the specific mention of the five provinces of Asia Minor was due to especial difficulties which Christians in that locality were suffering and which made this stirring appeal to play the part of a genuine Christian in the teeth of all persecution particularly appropriate; perhaps it was but a literary device to give the writing a certain resemblance to the earlier and now authoritative letters of Paul. One thing is clear. All of these little writings —to whomsoever they may be addressed—are concerned with the church in general. The contrast between them and the letters of Paul is so patent that the veriest tyro cannot fail to detect it. By anticipation it may be stated that they not only reveal the church in a much later situation than do the genuine letters of Paul, but that they owe their epistolary form to the Pauline correspondence. Paul had set the fashion for Christian writings. In contrast to him, the trail-blazer, these men were ready to follow on. For Paul the burning problem was the proclamation of the gospel, the salvation of mankind; for these authors the great task was the safeguarding of the church already established. Can there be reasonable ground for doubt as to which is the earlier, which the later?

Although these letters have been classed together from the earliest days, and although it will be convenient to discuss them together, for they have many points in common, it would be most misleading to consider them all of a piece. Each has its own purpose; each provides its own problem. Every critic realizes that there is a distinct connexion between I John and the Fourth Gospel. Very possibly they come from the same pen. To a certain extent it would be an advantage to consider them together. It has seemed wiser, however, to let each remain in the group in which it has reposed for so many centuries.

One final word of general introduction may not be out of place. These writings, despite their ambitious apostolic claims, were very reluctantly received into the canon. Apparently only I Peter and I John were generally considered canonical in the second century, and even they not universally. It was not until the fifth century, for example, that any one of the seven was translated into Syriac for the Syrian church, and then only James, I Peter, and I John. Marcion's canon contained none of them; the famous fragment of that second century Roman canon, commonly called the Muratorian, mentioned only Jude and two epistles of John. These three (II John, III John, and Jude) followed later, and were but doubtfully accepted; II Peter and James were completely ignored or rejected until well on in the third century. Origen, the earliest to cite James, is well aware that its recognition was far from general. Eusebius refers to them as commonly rejected in his day. It was not until the second half of the fourth century that James is mentioned in the Western church.[8] This pretty general reluctance to accept these writings—how great the contrast to the attitude toward the gospels and letters of Paul—must be kept in mind in considering their date and authorship. As a matter of fact, Jülicher may well be correct in his remark that probably one of the reasons that these writings eventually gained their niche in the canonical hall of fame while much more lengthy and pretentious writings like I Clement, Barnabas, and the *Shepherd* lost out was "the modest proportion . . . maintained between the value and the extent of the subject matter."

[8] By Hilary of Poitiers (*ob.* 366 A.D.).

Chapter XXXI

THE FIRST EPISTLE OF PETER

THE aim of the author of this short writing—it is about the same length as Philippians—is exclusively practical. His one desire was to inspire and encourage his readers in the face of severe persecution, or at least opposition. They are not to lose sight of the great prize; by their love and purity they are to advance the power of the gospel by provoking the admiration of their enemies. The true Christian is shown in suffering. This is the thesis of the epistle.

> Beloved, think it not strange concerning the fiery trial among you, which cometh upon you to prove you, as though a strange thing happened unto you; but insomuch as ye are partakers of Christ's sufferings, rejoice; that at the revelation of the glory also ye may rejoice with exceeding joy.[1]

Though the author's whole effort is devoted to this one end—to stiffen the backbones of those who may speedily be called upon to "suffer as a Christian," there is nothing pessimistic nor morbid from beginning to end. Rather the keynote is hope. In the opening words this note is struck with no uncertain hand:

> Blessed be the God and Father of our Lord Jesus Christ, who according to his great mercy begat us again unto a living hope . . . unto an inheritance incorruptible, and undefiled, and that fadeth not away. . . .[2]

Suffer they will, but, if it be not "as a murderer, or a thief, or an evildoer, or as a meddler in other men's matters, but . . . as a Christian," they have nothing to fear. For them hope need never wane.

> Wherefore let them also that suffer according to the will of God commit their souls in well-doing unto a faithful Creator.[3]

Following the address and salutation (1:1 f.) comes a paragraph of praise to God for his goodness in causing them to be born again to a glorious hope, undimmed by suffering, of salvation long sought by the prophets (1:3-12). Such a gift deserves the liveliest gratitude to God which will express itself in holy lives, at once free from vices and active in love: in short, conduct of a nature consonant with their new status as "an elect race, a

[1] I Pet. 4:12,13.
[2] I Pet. 1:3,4.
[3] I Pet. 4:19.

royal priesthood, a holy nation, a people for God's own possession" (1:13-2:10). Then follow more specific directions for such conduct: as it involves intercourse with unbelievers (2:11 f.), their attitude toward the government and those in authority (2:13-17), in the home—specific injunctions for slaves, wives, and husbands (2:18-3:7). This word to servants to be in subjection to their masters—the bad as well as the good—leads to a seeming digression, in which the example of Christ is cited (2:21-25). But actually this is not a digression. It simply buttresses the main note: It is not the fact of patient suffering, but the thing for which one suffers in patience that stamps the true Christian and puts to silence the ignorance of foolish men. Then (3:8-4:11) he comes again, this time not as an incidental point, to the central note: patience in unmerited persecution. The note is lyric: Who is he that will—can—harm you, if ye be zealous of that which is good? Again he buttresses his appeal by the example of Christ's suffering for sin—this time launching into the famous account of Christ's descent into the lower world to preach to the spirits in prison (3:19-21; 4:6). Such an example should lead them to arm themselves with the same mind in their fight against sin, and to be ready in the short time that ensues to act toward one another in Christian love. Then he stresses again the need of stedfastness in persecution—not one of the future but even then raging against them. Glorious as such a course can be, it is completely vitiated unless they conduct themselves in such a manner that it will be clear to all *why* they are suffering, not as evildoers but for "the name" (4:12-19). As he had warned them about the proper conduct toward those outside the church, he now turns to their behaviour toward fellow Christians—the elders are to be faithful shepherds untainted by greed; the younger in turn are to be subject to the elder. Each is to serve the other in humility; each to be on his guard against the common adversary, the devil. This section (5:1-11) closes with an appropriate benediction. A brief reference to "Silvanus, our faithful brother," salutations from her "that is in Babylon" and from "Mark my son," and the epistle closes (5:12-14).

The most striking thing in this writing is its dependence upon Paul. It is not an overstatement to say that it is saturated with Pauline ideas. In fact, it actually stands closer to Paul's thought than do some letters which bear his name. It is universally conceded that I Peter has used Romans and Ephesians freely. The resemblances and reminiscences are such that no reasonable criticism can deem them accidental.[4] In addition, the general make-up of the epistle: salutation, opening paragraph of thanksgiving, the series of domestic injunctions (technically known as *Haustafeln*), the salutation at the end, the reference to Silvanus "by whom" the author writes

[4] This evidence is assembled conveniently in Bacon, *An Introduction to the New Testament*, p. 154.

(which at once reminds the reader not only of the mention of Tertius (Rom. 16:22) but of such passages as Gal. 6:11; II Thes. 3:17), the compliment which Silvanus receives (cf. Paul's words about Timothy and Titus in the Corinthian correspondence)—all this suggests Paul, not Peter. Nor is it to be overlooked that the intimate and peculiarly Pauline phrase "in Christ" appears three times (3:16; 5:10,14). While the contention of the Tübingen school that Paul and Peter stand at opposite poles in regard to the gentile mission was overdrawn, Paul's own contrast—"he that wrought for Peter unto the apostleship of the circumcision wrought for me also unto the gentiles"[5]—does not lead us to see Peter in this new rôle, entirely unconcerned with the question of the validity of the law. Yet it is perfectly clear that the readers of this epistle are (at least predominantly) gentiles, not Jews. The phrase, "sojourners of the Dispersion," must not obscure that fact. This phrase, as its parallel in James, simply reflects the early Christian notion that heaven was the Christian's home; while on earth he was in a veritable dispersion. This notion—and Hebrews 13:14 is its best commentary[6]—may be couched in Jewish terms, but it must not be allowed to hide the clear testimony of the epistle that the readers had formerly lived "in the flesh to the lusts of man," but from their "former lusts" had been redeemed from their "vain manner of life handed down from [*their*] fathers," and had *become* (not continued to be) sons of Abraham.[7] Furthermore, the districts to which especial emphasis is given—Pontus, Galatia, Cappadocia, Asia, and Bithynia—were for the most part the scenes of Paul's labours. And finally, Silvanus—Acts prefers the variant Silas—had been a companion, not of Peter, but of Paul.[8] Mark, too, not only according to Acts, but as attested by Paul himself, had been at one time associated with Paul.[9] It is safe to say that were it not for the opening words, "Peter, an apostle of Jesus Christ, to the elect," Peter would never have been suggested as the author; rather it would probably have been considered the production of some later Paulinist. To be sure, Bernhard Weiss sought to maintain its authenticity by making it earlier than Romans and Ephesians—he freely admitted the literary dependence. This would entirely overturn our views of early Christian history. Paul's gospel would then have come from Peter; his claim in Galatians that he did not receive it from men would be grossly untrue; his proud boast that he had not laboured in another's province quite unfounded; his very habit of writing letters, as well as their form, borrowed; his characterization of Peter as an apostle to the circum-

[5] Gal. 2:7 f.

[6] Cf. also Hermas, *Sim.* i,1,1-11. This view finds its culmination in Augustine's conception of the City of God.

[7] I Pet. 1:14,18; 2:9 f.; 3:6; 4:2 ff.

[8] II Cor. 1:19; I Thes. 1:1; II Thes. 1:1; and the frequent references in Acts between Paul's departure from Antioch (Acts 15:40) and arrival at Corinth (18:5).

[9] Col. 4:10; Philm. 24.

cision absurd. This quixotic view has received no supporters and may be safely disregarded.

On the other hand, to consider it from the pen of Peter, but later than Paul, is scarcely less difficult. Almost nothing is known of Peter, despite the many legends that at an early date enveloped him. The friction between Paul and Peter at Antioch[10] should probably not be magnified into a life-long feud; none the less, that Peter later turned into a completely colourless and subservient Paulinist is, to say the least, improbable. Then again, there is an almost complete absence in the epistle of those references to the sayings and doings of Jesus, which, according to Papias, as quoted by Eusebius,[11] were wont to form the burden of Peter's preaching. Nor should this silence be construed a sober guaranty of genuineness; one of the reasons for challenging II Peter is not that that author refers to his pretended companionship with Jesus, but the way he refers to it. And finally, the diction of the epistle—it is excellent and idiomatic Greek, evidencing even fewer Hebraisms than do the letters of Paul—and the fact that for the author the Septuagint is the Bible discourage the notion that it was the composition of the Galilean fisherman who needed an interpreter on Greek soil. Nor is this difficulty to be side-stepped by assuming that this is a translation—perhaps by Silvanus—of Peter's Aramaic. It will indeed be a lusty translation enthusiast who will be able to detect the phenomenon here. Aware of these difficulties but reluctant to give up the traditional authorship, several critics have adopted a mediating position. Although Peter was the source of the writing, another—Silvanus, Barnabas, both names have been suggested—more skilled in writing was responsible for the actual composition. Not only does this conjecture—it is surely no more than this—leave unanswered Peter's readiness to appear in Pauline garb—presumably he would have had the letter read to him before it was sent!—but it is shivered by the manifestly late date of the writing. If any tradition about Peter is to be trusted, it is the one of his martyrdom in the days of Nero. To save the authenticity, Ramsay was ready to challenge this tradition. But since the epistle itself does not appear to be earlier than 100 A.D., this courageous skepticism appears unnecessary. By that date Peter was presumably neither dictating nor approving letters. Thus the epistle's claim—in any form—to be Petrine must be denied. The question as to how Peter's name became associated with it may be reserved for the moment.

The reasons for inclining to a date not earlier than 100 A.D. are easily stated. First, the clear use of the Pauline epistles, especially Romans and Ephesians. If the view of Ephesians, advocated in a previous chapter, be accepted, the matter is certain. But even if Ephesians be considered genuine, the difficulty is not removed. Individual churches might in the years shortly after Paul's death have such letters as he had written them, but it is far

[10] Gal. 2:11-14.

[11] *Hist. Eccl.* iii,39,15.

from likely that any considerable interchange or circulation of letters had taken place. Again, the warning that the elders are to tend the flock in a seemly manner, not for "filthy lucre," in so practical a letter suggests that this was not prompted solely by the fear that such misconduct *might* arise but that it actually had. It is precisely of a piece with the warnings in the Pastorals and the later Didache,[12] and sounds like the later days, when, as is unfortunately always the case with any new movement, positions of authority tend to attract those who would have kept aloof in the earlier days of privation. Perhaps the mythical descent of Christ into the lower world should be mentioned here. The theme is an old one. Had not Orpheus, Odysseus, Æneas, the Babylonian Ishtar, and the Mandean Hibil-Ziwa had similar adventures? That in this allusion we have simply the transference of an older story, common in the salvation myths, perhaps influenced by Eph. 4:9, to Jesus, is obvious; none the less, it appears to be the product of Christian reflection upon the scope and sweep of Christ's saving work, and is scarcely probable during the early years. Again, the burden of the epistle is the way Christians are to endure persecution. The author is no fanatic; he does not revel in the stupendous numbers of those who have died, as does the author of the Apocalypse. None the less, it is perfectly clear that the persecution which is even now raging[13] is directed against Christians *as such* (4:16), precisely as was the case in the days of Justin Martyr. Nor is there any reason to feel that this is a new attitude. Bacon is quite within the facts when he says, "No candid historical exegesis can remove the figure of the Roman magistrate from I Pet. c. 4 as the inflicter of such penalties."[14] Christians undoubtedly perished at Rome at the hands of Nero, but not so much because of their profession as to provide a scapegoat and thus to appease the infuriated Romans who were looking—justly or unjustly—at Nero as the one responsible for the burning of the city. To be sure, later Christians might—and did—see in this act of Nero a persecution of Christianity as such, but that that act of Nero's explains the attitude of I Peter is utterly improbable. It may, however, have been the cause of the Christian practice to refer to Rome as Babylon—surely that is what is meant in the words, "She that is in Babylon, elect together with you, saluteth you." Much has been written about the persecution of Christians by Domitian. In a previous chapter doubt has been expressed about the reality of this persecution. In the days of Trajan, however, we have definite and unimpeachable first-hand information that, in Asia Minor at least, the fact of being a Christian was considered a crime punishable by death. The correspondence between Pliny, the governor of Bithynia—one of the very provinces mentioned in the opening words of I Peter—and the emperor (about 111 A.D.) evidences that, while no system-

[12] Especially Did. 11-15. Cf. the same note in the Johannine epistles (see below p. 350).
[13] Cf. especially I Pet. 4:12,19.
[14] Bacon, *An Introduction to the New Testament*, p. 156.

atic persecution was being carried out, nor use made of spies or informers to smoke Christians out, when discovered by lawful means they were liable to punishment and were executed. This appears to me to give a definite clue to the date of the epistle. Although the epistle is most probably intended for all Christians everywhere, the fact that five provinces of Asia Minor are mentioned cannot be overlooked. It may well be that the mention of any distinct groups was suggested by this practice in the letters of Paul. None the less, the choice of precisely these Asia Minor provinces suggests the possibility that, while all Christians were being addressed, those in Asia Minor who were even then known to be undergoing the "fiery trial" were in the author's especial view. On the other hand, a date much later than 150 A.D. for the epistle has seemed to most scholars improbable because of its clear use in the epistle of Polycarp to the Philippians. Furthermore, Eusebius, when speaking of Papias, whose works have, unfortunately, disappeared, says: "The same author [*i.e.,* Papias] made use of testimonies from the first epistle of John and likewise from that of Peter."[15] Thus the most probable date for the epistle would appear to be between 95 and 115 A.D., perhaps nearer the latter than the former date. It is not impossible that the greeting already referred to, "She that is in Babylon, elect together with you,"[16] suggests that the author was a member of the church in Rome.

Thus it would appear to me probable that the author was a Roman Christian who, though he wrote nearly half a century after the death of Paul, had drunk deeply from that well. Desirous of nerving his fellow Christians, especially in view of the gloomy news from Asia Minor, he wrote them this stirring and inspiring message. In keeping with the tradition of his day the support of a great name from the past was of advantage. That of Paul would have been the natural one for him; Paul, however, had left too many letters behind; the differences in style would be too obvious. Peter too had suffered, and even more grievously than Paul. No letters from his pen were extant. Knowing the tradition of Peter's need of an interpreter, he allows Silvanus—a contemporary of both Peter and Paul—to occupy the rôle of amanuensis even as Tertius and others had been for Paul. Perhaps the same tradition which Papias knew joining Mark's name to Peter's explains the greeting—another Pauline touch—from "Mark my son." In a word, Paul's numerous letters provided him at once with the instrument and content of his message. The daring suggestion of Harnack that 1:1 and 5:12-14 were not from the author's pen, but later additions perhaps by the author of II Peter, has little to commend itself. It is, however, by no means impossible—in fact it is even probable—that the Roman presbyter has employed an earlier sermon which he has here revamped into this general epistle.

[15] *Hist. Eccl.* iii,39,17.
[16] I Pet. 5:13.

Chapter XXXII

THE EPISTLE OF JAMES

There are few more puzzling writings than this which bears the name of "James, a slave of God and of the Lord Jesus Christ," and consequently few which have provoked more widely divergent views. Although it did not gain an assured place in the list of accepted books until a very late date, it has been regarded by many, including not a few modern critics, as the production of James of Jerusalem, the brother of Jesus, and the earliest of all the New Testament writings. Emphasis has been laid upon fancied similarities to the gospels and the view not infrequently expressed that it preserves some of the sayings of Jesus in their most primitive form. Others have seen it as one of the latest writings to be produced and have dated it as late as 150 A.D. Its relationship to the thought of Paul has been constantly debated, but no unanimity of opinion has been reached as to the precise relationship between the two authors. Two penetrating critics[1] at the end of the last century independently urged that it was not the product of a Christian pen at all, but was a Jewish writing which was later given a Christian touch by interpolation at 1:1 and 2:1. Although this view has been mentioned by all subsequent critics, it has gained few, if any, adherents; none the less, the absence of distinctly Christian touches in the writing has been admitted by most critics. More recently A. Meyer argued that the framework is not only Jewish, but that it was originally a sort of onomasticon reading, "Jacob to the twelve patriarchs," and of much the same general nature as the *Testaments of the Twelve Patriarchs*, save that instead of the various characters being distinctly named they were represented (allegorically) by the meanings which their names had suggested to those who, like Philo, had laid great emphasis on this type of fanciful exegesis. Nor is this thesis so bizarre as a bare statement would suggest. That such work was done is abundantly proved by Meyer. The volume[2] is a lasting addition to the Jacobean literature.

As has been frequently pointed out, the writing is in no sense a letter. The barest salutation (that this is an original part of the writing has frequently been questioned) is followed by no greeting nor indication that any special group is before the writer's eye. Furthermore, the writing ends without

[1] F. Spitta, *Der Brief des Jakobus,* and L. Massebieau, "L'épître de Jacques est elle l'œuvre d'un Chrétien?" in the *Revue de l'Histoire des Religions,* xxxii, 1895, pp. 249-283.

[2] *Das Rätsel des Jacobusbriefes,* 1930.

warning, without even a pretext of conclusion. It may be called an epistle (in the technical sense, in contrast to a letter); actually perhaps the designation of it as a religious and moral tract is happiest.[3] That the writing is deeply indebted, so far as style is concerned, to the diatribe, the common form of popular moral address to be heard on the street corner of any Greek (or Hellenistic) city from the days of Bion of Borysthenes, and the almost habitual mode employed by the Cynic-Stoic preachers, is generally admitted.[4] It is destitute of structure as the many and different analyses painfully reveal. It is largely made up of pithy reflections or counsels for right living. These are but loosely strung together. Occasionally one suggests another. Thus the statement, "Of his own will he brought us forth by the word of truth" (1:18), probably accounts for the next paragraph in which after a mention of being "swift to hear" the "unplanted word" (1:21) is referred to and is made the basis for the repeated admonition to be doers of the word as well as hearers (1:22 ff.). Or again a play on words or the repetition of a previous word may occasionally account for the joining of two successive sentences.[5] On the other hand, there are other cases where no discernible connection is to be discovered. The most conspicuous of these is the warning against swearing (5:12), which joins naturally neither to what precedes nor to what follows.

Thus it may be safely said that there was no one great problem or crisis which called forth the writing, but that its purpose is simply to edify such readers as may chance to see it. None the less, there is one emphasis which recurs throughout the writing and which serves more or less to hold the various admonitions together, namely, a vigorous and blunt hatred of sham and smug pretence. One's profession and one's conduct must square. It is this which called forth the forthright and uncompromising criticism of what he calls "faith without works," or of being hearers of the word, but not doers. It is only as one keeps his feet solidly on the ground and shows his genuine acceptance of the law of God by his conduct that he can hope to draw nigh to God and thus keep himself "unspotted from the world." The severely practical purpose of the writer to shake his readers free from their quite unwarranted complacency is indicated by the hortatory style of the writing. In a bare 108 verses nearly sixty imperatives occur. Nor is it necessary to assume that all his admonitions are here coined anew. It has often been pointed out that the Greek which is back of "every good gift and

[3] This is the term employed by Ropes, *ICC James*. This is one of the finest volumes in this useful, if uneven, series.

[4] For a general description of this form of address, see *The Ethics of Paul*, pp. 41 ff., and for a detailed discussion of James as an example of the diatribe Ropes, *ICC James*, pp. 10-18.

[5] *E.g.*, χαίρειν ("greeting," 1:1) and χαράν ("joy," 1:2); λειπόμενοι ("lacking," 1:4) and λείπεται ("lacketh," 1:5). These examples could be multiplied, especially in the first part of the writing.

every perfect present"[6] is essentially a hexameter and is very probably a quotation. It appears to me quite probable that such words as "Blessed is the man that endureth temptation" (1:12), or, "Let no man say when he is tempted, I am tempted of God" (1:13), or, "But let every man be swift to hear, slow to speak, slow to wrath" (1:19), may well have belonged to the store of proverbs or familiar sayings known alike to the author and to his contemporaries. But to see the writing as a mere compilation of such proverbs is quite wrong.

While an ordered analysis of the argument is impossible—for there is none—and, as has been already said, the same material might have been articulated in almost any other order, the phrase, "my brethren," repeated nine times,[7] serves perhaps to mark the transitions, or at least provides as satisfactory a sign of division as any we could artificially make for this writing, of which Luther once exclaimed, "In one breath he talks of clothes, in the next of anger."[8] After the salutation (1:1) follows a word about the value of temptation which proves a man, making possible stedfastness, which in turn helps to produce completeness of character when accompanied by prayer which "nothing doubts." Far from poverty being a hindrance it is a distinct blessing, hence let the rich man glory when he is made low. Endurance in temptations—which are never to be ascribed to God, but always to the enticing power of man's own lusts—brings the crown of life which has been promised by God (1:2-18). Hearing is better than speaking, but hearing alone without doing is not enough. Genuine religion consists in good deeds and freedom from the taint of the world, especially present in the unbridled tongue (1:19-27). Yet these good deeds are useless if occasioned by toadying to the rich—who are actually your enemies—and a neglect of the poor. Such action cancels one part of the law and hence makes us guilty of all (2:1-13). But faith (which I have said is proved by temptation and must not be held "with respect of persons") without works is useless as is evidenced on the one hand by the faultless "faith" of demons, on the other by the fact that Abraham and Rahab were justified not by their faith, but by their works (2:14-26). The admonition, "Be not many of you teachers," serves to introduce another and fuller warning against the perils of the tongue, as illustrated (parabolically) from nature itself. Let one's wisdom be evidenced by a genuine goodness (rather than by talk) which is to be characterized by meekness and peaceableness, qualities which come from God, not from the world. "Draw nigh to God, and he will draw nigh to you" (3:1-4:10). Renounce alike quarrels with your brethren—God alone is judge—and the unwarranted confidence in the future evidenced by the merchant who ever embarks with-

– ⏑ ⏑ – ⏑ ⏑ – – | – – – ⏑ ⏑ – ⏑
[6] 1:17—πασα δο|σις αγα|θη και | παν δω|ρημα τε|λειον.
[7] 1:2; 1:19; 2:1; 2:14; 3:1; 4:11; 5:7; 5:12; 5:19.
[8] "Itzt sagt er von Kleidern, bald von Zorn."

out an "if the Lord will." To these warnings is appended another scalding denunciation of the rich (4:11-5:6). The nearness of the Lord's coming and the blessings which crowned the patient endurance of the prophets and Job alike encourage us to patience and mutual forbearance (5:7-11). Oaths are to be eschewed. In suffering, pray; in joy, sing praises; in sickness, call for the elders to enjoy their prayers and anointing which will aid and (if the sickness be a result of sin) will bring God's forgiveness, for prayer, as evidenced by Elijah, is a mighty power (5:12-18). He who converts a sinner from the error of his ways will himself be richly blessed (5:19-20). As already remarked, there is no conclusion.

That there is a surprising absence of distinctly Christian touches in this writing has been often commented upon. Jesus is named but twice, and in the latter passage (2:1) the reference is distinctly awkward. There is no mention, direct or by implication, of the death of Christ. That the coming of the Lord will bring blessing is clearly implied (5:7), although it is not specifically designated salvation. It is possible—to my mind probable—that most of the references to the Lord are to be understood of Christ rather than of God, but with the possible exception of 5:7 it is quite impossible to prove that they could not have been written by a Jew of Jehovah. As was remarked in the opening paragraph, this absence of distinctively Christian touches has led some critics to the view that the writing was from the pen of a Jew and that it was later adapted by a Christian. Much can be said for the view. The superficial resemblance to words in our gospels[9] is not impressive. The real objection lies in the assumption that any Christian who sought to take this Jewish writing over should have been content with such meagre and ambiguous additions. To my mind it is far easier to see the writing produced by a Jewish Christian, spontaneously stressing those qualities of life which appeared to him essential, and, since he knew himself to be a Christian, untroubled by the necessity of giving his products distinctive badges. Furthermore, it is to be observed that the absence of reference to dietary laws, Sabbath observance, circumcision, or duties peculiar to Judaism should not be overlooked by those who seek to classify the writing on the basis of superficial badges. Aside from the fact that the notion that this epistle was originally a Jewish writing and only later decked out with a few wisps of Christian finery is sheer assumption and without the vestige of external attestation, stands a positive indication that the epistle was from the pen of a Christian, namely, the obvious contrast in 2:14-26 to the Pauline view of faith and works. That the epistle is primarily an attack on Paul or that this section is the kernel of the writing may safely be denied. None the less, there is a contrast which is significant, and probably deliberate. Our author shows no comprehension of Paul's doctrine of salvation through faith. For him

[9] Notably Jas. 5:12; cf. Matt. 5:37.

faith and works are inseparable. It is not that he is denying the need of faith,[10] but that he is attacking those who were excusing themselves from works on the flimsy pretense of having faith. Faith without works is dead. Paul might well have agreed, for he emphasized ethical conduct as highly as did James, but he would have preferred to call these works "fruits of the spirit." Paul stigmatizes "works of the law," but these are not what James is contending for. Finally, what James derides as a dead faith Paul would have indignantly denied was faith at all. To see the words, "But wilt thou know, O vain man, that faith apart from works is barren?"[11] as an attack upon Paul is grotesque, and evidences a total ignorance of the style of the diatribe. The whole section is simply part of his attempt to stir from their smugness indolent Christians who are inclined to apologize for their disinclination to active works by citing their perfect faith. But that Christians were wont to make such apologies as a result of a mistaken understanding of what Paul had meant by faith and its sufficiency appears to me undeniable. In his own day Paul had found this teaching constantly misunderstood and requiring pointed correction. That James recognized that the source of this type of conduct was Paul's teaching and that accordingly he was setting himself either against Paul or against those mistakenly citing Paul appears to me far from certain. Surely his reference to Abraham and Rahab exactly reverses Paul's argument in Gal. 2:16 and Rom. 3:28, nor should the repeated denial that a man is "justified" (not "saved") by faith alone be overlooked; yet that he had these passages in mind or had ever read any letter of Paul's by no means follows. How any man could have read a dozen pages of Paul without realizing that they were in substantial agreement with his own position is to me inconceivable. Accordingly, I am inclined to feel that the contrast between faith and works evidences the fact that our epistle was written after Paul's death at a time when Paul's views were being misconstrued and that thus our epistle was written by a Christian, not a Jew—for surely then the attack upon Paul would have been unmistakable!—but that any attempt to see in this transparently honest hatred of sham and this attempt to get down to the brass tacks of religion more than an indignant protest against the habit of glossing over moral unfruitfulness by the repetition of pious but windy phrases—wherever culled—is totally unwarranted.

The writing purports to be from the pen of "James, a servant of God and of the Lord Jesus Christ" and to be directed to "the twelve tribes which are of the Dispersion." That this latter clause is to be interpreted in the sense of "Jews (or Christian Jews) living outside Palestine" is utterly improbable. The reference to the "twelve tribes" simply evidences the early Christian habit of referring to themselves as the spiritual Israel, the true descendants of Abraham, while the reference to the dispersion expresses the conviction

[10] Cf. for example, Jas. 1:3; 2:1.

[11] Jas. 2:20.

(already commented upon in I Peter)[12] that Christians, wherever they might dwell on earth, were absent from their true home. Ropes[13] has neatly paraphrased this clause of the greeting: "To that body of Twelve Tribes, the new Israel, which has its centre in Heaven, and whose members, in whatever place on the earth they may be, are all equally away from home and in the dispersion." Thus the writing is to be seen as intended for no particular group of Christians, geographical or racial, but for all Christians into whose hands it may chance to come.

The earliest opinion as to the identity of this "James" was expressed by Origen[14] in the early part of the third century. Origen's view that the author was James the brother of Jesus became the traditional one, although a few scattering votes have been registered for James the son of Zebedee or for James the son of Alphæus. For the latter two it is sufficient to say that this is sheer assumption without the slightest vestige of probability and that no Protestant scholar has ever sought to defend the thesis. On the contrary, it was long felt that Origen's view was correct. Was not James the head of the Jerusalem church? Had he not been out of sympathy with some of Paul's views? Was not its tone (at once strongly Jewish, but somehow reminiscent of words of Jesus) most natural in the mouth of the doughty head of the Jerusalem church who had caused Peter to risk a clash with Paul rather than incur rebuke? Yet there are so many weighty arguments against this hypothesis that most scholars have rejected it together with that of its early date. It is incredible that had James, who was not only an apostle and head of the influential Jerusalem group, but also the brother of Jesus, penned the letter that it would have remained unnoticed for nearly two centuries. Furthermore, traditions are preserved of James both by Josephus and Hegesippus; he appears to have been highly honoured in Ebionite circles; yet there is no trace of a tradition ascribing to him the authorship of this or any other writing. That James should have been acquainted with the style of the diatribe is perhaps possible, but that he should have written in Greek, and in such fluent and excellent Greek, second only to Hebrews among the writings of the New Testament, is scarcely likely. Nor is there the slightest probability that it is a translation from Aramaic. The free vivacious style, the occasional plays upon words, alliterations, and the general freshness of style are decisive. Another argument is more complex. If what has been said above with regard to the relationship between this writing and the thought of Paul is substantially correct, the traditional authorship is excluded. There is not the slightest sign of the clash or difference in attitude over the Jewish law which we are justified in seeing between Paul and the historical James

[12] See p. 323.

[13] *ICC James*, pp. 125 f.

[14] Perhaps the phrase "and brother of James" (Jude 1) is to be seen as evidencing a similar understanding.

not only in Acts, but in Galatians, but rather clear evidence of a decided opposition to a later current misinterpretation of one phase of Paul's teaching. Thus the notion that the epistle was written before Paul and James had come into conflict is manifestly absurd. James would then be reflecting a watered down view of Paul's before the latter had even enunciated it; would be doing it in a general epistle for all Christians everywhere before Paul's letters to individual churches had set the style for Christian writing; and, though a brother of Jesus with ample material at hand to point his admonitions, would hold himself so scrupulously aloof from any reference to that burning personality that his writing could seriously be considered non-Christian.

That actually the author's name was James, but that he was not the famous James of Jerusalem, has occasionally been suggested, but has little to commend it. If written after the first period of Christianity was over, the mention of James with no further qualifications would naturally have suggested but one figure. That the writing is, therefore, to be considered as pseudonymous and that the author intended for it the authority of this great name of the past, but without attempting to impersonate this James, appears to me probable.

There is little or no evidence which would justify more than a vague guess as to date. That it is *post*-Pauline and from a time when the clash between Jewish and gentile Christians has subsided may be taken for granted. Origen's guess that it was from the pen of James of Jerusalem would seem to indicates that it was written long before his time, hence not likely after 150 A.D. Many competent scholars are convinced that I Peter, I Clement, and (especially) the *Shepherd* of Hermas evidence knowledge of this epistle, and accordingly date it before 100 A.D. The evidence does not appear to me to warrant such a conclusion. Furthermore, if such is the case, the problem of its subsequent drop from view is made all the more inexplicable. To find indications of a very late date in the sorry, but not unusual, plight that some Christians are in is quite unwarranted. Paul was confronted with precisely the same problems, but the same can be said of all subsequent moralists. Again, the apparent expectation that the Parousia is near at hand does not incline one to too late a date. That view apparently had declined with the years. None the less, occasional Christians in the second century and even later gave expression to it. If it be felt that the author recognizes Paul as the source of the unfortunate break between faith and works, it would appear probable that that would preclude a date much if any below 125 A.D., for by that time Paul's fame was sufficient to cause a subsequent writer to be on his guard against appearing to clash with the great apostle. But even if, as argued above, this recognition is not likely, none the less each year after 125 A.D. renders unfamiliarity with the teachings of Paul the more surprising. Thus the evidence scarcely warrants a closer dating than the years between 70-125 A.D.

Nor can we be more definite as to the place from which he wrote. Both

Rome and some Palestinian city have been often suggested. The argument for Rome on the basis of fancied use of the epistle by I Clement or Hermas is, as already suggested, most uncertain. Nor does the strong Jewishness of the writer argue at all for Palestine. In all likelihood he was a Jew, but all Jews did not live in Palestine then any more than they do now. On the other hand, the allusion to the "early and latter rain" (5:7) appeared to Ropes to indicate Palestine, for "only in Palestine among the countries that come in question do the seasonal conditions produce the intensity of anxious hope to which this verse refers."[15] Is it too fanciful to see in the fact that Origen was the first writer to mention James a possible indication that he had discovered it in Cæsarea, where it had remained unnoticed, at least by the outside world, for a century?

In conclusion, the writing is to be seen as a tract in epistolary form, intended for no particular group of Christians, written by an unknown Christian teacher[16] who was himself of Jewish birth, perhaps from Cæsarea during the period of comparative quiet between the end of the Jewish war (66-73 A.D.) and the abortive rebellion under Bar Cochba (132-135 A.D.). Contemporary literary custom would make conceivable the publishing of the epistle under a false name, not to impersonate James, but solely to gain his authority. In this remote part of the empire it remained unnoticed for a hundred years; then, perhaps through the discovery by Origen, it became known to the Greek church and, with its claim of Jacobean authorship and with nothing unworthy of the name, it gradually came into use, and, though unmentioned in the West until the second half of the fourth century, soon thereafter became assured of a place in the canon by the work of Jerome and Augustine.

[15] *ICC James*, p. 42.

[16] "Be not many of you teachers . . . knowing that *we* shall receive heavier judgment"—Jas. 3:1.

Chapter XXXIII

THE EPISTLE OF JUDE

THE purpose of this brief and unpretentious writing is crystal-clear. It is a sharp warning to "them that are called" (1-2) to guard the faith "which was once for all delivered to the saints" against a group of *pseudo*-Christians who are bitterly denounced as basely denying "our only Master and Lord, Jesus Christ" (3,4). Their views and licentious conduct alike are abominable. Their impending doom, suggested by the fate of the evil workers—angelic and human alike—in the past (5-7) whom they actually surpass in baseness (8-11), is certain. Then after a further characterization of them couched in vivid pictorial language—"shepherds that without fear feed themselves," "clouds without water," "autumn trees without fruit" (12-16)—follows a brief warning to the faithful to remain unshaken in their obedience to the words formerly spoken by the "apostles of our Lord Jesus Christ" (17-23). An unusually impressive doxology (24-25) brings the writing to a close.

The two principal problems raised by this writing are: (1) its relationship to II Peter, (2) the identification of the errorists. That there is a real literary dependence between Jude and II Peter is certain. Although occasional attempts have been made to explain II Peter as the earlier writing, scholars are almost unanimous today in reversing the relationship and in regarding II Peter as the result of deliberate and barefaced copying. This question and its implications may be more profitably reserved for the next chapter.

Sure identification of the errorists is probably impossible, but some of their characteristics are clear. To see them as backsliding Christians is surely wrong. To be sure, their description as "hidden rocks in your love-feasts" (12) implies that they are not openly anti-Christian. The words,

> And on some have mercy, who are in doubt; and some save, snatching them out of the fire; and on some have mercy with fear; hating even the garment spotted by the flesh,[1]

would seem to imply that some of them at least are on the border line. This should not obscure the fact that they show indubitable similarities to the second-century Gnostics. The characterization of them as "they who make separations, sensual, having not the Spirit"[2] is surely not to be understood in the sense that they were mere trouble-makers, but that they classified

[1] Jude 22 f.

[2] Jude 19—Ψυχικοί, πνεῦμα μὴ ἔχοντες.

men as *psychikoi* (ordinary, unillumined men) and *pneumatikoi* ("spiritual," *i.e.,* Gnostics) in genuinely Gnostic fashion. If, as seems probable, the concluding phrase of verse 4 is to be translated "denying our only Master and Lord, Jesus Christ," it would appear that they held Docetic views, distinguishing between the man Jesus and the Christ who technically subsumed him.[3] The words, "set at nought dominion, and rail at dignities (glories),"[4] and "these rail at whatsoever things they know not,"[5] may plausibly be understood in the sense that they scoffed at the Old Testament and regarded the figures, including Jehovah himself, that those writings magnified, as of inferior position if not actually evil. Claiming a superior wisdom, they flattered the rich, trafficked in filthy dreams and visions, and were guilty of horrid immorality and unnatural vices. Thus there would seem to be little ground for denying that these reprehensible individuals are to be regarded as belonging to the groups generally dubbed Gnostic. On the other hand, the attacks are too general to warrant the application to them of the name of any of the famed Gnostic leaders known to us from the second- and third-century fathers, although this has not infrequently been attempted. Some have regarded them as akin to the Baalamites referred to in the Apocalypse,[6] others to the Cainites or Marcosians mentioned by Irenæus.[7] Clement of Alexandria, in describing the unbridled and promiscuous sexual practices of the Carpocratians, sees a prophetic reference to them in Jude 8-16a which he expressly quotes.[8]

The fact that these errorists may with all confidence be called Gnostics, although our too scanty knowledge of the exact views of the various groups, known to us only from vague and often probably ill-informed references by their opponents, makes it profitless to try for a closer designation, would seem to preclude for the epistle a date earlier than 100 A.D. Nor is this conclusion based solely upon the nature of those attacked. The apostolic age is now long past, as is evidenced by the admonition to "remember the words which have been spoken before by the apostles of our Lord Jesus Christ."[9] The fact that these errorists are spoken of as "*of old* written of beforehand,"[10] while not decisive, appears to point in the same direction. Even more significant is the fact that faith is referred to in the *post*-Pauline sense of the Pastorals as a deposit to be kept. Thus the author can speak of the "faith which was once for all delivered unto the saints."[11] An objective creed to be kept, it may be

[3] For a fuller discussion of this Gnostic distinction see pp. 344-346.
[4] Jude 8.
[5] Jude 10.
[6] Cf. Rev. 2:14,20,24.
[7] *adv.* Haer. i,31 and1,13-21.
[8] *Strom.* iii,2 (end).
[9] Jude 17.
[10] Jude 4.
[11] Jude 3.

referred to as "your most holy faith."[12] On the other hand, to try to force a reference to the destruction of Jerusalem from verse 5 is certainly unwise. Nor does the fact that both the *Assumption of Moses*[13] and the book of Enoch[14] are cited prove a late date, for since these writings were prechristian and, at least in certain circles, in high repute, there is no convincing reason why even an apostle should not have cited them. None the less, the fact that in the Christian writings which can with confidence be ascribed to the first century these apocrypha are not cited, while in this writing, which on other grounds appears to be late, there are at least two and perhaps four such allusions is not to be neglected. The first mention of the writing is in the Muratorian canon (*ca.* 170 A.D.). The earliest of the fathers to refer to it were Tertullian, Clement of Alexandria, and Origen. Thus we will hardly err in dating the writing in the period between 100 and 160 A.D. Any closer dating would appear sheer guesswork.

With regard to the author little more need be said. If the conclusions of the preceding paragraph regarding the date be accepted, Jude, the brother of James and hence of Jesus,[15] is definitely excluded. Eusebius[16] twice repeats "an ancient story," which he attributes to Hegesippus, which recounts how Domitian arrested the grandsons of Jude, but later, convinced by their obvious poverty and humble station that they constituted no menace, released them. Whether the story rests upon any foundation in fact or not, the words, "Now there still survived of the family of the Lord grandsons of Jude, who was said to have been his brother according to the flesh, and they were delated as being of the family of David," surely suggest that Jude himself and those of his own generation were not alive. Furthermore, the fact already commented upon that the first mention of the writing which we have does not antedate 170 A.D. and that even then it was but grudgingly accepted[17] is decisive against the view that it was penned by a man who was not only a brother of the famed James of Jerusalem, but of Jesus himself. Nor should it be forgotten that the reference to "the apostles of our Lord Jesus Christ" who had "spoken before" (v. 17) not only indicates a late date for the writing but renders improbable the notion that the author himself was one of that group or closely connected with it. It has occasionally been suggested that the words, "and brother of James," in the greeting are a later addition and that thus the author was actually a second century Christian named Jude, later mistakenly identified as the brother of the famous James of Jerusalem. This assumption of otherwise unknown individuals bearing the names of especially famous earlier heroes—Jude, James, John—who produced in their

[12] Jude 20.
[13] Jude 9. Origen (*de Princ.* iii,2,1) recognizes the dependence here.
[14] Jude 14 f.
[15] Mark 6:3.
[16] *Hist. Eccl.* iii,19 f. and iii,32,5.
[17] Eusebius, *Hist. Eccl.* ii,23,25; iii,25,3; Jerome, *de Viris inl.* 4.

own name writings which were later skilfully transformed by a word here or line there into apostolic writings appears to me far less probable than the assumption, surely no less arbitrary, that the writings were originally pseudonymous and that the several authors sought, in keeping with ancient custom, to gain for their productions the support of names from the past so revered that few epithets were necessary for them. Why the authors chose the particular heroes they did is impossible at this late date to settle. It is not unreasonable to assume that in the case of this epistle the author was a Christian to whom the memory of James of Jerusalem was most congenial. Nor does it appear to me unlikely that he may even have known the epistle that bore this name and on the basis of it modelled his own word of greeting, himself adding "and brother of James." It would be by no means impossible that this phrase actually was of weight in attaining for the later writing the place in the Muratorian canon that the earlier (James) failed to achieve.

We know far too little about the "realms of influence" in the early church to make particularly valuable or impressive any guess as to where this nameless enthusiast for James lived. Palestine, Syria, Egypt, Asia Minor have all been suggested. But, as to so many other questions, an answer would be sheer guesswork. The readers—"[they] that are called, beloved in God the Father, and kept for Jesus Christ"—are all Christians everywhere. That is, there would not seem any compelling reason to assume any especial group for whom the writing is particularly intended. The epistolary form is artificial. It is then a general tract, the outcome of the author's indignation at the antics of men who are outraging the church of God.

Chapter XXXIV

THE SECOND EPISTLE OF PETER

The purpose of this writing, too, is easily seen and as easily stated. It is not a mere attack on the false teachers described in chapter 2, nor is it, as is often said, the desire to prove Peter and Paul in substantial agreement. Rather, the purpose is to reëstablish faith in the Parousia, to stop the mouths of those who are sneering, "Where is the promise of his coming? for from the day that the fathers fell asleep, all things continue as they were from the beginning of the creation."[1] In the guise of the apostle Peter, whom the author seeks crudely to impersonate, the attempt is made to reëstablish this waning faith, in a clever but apparently quite unwarranted way. Instead of meeting his opponents on the real point at issue and attempting to refute them on intellectual or theological grounds, he inveighs against their character by applying to them the devastating attack which Jude had made on *his* opponents. Then after stigmatizing them in this stolen lampoon, which had been originally penned for a totally different set of men, he concludes: The views of such men are completely valueless. To be sure, he makes a half-hearted attempt to deny the validity of their skepticism. When they say, "All things continue as they were from the beginning of the creation,"[2] they are alike wilfully forgetful of the Flood and oblivious to the fact that the world will be destroyed in the future by fire. Then by a paraphrase of Psalm 90:4, "For a thousand years in thy sight are but as yesterday when it is past"—a word which has ever been of the greatest comfort to those whose religious calendars or sacred arithmetic has gone awry—he makes the best of a bad matter by the observation that the long delay in the expressly promised speedy return of Christ has been due to God's long-suffering. He has waited to give a few more a chance to share in it. But this long-suffering will soon be past. The Parousia will come unexpectedly as a thief in the night. Let his readers be prepared. The Transfiguration which he had attended "in the holy mount"[3] was a foretaste of this coming glory. All the apostles, even Paul, had been in harmony in this expectation.

This work purports to be the work of Peter. Not only do the opening words, "Simon Peter, a servant and apostle of Jesus Christ," attempt to gain the authority of a famous name for the views to be expressed—this was a

[1] II Pet. 3:4.
[2] II Pet. 3:4.
[3] II Pet. 1:18.

common practice in those days, as we have had occasion frequently to observe, and is not to be stigmatized as dishonest—but throughout the writing the author attempts to masquerade as Peter. He had been with Jesus in the "holy (sic!) mount";[4] was soon to die, "even as our Lord Jesus Christ signified unto me"[5]—in which latter word the reference to John 21:18,19 is evident; he had already written them a former epistle[6]—obviously I Peter—Paul is his beloved brother.[7] His attack upon his opponents, as has already been remarked, is simply Jude 3-18; but while in that epistle the author had opposed contemporaries and had phrased himself in the present tense when speaking of those who were then acting basely, our author, trying to be true to his masquerade, attempts to throw Jude's present tenses into the future, for these second-century skeptics would appear long after Peter's demise.

Little need be said in denying this unknown's claims to greatness. They break down completely at every point. That the two "Petrine" writings come from different pens needs no argument. Style, language, views, claims—all are totally different. Even Spitta, one of the very few modern critics who accepted the authenticity of II Peter, found it necessary to deny it to I Peter, for they were so completely at variance. I Peter, while not from the pen of Peter, is a writing which commands respect, being obviously the attempt to meet a distinct crisis in Christian history by a sincere Christian, confident that the historical Peter would have approved it. II Peter is a superficial highfalutin attempt to write elegantly by one who constantly displays a complete lack of even fundamental honesty. As has been already suggested, the dependence upon Jude is obvious. Practically the only differences are: (1) that II Peter has removed the quotations from the apocryphal writings which might have aroused suspicion had they occurred in the mouth of Peter; (2) that the later writing attempts to replace Jude's present tenses with futures to maintain the fiction of Peter's prophetic words.[8] In several passages II Peter's words are obscure until compared with Jude's. Then the obscurity vanishes. One example will suffice.[9] Jude had referred to Michael's unwillingness when contending with the devil to bring against him a "railing judgment."[10] II Peter,[11] by omitting this specific reference from the *Assumption of Moses*, makes a totally unintelligible reference to angels in general not daring to bring railing judgments against equally general dignities. Without further ado it may be safely said that the slavish dependence of II Peter upon Jude is one of the few theorems of early Christianity to which an unqualified

[4] II Pet. 1:18.
[5] II Pet. 1:14.
[6] II Pet. 3:1.
[7] II Pet. 3:15.
[8] One need only read 2:10-22 to see how unsuccessful he was in this respect.
[9] For an excellent summary of the material see Moffatt, *Introduction to the Literature of the New Testament*, pp. 348 ff.
[10] Jude 9.
[11] II Peter 2:11.

Q.E.D. may be suffixed. Were this the only point, it would be sufficient to establish the non-Petrine authorship. We do not need to stop to debate the point whether it would have been possible for Peter to have stooped to such plagiarism or to have sought to demolish folks with whose views he disapproved by attributing to them indiscriminately qualities which, while perhaps appropriate to another group, would certainly not have characterized all those who in the course of the years came to recognize the improbability of the near approach of the end. The matter of date is definitive. We have seen perfectly clear evidence that Jude cannot antedate 100 A.D. and probably is to be dated several decades later. Since II Peter used Jude it must be later, not improbably considerably later. But other clear indications of late date, quite apart from its dependence upon Jude, are present. By his quotation of his opponents' word, "from the day that the fathers fell asleep,"[12] he inadvertently reveals that the first generation has long since passed. Again, the mention of the "holy prophets . . . the Lord . . . and the apostles,"[13] the great source of authority for Christian truth and practice in the second- and third-century church, points in the same direction. Perhaps most impressive of all is the matter-of-fact reference to the letters of Paul. The word,

> Even as our beloved brother Paul also, according to the wisdom given to him, wrote unto you; *as also in all his epistles,* speaking in them of these things; wherein are some things hard to be understood, which the ignorant and unstedfast wrest, *as they do also the other scriptures,* unto their own destruction,[14]

reveals two highly important points. First, the letters of Paul have been collected and are known to Christians in general. Second, they have come to be regarded as Scripture and of equal weight with the Old Testament. Thus, on this point alone, any date earlier than 125 A.D. is absolutely precluded. On the other hand, the epistle was known to Origen, although it is by no means certain that he accepted it as genuine. Eusebius quotes him: "And Peter . . . has left one acknowledged epistle, and, it may be, a second also, for it is doubted."[15] Thus we cannot go below 200 A.D. in the range of possible dates. Probably we shall not err in dating it between 150 and 175 A.D.

Thus it is to be seen as the pseudonymous production by a writer posing as Peter and as the author of I Peter, who incorporates about all of Jude, probably then little known or almost forgotten, to demolish his opponents who, he believes, are denying the belief in the Parousia. Actually his obvious lack both of moral standards and of mental ability arouse some suspicion even as to the justice of his charge that they were denying the Parousia. By the time he wrote the notion of a speedy return in that generation, which, as we have already seen, had been the mainspring of early Christianity, had

[12] II Pet. 3:4.
[13] II Pet. 3:2.
[14] II Pet. 3:15,16.
[15] *Hist. Eccl.* vi, 25,8.

come to be modified. That orthodoxy[16] came even in the second century to a flat denial of the view is improbable. Rather the lapse of the years and the appearance and growth of organized Christianity caused the view to lose its central place and to withdraw to the pleasant limbo accorded religious views in every generation which have lost their value but not their sanctity. That the Lord would return was of course believed (as it is today by the majority of Christians), but that the expectation exerted any particular influence is doubtful. But then, as now, there may well have been individuals who considered the withdrawal of this view from the centre of religious thinking an unmitigated evil and who were ready to affirm that those who failed to preach every sermon from that text were not only guilty of denying the belief *in toto*, but were of necessity of filthy moral life. The present-day group, known as premillennialists, which still continues to afflict the church and to make it a laughing-stock to thousands repelled by their crudity and ignorance, may well be the spiritual descendants of this unknown author who penned this book which was not only the last to be written, one of the last (if not the last) to gain a place among the canonical writings, and by all odds the least deserving to have gained that place or to hold it today.

[16] There may have been occasional exceptions, as perhaps in the case of the Fourth Gospel. See below, pp. 448 f.; cf. also p. 242.

Chapter XXXV

THE FIRST EPISTLE OF JOHN

AT FIRST this unpretentious little writing appears to be a group of meditations or aphorisms without any strict logical sequence. The transitions are not clear; again and again the writer reverts to a previous thought with which he had apparently finished. This seeming lack of arrangement and plan, the constant admonition to love one another, and the frequent address to his readers as "my little children"[1] give the impression of the toothless babbling of an aged man. But under these soft and woolly verses is a real firmness of fibre. It is not a letter, although the occasional "I write" or "I have written"[2] might give that impression. Actually the term tract, manifesto, or homily would better describe it. It is apparently intended for no one church or group of churches but for all Christians everywhere, although—and this is of course true of all so-called general epistles—the particular circumstances of some one group may have led him to write to all. That the readers are Christians, not prospective converts, is clear from such passages as 2:12-14 or the express word, "I have not written unto you because ye know not the truth, but because ye know it."[3] Nor can there be any doubt as to the purpose of the tract. It is to urge upon Christians the recognition of the supreme and twofold requirement: true faith in Christ and true brotherly love. These two notes are constantly stressed, repeated, and—to change the figure—braided together. One might almost say that 3:23 is the text of the writing:

> And this is his commandment, that we should believe in the name of his Son Jesus Christ, and love one another, even as he gave us commandment.

Indeed, one scholar has suggested that the present writing is the combination of three short addresses (1:5-2:27; 2:28-4:6; 4:7-5:21), each of which is based on the two points: "fellowship (κοινωνία) is faith" and "fellowship is love." Whether this analysis is justified appears to me doubtful, but that these two themes are constantly stressed is obvious. Without attempting to add another to the many subtle analyses and supposed plans whose *hic jacet*'s are to be found in Moffatt,[4] a survey of the contents may be valuable at this point.

In the opening words the author sounds a note which is to be the burden of the writing, *viz.*, eternal life, which is fellowship with God and his son

[1] I John 2:1,12,18,28; 3:7,18; 4:4; 5:21; cf. also 2:13.
[2] Cf. I John 1:4; 2:1,12; 5:13.
[3] I John 2:21.
[4] *Introduction to the Literature of the New Testament,* p. 584.

Jesus Christ (1:1-4). The message to all Christians heard and known from the beginning is "God is light." If we walk in this light—and this entails recognition of sin—we have *fellowship* with him and forgiveness through his son Jesus Christ (1:5-2:2). (By these words by implication he makes clear that some are denying the possibility of their sinning, and hence are hopelessly denying Jesus Christ who came to cleanse from all sin.) Furthermore, we *know* him if we keep his commandments (2:3-6). He that is in the light loveth his brother (2:7-11). Do not ye—fathers, young men, little children—who have made so good a beginning allow yourselves to be beguiled by love of the world which is even now passing away (2:12-17). In this last hour be on your guard, especially against the many Antichrists who have arisen and who would lead you into the darkness by their denial that Jesus is the Christ. Against them stand firm, abiding in him by virtue of the anointing which you received (2:18-29). As children of God keep yourselves pure: do not allow yourselves to be led astray into sin; remember the ancient word that we should love one another and not be like Cain, not minding the hatred of the world but engaging in an active and practical love which finds its expression in deed and not in word alone. If we perform this double task—belief in the name of Jesus Christ and love toward one another—we have boldness toward God and receive from him whatever we ask (3:1-24). Then the line is drawn between those who confess that Jesus Christ is come in the flesh and those who by their denial show that they are not of God (4:1-6). Again he weaves his two requirements together in his repeated exhortation to love one another, for only so can we prove our love for an unseen God who first loved us and from whom our mutual love is made possible. Constantly these two themes are intwined and reëmphasized (4:7-5:13). Once more the boldness that the true Christian has in God is reaffirmed. This makes possible a very practical result, namely, the effective prayer for a brother "sinning a sin not unto death" (5:14-17). The writing closes with a reiteration of the obligation for those begotten of God to hold themselves aloof from the world and to guard themselves from idols (5:18-21).

It is clear that the tract was called forth by a definite circumstance, the existence of false teachers, and not by the mere fancy that this was wholesome advice. Their error was twofold. In the first place they were denying that Jesus was the Christ, the son of God. "Who is the liar but he that denieth that Jesus is the Christ?"[5] Apparently they were distinguishing between the man Jesus and the heavenly being, the Christ, who they maintained had come upon him (at the baptism?) to empower him temporarily.

This peculiar slant is called Docetism and was a consequence of the dualism incident to the Gnostic position. Gnosticism regularly identified its saviour with Jesus, but held to a peculiar Christology. Jesus was pure spirit; as such it was impossible that he should ever have come into contact with matter

[5] I John 2:22. Cf. also such passages as 4:2 f.,15; 5:1.

which was purely evil. Thus he had had no real body. It was only an appearance assumed by him to make it possible for him to reveal himself. Some Gnostics, like Cerinthus, asserted that only at the baptism did the Saviour unite himself with Jesus and that he left him before his death. Since the errorists against whom our writings is directed apparently shared this view, it is instructive to read Irenæus' statement of it:

> He [Cerinthus] supposed that Jesus had not been born of a virgin, but had been born from Joseph and Mary a son like all other men and had been more righteous and wise; and that after the baptism there had descended upon him from the Absolute, which is above all, the Christ in the form of a dove; and then he had proclaimed the unknown Father and had performed mighty deeds, but that at the end the Christ had withdrawn from Jesus and that Jesus had suffered and had been raised, but that the Christ had remained free from suffering since he was spiritual.[6]

This same notion is evidenced in the apocryphal *Gospel of Peter* with its famous "Ascent from the Cross" after the cry, "My *power*, my *power*, why hast thou forsaken me?" Others asserted that his body was pure phantom. For example, in the curious work known as the *Leucian Acts of John* he appears to John on the Mount of Olives during the crucifixion with the word,

> To the multitude down there in Jerusalem I am being crucified, and pierced with lances and reeds, and gall and vinegar is given me to drink, but unto thee am I speaking, and do thou hearken to what I say. I put it into thy mind to come up into the mountain, that thou mightest hear those things which it behoveth a disciple to learn from his teacher and a man from his God.[7]

A few paragraphs earlier in the same section John recounts:

> Sometimes when I would lay hold on him, I met with a material and solid body, and at other times, again, when I felt him, the substance was immaterial and as if it existed not at all.[8]

That these notions, which had as a common factor the conviction that he was neither born nor subject to death, constituted a serious problem to orthodox Christians at a comparatively early date is clear from the distinct antipathy to them in the four gospels. Such touches as the fact that the women "took hold of his feet";[9] the word, "See my hands and my feet, that it is I myself: handle me, and see; for a spirit hath not flesh and bones, as ye behold me having";[10] the eating of the piece of broiled fish;[11] the command to Thomas

[6] Irenæus, *adv. Hær.* i,26. 1.
[7] *Acts of John* 97.
[8] *Acts of John* 93. Here the reference to I John 1:1 is clear. This writing (§§ 87-105) provides an excellent exposition of the views of the Docetists. It is available in M. R. James, *The Apocryphal New Testament*, pp. 250-257.
[9] Matt. 28:9.
[10] Luke 24:39.
[11] Luke 24:42 f.

to touch his hands and side[12]—all these are most naturally explained as opposition to the growth of a view which was even then being regarded with alarm. It may be remarked parenthetically that one of the causes of the story of an empty tomb, apparently not an original part of the early Christian confidence, may well have been the desire to oppose this growing and popular view. There can be little doubt that the repeated emphasis of our writing upon the enormity of the sin of those who denied that Jesus Christ is come in the flesh, with the initial word—"that which we have heard, that which we have seen with our eyes, that which we beheld, and our hands handled"—is directed specifically against the cleavage between the man Jesus and the spiritual subsuming Christ, that is, against Docetism.

A second error of these opponents was their declaration of complete freedom from law. Their superior gnosis had raised them above law and prevented the possibility of their sinning. The writer's stinging words, "If we say that we have no sin, we deceive ourselves, and the truth is not in us"[13] and "If we say that we have not sinned we make him a liar, and his word is not in us,"[14] are obviously directed against this antinomianism or perfectionism which may well have had its origin in, or at least have drawn fresh strength from, a mistaken understanding of Paul's dangerous dictum of freedom. These individuals may well have had as a catchword the phrase, "I know him";[15] such a claim, when divorced from the keeping of his commandments, erased the power and even the need of Christ's death, and led to a supercilious contempt for those who strove to practise the kind of life the orthodox believed to be dear to God. Such men were obviously not of God, but of the world.[16]

Accordingly, the writing is to be seen, not as the comfortable word of an aged and gentle grandfather, but as a sharp polemic against this antinomian form of Gnosticism. To break from sin and to practise the law of love instead of hate, to recognize Jesus as the true son of God—this was essential. Our author is not content simply to demolish his opponents as Jude sought to do. In addition he strives to impart truth and thus to fortify his readers. The gospel is the true gnosis—"And ye have an anointing from the Holy One, and ye all know."[17] Its requirement is twofold: right living and right thinking, that is, the necessity of keeping God's commandments and of believing Jesus Christ was God's son. McGiffert has aptly phrased it: "A man cannot obey God's commands, the sum of which is love, unless he abides in God; and he cannot abide in God unless he recognizes Jesus Christ as his son and becomes one with him."[18]

[12] John 20:24-29.
[13] I John 1:8.
[14] I John 1:10.
[15] I John 2:4.
[16] I John 4:5.
[17] I John 2:20; cf. 2:27.
[18] *The Apostolic Age,* p. 618.

This writing is also of importance as casting some light on the question of sin. To a degree it seems to revolve about the contradiction, "In theory Christians are sinless; in practice they are sinners." Although in the opening paragraphs condemnation is heaped upon those who say, "we have no sin,"[19] later it is no less dogmatically announced, "Whosoever is begotten of God doeth no sin, because his seed abideth in him; and he cannot sin, because he is begotten of God."[20] It is often the case that views which we ourselves hold we consider most reprehensible when held by our opponents. And yet it can hardly be said that our author could deny that even Christians do sin, for in the last words of the writing it is urged that, "if any man see his brother sinning a sin not unto death, he shall ask, and God will give him life for them that sin not unto death."[21] Thus in the conflict between theory and experience—although the author does not attempt any formal reconciliation—this word about the efficacy of prayer serves to a degree as a connecting link, and, with his distinction between sins which are and those which are not unto death, provides the seed which soon developed into the theological distinction between venial sins, which weaken but do not destroy sanctifying grace, and deadly sins which do. By the closing decades of the second century Tertullian listed three sins as deadly on the basis of Acts 15. In the West, but not in Alexandria, these three were identified as idolatry, murder, and fornication. Later the three became seven. As we have already seen,[22] in Hebrews and in the *Shepherd* of Hermas the problem was wrestled with in a somewhat different manner.

The first point to observe in attempting to date the writing is that these false prophets—Antichrists—are present in large numbers.[23] This in itself suggests a date not earlier than the early years of the second century. While it is perhaps unwise to try to identify too exactly the sect to which the opponents belong, enough has been said to make it highly probable that they are akin to the second-century Gnostics. Furthermore, the implication of 2:20 ff. is clear that the gospel is available to all. The commandment "which ye had heard from the beginning,"[24] as Jülicher remarks, "represents the same idea . . . as does that of the tradition delivered 'once for all' . . . to Jude."[25] Paul's teaching is in the past; it has been absorbed by the writer as well as by his opponents. Eusebius says that Papias used quotations from this writing.[26] It is probable, but not absolutely certain, that Polycarp used it. The first absolutely unquestioned use of it is by Irenæus. Whether it is one of the "two of the aforementioned John" referred to in the famous Muratorian

[19] I John 1:8,10.
[20] I John 3:9.
[21] I John 5:16.
[22] Pp. 308 f.
[23] I John 2:18.
[24] I John 2:7,24; 3:11.
[25] *Introduction to the New Testament*, p. 246. 7th German edition, p. 229.
[26] *Hist. Eccl.* iii,39,17.

fragment[27] is perhaps open to question. That it was known to the framer of that early canon is obvious from his quotation of its opening words in his earlier reference to the Gospel of John.[28] There would not seem any good reason for questioning a date in the first quarter of the second century.

The question of pseudonymity does not arise. Although the writing has been from the earliest times known as the First Epistle of John, no such claim is made by the author. In fact, he says nothing of himself whatever, save in the intimation in the opening words[29] that he is a competent witness. But that these words imply a claim to be from an apostle appears to me questionable. Whether they do or not, it is evident that he was not. The complete absence of any traditional word of Jesus and the failure to quote the Old Testament as a buttress for his teaching not only suggest a late date, but exclude the notion that the author himself had been among the original followers.

That this nameless writer is the man who penned the Fourth Gospel is today regarded as highly probable by many scholars, although several entirely competent critics would prefer to identify him with the later reviser. In the gospel, too, the author conceals his name. Then again there are many striking parallels and similarities in vocabulary, style, and type of thought. A convenient survey of the material is provided by Moffatt,[30] who inclines to see the writer living and moving "within the circle in which the Fourth gospel originated," but with an "individuality and purpose of his own." To these parallels might well be added the common and noticeable fondness of both of these writings for the perfect tense.[31] Yet though the similarities are inescapable, there are equally clear differences—the polemic nature of the epistle in contrast to the calm, even flow of the gospel—which are perhaps most easily explained as the free parallels of the same writer, at work at a somewhat different time upon a quite different subject. A view not impossible is that the epistle is somewhat later than the gospel and is directed against those false teachers who by misusing the gospel were thus endangering Christianity and recommending themselves to the unwary. Further discussion of the author may be reserved until the discussion of the Fourth Gospel.

[27] *Muratorian Fragment,* lines 68 f.

[28] *Op. cit.,* lines 29-31.

[29] I John 1:1-5.

[30] *Introduction to the Literature of the New Testament,* pp. 589-593.

[31] Cf. my article in the *Journal of Biblical Literature,* Vol. LV (June, 1936), pp. 121-131, "The Perfect Tense in the Fourth Gospel."

Chapter XXXVI

THE SECOND AND THIRD EPISTLES OF JOHN

THESE two little epistles—each about the length of a note on a single leaf of papyrus—are so similar in form and structure that they must be regarded as coming from the same pen and at the same time or the one a slavish copy of the other. Whether they are by the same writer as I John is still debated. There are real similarities. The most noticeable contrast is in the form of address. The writer of I John, as we have seen, remains strictly anonymous; the author (or authors) of these two writings refers to himself as "the elder." Again, these latter are distinctly more epistolary in form. Although they achieved a place in the canon later, yet they breathe the same atmosphere as the longer writing and probably are to be seen as coming from the same period. For reasons which will appear in a subsequent paragraph I am inclined to feel that II John is from the same pen as I John and that the more epistolary form of the writing accounts for the difference of salutation, but that III John is by a different hand and was intended for ecclesiastical reasons to neutralize or at least safeguard the teaching of the letter copied.

The question as to the identity of "the elder" is interesting, but probably will never be completely solved. According to Papias, as quoted by Eusebius,[1] there was such an individual named John, and his tomb was in Ephesus. But whether the author of II John was this figure or was impersonating him is very hard to say. It would be rash to assume that the title "the elder" was restricted to any one individual. He would seem to be a person of some authority; none the less, Diotrephes dares to stand out against him[2] much as did the man referred to by Paul in II Corinthians. Tradition does not help us. Some of the fathers ascribed these letters to John the son of Zebedee, others to Papias' John, the elder (presbyter), still others were in doubt.

Written in the form of personal letters, they are none the less to be regarded as intended for general use. II John is addressed to "the elect lady and her children." From the salutation at the end—"The children of thine elect sister salute thee"—it is clear that she is not an individual (either named Kuria or addressed as Madam), but a church. But, as already remarked, it appears to me highly probable, although the epistolary form suggests an individual church, that this is fictitious and that the letter is truly catholic. Similarly,

[1] *Hist. Eccl.* iii,39,2-17.
[2] III John 9.

III John is directed to Gaius. In contrast to many scholars I am inclined to see this too as a fiction and the epistle purely general.

The purpose of II John is to warn Christians against extending an indiscriminate welcome to travelling teachers. False teachers are abroad. They are not to be received nor given Godspeed. Those that give these greetings partake in their evil works.[3] There seems little reason to question that they are part and parcel of the group denounced in I John. In this connexion it is instructive to read *Didache* 11-13 and *Shepherd* of Hermas, Mandate xi. These writings provide the background for an understanding of the warning of II John, and not only make all too clear that unworthy men were finding it profitable to pose as Christian teachers, but that the faithful had of necessity devised a pretty satisfactory method for unmasking the pretenders.

Under the guise of praising Gaius and Demetrius and of bitterly condemning Diotrephes—all to be seen as imaginary characters—III John urges as a sacred duty the cordial reception of travelling brethren and condemns unsparingly the lust for power on the part of local officers who were refusing to receive such kindly and to treat them with proper deference. It would appear to me probable that these writings come from the period of the development of the local church with its own bishop and other officers. A natural, if not commendable, rivalry arose between these local dignitaries and the wandering missionary teachers of the earlier days. Thus a natural interpretation of III John is to see it coming from a man who feared that II John might be construed as giving support for a rigorous exclusion of such wandering brethren. Hence, precisely as the later Paulinist produced II Thessalonians to neutralize the word of I Thessalonians which disturbed him, it is not unnatural to see the author of III John in a similar rôle. The obvious method would be to write another epistle so closely similar that it would appear evident that it was from the same author, and hence that the earlier epistle was surely not to be interpreted in the unwanted way. On this hypothesis the date of II John would be the same as I John; III John at a time somewhat later.

[3] II John 11.

Chapter XXXVII

APOCALYPTIC LITERATURE

FOR nearly three centuries (165 B.C.-120 A.D.) this curious and bizarre type of literature flourished in Judaism. Then it not only ceased to be produced, but seems largely to have dropped out of sight. Christians, however, found it highly acceptable and continued to make much of it. In fact, probably none of these writings except Daniel, which managed to gain canonical rank, would have been preserved had it not been for Christian zeal. As it is, since none of them save Daniel found a place in the Hebrew Bible, they are not extant in the original Hebrew or Aramaic; and since apparently few of them were ever considered by a majority of Greek-speaking Christians as quite on a par with the Old Testament writings they did not gain a permanent place in the Greek Old Testament of Christians. One of them, IV Ezra, was in the Old Latin Bible, that is, the Vulgate, and is accordingly to be found in the English Apocrypha under the title II Esdras, from the opening words: "The second book of the prophet Esdras."[1] The other apocalypses are known only in translation in the less-known languages. For example, Enoch is extant only in Ethiopic; the so-called *Secrets of Enoch*, a totally different work, for many centuries known only by name, in Slavonic, and is often styled Slavonic Enoch to differentiate it from Ethiopic Enoch, the apocalypse; Baruch in Syriac and to be differentiated from another writing, the so-called Greek Baruch.

It is no coincidence that these writings date from 165 B.C. to 120 A.D. These years embrace the period from the rise of Judas in opposition to the persecution of the Seleucids to the final subjugation of the nation to Rome. To a degree they were the revival of prophecy, and with it of national hopes. With the utter collapse of these hopes Judaism settled back into a patient waiting for God to work his will, and to a fresh study of the law. This should not suggest that during these three centuries this type of book occupied the

[1] There is considerable confusion as to the titles of the Ezra literature. The I Esdras in the English apocrypha is a writing of a totally different character. What is called II Esdras in the Septuagint is the combined canonical writings Ezra-Nehemiah. The difficulties in nomenclature may be lessened by the following lists:

LXX	English Apocrypha	Vulgate
I Esdras = I Esdras	I Esdras = I Esdras	I Esdras = Ezra-Nehemiah
II Esdras = Ezra-Nehemiah	II Esdras = IV Ezra	II Esdras = IV Ezra 1,2
		III Esdras = I Esdras
		IV Esdras = IV Ezra 3-14
		V Esdras = IV Ezra 15,16

centre of the stage in Jewish writing. Far from this being the case, they were totally ignored in the rabbinic writings. Undoubtedly some people found them acceptable, especially in times of tribulation, but that they reflect the general thinking of orthodox Judaism, educated or ignorant, is to be doubted. For Christians, however, it was quite different. From the very first the early disciples saw in Jesus the supernatural son of man of Daniel. His return upon the clouds of heaven was imminent. While for the Jew the inauguration of the golden age might come in any number of ways,[2] for the Christians this was the only way. Thus it was that the Christian eagerly appropriated them and even recast the material to form new ones—our Revelation of John, Apocalypse of Peter, Ascension of Isaiah.

The use of the term *apocalyptic* for this type of literature apparently comes from the opening words of the Revelation: "The Revelation (ἀποκάλυψις) of Jesus Christ which God gave him to show unto his servants, the things which must shortly come to pass."[3] The earlier name was *apocrypha*, that is, hidden, secret books. A passage in IV Ezra[4] reveals the common attitude toward them. In the destruction of Jerusalem the books of Scripture had been destroyed. Ezra prays to be enabled to reproduce them. In answer to his prayer he is inspired to dictate to five secretaries "everything that has happened in the world from the beginning." In forty days he dictates ninety-four books: the twenty-four canonical books and seventy others. While all, learned and ignorant alike, may use the twenty-four, the seventy are to be reserved, hidden for those competent to use them,

> For in them is the spring of understanding, the fountain of wisdom, and the stream of knowledge.

That the authors of this type of writing intended them for small circulation is most improbable. Rather, this notion of their having been hidden is most plausibly explained by the following consideration: These writings purported to be written by the great men of the past. But if so, why had they not been known earlier? The answer was easy. To be sure, these worthies had been recipients of the revelation of the things which would in the far future come to pass, but had been obliged to keep them secret, until just before the end, when they were revealed to those who would be able to profit by them. Thus all these writings are pseudonymous. They purport to be written by great worthies of the past—Ezra, Moses, Abraham, Noah, even Adam. Another characteristic of them is that the authors are always convinced that the things which they are announcing "must shortly come to pass." That is, the writer believed that *he* was living at the end of the age. To be sure, since the work is attributed to a hero of the past, this must be—and usually is—

[2] Cf. the commonplace: "The son of David coming with the clouds of heaven (Dan. 7:13) or lowly and riding on an ass" (Zech. 9:9)—Sanhedrin 98a.

[3] Rev. 1:1.

[4] IV Ezra 14:18-26,37-48.

veiled. Thus in such semi-apocalypses as the *Assumption of Moses* or the *Book of Jubilees* we have a long prediction of what is to come to pass, which is, as a matter of fact, largely a survey of history from Moses' time until the date of the actual author; or in the book of Daniel, the scene is laid in the Babylonian court where Daniel is supposed to have lived and written, but the real author is convinced that what the seer had long before foreseen is even now upon the world.

Again, it is obvious from the history of the period which produced these writings what their purpose was. They were in essence protests against the cruel fate which the nation was suffering and ringing cries of dauntless faith and hope. Evil is rampant; it is in the plan of God; its destruction none the less is certain. The promised day of the Lord is at hand. He will come when evil is at its height. Evil is due to the conflict in the angel world. The wicked adversaries of God have plunged the world into chaos. But their doom is sure. Power will be taken from those wicked nations, now Syria, now Rome—and from the demons who are inciting them—and will be restored to the people of God. Thus will God's plan be finally established, his power vindicated. And even now the clock has struck.

Certain elements of this type of thought, including distinct traces of apocalyptic imagery, are to be found also in the prophets. We at once think of the vision of the throne-room of God's palace in Isaiah 6, of the frequent visions of Ezekiel, especially those which he sees in ecstasy in chapters 40-48, of the visions and imagery of Zechariah. But there are also weighty differences. The prophets have been edited and revised with many and large additions. None the less, at the base they were the production of men who personally rebuked the nation, and they were uttered. The very opposite is true of the apocalyptist. He does not speak, but writes, and he does it not in his own name, but in the name of another. But there is an even greater difference in their attitude toward the origin of sin. The prophet denounces. Sin is rampant. Its cause is man's wicked ways, his deliberate disobedience to God. The prophets may at times foretell the future, but regularly they emphasize and stress the fact that man's conduct will determine to a large degree what that future will be. Thus their aim is to shape man's conduct. It is fair to say that to no little degree prophetism depends upon the notion of freedom of the will. Often the prophets raise their voices in protest in times of outward prosperity. Men are soft; in their comfort and luxury they have forgotten God; doom for their sins is certain. The handwriting is plain upon the wall, but men cannot see it or refuse to. Thus an Isaiah or a Jeremiah—the note of the prophet is essentially moral.

For the apocalyptist the emphasis is quite different. That he would deny that sin was ever a personal matter is not clear and appears to me improbable. None the less, it is clear that the evil fate which has befallen Israel is in no small measure due to the machination of evil spirits which have unleashed their forces. To that degree the apocalyptist is a determinist. Individual men may be good or bad; they will gain or lose on the basis of their character—

> As one year is more honourable than another, so is one man more honourable than another, some for great possessions, some for wisdom of heart, some for particular intellect, some for cunning, one for silence of lip, another for cleanliness, one for strength, another for comeliness, one for youth, another for sharp wit, one for shape of body, another for sensibility, let it be heard everywhere, but there is none better than he who fears God, he shall be more glorious in time to come.[5]

Whatever the vagaries, the stage properties, of the apocalypses with their terrible nightmares and lurid scenes, the ethical note is not expunged, for they all spring from the confidence that right will eventually triumph. In Daniel there is some emphasis on the probity of the three youths and of Daniel himself. In the semi-apocalypse, the *Testaments of the XII Patriarchs*, it is, of course, particularly clear. But they all voice the confidence, "Shall not the judge of all the earth do right?" although often the emphasis seems rather, "Shall he not ultimately triumph?" To a degree the words of the poet Lowell give expression to the confidence of the apocalyptist, be it a Daniel or a John, although, it must be admitted, in a chaster tone:

> Careless seems the great Avenger; history's pages but record
> One death-grapple in the darkness 'twixt old systems and the Word;
> Truth forever on the scaffold, Wrong forever on the throne,—
> Yet that scaffold sways the future, and, behind the dim unknown,
> Standeth God within the shadow, keeping watch above his own.[6]

But we should not read too much out of this emphasis. After all, the individual does not loom very large in his thinking. Forces far more powerful than he are at work. Thus instead of the word of condemnation and of doom so dear to the prophet, the word of the apocalyptist is one of encouragement. The times are in the hand of God. The forces of evil are rampant, but they are doomed. The darkest moment always presages the dawn. Thus for the apocalyptist the interest was not primarily to scourge the nation—still less the individual—for its sins, but, and this is particularly clear in Daniel and Revelation, to nerve men to stand firm. Together with the attempt at encouragement, this battle cry to faith and hope, and often obscuring it, is the ever-felt conviction that all history is the result of the interplay of the invisible but tremendously potent angelic forces, some with, some against, God—a curious "combination of creation and destruction."

For all these later apocalypses Daniel set the pace. The essential element is the series of visions in which what is transpiring in heaven and the situation on earth between Israel and the nations are brought into relationship. In all that Daniel sees, Israel occupies the central place; it is actually the history

[5] Slavonic (Secrets of) Enoch 43:2 f.

[6] *The Present Crisis,* lines 36-40.

of the Maccabean struggle, as the author sees it, thrown back superficially into the form of a prophecy of the hero Daniel. Beasts appear, three of them; then a fourth before whom the three fall. On his head is a horn in which are "eyes like the eyes of a man, and a mouth speaking great things." But then the heavens are opened with a vision of God, worshipped by the myriad angelic host. Judgment is set—this is an indispensable element of this type of writing—and Israel, seen as a "son of man," that is, a human being, in contradistinction to the awesome beasts who represent Babylon, Media, Persia, Greece, appears before the Ancient of Days and receives "an everlasting dominion, which shall not pass away."

Here are all the qualities of the true apocalypse—not only a vision as such, but the vision of the destiny of the world. The cosmic forces which have moved the nations about on the chessboard of the world are revealed. Again the book is pseudonymous, and the fiction, already referred to, whereby this supposedly ancient writing could have escaped notice for so long, is alluded to:

> And I heard, but I understood not: then said I, O my Lord, what shall be the issue of these things? And he said, Go thy way, Daniel; for the words are shut up and sealed till the time of the end.[7]

Another quality of the apocalypse, and this is true of all of them from Daniel to Revelation and IV Ezra, is their free use of symbolism and stereotyped material. In a word, the visions which the author claims to have seen he did not see with his own eyes, be they of body or of mind. This is simply a conventional and adopted symbol. That is, "vision" has become as conventionalized for the apocalyptist as "Thus saith the Lord" for the prophet. Each author appears to have employed older materials without scruple, although occasionally they found it necessary to edit or revamp them to make them fit the new time-table. One example will suffice at this point, although we shall have occasion to see it again and again in the Revelation of John. The fourth beast of Daniel is clearly Greece, but while Alexander and the later Seleucid successors were the especial thorn in the side of the author, in the succeeding centuries they were eclipsed by Rome. Hence in the later apocalypses, for example, Revelation and IV Ezra, this beast comes to be interpreted as Rome. This is explicitly stated in IV Ezra:

> And he said unto me: This is the interpretation of the vision which thou hast seen. The eagle whom thou sawest come up from the sea is the fourth kingdom, which appeared in a vision to thy brother, Daniel. But it was not interpreted unto him as I now interpret it unto thee or have interpreted it.[8]

But whatever their sources, they always produced one picture—a period of awful woe, with the hosts of the archfiend doing their worst; but these

[7] Dan. 12:8 f.

[8] IV Ezra 12:10-12.

woes invariably are to be succeeded by a period of joy and bliss, brought about supernaturally. Thus the earlier Jewish hope of a good time coming in the providence of God, when Israel, now scourged for his sins, would be deemed worthy of the fate that was in store: enemies conquered, scattered Jews brought back, Jerusalem rebuilt and glorious, no unbeliever in the land, the land itself flowing with milk and honey and with God all in all—this gave place in these writers to a supernatural deliverance, and came to be depicted in terms of heaven instead of a glorious future on this earth. That is, there becomes increasingly clear a distinct "two age" conception, this age and the "Age to Come"; and the writings breathe a bitter and passionate hatred of this world in which the righteous go constantly sorrowing, and must so long as the present order maintains.

This clear-cut dualism (and consequent asceticism) is distinctly not characteristic of Judaism. Hence the question is natural: Is this type of writing a legitimate child of Judaism? As has been indicated, elements of it are found in the prophets; but though the building-stones are there, who is the architect? There is much to commend the view expressed by many scholars that this type of thought is not to be seen as Jewish, but as Persian in origin. Persian thought was frankly dualistic. The twelve-thousand-year struggle between Ahriman (Angra Mainyu) and his hosts and Ormuzd (Ahura Mazda) and his angels provides a real explanation of the clash between Satan and Michael. Shaoshyant, the last of three Persian saviours, who appeared at the end of the twelve-thousand-year cycle and had as his function the preparation of men for the new age, the rousing of the dead, and the setting up of the final judgment may well be seen as the source of the figure of the final judge in the apocalypses, Jewish and Christian. In fact, I think it can be maintained that the whole concept of the final judgment, at least in the cosmic sense—not simply for Israel's enemies, but for all men—is distinctly Persian, not Jewish in origin. Yet even if the sheer to apocalypticism came from Persia, one thing is clear: the seed fell into congenial soil, and Israel appropriated it as its own. Whether or not the more staid Jews of the period in which this literature flourished found the complicated and lush development congenial or not, certain elements of this dualism, notably the belief in resurrection, were taken over and woven into the veriest orthodoxy.

While much in this field is obscure and will probably remain so, and accordingly too definite statements are rash, it appears to me highly probable that however much the earlier thinking of Judaism may have led to the adoption and adaptation of apocalypticism, yet, none the less, it is not the native product of Judaism. Pure Judaism never produced it. An outside and mighty alien religion had a distinct part in its birth. For the want of a better name we can style it the product of religious syncretism.

Chapter XXXVIII

THE REVELATION OF JOHN

THE Revelation or, as it is often called, the Apocalypse is not a unique book, but belongs to the class of writings discussed in the preceding chapter which flourished between 165 B.C. and 120 A.D. Like Daniel, this work was written in a time of distress. Whether actually the danger was as menacing as that which produced a Daniel we can leave for the moment. That the author *thought* it was is certain. True religion was being endangered by the heathen power which was momentarily in the saddle. The writing is to nerve the faithful to stand firm, to awaken new courage in the dispirited. God will intervene—in the coming of Christ as avenger and judge. Not only will the evil power—for the author the menace is Rome—be overthrown, bound, destroyed, but there will be a scrutiny of Christians to separate the genuine from the pretenders. Those who have died, who have sealed their faith with their blood and who are even now crying for vengeance, will reign with Christ during his thousand-year rule. How the overthrow would take place—would it be at the hands of warring nations, as the Parthians,[1] or by a literal earthquake,[2] or by the returning Christ?[3]—is not clear, for all three of these images occur. But take place it will, and will include with it the complete discomfiture of the wicked spiritual powers which stand behind the blasphemous Rome.

Thus, like Daniel, the book moves in the realm of the catastrophic. Furthermore, it abounds in the same fantastic and terrifying imagery—beasts, angels, visions interpreted by angelic voices—met with in all this kind of writing, and which must be viewed with discrimination. That is, it is necessary to distinguish sharply between the "machinery of apocalypse," the stage properties which are to be found with little variation in them all, and the personal notions and sober beliefs of the author. Thus it is quite unnecessary and unwarranted to assume that in this writing we are in a different circle of thought, that in contrast to the Jewish apocalypses we are here confronted with Christian "prophecy," perhaps of the kind produced by the prophets of whom Paul repeatedly speaks. All the qualities of apocalyptic eschatology are to be found in the canonical Revelation—the concept of two ages, the catastrophic manner of the end, the resurrection of the dead,

[1] Rev. 9:13 ff.; perhaps at the instigation of the returning Nero (*i.e.,* Nero *redivivus*), chap. 17.

[2] Rev. 6:12-17; 16:17-21.

[3] Rev. 19:11 ff.

reprisal of individuals, sway of the devil in this age and his ultimate defeat at the end of the world, the world judgment, the new world rising out of ruins of the old. Each apocalypse has its own peculiar touches and slants, and this is true of the Revelation of John, but the general qualities are too like all the others to allow for question.

Certain unique elements may be mentioned. (1) Jesus is introduced into the apocalyptic framework, and with him a Christian symbolism, but there is less distortion than is sometimes assumed. Probably a good bit of what passes for distinctly Christian phantasy is actually far older, and is simply inserted, perhaps without always being definitely intended to represent Jesus; surely without having been produced *de novo* because of traditions about him. Notably this is true of the section about the woman in travail and the defeat of the dragon (chapter 12). (2) The presence of the seven letters to churches in Asia Minor (chapters 2 and 3). These, however, are not real letters which were ever separate from the rest of the book or intended to be delivered. Furthermore, they are steeped in apocalyptic imagery. Nor should it be overlooked that it is no accident that seven and only seven churches are addressed. Few, if any, of the apocalypses lay a greater weight on the significance of the number seven than does this writing. (3) Again, this writing does not purport to be from the pen of some hero of the distant past as Ezra, Daniel, or Moses, but is written in the name of a man called John. We can profitably reserve the question of authorship for the moment. We should not, however, infer that the writing is not pseudonymous. Christians now had their famous "names"; it was not necessary to revert to those of the remote past. The *Apocalypse* (or *Revelation*) *of Peter* claims to be by Peter; demonstrably this is fictitious. It is thus not unlikely that the same is true here. It is to be observed, however, that the author does not purport to allude to his earlier life or to give a vision of the time between his time and the "now" in which he is writing. Instead of the word to Daniel, "for the words are shut up and sealed till the time of the end,"[4] the one to our writer is quite different: "And he said to me, Seal not up the words of the prophecy of this book; for the time is at hand."[5]

Two other characteristics of the mechanics of apocalypticism may be mentioned which the Revelation of John shares, but with certain emphases of its own—the matter of dreams and visions, and the function of angelic interpreters and guides. Dreams played an important part in the earlier Jewish apocalypses. Nebuchadnezzar's dreams of the great image[6] and of the mighty tree in the midst of the earth[7] are cases in point. The four

[4] Dan. 12:9.
[5] Rev. 22:10.
[6] Dan. 2:1 ff.
[7] Dan. 4:10 ff.

beasts appeared to Daniel himself in a dream;[8] perhaps the same is true of the ram and the he-goat which he saw "in Shusan the palace," although it is not said that it was a dream.[9] In Enoch, too, dream visions occur.[10] So, too, the book of the *Secrets of Enoch* begins with a vision which Enoch had upon his bed.[11] To these may be added IV Ezra 11:1; 12:3; 13:1,13, the visions of the cedar trees[12] and the clouds[13] and that which came to Levi,[14] for all these are in the form of a dream. But in contradistinction to the dream the straight vision plays an important part. Thus the vision of the man which Daniel saw came as he was standing "by the side of the great river, which is Hiddekel."[15] Similarly, Baruch sees the heavens opened as he stood upon Mt. Zion.[16] It would appear that as Jewish apocalypticism developed there was a tendency more and more from the dream vision—dreams had always played a large part in Jewish thinking, as in the case of those of Joseph—to the ecstatic vision. In the Revelation of John it is to be observed that the dream plays no part; here we have simply the pure vision often introduced by the phrase, "I was (or became) in the spirit."[17] Closely connected with the vision is the mention of being snatched up and carried away. In ecstasy it is not impossible that occasionally the seer believed that these experiences of walking about from one place to another, often by divine assistance, had been real experiences. A case in point occurs to Ezekiel:

> And he put forth the form of a hand, and took me by a lock of my head; and the Spirit lifted me up between earth and heaven, and brought me in the visions of God to Jerusalem, to the door of the gate of the inner court that looketh toward the north.[18]

The same theme is expanded in the story of *Bel and the Dragon* 33-39. It is also to be found in the snatching up of Baruch;[19] a similar story is recounted of Jesus in the fragment usually ascribed to the lost Gospel of the Hebrews and quoted by Origen.[20] It is possible that the legends about the translation of Enoch may lie back of this conception. To some investigators, notably Bousset, this evidences a new development in the later apocalypticism in which the theme of the supernatural catching up of various

[8] Dan. 7:1 ff.
[9] Dan. 8:1 ff.
[10] Enoch 83 f. and 85-90.
[11] Slavonic (Secrets of) Enoch 1:1 ff.
[12] Baruch 36:1 ff.
[13] Baruch 53:1 ff.
[14] *Test. XII Patriarchs, Levi* 2:5.
[15] Dan. 10:1 ff.
[16] Baruch 22:1 ff. (cf. 13:1 ff.).
[17] Rev. 1:10; 4:2.
[18] Ezek. 8:3.
[19] Syr. Baruch 6:3 ff.
[20] M. R. James, *The Apocryphal New Testament,* p. 2.

heroes (Isaiah, Baruch, Moses, Levi, Abraham—to cite but a few) came to be more and more stressed and even to be an end in itself. In the Revelation of John the seer is caught up—"And he carried me away in the Spirit"[21]—but there is more restraint; at any rate, it is never an end in itself, but simply the convenient way whereby he is enabled to "see" what he wishes to describe.

The other characteristic has to do with angelic guides, often introduced with no other description than "an angel" or "the angel" or "another angel." In Daniel there is "a watcher and a holy one" who came down from heaven to order the pruning of the tree;[22] in later chapters Gabriel interprets to Daniel the visions.[23] Enoch is regularly accompanied by an angel—Uriel, Raphael, Raguel, Michael. Uriel gives Enoch the explanation. In IV Ezra Uriel occasionally appears but melts into God,[24] while in Baruch the seer is in direct converse with God. In the Revelation of John angels play but little part in the earlier chapters. It is Christ himself who appears to the seer. The voice which is heard in 1:10 and 4:1 is that of Christ. In 10:1 ff. the angel plays a part, while in 17:1 the great harlot of Babylon and in 21:9 the new Jerusalem are shown by the angel. That is, in the passages which appear to be borrowed more or less ready made from conventional apocalyptic imagery the function of the angel is clearer. The representation of Jesus as the angel of interpretation is, of course, a distinct Christian touch, but is simply an obvious adaptation of apocalyptic imagery and usage.

Since this book is thus a genuine apocalypse, although with some minor variations, several earlier avenues of interpretation are definitely closed. It is failure to observe this which has led to so many misconceptions of the nature of the book which in turn prompted the English preacher, Adam Clarke, to exclaim in one of his sermons: "The more it was studied, the less was it understood, as generally either finding a man cracked or leaving him so." Nor would the English divine, if still alive today, find it necessary to modify his remark.

These predictions are not to be seen as having to do with a far-distant future; they are to be realized at once. This is the essence of all apocalyptic, and is specifically emphasized in this writing.[25] Thus, taking the hint from the genius of apocalypticism, we are to see the book concerned with the *present* crisis confronting the Christian churches, a crisis caused by the hostile ruling nation, Rome, who, of course, is being incited by the invisible

[21] Rev. 17:3; 21:10.
[22] Dan. 4:13,17.
[23] Dan. 8:16 ff.; 9:21 ff.
[24] IV Ezra 5:43 ff.
[25] Rev. 1:1,3; 22:10-12,20.

but potent powers of evil. In other words, the purpose of the book was solely to nerve Christians to stand firm in their hour of crisis.

Methods of interpretation which fail to observe this patent fact may be safely disregarded. Three of them may be mentioned. (1) *The church historical method.* Those who hold this view see in the book a real prophecy of the unfolding history of the church from the writer's time to that of the particular interpreter. Thus Mohammed, the Pope, Luther, Napoleon, Hitler are all seen depicted. In this type of interpretation the situation is exactly inverted. When viewed as an apocalypse we see the *author* convinced that the end is near; from this curious angle of interpretation, however, each interpreter feels that *he* (not the author) is living at the end of the age. Thus even to the present-day fervid but misguided individuals give away their possessions, put on their ascension robes, and—spend the rest of their days in the poorhouse or insane asylum. (2) *The futurist method.* Advocates see in the book a prophecy of what is to come to pass at the end, but, unlike those who hold the view just described, these individuals do not regard it as a recapitulation of the past but as a real prophecy, the time of whose fulfilment has not yet started. None of the things portrayed has yet occurred. They will arise—immediately before the second advent—and then men will know them for what they are. (3) *The symbolical method.* This is much like the church historical, save that everything is taken from the realm of history and interpreted as a pictorial struggle between good and evil.

As has been frequently remarked in the preceding pages, all sound interpretations must start with the recognition that it is the Roman nation which is the immediate source of the persecution being endured and that the author is writing to nerve his followers—not us—to make their stand. That is, it arises from the historical circumstances in which the author finds himself; the materials which he revises or produces anew are to be seen as largely depicting these circumstances. But at once difficulties arise when we attempt to interpret the book from this sound point of view. All the material does not seem to fit into the scheme. That emperor worship, which was flourishing in Asia Minor at the end of the first century, is the particular *bête noire* to the author is clear; that in the latter days of Domitian this received a fresh impetus is generally, and probably rightly, assumed. None the less, there seems to be material in the book pointing to earlier periods. For example, when the seer is given a reed and told to measure the temple,[26] it is reasonable to see an indication that the temple is still standing, hence, that it antedates 70 A.D. Or again, there is a curious oscillation with regard to the destruction of Rome. In 14:8 the words, "Fallen, fallen is Babylon the great, that hath made all the nations to drink of the wine of the wrath of her fornication," suggest that

[26] Rev. 11:1 ff.

this has already taken place; yet three chapters later it is predicted (17:16). In 18:2 it is announced as having occurred, while in 18:21 and 19:2 f. again it is predicted. It is not until 19:11-21 that it is finally effected.

This has seemed to many interpreters evidence that the book is not the product of one man but that at the most he is to be seen as an editor who has used earlier material without a thorough reworking. In 1886 E. Vischer in an important study[27] argued that our writing is a Christian second edition of an earlier Jewish apocalypse. To the Jewish section (4:1-22:5) were prefixed and appended a Christian introduction (1:1-3:22) and conclusion (22:6-21); slight modifications and alterations were also made to the original.[28] Vischer's analysis led to several others. Today the view that it is largely an unmodified Jewish apocalypse is not generally held; none the less, the work of these investigators has forced the recognition that in the writing, or in its materials, various strata and different authors are to be seen. The degree to which it is broken up varies from the intricate analyses of Spitta, Johannes Weiss, and R. H. Charles to the view that while the author is an author (not a mere editor) he has made use of materials from the past, that these materials naturally reflect the crises which produced them, and that the author did not always work them over so thoroughly as to obliterate the older distinctive (and disharmonious) traces, although he occasionally sought to bring an older (and still unfulfilled) prophecy up to date. As evidence of this it is possible to point not only to the patent fact that since the author shared the view common in his day that the beast of Daniel was Rome, not Antiochus Epiphanes, he revarnished that material,[29] but also to the equally clear touch in 17:11. One can scarcely doubt that the awkward phrase, "And the beast that was, and is not, is himself also an eighth, and is of the seven," is a later addition to a prophecy built upon the number seven in regulation apocalyptic style. Unfortunately, at the time of writing, however, an eighth emperor was reigning. Prophecy uttered before the fact has in every age squeaked. While I am not convinced that either the intricate analysis of Charles or the twofold division of Vischer is necessary or probable, it does appear to me beyond reasonable doubt that the author—and I prefer this as a designation for him to editor—has taken over among other materials older oracles, perhaps some of them Jewish, and has incorporated them at times with little or no alteration.

But another insight was prompted by Gunkel, who in 1895 in his very important study, *Schöpfung und Chaos*, sought to explain the inconsistencies in a different way. Literary criticism had gone too far. It was also quite

[27] *Die Offenbarung Johannes, eine jüdische Apokalypse in christlicher Bearbeitung.*

[28] The following passages were regarded as Christian additions: 5:9-14; 7:9-17; 11:8b; 12:11; 13:9-10; 14:1-5,12-13; 15:3; 16:15; 17:14; 19:9-10,11,13; 20:4-6; 21:5b-8. There were other minor changes.

[29] Contrast Rev. 13:1 ff. with Dan. 7:1-7.

impossible to explain everything in the book by contemporary history; indeed, the absurdities of the allegorists and symbolists lay at the door of the contemporary historical method. The real cause of the manifest inconsistencies was due to the growth of the tradition itself which the author had incorporated without really understanding it. Though Gunkel admitted the *final* interpretation of the beast to be Rome, the bulk of the material was not produced anew for this purpose by this author or even by a group of immediate predecessors. Rather, it was for the most part very old material—old myths—which we find in the book; and they had been altered but very little. Chapter 12 occupied Gunkel's particular attention. This is not a Christian or Jewish creation depicting the birth of the Messiah, but is an ancient Babylonian creation myth which had been adopted for eschatology. All of this material has a long history extending over hundreds of years. The apocalyptist is not the inventor but the user, at times perhaps the adapter, of this old stuff.

The most promising method of interpretation is a combination of these last three. Surely the book reflects contemporary history. At times the identifications are unmistakable. On the other hand, while the intricate analyses are improbable, we can see different layers of material—the stratification of various documents or material, large sections of which are probably Jewish—although it may well have come from the author's hand essentially as we have it. Finally, while Gunkel and his pedisequi are wrong in their view that this "religionsgeschichtliche Methode" *replaces* the contemporary historical and literary critical, it is futile to deny that some very ancient material, in part at least antedating apocalypticism as such, has been incorporated.

Thus it should be perfectly clear that the book is in no sense a source of authentic history—past, present, or future. Its value lies simply in the intensity of faith, the unshaken confidence in the power of God which guarantees the final triumph of the righteous cause. To nerve his followers to stand firm he writes in this peculiar style. It is quite a mistake to try to identify each element of each vision, as if it were reflecting some historical event. Occasionally this can be done. The scarlet woman, wherever the author got the figure, is Rome who is even now drunk with the blood of the saints. Similarly, the two beasts of chapter 11—one is the Roman empire, the other the priesthood of emperor worship. The author may well have employed earlier figures, but he obviously employs them in this sense. Very often, however, the apocalyptic tubes are squeezed simply to contribute to the general picture. None the less, it should be clearly recognized that, although it is couched in all the imagery of apocalypticism, it is for a definite purpose. It is not merely an extravaganza from the mind of a religious fanatic running wild.

Again, the book is solely the product of study and reflection. No living man, even in the wildest vision or nightmare, actually *saw* the things he describes. They are simply paper descriptions. Again and again the same event is portrayed in different visions—as is also notably the case in Daniel—or, as has already been remarked, he *sees* it again in preparation. Nor is it out of place to remark that, even if he had actually *seen* them, the mind of man is such that he could not have remembered them all in this welter of detail. He may well have been an ecstatic. But his *seeing* is simply the conventional means of describing what he wants to represent.[30] So conventional is the phrase that the author naturally "turns to *see* the voice" which was talking to him (1:12); he *sees* a book sealed with seven seals, but *sees* that it is written within and on the back (5:1). He *sees* the new Jerusalem in the form of a perfect twelve-thousand-furlong cube,—fifteen hundred miles! (21:16). He *sees* the son of man holding seven stars in his right hand, yet placing that same right hand on his (the writer's) head (1:16 f.). He *sees* the four-and-twenty elders prostrating themselves before the Lamb, seemingly unencumbered by the bulky golden harps and shallow bowls filled with incense which they were at that moment balancing in their hands (5:8). The use of the numbers 7 and 3½; their reference and correspondence to other visions; the sudden shifts of scene, now in heaven, now on earth; the almost monotonous "and another angel"—all these are simply stage properties. This is no hastily thrown off pamphlet or chronicling of some weird dreams, but a carefully studied product of tremendous, if sensational, imagination. Furthermore, as has already been remarked, although he has used freely earlier materials, much of which may well be pre-Christian, and has not always revamped or revised them thoroughly, he is not to be viewed as an editor or compiler. The only just term is author.

When shall we date the writing? The most noticeable emphasis in the book is the hatred of Rome. The contrast with Paul's sober words (especially Rom. 13:1-7) is striking. I Peter 2:13-17, too, urges obedience to Rome, but with the additional note that Christians are not to think it strange if the fiery trial be among them (4:12). That is, while there is no intimation in Paul—or in Acts—of persecution by Rome, as such, yet in I Peter it appears to me present, although I Peter has none of the incendiary character of Revelation, but is far more at one in this respect with Paul, although many years later. None the less, I see no difficulty in dating I Peter and Revelation from the same period. There is no reason to assume that all Christians viewed the future alike. The Revelation of John moves in the field of the exaggerated with its thousands and ten

[30] Failure to observe this elemental fact of apocalypticism has led to many unfortunate consequences, perhaps the worst of which has to do with the Jewish view of the Messiah. Because occasional writers had occasion in their chronicles of personally conducted tours of heaven to *see* the Messiah, modern scholars have evolved the remarkable theory of the "Jewish doctrine of the preëxistent Messiah"!

thousands. There is little reason to assume that the number of martyrs had been numerically large. But for this author there is only earthly woe and sorrow in sight; in short, he is an alarmist. I see no ground for doubting that at any time after Nero's burning of Christians in Rome or, for that matter, after Caligula's attempt to set up his statue in Jerusalem, some Christians and some Jews may have been fanned to fury and may have regarded Rome as determined upon the annihilation of true religion. That all, however, shared these views is preposterous.

It is generally felt, and rightly, that emperor worship is the source of our author's wrath. Although emperor worship had been the spontaneous act of provincials in Asia Minor accustomed to the earlier worship of Alexander the Great, evoked by the lively sense of gratitude for the improved conditions which the Augustan reform had produced and not forced upon unwilling subjects by the emperors themselves, it had been from the start an unmitigated offence to Jews and Christians alike. Jews had fared far better than Christians because of their recognized status. To Christians, equally unreconciled but not exempted, it was an impossible demand. Their refusal always exposed them to possible persecution. Apparently Domitian (81-96 A.D.) in his later days took this worship more seriously than any of his predecessors save Gaius (Caligula). But though it is commonly said that he conducted a persecution of Christians because of their refusal, there is no evidence of an imperial edict from him enforcing the cult against Christians. The correspondence between Trajan and Pliny in Bithynia in the early second century indicates that Christians were under suspicion and had occasionally at least been executed. Ignatius' well-known difficulty in becoming a martyr indicates, however, that even in his time there was no sweeping attempt. But to a man of the obviously morbid outlook toward Rome of our author no especial time of real crisis need be assumed. Any date after Nero might well have seemed to him as critical a moment as had the impious act of Antiochus Epiphanes to Daniel. Christians could do no less than repudiate absolutely the whole ungodly system.

On the other hand, there seem to be definite indications of a date at the end of the century, which date, although not demanded by the alarmist tone, is perfectly congenial to it. The two beasts of chapter 13, respectively the Roman empire and the priesthood of the imperial cult, are the very embodiment of evil. The devil has given Rome his authority over the world. The reference to the head "as though it had been smitten unto death" (13:3) may plausibly be the author's reinterpretation of an older view and thus evidence the Nero *redivivus* legend current at the end of the first century. Again 17:11 can scarcely be earlier than Domitian, and appears to be an obvious attempt to bring an earlier prophecy written in the time of Vespasian or Titus up to date. No interpreter of the book appears to feel he has done his full duty without a discussion of the famous "number of a man" in 13:18. In spite of somewhat over-optimistic "solutions," there appears to me nothing certain or definite about it—even the number itself is uncertain; for, though 666 is the customary reading, there is ancient evidence favouring 616. It may be that it is a riddle to be solved by supplying letters in such a way that they spell the required name and that their numerical values total the required 666 (or 616). It would be fruitless to review in detail the various attempts. Among them may be listed "Nero Cæsar" (written in Hebrew characters), "lateinos" *i.e.,* "the Roman" (written in Greek), "Gaius Cæsar" (in Greek), "Chaos of Old." Others view it not the riddle of a man's name but a play upon the values which certain numbers had in Hebrew imagery. "Six" carried a sinister meaning. It fell just short of "seven," the sacred number of perfection. Thus six upon six upon six represents the apotheosis of evil, and also its ultimate defeat, failing as it does to reach seven. Others point to the fact that 666 is a triangular number, that is, the sum of the arithmetic progression 1 + 2 + 3 + 4 + . . . 36. Again this 36 is the triangular number of the series 1 + 2 + 3 + 4 + . . . 8. And since a triangular number shares the meaning of its last component, 666 is the equivalent of 36 and hence of 8. Thus 666 represents the eighth emperor of 17:11. Perhaps the true meaning of the passage lies in the result of one of these various excursions into the realm of sacred arithmetic. Personally I should be most disinclined to use as a foundation a spherical stone which seems to be ready to roll in any direction of the compass.

A date at the end of the first century appears to be in keeping with the picture of the seven churches in the letters of chapters 2 and 3. Ephesus has forsaken her first love, Sardis is practically dead; Laodicea's spiritual life is extinct. In Pergamum are Balaamites and Nicolaitans with antinomian teachings akin to those of the errorists rebuked by Jude and I John. Again, the tradition from Irenæus down—whatever it may be worth—is that "it [the vision] was seen not a long time ago, but almost in our own generation, at the end of the reign of Domitian."[31]

Several scholars have seen in 6:6 evidence for an even more exact dating. In 92 A.D. Domitian forbade the cultivation of vines in the provinces, tacitly to encourage grain culture, but probably actually to serve as a protective measure for Italian producers of grapes. Because of the widespread opposition which the edict aroused it was reversed the next year.[32] S. Reinach argued that the book was written in 93 A.D., and that in the words, "A measure of wheat for a denarius, and three measures of barley for a denarius; and the oil and wine hurt thou not," the author is protesting against the removal of this edict which to him (because of his ascetic

[31] Eusebius, *Hist. Eccl.* iii,18,3.
[32] Suetonius, *Domitian* 7 and 14.

leaning) was wholesome. As a consequence the necessities of life will be dear, the luxuries cheap.

On the other hand, there are indications of an earlier date. Many of those so regarded are not probable. For example, the figure of the woman with her son fleeing from the dragon to the desert for three and a half years is scarcely to be seen as an allusion to the flight of the Christians from Jerusalem to Pella during the fateful siege of the city. Not only is it most unlikely that a Christian writer would call the Jerusalem church the "mother of Christ," but the whole figure is probably borrowed by the author from older material. On the contrary, as has been already remarked, the command to the seer to measure the temple of God, but not the outer court (11:1 f.), does imply that the temple is still standing and hence a date before 70 A.D. But this does not demand that the book *as a whole* was then produced, but simply that the author has incorporated a fragment from that time. Again, the passage 17:9-11, to which I have already referred, suggests that though in its present form it is from the time of Domitian the latter verses are simply additions to an earlier passage in which the *seven* heads had been mentioned. The presumption is that it was written during the reign of the sixth, Vespasian[33]—"the five are fallen, the one is, the other is not yet come." The additional word of the eighth who is also "of the seven" does not appear to me a part of the original seven scheme, but a later touch intended to bring it up to date. Whether the last part of verse 10, "and when he [*i.e.*, "the seventh"] cometh he must continue for a little while," is to be seen a part of the original prophecy—the author is sure that the end is near; hence Vespasian's successor will remain but a short time—or is also an addition written at the time of verse 11 and thus reflecting the fact that Titus did reign but two years appears to me impossible of decision.

Thus, as I see it, the evidence is by no means uniform. However we interpret it, one thing is certain. There are strata of different material in the book, but the unity of style inclines me away from partition theories. The book as a whole is a unity—that is, the author has welded all the stuff together. I am inclined to feel that the traditional date is the more probable, that is, that the author himself was the one who made the later additions, rather than to see it as composed as a piece at the earlier date, with later touches added by different and subsequent hands.

The identity of the author of this book is but one of the many New

[33] Augustus 31 B.C.-14 A.D., Tiberius 14-37, Gaius (Caligula) 37-41, Claudius 41-54, Nero 54-68, Vespasian 69-79, Titus 79-81, Domitian 81-96.

Julius was not usually included in the list of the emperors. It is scarcely probable that the rivals Galba, Otho, or Vitellius, who contended for the throne through the terrible year 68-69, would be reckoned in the line.

Testament puzzles which will probably continue to entice investigators and to elude their investigation. Some things about him, however, are reasonably sure. That he was a Jewish Christian has usually been assumed, and probably rightly. Not only is he familiar with the Old Testament—this in itself would prove little, even though it must be admitted his acquaintance, especially with apocalyptic passages, is minute and exact—but his references to gentiles[34] exhibit the natural attitude of the Jew, while the term "Jew" is one of honour and not to be abused.[35] Hebrew he understands. The Greek is a barbarous and wretched jargon written with no regard for the most elemental rules of syntax. Perhaps it is to be explained as the production of a man whose mother tongue was Semitic. The real objection to it being translation Greek appears to be the difficulty in finding a translator whose knowledge of Greek was so near nil. Actually at times it appears as if the barbarisms were intentional. The frequent coördination of participles with finite verbs; the treatment of ὁ ὢν as an indeclinable noun; the production of ὁ ἦν to parallel it—these are but a sample of what one may expect. In this present study it appears pointless to clutter the page with a list of these solecisms. A half-hour's reading by one competent to judge will be far more profitable, while for one unable to make such an examination for himself the evidence would, of course, be meaningless. Suffice it to say that the mellifluous prose and poetry of the King James Version—as in so many other portions of the Bible, notably Isaiah 53—is vastly different from the original it portrays.

The Tübingen school regarded the writing an attack upon Paul. In 2:9 and 3:9 they saw Paul lampooned among those "who say they are Jews and are not," and again in 2:2, "who call themselves apostles and are not." The reproof of the Pergamites who eat things sacrificed to idols was viewed as a criticism of Paul's word in I Cor. 10:25-30. The woman Jezebel in Thyatira who called herself a prophetess (2:20), and who has so puzzled commentators, was easily recognizable to them: she was of course a burlesque of Lydia whose conversion is recorded in Acts 16:14-15. Was she not of the city of Thyatira and a friend of Paul's? Since not only Peter and James but even Paul had had visions of Jesus, these scholars found little difficulty in the assumption that a group of Christians felt it but natural for John to have had one too. (And in this point, it may be parenthetically remarked, they were probably correct, although not in the conclusion they drew from it.) Today this view has been largely abandoned. There is no slightest evidence of any of the distinctly Pauline emphases: he neither affirms nor denies but simply ignores them.

Is there evidence pointing to his identity? Four times he calls himself

[34] Cf. Rev. 11:2; 20:3,8.

[35] Rev. 2:9; 3:9.

John,[36] once "the slave of Jesus Christ,"[37] once "your brother and partaker with you in the tribulation and kingdom and patience which are in Jesus."[38] Asia Minor may well have been his home, since he not only appears to feel a responsibility for its various churches (or at least selects seven of them to epitomize Christians), but also shows an apparent familiarity with their condition. That he was an apostle is nowhere affirmed, nor does he suggest that he had ever been with Jesus. To be sure, his tone is severe to those who would add to or detract from his book,[39] but surely this is no indication of apostleship. His words are a revelation from God; he is warning against a mutilation of them. That the reference to "ye apostles" in 18:20 proves that he was *not* an apostle appears to me doubtful since it is quite parallel to the words which immediately follow, "and ye prophets." Surely he considered himself a prophet. On the other hand, the matter-of-fact reference to the "twelve apostles of the Lamb" (21:14) suggests that he was not one of them.

Thus the tradition which from the time of Justin Martyr usually (but by no means universally) ascribed this writing to John the son of Zebedee finds little support from the writing itself, while the extreme difficulty the book had in the whole East (with the sole exception of Asia Minor) in commending itself to readers as worthy of a place in the sacred writings, even though it purported to be by "John," which must surely have suggested the famous apostle who bore that name, is not to be minimized or disregarded. Furthermore, it is apparently definitely excluded by the high probability that although, as we have seen, the book was not written until the very end of the first century, and quite conceivably two decades later, John the son of Zebedee was martyred before 70 A.D. This evidence has been frequently printed in recent years, and may be briefly summarized. (1) George Hamartolos in his ninth century *Chronicle*, as preserved in the codex *Coislinianus*, states that John "was deemed worthy of martyrdom," and quotes Papias' words (which he then amplifies and comments upon) that "he was killed by the Jews." (2) In spite of the apparent errors in this passage from George, the fact that Papias actually did so write appears from the so-called de Boor fragment of an epitome (600-800 A.D.) of the *Chronicle* of the fifth-century writer, Philip of Side. Here, too, Papias is quoted: "Papias in the second book says that John the divine and James his brother were killed by Jews." (3) That Papias' source of information is simply an inference from Mark 10:35-40 or its parallel, Matt. 20:20-23, is possible. None the less, this Marcan passage itself affords solid ground. No reasonable interpretation of these words can deny the high probability

[36] Rev. 1:1,4,9; 22:8.

[37] Rev. 1:1.

[38] Rev. 1:9.

[39] 22:18,19. It need scarcely be reminded that these words apply solely to this book and not to our whole Bible, of which he had never heard.

that by the time these words were written both brothers had "drunk the cup" that Jesus had drunk and had been "baptized with the baptism" with which he had been baptized. Furthermore, while in contrast to many scholars I am disinclined to date Mark before 70 A.D., it appears unjustifiable to place it many years after. (4) In Heracleon's list of the apostles who did not suffer martyrdom, as quoted by Clement of Alexandria,[40] are Matthew, Philip, Thomas, and Levi, but not John. It may be also remarked that in a fifth century Syriac martyrology the joint martyrdom of James and John was celebrated on December 27. From this evidence it would appear highly probable that the story which is popularly told of John the beloved disciple being the only one of the twelve to die a peaceful death has very little to commend it, but that he had been dead many years when the Revelation was composed. Furthermore, it is to be observed that while, as has been already observed, the Revelation appears to have been produced by one who lived in Asia Minor, there seems little evidence that John the apostle had laboured there. Thus in the *Martyrium Andreæ* the story of the apostles casting lots shortly after the Ascension to see where they were destined to go records that to James and John was assigned the East. That the story is unhistorical is of course obvious. None the less, it evidences no knowledge of any tradition connecting John with Asia. Again the silence of Ignatius about John (although he mentions Paul) in his letter to Ephesus and the similar silence of all the sub-apostolic writers until 180 A.D. would seem to make a residence of John in Ephesus most improbable.

Nor is it accurate to say that this skepticism runs counter to the uniform tradition, for there was no uniform tradition. In addition to the material already cited it is to be observed that by the end of the second century a tradition was current that John had been exiled to Patmos. All the Revelation says is that he was "in the isle that is called Patmos."[41] As the various guesses of the commentators make evident, the subsequent words, "for the word of God and the testimony of Jesus," can be interpreted in many ways. Both Clement and Origen refer to the "exile," but do not indicate which "king" it was who had caused it. Irenæus, on the other hand, states that he wrote during the last years of Domitian, but does not refer to it as done while in exile. Probably the notion that he had been exiled by Domitian is due partly to a natural (but not necessary) inference from the book itself and partly to the words of Irenæus. Other traditions, too, were common. Tertullian remarks that in Rome "John was first plunged, unhurt, into boiling oil and thence remitted to his island-exile."[42] This legend was apparently due to a fanciful interpretation of being "baptized" (Mark

[40] *Stromata* iv,9.
[41] Rev. 1:9.
[42] *de Præscript. Hær.* 36.

10:39). Other late legends are occasionally told, as that of his drinking a cup of poison or his meeting with the archheretic Cerinthus in the bathhouse. Thus one negative conclusion seems justified. The author of Revelation—John though he may possibly have been—was not John the son of Zebedee.

The other definite conclusion about authorship is also negative. The author was not the author of the Fourth Gospel and I John, and probably not of II John or III John, although this is not so glaringly impossible. From an early date the glaring dissimilarities between this gospel and the Revelation have been recognized. Dionysius of Alexandria (*ca.* 190-265 A.D.) states the case with scholarly precision and accuracy.[43] Style, vocabulary, ideas, and point of view are quite different. Nor should the contrast between the silence of the writer of the gospel with regard to himself and the repeated reference, "I, John," in the Revelation be disregarded. Thus attempts to explain these differences as being due to a considerable lapse of time between the writings are unjustified for various reasons. First, there appears to be no adequate reason to postulate the lapse, since both writings are to be dated at the very end of the first century or in the early years of the second. Second, the relationship between the two writings is distinctly not that of elementary or immature to mature. To mention but one point—the Greek of the gospel is not that of an improved Apocalypse. As H. B. Swete remarked, "The difference is due to personal character rather than to relative familiarity with Greek." The Revelation is easily the most strongly Jewish book in the New Testament; the Fourth Gospel is, on the contrary, philosophical and contemplative, revealing a debt both to Alexandrian thought and to Paul. Similarities do exist, and have often been tabulated,[44] but are not of a quality to neutralize the greater differences. Both writings exhibit a fondness for such words as "witness" and "to bear witness"; for such figures of speech as "water of life," "vineyard," "shepherd," "bride." "As I also have received of my Father" (Rev. 2:27) may be compared with "This commandment received I from my Father" (John 10:8); or again, "And he that is athirst, let him come" (Rev. 22:17) with "If any man thirst, let him come unto me and drink" (John 7:37). That these similarities are purely accidental is not probable, but that they indicate literary dependence in the terms of common authorship even less so. It would appear to me that they may be accounted for on the assumption (1) that both writings came from the same locality and thus are tinctured with similarities, or (2) that the Revelation had had sufficient influence upon the later writings—

[43] Eusebius, *Hist. Eccl.* vii,25,1-27. This section, unfortunately too long to reprint here, should be read and pondered. All modern treatments are essentially a restatement of this able argument.

[44] R. H. Charles, *ICC Revelation*, Vol. I, pp. xxix-xxxiv; Jülicher, *An Introduction to the New Testament*, pp. 281 f. (German, pp. 259-261); W. Bousset, *Die Offenbarung Johannis*, pp. 177-179.

a very brief interval would be quite adequate—to cause an occasional striking but superficial resemblance. Other questions pertaining to authorship including the extraordinarily difficult one, Why did the notion arise that all five writings were Johannine? may profitably be reserved for the chapter on the Fourth Gospel.

Chapter XXXIX

THE GOSPEL ACCORDING TO MARK

In approaching a study of the four gospels which for nearly nineteen centuries have occupied a unique place in Christian circles certain facts stand out. Three of these gospels stand very close together. They have a common plan; the same incidents occur in each; again and again events are described in all three in essentially identical language. For over a century it has been customary to refer to them as the Synoptic gospels. This designation does not mean that from them (in contrast to the fourth) one can gain a synopsis of the life of Jesus, but that they are so related one to the other that they can be printed in parallel columns with amazingly little distortion. In contrast to these three—Matthew, Mark, and Luke—stands the fourth, John. To be sure, it, too, purports to tell about the central figure of Christianity, but the picture it gives is quite distinct. Not only does it differ totally in arrangement and phraseology, but the material itself is almost entirely unique. Thus the student is tempted to arrange the writings in two sharply separated classes—Synoptic gospels and John—and to focus his attention upon the agreements of the first three and the contrast between them and the fourth. To a large extent this division is justified and useful. No solid or adequate treatment of the Synoptic gospels is possible without a clear recognition of their mutual similarities or resemblances and an attempt to explain them. And it is no less clear that the old attempts to print all four gospels in parallel columns is worse than useless. On the other hand, there has been a tendency in recent years to over-emphasize both the similarities of the Synoptics and the uniqueness of John. Actually Matthew, Mark, and Luke—despite agreements so amazing that any theory which denies literary dependence of two upon the third is unthinkable—are by no means of a piece. Each has its own very distinct peculiarities which must not be overlooked. While it is essential to read them in the parallel columns of a harmony, it is no less true that if that is the only way in which they are read we fail almost utterly in appreciating them. Each was written to be read as a whole, not to be compared and collated with others. Then again, a word of warning is necessary against the popular practice today of magnifying the contrast between the Synoptists and John. Actually it appears to me that it is becoming increasingly clear that the Synoptic gospels stand distinctly closer to John than had been recognized, that is, that their purpose is by no means limited to a simple chronicle of the sayings and deeds of their hero, but that they share—at times, as in

Mark, very distinctly—the theological or doctrinal interest of John. In a word, although they attempt it from different angles, all four of these writings are intended to arouse and keep alive faith in Christ, to make him live in the hearts of men, to provide a polemic against the outside world, and in no little degree to establish and demonstrate convictions and beliefs that had become sacred.

Students find it comparatively easy to memorize the main facts incident to the Synoptic problem and to the Johannine; they talk (or write glibly) about the priority of Mark, the nature of Q, the ways in which the two junior Synoptists modified the elder, the total unlikeness of the Fourth Gospel; but when given a list of the passages from the four gospels from which scholars have reached these various conclusions, they are as likely to ascribe the Raising of Lazarus to Mark as to John, have no opinion at all as to where such parables as the Talents and the Pounds are to be found, and seem quite surprised to discover that the Cleansing of the Temple occurs in a different situation in John than in the other three. Since it is manifestly impossible to have an opinion about the four gospels without a reasonably exact knowledge of the aims (and subject-matter!) of each of them, it has appeared wise to consider somewhat in detail each of the three Synoptists as separate units before attempting to discuss in orderly style the thornier questions of literary relationship. But though the Synoptic problem, as such, will be reserved for a later chapter, it will, of course, be quite impossible to avoid all reference to it in a discussion of the nature and methods of Matthew and Luke and the use they made of Markan material. That Mark is anterior to Matthew and Luke is so much a matter of common knowledge to laymen as well as to professional students that it would appear unnecessary at this point to justify the discussion of Mark before Matthew.

Mark is a brief but highly dramatic narrative or sketch. It is in no sense a biography or life of Christ. One point alone is of superlative interest to the author, the hostility against Jesus which ended in his crucifixion—whereby he gave his life a ransom to many—and which was succeeded by his resurrection and expected second coming, as a consequence of which the cause of God is made ultimately triumphant. This motif governs everything in the gospel. There is no prologue or introduction. The book starts *in medias res.* It treats only the critical period, and contains none but significant events. Far from being loosely thrown together, it is tightly articulated, and with a distinct progress. The style is rapid and terse; the adverb "immediately" occurs again and again to connect one section with the preceding. Constantly the author falls into the historic present, so real to him is the scene. The paratactic "and" is very noticeable, but by no means lessens the dramatic quality. As the narrative proceeds, the tone of excitement heightens, until in the last pages—the dreadful days in Jerusalem—

there is no let-down or breathing-space till the very end, the death. His enemies are victorious; his body is put in a rock-cut tomb. The curtain falls with the audience speechless. Then after a quick moment the curtain rises again for an instant. No longer is the sky grey and forbidding. In the light of the Easter morning the tomb is seen open and empty. An angel gives the glad tidings: "He is risen; he is not here . . . he goeth before you into Galilee; there shall ye see him, as he said unto you."[1] The curtain falls. It is only as we sense this tremendous dramatic quality—in many ways the gospel may be compared with one of the operas of Wagner—that we really grasp the nature of this writing. There is only one way to read this gospel, and that is at a sitting, and it leaves one tense and exhausted.

The sayings of Jesus, comparatively few in Mark, are introduced solely on the basis of this idea—the inception and development of the conflict. They are no mere illustrations of his teachings, but they regularly strike the note of success in spite of opposition. Thus in chapter 4 the parable of the Sower makes clear that some of the seed will produce its abundant harvest despite all mishaps. The lamp is not—cannot be—placed under the bushel or the bed; its place is on the stand, for it is to give light. The seed grows secretly; the sower need not worry, for the earth must bring it forth. Small though the mustard seed be, it will produce its great plant. Similarly the attacks on the Pharisees are introduced as the clash becomes more intense. The eschatological section is thus seen to be a genuine part of the fundamental problem; it provides the only solution to the tragedy, a veritable *deus ex machina*. This section may well be wrought from different sayings, some of them already grouped, and put ready-made into Jesus' mouth. But it is no patch on the garment. It stands the great prophecy of ultimate victory even through disaster, and makes possible the great crescendo to the book: "Verily I say unto you, This generation shall not pass away, until all these things be accomplished."[2] Victory and reward, and they are soon to come!

Thus it is surely fair to say that the book was written to meet the objections and attacks aroused by the death of Jesus. But this is not the only purpose, for together with the central note of the developing hostility another may be discovered closely intertwined with it, *viz.,* the belief that Jesus had been anointed by God for a special service, and is thus the "son of man." His purpose is not to prove that this was true, but rather to explain *how* it could be true in the face of the stubborn fact that he had been crucified. Thus the gospel is distinctly theological in purpose, and hence to a measure resembles John. Two strands are woven together: the one revealing the nature of the quarrel, and showing that Jesus was innocent of any just charge; the other making clear that Jesus' death had been no accident, but was divinely appointed. God's anointed had come, had been recognized, had gone to his

[1] Mark 16:6 f.
[2] Mark 13:30.

rightful place at God's right hand, but in the near future will return to gather his chosen to the glories of participation in the coming kingdom.

Two other interests may also be discerned, although both of them are quite subordinate. The first may be called a geographical interest. He has arranged his material into two sharply defined periods—one in Galilee (chapters 1-9), the other in Jerusalem, whither he had gone from Galilee through the Perea (10-16:8). Nor are these essentially duplicates. They are portrayed in a very different way. It is not until the end of the first that the disciples grasp—and then only dimly, for, like the man in the highly significant story, they see "men as trees, walking"—who he really is. Then in the second period he devotes himself almost exclusively to his disciples, and starts his teaching of the impending tragedy and triumph, a teaching which they fail to appreciate fully until they see it reflected by the Easter light. The other interest lies in the attempt to establish the position of the apostles as legitimate, the true representatives of Jesus in the church. Thus he describes their call, lists their names, and paints a picture of the mission upon which Jesus sends them. Why the author introduces this emphasis is perhaps not quite clear. It appears to me not improbable that it is in the form of a tacit reproof of the earlier claims of Jerusalem to leadership, based upon the fact that James was the brother of Jesus. However that may be, Mark finds himself involved in difficulties here, for his view of the "Messianic secret" leads him constantly to make Jesus disparage their insight and to stress their failure to believe.

Since Mark's order was taken over bodily by Matthew and Luke, it is easy to be beguiled into thinking that it is the actual order of events. Obviously, if the baptism story is historical, it came at the beginning of the ministry; it is equally clear that the ministry in Galilee preceded the shameful death on Calvary, and probably the sojourn in Jerusalem, but it is equally clear that Mark's reason for arranging them thus was not to produce a biographical sketch nor even to conform to a definite chronology. As will be suggested in a later chapter, it is highly probable that there were few if any clear indications in the various separate stories and traditional words which formed the bulk of his material as to when or where this or that was said or done. Occasionally an incident may be chronicled in its actual sequence, but there seems little reason for feeling that this was of particular concern to the evangelist. Even the earliest scenes are placed in this position consciously, not to conform to any tradition but rather for a very practical purpose. The Baptist appears to announce the coming of his greater successor. This serves to introduce Jesus into the scene and to sound the note all important *for the reader*. He is baptized, and receives visible evidence of the Father's choice. He now knows his function, and in quiet confidence returns to Galilee after the wilderness temptation. Nor should it be overlooked that the temptation story is of the utmost importance for the evangelist's notion of the

"Messianic secret" so scrupulously kept by Jesus. The demons have learned it when he bested them in the wilderness, and hence regularly recognize him.[3] This is one of the ways whereby the evangelist lets his readers into the great secret. Not only do they hear the demons' cries of recognition, but they too have heard the word, "Thou art my beloved son." Thus we can watch Jesus exercising his power without sharing the astonishment of those in Capernaum (1:21-28), for we know the secret. Furthermore, it is by no means clear that the events recorded as occurring in the early days are so to be placed. One example will suffice. Following the healing of the leper it is said that his fame was now such that he "could no more openly enter into a city, but was without in desert places: and they came to him from every quarter" (1:45). But that this would appear to come from a later period is implied by such passages as 2:1; 3:1; and 6:1-6, where he is represented as still teaching openly in synagogues and cities. These events are placed as they are not for chronological accuracy but to reveal Jesus' increasing fame—"And the report of him went out straightway everywhere into all the region of Galilee round about" (1:28). But in view of his belief that Jesus scrupulously hid his secret from the populace, the evangelist asserts that Jesus' word to any who might have an inkling of it—as the healed leper,[4] or the demons[5]—was to keep silent. This has a twofold purpose: it warns us that Jesus was not responsible for the charge soon to come that he was a seditious man; it also serves to explain why it was that, if Jesus had performed such deeds, it had not become clear to all who he was.

Furthermore, in the Galilean ministry the materials were brought in skilfully to heighten the picture of the developing opposition from the Pharisees. He heals the paralytic (2:1 ff.), and more than that declared his sins forgiven; he violated without qualm the sanctity of the Sabbath. Whatever the original *pre*-Markan form of these narratives may have indicated concerning Jesus' notion of his own power and authority in these cases,[6] it is clear that in the judgment of Mark Jesus' attitude appeared presumptuous in the extreme to his critics. Opposition to him is rising even as his fame is increasing. Why is the story of the fasting of John's disciples and the corresponding failure of Jesus' disciples to fast introduced so early? Surely there is no chronological sequence between 2:15-17 and 2:18-22, although the former with its reference to Jesus and his disciples at table provides a setting for the next section. The latter passage serves to strike the prophetic note, "But the days will come, when the bridegroom shall be taken away from them, and then will they fast in that day." Opposition had already occurred (2:6,16). Soon (3:6) the sharper note is struck, "And the Pharisees went out, and straightway with the Herodians took counsel against him, how they

[3] See above, p. 157.
[4] Mark 1:43 f.
[5] Mark 1:34.
[6] See above, p. 162.

might destroy him." They accuse him of Satanic power, and he turns the tables upon them (3:22 ff.). But worse than this, the even more ominous note had been struck—the Twelve have been selected—"and Judas Iscariot, who also betrayed him" (3:19). Even his own family are unresponsive, even downright suspicious, and think him crazy (3:21). This mention of his family makes natural the reference to his mother and brethren and provides the setting for his portentous answer: "Whosoever shall do the will of God, the same is my brother, and sister, and mother" (3:35).

In chapter 4, as has already been suggested, a few parables are included. Their significance at this point is obvious. They are placed here, not because this was the time chronologically that he had uttered them, but to strike a note of encouragement for the reader. The clouds are heavy, but the day of victory will come. What more appropriate than that on that very day (4:35) he crossed the lake and stilled the menacing wind and waves? Surely a glorious climax to the note of victory which he had just sounded. It is as if the author were whispering: "As he stilled the waves and was victorious over storms, so we shall see him victorious over his more dangerous enemies." So we could carry the story of the developing conflict straight to the awful end. There seems, accordingly, little valid reason to question the fact that the gospel structure bears indisputable evidence of intentional and studied arrangement and pointing of blocks of material originally quite detached and separate.

A little further on in the narrative the disciples are rebuked for their blindness: they have seen the two miraculous feedings, of the five thousand and of the four thousand, and yet, although Jesus is in the boat, they can bewail their lack of bread (8:14-21)! Is it simply coincidence that this incident is immediately followed by the story of the blind man, who gains his sight, but at first only in part, so that he sees men "as trees, walking" (8:22-26)? Whatever the original nature of the story is—as the sober account of an actual event there are obvious difficulties: how did the blind man know what either trees or men looked like?—as Mark has utilized it it marks the turning point of the gospel. It is immediately followed by the similar experience of Peter. From his eyes, too, at Cæsarea Philippi the scales fall and he makes his famous confession (8:27-30). But like the man in the story his sight is at first not clear, and he must be rebuked for his failure to see that suffering and death were a necessary part of Jesus' task (8:31-33). Then follows the Transfiguration, "after six days." Why telescope these two events—did nothing happen during the six days? There appears to me little question that this too is simply the result of Mark's arrangement of material. The origin of the story itself may well be quite distinct.[7] There would appear to me adequate reason for considering it but one of the many

[7] It should be compared with the strikingly similar story of Moses in the mountain, with its reference to the lapse of six days, the veiling clouds, and the vision of Jehovah (Exod. 24:12-18).

resurrection stories which circulated in the early days,[8] but which eventually dropped out of sight. For Mark, however, it is the necessary sequel to Peter's confession. Peter has made his statement; God's answer comes from heaven. Peter was right. "This is my beloved Son: hear ye him."[9] The first word from heaven, at the time of the baptism, was for Jesus' information, and had been addressed to him personally; the later word is appropriately addressed to the disciples, and comes to confirm their dawning faith. Again Peter sees "men as trees, walking"—"Let us make three tabernacles; one for thee, and one for Elijah, and one for Moses!" (9:5). Then follows a series of pathetic instances of blindness—the dispute of the Twelve as to preëminence (9:33 f.), the presumptuous request of James and John (10:35 ff.), the faithlessness of Judas (14:10 f.), the sleeping disciples in the garden (14:32 ff.), their cowardly flight (14:50). Even Peter sits down by the fire of his enemies (14:53 ff.)!

Other instances of the blindness of the disciples—both before and after their partial illumination—occur: their perplexity after the stilling of the sea (4:41); their failure to comprehend the nature of Jesus' question regarding the woman with the issue of blood (5:31)—and of course the reader understands as the disciples do not, what the question really means[10]—their failure to "understand about the loaves (6:52); their attitude towards other exorcists (9:38 ff.); their attempt to prevent the folk from bringing the children to Jesus (10:13 ff.); their perplexity at Jesus' words about riches (10:23 f.); above all their inability to understand parables (4:10-20,33 f.). These many and striking examples—many of which are either omitted or toned down by Matthew and (or) Luke—are intentionally employed by Mark because of his view of the Messianic secret of Jesus, and form his answer to the larger query, Why this hostility to Jesus? Mark's answer is: Jesus had not revealed it to his hearers, even to the Twelve, although upon them it had gradually and partially dawned, due in part to their frequent observations, but principally to their private instruction, for it was theirs to know the mystery of the kingdom (4:10 f.). This, of course, involves Mark in the distinct historical difficulties already mentioned.[11] How could the disciples be so obtuse? If they had been privileged to enjoy such intimate views of his power and his private instruction, why did they not see? How could they continue to misunderstand his explicit word about his suffering and coming glory? The crowd, on the other hand, is prevented by God from seeing it. This necessitates his artificial explanations of the purpose of Jesus' parables—

[8] Cf. I Cor. 15:3-7.

[9] Mark 9:7.

[10] For John's use of this familiar literary device, see pp. 443-445.

[11] See pp. 165, 167.

Unto you is given the mystery of the kingdom of God: but unto them that are without, all things are done in parables: that seeing they may see, and not perceive; and hearing they may hear, and not understand; lest haply they should turn again, and it should be forgiven them[12]—

and also of the injunction to "tell it to no man," although occasionally, as in the case of Jairus' daughter, any such word of secrecy is, of course, quite artificial in view of the attention that the child's death has already aroused (5:21-43).

In Jerusalem the obvious arrangement of incidents by Mark is to be seen, especially since some of them are sheerest legend: the Cursing of the Barren Fig Tree (11:12-14,20-23), prophetic of the fate of the fruitless nation; the Cleansing of the Temple (11:15-18); the even clearer prophecy of the merciless irony of history in the parable of the Wicked Husbandmen (12:1-12); the plotting and questions to lure him into a trap (12:13-27); his orthodox answer regarding the law (12:28-34)—no insurgent or blasphemer he, in spite of his shameful death!—his final silencing of his opponents by the question regarding David's son (12:35-37) and his warning against them (12:38-40); the touchingly significant contrast shown by the Widow and her two Mites (12:41-44).[13] Then, as the opposition reaches its height, the words of the coming triumph in the eschatological chapter. Following this interlude, which serves not only to heighten the picture but to give the disciples the information which they need and can use when once their eyes are really open, comes the final tragedy to which all else has led up and the quick glimpse of the glorious victory which has been so often hinted to the disciples—but with their half-closed eyes they had been unable to see it—and so explicitly revealed to the reader.

There is order and progress in the gospel, but it is the order produced by an efficient and able artist, not the order of history. All this should warn us against the notion that the gospel is the rough-and-ready product of a half-illiterate Galilean fisherman. Perhaps the Greek is in spots rough—although not nearly so bad as many modern critics, whose command of Greek is largely due to *Hadley and Allen* or *Goodwin*, maintain; if so, it simply makes the more dazzling the superlative beauty of the picture it presents.

The question of the original language of the gospel has been debated periodically for centuries. Recently it has been raised afresh. Our gospel stands in Greek; on the other hand, not only did Jesus obviously use Aramaic, but there are distinct Semitisms in our Greek Mark. The question then is, Was our gospel written in Greek or do we have a translation of an

[12] Mark 4:11 f. Hence such a private explanation of a parable as 4:14-20 is surely secondary, although it may not have been produced by Mark afresh, but simply utilized in accord with his view.

[13] This last story may well be suggested by the reference to "widows" in the preceding verse.

earlier Aramaic version? Opinions differ, although by far the greater number of scholars today scout the suggestion of an Aramaic original, some—notably in the University of Chicago—seeming to consider the suggestion a personal affront. C. C. Torrey, the veteran Semitist of Yale, on the contrary, feels that it is certain.[14] There is no question that there are crabbed and infelicitous turns in the Greek quite contrary to the manifest literary skill of the author, who is, as we have seen, no ill-educated or half-educated man. It has been maintained that he thought in Aramaic and translated as he wrote. This, while far from impossible, is only a conjecture; but for that matter the same is true for all the rival views. The fact that the Old Testament is regularly quoted from the Septuagint does not constitute direct evidence that Greek was the original language, for even if the author were translating from either a written document or "in his head," he would naturally make use of the version his readers employed. To me the superlative difficulty underlying the notion of an Aramaic original is the question of date. The early date which Torrey is obliged to postulate—to be sure, he makes virtue of necessity—appears to me grossly improbable if not downright impossible. Hence I am inclined to feel that the appearance of translation Greek is probably most plausibly explained as due to the wide use of Aramaic sources, written or oral. If, however, the exponents of form criticism, notably Dibelius,[15] are correct that many at least of the pericopes from which the gospel is framed were produced in mission preaching to gentiles, even this concession is not free from difficulties. It would be rewarding if a scholar at home in the literary criticism of the gospels and at the same time equipped with a competent knowledge of Aramaic were to examine the Markan text with an eye to determining whether there are sections of pericopes in which the *bona fide* Aramaisms are most evident and then, if this be true, to determine the nature of these sections.

Recently the question of a Latin original has been raised afresh.[16] Appeal is made to the tradition that Mark was Peter's interpreter. Why, queries West, should Peter need an interpreter to Greek-speaking people after thirty years' preaching, especially in view of his earlier activity in Antioch (Gal. 2:11 ff.)? The presence of numerous Latinisms in the gospel[17] is stressed, together with such interpretations as "two *mites*, which make a *quadrant*" (12:42) and "within the *court*, which is the *Prætorium*" (15:16), in both of which cases Greek words are given their Latin equivalents. Couchoud

[14] C. C. Torrey, *The Four Gospels* and *Our Translated Gospels*.

[15] M. Dibelius, *From Tradition to Gospel* and *A Fresh Approach to the New Testament and Early Christian Literature*.

[16] Cf. the articles by J. C. West in the *Interpreter*, Vol. 20 (July, 1924), and P.-L. Couchoud in the *Crozer Quarterly*, Vol. 5 (January, 1928).

[17] λεγιών (5:9,15); δηνάριον (6:37; 12:15; 14:5); ξέστης (7:4); κῆνσος (12:14); κοδράντης (12:42); φραγελλόω (15:15); πραιτώριον (15:16); κεντυρίων (15:39,44,45); σπεκουλάτωρ (6:27).

further gives an elaborate and ingenius argument intended to show that the meaning of Mark is frequently unintelligible and the phraseology unnatural save on this hypothesis.

This view has never enjoyed any great popularity, although several manuscripts carry the legend that the gospel was written in Latin, and in the subscription to the Peshitto and Harclean Syriac it is expressly stated, "written in Latin in Rome." Some scholars, notably Bacon, have urged that while this evidence does not warrant the assumption of a Latin original, it does tend to strengthen the tradition that Mark is a Roman gospel. The probability that it was written in Greek, not Latin, does not invalidate this hypothesis, for Greek was freely used in Rome in the first two centuries of our era. On the other hand, there is no direct evidence from the gospel itself for Rome. The additional clause about divorce (10:12) certainly implies acquaintance with Roman law, and can scarcely be attributed to Jesus,[18] but does not demand Rome. Surely it is precarious to see in the reference to Rufus (15:21) proof, simply because a Rufus is greeted in Rom. 16:13, since the name was a common one, and the last chapter of Romans was apparently sent to Ephesus (not Rome). And finally, to argue for Rome as the place of origin because of two traditions, one connecting the author with Peter, the other Peter with Rome, has little to commend it. All that it appears to me legitimate to conclude from these comparatively infrequent Latin words, phrases, and practices is that they imply some familiarity with the Latin tongue and with Roman jurisprudence. But this could indicate Alexandria—to mention but one locality—quite as easily as Rome, for during the first pre-Christian century Roman culture had spread widely in Egypt as is abundantly attested by the Latinisms in the Egyptian papyri.

On the other hand, the gospel—at least in its present form—definitely presupposes gentile readers who are not particularly well informed with regard to affairs in Palestine. What Palestinian would need to be told that Nazareth was in Galilee (1:9)? It is necessary to translate such names as *Boanerges* (3:17), *Bartimæus* (10:46), *Golgotha* (15:22), as well as the phrases *Talitha cumi* (5:41), *Ephphatha* (7:34), *Eloi, Eloi, lama, sabachthani* (15:34), and to explain not only the meaning of "common" hands, but to state that "the Pharisees, and all the Jews, except they wash their hands diligently (?) eat not, etc." (7:2 ff.). The significance of the Jewish "corban" must be explained (7:11); not only must the readers be told that the day before the Sabbath was called *Preparation* (15:42), but that the Passover lamb was wont to be slain on the first day of the Feast of Unleavened Bread (14:12), and that the Sadducees denied the resurrection (12:18). Thus we can be reasonably certain that the gospel was written for gentiles living outside Palestine from some one of the many cities or localities in the Roman world

[18] See Enslin, *The Ethics of Paul*, pp. 109 f.

into which some familiarity with things Roman had come. But to attempt a more specific statement would appear unwarranted.

Nor is it possible to make any exact statement as to the author. This gospel—and the same is true of the other three—is anonymous. Not only is there no statement of authorship, but there are also no hints. Thus they are not to be called pseudonymous despite the titles "According to Mark," "According to Matthew," etc., which stand regularly in the manuscripts and modern editions. These titles are not part of the original writings, but were prefixed apparently at a time when a collection of gospels was being made, and it thus became necessary—as it had not been earlier—to distinguish between them. The tradition which ascribes the gospel we are now considering to Mark is ancient—our earliest mention of it is in the lost writing of Papias—but is by no means convincing. Papias, an early bishop of Hierapolis, who wrote some time before 160 A.D., quotes a tradition which he had learned about this gospel and makes some further deductions. His writing has not been preserved, but this section was incorporated by Eusebius in his *Church History*. The passage reads as follows:

> And the presbyter used to say this, "Mark became Peter's interpreter and wrote accurately all that he remembered, not, to be sure, in order (?), of the things said or done by the Lord." For he had neither heard the Lord nor followed him, but later, as I said, followed Peter, who used to give (his) teachings as the need arose but without making an arrangement of the Lord's oracles, so that Mark did nothing at all wrong in thus writing down some things as he remembered them. For for one thing he gave concern, to omit nothing of what he had heard or to falsify anything therein.[19]

This oft-quoted passage fairly bristles with difficulties. Is Papias quoting the "presbyter" throughout, or, as suggested by my punctuation, is the quotation limited to the first sentence and the remainder his own interpretation? What is meant by the puzzling "not, to be sure, in order"? To what extent was Mark Peter's interpreter? Many answers have been given to these and other questions. One thing would appear reasonably certain. Papias' word is for the purpose of defending the gospel against accusations or criticisms of some sort or other. That by his word "not in order" he means "not in chronological order" is not impossible, but is scarcely likely. It would appear to me more probable that he is contrasting this gospel with some other writing, and is attempting to excuse the contrasts. It has often been assumed that this other standard was the Gospel of John. I am inclined to feel that it is more probable that the standard was the Gospel of Matthew, and that Papias is concerned, not so much with variations of chronology or even of arrangement, but with regard to comparative fulness in the accounts. The puzzling word *taxis* may well denote completeness,

[19] *Hist. Eccl.* iii, 39,15.

and thus may stand as almost the exact equivalent of "list." Thus I incline to the translation, "but not with the completeness of a list," suggested by the Catholic scholar, Father Kleist, although without the conclusion he draws from this view.[20] The fact that this gospel not only contained so few of the sayings of Jesus, but lacked other material, notably stories of his supernatural birth and of his resurrection appearances, aroused attention as soon as the several gospels were compared, and may conceivably have played no little part in the almost universal disparagement of this, the oldest of our gospels, from the second century until the rediscovery of its importance in the nineteenth. Papias may well have thought that it was this lack in material which led the presbyter to write *ou mentoi taxei*, and it is not inconceivable that Papias was right.

From this statement of the connexion between Peter and Mark many conclusions and inferences have been drawn. Peter was the real author of the gospel; Mark merely transmitted it. Thus we have the essential content of Peter's habitual preaching. The homely little incident of the youth who fled naked at the time of Jesus' arrest (14:51 f.), which is omitted by Matthew and Luke, has been regarded a personal reminiscence of Mark's, who was that young man. This has been given a specious probability by the fact that, according to Acts 12:12 Mark's mother Mary had a house in Jerusalem frequented by the early Christians, and which had served as a haven for Peter himself when released by the angel from prison. It was further deduced that this had been the house in which the Last supper had been held. What more natural than that Mark, while not present at the meal, had hovered in the background? Furthermore, does not I Peter 5:13 attest the bond between Peter and Mark? A full discussion of these details would lead us far afield, without resulting in any real enlightenment.

Whatever the tradition upon which the elusive presbyter relied which connected the name of Peter with the gospel, one point appears to me inescapable: neither Peter nor any other personal attendant of Jesus was in any sense its author. That some of the material emanated from a circle which held Peter in reverence is quite possible. But what Christians in the last decades of the first century failed to do this? There is an emphasis upon Peter in this gospel. In the legend of the Cursing of the Fig Tree Peter is the one who said to Jesus, "Rabbi, behold, the fig tree which thou cursedst is withered away."[21] To be sure, in Matthew's version there is no especial mention that it was Peter who spoke.[22] But it would surely be precarious to see such a palpable legend coming from an eyewitness. Again in 16:7 Peter is singled out—"But go, tell his disciples *and Peter*"—but if this touch, perfectly natural in the light of the place which Peter had presumably

[20] J. A. Kleist, *The Memoirs of St. Peter,* pp. 17-22.

[21] Mark 11:21.

[22] Matt. 21:20.

played in the revived hopes of the disciples, be considered a Petrine touch, what is to be said of John 21:7-23? Despite these unique Petrine touches the emphasis upon Peter is actually less pronounced in Mark than in Matthew, while much of the material of the gospel, not to mention the use made of it, surely rules out an eyewitness. If anything is certain, it is that the stories of the miraculous feedings of the Five Thousand and of the Four Thousand are doublets, that is, two independent versions of the same story, a story which apparently had been earlier told of other persons beside Jesus.[23] Is it probable that an eyewitness would not only thus chronicle them as two separate events, but would make Jesus himself refer to them as independent? The careful and studied arrangement of materials—some of them legendary—the unconcern for chronological sequence, the use of doublets, the indication of a comparatively late date which will be considered in a subsequent paragraph—all this renders any ascription of it to the Galilean fisherman unthinkable. To attempt to prove that a Mark did not write it would be a thankless task. None the less, it is very clear that the author, whatever his name was, did not achieve this result through compiling, under dictation or otherwise, the reminiscence of any one man, the authority of whose name would of necessity have laid cramping restrictions through making the thought of deviation or alteration presumptuous. Our author was not writing under the shadow of any one; on every page he betokens his full and conscious freedom to gather his material whence he could and to arrange it as seemed to him best. What he sought to achieve was *the gospel*, not *the gospel according to Peter* or to anyone else. To some this may seem a ruthless, even reckless, disregard of tradition. Those who have delved at all deeply into history will, however, not need to be reminded that traditions, in every age, are remarkably hardy and fast-growing plants and often, though starting from a seed as tiny as the mustard's, achieve a rapid and luxuriant foliage in which many strange birds can lodge.

There are distinct touches in the gospel which would seem to preclude a date before the destruction of Jerusalem. The reply of Jesus to the disciples who had exclaimed, "Teacher, behold, what manner of stones and what manner of buildings!" "Seest thou these great buildings? there shall not be left here one stone upon another, which shall not be thrown down,"[24] is most naturally understood as written in the light of the fall of the temple. Surely the allegory of the Wicked Husbandmen apparently reflects the actual circumstances which Christians came to see as the punishment of the Jews for having killed the beloved son and heir, *viz.*, the giving of God's vineyard to the gentiles.[25] Whether 13:9-10 is to be understood as a reflection of Paul's experiences is by no means sure. At any rate, the concluding words,

[23] Cf. II Kings 4:42-44.
[24] Mark 13:1 f.
[25] Mark 12:1-12.

"And the gospel must first be preached unto all the nations," clearly reflects the well-established gentile mission, as does the story of the rending of the veil of the temple (15:38). This can only be explained in terms of the conclusion which Christianity eventually reached, that Jesus' death had broken down every barrier and distinction, the burden of such writings as Ephesians and Hebrews.[26] Nor is it improbable that the author saw in the admonition to them in Judea to flee unto the mountains (13:14) a fulfilment in the flight of the Christians to Pella during the awful siege by the Romans. It may very well be that the nucleus of chapter 13 was produced during the excitement incident to Caligula's attempt to set up his statue, but the chapter as a whole appears to me to postdate the year 70 A.D. It is possible that in the story of the death of John the Baptist there is another indication of a date after 70 A.D. As has already been remarked, there are very decided difficulties in this story of the denunciation of Antipas' adulterous union with Herodias. Dio Cassius records the following:

> Berenice was at the height of her power and consequently came to Rome with her brother Agrippa. The latter was granted prætorial honors, while she lived in the palace and cohabited with Titus. She expected to be married to him and acted as his wife in every way. But he, perceiving that the Romans were displeased at this situation, sent her away; for all sorts of rumors were being noised about. At this time, too, some sophists of the cynic school contrived to get into the city. First came Diogenes into the theatre when it was full of men and denounced them in a long and abusive speech; for this he was flogged. Heras followed him, and showing no greater intent of being obedient, uttered many senseless yelpings in a genuine cynic [*i.e.,* dog-like] wise; for this behavior he was beheaded.[27]

Is this event of the year 75 A.D. simply a strange parallel, or did it provide Mark the background for his story?

On the other hand, it should be stated that while many scholars incline to a date after the year 70, some stressing one argument, some another, there are several able critics who incline to a much earlier date. Among those is the Berlin historian, Harnack. He was led to this conclusion through his changed views of Acts, which he had come to see as written by a companion of Paul before the latter's death. But Luke must precede Acts, and Mark was one of the sources of Luke. Therefore of necessity Mark must have been written well before 60 A.D. As mentioned above, Professor Torrey minimizes the significance of the various indications of a late date and considers the Aramaic gospel produced in the year 40 A.D.

Tradition is by no means uniform about the date. Irenæus[28] states that it was written by Mark *after* Peter's death, that is, after 64 A.D. On the other hand, Eusebius recounts the tradition known to him that Mark wrote it

[26] Eph. 2:11-18; 3:12; Hebr. 10:19 ff.
[27] Dio Cassius, *Hist. Rom.* lxvi,15.
[28] *adv. Hær.* iii,1,1.

before Peter's death, and that the latter "knowing by the revelation of the spirit to him what had been done, was pleased at their zeal and ratified the scripture for study in the churches," and remarks, "Clement [of Alexandria] quotes the story in the sixth book of the *Hypotyposes*, and the bishop of Hierapolis, named Papias, confirms him."[29] In my own opinion the most probable date lies between the years 70 and 85, and probably nearer the earlier than the latter. No one passage or verse would appear to me decisive in determining this date; rather the general tone of the whole writing inclines me to feel that a deal of water had flowed beneath the bridge before the author took pen in hand to record his "gospel of Jesus Christ, the Son of God."

A final word may be added with regard to the end of the gospel. Our gospel ends with 16:8—"And they said nothing to any one; for they were afraid." The two manuscripts B and א, the very valuable Sinaitic Syriac, many of the manuscripts known to Eusebius, and some of the versions, notably the Armenian, end with 16:8. Other manuscripts have the verses 9-20, with indications of a break, such as spaces or symbols of various sorts. Still other manuscripts have another and shorter conclusion:

> They reported briefly all the commandments to the companions of Peter. After this Jesus himself sent through them from the east to the west the holy and incorruptible preaching of eternal salvation.

Both endings must be regarded on internal and external grounds as later additions. This fact is so universally conceded that it is unnecessary to belabour the point.[30] The longer ending, regularly printed in most of the modern versions (although with suitable warning in the later ones), by its account of appearances in the environs of Jerusalem flatly contradicts the earlier warning, "Howbeit, after I am raised up, I will go before you into Galilee" (14:28), starts with an intolerable abruptness in the Greek, and is simply an amalgam of material from the other three gospels.[31] The great majority of scholars, while conceding the spuriousness of the two rival endings, do not consider 16:8 the original ending. Such an ending would provide impossible Greek, while the abrupt end of the narrative without resurrection appearances is equally unsatisfactory. Hence it is customary to assume another ending which for reasons to us unknown almost immediately disappeared. To me this reasoning is entirely unconvincing. I have already endeavoured to show that many of the statements regarding the "impossible

[29] *Hist. Eccl.* ii,15.

[30] For the classical discussion of the whole problem the student is referred to an essay by Dr. Hort in Westcott and Hort, *The New Testament in Greek*, appendix to Vol. II, pp. 28-51.

[31] Mark 16:9-10; cf. John 20:11-18;
12 f.; cf. Luke 24:13-35;
14; cf. John 20:19-20;
15,16; cf. Matt. 28:16-20;
19; cf. Luke 24:50,51.

Greek" are unwarranted.[32] Nor does it appear to me that the present ending is unsatisfactory. Is it not possible that our tastes have been set by the other gospels which do end with resurrection stories? Is the ending any more abrupt than the beginning? To me, as I have already indicated in the analysis of the gospel, this forms a highly dramatic and magnificent conclusion. The reader has already been informed that appearances had been promised. Instead of attempting a description that might easily have been banal, he lets the curtain fall on this brief, but triumphant, epilogue with the last word freighted with delightful and portentous irony.

[32] See my article "Ἐφοβοῦντο γάρ" in the *Journal of Biblical Literature*, Vol. 46, 1927, pp. 62 ff.

Chapter XL

THE GOSPEL ACCORDING TO MATTHEW

THE gospel of Matthew has been described as a "manual of the life of Christ and of biblical theology." This is a singularly apt designation, for it emphasizes the characteristic of the writing which is most obvious, namely, that it is at once systematic and comprehensive and intended for church use. It is carefully arranged, with topics easily remembered. Of all the gospels its outline and content are the most easily remembered. It implies an organized church life with a well-defined moral code. Throughout the book the comparison between the first great lawgiver, Moses, and his far greater successor are too apparent to be accidental. Both had been miraculously preserved at the time of their birth from the machinations of a wicked and suspicious king; both had given their God-inspired legislation from the mountain top. In a word, the Gospel of Matthew may be styled the New Law. As one reads this gospel he feels it is the work of the evangelist. Furthermore, the designation *editor* is a most unhappy one; in every sense of the word he deserves the term *author*. He has used sources, probably more completely than has often been admitted, but he clearly felt perfectly free to interpret, to rearrange, to rewrite drastically, and to suppress. Though his readiness to rearrange is everywhere evident, his fondness for preserving the exact phraseology of his several sources, if at all possible, is equally noticeable. It may be remarked parenthetically that in both these latter respects his habit is precisely the reverse of Luke. He skilfully combines Jesus' sayings into units. The Sermon on the Mount is an excellent example. Here various detached sayings of Jesus—many of which are also preserved in Luke, but for the most part are scattered through that gospel—are assembled into an artistic, closely compacted whole to serve as a sample of Jesus' "teachings." Chapter 13 presents a series of parables, illustrative of another phase of his threefold ministry,[1] *viz.,* "preaching the gospel of the kingdom."

Unlike Mark, who has arranged his material to present vividly the problem of Jesus' death—its historical occasion and its theological purport—and to provide occasional materials, almost in the nature of asides to the reader, to keep this emphasis clear, Matthew's purpose is quite different. Although he utilizes Mark's material almost *in toto*, and thus of necessity preserves many of Mark's emphases, he is not concerned with them. One of the fea-

[1] Cf. the clear-cut statement in Matt. 4:23, expanded and illustrated by the remainder of the book.

tures of this gospel is its structure, noticeably its arrangement in numerical groups—three's, five's, and seven's. Among these may be mentioned the curious arrangement of Jesus' ancestors in three divisions each of fourteen generations;[2] the three temptations; three illustrations of the implicates of Christian righteousness[3] (alms, prayer, fasting); three prohibitions[4] ("do not lay up treasures on earth," "do not judge," "do not give that which is holy to the dogs"); three commands[5] (ask, enter, beware of false prophets); three healings[6] (the leper, the centurion's servant, Peter's mother-in-law); three "fear nots";[7] three prayers in Gethsemane;[8] above all the threefold nature of the ministry—"And Jesus went about in all Galilee, teaching in their synagogues, and preaching the gospel of the kingdom, and healing all manner of disease and all manner of sickness among the people."[9] There are seven woes in the blistering attack on the Pharisees;[10] seven beatitudes;[11] and seven parables in chapter 13. Even more conspicuous is the arrangement of Jesus' words into five blocks of extended sayings, each one followed with a colophon:

> And it came to pass, when Jesus had finished these words, the multitudes were astonished at his teaching: for he taught them as one having authority, and not as their scribes (7:28).

> And it came to pass when Jesus had finished commanding his disciples, he departed thence to teach and preach in their cities (11:1).

> And it came to pass, when Jesus had finished these parables, he departed thence (13:53).

> And it came to pass when Jesus had finished these words, he departed from Galilee, and came into the borders of Judea beyond the Jordan (19:1a).

> And it came to pass, when Jesus had finished *all* these words, he said unto his disciples, Ye know that after two days the passover cometh, and the son of man is delivered up to be crucified (26:1,2).

[2] It has been pointed out that in the genealogy the emphasis upon Jesus as the son of David is pointed. Furthermore, the name David in Hebrew consists of *three* letters DVD whose numerical value is *fourteen* (4 + 6 + 4 = 14). Is it conceivable that in this we have an early Christian riddle?

[3] Matt. 6:1-18.

[4] Matt. 6:19-7:6.

[5] Matt. 7:7-20.

[6] Matt. 8:1-15.

[7] Matt. 10:26,28,31.

[8] Matt. 26:39-44.

[9] Matt. 4:23; cf. 9:35.

[10] Matt. 23:13-36.

[11] The beatitude, "Blessed are the meek: for they shall inherit the earth," which in many Mss. follows, in others precedes, "Blessed are they that mourn," is probably to be seen as a later addition on the basis of Psalm 37:11.

That to some degree at least these sections were considered parallel by the author is obvious from the strikingly similar phraseology of these colophons. It will be necessary on a later page to consider the question of whether this fivefold division goes even deeper into the structure of the gospel, and whether it is more than an accident that we have five (not four or six) such divisions. The significant point at this juncture is that the combination and arrangement of material into blocks was due to Matthew[12] himself and not to any source.

One example will suffice. Chapter 13 contains seven parables. The first (Sower) and third (Mustard Seed) are taken from Mark. It is usually stated that the parable of the Seed Growing Secretly (Mark 4:26-29) which follows that of the Sower and precedes that of the Mustard Seed is omitted by Matthew. It appears to me far more probable that Matthew's second (the Wheat and the Tares) is Matthew's own adaptation of the Markan parable which he places in the same relative position. The fourth (the Leaven) occurs also in Luke and is usually ascribed to the source from which Matthew and Luke independently drew. The remaining three (the Hidden Treasure, the Merchantman and the Pearl, and the Drag-net) are unique to Matthew. Perhaps all three are to be ascribed to other sources available to him, very possibly in oral form, although it appears to me highly probable that the last of these three, because of its identification of the kingdom of heaven with the Christian church, is to be ascribed to Matthew himself, and was suggested to him by such a word as that in Mark 1:17. To these seven he appends another.[13] Its purpose is not further to amplify the mystery of the kingdom, for its introduction and nature are quite different from the preceding. In these concluding words regarding the disciple who grasps in full the teaching it may well be, as Bacon remarks,[14] that we have "an unconscious portrait" of the evangelist himself.

In these parables another trait of the evangelist is revealed—his excessive fondness for identity of phrase and balanced statement. The parables of the Mustard Seed, the Leaven, the Buried Treasure, the Pearl, and the Drag-net all begin with the same phrase "The kingdom is like unto . . ." To the second, third, and fourth of the seven is prefixed either "Another parable set he before them saying" or "Another parable spake he unto them." Precisely the same word—"Repent ye: for the kingdom of heaven is at hand"—stands as the message of both John the Baptist and Jesus.[15] In the Markan story of the calling of the first four disciples the same trait is seen.[16] In the

[12] Such references, here and in other sections, to the authors of the gospels by the names which the books now bear, are solely for the sake of convenience and imply nothing as to the identity of the authors.

[13] Matt. 13:51,52.

[14] B. W. Bacon, *Studies in Matthew,* p. 131; cf. p. 217 and frequently. This volume, while highly technical, will prove very rewarding to the serious student of the gospels.

[15] Matt. 3:2; 4:17.

[16] Matt. 4:18-22; Mark 1:16-20.

case of both pairs of brothers the inconspicuous parallel, "and . . . *his* brother," should not be overlooked. More striking is the double conclusion,

"And they straightway left {the nets, / the boat and their father,} and followed him."

In the case of the former Matthew has adopted the Markan statement. His love of balance leads him to repeat it at the end in preference to Mark's slightly different phrase. In the temple, Matthew tells us, the children cried out, "Hosanna to the son of David,"[17] thus repeating the shout of the crowd at the Triumphal Entry—in the form which Matthew had there used.[18] Even more noticeable is the repeated word, "Ye have heard that it was said . . . ,"[19] or the balance, "Ye are the salt of the earth" . . . "Ye are the light of the world."[20] Closely allied to these—and the list could be greatly increased—is the fondness for balanced statement. For example, to the statement that Jesus was in the wilderness forty days, Matthew alone feels it necessary to add "and forty nights."[21] To the word, apparently taken from Mark 11:25, which Matthew suffixes to the Lord's Prayer—"For if ye forgive men their trespasses, your heavenly Father will also forgive you"[22]—he provides the balanced opposite, "But if ye forgive not men their trespasses, neither will your heavenly Father forgive your trespasses."[23]

Matthew is dependent upon Mark not only for his general outline, but for his narrative material. He utilizes all of Mark and has practically no other narrative material. The only two incidents *outside* of Mark are (1) the genealogy and birth story, and (2) the curious legend of the Coin in the Fish's Mouth (17:24-27). All the other additions are simply expansions of Markan material, and are joined to it as the "mistletoe to the oak" (Streeter). Examples of this are the stories of Peter walking on the water (14:28-31), the end of Judas (27:3-10), the message and dream of Pilate's wife (27:19), Pilate's washing his hands (27:24,25), the raising of the bodies of the saints who had fallen asleep (27:52,53), and the guard at the tomb (27:63-66). All of these are simply haggadic expansions of the Markan narrative and indicate no independence of origin. From this a general working principle emerges: While Mark's narrative is not to be accepted uncritically as a plain chronicle of actual facts, but must be closely examined, Matthew's additions are palpably legendary.

The two exceptions mentioned in the last paragraph are somewhat different and deserve a special word. His inclusion of the genealogy and birth story is certainly not due to any desire to write a fuller biography—if pos-

[17] Matt. 21:15.
[18] Matt. 21:9.
[19] Matt. 5:21,27,33,38,43.
[20] Matt. 5:13,14.
[21] Matt. 4:1.
[22] Matt. 6:14.
[23] This latter word, while occurring in some Mss. as Mark 11:26 is demonstrably an interpolation from Matthew. See below, p. 478.

sible, Matthew is even less a biography than Mark. It is probably fair to call it a reply to calumny. Not only the reference to the fulfilment of prophecy (1:22) but the mention of the women—Tamar, Rahab, Ruth, Bathsheba—appear to be an attempt to answer anti-Christian slander, notably Jewish, of Mary.[24] For suggestions as to the ultimate sources of the story and the possibility of its being an "international myth," the student may be referred to Bacon's *Studies in Matthew*, pp. 145-154. His story of the Coin in the Fish's Mouth is apparently a bit of Jewish Christian Haggada, reflecting the problem which Jewish Christians faced in regard to the temple tax. Should they refuse to pay it, on the ground that they were no longer Jews, they would become involved in all sorts of difficulty, especially with their Jewish friends. Nor is this (necessarily) an indication that the story antedates the year 70, for after the destruction of the temple the tax was still collected by Rome for her own purposes. On the other hand, that Matthew is the author of this fable is by no means necessary nor perhaps even probable.

For the rest of his narrative material Mark is the sole source of information,[25] but, though he uses it almost in its entirety, he not only often compresses the narrative, omitting many picturesque details,[26] and by no means preserves the vividness and dramatic quality of the earlier account, but also has no hesitation at all in revamping it drastically so that at times its final form is superficially quite different from its source. That the parable of the Wheat and Tares is to be seen as the Matthæan adaptation of Mark's parable of the Seed Growing Secretly which occurs in the same relative position—between the parables of the Sower and the Mustard Seed—has already been suggested. Occasionally the shortening of a narrative or the rearrangement of material involves Matthew in difficulties. A case in point is the statement of Antipas' judgment about Jesus. In Mark the story of Jesus' rejection in Nazareth because of the people's unbelief (Mark 6:1-6a) is followed by the story of the sending out of the Twelve and their success (6:6b-13). Then appropriately enough comes the mention of Antipas' concern because of this fame of Jesus (6:14-16), which of course had been noised abroad by his disciples. But Matthew has followed the story of the call of the Twelve by that of their mission, and thus passes directly from the incident of the rejection of Jesus at Nazareth to Herod's amazement at his fame (Matt. 13:53-58; 14:1,2). Without the Markan clue there is thus the patent absurdity in Matthew's account: Antipas thinks Jesus is John the Baptist risen from the dead, because Jesus had been rejected! The exorcism of Mark

[24] For evidence of such slander see the material assembled by Herford in his volume, *Christianity in Talmud and Midrash,* and also Origen, *c. Celsum* i,28,32,33,39.

[25] The evidence that this source was the canonical Mark, not an earlier version or a source common to both Matthew and Mark, will be presented in chapter 43.

[26] Cf., for example, the abbreviation in Matthew's version of Mark 1:29-31; his omission of the word that Jesus was "in the stern . . . on the cushion" (Mark 4:38); that the swine numbered "about two thousand" (Mark 5:13); and that the grass was "green" (Mark 6:39).

1:23-28 is omitted by Matthew in his shortening of the whole Markan section (1:16-39), but is compensated for, since in his version of the story of the Gadarene demoniac (Mark 5:1-20) he has two demoniacs cured (8:24-34). Or again, he omits the story of the blind man (Mark 8:22-26)—was it because it was too gradual a miracle?—but has Jesus heal *two* blind men for Mark's Bartimæus (20:29-34 = Mark 10:46-52). Similarly he omits Mark's story of the Deaf Mute (Mark 7:32-37), perhaps because in the story the mechanics of the miracle were stressed, but in 12:22-24 he gives a parallel story and states that this man was also blind. Thus none of the Markan material is actually neglected, although it is often distinctly revamped. To this there is one exception. The story of the Widow's Mites (Mark 12:41-44) is omitted. This was perhaps dropped out between the two great apocalyptic sections as an inconsequential matter. At times he disapproves of a slant of Mark's, and makes a real substitution. A good case in point is in the story of John's reproof by Jesus for attempting to hinder those "who followed not us"—"For he that is not against us is for us" (Mark 9:38-41). This Matthew omits, apparently disapproving of such an attitude, opposed as it is to the teaching of Matt. 7:21-23. But it is to be observed that in 12:30 he has the converse of Mark 9:40, that is, "He that is not with me is against me," which is precisely the attitude which Mark has Jesus reprove; while, furthermore, Mark 9:41 is salvaged and appears in Matt. 10:42, which in turn follows hard upon 10:40, which is adapted from Mark 9:37 (the verse immediately preceding the "omitted" Markan section). Thus Matthew cannot be said to have neglected the section. He salvaged as much of it as he could, and then continued with the Markan narrative (Matt. 18:6 = Mark 9:42).

Matthew's free use of Markan material is seen in the way he tends to omit such touches as those which savour too much of human emotion on the part of Jesus or of his need of asking questions. This material is so readily available that a few examples will suffice.[27] He omits the words, "And being moved with compassion" (Mark 1:41), the puzzling "And he strictly charged him [lit. "was angry with him"] and straightway sent him out" (Mark 1:43), and the words, "with anger" (Mark 3:5); substitutes for Mark's "Teacher, carest thou not that we perish?" (Mark 4:38) "Save, Lord; we perish" (8:25), for "Is this not the carpenter?" (Mark 6:3) "Is not this the carpenter's *son*?" (Matt. 13:55). For Mark's blunt statement—"And he *could* there do no mighty work, save that he laid his hands upon a few sick folk and healed them. And he *marvelled* at their unbelief" (Mark 6:5,6)—Matthew writes: "And he *did* not many mighty works there because of their unbelief" (13:58). He omits Mark's phrase, "And he would have passed by them" (Mark 6:48), "And he sighed deeply in his spirit" (Mark 8:12), and by his omission of Mark's significant "And he would not that any man

[27] See W. C. Allen, *ICC Matt.*, pp. xxxi ff.

should know it" (Mark 9:30) evidences his disagreement with Mark's notion of the Messianic secret. Had not God revealed it *openly* at the time of the baptism, "This is my beloved son," not, as Mark had recorded, "Thou art . . . ," *i.e.,* as a word to Jesus only? Perhaps the best known of these alterations is in the story of the Rich Young Ruler. Mark recounts that the man had approached Jesus with the word, "Good Teacher, what shall I do that I may inherit eternal life?" and had received the answer, "Why callest thou me good? none is good save one, even God" (Mark 10:17,18). Matthew's recasting is significant: "Teacher, what good thing shall I do, that I may have eternal life? . . . Why askest thou me concerning that which is good? One there is who is good" (19:16,17). The objectionable element incident to Jesus' denial that he was good is removed, but with the least possible verbal alteration. Nor should his substitution in the same verse of "Keep the commandments" for Mark's "Thou knowest the commandments" be overlooked. For Matthew Christianity is the new law; thus he can conclude his gospel with the words, "teaching them to observe all things whatsoever I commanded you." This list could be enlarged. A similar note is to be seen in his attitude toward the apostles. Instead of the rebuke, "Know ye not this parable? and how shall ye know all the parables?" (Mark 4:13), which, as we have seen, evidenced Mark's view that Jesus was constantly waiting for the truth to dawn on the disciples, Matthew prefixes a blessing (13:16-17). Similarly, Mark's "Have ye not yet faith" (Mark 4:40) is modified to "O ye of little faith" (8:26). Again, Matthew rewrites the end of the story of the Walking on the Sea, omitting Mark's concluding word, "For they understood not concerning the loaves, but their heart was hardened" (Mark 6:52), and substituting for "and they were sore amazed in themselves" the more acceptable "And they worshipped him saying, Of a truth thou art the Son of God" (14:32). Sometimes the alterations are only skin-deep. In the story of the ambitious request of James and John (Mark 10:35-45), Matthew recasts it a bit (20:20-28). In his version *their mother* came and made the request. Impossible that apostles could have made a request which would have laid them open to this criticism! Far better from the lips of the doting mother! Unfortunately his desire to preserve the phraseology of his sources as closely as possible causes him to leave Jesus' answer in its Markan form—"*Ye* know not what *ye* ask. Are *ye* able, etc."

In the case of miracles there seems a deliberate tendency to heighten the miraculous. The fig tree, when cursed, immediately withered away (21:19). In three miraculous cures the touch is added that they were made whole "from that hour" (9:22; 15:28; 17:18). In the second of these, this touch necessitates a slight rephrasing of the story; in the case of the story of the Epileptic Boy, by the omission of Mark's full and vivid touches the impression is given: he speaks and it is done. In the case of the two miraculous feedings, Matthew is careful to add (either to heighten the miracle by increasing the number fed or because of his fondness for balanced and full statements) "besides women and children" (14:21; 15:38). Had not Mark said that those who were fed were five thousand *men*? These various alterations serve to make clear not only that it is Matthew who has used Mark (and not the reverse), but that he has not scrupled to revise as seemed good to him. Often the alterations are so mechanical that the experienced student will know from the Markan account what alterations Matthew employed (without examining the parallel version). At other times they are not so superficial. Generally, however, it is possible to see *why* it was that Matthew altered as he did. Of all the evangelists, it is easiest to "think Matthew's thoughts after him."

But though Matthew is dependent upon Mark for narrative material and, as will be seen in a later chapter, for his general order or framework, this accounts for only about half of the gospel. In addition to narrative he presents a large quantity of the sayings in the form of discourse and parable, grouped into five blocks, each of which concludes with a set phrase, "And it came to pass, when . . . ," which, according to Bacon, also serves to introduce the next block of narrative, which latter in turn leads up to the next discourse. It is widely conceded that these five discourses are composite. (1) The first comprises chapters 5-7 and is popularly known as the Sermon on the Mount. This designation has contributed to the widespread notion that it is essentially a sermon preached by Jesus, and many fanciful and unfounded conclusions have been drawn. The sermon deserves careful study, but as an example of the homiletic skill of Matthew, not Jesus. Bacon designates it "Concerning Discipleship";[28] Ropes, "Life of a Disciple of Jesus."[29] Both of these descriptions are apt and free from ambiguity. I am inclined, however, to call it the "Essence of the New Law." To a degree it is similar to the section in Luke 6:24-49, but with a quite different emphasis. Actually the conclusions one reaches regarding the relationship of these Matthæan and Lucan sections are of the utmost importance in the perplexing larger question of the relationship of the two gospels. Bacon has caught the exact difference between the two in his word: "Matthew legislates; Luke proclaims glad tidings." Matthew insists that the great reward in heaven is promised *in consequence* of the scrupulous keeping of the new law by Christians, a law characterized by a righteousness superior to that of the Pharisees. Luke, on the contrary, stresses the fact that in spite of the present difficulties they will gain the kingdom; that is, as over against those who are apparently now in high favour, the Christians are the true elect of God. (2) Chapter 10. The call and sending out of the disciples (based upon Mark 3:14-19 + 6:6-13) is developed into a great mission discourse, which apparently reflects and gives insight into the missionary methods and experi-

[28] *Op. cit.*, p. 269.

[29] *The Synoptic Gospels*, p. 48. The student will find this little book of immense value.

ences of the church and the difficulties Christians had found (and were still finding) themselves confronting. This latter note is especially clear in such a section as 10:17-25 (which in turn should be compared with 24:9,13) and 10:37-39. That occasional words of Jesus may be imbedded in this section is not to be denied, but that much of the material reflects the experiences of early missionaries in the gentile world, and that the final form is definitely sub-apostolic appears to me beyond reasonable doubt. It is actually a little handbook on "How to be a Christian Missionary." (3) Chapter 13. Little additional need be said of this discourse, composed, as we have seen, to illustrate Jesus' teaching about the kingdom and stressing the note of the rejection of Israel. (4) Chapter 18. In this discourse the theme is clearly the duties and responsibilities of members of the church which Jesus had just said was to be built upon Peter. The churchly tone is especially clear in 18:15-17. That here we have a page from the "constitution and by-laws" of any early church would appear highly probable. Furthermore, it is to be observed that to the disciples as a whole (18:18) is promised the power previously promised to Peter (16:19). Throughout this section Matthew's handiwork is especially evident. The parable of the Thankless Servant (18:23-35), appropriately introduced by the question of Peter (18:21,22), may well be Matthew's own expression of the saying earlier recorded (6:14,15), which, as has been suggested, was ultimately derived from Mark 11:25. (5) Chapters 23-25. This intense closing discourse falls into two parts. First comes the blistering attack upon the Pharisees with the seven Woes, clearly revealing the hostility between the Church and the Synagogue in the author's day. Furthermore, his expansion of Mark's *three* verses (Mark 12:38-40) into this bitter tirade is quite in keeping with Matthew's view that the Scribes and Pharisees were responsible for the whole catastrophe. The first half closes with the lament over Jerusalem (23:37-39). Then follows the lengthy eschatological section (24:1-25:46), which is based on Mark 13, but is expanded to double the Markan length through the introduction of parables, the longest of which are the Ten Virgins, the Talents, and the Judgment of the World.

The question as to the source or sources of the sayings out of which these composite discourses have been built by Matthew is decidedly not easy, and the views of competent scholars are widely different. It will perhaps be better to reserve further discussion of this question until the chapter on the Synoptic problem as such, for it is inextricably intertwined with the larger problem of the relationship between Matthew and Luke.

One other characteristic of Matthew deserves attention. He is obviously profoundly impressed by the correspondence between Christian events and fancied prophecies in the Old Testament. He may well be compared with *Barnabas* and Justin Martyr in his concern to show the truth of the "prophetic equation." Thus in 1:22 f. he finds a prediction of the supernatural birth of

Jesus from a virgin mother from the word in Isa. 7:14, due to the unfortunate choice of the Greek word employed to translate the Hebrew word meaning "young woman" or "young matron." He knows that Jesus was born in Bethlehem (2:6) because of Micah 5:2. The legend of the flight of Joseph and Mary to Egypt rests upon Hosea 11:1—"Out of Egypt I called my *son*." Who was God's son save Jesus? Hence it must have been predictive. If called *from* Egypt, he must previously have been *in* Egypt. That Hosea's word was not prophetic, but a back-glance to the Exodus under Moses, was quite neglected by Matthew, and probably by the majority of Christians in his day, who saw the Christ portrayed on every page. Why did Jesus go to Capernaum—not Nazareth—upon his return to Galilee as Mark asserts he did (Mark 1:14,16,21)? Matthew finds the answer (4:12-17) in the reference to the "way of the sea" in Isa. 9:1,2. To be sure, he mechanically repeats Mark's word, "And he charged them that they should not make him known" (12:16 = Mark 3:12), but the word which immediately follows, "that it might be fulfilled which was spoken through Isaiah the prophet," has nothing to do with the injunction to silence, but provides a prophetic contrast between the one who "should break no bruised reed" and the opponents whom the preceding section had revealed doing precisely that. Psalm 78:2 provides the explanation of Jesus' fondness for parables,[30] although his ascription of the passage to "the prophet"—some Mss. read "Isaiah, the prophet"—bears evidence that his quotations were made from memory, and that occasionally the memory slipped. Zechariah's mention of the king riding upon an ass (Zech. 9:9) provides him with his prophecy of the triumphal entry, although his literal rendering of the Zechariah text and his failure to recognize the Hebrew parallelism incident to the words, "riding upon an ass, *even* (not "and") upon a colt the foal of an ass," led him to alter Mark's account so that Jesus sat down and rode on two beasts at the same time (21:7), while the opening words of his quotation, "Tell ye the daughter of Zion," is due to Isa. 62:11, which he confuses with the similar word of Zech. 9:9. So, too, while Mark mentions no stated sum paid to Judas, Matthew knows it was "thirty pieces of silver" (26:15). This "knowledge," too, came from Scripture: "Then was fulfilled that which was spoken through Jeremiah the prophet" (27:9), but, of course, it was not Jeremiah but Zechariah (11:12,13) who made the statement. Again Matthew's memory is here confusing two incidents—one about the thirty pieces of silver cast unto the potter (?) in the house of Jehovah, told of by Zechariah; the other about the buying the field of Hanamel, the son of Shallum, Jeremiah's uncle (Jer. 32:6-15). Probably Jeremiah's earlier reference to a visit to the potter's house (Jer. 18:2-4) accounts for Matthew's confusion here. In this concern for prophetic parallels Matthew shares the view common at the end of the first century—and not entirely outgrown even yet—that the

[30] Matt. 13:34,35.

Old Testament was to be wrested from unbelieving Israel and given to the gentiles. Christianity had been offered to the Jews first, but they had rejected it.

Another reason for the strong anti-Jewish feeling of the author, the heightening of the woes against the Pharisees, the story of Pilate's gesture of innocence (27:24), and the awful cry of his Jewish accusers, "His blood be on us, and on our children," may be found, if, as seems reasonable, Matthew himself was a converted Scribe, for it is always the convert who is the bitterest about the faith he has left. At any rate, Matthew has the universal tone, although at times he is most intensely Jewish. In his reputed emphasis upon the rejection of unbelieving Israel and the call of the gentiles—cf. such parables as those of the Two Sons (21:28-32), the Wicked Vineyardmen (21:33-46), the Wedding Feast (22:1-14) with its curious appendage about the man without the wedding garment—he strikes a note which led the eminent French critic, Renan, to style this gospel "the most important book ever written." He knew how to write a Catholic gospel, expressing the emancipated spirit of the growing universal church.

All this warns against an early date. In 22:7 we have an almost conclusive evidence for a date later than 70 A.D. This touch of the king's wrath, his sending out his armies, and his burning of the city, cannot reasonably be interpreted save in the light of the destruction of Jerusalem. Not that the story may not have been current earlier, but it is here an obvious insertion in the rest of the parable, and a grotesque one at that. People reject a dinner invitation. The king is aroused to such a paroxysm of wrath that he burns the city down (using *armies* to do it), but then a few moments later invites more people (from the devastated area) to the palace which has in some wise escaped the general conflagration. That Matthew went out of his way to introduce such an addition to his story, except for the purpose of making it an allegory of the one point which he is stressing throughout—God's punishment of Israel for its blindness—is to me incredible. Again, in the reference to the master who tarried (24:48) or to the bridegroom who tarried while those awaiting him slumbered and slept (25:5) one surely does not err in detecting the wistful longing of the church, obliged to wait so long for the promised return of its Lord. Finally the concluding words of the gospel—the so-called "Great Commission" (28:19,20)—stand an insuperable barrier to an early date. The world-wide vision, now ascribed confidently to Jesus; baptism with the use of the trinitarian formula; "teaching . . . all things which I have commanded you"—surely thus a more-or-less objective teaching, and precisely capping the emphasis which Matthew alone of the evangelists gives, that Jesus' teaching was a new Law—all this makes any date much earlier than the opening decades of the second century to me unthinkable. Thus 100 A.D. is a convenient figure for those who desire a specific date; but there would appear no insuperable difficulty in extending the limits a decade in either direction.

As is the case for most anonymous writings, it is a hopeless task to try to discover the name of the author. To be sure, Eusebius preserves the following statement from the lost writings of Papias:

> Matthew collected the oracles in the Hebrew language, and each interpreted them as he was able.[31]

That Papias is here referring to our gospel and not to some one of its sources appears to me certain.[32] His remark that it was originally written in Hebrew seems to have been his own conjecture or deduction, and has little to support it. If anything is clear, it is that the present Matthew is directly dependent upon the present Greek Mark. Again, his ascription of the gospel to the apostle Matthew, whether that too was his own conjecture—which is scarcely probable—or due to some tradition known to him, is quite impossible. That Matthew, an eyewitness of the ministry, should have leaned so heavily upon the writing of Mark, who had his information at best at second hand, is unthinkable. Nor it is to be asserted that Matthew is simply employing his colleague Peter's notes, for, as we have seen, Peter's connexion with the Gospel of Mark is very tenuous. Again the notion of Matthew or of any other eyewitness is ruled out not only by the freedom shown in revamping and rewriting but by the late date. The gospel is not directly or indirectly a primary or apostolic source; and all attempts to accord it a halo of apostolic authority by playing with the notion that it is a second and modified edition of an earlier Aramaic gospel simply confuse the issue. To be sure, Jerome claims to have seen and translated an Aramaic gospel of Matthew. This is rightly considered by modern scholars preposterous, and to be rejected without qualification. But how did the name of the obscure Matthew become attached to this writing? There is one conjecture which is ingenious and to my mind quite possible. It was first suggested by Bacon in an article in 1920, and later restated in his *Studies in Matthew*. In Mark 2:13-17 we have the call of the tax gatherer, Levi, son of Alphæus. He is thus the fifth to be called. But in the subsequent list (Mark 3:13-19) although the other four (Peter, Andrew, James, and John) reappear, Levi does not, but a James, "the son of Alphæus," does. Luke follows Mark in this puzzle. But Matthew (9:9), in his parallel to Mark 2:14 substitutes "Matthew" for "Levi, son of Alphæus." This has often been considered an indication that Matthew was really the author of the gospel and was here whispering in the reader's ear, "I am the Levi of whom Mark is speaking; I have two names, one Levi, the other Matthew." But there are fatal difficulties to this traditional explanation quite aside from the nature of the

[31] *Hist. Eccl.* iii,39,16

[32] See also p. 431.

gospel itself. At a very early date the failure of Levi in the later Markan list was noticed, and in the Western text in Mark 2:14 Levi was changed to "James"—thus conforming to Mark 3:18. There are good reasons for thinking that Matthew's copy of Mark had this reading, thus telling the story of the call of the tax gatherer *James*, son of Alphæus, and that Matthew repeated the story. But later in the gospel of Matthew the name *James* in 9:9 was altered to *Matthew*, not because of any tradition that a Matthew wrote it, but simply to conform to his later list (10:1-4).

The reasons for this change were two: (1) the words "the tax gatherer," which stands in our texts after the name Matthew in Matt. 10:3, may well be a gloss or comment written by some scribe *in the margin* and intended by him to apply to *James, the son of Alphæus,* whose call had been described in 9:9; (2) but a later copyist of the manuscript thought the words an omission, and wrote them *in the text*, but by error applied them not to James, for whom they were intended, but to the preceding name which chanced to be Matthew. Then later for conformity in the Matthæan text *Matthew* replaced *James* in 9:9. It is not impossible that it was from this curious harmonization of readings that the tradition "according to Matthew" arose. At any rate, as Bacon points out, the popular assumption that Matthew was particularly fitted to write a gospel because he was a tax gatherer is thus nullified, for it was Levi, not Matthew, who held that office.

But though we do not know his name, we can see the sort of man he was, or at least some of the points which he considered important. Attention has already been called to his emphasis upon Christianity as the new law and to his repeated contrast between Moses and Jesus. In this connexion the fivefold division is of interest. Was this accidental or was it a deliberate attempt to frame his gospel after the plan of the Pentateuch? Bacon has strenuously argued for this view. The colophon which stands at the end of each discourse was "not so much a rounding-off of the preceding discourse, as *a link by which the narrative which follows* [*was*] *coupled on*."[33] This he seeks to demonstrate by a painstaking analysis of Matthew's editorial rearrangements, and also finds a paper manuscript of the sixteenth century, recently discovered on Mt. Athos, an important support for his theory. In this manuscript stand six iambic verses:

> Matthew curbs the audacity of the Jews;
> Checking them in five books as it were with bridles.
> Now whoever the infamous error of these
> (Pure error it is) shall in arguments refute
> Destroys at a stroke all the heresies together;
> For the mother of these is the strife of the deicide people.

[33] *Expositor*, Vol. 87, 1918, "The 'Five Books' of Matthew against the Jews," p. 65. The thesis suggested in this article is expanded in the later book, *Studies in Matthew*. This latter volume is not easy reading, but will repay the serious student.

These verses did not apply to the present paper manuscript which chanced to be in five books, but to our gospel, which from the second century had been regarded—and rightly—as written with a special eye to the Jews. Furthermore, the fact that Papias had considered our gospel the product of Matthew himself, had used it as the standard for judging Mark, and had himself written his commentary *in five books* appeared to Bacon to justify the view that not only had second-century Christians recognized the five-fold nature of the gospel, but that the author, himself "a scribe made a disciple of the kingdom of heaven," had consciously used the Pentateuch as a model for his representation of the words of Christ which Christian missionaries were to enjoin on all the nations. And it appears to me not unlikely that in this view Bacon was right.

The few available indications of the place of origin of the gospel would seem to suggest Antioch. From the first it enjoyed a great popularity in that centre, as is reflected by Ignatius, an early bishop of that city. Furthermore, the verses 16:17-19, with their signal claims for Peter inserted into the earlier Markan narrative and standing in such contrast to the retained rebuke, must emanate from a circle which held Peter in high esteem. This was true of Antioch, to which city tradition ties Peter's name. The view, occasionally suggested, that in this passage we have a hint of the rivalry between Antioch and Jerusalem and of Antioch's retort to the supporters of James, appears to me to have much to commend it.

Chapter XLI

THE GOSPEL ACCORDING TO LUKE

THE Gospel of Luke, quite unlike the two discussed in the preceding chapters, is definitely cast in biographical form. Yet to speak of it as a biography may well be misleading, for it is not, and was not intended to be, a writing complete in itself. Rather, it forms with the book of Acts, part of a carefully conceived and developed history. It is distinctly unfortunate that through the years these two halves of a single whole have been divorced from one another, for it is only as we view them together that we gain the true force and significance of each half. Throughout the whole writing the touch of the littérateur is clearly seen. This is no hit-or-miss work, but a carefully and artistically prepared account. As the student examines and ponders the Lucan writings, he can scarcely fail to be struck with the truth of the quip: "The simple gospel is not nearly so simple as simple people sometimes think." In the opening words—the much-discussed preface (1:1-4)—the classical student finds himself at once at home. What the precise force of these words is—whether they are to commend or to disparage these earlier attempts—is not clear.[1] It is interesting to compare it with the opening words of Arrian's *Anabasis of Alexander*:

> If any one wonders why, after so many historians this work of history occurred also to me, when such an one has both read through all their works and perused also this of ours, so let him wonder.[2]

At any rate, the use of such a preface indicates not only that Luke was familiar with the literary forms of his day, but was desirous that his work should take its place among the volumes read by cultivated men. The first half of his writing, our gospel, may then be described in words largely of his own choosing as a biographical "treatise concerning all that Jesus began both to do and to teach." All the evangelists had as a prime purpose the glorifying of Jesus, the arousing of admiration for their hero. John gives the classic expression of this aim: "These are written, that ye may believe that Jesus is the Christ, the Son of God; and that believing ye may have life in his name."[3] The several writers achieve this goal by different means and emphases; none the less, they all share this one purpose.

[1] Eusebius (*Hist. Eccl.* iii,24,15) understood it as a disparagement of the earlier attempts.
[2] Quoted by H. J. Cadbury, *The Making of Luke-Acts*, p. 303.
[3] John 20:31.

At the head of the gospel stands the story of the Rejection at Nazareth (4:16-30). In this passage the theme or motif is expressed which is to occur again and again through not only the gospel, but its sequel, the book of Acts. To a real degree it may be called apologetic. Throughout the gospel he is at pains to prove that Jesus was the true Jewish Messiah. He had appeared to the Jews, had been born of the seed of David; but they had rejected him. Christianity was the new Israel. Gentile Christianity had arisen not through wanton neglect on the part of Jesus to go to the Jews. Far from it, he had gone to them, but they had rejected him. This is the framework for the whole Lucan writing and the reason it stands at the head of the gospel. From the materials of Mark 6:1-6[4] and a quotation from Isaiah Luke reconstructs this incident with a speech in Jesus' mouth to sound the note: "Salvation has come to men." This is quite different from Mark's view that it is a future task to be realized. In the judgment of Luke it had been present in the world from the moment of the Messiah's birth, and had been hymned by the heavenly host (2:14); now it was openly and clearly fulfilled. Although those to whom Jesus preached—even his immediate followers—failed to realize that this salvation was for all men, irrespective of race or status—Jew or gentile, strict adherent of the law or outcast—such it was. Thus Jesus can refer to the experiences of Elijah and Elisha—the one with the widow of Sarepta, the other with Naaman the Syrian. Thus Luke strikes the chord which is to sound again and again through the whole story of the rise and development of Christianity and which is more fully orchestrated in the later score. At the time of Stephen's death a real break comes: the start of the gentile mission is clearly made. But, as he takes pains to point out, this is no essentially new, that is, unhinted, development. At Pentecost there had been a foretaste of it; furthermore, even in Jesus' ministry the start had been made. Jesus had clearly revealed his attitude, not only by the choice of Samaritans—the only gentiles with whom he could have come into contact—but in his first address. Thus at the very opening Luke strikes this melodic note and continues it to the last page of the work (Acts 28:23-28), where Paul, after quoting the apposite words of Isaiah, is made to conclude: "Be it known therefore unto you, that this salvation of God is sent unto the gentiles; they will also hear."

But it is to be observed that, while this conviction is central in Luke's own thinking and while he feels it imperative to give expression to it at the

[4] That the Markan passage has been utilized by Luke is indubitable. Jesus preaches in the Nazareth synagogue; the people take offence and disparage him personally; he retorts that prophets are not acceptable in their own country; the absence of miracles in Nazareth is stressed, in Luke somewhat lamely, for here the incident stands as the opening event of the Galilean ministry, and the mention of miracles already performed in Capernaum (and recorded in an early page in Mark) throws into the sharper relief that in Luke's account it is only *after* the rejection at Nazareth that Jesus goes to Capernaum (4:31).

outset of his "continuous" account, he does not make it too obtrusive. It is also present as an undertone, especially in the Samaritan touches (cf. the Good Samaritan[5] and the grateful Samaritan leper[6]) and the omission of such a section as the seemingly harsh word to the Syrophœnician woman,[7] but he does not venture to obtrude it in the Markan account. Did we not unconsciously read each gospel in the light—often hazy—of the others, we could scarcely fail to discover a difficulty at precisely this point. Mark finds no especial need to tell the reader *why* Jesus was arrested and executed. His skilful weaving of the story has made that self-evident. Luke, on the contrary, does not stress this quarrel nearly so much as does Mark (for him the issue is a greater one), but he does not venture to insert material at the arrest to make it clear that Jesus' arrest was due primarily to his view of a salvation destined for all. Thus to a degree the reader is left without an adequate cause for Jesus' arrest, or at least without an adequate explanation of it. He is content to paint in the latter pages of the gospel an increasing cleavage between Jesus and the nation. The Pharisees are represented as being constantly perplexed as to why Jesus does not pay more attention to them (cf. 7:36; 15:1,2). Also Jesus' tone is not that of bitter criticism—the contrast with Matthew is here especially noticeable—so much as of regretful sorrow that they will not hear and recognize God's great gift which embraces all alike, them as well as gentiles. Here in this skilfully wrought undertone we can scarcely fail to hear the apologetic note of later Christianity, hard put to answer Jewish criticism.

That this explanation of the real point of cleavage, always present in the gospel but usually without over-emphasis, is actually true to the facts is extremely doubtful. Rather, in it we see the point of view of Christians far enough removed from the early days to be trying to evaluate and understand the course of the past half-dozen decades, confident that all that has happened has been in accord with God's plan. Here we find a subtle but significant difference between the emphases of Matthew and Luke. For Matthew, all that has happened has been prophesied; for Luke, on the contrary, all that has happened has been foreseen and purposed by God, and was of necessity implicit in the work and outlook of the Messiah.

The reluctance of Matthew to represent Jesus as moved by human emotions, as sorrow, anger, love, and his frequent omission of those touches in his revision of the Markan account have already been noted. An even more careful pruning out of these is to be seen in Luke, who cancels several which had not offended Matthew. For example, he omits Mark's word that at the feeding of the Five Thousand Jesus was moved with compassion (9:11 = Mark 6:34). Following Peter's confession the disciples as a whole are

[5] Luke 10:25-37.
[6] Luke 17:11-19.
[7] Mark 7:24-30.

bidden to keep silent, but the specific rebuke to Peter with which the Markan section closes (Mark 8:32,33) is entirely omitted from the Lucan version. In the account of the Passion Luke takes care to tell the story in such a manner that it will be clear that Jesus was condemned not as a malefactor, as were the two who were crucified with him (23:32), but as the Messiah. In the trial before the Sanhedrin there is no mention of the alleged threat to destroy the temple as in the Markan account (Mark 14:55-61), but simply the query, "If thou art the Christ, tell us" (22:67). Similarly, in place of the gibe of the bystanders at the cross, "Ha! thou that destroyest the temple, and buildest it in three days, save thyself, and come down from the cross" (Mark 15:29), Luke has "If thou art the king of the Jews, save thyself" (23:37). The vivid story in Mark of the Cleansing of the Temple, the overturned tables and benches, the refusal to allow any man to carry a vessel through the temple (Mark 11:15-19), is drastically shortened and presented without any show of violence (19:45-48). The spitting on Jesus (Mark 14:65) and the scourging by command of the Roman governor (Mark 15:15) go unnoticed. Furthermore, he recasts Mark's account of two meetings of the Sanhedrin (Mark 14:53 ff. and 15:1) to one, occurring in the early morning. To this, however, he adds the story of another trial before Herod, quite unnoticed by Mark. It was at this meeting that Jesus was decked out in royal garb and insulted (23:6-16; contrast Mark 15:16-20). That in this alteration we are to see evidence that Luke is drawing on extra non-Markan material appears to me improbable. Acts 4:25 ff. with its quotation of Psalm 2, which refers to "the *kings* of the earth and the *rulers* in array against the Lord and against his Anointed," would appear to provide a sufficient ground for the alteration.

The gospel is carefully written, and is far harder to remember than Matthew, where the systematic—one might almost say, the bony—structure is always evident. These corners and joints are all painstakingly smoothed down into a literary whole. It is written in excellent Greek. The preface is classical Greek, while the rest of the gospel is idiomatic and smooth. That it is the translation of an Aramaic original is quite unlikely. There are frequent traces reminiscent of the Semitic genius, but these appear to me adequately explained as due to the author's use of Aramaic sources. Nor should we neglect the possibility that the author has deliberately sought to give to his narrative local colour.

That Luke had become possessed of some new materials, notably in the story of the Passion, is often asserted, and to a limited degree is perhaps not improbable. But it is very easy to overemphasize this element and to seek to explain the variation from Mark as due to his use of some substantial parallel non-Markan account. This appears to me highly questionable. The striking thing—and this is perhaps even truer of Matthew—is the apparent paucity of non-Markan material available to our author. As one studies the gospels he is more and more impressed by the almost complete dependence of the latter two upon the former. It is very easy to overstress the "many" who Luke says had preceded him. Today it is the fashion to talk about "editors," and to explain all variations as being due to a different source, of which "sources" ingenious scholars have discovered a surprisingly large number which give them great aid and comfort.

For the most part Luke has reproduced the Markan order, has incorporated or compensated for most of the Markan material, and except in the Passion and Resurrection narratives has limited his changes for the most part to abbreviations of the fuller Mark or to improvements of the style. Several Markan sections are omitted, usually, however, because Luke appears to have had a parallel narrative available which he preferred. Nor should it be overlooked that, occasionally, at least, his own ingenuity had been solely responsible for the preferred parallel. A few examples will suffice: He omits Mark 6:1-6 because he has already made use of the incident in an earlier connexion (4:16-30). The question of the Scribe in Jerusalem, which Mark[8] presents as the third of a similar series, is omitted because he has already utilized it as the setting for the parable of the Good Samaritan (10:25-28). It is to be noted, however, that he has not scrupled to use the *Scribe's* reply (Mark 12:32) as the pleased rejoinder of the *Scribes* to Jesus' neat tripping of the Sadducees (Luke 20:39), while Mark's final word, "And no man after that durst ask him any question,"[9] is drawn forward similarly to close Luke's shortened series (20:40). Surely the use of this dialogue to introduce the parable is obviously secondary. The Scribe has asked for a definition of his neighbour: Who is the man whom he is to love as himself, that is, who is to be the *object* of his benevolence? This the parable does not answer. Rather, as the query, "Who showed himself neighbour?" reveals, the matter is inverted. "Neighbour" is used in the sense of one who himself showed benevolence, that is, the *subject* of the action. It would hence appear that Luke had himself built this setting to "tie" the parable in to his narrative.

An essentially similar situation is found in the Markan story of the Anointing at Bethany (Mark 14:3-9). This Luke omits, for he has used the material earlier in a story which he constructed to serve as the situation for the parable of the Two Debtors (Luke 7:36-50). Apparently the reason for the Lucan location is the reference, two verses earlier, to Jesus eating and drinking (7:34). The secondary nature of the resulting story is evident: strange, indeed, is the behaviour of the host who invites Jesus but is neglectful of the ordinary duties of a host; unnatural, too, is the discourtesy involved in the comment of Jesus, a guest in the house, regarding his host's omission. But more serious than this is the confusion in the story. Plainly the teaching

[8] Mark 12:28-34.
[9] Mark 12:34b.

of the story is: The woman anointed Jesus because she loved him, and hence because of this love was forgiven. But the parable strangely inverts the point: The debtors love the master because he had forgiven them. And again, had Simon provided water and oil, this would not have exhibited his love, great or small, but would have been simply part of his duty as a host. That Luke was not dependent upon Mark for the story, but simply utilized it and cancelled its later Markan doublet is perhaps not impossible, but appears to me on the whole improbable. He is always anxious to tie in his extra-Markan material (here the parable of the Debtors); this story provides the means. The host in each case is Simon. Luke makes him a Pharisee, and places the story in Galilee instead of Bethany in Judea. Simon's leprosy is not mentioned; the "woman" of Mark is made a "sinner," apparently because the debtors were "forgiven."[10]

The Markan story of the Cursing of the Fig Tree (Mark 11:12-14,20-25) is omitted, perhaps in part from Luke's unwillingness to chronicle such an act of Jesus, but is compensated for by the parable of the Fig Tree (13:6-9) which may very plausibly have been the nucleus of the later story. Luke most appropriately appends this parable, which for him symbolizes the Jewish nation and the short time allowed it for repentance, to the call for repentance (13:1-5) which ended, "Except ye repent, ye shall all likewise perish."

The ambitious request of James and John and their subsequent rebuke (Mark 10:35-45), which was toned down by Matthew, is omitted by Luke, but apparently compensated for by 22:24-27. This Lucan setting is apparently due to the contrast (suggested by Mark) between the servant who waits on table and the master who is waited upon. Though there is thus a specious connexion, the setting is obviously secondary and not precisely happy, for Jesus is not strictly waiting on table as a servant, but presiding as master of the feast.

Thus with the exception of the Markan section 6:45-8:26 the only Markan materials completely ignored by Luke are (1) the charge of insanity (Mark 3:20-22) which was presumably distasteful to him; (2) the tiny parable of the Seed Growing Secretly (Mark 4:26-29); (3) the story of the death of John the Baptist (Mark 6:17-29), which he had already hinted at earlier (3:19 f.); and (4) the identification of John as Elijah (Mark 9:11-13), perhaps because he felt he had adequately spoken of John's significance elsewhere (7:24-35). One large block, however, (Mark 6:45-8:26), he does cut

[10] The Johannine version of this story (John 12:1-8) is dependent upon both Mark and Luke. It occurs in Bethany toward the end of the ministry (Mark), but in the home of Lazarus, and the woman is not a sinner, but Mary. (Is the Lazarus touch due to the blending of the elements, Simon "the leper" with a Lazarus, "full of sores" (Luke 16:20)?) John is dependent upon the Lucan account for the touch that the woman anointed Jesus' *feet* (not his *head* as in Mark), but though she wipes them with her hair, there is no mention of her tears—why should she weep? she is no sinner—which had made the act natural in Luke.

entirely from the Markan narrative, as is evident from a glance at a harmony: Mark 6:42-44 is Luke 9:17; Mark 8:27 is Luke 9:18. And plausible reasons are found for this cancellation. The Feeding of the Four Thousand (Mark 8:1-9a) is a mere doublet of the Feeding of the Five Thousand (Mark 6:34-44). But this omission would have necessitated a drastic rewriting of the following material, especially Mark 8:14-21. The discussion with the Syrophœnician woman (Mark 7:24-30) would naturally have been distasteful to gentile readers, while the preceding section regarding the dispute with the Pharisees about the niceties of the Jewish law (Mark 7:1-23) may well have seemed to him irrelevant. The two miracles of healing (Mark 7:31-37 and 8:22-26) were performed with difficulty; the Walking on the Sea (Mark 6:45-52) may well have seemed more or less parallel to the Stilling of the Storm, already recounted (8:22-25). Thus a plausible explanation for the omission of the whole block of material can be found without recourse to the theory that this whole section of our Mark was not in Luke's copy of Mark, which theory is involved in the very real difficulty that in that case Luke's mention of Bethsaida (9:10) is quite inexplicable, since it is only in Mark 6:45 that the town is mentioned.

His treatment of Mark, which might seem from these examples occasionally cavalier, should not lead the reader to the unjustified conclusion that he was an irresponsible writer, wilfully perverting history. On the contrary, although his primary purpose was religious—like the other evangelists he was trying to make saints, not historians—he had a very real feel for history, and to a far greater degree than his fellow writers was seeking to paint the picture of the Christian beginnings. In the long range that he is trying to cover, his aim apparently was to follow the main currents and to show the logical development. His view is the broad one of the man looking back over a long period, after the events have assumed their positions of relative importance. In a word, Luke's production has few of the qualities of a series of photographs—each correct in every minute detail—but, as was already remarked on an earlier page, is rather a panorama of significant events, so arranged and so interpreted as best to show the unfolding purposes of God at work below the events described. In the preface he makes this aim clear with the words, "it seemed good to me to write unto thee *in order*." The word translated "in order" does not signify "in chronological order," as is often assumed, but rather "continuously" or "in a logically unbroken sequence." And this is precisely what he has accomplished. One step leads logically and continuously to the next. In earlier articles[11] I have tried to show how this dominating interest led him to produce narrative material from the scantiest sources. Is it necessary to assume that he had before him a source which told of the trip from Nazareth

[11] "Paul and Gamaliel," *Journal of Religion*, July, 1927; "The Ascension Story," *Journal of Biblical Literature*, 1928, Parts 1 and 2.

to Bethlehem made necessary by an imaginary census? Is it not more probable that the account is his own creation in order to harmonize the two variant traditions, both of which he accepted, that Jesus' family had from the earliest years lived in Nazareth and yet that their child had been born in Bethlehem? Or again, it appears to me that the account in Acts of the connexion of Paul with the stoning of Stephen has no historical foundation. It was in Jerusalem that the Christian mission to gentile lands arose, and it was Stephen's death that had caused this beginning. Paul was the one who above all others was instrumental in the movement. Therefore Paul is transferred from Damascus to Jerusalem and enters the story at this crucial moment. Similarly his desire to show "continuously" the successive great stages of the Christian movement led him drastically to rewrite Mark's account of the Passion and, by omitting the flight to Galilee[12] and appearances there (implied at least by Mark), to make the transfer from Galilee to Jerusalem absolute. When the Galilean pilgrims in company with the Master reached Jerusalem, to which he had set his face stedfastly, that city became the next theatre of the Holy War.

This is true not only in great turning-points—the successive stages in the birth and growth of the new religion from its inception in Palestine to its establishment in Rome—but in all the material. There are no loose ends. All the material is closely articulated, or, to change the figure, forms one long rope whose various sections are united by long splices to keep the diameter constant. Thus he regularly prefaces each narrative or saying with an introduction showing under what circumstances it was said or done, as, "And as they heard these things, he added and spake a parable, because he was nigh to Jerusalem, and because they supposed that the kingdom of God was immediately to appear" (19:11). An examination of such introductions as 9:37; 13:1; 15:1,2; 18:1; 19:11 can scarcely fail to convince the student that these are all Lucan splices, but should warn him that they are also simply Luke's judgment, as to why or for what purpose this parable or that was spoken.

Or again, while generally holding to the Markan framework and skilfully splicing in his non-Markan additions, in two sections he varies this by inserting two long non-Markan sections (6:20-8:3 and 9:51-18:14). The latter is of particular concern, for it appears to illustrate one of his literary habits. It is usually designated "The Perean Ministry," not very happily since 9:52 would appear to suggest that in Luke's judgment the trip south was through Samaria, not the Perea. Some critics think that Luke took this section over more or less ready-made from another source—"the Perean document." It appears to me far more probable that the section is of his own construction, and served as a sort of scrap basket for materials which he found it difficult to insert separately into the Markan frame. The departure from Galilee af-

[12] See pp. 170 f.

fords a breaking-point in the narrative, and thus an excellent and non-confusing place for the preservation of these important incidents. Thus he breaks Mark open at 9:40, inserts the long catena of material, and resumes Mark at 10:13. He thus omits Mark 10:1-12, apparently because he feels that his previous word (16:18) is adequate to show Jesus' attitude to divorce.

One further evidence not only of Luke's desire for a continuous and connected account, but of his artistic ability, is to be seen in the opening pages of his writing. Instead of the abrupt start of Mark, unconcerned with anything approaching a biography, or of the singularly inartistic way in which Matthew opens his account, Luke projects his story back to the annunciation to Elisabeth, makes clear the significance of the strange John who appears in Mark's opening sentences, introduces Jesus so skilfully that one does not feel the transition from the wonder child to the mature man, and then, while Jesus is now occupying the centre of the stage, with the words from heaven still resounding, traces his lineage back to the foundation of the world, not to prove that he was the Son of God—that is already obvious—but to show that Christianity is no new upstart, but the culmination of the eternal purposes of God.

The question of the identity of this author, whose gospel, according to Renan, is "the most beautiful book ever penned," must be reserved until the discussion of the second half of his writing, the book of Acts. It is only in the light of this later section that one can consider profitably the justice of the tradition which has from the earliest days ascribed these writings to Paul's friend and fellow labourer, Luke, the beloved physician. Furthermore, a more detailed examination of what sources of information were available to him when he determined to write for the benefit of most excellent Theophilus must remain for the chapter on the Synoptic problem. While the question of date is intertwined with both of these considerations, a few tentative conclusions may be drawn from the gospel itself. In spite of the early date for Luke-Acts which has been urged occasionally in recent years, it would appear to me certain that 70 A.D. is the *terminus a quo*. That the description of the destruction of Jerusalem, with the precise method of its destined accomplishment,[13] is a prophecy, made natural by the repeated words of the Old Testament prophets, seems far less likely than that it is a later reflection of Titus' siege, during which the wall to the north was thrown up to starve the city into surrender. Again, while many critics are convinced that the mention of the "abomination of desolation standing where he ought not" in Mark 13:14, whatever its ultimate origin may have been, was prompted by those awful days, the deliberate substitution by Luke of the words, "When ye see Jerusalem compassed with armies, then know that her desolation is at hand,"[14] appears to me conclusive. The anti-Docetic

[13] Luke 19:42-44.
[14] Luke 21:20.

emphasis in such a passage as 24:39-42; the matter-of-fact mention of the Old Testament as a continuous prophecy of Jesus;[15] more important, as in the case of Matthew, the whole tone of the writing, and the impression that the author is looking back over a lapse of many years and is evaluating the events of the far past—all this inclines me to a date little if any before the end of the first century. And by anticipation it may be remarked that further evidence pointing in the same direction is available in the second part of the writing which followed hard upon the tracks of the gospel, if indeed there was any appreciable interval between the two parts of the single whole.

[15] Luke 24:25-27,44.

Chapter XLII

THE ACTS OF THE APOSTLES

THAT Acts is the continuation of the story of the rise and spread of Christianity, the first half of which is the Gospel of Luke, is so universally accepted today as to require little argument.[1] The common dedication to Theophilus; the resumption of the narrative in these later chapters precisely at the point at which the gospel concludes, the final departure of Jesus from his disciples; a subtle but none the less unmistakable oneness of purpose, attitude, emphasis, and phraseology—all these can hardly be accidental. Thus the real question is not "Were the two writings by the same pen?" but rather "Are we justified in assuming that the second part was written after an appreciable interval?" or "Were these originally but successive chapters to the gospel, which, for reasons best known to the author, he (or perhaps some later Christian) later made into a second volume of approximately the same length and to which he provided an introduction by a slight recasting of the opening pages and the insertion of a duplicate list of the apostles (1:13)?" It is by no means easy to decide between these alternatives, each of which has points of strength. There is one obvious clash between the gospel and Acts, and precisely at the point of cleavage, namely, regarding the departure of Jesus. In the gospel he parts from them apparently on the resurrection evening and (in the primitive text) without the mention of an ascension to heaven. In the Acts, on the contrary, not only is the ascension story told in detail, but it is also asserted that it occurred forty days after the resurrection. That this contradiction requires the assumption of different authors for the two books is by no means the case. It simply indicates that new information of some sort or other had come to the author which led him to change his earlier view. But was this during the interim between the composition of the gospel and the appearance of Acts, or was it prior to his revision, and perhaps one of the reasons leading him to revise and divide the narrative? This appears to me an open question.[2]

The title, (The) Acts of the Apostles, almost surely not from the hand of the author, is not strictly a happy one, for only in the loosest sense does it

[1] A notable exception is found in A. C. Clark, *The Acts of the Apostles,* especially pp. 393-408. He decides against the view of a common author for Luke and Acts, largely on the basis of linguistic differences.

[2] For a more detailed study of this problem see my article, "The Ascension Story," *Journal of Biblical Literature,* Vol. 47, 1928, pp. 60-73; cf. also Jackson and Lake, *Beginnings of Christianity,* Vol. V, pp. 16-22.

describe the content. As Jülicher has aptly remarked, its real theme is "The History of the Power of God in the Apostles." A brief but pointed table of contents for the writing is on the first page—"But ye shall receive power, when the Holy Spirit is come upon you: and ye shall be my witnesses both in Jerusalem, and in all Judea and Samaria, and unto the uttermost parts of the earth" (1:8). It opens with a little group of disciples in Jerusalem. It ends with churches established in strategic centres throughout the Roman empire, and with its doughty champion Paul at Cæsar's court in Rome. The significance of this enormous change is fully stressed. It had been made possible by the establishment of Christianity as a religion for gentiles, but (as was also stressed in the gospel) not out of wanton neglect of the Jews.[3] The attempt to limit its scope to Jews had been successfully defeated. Nor was this change unprecedented. As we have seen, Luke had prefixed to his whole story the incident in the Nazareth synagogue where Jesus had proclaimed the ringing words of Isaiah:

> The Spirit of the Lord is upon me,
> Because he anointed me to preach good tidings to the poor:
> He hath sent me to proclaim release to the captives,
> And recovering of sight to the blind,
> To set at liberty them that are bruised,
> To proclaim the acceptable year of the Lord.[4]

When Jesus had healed ten lepers, had not the lone Samaritan been the only one to give thanks (Luke 17:11-19)? But this note is even more clearly sounded in Acts in the word of Peter to Cornelius (10:34-43), of James to his hearers in Jerusalem (15:14), and of Paul on Mars Hill at Athens (17:22-31). And it was Paul more than any other who by his sturdy defence of freedom had made this spread and growth possible. As has been already remarked, Paul is thus appropriately introduced in the incident which serves for the author as the real start of the broader work.

But these emphases, which, for want of a better name, may be called historical, are but a part of a larger purpose, the desire to preserve Christian history for Christians, that is, to edify and strengthen. As in the gospel, so in the book of Acts there is a constant stress on the divine guidance of the whole movement, of the power of God which had always attended the efforts of the earlier heroes and was still leading them on. Thus Peter could assure Cornelius that it was God who had sent the word unto the children of Israel, preaching good tidings of peace by Jesus Christ (10:35,36). The Spirit had been a constant source of supply, not only enabling Peter to confound the faithless Ananias and Sapphira (5:1-11) or Paul to strike the sorcerer Elymas blind (13:6-12), but guiding the steps of Paul through Asia Minor, forbidding him to speak the word in Asia and preventing him from

[3] Cf., *e.g.*, Acts 7:51.

[4] Luke 4:18,19 (Isa. 61:1,2).

entering Mysia (16:6,7). It is scarcely a coincidence that Luke, both in the gospel and Acts, evinces such a fondness for the auxiliary "must" or "it is necessary." Throughout the whole course of Christian history runs an undercurrent of divine necessity.

Throughout the narrative is clearly to be discerned a genuine apologetic to Jew and Roman alike. John the Baptist, Jesus, Timothy, had all been circumcised. Was not Jesus constantly in the synagogue? Although his friends must have been most eager to pay their last respects to their crucified Lord, had they not "rested on the Sabbath according to the commandment" (Luke 23:56)? Paul had ever been most careful to observe Jewish requirements, had regularly turned first to the Jews in each community in which he had visited, had helped orthodox Jews in Jerusalem to keep the strictest vows (Acts 21:23-26), had faced death in the face of the prophecy of Agabus in order to be at Jerusalem on the day of Pentecost (20:16; 21:7-14). Even James, whose orthodoxy was unimpeachable, had declared to Paul his confidence that the charge that he was "teaching all the Jews who are among the gentiles to forsake Moses, telling them not to circumcise their children, neither to walk after the customs" (21:21) or was not himself walking in an orderly manner, keeping the law (21:24), was quite unfounded. Had not Gamaliel, himself not a Christian, urged his fellow Jews to cease their attacks (5:33 ff.)? This emphasis, although specifically against Jewish charges, was not without its value to Roman critics as well. Christianity was not an *advena*, a *religio illicita*, as was often being asserted, but actually the true and legitimate Judaism. None the less, there was the stubborn fact that Jesus had been crucified at the hands of Romans; Paul had been often arrested and had been sent to Rome for trial. But had not Pilate three times asserted his confidence that Jesus was innocent? Had not the Roman authorities—the magistrates at Philippi, Gallio in Corinth, the Roman captain, Felix, and Festus in Jerusalem—regularly released Paul, repeatedly arrested through Jewish malice? Had not Festus and Agrippa agreed, "This man doeth nothing worthy of death or of bonds . . . he might have been set at liberty, if he had not appealed unto Cæsar" (26:31,32)? Jewish malice, not the breaking of Roman laws, had sent Jesus to the cross, and had dogged the steps of Paul. Nor should it be overlooked that in the gospel Luke had carefully pruned out all words and deeds of Jesus which might be distorted to show him a seditious and violent man. And it is not without interest to observe that, although all the evangelists record the act of cutting off the ear of the servant of the high priest by one of the disciples in Gethsemane at the time of Jesus' arrest, Luke alone records that Jesus at once counteracted this act of violence by a miraculous and instant cure (Luke 22:50,51). In Paul's word to Festus the innocence, not only of Paul himself, but of all his comrades, finds expression: "Neither against the law of the Jews, nor against the temple, nor against Cæsar, have I sinned at all" (25:8).

That the book of Acts falls into two more or less clearly differentiated halves has often been suggested, but opinions have differed as to the place of division. Some have seen it at the end of chapter 12; in the earlier chapters Peter is the particular hero, in the latter Paul. For others, the turning-point is 15:35. Professor Torrey, for example, argued that 1:1-15:35 was not composed by the author of the second half, but was translated by him from Aramaic.[5] Other scholars, although unconvinced by the linguistic phenomena so clear to Torrey, have been led to make the division at this same point because of the peculiarly baffling phenomenon which makes its appearance without warning in the story of the missionary journey of Paul which starts at 15:36—the so-called "We passages." These may be tabulated as follows: 16:10-17; 20:5-15; 21:1-18; 27:1-28:16, although the lines of demarcation are not precisely certain. Other scholars, notably Lake, see not four, but three, passages, and, by combining the second and third (20:5-15 and 21:1-18) through the inclusion of Paul's speech at Miletus and appending the story of Paul's conversation with James and its consequences (21:17-26), make the second passage extend 20:5-21:26. The first begins at Troas and ends with the arrest of Paul and Silas at Philippi; the second begins again at Philippi on a later journey and extends to the arrival in Miletus en route to Jerusalem; the third resumes the narrative at the departure from Miletus and carries Paul to Jerusalem; the fourth begins with Paul's departure from Cæsarea, and ends with his arrival at Rome.

That these sections come from the diary of a companion of Paul's is almost universally admitted. It has seemed difficult, if not impossible, to explain the surprising shift from *they* and *them* to *we* and *us* on any other hypothesis. One example will make the abruptness of the transition clear:

> And *they* went through the region of Phrygia and Galatia, having been forbidden by the Holy Spirit to speak the word in Asia; and when *they* were come over against Mysia, *they* assayed to go into Bithynia; and the Spirit of Jesus suffered *them* not; and passing by Mysia, *they* came down to Troas. And a vision appeared to Paul in the night: There was a man of Macedonia standing, beseeching him, and saying, Come over into Macedonia, and help us. And when he had seen the vision, straightway *we* sought to go forth into Macedonia, concluding that God had called *us* to preach the gospel unto them. Setting sail therefore from Troas *we* made a straight course to Samothrace. . . .[6]

But the decisive question is: Was the author of these "We passages," who admittedly had participated with Paul in at least these few doings, the author of the book as we have it; or are these sections merely incorporated by the

[5] *The Composition and Date of Acts.*

[6] Acts 16:6-11.

author into his narratives from one of his sources? Many and varied have been the answers to this basic query.

The so-called "external tradition" about the author, that is, the observations of the early writers, is singularly inconclusive, despite the fact that from the latter half of the second century it is regularly stated that both gospel and Acts were composed by Luke the physician and friend of Paul. The famous Muratorian fragment provides the earliest statement of this tradition. All the later writers—Irenæus, Clement of Alexandria, Tertullian, Origen, Eusebius, and Jerome—simply attest in essence the same view:

> The third book of the gospel, according to Luke, Luke that physician, after the ascension of Christ, when Paul had taken him with him a devoted helper [or perhaps, "as a travel companion"], composed in his own name from hearsay. Yet he himself did not see the Lord in the flesh and therefore (?), as he could follow, so [he set them down (?)], and began to speak from the nativity of John. . . . But the Acts of all the apostles were written in one book. Luke compiled for "most excellent Theophilus" the several events done in his presence, as he clearly reveals by his omission of the death of Peter and the departure of Paul from the city, on his departure for Spain.[7]

While certainty is, of course, impossible, the nature of the tradition suggests that it rests simply upon conjectures and inferences drawn at an early date from the gospel and Acts themselves and therefore, as Cadbury rightly remarks,[8] may well be neither "external" nor "tradition" at all. The surprising shift from *they* to *we* which first makes its appearance in connexion with the journeys of Paul; the fact that in the preface to the gospel the author disclaims personal acquaintance with the earliest happenings, but declares that he was in a position to have accurate knowledge for a considerable time; the fact that the first "We passage" finds Paul at Troas, ready to go to Philippi, and the last one leaves him in Rome—these data plus the list of Paul's companions who were with him in Rome,[9] for these letters were considered written from Rome during his two years in prison, perhaps aided by the word, "Only Luke is with me" (II Tim. 4:11), may quite conceivably have led to the selection of Luke as the probable author. The significant thing is that there is nothing in the "tradition" which could not be inferred from the writing, and hence to consider it as a certainty, in itself not open to examination, appears to me quite unwarranted.

Thus the whole problem of authorship really turns on the one question: Does the book as we have it contain material which could not have come from the pen of a companion of Paul's? or, perhaps better stated, Does the

[7] *Muratorian Fragment,* lines 2-8,34-39. I have tried to reproduce the obscure and slovenly Latin in this painfully literal rendering.

[8] Jackson and Lake, *The Beginnings of Christianity,* Vol. II, p. 263. Professor Cadbury has here collected the pertinent "traditions" and has subjected them to a penetrating and judicious examination.

[9] Col. 4:10 ff., Philm. 23,24.

account diverge so manifestly from historical events that only one who did not know Paul personally could have accepted the tradition and have penned the resultant narrative? That in the earlier chapters of Acts the author is obviously far removed from the events and is dependent upon sources, including doublets of the same events which he has drastically rewritten,[10] and upon legendary material, as the wonder stories of Peter at Joppa and Lydda, his two miraculous releases from prison, the variant and coarser tradition of Judas' tragic end,—all this is perhaps not definitive, but would nevertheless suggest that he was not in a position to gain much primitive tradition. Perhaps even the manifest contradiction between the account in Acts and Paul's own statement that Timothy joined him in Athens[11] might be explained as due to the fact that Luke had not accompanied Paul south from Philippi; but the wonder stories of Paul's release from the Philippian prison (16:25-39) and of his preservation and doings on the island of Malta (28:1-10) cannot be so easily accounted for. For those who accept the reconstruction of the visits of Paul to Jerusalem and of the consequent journeys, suggested in an earlier chapter,[12] the view that the account in Acts was penned by one who had known Paul personally is by no means easy. Is it probable that one who knew Paul personally and his views that while Peter had been entrusted with the gospel for the circumcision he had been entrusted with the gospel for the uncircumcision (Gal. 2:7 f.), would have allowed Peter to declare, "Brethren, ye know that a good while ago God made choice among you, that by my mouth the gentiles should hear the word of the gospel, and believe" (15:7)? Of course, it is possible that due to Paul's letters we may be inclined to overemphasize his departure from Judaism. He may well have remained far more a Jew than he realized. At least, many of his converts apparently thought so. To a gentile, even though a companion and friend of Paul's, these Jewish traces may well have been all too apparent, and may have led him to see no incongruity in representing Paul—as he had Jesus—as actually an apostle to Jews and regularly turning to gentiles only when Jewish opposition made this step necessary; or of penning such a story as that of Paul in Jerusalem (21:17-26), which is scarcely what we would have expected of the Paul known to us only from his own letters.

What appears to me the most serious difficulty in believing that the picture of Paul drawn in Acts was produced by a friend and companion is the curiously unsatisfactory way the story of his conversion is told. Three times the story is given.[13] Not only are the details different and mutually contradictory in the three accounts, but they minimize, or at least fail to emphasize, the one point that Paul apparently felt all-important, *viz.*, that he had *seen*

[10] See pp. 228 f.

[11] See p. 234.

[12] Pp. 226-230.

[13] Acts 9:1-19; 22:6-16; 26:12-18.

the Lord.[14] In the Acts account he hears a voice, a light shines forth, but there is a complete silence as to the actual vision. This to me is very serious. To be sure, it is possible to harmonize the pictures by stressing the word that the *men with him* beheld no man (9:7)—hence that Paul did—but that a friend of Paul's should have so subordinated this all-important point and should have been so vague about the whole happening appears to me quite unlikely.

Nor should it be overlooked that there is a complete silence in the Acts account about the very considerable collection which Paul had been at such pains to collect for the poor saints in Jerusalem. Could a companion of Paul have overlooked this or have considered it so incidental as unworthy of mention? It does not appear to me legitimate to lay much stress on the author's failure to understand Paul's theology. Few early Christians did. But the completely different emphasis throughout the book on the significance of Jesus' death is after all surprising. In Acts it is simply a horrid crime which the Jews had wrought, and quite in keeping with the earlier acts of their fathers. For Paul it was the all-central point: the means of salvation. That the author should have failed to incorporate that distinctive note in the earlier pages of his book is perhaps not surprising. He might well have sought to preserve the flavour of the earlier, pre-Pauline, preaching. But that there should have been no hint in the speeches in the mouth of Paul himself of the one point that he apparently never ceased to stress and which any travel companion must have heard so often is to me most unlikely. And finally, there is the amazing failure even to hint that Paul had ever written letters to his churches. Surely he must have known that Paul had carried on an extensive correspondence. Why did he fail to mention it? This point, rarely considered in modern discussions of the identity of the author, appears to me of great significance as a weighty, if not fatal, objection to the view that he was a travel companion of Paul's.

Thus I find myself forced to feel that the lack of exact knowledge of the details of Paul's career even in the period during which the author of the "We passages" was with him and the evident readiness to transform and rewrite his sources of information in the light of his philosophy of history exclude the author from having been the companion of Paul, who penned the diary notes. Rather the author used various sources from which he produced his writing. One of them was a series of entries, quite fragmentary in extent, from a diary of an erstwhile travel companion, which he skilfully utilizes, choosing, for reasons about which we can raise guesses but can never know, to preserve the personal "we" touch. It may perhaps be remarked that had the author with his obvious literary skill meant by this touch to indicate his own appearance in the story, he might well have done it in a more finished and natural manner. Nor is it fair to say that in the "We

[14] I Cor. 9:1; 15:8; and probably Gal. 1:12,16; II Cor. 12:1-5.

passages" we find a fresher, more vivid tone. Aside from the curious *we's* there is nothing in the accounts which might not well have come from one who knew the country he was describing and knew how to write convincingly.

Several scholars, notably Hobart and Harnack, have seen distinct traces in Luke and Acts that the author was a physician; hence, since the Luke who had been with Paul was a physician,[15] have discovered fresh proof of the justice of the traditional view that it was this Luke who wrote the books. Professor Cadbury has, however, completely exploded this fallacy of the alleged medical language in Luke-Acts[16] by demonstrating that there was no technical phraseology available for the ancient physician, comparable to that of the present-day medical jargon, and by showing that all of the words and phrases eagerly pounced upon by Hobart and his pedissequi were in common use by such writers as Aristophanes and Lucian, who, to say the least, had never received a doctor's degree. Were it not for the accidental reference of Paul to "Luke, the beloved physician," it is extremely possible that the famous but enigmatic author might have come down to us not in doctor's robes, but in the garb of a sea captain.

One final word with regard to the literary craftsmanship of the author must be mentioned. No classical student will need to be warned that the speeches in the book of Acts are the free composition of the author, precisely as are those of Josephus, Philo, Thucydides, or Livy. Thucydides gives us a terse but frank statement of this ancient custom:

> As to the speeches that were made by different men, either when they were about to begin the war or when they were already engaged therein, it has been difficult to recall with strict accuracy the words actually spoken, both for me as regards that which I myself heard, and for those who from various other sources have brought me reports. Therefore the speeches are given in the language in which, as it seemed to me, the several speakers would express, on the subjects under consideration, the sentiments most befitting the occasion, though at the same time I have adhered as closely as possible to the general sense of what was actually said.[17]

In the light of this statement the student will not be perplexed by the marked similarities between all the speeches—be they of a Peter, a Stephen, or a Paul. It will not be necessary to debate whether Paul has been "petronized" or Peter has been "paulinized"; rather, it is clear that all of them have been "lucanized." Their marked sameness of tone, their smoothness and freedom from the little idiosyncrasies which stamp the man himself, the surprising fact that the author knows on occasion what was said in secret

[15] Col. 4:14.

[16] *The Style and Literary Method of Luke*, pp. 39-72; *Journal of Biblical Literature*, 1926, pp. 190-209.

[17] *de Bello P.* 1,22 (quoted by Cadbury, *The Making of Luke-Acts*, p. 185).

council (4:15-17), the providential preservation of the letter of Claudius Lysias to Felix with its highly satisfactory and sympathetic statement of Paul's innocence (23:26-30) require no *tour de force* of laboured explanation. These speeches may well give us a fair picture of early Christian thought and even of the kind of preaching that the early Christians heard—or that Luke thought they ought to have heard—but the cautious student will be slow to use them as sources of knowledge for reconstructing a life of Peter or of Paul. As was remarked on an earlier page, Stephen's famous speech to his accusers does not remotely answer the charges brought against him. It is simply a tirade—whether justified or not is of no consequence at the moment—against the Jews who had from the beginning persecuted God's saints. This theme was very likely a favourite one in early Christian preaching and finds constant expression not alone in the speeches of Peter—

> Let all the house of Israel therefore know assuredly, that God hath made him both Lord and Christ, this Jesus *whom ye crucified*[18]—

but in many of the words now found in the mouth of Jesus, especially as recorded by Matthew.

Occasionally Luke's desire to use the speeches as a convenient means for providing necessary information for the readers gives a distinctly artificial appearance to the utterance. Thus in Peter's first speech he is made to describe to his fellow Jews in Jerusalem an incident which had purportedly just happened and which they must have known as well as did he in the following amazing language:

> And it *became known* to all *the dwellers at Jerusalem*, in so much that *in their language* that field *was called* Akeldama, that is, The field of blood.[19]

None of the speeches attributed to Paul reveal the Paul known to us from the letters. This fact, as has been remarked, is of no small weight in the problem of authorship. Even in the farewell speech of Paul to the Ephesian elders at Miletus (20:18-35)—a speech regarded by some critics as distinctly different from the others and perhaps an actual part of the "We source"—the stereotyped prophecy of impending evil—

> I know that after my departing grievous wolves shall enter in among you, not sparing the flock; and from among your own selves shall men arise, speaking perverse things, to draw away the disciples after them—

is so precisely similar to the tenor of the Pastoral Epistles, Jude, II Peter, Matt. 5:10-12; 10:16-23 that it does not appear rash to consider it a prophecy *post eventum*.

Nor should it be overlooked that occasionally in the mouths of the speakers are found both improbable sentiments and impossible statements. The

[18] Acts 2:36; cf. 2:23; 3:15; 4:10.
[19] Acts 1:19.

speech of James at the council in Jerusalem (15:13-21) is an example of the one; the temperate and oft-cited advice of Gamaliel (5:34-39) of the other. James is made to quote Amos 9:11,12 in very free paraphrase of the Septuagint. The Hebrew read:

In that day will I raise up the tabernacle of David that is fallen, and close up the breaches thereof; and I will raise up its ruins, and I will build it as in the days of old; that they may possess the remnant of Edom, and *all the nations that are called by my name*, saith Jehovah that doeth this.

That is, that Israel may possess Edom and the other nations. But James is made to say,

. . . *that the residue of men* may seek after the Lord, and *all the gentiles, upon whom my name is called*. . . .

That the historic James used the Septuagint is most unlikely; surely Gal. 2:11 ff. makes it highly improbable that this utterance represents James' attitude, to say nothing of his words.[20] In the other passage Gamaliel is made to refer to the rebellion of Theudas which had occurred "before these days" and which, he goes on to say, was later followed by the insurrection and death of Judas of Galilee. Now Theudas raised his rebellion in the days of Fadus and not earlier than 44 A.D., that is, several years *later* than the difficulty which prompted Gamaliel to speech. Furthermore, Judas of Galilee raised his rebellion not *after* Theudas, but nearly forty years *before* (6 A.D.). Why Luke made this historical error may be deferred to a later paragraph; that this speech can scarcely be construed as a verbatim record of Gamaliel's word is evident. Thus the only safe conclusion with regard to the several speeches would appear to be that they are the author's free composition, as was true of those of all ancient historians. They are not to be used as source material in any moot point. They may occasionally have historic value, but we are not safe in using them unless they agree exactly with something else, the authority for which is unquestioned, and in that case they are superfluous.

Little more need be said about the probable date of Acts. As has already been argued in the previous chapter, there appears good reason to date the Gospel of Luke about 100 A.D. The book of Acts is at least not earlier. The apologetic tone, which is even clearer in Acts than in the gospel, suggests a date when it was necessary to justify Christianity in the eyes of Rome. Thus the unwillingness of the author to chronicle the deaths of Peter, and especially of Paul, without any corresponding story of their subsequent resurrection triumph may well provide as satisfactory an explanation of the enigmatic end of the book as does the assumption of Torrey and Harnack that the silence was due to the fact that Paul's death had not occurred when Luke for the last time dipped his pen in the inkhorn. The representa-

[20] This is a powerful argument against the contention that Luke is dependent upon Aramaic sources, not to mention a continuous Aramaic document.

tion of the apostles as a college of officials charged with oversight over the other groups; their refusal to leave Jerusalem under pressure (8:1); the interpretation of the incident of Peter and Cornelius in the light of the later "open membership" practice; the indications of the organized form Christianity was coming to possess, with presbyters (11:30; 14:23) and ordination (6:6); the legendary accretions, already mentioned, even to the figure of Paul—all this suggests the lapse of many years. And finally, there is always the lingering possibility—some scholars consider it a probability—that Luke had some familiarity with the *Antiquities* of Josephus (93-94 A.D.). This assumption rests on two misstatements—one in Acts, the other in Luke. The first, Gamaliel's strange confusion regarding the dates of Theudas and Judas of Galilee, has already been remarked. How could Luke have made such a mistake? It is to be observed that in the *Antiquities* the account of the downfall of Theudas is immediately followed by the words:

> The *sons of Judas of Galilee* were now slain; I mean of that Judas who caused the people to revolt when Quirinius came to take an account of the estates of the Jews as we showed in a former book.[21]

Is not a careless reading (or faulty memory) of this section responsible for Luke's anachronism and mistakes in order—that is, he failed to remember the fact that it was not *Judas* but *Judas' sons* whose deaths were mentioned as subsequent to Theudas? Luke's apparent error with regard to the date of the census would suggest that, however diligent he may have been in his search for the facts, he may yet have slipped occasionally on his dates, as has every other historian both before him and after. The other misstatement occurs in the famous synchronism:

> Now in the fifteenth year of the reign of Tiberius Cæsar, Pontius Pilate being governor of Judea, and Herod being tetrarch of Galilee, and his brother Philip tetrarch of the region of Iturea and Trachonitis, *and Lysanias tetrarch of Abilene. . . .*[22]

The only Lysanias of Abilene about whom we have any knowledge was executed by Mark Antony in 36 B.C. But Josephus[23] mentions that in 53 A.D. Claudius in his twelfth year gave to Agrippa II Abila, which "*had been* the tetrarchy of Lysanias." It is only fair to state that our confidence that in these words we find the explanation for Luke's careless statement is lessened by the fact that in the *Wars*[24] Josephus in mentioning this same transaction refers to Abilene as that kingdom which *was called* the kingdom of Lysanias. If this was a general appellation for it in later times, of course Luke may have learned it from other channels than Josephus. This possibility should not

[21] *Antt.* 20,5,1.
[22] Luke 3:1.
[23] *Antt.* 20,7,1—the same book from which the other misstatement conceivably arose.
[24] *Wars* 2,11,5.

obscure the fact that Luke was wrong in his assumption that Lysanias was actually the tetrarch in the fifteenth year of Tiberius. These two cases are interesting. Other possible examples might be cited.[25] They do not amount to a mathematical demonstration; it is perhaps surprising, if Luke knew the source of information at all, that he made such scanty and desultory use of it. None the less, I cannot escape the lingering suspicion that the coincidences are not accidental and that both gospel and Acts are definitely thus to be dated after 95 A.D. The *terminus ad quem* can in no case be later than 150 A.D.—for Marcion included the gospel of Luke in his canon—and in all probability considerably earlier, since the gospel was almost surely known and used by the author of the Fourth Gospel. While I thus would be disinclined to set the latest possible date for the joint work much, if any, below 105-110 A.D., I feel little force in the usual argument that every year subsequent to 100 A.D. makes the failure of Luke to know and utilize the Pauline letters the more amazing. There can be no doubt that such would be the case if the author is, as is today generally considered axiomatic, actually ignorant of them. As has been suggested in the discussion of the several letters,[26] it would appear to me that the axiom needs reëxamination and that there are distinct indications that the author did know and made occasional, if fragmentary, use of at least some of them.

There seem few indications in the gospel or Acts as to the exact place in the Roman world in which they were written, nor are the traditional statements such as to arouse much confidence. In one passage Jerome remarks that it was written from Rome, basing this opinion upon the fact that the book ends with Paul still in that city;[27] in the preface to his *Commentary on Matthew*[28] he remarks that Luke "composed his book [that is, the gospel as distinct from Acts] in the districts of Achaia and Bœotia." Priscillian, to whom is attributed the so-called *Monarchian Prologues*, mentioned Achaia as the place of composition for the gospel. This tradition is apparently due to the inference that, since the "We passages" begin just prior to Paul's advent in Greece, it was there that Luke, an Antiochian,[29] had joined Paul. Whether this early and general ascription of Luke to Antioch is based upon an actual tradition or is an inference from the prominence that that city received in the Acts account is impossible to decide. It is of interest, perhaps of importance, to observe that in the so-called *Western* text of Acts there is another "We passage." In this type of text, which is surely primitive,

[25] See Moffatt, *Introduction to the Literature of the New Testament*, pp. 29-31. Cf. also Lake's observations with regard to Acts 21:38 and *Wars* 2,13,3-5 in *Beginnings of Christianity*, Vol. II, p. 357 and Vol. IV, pp. 276 f.

[26] See my article, " 'Luke' and Paul," *Journal of the American Oriental Society*, Vol. 57, No. 1, (March, 1938).

[27] *de Viris inl.* 7.

[28] Migne, *Patr. Lat.* xxvi,18.

[29] So Eusebius (*Hist. Eccl.* iii,4,6) as well as Jerome and Priscillian in the above-cited passages.

although probably not preserving the original reading, there is prefixed "And when *we* were assembled together" to the words, "there stood up one of them named Agabus" (11:28). It may well be that this variant reading was the source, not the result, of the tradition ascribing the writer of Luke and Acts to Antioch, and may reflect a real tradition that that church had been the first to use these writings. At any rate, it suggests that the one who phrased the gloss—if gloss it be—considered Antioch the place of composition, and it is by no means certain that he was not correct.

Chapter XLIII

THE SYNOPTIC PROBLEM

It is very easy to state the problem; the difficulty lies in finding a solution which will account for all the facts without recourse to the famous bed of Procrustes. That Matthew, Mark, and Luke stand in some very close relationship, as regards both order of material and phraseology, is self-evident and needs no argument. As was indicated in the chapters regarding Matthew and Luke, in each of these two gospels almost the whole of Mark is preserved, occasionally in altered form, not infrequently drastically rewritten, but none the less unmistakeably present. And if, as has been argued in the chapter devoted to Mark, the order and casting of material in that gospel is not to be seen as the simple tying together of incidents in chronological order but rather as a deliberate and purposeful arrangement of materials to present a decisive answer to a question which the author considered all-important, it is surely highly improbable that two other writers, unacquainted with this arrangement, and themselves bearing clear evidence that their own purposes were quite different, should have independently hit upon the same outline. Occasionally a deviation occurs. Thus, for example, as we have seen, Luke parts company with Mark at Mark 9:40 and continues for several chapters (Lukc 9:51-18:14) with non-Markan material. But at the end of this unique section he is once more running exactly parallel with Mark, and—what is more important—the resumption of Mark continues the Markan narrative at precisely the point where it had been temporarily left. Or again, a glance at a harmony of the gospels reveals that generally when either Matthew or Luke has an order of material different from Mark the other runs parallel to Mark. In a word, throughout the whole story Mark appears as the outline which both the others consciously and systematically used. It has already been suggested that the Markan section 8:27-9:32, comprising three separate incidents—Peter's Confession, the so-called Transfiguration, and the Healing of the Epileptic Boy—was so arranged for a definite purpose, not simply because the events happened chronologically (and that in the week's interval between the first and the second Jesus had done nothing worthy of record). The Transfiguration is a scene built up from materials—perhaps a resurrection story—to impress the heavenly seal upon the dawning confidence of Jesus' followers as expressed by their spokesman Peter. Jesus' absence in the mountain provides a setting for the story of the cure of the epileptic boy—the disciples were unable to perform the cure; Jesus was able. Obviously for such a story Jesus must be absent at first from the scene. Now that three independent writers should have chanced to see the aptness of precisely this artificial arrangement is of course utterly improbable. In the Markan section 2:23-3:6 two incidents are joined—Jesus and his disciples in the grain-field and the Cure of the Withered Hand. Their connexion is obviously not due to an actual sequence of events, but because both illustrate Jesus' conduct on the Sabbath. But Matthew (12:1-14) and Luke (6:1-11) both preserve the events in the same order, and essentially at the same point in the story. Did all three writers independently conclude, not only that it was necessary to show Jesus' attitude on this point, but that these were the two incidents especially apt?

Nor is this amazing similarity seen only in the selection and arrangement of the material, but in the very phraseology. An excellent case in point is found in the case of the paralytic. In answer to his critics Jesus replies: "But that ye may know that the son of man hath authority on earth to forgive sins." Then follows a curiously infelicitous parenthesis, "he saith to the sick of the palsy."[1] And all three evangelists, agreeing without variation in the exact wording of Jesus' utterance, interrupt it at precisely the same spot with this parenthesis. That three independent writers should have couched their narrative in such a wise as to make this awkward interruption necessary is quite unthinkable. It would be possible to print long lists of sections where the phraseology of the evangelists—now of all three, now of two—is identical, but it is unnecessary. Two hours' thoughtful reading by the student himself in a harmony (preferably in Greek) will allow him to be convinced at first hand. And the point to be kept closely in mind is: These agreements in phraseology are in our Greek gospels. Jesus spoke Aramaic. Surely it is incredible that three translators chanced to employ precisely the same renderings from one language to another. And it may be remarked that in these readings not infrequently highly unusual and rare Greek words are to be found. Lists of these have often been compiled and are readily available to students who use Greek. Two particularly striking ones may be added: In Mark 9:42 the phrase translated "millstone" is literally "a millstone turned by an ass" (μύλος ὀνικός)—a very unusual term. Matthew reproduces it (18:6). Similarly in the apocalyptic discourse Jesus is made to say "and except the Lord *had shortened* the days" (Mark 13:20). The word translated "had shortened" literally means "had mutilated" or "cut off," and is not only a rare word, but is only here employed of anything except physical mutilation, as cutting of the feet (so Aristotle) or the nose (so Diodorus Siculus). But in the parallel section in Matthew (24:22) precisely the same rare word is employed.

On the other hand, the differences, in the form of alterations and con-

[1] Mark 2:10 = Matt. 9:6 = Luke 5:24. (Luke inverts "son of man" . . . "has authority.")

tradictions, are no less clear, and prevent the otherwise convenient explanation that since our gospels are unique books they are not to be judged by ordinary literary standards, but that the authors had been divinely guided, even in the perplexing matter of translating Aramaic utterances into Greek. But surely such a divine control could not have brooked contradictions. Many of Jesus' utterances occur in Matthew as parts of long compactly built discourses, while in Luke they appear under quite different circumstances and in different settings. More perplexing would be the definite contradictions. For example, all three evangelists record in substantially the same Greek words that at Jesus' baptism a voice was heard from heaven.[2] But while all three agree that the purport of the word was that Jesus was the beloved son in whom God was well pleased, Mark and Luke say that this word was to Jesus: "Thou art . . . ;" Matthew, on the contrary, implies that it was to those who needed the information: "This is . . ." Surely the voice did not speak twice; nor would it be easy to explain how, under a mechanical view of verbal supernatural guidance, the evangelists had been allowed to make this contradiction. Or again, in the story of the Cure of the Man with the Withered Hand,[3] all three evangelists agree that the question was asked, "Is it lawful on the sabbath day to do good, or to do harm? to save a life, or to kill?" (Matthew reads simply, "Is it lawful on the sabbath day to heal?") But who asked this question? Mark and Luke state that it was Jesus; Matthew, on the contrary, that it was his opponents. Near Jericho, say all three evangelists,[4] a healing of the blind took place. The many verbal identities in the three accounts, as well as the representation of the scene in general, allow no question but that it is the same incident. None the less, Mark asserts that Jesus healed one man on his departure from Jericho; Luke that it was as he drew near to Jericho; Matthew agrees with Mark that it was as Jesus left Jericho, but asserts that it was not one man but two who were healed. The disagreement between Matthew and Mark as to who made the request for James and John—was it the two disciples themselves or was it their mother?—has already been mentioned.[5] In the same connexion the differences the evangelists evidence in the treatment of the query of the rich young ruler[6] or of the question with regard to the great commandment[7] may well be pondered. And when we examine Matthew and Luke for that part of Jesus' life which was not treated by Mark—genealogies and birth stories, on the one hand, and his resurrection appearances to his disciples, on the other—it would appear somewhat less laboured to agree that the spirit

[2] Mark 1:11 = Matt. 3:17 = Luke 3:22.
[3] Mark 3:1-6 = Matt. 12:9-14 = Luke 6:6-11.
[4] Mark 10:46-52 = Matt. 20:29-34 = Luke 18:35-43.
[5] See p. 395.
[6] See pp. 160 f., 395.
[7] See p. 407.

which guided Matthew's pen was not the one which performed a similar function for Luke's.

During the past century an immense amount of labour has been expended on the problem of these agreements and differences, and, while there is still much that is uncertain and which leads equally competent and unprejudiced investigators to very different conclusions, one point has become so clear as to be universally accepted, *viz.*, the priority of Mark. For centuries this was denied, and Mark was regarded, as it had been by Augustine, a colourless epitome of Matthew and Luke. This view became the corner stone for the views of the Tübingen scholars, who saw Mark as the bridge thrown by later builders across the gulf between the Jewish Matthew and the gentile Luke. On other grounds, but no less vehemently, the keen and gifted Strauss, even as the smoke of the battle he had so successfully waged against the rationalists was clearing, continued to level his heaviest, at least his noisiest, guns against the "lions of St. Mark." But his guns fell short. By the end of the past century it had become perfectly clear that no explanation was adequate which denied that Mark was anterior to Matthew and Luke. This does not mean that there were not sources of material, probably in written form, from which Mark drew; but simply that of our three gospels Mark is the oldest and that upon it Matthew and Luke depended for a large part of their material. The many grounds for this conclusion need not be repeated here in detail. Many of them have already been considered in the preceding chapters, since it was quite impossible to discuss Matthew and Luke without indicating their Markan base. In the last analysis the whole matter boils down to one question: If Mark is the epitome of Matthew and Luke, why did he write at all, since there is nothing of any consequence in his gospel not found in either the one or the other? Mark's brevity is not due to boiling Matthew and Luke down—regularly his narratives are the longer and more detailed—but to the almost entire absence of discourse material. Again, the alterations in style or phraseology regularly show Mark's the more vivid and the rougher. Frequently a crabbed expression in Mark is resolved by Matthew and Luke in different ways, but in both more smoothly and felicitously. To conceive of Mark reversing the process and achieving a result which nevertheless would explain both the other variants is quite impossible. Or again, in Mark 1:32 we find the statement, "And at even, when the sun did set," as the prelude to the account of the healings. In Matthew's account of the incident (8:16) we find the former of these phrases, in Luke's (4:40) the latter. It is easy to see why the subsequent writers preferred the single unredundant statements; but to conceive of Mark's construction of the narrative by prefixing the two equivalent phrases—one from Matthew, the other from Luke—is as difficult as it is to see both Matthew and Luke independently chancing to start the narrative with similar notes of the time of day. Furthermore, in the same sections the other verbal resemblances in which now Matthew, now Luke, agrees with Mark should not be overlooked. Or in the story of Joseph of Arimathea's part in the burial of Jesus the Markan account is obviously the original.[8] The additional details in the other two are obviously simple elaboration. Thus Matthew infers that he was rich, for had not Mark told of his owning a tomb and of his purchase of burial materials? That he was also a disciple of Jesus' he felt implied in Mark's "who also himself was looking for the kingdom of God." Similarly Mark's reference to his being a councillor and of honourable estate leads Luke to infer that of course he "had not consented to their counsel and deed." To have culled from Matthew and Luke, and from this material to have produced the natural and effective outline, constantly to have achieved a rougher, more primitive, and more unfinished style, but at the same time with more graphic and telling effect, would demand a literary miracle which would be simply incredible. The reverse of the process, however, is both simple and natural.

While considerations of this character gradually led scholars to the recognition of the priority of Mark, it was long argued that the Mark which Matthew and Luke employed was different—to what extent scholars were not agreed—from our present Mark. This, in a word, was the theory of an earlier form of Mark—the so-called Urmarcus or proto-Mark—which, while occasionally cropping up today, has been given up by the great majority of students. The principal justification for this view was the phenomenon which is confessedly the most baffling and probably the crux of the whole problem of the relationship of our gospels, namely, the fact that frequently Matthew and Luke in passages for which they are dependent upon Mark none the less agree in minor details as against Mark. Of course, the obvious explanation might seem: Their copy (or copies) of Mark differed from ours and contained these touches. But when those passages are examined, the unsatisfactory nature of that hypothesis is apparent. By no means infrequently these minor agreements exhibit a tone and outlook distinctly not primitive but more sophisticated. This is to my mind the most decisive objection to the whole hypothesis. On this assumption the earlier edition of Mark contained frequently a later flavour than the one which subsequently supplanted it. On a later page we shall have to consider other more probable explanations of these minor agreements. For the moment the point of significance is that it was essentially our Mark[9] from which Matthew and Luke drew nearly their entire narrative matter, approximately half their whole content. This material is commonly styled the "triple tradition," *i.e.*, the matter common to all three. Mark was the source for it,

[8] Mark 15:42-47 = Matt. 27:57-61 = Luke 23:50-56.

[9] The word "essentially" is employed because the text of Mark, as of the other gospels, may well have undergone certain corruptions due to errors in copying, both accidental and intentional.

and the only guarantee of its historical accuracy. That Matthew and Luke subsequently repeat it by no means gives it the threefold attestation so often enthusiastically supposed.

In addition to the material which occurs in all three Synoptists (or in Mark and either Matthew or Luke) there are numerous passages where Matthew and Luke agree but where Mark is wanting. And not infrequently in these passages, styled conveniently the "double tradition," the verbal agreements are very striking. Thus, to take but one example, the scalding word of John the Baptist, save for three trifling variations, is reported in identical words by Matthew 3:7-10 and Luke 3:7-9. How are these agreements to be explained? The explanation in favour with the great majority of scholars today is a second source from which both Matthew and Luke independently drew, and which is ordinarily styled Q. Many attempts have been made to reconstruct this hypothetical source by gathering all the non-Markan passages which occur in both Matthew and Luke. Since all save two of these passages are in the form of discourse, it has become the habit to speak of Q as "the discourse source," and then to find an external guarantee for it in the oft-cited word of Papias: "Matthew collected the logia (oracles) in the Hebrew language, and each interpreted them as best he could." Thus the terms "the logia," or "the Matthæan logia," or "the logia referred to by Papias," or Q were treated as parallel titles for the same source, and quite unwarranted conclusions were drawn. This was very unfortunate. As stated in Chapter 40, there is a very high probability that Papias is not referring by these words to anything save our canonical Matthew. To press "logia" to refer to a catena of Jesus' sayings is utterly unwarranted, for the Greek word can equally well refer to narrative stories or to a connected account embracing both narrative and discourse. For scholars to continue to use the term logia in reference to the purely hypothetical Q is in every way deplorable and cannot fail to lead to confusion and misstatement. That Matthew and Luke independently used a second source and from it drew material which was in the main—but not exclusively—linked to sayings of Jesus is conceivable, but it should be kept clearly in mind that this is simply a deduction drawn from the nature of Matthew and Luke. There is absolutely no reference to this hypothetical source in Papias or any other writer anterior to the nineteenth century. In the language of Harnack, one of the many scholars to try his hand at reconstructing its contents, "it found its grave in Matthew and Luke." We know that Matthew and Luke used Mark because we have Mark; the situation is utterly different in the case of Q, and all attempts to gauge its exact content—whether it was simply a catena of sayings, or whether the presence of the two narratives (the Temptation story[10] and the Healing

[10] Matt. 4:1-11 = Luke 4:1-13.

of the Servant of the Centurion in Capernaum[11]) plus some material regarding John the Baptist suggest that it was in some sense a gospel or at least was provided with a modicum of narrative to hold the sayings together—and to debate with regard to the comparative fidelity of Matthew and Luke in the use of it appear to me precarious if not actually futile.

The very existence of this hypothetical source depends solely on the assumption of the independence of Matthew and Luke. If either used the other, there is no need to postulate a Q to explain the so-called "double tradition." The great majority of scholars consider the two junior Synoptists independent, and support the contention by various arguments. To me the evidence adduced is far from convincing. It may be frankly conceded that there are very real differences. The birth stories are quite irreconcilable; most of the parables found in the one are absent from the other. There are many contradictions and omissions. If Matthew and Luke be considered editors whose function was to preserve for posterity all the material available to them, these arguments would be of weight; but if, as has been argued in the preceding chapters, they were authors who approached their task with definite purposes and objects, much of the weight of this oft-repeated argument vanishes. To us the content of each of the gospels has become so precious that we naturally find it hard to conceive that an author could have omitted it had he known it. But the use of Mark by both Matthew and Luke reveals that it was by no means sacrosanct to them. Although Luke had Mark's story of the Passion before him, he was none the less quite ready to rewrite it so drastically that many scholars find it necessary to assume a different source for his version. Accordingly, it appears to me that a frank recognition of the fact that both of these writers were authors in the truest sense of the word—but authors who lived in the first century, not the twentieth—deprives the argument that each must have worked independent of the other, because of their omissions and substitutions, of most of its force, and enables us to see the matter of their so-called agreements in a different light. In the Markan story of the Cure of the Leper[12] there are several minor agreements between Matthew and Luke as against Mark. All but two of them—the addition of "lord" and "behold"—are simply to remove disagreeable elements—Jesus' unexplained anger—or to improve the style. The use of "lord" and "behold," as reference to a concordance will reveal, is characteristic of both of these authors, not of their sources. Hence it is quite unwarranted to use such material as evidence that Matthew and Luke were employing an earlier version of Mark which had these touches, for the significant point is that the touches are not primitive. A few other examples may be mentioned. To the word of reproof uttered by Jesus, "O faithless generation" (Mark 9:19), both Mat-

[11] Matt. 8:5-13 = Luke 7:1-10 + 13:28-30.
[12] Mark 1:40-45 = Matt. 8:1-4 = Luke 5:12-16.

thew and Luke add "and perverse," and to the command of Jesus, "bring him to me," add "hither." Similarly in the story of Judas' defection they agree in a slight variation, "he sought opportunity . . . ," instead of Mark's "he sought how he might conveniently . . ." (Mark 14:11). In the story of the mockery and insults suffered by Jesus they agree in adding "Who is he that struck thee?" to Mark's simple "Prophesy" (Mark 14:65). Or again, both agree that the appearance of the angel (s) was "lightning-like,"[13] although this agreement is obscured in the English translation. In and of themselves these points are of trifling importance. But to the student they cannot be overlooked, for they evidence some sort of contact between Matthew and Luke, either at the time of composition or at least prior to our earliest manuscripts. Today it is frequently argued that Mark used Q, or rather the source of which Q is a part, and that thus the minor agreements between Matthew and Luke in a Markan section are to be explained as cases where Matthew and Luke preferred the Q form to that of Mark. The view is conceivable—although it appears to me utterly improbable—but is far from proved. For convincing proof of the dependence of Mark it would be necessary to have frequent instances where all three evangelists preserve the same incident and where Matthew and Luke agree against Mark in so striking a manner that the possibility of accidental coincidence or textual harmonization is ruled out, and where this agreement of Matthew and Luke shows conclusively a more primitive form—else all we could say would be that Mark and Q occasionally overlapped. This evidence I cannot discover. Hence the assumption appears to me sheer surmise and incapable of proof. Even on the hypothesis that there were a Q, it would appear to me that its version of the threefold temptation, replete with apt scriptural citations, offers little presumptive evidence that it is prior to Mark's brief and sober account. Nor does this other narrative section, the Healing of the Centurion's Servant, with its account of the magical cure at a distance, evidence a primitive flavour.

But I find myself more and more skeptical not about the age of Q but of its very existence, and am inclined to feel that it is an unnecessary and unwarranted assumption serving to account for material common to Matthew and Luke which can be more satisfactorily explained on the hypothesis that one of them used the other. And it appears to me highly probable that Luke was the one who did the borrowing. To be sure, the reference in his preface to the many who had "taken in hand to draw up a narrative" does not demand that our Matthew was one of them. On the other hand, it is not unlikely. But there are distinct touches which appear to me to suggest that Luke's is the later production. It is easy to see how the despairing cry of Jesus on the cross, which Matthew preserves from Mark, should have been supplanted or at least supplemented by the word,

[13] Matt. 28:3 = Luke 24:4.

"Father, into thy hands I commend my spirit" (Luke 23:46), but the cancellation of this word of quiet dignity would be surprising. The legendary expansion of the story of the two dying thieves or the story of the twelve-year-old Jesus in the temple might not have appealed to Matthew, but I find it impossible to believe that had he read Luke he could have failed to have been impressed by the Lucan interpretation of Jesus as the "suffering servant." With his eagerness to present prophetic indication of the coming Messiah, that would have been a pearl of price. Matthew's silence upon this point appears to me highly important and to incline the balance distinctly in favour of his priority.

After removing the "triple tradition" from Matthew and Luke as coming from Mark and the "double tradition" as due to Luke's use of Matthew, or, as the majority of scholars would say, from Q, there remains a considerable residue in Matthew and Luke. While parts of this material can safely be classed as legendary, in some cases probably haggadic expansions of the earlier narrative made by the evangelists themselves, that accounts for but a part of the special material. There seems no good reason to doubt that both Matthew and Luke had special sources of information from which they drew. The nature of these sources, however, is by no means clear. Recently there has been a tendency on the part of critics to see evidence that each writer had written sources—pre-gospels, as it were. Thus Streeter, in his highly important volume, *The Four Gospels,* discovers a Jerusalem source, M, which Matthew employed and a Cæsarean source, L, employed by Luke. This M source has not secured many champions, and has little to commend it, but several competent scholars are agreed that Luke did make use of a connected source which at times, as in the Passion narrative, he preferred to Mark. But, after all, the whole matter of L depends on the question as to the extent to which Lucan differences can be explained as the work of Luke himself. It appears to me that the sole value of L is that it gives relief to puzzled interpreters of Luke who cannot bring themselves to allow Luke to make (or make up) history, but find it necessary to postulate another source for him to draw upon. Accordingly, it appears to me that the present fondness for multiple sources—scholars in the University of Chicago have discovered many such—is simply but one more consequence of the mistaken emphasis upon editors. The researches of these scholars have been of profound value—not so much for their results but for the incidental light they have thrown on the larger problem—but it would appear to me probable that in the coming years both Matthew and Luke will be obliged to accept responsibility for forsaking Mark when they each thought they could pen better stories. Furthermore, just as considerable material which was formerly marked "Matthew special" or "Luke special" may not unreasonably be considered the evangelists' own revamping or rewriting of Markan matter, so I am inclined to feel that a fresh study of the special material of Luke in the light of its being a possible adaptation of Matthew would not be wasted. Thus, for example, it might well be considered if Luke's parable of the Prodigal Son is not actually his own revision of the parable of the Two Sons, as recorded by Matthew (21:28-32). Or again, I find it quite unnecessary to see in Matthew's Sermon on the Mount the conflate of two sermons—one from Q and substantially preserved in that form by Luke, the other from M. On the contrary, the arrangement of material is so distinctly Matthæan that it is far easier to allow him entire responsibility for its form and to see Luke's Sermon on the Plain his own revision of Matthew's combination, in which he preserved the skeleton—beatitudes at the beginning, the parable of the Two Houses at the end—but preferred to arrange much of the material elsewhere. On the other hand, it may well be that occasionally he may preserve material parallel to that of Matthew in a different form which he preferred. All Christian tradition was not restricted to sources as we so easily imagine. Knowledge of the Lord's Prayer was available to Christians who had never read either Matthew or Luke. That some of this floating material had come to assume definite written form before Mark on the one hand or Matthew and Luke on the other is possible, but I see little evidence for it. We may well consider Matthew and Luke masterpieces, and without exaggeration; yet despite the fact that the church soon considered them distinctly superior to Mark, Mark was none the less preserved and included in the canon. It is hard to conceive the disappearance of earlier writings without even so much as a trace of their presence left behind them. Behind not only Matthew and Luke but Mark there were sources of knowledge available, but their complete disappearance suggests that they were in no very permanent form. To what extent we can ever hope to reconstruct them appears highly questionable. Form criticism is the most recent endeavour to pierce the mists behind our first gospel—and incidentally of the other two. This study is still in its infancy. In spite of its staggering nomenclature, bristling with paradigms or apothegms, miracle stories and *Novellen*, and the insistence that the form was originally more important than the content, it has already cast a deal of light upon the Christian message before it became solidified into gospels. Their stress that the first traditions of the early church would scarcely have been in written form nor in the form of connected narrative, but rather would have existed as vivid memories, scattered sayings, separate stories, free to develop and to change as they were used over and over by the early missionary preachers; that in the course of these pre-literary years these materials often took on quite new aspects; that older stories originally not told of Jesus at all gradually came to occupy an honoured place—all this is far from improbable. It would appear to me not unlikely that not only was it from these mines that Mark drew much of his ore, but that they were still being worked when Matthew and Luke girded themselves for their task, and that they provided these later workmen with much so-called "unique material."

Chapter XLIV

THE GOSPEL ACCORDING TO JOHN

WHILE Matthew, Mark, and Luke stand so close together, despite their many differences, that the thoughtful reader, even without any technical knowledge of Synoptic criticism, is struck by their similarity of expression and choice of material, the Gospel of John, or as many writers prefer to call it, the Fourth Gospel, is widely different. More than ninety per cent of its material falls outside the Synoptist tradition. This one fact alone makes it valueless to attempt a "harmony" of the four gospels. In former years such were made, but they are not worth the paper they are printed on, unless the few Johannine parallels or reminiscences be subordinated to footnotes or appendix. The attempt to weave all four together is utterly perverse and cannot fail to result in complete confusion.

Nor is this recognition of the essential dissimilarity of the Synoptists and John any new discovery. The fathers recognized it as clearly as do we, and sought to explain the obvious fact. Clement of Alexandria (*ca.* 200 A.D.) gave the classic answer:

> But that John, last of all, aware that the bodily (*i.e.,* external) facts had been revealed in the gospels [he has just spoken of Matthew, Luke, and Mark], was urged on by his acquaintances, and, under the inspiration of the Spirit, wrought a spiritual gospel.[1]

To this day the differences continue to be explained.

Who the author was will probably always remain veiled in mists. One thing, however, may be said of him with confidence: he was a profoundly religious man. He had had a real communion with the Christ about whom he wrote, and, though the portrait he painted differs radically from those of his fellow artists, he believed this Christ to be the Jesus of history. Allegory and theology abound in the book; none the less, the resultant gospel is not intended to be an allegory. Although he wrote many years after the events, and in all probability had never seen with the eyes of the flesh the one he described, he knew that he had had direct fellowship with this Jesus who by his life had become the deathless, changeless possession of the church. If Paul stressed the point that his gospel was not from men, but was a direct revelation from God, so our author was convinced that in the deeper, more abiding facts of this life of lives he had direct and first-hand information. He had himself communed with Christ and testified to the things he had

[1] Quoted from the *Hypotyposes* by Eusebius, *Hist. Eccl.* vi,14,7.

himself seen and heard. He describes the one whom the church has come to regard as the saviour of the world (4:42) not merely as he was within the narrow limits of his life on earth, but as he is for ever to those who have known and loved him. If we fail to keep this emphasis to the fore, we shall fail completely to understand either the gospel or its author.

The Fourth Gospel, although totally unlike Mark in outward form, yet shares with it a definite theological interest and purpose. And this purpose is distinctly not to provide a biography of Jesus or to supplement the accounts already written which he apparently knew and to a degree used; it is to demonstrate something about Jesus, namely, his supernatural character. In the opening word the note is struck: Jesus is the Logos, the preexistent Son of God. Everything in the gospel tends to make the truth of this proposition obvious. Jesus is of course conscious of his true nature from the outset. All about him, friends and enemies alike, recognize it. John the Baptist is made explicitly to refuse the title, Christ, precisely for the purpose of making it the clearer that there is one whose claim to that title is above dispute.[2] The miracles are frankly and avowedly signs—stupendous, marvelous manifestations of power intended to compel this belief. The theory of Mark that Jesus deliberately sought to hide his power from the outside world, and constantly bade those upon whom cures had been wrought, "Tell it to no man," is completely reversed in John. Rather, Jesus always performs his miracles at the precise moment when their effect will be the greatest. Finally Thomas, who had been represented as the type of man naturally cautious and skeptical, unwilling to believe save in the light of the clearest proof, is forced by the sheer magnitude of the evidence to acknowledge it—"My Lord and my God" (20:28). To this confession—a confession not alone of Thomas, but of the many Thomases of the author's own day—Jesus responds: "Because thou hast seen me, hast thou believed? blessed are they that have not seen, and yet have believed" (20:29). This climactic note is the logical place for the gospel to close, and it does[3] with the word:

> Many other signs therefore did Jesus in the presence of his disciples, which are not written in this book: *but these are written, that ye may believe that Jesus is the Christ, the Son of God; and that believing ye may have life in his name.*[4]

The genuine contrasts with the Synoptists are many and significant. Perhaps the most striking is the totally different order of events. In the Synoptists Jesus' ministry is confined to Galilee. Apart from a few obscure references which probably can be explained there is no trace of any visit to Jerusalem during the ministry until the final tragic journey which ended in his death. The length of the ministry appears also to have been brief—at least they indicate nothing to lead the reader to assume that it was more

[2] John 3:28; cf. 1:19-23.
[3] For the evidence that chapter 21 is a late appendix by another writer see below, pp. 448 f.
[4] 20:30 f.

than a few months. In the Fourth Gospel all is changed. The scene has been shifted from Galilee to Jerusalem and its environs in Judea. From Jerusalem there are a few brief excursions up into Galilee,[5] but regularly concluded with a return to Jerusalem to this feast or that. Indeed, Jesus' word about a prophet having no honour in his own country and the implied favour of the Galileans (4:44 f.) might even suggest that Judea, not Galilee, was his *patris*. Against this, however, is the query of Nathanael (1:46) and the repeated reference to Jesus of Nazareth.[6] Again, his family appears at home, or at least with him, in Galilee.[7] The mention of at least three, perhaps four, Passovers suggest that the ministry was of two or three years' duration.

Then again the events are quite different. Stories as of the Feeding of the Five Thousand and of the Walking on the Sea occur; an occasional word of Jesus, as that about the ubiquitous poor,[8] appears quite as in the Synoptists. But these are very few in comparison with the bulk of the material. There is no story of the baptism. The author is familiar with the account, but is obliged to recast it entirely. He is pointed out at once as the Messiah by the Baptist. A few follow him. Then he goes to Galilee and performs a miracle at Cana. From here he returns to Jerusalem to a Passover and cleanses the temple. By shifting the time of this event—in the Synoptists it is at the close of the ministry and precipitates the tragedy—John is obliged to find another event which serves as the immediate occasion of the end, namely, the Raising of Lazarus (11:45-57). Then follow the episode with Nicodemus and the interview with the woman in Samaria. Returning from Galilee, he heals the impotent man at the pool of Bethesda. After another trip to Galilee he returns to Jerusalem, this time to attend the Feast of Tabernacles. The man born blind is healed. After the Feast of Dedication he goes across the Jordan, whence he returns to perform his stupendous miracle, the Raising of Lazarus. All of these incidents are quite unnoticed in the other gospels. Following his raising of Lazarus he remains in Jerusalem until his death. The older harmonists sought to work these episodes into the other strain. John was used as the framework, and between these various feast journeys they attempted to sandwich in the Galilean material, practically absent in John. But this attempt was futile. The two cannot be harmonized. One is a Jerusalem ministry, the other a Galilean.

Again there are very marked differences in the representation of Jesus in the two strains, although these differences have been unnecessarily exaggerated. All three Synoptists represent Jesus as coming to John the Baptist and being baptized by him. Matthew feels a difficulty in Mark's probably unintentionally crisp account of this event and seeks to soften it by his dia-

[5] John 2:1-12; 4:43-5:1; 6:1-7:14.
[6] John 18:5,7; 19:19; cf. also 7:41,52.
[7] John 2:1; 7:3.
[8] John 12:8 = Mark 14:7 = Matt. 26:11.

logue between Jesus and John. None the less, at Jesus' bidding John baptizes him. At this moment Jesus realizes his call (Mark). In John it is quite different. In the prologue Jesus is identified with the preëxistent Logos. It is quite unthinkable that such an one could be baptized. John is introduced simply to bear witness that the Christ is coming. This he does before he even sees Jesus. Jesus passes by. Instantly John proclaims that Jesus is the Christ. The Synoptist imagery of the descending dove and the voice from heaven are preserved. But their function is simply to warn John that the expected one has appeared. In obedience to the sign from heaven John makes public pronouncement. This, of course, leaves no place for the later query of the Baptist, "Art thou he that cometh, or look we for another?"[9] On the next day—the phrase, "on the morrow," is as characteristic of John as is "straightway" for Mark—two of John's disciples recognize him as the Lamb of God and follow him. Thus from the very beginning his position is recognized. How different the Synoptists. Mark carries the theory forward without contradiction: Jesus knew his destiny, but hid it from all. Gradually his disciples came to catch a glimmer of it at Cæsarea Philippi. Matthew and Luke follow Mark in part. They too record Peter's confession, but by no means agree with Mark's theory of the Messianic secret. Thus they are involved in some difficulties which they never seek to remove. In John, on the contrary, all is known from the first. There is no place for Peter's confession. The incident, however, is known to John, and he revamps it completely. Thus following the falling away of the crowd, Jesus inquires, "Would ye also go away?" and Peter replies, "Lord, to whom shall we go? thou hast the words of eternal life. And we have believed and known that thou art the Holy One of God."[10] In this account there is no progression; no start in hope for Jesus; no gradual recognition that "narrow is the gate and straitened the way, that leadeth into life, and few are they that find it"; no expectation of winning the Pharisees and the nation at large. From the beginning he knows how it will end. At the very first a sharp line is drawn between believers, enemies, and waverers. His enemies are as hot against him at the first as at the end, but they cannot lay hold of him *because his hour is not yet come*. Their attempts to arrest him fail;[11] their plots to kill him miscarry.[12] Jesus is protected by a miraculous power that keeps him safe until the hour comes. Thus when his enemies seek to stone him it is said, "But Jesus hid himself, and went out of the temple" (8:59). This is surely not to be understood that he skulked away. Rather he miraculously disappears: *his hour had not yet come*. Thus the early Cleansing of the Temple provides no problem for the author.

The picture of Jesus is that of a figure quite distinct from all around him.

[9] Matt. 11:2-6; cf. Luke 7:18-23.

[10] John 6:66-71.

[11] John 7:30,32,44; 8:20; 10:39; cf. 12:36.

[12] John 5:16-18; 7:25; 8:59; 10:31.

The "Jews" are his enemies; this term, constantly on the lips of the author,[13] is always a reproach and with no suggestion that Jesus himself was a Jew.[14] At the very beginning it is announced: "He came unto his own, and they that were his own received him not" (1:11). So he speaks of "your" law (8:17; 10:34); he can even say: "But this cometh to pass, that the word may be fulfilled that is written in *their* law. They hated me without a cause" (15:25). He is in the world, but is not of the world. Even to his disciples he never speaks of "Our Father"; it is always "My Father" or "Your Father." To Mary Magdalene he can say, "Go unto my brethren, and say to them, I ascend unto *my Father and your Father, and my God and your God*" (20:17).

So it is with the miracles. As has been remarked, the author aptly designates them as *signs* intended to compel belief. The kind-hearted teacher—whom at least modern ingenuity has discovered in the Synoptists—who walks about the Galilean hills and lays his hand in sympathy upon the sick and distressed because his Saviour heart was stirred by their suffering, has vanished. Instead there walks about a majestic and almost aloof figure whose miracles are tremendous signs, not called forth by any sympathy for the afflicted, but precisely to show his tremendous power. Thus it is to be noted that Jesus never takes advice from those about him. Even if he later does precisely what he is advised to do, he is yet made to do it in such a way that it is evident he is doing it solely on his own initiative. Examples of this may be seen in his rejoinder to his mother at Cana (2:4) or in his attitude at learning of the sickness of Lazarus (11:6). The most striking is his attitude toward his brothers' advice: They urge him to go to the feast; he replies, "Go ye up unto the feast: I go not up unto this feast." Then after their departure he went up also.[15]

When word comes that Lazarus is sick, instead of hastening to his friend, he waits, lets him die, waits again until he is three days dead, then comes and raises him. The author's reason for this delay is transparent. The Jewish view about death is revealed in one of the Midrashim:[16]

> Bar Qappara taught: The entire intensity of the mourning is reserved for the third day. Three days long the soul hovers about the grave. It thinks that it will return (into the body). When, however, it sees that the colour (appearance) of its face has changed, then it departs and leaves it.

Thus Martha is made to say, "Lord, by this time the body decayeth; for he hath been dead four days."[17] No reader may object that the raising of Lazarus was that of a man who had not actually died. To the gratuitous

[13] It is employed seventy times in John as against five in Matthew, six in Mark, and five in Luke.

[14] Cf. John 2:18,20; 5:16; 6:41 and frequently.

[15] John 7:1-13, especially verses 8 and 10.

[16] Genesis R. 100,64a, cited by Strack und Billerbeck, *Kommentar zum Neuen Testament aus Talmud und Midrasch,* Vol. II, p. 544.

[17] John 11:39.

remark, often made, that the word, "Jesus wept" (11:35), suggests Jesus' sympathy for Lazarus, it need only be remarked that the author reveals quite the contrary by his explicit rejoinder: "The Jews therefore said, Behold how he loved him!" No clearer evidence could be desired. The Jews invariably misunderstood and misinterpreted every word and deed of Jesus. His tears are not of sorrow, but of anger: These Jews in their unbelief have dared to weep for the dead in the presence of him, the Lord of life. The whole point to the story is given in Jesus' words:

> I am the resurrection and the life: he that believeth on me, though he die, yet shall he live; and whosoever liveth and believeth on me shall never die.[18]

By their tears the Jews have shown their unbelief. Thus Lazarus is raised, not out of love for Lazarus, but as Jesus is made expressly to say, "that they may believe that thou didst send me" (11:41-43). The whole scene is one of slow and impressive dignity. The same may be said of the curiously artificial story of the miracle at Cana.[19] The emphasis upon Jesus' aloofness and the lavish display—150 gallons of wine when the feast was drawing to a close!—but express the author's confidence that the old system was being supplanted by the new at the touch of Jesus.

The miracles are few in number—only nine in all—but tremendous in nature. The impotent man at Bethesda had been ill thirty-eight years;[20] again and again it is emphasized in the case of the blind man that he had been born blind.[21] When Jesus walks on the water, he either walks across the whole lake or else, more probably, the author means that by miraculous power the boat was propelled instantaneously to the other shore: "They were willing therefore to receive him into the boat: and straightway the boat was at the land wherein they were going" (6:21). The son of the nobleman was sick in Capernaum. Jesus was in Cana. A spoken word was sufficient, and the child lived.[22] It is unnecessary longer to dwell on this phase of the portrait. Suffice it to say that in this gallery of signs one looks in vain for such an incident as that told by Luke, "And when the Lord saw her, he had compassion on her, and said unto her, Weep not."[23]

It is by no means against his will that he dies. There is no Gethsemane incident, no agony of prayer that the cup pass from him. The author knows the story of a period of agony just prior to the crucifixion, but for various reasons finds it impossible in his account. The fact that it is just after the

[18] John 11:25,26.

[19] John 2:1-11. Note (1) the mother's confidence, although it is later stated that this was the first miracle performed by Jesus; while in Mark 3:21 it is implied that his mother had no lively confidence; (2) the unfilial word of Jesus; (3) the presumption of the visiting woman in giving orders to the servants; (4) their obedience to her.

[20] John 5:5.

[21] John 9:1-40; contrast Mark 8:24.

[22] John 4:46-54.

[23] Luke 7:13.

high-priestly prayer, which ends in the lyric burst of serene confidence, that Jesus is arrested would make such an episode as that in Gethsemane's garden unthinkable. For it, directly after the all-important Coming of the Greeks—emblematic of the success of the gentile mission—and the portentous, "The hour is come, that the son of man should be glorified," he substitutes the words, "Now is my soul troubled; and what shall I say? Father, save me from this hour? But [*i.e.,* "precisely"] for this cause came I unto this hour. Father, glorify thy name."[24] The analogy of the prayer at the grave of Lazarus (11:41 f.), already commented upon, indicates the author's meaning. The emotion of Jesus had been *for this* cause, *i.e.,* to direct this prayer to God and that God might answer it by a voice from heaven, which, Jesus goes on to say, "hath not come for my sake, but for your sakes." That is, the prayer reveals Jesus' union with God; the emotional outburst is simply the necessary prelude to the prayer.

Instead of a rabble sent hastily with swords and staves a whole cohort (two hundred men!) come out. When they approach him, they are miraculously felled to the ground by his word, "I am he." Surely we can hear our author whispering: "It was not against his will that he was taken." At the examination before Pilate Jesus is not silent, but makes his proclamation of power. To Pilate's question, "Art thou a king then?" Jesus replies, "Thou sayest that I am a king. To this end have I been born, and to this end am I come into the world, that I should bear witness unto the truth."[25] Again in emphasis that his death was voluntary, to Pilate's querulous question, "Speakest thou not unto me? knowest thou not that I have power to release thee, and have power to crucify thee?" Jesus makes dignified response: "Thou wouldest have no power against me, except it were given thee from above" (19:10 f.). The dying cry, "My God, my God, why hast thou forsaken me?" was qualified by Luke. From John it is entirely absent. In its stead is the sublime word, "It is finished" (19:30).

The essential dissimilarity between the portraits of Jesus in the Synoptists and that in John is perhaps most clearly revealed in his discourses. The effective and apt parables so prominent in the former are totally absent in the Fourth Gospel. In their place are long colourless allegories and cryptic statements frankly intended to puzzle his listeners. The evangelist is obviously using this means to reveal the essential difference between Jesus and those about him. Thus everything he says is misunderstood, not alone by the Jews, but even by his disciples, *and the reader knows that they misunderstood him.* Thus in the interview with the Samaritan woman Jesus speaks of the water he could give, of which, if one drank, he would never thirst again. The *reader* knows that he is speaking of something quite different from physical water, and knows it before the evangelist explains, but the

[24] John 12:27, reminiscent of Psalm 6:3.
[25] John 18:33-38.

woman does not.[26] Or, in the same story, the disciples return and ask Jesus if he is not hungry. He replies, "I have meat to eat that ye know not." The *reader* knows that he is referring to something far different from physical food. The disciples, on the contrary, naïvely ask: "Hath any man brought him aught to eat?"[27] This motif extends through the gospel for the sole purpose of exalting Jesus. The questioners ask the most obvious and artificial questions, simply for the purpose of providing Jesus with an opportunity to speak. The whole structure of both speeches and settings is artificial. When does Jesus end and the evangelist begin? For example, in the interview with Nicodemus, the ruler of the Jews is off the stage in an instant, and Jesus is left discoursing about the one great subject in the gospel—himself. But is it Jesus speaking for the benefit of Nicodemus, or is it the evangelist addressing his own readers? Surely such a word as "Verily, Verily I say unto thee, *We* speak that which *we* know, and bear witness of that which *we* have seen; and *ye* receive not *our* witness" (3:11) inclines one to the latter view. So also Jesus is made to say to Nicodemus, "Marvel not that I say unto *thee*, *ye* must be born anew" (3:7). The whole tone is of theological speculation; the pithy common sense that characterizes so many of the parables and other sayings of the Synoptists is gone. Jesus never speaks to help his hearers to solve the riddle of life, but always to reveal his own omniscience or to discuss the central point, his own nature. While in the Synoptists he regularly speaks of the kingdom of God, in John the emphasis is not on the kingdom at all—only twice is the phrase used, and then quite incidentally (3:3,5)—but on himself, the king.

Thus we surely will not err in regarding these speeches as entirely the compositions of the evangelist himself, who uses them to make Jesus speak the way he wants him to speak. In a word, they evidence all the characteristics of the speeches found in ancient writers. The freshness and spontaneity are gone; they are all far removed from any real contact with the actual scenes described. I have alluded to the surprising sameness of the several speeches in Acts—be they from the lips of a Peter, a Stephen, or a Paul. This quality is even more noticeable in John. The interviews are all built from the same blueprint. Some one asks a question. Jesus makes an ambiguous reply which the questioner—but not the reader—misunderstands, and which Jesus corrects. This provokes another question. If this indicates that the questioner is now on the right track, all is well. Jesus speaks, and as he continues the whole stage setting vanishes, the questioner disappears, and a long discourse, often distinctly not apposite to the introductory question, follows. Not infrequently there is an almost verbatim sameness to the questions. The Samaritan woman beseeches: "Sir, give me this water that I thirst not, neither come all the way hither to draw" (4:15); the Galileans

[26] John 4:10-15.
[27] John 4:31-34.

make the identical request: "Lord, evermore give us this bread" (6:34). Often the answer does not answer the question. Thus Peter queries: "Lord, to whom shall we go? thou hast the words of eternal life. And we have believed and know that thou art the Holy One of God." Jesus replies, "Did I not choose you the twelve, and one of you is a devil?" (6:68 ff.). I have sought in an earlier article[28] to show that the excessive fondness for the perfect tense (with its emphasis upon the existing result of a past action), evidenced by the author of the Fourth Gospel (and of I John), is a clear evidence of reflection on the part of the author. What Jesus had said and done—to a measure what his contemporaries had said and done to him—had been freighted with what for want of a better name can be loosely styled "cosmic effect." The ageless, timeless manifestation of the divine wisdom has spoken; his words thus "stand spoken."

These many and sharp contrasts and differences between the portraits in the Synoptists and the Fourth Gospel cannot be disregarded.[29] If Jesus spoke as he is reported to have spoken on the Galilean hillside, he did not speak as John 14-16 portrays him. If his attitude toward those about him was that which Mark suggests, it was not that of John. A person alternately appearing now in one garb, now in the other, would be psychologically impossible. This the alienists recognize, and hence have produced their chromos of the mentally sick Galilean, swinging back and forth between megalomania and micromania. The absurdity of their result is simply due to their entire ignorance of the literary problem involved in the study of the gospels. Oil and water will not mix, although they can be churned together into a sticky mess. But oil and water when kept separate are both of the greatest value.

The Synoptists, as has been argued at length in the foregoing chapters, are far from being photographs of Jesus of Nazareth, but, on the contrary, bear clear evidence on every page both of studied reflection and of the growth of tradition and legend. But even so, there can be little question that their portraits are closer to that of the historic Jesus of Nazareth than that of the Fourth Gospel. Occasionally John has used their material as the basis of some of his stories. There may be genuine traces here and there, although it would appear to me hazardous to attempt to localize any of them, so completely is the whole the product of the evangelist himself. The writing is priceless as an indication of the type of thought early Christianity produced, well nigh worthless, however, for the historian who desires to glimpse the Jesus of history. That in the date of the Last supper the Gospel of John preserves the correct date—namely, that this meal was not the Passover, but held on the evening before—is probable. But this alteration of the tradition was not due to a desire for historical accuracy, but solely because it

[28] "The Perfect Tense in the Fourth Gospel"—*Journal of Biblical Literature,* Vol. LV, 1936, pp. 121-131.

[29] See also E. C. Colwell, *John Defends the Gospel.* This excellent volume appeared too late for me to make more detailed use of it.

suited his theological purpose to make Jesus—the true Lamb of God, the Christian's everlasting Passover—die just as the paschal lambs were being slaughtered. The geographical and chronological touches might at first seem to evidence an accurate knowledge on the part of the author. Thus the references to "Bethany beyond the Jordan" (1:28); to "Ænon near to Salim, because there was much water there" (3:23); to Jesus walking about in "Solomon's porch" (10:23); to his two-day visit in Samaria (4:40,43), to its being the "midst of the feast" when Jesus went up to Jerusalem (7:14)—these might tempt one to assume familiarity with the events described. But they are far from conclusive and prove little. Any pilgrim to the holy sites in Palestine at the beginning of the second century—an ancient forerunner of the modern Cook's tour—could easily have acquired such local colour. The thrice-repeated statement that Caiphas was "high priest for that year" (11:49,51; 18:13) would certainly imply that his knowledge of things Palestinian was not profound. Nor should it be overlooked that the later incidents are referred back to the earlier ones in a purely literary—not historical—connexion. Thus in 7:21-24, at the Feast of Tabernacles Jesus justifies himself without preamble for the Sabbath healing of the impotent man at Bethesda, mentioned in a previous chapter (and hence perfectly familiar *to the reader*). But according to John's own statement this event had taken place more than six months before and in the interim another festival had occurred. In 10:26-28, without warning, a discourse about sheep is continued. To be sure, it had begun earlier in the same chapter, but in a different locality and to different hearers. In 6:15, Jesus is said to have gone up "again into the mountain . . . alone," but in 6:3 he had gone up into the mountain and had not come down. The list of these "rough spots" could be easily lengthened. None accept the witness of Jesus;[30] yet all flock to him.[31] Jesus did not come to judge the world,[32] yet does precisely that.[33] Jesus refers to his *one* work in Jerusalem[34]—the Sabbath miracle of chapter 5—quite ignoring his previous signs to Jerusalem.[35] He answers his disciples, "*All things* that I heard from my Father I have made known unto you";[36] yet a little further on refers to the many things he has yet to say which they cannot bear now.[37] He is surprised that no one asks whither he is going[38] despite the fact that Thomas had asked precisely that.[39] In 14:31 it is said, "Arise, let us go hence"; but it is not until 18:1 that they actually go. In the interview with

[30] John 1:5,10; 3:11,12,32.
[31] John 3:26,29 f.
[32] John 3:17; 8:15; 12:47.
[33] John 5:22.
[34] John 7:21.
[35] John 2:23; 7:31.
[36] John 15:15.
[37] John 16:12.
[38] John 16:5.
[39] John 14:5; cf. also 13:36.

Nicodemus Jesus refers to his ascension as if it had already taken place.[40] Of course it had for the one who actually uttered the word. Attempts have occasionally been made to remove some of these infelicities by rearranging the material—chapter 6 before chapter 5; the removal of chapters 15 and 16 as a later addition, and the view that chapter 17 was spoken while standing in the room, thus bringing 14:31 and 18:1 together—and may be studied in detail in Moffatt.[41] But these alterations all attempt to give a chronological consistency to a writing entirely indifferent to such matters. On the other hand, the famous story of the Woman Taken in Adultery (7:53-8:11) is universally regarded as a comparatively late interpolation. The textual evidence leaves no question. The four earliest uncial manuscripts omit it, as do many of the minuscules; such fathers as Origen, Eusebius, Chryostom, Cyril of Alexandria, and Theophylact did not read it in their copies of John. Euthymius (*ca.* 1100 A.D.), the first of the Greek expositors to consider the question, states,

> It is necessary to observe that the section is either not found in the accurate manuscripts or is obelized. From this it appears to be an addition and appendage.[42]

A whole group of manuscripts—the so-called Ferrar group—have it not in John but after Luke 21:38. Other manuscripts and versions place it after John 7:36 or 7:44, or at the end of the gospel. Furthermore, the style is utterly unlike that of the Fourth Gospel. Eusebius says that Papias expounded "a story about a woman who was accused before the Lord of many sins, which the Gospel according to the Hebrews contains."[43] How this story came to lodge in the Western text at this point is one of the many enigmas as yet unanswered.

In concluding this section upon the nature and characteristics of the Fourth Gospel it may be repeated that it has a heaviness and artificiality vastly different from the Synoptic accounts. The reason why this gospel is so popular despite its turgidly, often tiresomely, repetitious style is partly due to its several favourite quotations, partly to the fact that we read it in the light of the Synoptists. The simple, unaffected, generous, tender-hearted figure discerned in those accounts is read into the statelier, more tremendous, but not in itself especially pleasing, figure of the Johannine Christ. What we admire is not the Jesus of the Fourth Gospel but the conflate of the two. Should we by a miracle lose our Synoptists and all remembrance of them, I believe many would find the Gospel of John shorn of much of its former charm.

When we approach the question of authorship, we find ourselves in a very deep fog. The problem fairly bristles with difficulties, three of which are very

[40] John 3:13.
[41] *Introduction to the Literature of the New Testament,* pp. 550-563.
[42] Quoted by W. Bauer, *Das Johannesevangelium, in loc.*
[43] *Hist. Eccl.* iii,39,17.

perplexing. (1) Why the Johannine tradition? If the position maintained in the preceding pages is correct, the possibility of an eyewitness is ruled completely out of court. Furthermore, as was argued in a preceding chapter,[44] there is a real probability—many scholars would feel it a certainty—that John the son of Zebedee was martyred before 70 A.D., and every critic, whatever his views as to the author, agrees that the gospel cannot antedate the year 100. Furthermore, all of these "Johannine" writings appear to emanate from the environs of Ephesus, and yet there seems no valid evidence that John the son of Zebedee ever laboured there.[45] Why then the persistent tradition which runs in the face of all this evidence and claims the son of Zebedee as author? (2) Whom does the author mean by "the beloved disciple," who is frequently referred to in the gospel in this enigmatic way? (3) What is the relation of chapter 21 to the rest of the gospel? That it is an appendix is obvious. The main body of the book closes with 20:31. But is the appendix an afterthought by the same author—if that is the case, obviously its concluding verses (21:24,25) must be by a different hand and in the form of an early gloss—or by a different author who felt impelled to add the additional material? These problems are all so interrelated and tangled that any verdict about one will of necessity affect the others. It will be convenient to consider the last first.

There are at least three distinct purposes revealed in this appendix. The first is the rehabilitation of Peter (21:1-19, esp. 15-19). This section, which would seem to contain the *first* of a cycle of post-resurrection appearances, is brought in very lamely after 20:24 f., and must be referred to as the "third" appearance.[46] Then there is the desire to correct the tradition that Jesus had said that the "beloved disciple" would not die before the Parousia. Obviously the disciple has died; hence this attempt to show that Jesus' words had been misconstrued. Then finally is the wish to stress the authorship of the gospel by ascribing it to the "beloved disciple." Thus 21:24 is to explain the enigmatic 19:35, and to make clear that the beloved disciple is the one there referred to; 21:25 appears a simple expansion of 20:30.

Deductions from the style and language of the chapter are probably uncertain, although the complete absence of the use of the perfect tense is suggestive. But the incorporation here of a tradition of an appearance in Galilee, quite out of harmony with the concluding chapter of the gospel, would appear to suggest that it was added by a later hand anxious to harmonize this gospel with Matthew and Mark. More important is the indication of a different view about the Parousia in this appendix from that in the gospel proper. In the gospel one of the author's aims is to provide an answer to the doubts aroused by the failure of the Parousia. His word is clear: Jesus has

[44] Pp. 369-371.
[45] See p. 370.
[46] For the importance of this bit of tradition see pp. 170 f.

already come: his coming was in the form of the Comforter. But in the appendix the reference to Jesus' word, "If I will that he tarry till I come," shows that the author does not share this view. Thus I am definitely inclined to feel that the appendix was added by a later hand. Whether, as some scholars affirm, he also attempted a revision of the whole gospel, and that this accounts for some of the seeming dislocations of material is to me not clear. At any rate, the concluding verses of the appendix would appear to be by the later hand and to be intended to give information about the authorship of the gospel. Without this word the whole problem of authorship might well have been different, for, although 19:35 *could* be understood as a reference to the beloved disciple—and of course *is* by the author of the appendix—it is by no means certain that the author of the gospel so intended. At most it would appear that he appeals to this figure as the guarantor of the truthfulness of his account. That he is thus referring to himself, that is, is designating himself by this term, is far from probable. It is far easier to see the word as penned by a disciple of that beloved intimate. It may be, as several have supposed, that the author means by the beloved disciple, John the son of Zebedee, and is thus indirectly citing him as the ultimate source of information. But, on the other hand, that John the son of Zebedee had actually been the teacher of this man is by no means an easy assumption. The further one delves, the deeper grows the uncertainty.

Nevertheless, it is quite possible to suggest a plausible explanation of the quite incorrect tradition that John, the son of Zebedee, was the author of all five of the Johannine writings. Several consecutive steps may be listed. 1. Throughout the gospel the beloved disciple is given a place of prominence —at the Last supper he leaned upon Jesus' breast; at the cross he alone was faithful and was entrusted with Jesus' mother, thus actually becoming Jesus' foster brother. As we have seen, 19:35 can be construed so as to refer to this figure, while 21:24 asserts that he was the author of the book. 2. The similarities between the gospel and I John are unmistakable and were recognized by the early Christians as well as by modern critics. The opening words of this epistle can be construed to mean (although it is apparently not what the author means) that the author had himself been an eyewitness of Jesus. If he was, so was the author of the gospel. 3. The beloved disciple must obviously have been one of the most intimate of Jesus' disciples. Early Christians had read the Synoptic gospels and knew the priority given to Peter, James, and John. The beloved disciple must have been one of these. But Peter is excluded, since he is several times referred to by name in this gospel. It was he, for example, who had urged the beloved disciple to question Jesus as to the identity of the traitor. Neither James nor John was mentioned by name in the gospel. Accordingly, either might be the enigmatic beloved disciple, but Acts explicitly refers to the early martyrdom of James at the hands of Agrippa. Only John is left. And does not his close association with Peter in the early chapters of Acts make it natural for Peter to have been the one who asked the question of his close friend and comrade? 4. Finally, a *John*—to be sure his other name was Mark, but details of that sort are of little moment in the growth of tradition—had a mother *Mary* living with him in Jerusalem (Acts 12:12). Might this not well be remembered in connexion with the word of Jesus on the cross to the beloved disciple to take *Mary* to his home? It appears to me that from some such line of reasoning the tradition arose connecting John's name with the gospel and First Epistle. 5. But we can go on. II and III John both purport to be written by "the elder." Now the only reference, at least the only one known to me, to a specific figure bearing that title is Papias' oft-cited one to the "elder *John*." 6. The book of Revelation explicitly claims to be written by a *John*. Thus it is possible to see how to uncritical folk, who had the will to believe, a halo of Johannine authorship came to rest upon all five books despite the glaring and patent contradictions between some of them, as the gospel and the Revelation. This is frankly conjecture, but so are the most complicated and learned discussions of the Johannine problem.

Thus I am definitely inclined to the view that tradition tells us nothing about the actual author, and that all attempts to see the Galilean fisherman as author, in any degree of remove, of this highly theological and apologetic brochure are unwarranted and misleading. The little that we can learn about the personality of the author does not come from surmises, but from the gospel itself—and it is surprisingly meagre. He is a deeply religious man; is acquainted with the Alexandrian philosophy (at least he makes use of the concept of Logos, popularized by Philo, and expanded by the Christian catechetical teachers of that city: Pantænus, Clement, and Origen); knows the Synoptic gospels and occasionally utilizes some of their material, but without evidencing the slightest feeling that they are inspired Scripture; is influenced, probably deeply influenced, by Paul, although he does not scruple to alter some of that master's central notes. For example, he lays his emphasis on the life of Christ rather than on his death. Thus for him the resurrection was not the proof of Jesus' divine character as it had been for Paul. His life had proved this beyond the peradventure of a doubt. The resurrection marked the beginning of the ever-widening and abiding activity of Jesus. From all these sources he drew, but he drew far more deeply on his own deep and abiding convictions. Today we find it necessary to find a definite "source" for every utterance and idea that our gospel writers expressed, and we hesitate to postulate any originality of thought for any of them. If we deprive our author of *this* source, we simply fail to understand him. In the last analysis the kind of Jesus whom he is depicting is the kind of Jesus whom he knows and whom the church knows. To do this he may at times utilize materials, which because they are earlier than he, we call "historic"; but he does not hesitate to rework and recast them to make his portrait the clearer. That he was a Jew is possible, and is generally assumed; but there is surprisingly little direct evidence of it. Such a view would explain the smug observation, "Salvation is from the Jews" (4:22), but is neutralized by his no less obvious hatred of the word Jew, for whom he has nothing good to relate. Palestine was certainly not his home; his evident desire completely to subordinate John the Baptist has led some to feel that there were followers of that dead teacher independent of, if not in rivalry to, the Christians in the place where the author wrote. Acts 18:24-19:7 has been often thought to indicate such a situation in Ephesus. At any rate, by far the great majority of critics are accustomed to style this writing the "Ephesian Gospel." The hypothesis has one point of obvious strength. There is no stronger rival. That he wrote in Greek appears to me highly probable despite the arguments of occasional champions of an Aramaic original.

Enough has been said to make argument unnecessary that the date of the gospel cannot be set before 100 A.D. Its use of the Synoptic gospels, its obvious antipathy to the Docetic heresy, its utter recasting and evaluation of the earlier traditions are definitive. On the other hand, it is known and quoted by the Muratorian fragment (*ca.* 170 A.D.). That it was used by Valentinian Gnostics, and so not later than 130 A.D., is felt by many critics probable, although the thesis has been expanded to unjustified lengths. Some have seen a probable reference to the ill-fated rebellion of Bar Cochba (132-135 A.D.) in the word, "If another shall come in his own name, him ye will receive" (5:43). Certainly Bar Cochba did claim to be the Messiah, and did receive a large support. That either Justin Martyr or Ignatius knew and used the gospel appears to me at least debatable. On the other hand, the spurious Markan appendix (Mark 16:9-20) does utilize it. By the last quarter of the second century its place in Christian Scripture was undoubted. It would seem most likely to have been penned during the first three or four decades of that century. The recent discovery of two papyrus fragments,[47] both of which are dated provisionally by experts about 150 A.D., would seem definitely to confirm this date as the *terminus ad quem*.

[47] See pp. 486 f.

PART III

THE LITERATURE OF THE CHRISTIAN MOVEMENT

SECTION II

ITS INCREASING SANCTITY AND TRANSMISSION

Chapter XLV

ON THE WAY TO A CANON

FEW problems which confront the student of Christian beginnings are more perplexing than those which involve the evolution of a canon of distinctly Christian writings.[1] How the separate writings arose is reasonably certain, although, as the preceding pages have made all too clear, many points are still obscure. That before the time of Eusebius several of these writings had come to achieve an assured position as inspired Scripture, equal in authority to those of the Old Testament, if not actually superior to them, and that they could be referred to as parts of a *New* Testament is sure. That Athanasius gives a list in 367 A.D. exactly coinciding with ours—no more, no less—is well known. A few fixed points like these are of inestimable assistance to the historian, but they also serve to reveal to him that far more is obscure than known. A vast degree of separate and fragmentary information about the different writings and the use different individuals and groups made of them is available. The problem lies in the assembly of these materials. How difficult a task this is is seen in the widely different results achieved by the many and competent scholars who have laboured with the problem. It is vastly easier to raise questions than to find adequate answers.

The one point about which no debate would seem possible is that throughout the first century and well into the second the Old Testament, Jewish Scripture, had remained the sacred book of the new religion. During these years letters and other writings had come from Christian pens, but had not been intended by their authors to rival or even to supplement the things which stood written. Eventually some of them came to achieve this status; but it was not overnight, but only as the result of a very gradual process that could scarcely have been foreseen in those early days.

From its beginning Christianity was a missionary religion. Prophets, teachers, missionaries—their title is of little moment—had been at work proclaiming their message. Christian groups were springing up like mushrooms through Asia Minor and Greece. Occasionally these teachers seemed to have felt a responsibility over the churches they had been instrumental in forming. At least this was true of Paul. When problems of difficulty arose, he wrote to his churches letters for their guidance and advice. Whether other teachers did the same in the early years we do not know. Only Paul's letters

[1] At this point pp. 203-205 should be reread. The first half of this chapter has appeared as a separate article in the *Crozer Quarterly*, Vol. 14, No. 2 (April, 1937).

have been preserved, and of them only a part. Some of these seem to have been felt by their recipients of sufficient worth to be preserved, and probably to be reread from time to time. While they were each specific in their purpose, occasionally they might prove of value to another, too. Thus the Colossians are to allow the Laodiceans to read their letter and are themselves to read the letter "from Laodicea."[2] It is very possible that an occasional letter may have been written by Paul with more than one church in mind, or at least have been sent by him to several.[3] Surely for those who consider Ephesians genuine no other hypothesis is feasible. There seems no evidence available that during Paul's lifetime formal copies of the letter received by one church were ever made for another. None the less the several churches must have known that such letters were in existence. Eventually Paul went to a martyr's death. Did that raise his prestige? Did that lead to the speedy desire on the part of his converts to get other memorials of him? It is impossible to say. At any rate by the opening decades of the second century, and perhaps earlier, Clement in Rome not only knows that the Corinthians had received a letter from Paul, but can direct them, "Take up the epistle of the blessed Paul the Apostle."[4] It was still in their possession. Ignatius of Antioch, in his letter to the Ephesians, refers to the apostle's mention of them "in every epistle."[5] To maintain that this *proves* that he had a collection of Paul's letters is absurd. On the other hand, since he appears to have been familiar with at least several of them, notably I Corinthians, Ephesians, Romans, Galatians, II Corinthians, and Philippians, it is possible, and even probable, that by this time some sort of collection of them had been made. Whether titles for them—"to the Romans," "to the Galatians," etc.—had by this time been produced cannot be said; at any rate, neither Clement nor Ignatius makes use of such titles. That such designations, however, must have arisen shortly after the letters had been collected is probable. The oft-cited word of Polycarp to the Philippians, that Paul "when he was absent wrote letters to you, from the study of which you will be able to build yourself up into the faith given you,"[6] by no means proves, as it has been often asserted, that Polycarp knew at least two letters to the Philippians from Paul's pen. Even less is it to be taken as an indication that our Philippians is an amalgam of two letters, separate in Polycarp's day but subsequently joined. On the other hand, the remark does confirm what was said of Clement's reference. The Pauline churches were still making use of Paul's letters. Futhermore, the fact that Polycarp's letter serves as a cover letter for a collection of the Ignatian letters which he (Polycarp) is sending to the Philip-

[2] Col. 4:16.
[3] Notably Romans; cf. pp. 231 f., 267 f.
[4] I Clem. 47:1.
[5] *ad Eph.* 12:2.
[6] *ad Phil.* 3:2.

pian church at its request,[7] and "from which [they] will be able to benefit greatly," leaves it scarcely open to question that similar collections of Paul's letters were now in use, and had prompted the desire for a collection of the letters of Ignatius. But indications are not wanting that many years earlier than this[8] such collections were available. That in the Apocalypse we have a collection of seven letters, ostensibly to churches in Asia Minor, but actually for all Christians everywhere, is in all probability due to the fact that Paul's letters by this time had been collected and were in wide use. Or again, while most of the Catholic epistles did not gain wide acceptance until many years after their composition, the thought of writing such epistles was not improbably prompted by a similar consideration. Does Acts give us any help in the matter of the collections of Pauline letters? Goodspeed thinks that it does. His thesis is that Acts served to arouse interest in Paul, and that as a consequence a reader who already knew two such letters (Colossians and Philemon) was prompted to go to the churches mentioned by Acts as founded by Paul to search for more; that having found these, he prefixed a cover letter of his own (Ephesians). Thus Goodspeed definitely dates the first collection of Paul's letters between the time of the composition of Acts and that of Revelation. Since I do not share his confidence that Acts evidences no trace of knowledge of the Pauline letters, I am inclined to hazard the guess that Acts did not create a new interest in Paul and the desire for more knowledge about him, but was rather a reflection of the already keen interest felt by Christians in the martyred Paul and is to no little degree indebted to the Pauline letters for information regarding Paul's itineraries and churches. Thus I find myself irresistibly drawn to the conclusion that by the end of the first century—pehaps even sooner—informal collection of Paul's letters might well have been found in the larger and more influential Christian centres, and have been read from time to time in the church services. This is not to imply that they had become canonical or were even considered inspired; simply that they were treasured and read. Before we raise the question as to what lifted them from this status to that of Scripture, it will be necessary to consider the rise of a quite different kind of writing.

Behind our gospels is a long story, but one which is still vague and for the most part unknown. Recently several German scholars have sought to pierce this unknown by their excursions back into the days before the gospels on the assumption that during those days Christian traditions were taking form, or, better said, that traditional words of Jesus and the story of an occasional act of his were being cast in the moulds or forms then in vogue, and in this form were being widely used in early preaching. Not infrequently older stories, which had been told first of one hero, then of an-

[7] *ad Phil.* 13:2.
[8] Polycarp was martyred 155 A.D.

other, had been given a distinctly Christian touch by turning them into exploits of Jesus. That these explanations of form criticism not infrequently cast genuine light is not to be denied; that they will serve as the key to unlock all the doors is far less certain.

Jesus himself never wrote anything, and few traditions to the contrary are known. To be sure, Eusebius preserves the curious story of Abgar, "monarch of the nations beyond the Euphrates," who sent a letter to Jesus requesting a cure, and of the letter which Jesus wrote in reply, promising to send one of his disciples.[9] Obviously a late and completely untrustworthy legend, it but heightens the wonder that no more of them came to be produced. On the other hand, apparently traditional words or sayings of Jesus and stories of his exploits were passed on by word of mouth from the earliest days as possessing especial value and significance. Occasionally Paul refers to such a word, and indicates that it was of the utmost importance. But these references are few and far between. Jesus is but rarely cited by him as an example; never is a gospel story appealed to or even mentioned.[10] It would thus seem hazardous in the extreme to infer that he possessed any sort of compendium of Jesus' words or deeds. And for many years much the same situation apparently prevailed. By the beginning of the second century we begin to find more frequent reference to "Synoptic tradition," but for the most part it is too vague to allow one to say from which gospel (if any of them) it comes. Occasionally this is very surprising. Apparently Mark was written well before the end of the first century; according to many scholars was especially intended for Rome. Yet Clement of Rome makes no quotation from it. All one can say is that he evidences a knowledge of Synoptic tradition.[11] Much the same is true of Ignatius, although, as will be mentioned in a moment, he apparently did know and use Matthew. The apparently scanty use by Christians, even a hundred years after Jesus' death, of the written gospels is amazing, and would appear to justify the view that when these gospels appeared (70-125 A.D.) they were by no means accorded universal acclaim. Independent evidence for this is often found in the word of the puzzling Papias, quoted by Eusebius. In the preface to his *Interpretations of the Oracles of the Lord*, a five-volume work which is now unhappily scarcely more than a title, but which was extant in the days of Eusebius, Papias is said to have remarked:

> And I shall not hesitate to append to the interpretations whatever I well learned from the elders and well remembered, for I have confidence in their truth. For unlike the majority of men I have not been wont to rejoice in those who talk much, but in those who teach the truth; not in those who recount the commands of others, but in those who bring to remembrance those commands given to the faith from the Lord and derived from the truth itself. And if there came one who

[9] *Hist. Eccl.* i,13.

[10] Cf. my *Ethics of Paul*, pp. 107-116.

[11] Cf. *The New Testament in the Apostolic Fathers*, especially the tabulations on pp. 137 f.

> had followed the elders I was ever wont to ask about the words of the elders, what Andrew or Peter had said or what Philip or Thomas or James or John or Matthew or any other of the Lord's disciples had said, and the things which Aristion and John the elder (*i.e.*, presbyter) were saying. For I was never wont to consider material from books as much benefit to me as that from a living and abiding voice.[12]

Perhaps this preference for the oral tradition was shared by others and may aid us in accounting for the absence of more detailed use of written gospels. On the other hand, it must not be overlooked that whatever preference he may have had for the living voice he himself was not only familiar with at least two of our gospels—Matthew and Mark—but also wrote a five-volume commentary on the "Oracles of the Lord." Furthermore, it appears to me highly probable that these "oracles" were our canonical Matthew. If this is the case, it would indicate that he must have prized it highly to devote so much attention to it.

And again it seems scarcely open to question that Ignatius did know and quote, not only Synoptic tradition, but the Gospel of Matthew. His reference to "the gospel"[13] may well evidence his belief that the gospel is what is contained in the book. The absence of distinctive titles for the several books surely was due to the authors' belief that what they were compiling was the Gospel of Jesus Christ—not of Peter or of Mark. These titles were later prefixed to distinguish the one from the other when they came to be used side by side by various churches. It is probable that before such collections were made a particular church or individual would not have had more than one such available. A title was superfluous. But was not even this stage preceded by one in which for the most part only the churches for which the particular gospels had been written had such instruments? Of course it is easy to overemphasize this unfamiliarity with written gospels. Obviously the framer of our Matthew had a copy of Mark or at least knew it thoroughly. Similarly Luke knew not only Mark, but other gospels as well, among which, I am inclined to believe, was probably Matthew. But with all allowances made, it still appears to me probable that when written gospels were beginning to be copied and made available for various churches, these various churches had their distinct preferences for one gospel or another. Eventually, and probably this was not much if any later than 150 A.D., collections of gospels arose. What led to this new move is not easy to say. That it was to combat Marcion's exclusive use of Luke has often been asserted, and is not impossible. On the other hand, it would appear that the comparatively wide use of the fourfold gospel shortly after the time of Marcion would make it more probable that this was no new development. It can scarcely be doubted that the appearance of the Gospel of John caused

[12] *Hist. Eccl.* iii,39:3 f.
[13] Cf. *ad Philadelph.* 9:2.

much difficulty and uncertainty among early Christians. It was so different, not only in form, but in content and emphasis, from the other gospels and from the oral traditions. The many statements still preserved, which seek to explain and justify the differences between them, bear significant testimony. In the Muratorian fragment[14] the lavish commendation of this gospel—it had been authorized by divine revelation and had been approved by John's fellow disciples and bishops—and the express statement, "Thus while different ideas are taught in the various books of the gospels, yet there is no difference in the faith of believers, since in all everything is declared by one principal spirit, concerning the birth, passion, resurrection, conversation with his disciples, and his twofold advent," suggest an earlier period of conflict and of opposition to this *advena*. Thus it may very well be that the earliest move to collect the gospels into a unit was the work of those who were zealous for the Fourth Gospel and who hoped in this way to gain for it a wider reading than it might have achieved alone.

This early selection of gospels—if the above suggestion which has commended itself to many scholars be accepted, the scene of this collection would most probably be in the environs of the Fourth Gospel itself, probably Asia Minor—was not intended as a body of inspired Scripture. It served a twofold purpose: First, it would gain for John a wider recognition by allying it with the other writings which were coming to be looked upon with favour and to be read in the church services. Second, by this gathering of the separate accounts into something of a unit, if not a unity, the prejudice of the various churches against several and different gospels would be in a measure overcome.

The Old Testament still remained the sole Scripture; prophetic in every page of him whose sayings and doings were now being read in the various churches, it continued to be the great authority. In a curious and perplexing passage Ignatius apparently says:

> For I heard some men saying, "If I find it not in the charters, I do not believe (it?) in the gospel;" and when I said to them that it is in the Scripture, they answered me, "That is precisely the question." But to me the charters are Jesus Christ, the inviolable charter is his cross and his death and resurrection and faith through him; by these I desire to be justified by your prayers.[15]

In the opening sentence a change in punctuation would alter the meaning by making the "charters" identical with the gospel. But apparently Ignatius is referring to a group to whom the Old Testament is the sole authority. Unless its prophecies coincide with the gospel stories, the latter are not valid for them. Ignatius, on the contrary, would appear to attach some independent value to the latter as embodying the real Christian gospel. Does this reference

[14] *Muratorian Fragment,* lines 9-23.

[15] *ad Philadelph.* 8:2.

to the "gospel" indicate one of the books we know as gospels, perhaps Matthew, or is it simply a reference to the Synoptic tradition? While I am inclined to think the former is not impossible, any dogmatic statement is unwise. Whatever Ignatius' own attitude to these later writings may have been, it would appear that he witnesses the prevailing authority of the inherited Bible.

Probably much the same situation is to be seen in the writings of Justin Martyr. That he knows written gospels is scarcely debatable. Several times he refers to the "memoirs" composed by the Apostles, once specifically adding, "which are called gospels."[16] He never cites them by name, although once he apparently refers to the Gospel of Mark as the memoirs of Peter.[17] How many such gospels he knows cannot be said with entire confidence. His quotations from the Old Testament are often inexact and occasionally are referred to the wrong prophet. This informality of quotation must be borne in mind in the matter of possible gospel quotations. That he knew and cited Matthew, Mark, and Luke is reasonably sure; with regard to John the matter is much more doubtful. Any detailed statement would lead us far afield. Suffice it to say that it would appear to me probable that while he did know the writing, his failure to cite it to buttress an occasional argument, when such citations lay ready at hand—especially in regard to his belief in Christ's preëxistence—preferring to use a far less apt word from one of the other gospels, bears clear evidence that either he himself considered it of less authority or recognized its less secure status in Christian circles generally. It is furthermore to be observed that his several references to incidents in the life of Jesus not recorded in any of our canonical gospels—the birth of Jesus in a cave,[18] the fire in the Jordan at the time of the baptism,[19] the word, "This day have I begotten thee"[20]—suggest that he was familiar with and used other written gospels or oral traditions. Thus Justin cannot be legitimately cited to prove that in his day our four gospels and they alone had achieved a unique place in Christian circles. Nor does his statement that they were read with the Prophets in the Sunday services indicate that they were as yet regarded as inspired Scripture. On the other hand, this regular practice of reading them in the church services together with canonical Scripture was to be of greatest significance. Let these canonical Scriptures be challenged by a heretic and the attempt be made to substitute distinctly Christian writings for them, and scandalized orthodoxy would be confronted by a twofold problem: the necessity of defending the old Scriptures; the impossibility of giving a lower estimate to the distinctly

[16] *Apol.* i,66,3.
[17] *Dial.* 106.
[18] *Ibid.*, 78.
[19] *Ibid.*, 88.
[20] *Ibid.*, 88 (end).

Christian writings than the heretic had done. By doing precisely this, Marcion precipitated a crisis which resulted in a canon of Christian Scripture.

The significance of Marcion in the emergence of a Christian canon of Scripture cannot be over-emphasized. It is difficult fairly to appraise the man, for almost all that we know of him comes through those who bitterly hated him. His particular enemy was Tertullian who devoted five books to the refutation of his views, thereby, of course, immortalizing the notions he sought to destroy. Despite Tertullian's often lurid rhetoric and the legends that soon grew up about this archheretic, it is safe to say that he was not only the most influential of second-century heretics, but far superior in critical insight to most of his orthodox contemporaries. He was a native of Pontus,[21] born about 100 A.D., and came to Rome in the middle of the second century. Soon his relations with the Roman church became strained, and he was eyed askance. The story that by seducing a virgin he incurred the displeasure of his father, a bishop in Sinope, and despite his entreaties failed to gain absolution is probably to be set down as a legend arising from his "seduction of the church." Equally improbable is the story that his break with the Roman church was due to his anger at not being appointed bishop. Few facts about his life are known. Apparently he traveled a great deal. Ephraem the Syrian compares him to Cain the wanderer; Tertullian frequently styles him *nauclerus.*

Apparently he considered himself an orthodox and Pauline Christian. Not the mythical speculations so stressed by other Gnostics but the Christian revelation was central in his thinking. His real point of cleavage with orthodox Christianity lay in his denial of unity to the First Principle. There were two gods, a just God depicted in the Jewish Scripture and a good God revealed in Christianity. The one demanded "an eye for an eye and a tooth for a tooth," the other "To him that smiteth thee on the one cheek offer also the other." The God of the Jewish Scripture could say, "I create evil" (Isa. 45:7; cf. Amos 3:6). Since a good tree cannot bear evil fruit, such a God cannot himself be good. Thus for Marcion the true word of Jesus read "I am not come to fulfil the law, but to destroy it." Nor was this God of the Jews the Supreme Intelligence: he could not find Adam when the latter hid from him. The just God was the creator of the material universe; the good God remained undivulged until, taking pity on mankind brought as it was into such woe by the creator, he interfered for its redemption. This interference was all the more startling for it was completely unheralded in the Scriptures. In the Old Testament a deliverer was foretold, but this Christ of the prophets was not the Christ of the Christians, but a deliverer of the Jews, a man of war, not the Christian man of peace.

[21] For a good example of Tertullian's power in invective the student may be referred to the preface of his *adv. Marcion.* (i,1).

Thus Marcion was irrevocably opposed to any Jewish note in Christianity. The Old Testament which until his time had been the sole authoritative and inspired Scripture for Christians was rejected *in toto*. This necessitated a new canon in its place. Paul was his hero; he too had been in conflict with the Jews. Thus Marcion took as the nucleus of his Scripture the ten letters of Paul which he considered genuine and arranged them in order of their apparent anti-Jewishness—Galatians, I and II Corinthians, Romans, I and II Thessalonians, Laodiceans (Ephesians), Colossians, Philippians, and Philemon. It is probable that he subjected them to some sort of editing to prune out the too-favorable references to Judaism. To what extent this was done is not certain. The Pastoral Epistles he did not include. A not improbable reason for this exclusion was his sound belief that they were not from the pen of Paul; recently, however, Professor Riddle has made a strong case for the view that the Pastorals were not known to Marcion, but produced at a later time to combat him.[22] In addition to this *apostolicon* he accepted the Gospel of Luke, in a somewhat altered form. The precise degree of alteration is not certain. That he omitted the birth story is clear. Apparently the gospel was made to begin, "In the fifteenth year of Tiberius he (or God?) came down to Capernaum, a city of Galilee, and taught on the Sabbath days." But that his text, by and large, of the gospel was not a fair approximation of the one he had inherited is not lightly to be assumed. Tertullian charges him with refusing to accept the writings of apostles, that is, the other gospels,[23] because Paul had accused these apostles of perverting the gospel of Christ. He further waxes caustic: "Marcion . . . ascribes no author to his Gospel, as if it could not be allowed him to affix a title to that from which it was no crime to subvert the very body!"[24] To what extent the titles had become commonly employed for the different gospels in Marcion's time is hard to say. If, as has been suggested above, a collection of them had been already made, it is probable that at that time the titles had been affixed. Furthermore, that Marcion did not accept the book of Acts is no particular source of surprise. When the gospels were collected, that would of necessity have required the separation of the second half of the "writing to Theophilus"; the early pages of this writing might well have seemed to Marcion to overbalance the later enthusiasm for Paul. In addition to this gospel and *apostolicon* he composed his own writing, the *Antitheses*, in which he argued by a series of antithetical passages that not only was the Old Testament contradicted by the Christian Scriptures, but that it was in constant contradiction to itself. Whether Marcion gave to this composition a rank equal

[22] D. W. Riddle, *Early Christian Life*, pp. 195-216.

[23] This would also account for his disregard of those of the so-called Catholic epistles which he knew.

[24] *adv. Marcion.* iv,2.

to his canonical Scripture is perhaps not clear. If Tertullian is to be believed, his followers apparently regarded it very highly.[25]

The importance of this step of Marcion's cannot be too highly stressed. Hitherto Christian writings had been slowly gaining in favour. It is by no means improbable that the gospels and the letters of Paul were coming to be read in the Christian services as providing valuable information and instruction. Surely this was the case by the time of Justin Martyr and II Peter; nor is there any indication that this practice had arisen overnight. But, none the less, whatever use had been made of them prior to Marcion, they were distinctly subordinate in authority to the Old Testament; at most they were read *with* them. Justin's statement to Trypho the Jew reflects the Christian attitude to the Old Testament which had prevailed from the earliest day:

> For these words have neither been prepared by me, nor embellished by the art of man; but David sang them, Isaiah preached them, Zechariah proclaimed them, and Moses wrote them. Are you acquainted with them, Trypho? They are contained in your Scriptures, or rather not yours, but ours. For we believe them, but you, though you read them, do not catch the spirit that is in them.[26]

Marcion's polemic against them and his substitution of other writings forced the issue. If his new canon had been simply his own writings, it might have been contemptuously dismissed. By his choice of writings already highly esteemed the matter became more serious. Could the orthodox afford to accord less reverence for their own writings than did Marcion? His enthusiasm for the epistles of Paul may well have led his contemporary Justin to tactful silence about them, but even this caution soon yields to an equally enthusiastic acceptance not only of the ten, but also of the Pastorals, and, in some circles, of Hebrews. For example, in the first year of Commodus (180 A.D.), in the North African town of Scili, to the query of the Roman proconsul, "What kind of thing have you in your (church) case?" the Christian Speratus retorts, "Books and the epistles of Paul, a just man."[27] Just what is to be understood by "books" is perhaps debatable, although it is highly probable that it would include one at least of the Christian gospels together with some of the Old Testament Scriptures. But it is also to be noted that in this collection of writings to be used in the church services were some at least of the Pauline letters.

Although orthodox Christians could not afford to ignore or deny the writings which Marcion selected, they did find an answer ready at hand. Not only had he perversely rejected the Scriptures, prophetic on every page of the Christ, but had also dishonoured and misused even those writ-

[25] *adv. Marcion.* iv,4: "They receive his *Antitheses*; and more than that, make ostentatious use of them."

[26] *Dial.* 29.

[27] *Passio Sanctorum Scilitanorum* in *Texts and Studies,* Vol. I, No. 2 (1891), p. 114.

ings which he professed to revere. He had shamefully mutilated the letters of Paul, and with them and an emasculated Luke was seeking to attack Christians with their own writings. Thus naturally, precisely these writings which he either had denied or dismembered must now become for an outraged orthodoxy weapons both of defence and offence. A single front was necessary. There had been too much individual action, too many independent opinions, in the past. A common foe demanded a common answer. The faith which had been delivered once and for all was under fire; all must rally to its defence. This crisis may well have led may conservative Christians who had still retained a preference for the "living voice" as against written books to rally to the defence of the latter. And the union of the separate gospels, each endeared to various churches, was no longer seen as an effort to let one of them ride into popularity on the crest of the others. It was the God-given answer to those who would try to put asunder what God had joined together. This temper is exactly illustrated by Irenæus. After deploring the attitude of a Marcion or a Valentinus—the one perverting Luke, the other torturing John—he reveals the answer of orthodoxy:

> It is not possible that the gospels can be either more or fewer in number than they are. For, since there are four zones of the world in which we live, and four principal winds, while the church is scattered throughout all the world, and the "pillar and ground" of the church is the gospel and the spirit of life; it is fitting that she should have four pillars, breathing out immortality on every side, and vivifying men afresh. From which fact, it is evident that the Word, the Artificer of all, he that sitteth upon the cherubim, and contains all things, he who was manifested to men, has given us the gospel under four aspects, but bound together by one Spirit. . . . These things being so, all who destroy the form of the gospel are vain, unlearned, and also audacious; those who represent the aspects of the gospel as being either more in number than as aforesaid, or, on the other hand, fewer.[28]

That for Irenæus the four gospels are inspired Scripture, canonical in all save name, few will deny. Essentially the same attitude is seen in the word of Theophilus of Antioch (177 A.D.):

> Moreover, concerning the righteousness which the law required, confirmatory utterances are found both with the prophets and in the gospels, because they all spoke inspired by one Spirit of God.[29]

That of these gospels John's was one is evident from his express reference on an earlier page of the same writing (ii,22).

But Marcion had done more than to force orthodox Christianity to a clear-cut attitude toward the various gospels and letters of Paul. He had thrust Paul forward as an opponent to the other apostles—as Matthew,

[28] *adv. Hær.* iii,11,8 f.
[29] *ad Autolycum* iii,12.

Peter, John. Is it surprising, then, that Irenæus quotes extensively from Acts and constantly emphasizes the harmony that existed between Paul and the other apostles and the impudence of those who assert that Paul alone knew the truth? It is very possible that the attitude of Marcion brought Acts back into prominence. When first produced, it had enjoyed whatever favour the Gospel of Luke had gained. It was a part of that writing. When, however, the four gospels had been collected, the second half of the Lucan writing had of necessity been separated. Just what was its status as a separate writing? Apparently for some decades it occupied a sort of limbo, although it may well have set the fashion for other writings which purported to chronicle the doings of this apostle or that. Now toward the end of the second century it once more achieves a popularity which it was never again to lose. It served as a very valuable link between the gospels on the one hand and the epistles of Paul on the other. The fact that it not only gave a connected story of Paul's activity but portrayed him as a friend of the other apostles must have seemed a powerful answer to the assertions of Marcion. Furthermore, it filled an obvious gap. Many of the apostles had left no writings behind them. On the other hand, during the second century several writings had been produced which either purported to be by members of the Twelve or at least were so regarded by some Christians. Here too, Acts was a valuable book. It provided a sort of link whereby these apostolic writings could be joined not only to the gospels—in which their several authors were described—but to the somewhat similar letters of Paul, their fellow apostle. Thus the book seems to have been of value in many ways in the formation of definite and distinct collections of Christian Scripture out of originally separate groups of writings. With regard to these letters of apostles much latitude of opinion existed. Irenæus refers to I Peter and a letter of John (I and II John); others, as Clement of Alexandria and Tertullian, would also include Jude. On the other hand, while Jude and at least two epistles of John, of which I John is certainly one, are referred to in the Muratorian canon, I Peter is ignored. And, as will be mentioned in a moment, the Assyrian churches disregarded all of them.

One other type of writing must be briefly mentioned here—the apocalypses. The Revelation of John was known and cited with approval by Justin. Irenæus quotes it extensively and as Scripture. It has its place not only in the Muratorian canon, but in the writings of Clement of Alexandria and Tertullian. Later it was to prove a storm centre, but during the second century it was highly popular and apparently shared the increasing reverence which the books already mentioned were receiving. In a word, there is no evidence that during the second century any orthodox collection of Christian writings omitted the Revelation.[30] Nor did it stand alone. The *Revelation of Peter* and the *Shepherd of Hermas* were also known and

[30] But see the next footnote.

popular. Clement of Alexandria accepted both of them on the same plane with the Revelation of John. In the Muratorian canon, however, it is stated that since the *Shepherd* was recently written it is not to be read publicly in church, but may be read privately; the *Revelation of Peter* is joined to that of John, but with a warning note:

> We receive also the Apocalypses of John and Peter, although some among us are unwilling to have [the latter?] read in the church.[31]

Tertullian, although he had earlier been attracted to the *Shepherd*, bitterly condemns it as the "shepherd of adulterers" in his later writings. The *Revelation of Peter* he never mentions. Thus the evidence would seem to indicate that this type of writing soon lapsed into disfavour, although the one bearing the name of John remained in favour in the West.

Toward the end of the second century a situation had arisen which would have scandalized the first generation of Christians. The Old Testament no longer stood alone as Scripture. Other writings of different kinds had come to invade that sacred precinct: (1) Four gospels, (2) thirteen letters of the apostle Paul, (3) the book of Acts known at least in some circles as the "Acts of all the Apostles," (4) a few letters bearing the names of members of the Twelve, and (5) several apocalypses attributed to John, Peter, and Hermas.

By no means entire unanimity of opinion prevailed. So far as the gospels were concerned, our present four held undisputed sway. Other gospels were known and continued to be used by occasional groups. Clement of Alexandria bears evidence to the popularity of the Gospels of the Hebrews and of the Egyptians, but, while not condemning them himself, shows that in his estimation they did not occupy an equal position with the other four. Serapion, bishop of Antioch (190-203?), is said by Eusebius to have heard that the Gospel of Peter was in use by Christians in the town of Rhossus. He himself was not at the time familiar with its contents, but later read it and discovered that "most of it belonged to the right teaching of the Saviour, but some things were additions." What his final judgment was is not reported. This indicates, however, that the writing was in use in some circles, but was by no means universally known. During the second half of the second century the Assyrian Tatian, who had become a Christian in Rome, and a pupil of Justin Martyr, made a harmony of the four gospels for the Assyrian church. This work, known as the *Diatessaron*, was all but universal in the Assyrian church until the fifth century, despite the fact that its compiler was adjudged (on other grounds) a heretic by all save the Assyrians. This evidence would appear to cut in both directions. Tatian's selection of the four gospels evidences their dominance in

[31] *Muratorian Fragment,* lines 71-73. Probably this is the meaning, but the translation "them" is certainly allowed by the ambiguous Latin.

Rome; on the other hand, his freedom in recasting the material, his use of John as the framework, with his rearrangement of such incidents as the interview with Nicodemus which he placed in the last winter of Jesus' life, his recognition of the fact that divergent accounts (as the Cleansing of the Temple or the Healing of the Blind at Jericho) do not mean separate incidents—all this indicates that the gospels had not achieved a sacrosanctness which precluded change or rearrangement.

The Pastoral Epistles were now regularly a part of the "Apostle" in all circles. Hebrews is mentioned for the first time by Clement of Alexandria as Pauline, although he recognizes a difference in style which he feels obliged to explain as due to translation. The East followed his judgment, but without sharing his scholarly qualms. At least, Hebrews appears subsequently in all lists of Pauline letters. The West, however, did not finally accept it as Pauline for more than two centuries. It is unmentioned in the Muratorian canon. Tertullian knows it, but ascribes it to Barnabas, "a man sufficiently accredited by God, as being one whom Paul has stationed next to himself in the uninterrupted observance of abstinence."[32]

Of the Catholic epistles I Peter and I John appear to have been in pretty general use in all save the Assyrian churches, although, as has already been remarked, I Peter is not included in the Muratorian canon. Curiously enough, the little Epistle of Jude seems to have gained early favour in the West. II Peter and James, however, remain unmentioned. On the other hand, the epistles attributed to Barnabas and Clement (I Clement) apparently possessed equal weight in the eyes of Clement of Alexandria with I Peter and I John. Tertullian remarks, "The Epistle of Barnabas is more generally received among the churches than that apocryphal 'shepherd' of adulterers" [*i.e.,* Hermas]. The fact that Barnabas and I Clement are found in two early manuscripts further attests their early popularity which sustained itself in some circles at least.

Thus by the end of the second century the Church had produced a group—or, better said, various groups—of writings which were not only highly prized and read regularly in the service alongside the Old Testament, but which had come to be regarded as authoritative and inspired. That each Christian or group of Christians regarded each particular writing which it chanced to have as equal in authority to every other is by no means clear. Did the Catholic epistles or even Acts appear to Clement of Alexandria as equal in authority to the gospels and the Apostle? None the less they are Scripture. Regularly they are cited or referred to in the precise terms ascribed to writings of the Old Testament. Furthermore, it is to be observed that for Irenæus there are precisely twenty-two writings in the distinctly Christian Scripture, just as there is the same number of books in the Old Testament. He does not indeed give to this

[32] *de Pudicitia* 20.

collection any specific designation, but apparently even the title *New Testament* had been born before the end of the century. A letter by Melito, bishop of Sardis (*ca.* 180 A.D.) is preserved by Eusebius[33] in which a specific reference to the "books of the Old Testament" is made. This term certainly implies a contrast with a *New* Testament. No such word by Melito is preserved. On the other hand, Eusebius refers to a nameless writer against the Montanists, in the time of Apolinarius, who expressed his own hesitation to write "from timidity and scruples lest I might seem to some to be adding to the writings or injunctions of the word of the new testament (covenant) of the gospel, to which no one who has chosen to live according to the gospel itself can add and from which he cannot take away."[34]

The work had been done. The new religion was now equipped with its Scripture. The older writings had not been displaced. Marcion's shafts had failed. But alongside these writings were now others. Years of usage in the various churches had given them an increasing sanctity. By his attempt to oust the older writings and to replace them by some of his own choosing Marcion had written unwittingly an important page in church history. His challenge could not pass unnoticed. The writings which he had stolen and garbled were already precious. His collections gave rise to others. In this there seemed to be no new or radical step. As the various writings, long prized by the great majority of Christians severally, came to be generally recognized, it must have seemed to Christians everywhere simply a vindication of their own judgment, a clear and definite expression of what had been perhaps vague and what they had not said in so many words, but to which none the less they could respond with a simple "Of course."

Uniformity, however, does not arise overnight. However valuable it might be for all Christians to present an unbroken front to their enemies, however they might agree that "every scripture inspired of God is also profitable for teaching, for reproof, for correction, for instruction which is righteousness," there was as yet no complete agreement as to just which scripture had been inspired and which not. Three classes of books had come into view: (1) Those that all save occasional heretics like Marcion accepted. These writings comprised the bulk of our present New Testament, *viz.,* four gospels, Acts, and thirteen Pauline letters. (2) Books challenged by some (or even quite ignored) but later received. These comprised Hebrews, James, II John, III John, Jude, II Peter, and even I Peter and I John. Whether Revelation should be placed in this class or in the preceding is debatable. Apparently it was not until the beginning of the next century that it fell into general disfavour in the East; but that it was accepted in the Assyrian churches in the second century would appear utterly improbable. (3) Those received and read by some but ultimately rejected.

[33] *Hist. Eccl.* iv,26,13 f.
[34] *Ibid.,* v,16,3.

Among this more fluid group were the Gospel of Peter, the Revelation of Peter, the Shepherd of Hermas, Barnabas, I Clement, and II Clement. The century had been a period of individual circulation and gradual collection, first by sections, as the four gospels, the Pauline body, a group of Apostolic letters to which the Acts was appended, and a group of apocalypses. Then, as I have tried to sketch out, came a collection of the various sections into a more or less flexible group which speedily assumed its place as such beside the similar group of older writings. The whole was the result of the judgment first of individual Christians, then, if I may so phrase it, of organized Christians, as to which books were and which were not of value, that is, were or were not to be read in the churches.

What did these New Testaments look like? Probably in the great majority of cases they were comprised of a series of parchment rolls, each containing but one of the various books, save perhaps in the case of the shorter letters. On the other hand, it is not possible to be dogmatic even here. Until recently it was considered axiomatic that the earliest appearance of the fourfold gospel in one book could not antedate the third century. No parchment roll could contain more than a single gospel. And there was no evidence that the codex was in use before the third century. But in 1931 twelve biblical papyri were discovered in Egypt; they threw a new light on the whole matter. These papyri were codices, *i.e.,* books not written on a roll made up of a continuous sheet, but with quires of pages as in a modern volume, and thus able to contain vastly more material. And one of these codices has been dated by experts as not later then the second century, perhaps as early as 150 A.D. To be sure, this codex does not happen to contain the gospels, but Numbers and Deuteronomy; but it proves that the much more inclusive codex was known and used by Christians in the second century. Apparently then there would be no real ground to deny the possibility that Irenæus may have had, not a collection of four rolls, but a single volume containing all four gospels in its pages. This is of course only a possibility, but it is not to be ignored. That such copies were common is not for a moment to be thought. Their cost must have been far too great. On the other hand, the existence of the codex form of volume, making possible the inclusion of a far greater amount of material, may well have been a distinct aid in collecting and combining the hitherto separate writings.

The remainder of the story of the formation of the canon must be briefly sketched, for while of distinct interest it is of far less importance than that already told. During the next two hundred years not only were the various writings quoted copiously, but the lines were more sharply drawn. What were the conclusions reached in the various sections of the church?

Popular practice in Alexandria was quite different from that in the more conservative West and also from that in the East, as is illustrated by remarks of Origen in his homilies. As a scholar he had classified various writings as "acknowledged" and "disputed." The former comprised the four gospels, Acts, fourteen letters of Paul—like his predecessor Clement he here included Hebrews, although more cautiously—the Revelation of John, I Peter, and I John; which, totalling twenty-two, exactly matched the Old Testament. Among the "disputed" books were James, II and III John, II Peter, Jude, Barnabas, and the Shepherd of Hermas. Although as a scholar Origen had drawn his line between the two classes of writing to conform to the practice of Christians in other parts of the church, it would appear that in his own judgment all twenty-nine were worthy of their place in Christian Scripture. Thus in a homily on Joshua he writes:

> So too our Lord, whose advent was typified by the son of Nun, when he came sent his apostles as priests bearing well-wrought trumpets. Matthew first sounded the priestly trumpet in his gospel. Mark also, Luke and John, each gave forth a strain on their priestly trumpets. Peter, moreover, sounds loudly on the *twofold* trumpet of his epistle; so also James and Jude. Still the number is incomplete and John gives forth the trumpet-sound in his *epistles* and apocalypse; and Luke while describing the Acts of the apostles. Lastly, however, came he who said, "I think that God hath set forth us apostles last of all," and thundering on the fourteen trumpets of his epistles threw down even to the ground the walls of Jericho, that is to say, all the instruments of idolatry and the doctrines of philosophers.[35]

For many years the Assyrian church went its own course. The four gospels in their combined form (*Diatessaron*) had formed the nucleus of the sacred writings. To these and Acts Paul's fourteen letters were added; whether or not Tatian had translated them into Syriac is by no means as certain as many modern statements would suggest. A list from about 400 A.D. gives these nineteen (by this time the separate gospels were beginning to displace the *Diatessaron*) and adds the word, "This is all."[36] Not until the first quarter of the fifth century were any of the Catholic epistles in use, and then only James, I Peter, and I John.[37] A century later the remaining four epistles were translated together with the Revelation of John. But even then many Syriac-speaking Christians preferred the earlier translation with its more limited list.

Eusebius followed Origen in attempting to be faithful to the varying attitudes of different branches of the church. In addition to these writings which were either "acknowledged" or "disputed"[38] were the "spurious" (*nothoi*) or "rejected," which included the Acts of Paul, Hermas, the Revela-

[35] *Hom. in Jos.* vii,1 (quoted by Westcott, *On the Canon of the New Testament,* 7th ed., p. 368).

[36] In this list I Timothy is accidentally omitted.

[37] Namely in the Peshitto, for an account of which see pp. 501-503.

[38] The latter included James, Jude, II Peter, and II and III John.

tion of Peter, Barnabas, the Didache, and "perhaps the Revelation of John." It is not without interest to observe that he follows his preceptor Origen in ignoring I Clement, although Clement of Alexandria had used it along with the other Catholic epistles. Just as in the East there was a distinct animus against the Revelation and at least a coolness toward many of the Catholic epistles—for example, Chrysostom used but three of the Catholics and rejected Revelation; Theodore of Mopsuestia ignored all eight—so in the West for many years there was a tendency to accept only two or three of the Catholics and to reject Hebrews entirely. In fact, Hilary of Poitiers (died 367 A.D.) was the first in the West to accord Hebrews a place in Christian Scripture. But gradually these difficulties were ironed out. The prestige of names like Augustine, Jerome, and Athanasius was great. The letter of Jerome to Claudianus Postumus Dardanus well reveals the growing attitude to uniformity and suggests that the story is drawing to a close. In this letter, written in 414 A.D., he remarks:

> This is to say to our friends, that this epistle which is inscribed "to the Hebrews" is received not only by the churches of the East, but also by all church writers of the Greek tongue before our day, as of Paul the apostle, although many think it is from Barnabas or Clement. And it makes no difference whose it is, since it is from a churchman, and is celebrated in the daily readings of the churches. And if the usage of the Latins does not receive it among the canonical Scriptures, neither, indeed, by the same liberty do the churches of the Greeks receive the Revelation of John. And yet we accept both, in that we follow by no means the habit of today, but the authority of ancient writers, who for the most part quote each of them, not as they are sometimes accustomed to do the apocrypha, and even also as they use rarely the examples of the profane books, but as canonical and churchly.[39]

Nearly a half-century before, Athanasius of Alexandria in his famous *Festal Letter* had listed the writings of the Old Testament and of the New. The latter list agrees precisely with the twenty-seven writings in use today. Following the lists he remarks:

> These are the springs of salvation so that the thirsty may be filled with the utterance within them. In these alone is proclaimed the good news of the teaching of true religion. Let no one add to them nor remove aught from them. Concerning them did the Lord in shame of the Sadducees say, "Ye do err, not knowing the Scriptures," and exhorted the Jews, "Search the Scriptures because these are they which bear witness of me." But for the sake of greater accuracy this also I add, writing of necessity, that there are other books apart from these, not to be sure in the list (κανονιζόμενα), but produced by the fathers to be read by (to?) those who are on the point of coming forward to be instructed in the word of true religion: the Wisdom of Solomon and the Wisdom of Sirach and Esther and Judith and Tobit and the so-called Didache of the Apostles and the Shepherd.

[39] *Epist.* 129.

And nevertheless, beloved, although the former are in the list and the latter are read, there is absolutely no mention of the secret writings (τῶν ἀποκρύφων), but they are a contrivance of heretics, writing them when they will, bestowing upon them and adding to them times in order that they may have the excuse for deceiving those as yet undefiled by producing them as though they were ancient.

These utterances, however, were not revolutionary. Bishops and clerics then as now rarely set the fashion. They simply affirm in ponderous tones what the majority of their constituents are taking for granted. The councils obediently ratified what the churches had decided, and penalized any variations. Thus the third Council of Carthage in 397 A.D. declared that "none except canonical writings were to be read in church under the title of divine Scripture." But even yet no absolute agreement existed. Still some in the East omitted one book or another. In the West Cassiodorus (560 A.D.) revealed his conservatism by omitting four of the Catholic epistles and also Hebrews.[40] Though a native of Italy, he may well have been influenced in part by his Syrian forbears. On the other hand, the Ethiopian church preferred a long list of thirty-five books. But these were simply aberrations. The work had been done; and it had been done by the end of the second century. From then on it is to be remembered that not only had a very general agreement been reached as to which books belonged in the canon, but, far more important than that, the revolutionary view had become orthodox that in this canon distinctly Christian writings had their place.

For a thousand years after the age of the councils there was little or no new work. Then in the fifteenth and sixteenth centuries new investigations were started in the course of which it became all too clear that the position of the earlier disputed seven (Hebrews, Revelation, James, Jude, II Peter, II and III John) was none too solid. Erasmus (1466-1536) raised cautious questions about Hebrews, Revelation, II and III John. Luther (1483-1546) placed James, Hebrews, Jude, and Revelation in a distinctly lower class than the other twenty-three. Others, like Karlstadt (1480-1541), Œcolampadius (1482-1531), and Calvin (1509-1564), showed clearly that they felt far less awe toward these "disputed" books than to the others. For the Roman church the Council of Trent (1546), although not a general council, uttered the final word (although its word regarding the "authentic text" caused no little scholastic heartburn).[41] Partly to defend the Word, but more particularly to oppose the reformers, it declared the Old Testament (including the Apocrypha, that is, Tobit, Judith, Wisdom, Ecclesiasticus, I and II Maccabees) and the New Testament *sacri et canonici*, and invoked a curse on

[40] *de Inst. div. Litt.* xiv,2. Some scholars would dispute this statement, since some texts add Hebrews.

[41] See pp. 501 f.

all who failed so to regard them. The concluding words of the decree are of interest:

> If, however, anyone does not receive the entire books with all their parts as they are accustomed to be read in the Catholic Church and are found in the old Latin Vulgate edition as sacred and canonical, and knowingly and wittingly despises the aforesaid tradition, let him be anathema.

Although for the multifarious branches and twigs of Protestantism there can be no such convenient pronouncement, the matter is as surely closed. Occasionally "shorter Bibles" continue to make their appearance; now and then some enthusiast gets a brainstorm and plans a new Scripture which will include all the things of value in all the sacred writings of the various religions. Some of these undertakings are not without value, but it would appear that the twenty-seven writings which were hammered out on the primitive anvils and scrutinized and tested for many years by many groups before they received their final approval, that is, unquestioning use, will continue for many a decade for better or for worse to occupy the place they achieved.

Chapter XLVI

MANUSCRIPTS AND MEN

Brief mention has already been made of the reason for the study of the text of the various New Testament writings, namely, the fact that the original books themselves, technically known as autographs, are not (known to be) in existence and that in their place are thousands of copies, many in Greek, more in other languages into which at different times the Greek had been rendered.[1] As will be mentioned presently, occasional tiny papyrus fragments dating perhaps from the second and third centuries have been discovered. Their value is immense, but they preserve but a few verses and are of little significance for reconstructing the text as a whole. To this there is one exception. In 1931 the discovery of a group of papyri obtained in Egypt by A. Chester Beatty was announced. The discovery of these papyri, twelve in number, throws a great deal of new light. Three of them, dated by experts in the third century, contain substantial parts of the whole New Testament. One of these originally contained all four gospels and Acts, another the Pauline epistles, a third the Revelation of John.[2] Save for these various papyri the oldest manuscripts are not earlier than the fourth century. Two of them, B and ℵ, in many ways the most valuable textually as well as the oldest, are generally dated in the fourth century. Perhaps fifteen more may be dated in the fifth or sixth century. The great bulk of Greek manuscripts giving in whole or part the New Testament, rather more than three thousand in number, are much later.

All of them were of course written by hand. Thus it is not surprising that no two of them are identical. In the first place it is humanly impossible to copy any considerable piece of writing without introducing many unintentional changes. Recently I had occasion to transcribe a paragraph. Upon rereading it I discovered I had written "Jerusalem" for Rome. What mental quirk caused that error must be referred to the psychologists. Some years ago I prepared typewritten copy of proposed courses for the seminary catalogue. In the description of one of the courses it was unfortunately necessary to write "Reading of the Greek text will not be required." The catalogue appeared with its surprising information, "Reading of Greek textbooks will not be required." Here the apparently unintentional alteration of "text" to "textbooks" had introduced the intentional deletion of

[1] At this time pp. 206, 208 should be reread.

[2] For their significance see pp. 470, 487.

"the." But these examples—and the list could, of course, be indefinitely extended—embraced errors in copying perfectly legible printed or typed copy. In the case of ancient manuscripts many other elements enter the picture. Words were not written separately, but with unspaced letters. Thus it was very easy to make faulty divisions in copying. For example, an ancient Latin text read . . . *palam includi; turpia enim,* but the letters PALAMINCLUDITURPIAENIM . . . were regularly misdivided *palam includitur pia enim.* One editor "corrected" *pia* to *piacula!* The child who misread THISISAWORMDONOTSTEPONIT as "This is a warm doughnut; step on it" unconsciously illustrated a type of error as old as writing. Another common error was the accidental repetition of a letter, syllable, word, or even a whole phrase. Thus the Latin side of one bilingual manuscript reads *et repleti sunt et repleti sunt omnes spiritu sancto*;[3] surely the words *et repleti sunt* are to be deleted as an accidental repetition, technically called *dittography*. The opposite of this, that is, the failure to repeat, as writing a single "verily" for "verily, verily," is even more common and is known as *haplography*. Occasionally this occurs in the midst of a word;[4] not infrequently the habit of writing common words as abbreviations leads to the same confusion. At times it is impossible to say which reading was the original, which the correction. The reading which several manuscripts give in Matt. 27:17, "Whom will ye that I release unto you? Jesus Barabbas, or Jesus who is called Christ?" is a case in point. The name Jesus was regularly written as a two-letter abbreviation. In this sentence the syntax would demand the accusative case. This abbreviation would then be the same as the last two letters of the preceding word "to you."[5] Are the few manuscripts which preserve the strange reading correct and the change of "Jesus Barabbas" to "Barabbas" due either to haplography or to the notion that the letters in question were a dittograph and so (intentionally) cancelled? (The horizontal line which was regularly written above abbreviations could thus easily have been mistaken for the dot a corrector wrote above a letter to be deleted.) Or is the shorter reading the correct one and the reading "Jesus Barabbas" due to dittography and the resultant expansion of the repeated two letters into the proper name Jesus? Both views find their supporters. Another very common error is due to two phrases of identical form in the copy. When mechanically copying, it is very easy for the scribe having copied through the first to let his eye fall on the *second* when he looked back to his examplar and thus to omit the intervening material. This error is known as *homoioarcton* if the two phrases begin alike, *homoioteleuton* if their endings are identical. An excellent example is found in Codex B. In John 17:15 the text reads, "I pray not that thou shouldest take them *from*

[3] Lake, *The Text of the New Testament,* 6th ed., p. 3.

[4] For example, επεμψε for επεπεμψε.

[5] $\mathrm{\Upsilon MIN}\overline{\mathrm{IN}}$.

the world, but that thou shouldest keep them *from the* evil one." But the scribe let his eye slip from the first "from the" (ἐκ τοῦ) to the second, thus omitting the intervening material and resulting in the amazing prayer, "I pray not that thou shouldest take them from the evil one."

All of these types of error are timeless and are possible even when operating with printed texts. Another class—and a very annoying one—was the peculiar property of handwritten manuscripts, although once this error had been made it became a part of the text. This is known as the *marginal gloss*. Occasionally a scribe would write some comment of his own in the margin, much as a certain type of reader annotates his books. The annotator might be the scribe himself or some later reader. He might simply write his comment or he might mark the word or phrase and opposite his marginal observation place the same symbol to show the connexion. A later scribe copying that manuscript (more or less mechanically) would see the marginal word or phrase and might well think that it had been accidentally omitted by the original scribe and later inserted either by him or by the professional proof-reader (*diorthotes*). The result would be that the copyist would insert it as a part of his text, and thus the extraneous reading might well continue as the reading of all subsequent descendants of that particular manuscript. Marginal glosses are of different kinds. Sometimes they are merely synonyms of unusual words; at other times they are comments. It has already been suggested[6] that the words, "the publican" (Matt. 10:3), are such a gloss intended to refer to James, and which were incorporated by a later hand in the wrong place. Others have seen the words, "Sinai is a mountain in Arabia," as a scribal gloss which eventually got into the text in Gal. 4:25. It is not necessary to mention the other examples which one scholar or another has thought he has detected. Then there is what is known as *itacism*. Strictly this means the substitution of the Greek letter iota for other vowels, but it is commonly used to cover the various misspellings due to similar pronunciations of vowels. Many vowels and diphthongs came to be pronounced alike; the result is that frequent alterations are only too common. These corruptions could arise when the scribe was copying a manuscript and reading it aloud to himself. But that was not the only way manuscripts were copied. Frequently several scribes would work in the same *scriptorium*, writing from the dictation of a reader. As a consequence many variations, especially itacism and other misspellings, were easily introduced, particularly if the scribe was inattentive. Particularly frequent and annoying are the variants "you" and "we" (ὑμεῖς and ἡμεῖς) which came to be pronounced alike. The first task of the textual critic is to remove as many as possible of these errors from the individual manuscripts. Some, of course, are obvious; others are by no means easy to discover. Similar but different errors would arise in the manuscripts of the

[6] Pp. 400 f.

versions. One example may be mentioned. For years *Barnabas* was known only in Latin translation. In 4:9 occurred the words *Sicut dicit filius Dei "Resistamus . . ."* ("thus says the Son of God, 'Let us resist etc.' "). No such traditional word of Jesus was known. When the Greek manuscript ℵ was discovered (which beside the Old and New Testament contained the text of Barnabas as well as of Hermas) it was found that the reading was "unless we resist as becomes the sons of God."[7] At once the difficulty was explained. The perplexing *dicit filius* was seen to be a corruption of *decet filios*, and so not a saying of Jesus at all. Here is a confusion which could arise only in Latin, not in Greek. On the other hand, there are other cases which could give rise to confusion in Greek but not in Latin. For example "God" (regularly written in abbreviation $\overline{\Theta\Sigma}$) could easily be confused with the relative pronoun (OΣ). In Latin this particular uncertainty could not occur, as *DEUS* ($\overline{DS}$) and *QUI* bear no resemblance to each other.

So far we have been considering unintentional alterations. But scribes not infrequently sought to correct some mistake they fancied they had discovered or to simplify something not easily understood. These intentional alterations are legion and are due to various causes, such as hopeless obscurity (often through the emergence of unintentional alterations), the desire to smooth up mistakes, harmonization of one writing with another where both gave the same incident or saying in similar but different language. This last is particularly common in the text of the gospels. There was the tendency (sometimes it was apparently unconscious) to make the two accounts identical either by inserting a phrase into the shorter or by accommodating the phraseology of the one to the other which the scribe preferred. Although Mark, as we have seen, was the earliest of the four and provided the framework for Matthew and Luke, Matthew soon surpassed Mark in popularity at least in some circles. The consequence was that frequently the text of Mark was brought into conformity to that of Matthew. One example may be cited. On p. 392 I suggested that the word, "For if ye forgive men their trespasses, your heavenly Father will also forgive you," which Matthew appends to the Lord's Prayer,[8] was apparently taken by him from Mark 11:25. To this word he provides the balanced opposite (Matt. 6:15). The interesting thing to observe is that some manuscripts of Mark have this Matthæan addition as Mark 11:26; that is, the Markan text has been intentionally harmonized with that of Matthew. Or again intentional alterations not infrequently were due to doctrinal likes or dislikes. Occasional examples have been cited in the earlier discussions of the several writings of the New Testament and reference has been made to the changes introduced by such figures as Marcion. A notorious case is to be found in the several rival readings in Matt. 1:16. Another not so well

[7] ἐὰν ὡς πρέπει υἱοῖς θεοῦ, ἀντιστῶμεν.
[8] Matt. 6:14.

known occurs in John 1:13. Here the Latin Ms. b and the writings of Irenæus and Tertullian have the reading, "who was born," indicating that on doctrinal grounds a slight alteration of the text had been made to make John attest the virgin birth.

Not infrequently unintentional and intentional alterations unite, that is, an accidental change occurs which introduces a difficulty which a later scribe attempts to remove. Souter[9] cites an excellent example from Juvenal (*Sat.* 8,148). The poet certainly wrote:

Ipse rotam adstringit sufflamine mulio consul,

that is, "The consul, himself a muleteer, with dragchain binds the wheel." The comparatively uncommon word *mulio* was misread *multo.* This introduced no difficulty in meaning. "With mighty dragchain" was tolerable. The metre, however, was thrown out. A later scribe observed this infelicity and sought to remedy it. Naturally it never occurred to him to substitute *mulio* for *multo.* He observed, however, that by changing the order of the two words, *sufflamine multo,* the limp in the metre would be removed. This he did and the resulting corruption,

Ipse rotam adstringit multo sufflamine consul,

persisted for centuries. This is a particularly good illustration of the fact known by every textual critic that intentional alterations are almost invariably wrong and often remove the original mistake in such a way as to make its discovery by scrutiny of the individual manuscript impossible. It is only by the comparison of manuscripts (into some of which the particular error did not chance to go) that it can be detected. Thus it should be clear that the removal of obvious errors from individual manuscripts is but one step toward the goal of the textual critic, namely, the recovery of the text which the original authors penned.

The next step is to compare the various manuscripts and to arrange them in families or classes. This will not only serve to reveal many errors which would otherwise pass unnoticed, but often to explain others which, while observable, might have arisen through various corruptions. But even more important, the arrangement of individual manuscripts into families relieves immensely the burden of trying to operate with thousands of individual manuscripts. Obviously if B, C, D, and E can be proven to be mere copies of A, it is unnecessary to concern oneself further with B, C, D, and E.[10] In drawing up the genealogies of separate manuscripts various clues are of value. The most certain is technically called *community of error.* If several manuscripts have a common mistake, it evidences a taint in the blood or,

[9] *The Text and Canon of the New Testament,* pp. 112 f.

[10] These letters are chosen arbitrarily here and do not refer to any particular manuscript.

to speak theologically, inherited guilt. In this way it is in general possible not only to arrange the manuscripts into families, but to detect which are ancestors, which descendants. Of course very frequently it will become clear that several manuscripts stand in the relation of brothers, and that the father has disappeared. The text of the missing parent can be reconstructed with reasonable probability by attributing to him all the sins which his children possess in common, but freeing him from those which are not the common possessions of them all. Each child, unfortunately, has his own peccadillos.

In theory this is easy; in practice it is far more complicated, for scribes did not always copy direct from one manuscript to another, but from several, sometimes following one, sometimes another. Thus allowances must be made for what the critic calls *mixture*. The result is of course an eclectic text. But mixture occurs in other ways, too. A manuscript may be (and generally was) corrected. At times the scribe himself would introduce the alterations as he was writing. At other times it would occur later at the hands of subsequent readers or correctors. One example will suffice to illustrate. It is now generally agreed by textual critics that about the beginning of the fourth century a revision of the text was made, probably in Antioch, to bring the various widely differing texts which had arisen during the previous centuries into conformity, and thus to provide a standard or ecclesiastical text. This revision speedily became very popular, and by far the majority of later manuscripts attest its sway. We shall have to consider its value later. For the moment the important thing to be observed is its effect upon earlier manuscripts in use at the time of the revision. Manuscripts cost money. Even though the new and authoritative text was desired by this or that church or monastery, it was not practical to throw their copy away and buy a new. Instead it is highly probable that the old manuscript would be brought to a near-by church which had a copy of the approved text, compared with it, and numerous corrections made by erasure, alteration, or marginal changes. Naturally all the changes would not be made. Slight alterations of spelling or of order might occasionally seem insignificant or be overlooked. Then if this partially "corrected" manuscript chanced later to be copied, the alterations would go into the copy being made, and the resulting manuscript would have a distinctly mixed text. Now it is to be remembered that this would be happening frequently and in different centres. The various correctors would not happen to make the same corrections. Furthermore, even though a standard text had been made, no two copies of it would be in entire agreement, for scribes were human and fallible. Hence the phenomenon already referred to that no two copies in existence are precise duplicates. Despite all these difficulties which confront the critic and which require the most profound knowledge not only of manuscripts and of the common errors of scribes, but of church history in its broader aspects, the patient endeavor of experts has made long strides toward accomplishing this second step. As new manuscripts are discovered or older ones are edited, it is possible to place them in their proper niche.

But this too is but another step, important though it is. It is now necessary to compare the ancestors of these various families or classes. By anticipation it may be remarked that critics today are in general agreement that there are three or four main groups into which the various families fall, although there is no entire agreement as to the exact lines, and some, notably Canon Streeter, in accord with his theory that each important ecclesiastical centre produced its own characteristic local text, are inclined to see even a larger number of distinct types. Discussion of these various types, be they three or five, may be reserved for the moment. The next step in the process which I have been trying to sketch is the comparison of the ancestors of the various groups. Naturally these ancestors, technically known as the *archetypes*, do not exist, but can, as has been indicated above, be reconstructed with reasonable certainty from the common agreements of their various heirs. The next step is obviously a comparison of them, for, if the genealogical tree has been correctly made, the variants in each particular case have all resulted from alteration of the original. Frequently of course all the reconstructed archetypes agree; those readings are in all probability original. The problem comes when there are disagreements. Which reading is to be considered original? Obviously the number of the manuscripts attesting the one reading or the other is not particularly significant, for in theory at least the number of children and grandchildren a particular man or manuscript has had is not necessarily in proportion to the purity of his blood. The genealogical method demands that the rival readings of the archetypes be dispassionately compared, heedless of the comparative clamour their progeny can raise. To decide between readings two types of evidence are important: *intrinsic* and *transcriptional probability*. By *intrinsic probability* is simply meant: Which of the variant readings is it the more probable the author wrote? Obscure or ungrammatical constructions are not necessarily wrong. He may have written that way. In fact, the tendency of scribes to try to remove obscurities would, as will appear in an instant, often suggest that such a reading is probably correct. On the other hand, the obscurity may have been due to unintentional error by some copyist, and hence wrong. Thus intrinsic probability, while a valuable tool, is also often an uncertain one. It is only when the one or other is strongly to be preferred as intrinsically the more probable that it is much good. *Transcriptional probability,* on the contrary, has to do with the habits of the scribes, *i.e.,* which of the rival readings is probably due to scribal error? In deciding that, several criteria are valuable. Years ago Bengel, one of the great critics, laid down the criterion: *proclivi scriptioni præstat ardua,* that is, "the harder reading is to be preferred." When stated absolutely this is often faulty, for a reading may be so "hard" that intrinsic probability is clearly against it.

Errors due to homoioteleuton may produce sheer nonsense. If, however, one can be reasonably sure that the variations can be explained as due to intentional alteration, then Bengel's canon is of value, for the tendency of scribes was to smooth out the text, not to make it more difficult. In line with this criterion is another: "Prefer the shorter reading." This, too, must be used with care. Its overuse has brought protests from many competent critics, notably those operating with classical texts, who point out that not infrequently the scribe tended to omit the superfluous and to condense. Be that as it may, in the New Testament it not infrequently holds. As has already been remarked, the shorter text of Luke's story of the Last Supper is distinctly more likely to be the original, for it is inconceivable that had the text contained the familiar words, "which is given for you . . . which is poured out for you" (Luke 22:19b,20), which so exactly agreed with early practice, it would have been omitted. Or again there can be no question that the words, "For thine is the kingdom, and the power, and the glory, for ever. Amen," were added at a later date and not omitted by those manuscripts which do not carry them. More important, however, than either of these two criteria is a third which may be easily stated, although it is not always easy to apply it: "That reading is to be preferred which most completely explains the variants." That is, if of several rivals only one is of such a character that it is possible to see how by various plausible alterations or variations each of the other readings could have been produced, the probability that that reading occurred in the autograph is very high.[11] It is conceivable that occasionally it would be impossible to decide between rival readings. In that case generally the decision would have to be on the basis of which part of the apparatus had the highest average of primitive readings.

Our final step may be briefly mentioned. After the various individual manuscripts have been cleansed of obvious errors, have been arranged into

[11] So excellent an example of this is found in Luke 19:37 that I venture to mention it, in part to whet the appetites of those who unfortunately in school considered Greek a dispensable luxury:

(1) *περι πασων ων ειδον δυναμεων*
(2) *περι παντων ων ειδον δυναμεων*
(3) *περι παντων ων ειδον γεινομενων*
(4) *περι πασων ων ειδον γινομενων δυναμεων*
(5) *περι παντων ων ειδον*
(6) Omit.

The reasons for considering (5), although attested only by a Syriac version, the original are as follows: All combinations of the neuter *παντων* and feminine *δυναμεων* are unlikely. *δυναμεων* was probably a marginal gloss to explain what "all things" meant. This became incorporated as part of the text. *παντων* was replaced by *πασων* to improve the grammar. *γεινομενων* (note the itacism) was a variant expansion. (4) is obviously a later blend. (6) was apparently a counsel of despair caused by the various claimants. Thus on the assumption that (5) was the original all the variants can be accounted for; this would be true for none of the others, particularly for (1), which is approved by most modern editors as well as by the bulk of the manuscripts.

families, and their conjectured archetypes compared, occasionally there will be readings which are either obviously wrong or at least suspicious. There is no further criterion available in such cases. If a further step is to be taken, it can only be a guess as to what the original reading was. This process is technically known as *conjectural emendation*. Editors differ as to the justice of printing such resultant readings. It is easy to lean over backward here, for it may well be that some of the readings which now have strong manuscript support were originally conjectural emendations by early scribes whose knowledge of textual matters was far less solid than that of modern scholars. On the other hand, there is no tool that should be used with greater care. Once the critic becomes enamoured of it, all restraint vanishes and all difficulties sweetly yield. Subjectivism at its worst is sure to result. Personally I should be most loath to indulge in it. It appears to me a far safer policy to indicate such suspicions by symbols suggesting "probable primitive corruption." If the editor feels it imperative to add his guess as to the source of the error, he can do so in the form of a plainly marked marginal note. This may be ultra-conservative; at least it will avoid many pitfalls and prevent textual criticism from being turned into guesswork.

It has already been remarked that with one exception the earliest copies of the New Testament—save for occasional tiny fragments—come from the fourth century. Nor is this surprising. It was not until that time that parchment came into general use. Previously papyrus had been the almost universal material, and papyrus was a perishable substance in all save very dry climates. The story of the preparation of papyrus for the market—the cutting of the stem into sections, the splitting of these sections lengthwise into strips, the building up of the sheet by two layers glued together and pressed until dry, the smoothing with mallet, scraper, and pumice—need not be told here in detail. Pliny gives a full and detailed statement in his *Natural History*,[12] which is readily available, while most of the books on textual criticism treat the subject fully.[13] Although the papyrus sheets were normally glued together to form a continuous strip perhaps thirty-five feet in length, written on one side, with the two ends glued to rollers upon which it was rolled up, it became increasingly common to form codices, that is, books, by folding the single sheets once through the middle to form four pages. This more convenient codex gradually ousted the roll which was inconvenient to handle and wasteful, since but one side was to be used. Although the roll remained standard in most circles until the fourth and fifth centuries, Christian writers appear to have used the codex

[12] *Nat. Hist.* xiii,11 and 12(20-26).

[13] An excellent statement is given by Kenyon, *Books and Readers in Greece and Rome*, together with a great deal of other information about ancient books, their preparation, appearance, and use.

regularly in the third century. The Chester Beatty papyri, already referred to, suggest that even in the second century it was known and at least occasionally used by Christians. But at best it was perishable, and, since it was not practical to fold the narrow and brittle sheets in both directions, it gradually yielded to the more convenient parchment or vellum made from the skin of goats, sheep, antelopes, calves, and swine. Vellum—distinctly different from tanned leather—was made from carefully washed skins which were scraped to remove all flesh and hair, rubbed with pumice, and dressed with chalk. Both sides (called technically the *recto* and the *verso*) could be used; furthermore, they could be laid up in quires as in modern books. Although parchment did not supplant papyrus overnight, the fourth century saw its decline. It is reasonable to suppose that our two earliest manuscripts (B and א) were actually among the earliest to be written on vellum. The fact that they are written in three and four columns, respectively, to the page suggest that they were copied from papyrus rolls (not codices) which regularly employed the narrow column. Gradually it became recognized that a wider column was more convenient. In the fifth century Codex A two columns were employed. This soon became normal in the large vellum codices, although occasionally a manuscript (as D) had but one wide column to the page.

Although the codex could hold far more than the earlier roll, only infrequently were copies of the whole New Testament made in the early days. To be sure copies still exist. B, א, A, and C originally contained not only the whole New Testament but the Old as well. These were distinctly rare and obviously produced for wealthy individuals or churches. It was not until the twelfth or thirteenth century that such comprehensive codices became common. In their stead were those containing the gospels, the Acts and Catholics, the letters of Paul, and the Apocalypse. Some have combinations of these, as Acts and Paul and the like.

The first thing that catches the eye of the student who for the first time examines ancient manuscripts is the difference in the styles of writing. Some manuscripts were written in capital letters, others in a flowing connected hand akin to our type of writing. The difference is significant, but since it has not infrequently been unduly stressed a brief statement is wise. Until about the year 800 A.D. books were written in what is called the *uncial* hand, that is, in capital letters not connected with one another (and of course with no spaces between words). Although this was the regular literary hand, it was not the only type of writing, as a glance at the thousands of papyri show. From the earliest times there existed also a flowing or cursive hand, commonly employed for non-literary purposes. It is highly probable, as a matter of fact, that early copies of some of the Christian writings may have used it, although no definite evidence exists. It is at any rate probable that Tertius employed it when writing at Paul's dictation to Rome. But in the ninth century a new and elegant type of flowing hand was invented which speedily supplanted the older uncial literary hand. This did not happen overnight. Uncial manuscripts continued to be made for two centuries—in fact, the majority of uncials which we have are from this period of change—but the new literary cursive hand, connected with ligatures, had come to stay. It is becoming increasingly common to reserve the term "cursive" for the older non-literary flowing hand, and to use the term "minuscule" to refer to the new literary form of connected writing.

For over two hundred years it has been customary to distinguish between manuscripts by employing totally dissimilar symbols for the two styles of writings. Uncial manuscripts are regularly referred to by the capital letters of the English, Greek, and Hebrew alphabets. The order of letters does not indicate the comparative age, but the time of discovery. Thus Codex Alexandrinus was known and named before the older Vaticanus and so received the letter A. Codex Sinaiticus, one of the oldest manuscripts in existence, was not discovered until the middle of the last century. Since the early letters of the English alphabet were exhausted it was christened א, (Aleph) the first letter of the Hebrew alphabet. It might have seemed expedient to refer to minuscules by the small letters. This, however, was not done, and, fortunately, for a tiny fraction of them would soon have exhausted all the alphabets. Small letters—a, b, c, and the like—are instead used for a totally different purpose, *viz.,* to refer to manuscripts of the Old Latin versions. Instead, Greek minuscules are referred to by Arabic numbers. Nor are they chronologically numbered. For example, 1 is a twelfth-century minuscule containing the whole New Testament save the Revelation, 1739 a much older (tenth-century) codex now containing the Acts and the epistles. One difficulty with this nomenclature is that it is often misleading. Thus D is used not for one manuscript, but for two; one, Codex Bezæ, containing the gospels and Acts, the other, Claromontanus, containing the letters of Paul. B is used not only for the fourth-century Vaticanus, but for the totally different eighth-century manuscript of Revelation, which to be sure is now coming to be referred to by the new symbol 046 to avoid confusion. Among the minuscules the confusion was even greater. These were arbitrarily numbered on the basis of gospels, Acts, Paul, and Revelation. Thus not only could the same number refer to (parts of) four different manuscripts, but a manuscript containing all four parts could have thus four different numbers. A further infelicity of this system is that it throws into unnatural relief the difference between uncials and minuscules, and gives the natural impression that the former are vastly more significant. As a matter of fact, after the sixth century the value of a manuscript is by no means in proportion to its age, and the text of a minuscule may be, and not infrequently is, of distinctly greater value than that of an uncial, equipped with an imposing-looking capital letter though it be.

To remedy this confusion two different systems have been propounded. The one by von Soden is a radical change and completely ignores the distinction between uncials and minuscules. Instead it indicates the age and content of the manuscript. This ingenious but complicated system does not appear to have gained any large number of supporters. For the critic knowledge of it is essential to enable him to use von Soden's apparatus. The student who desires to learn it will find it described in detail in the first volume of von Soden's own work[14] and clearly summarized by Lake.[15] The other system was proposed by Gregory,[16] and embodies the minimum number of alterations consonant with clarity. All uncials are given numbers, the first digit of which is 0, and are printed in full faced type, as **01** or **0161**. The more familiar of the uncials, although they have their number, will probably continue to be cited by letter. The minuscules are similarly brought into one list. Gospel manuscripts regularly retain their old numbers; those containing other parts have in general new numbers assigned. It is to be hoped that this nomenclature will be universally adopted in new publications.[17] Gregory provides a full table of the old numbers and their new equivalents. This makes available older studies as Tischendorf's famous eighth edition, which followed the older system.

Although it would of course be impossible and senseless to print here a description of all the known manuscripts, a few of the more valuable may be briefly described. The great majority of known manuscripts contain essentially the same text, *viz.*, that referred to on p. 480 as produced in the early fourth century. Hence it is totally unnecessary to print the full list of manuscripts attesting a particular reading. What is desired is to know the rival readings of the various families of manuscripts. Generally this is obtained by citing the leading authorities for each type. Only when the best witnesses in each group differ among themselves is it of value to cite their less illustrious relatives.

Of the fragments of Greek papyri, save for those that bear the name of Chester Beatty, little need be said. Until their discovery the oldest fragment was the one in the University of Pennsylvania. This is dated from the third century and contains Matt. 1:1-9; 12,13,14-20. In Gregory's notation it is $\mathfrak{P}^1$. A still older fragment, P. Ryl. Gk. 457, has been published by C. H. Roberts,[18] who dates it in the first half of the second century. It is of great interest to note that it is a fragment of a codex (not a roll) and thus, if this dating which has approved itself to such an expert palæographer as Kenyon be accepted,

[14] *Die Schriften des Neuen Testaments*, Vol. I, Part 1, pp. 37 ff.

[15] *The Text of the New Testament*, pp. 89 f.

[16] *Die griechischen Handschriften des Neuen Testaments.*

[17] This is being done in the admirable new publication, *Novum Testamentum Græce*, by S. C. E. Legg, which is intended to do for our generation what Tischendorf's notable edition did for his. The first volume (Mark) has appeared. Others are in preparation.

[18] *An Unpublished Fragment of the Fourth Gospel*, 1935.

affords confirmatory evidence to the existence of Christian papyrus codices in the second century. Its content is so small (John 18:31-33,37-38) that it is of small value as a witness for the text, but its importance is none the less tremendous both to the textual and literary critic. Another Christian gospel fragment, P. Eg. 2, is also dated provisionally in the second century. Since it is not a part of any of the four canonical gospels, it is unnecessary to describe it in any detail. A full description is given by its editors[19] and also their hypothesis as to its nature. Von Dobschütz's convenient revision of Nestle's *Introduction*[20] lists thirty-one other papyrus fragments, including the fourth century $\mathfrak{P}^{13}$ which contains the largest amount of text (save in the Chester Beatty papyri) yet discovered, namely, Hebr. 2:14-5:5; 10:8-11:13; 11:28-12:17. To this list others are constantly being added.

The three Chester Beatty papyri containing sections of the New Testament have all been dated from the third century. They are written by different scribes in widely divergent hands. Thirty leaves of $\mathfrak{P}^{45}$, which originally held the gospels and Acts, are extant and contain a few verses of Matthew and large blocks of the other four works. At first, only ten leaves of $\mathfrak{P}^{46}$, the Pauline codex, were found. Later thirty more leaves were published by the University of Michigan. Scarcely were those published when word came that Mr. Beatty had acquired forty-six more. As a result no less than eighty-six leaves of the original 104 of this manuscript, a century older than any other known copy, were made available to students of the Pauline text. Hebrews surprisingly enough follows Romans in this collection. This would appear to indicate that this generally disputed writing was held in high esteem in Egypt in the third century. After these two come the other letters in the unprecedented order: I and II Corinthians, Ephesians, Galatians, Philippians, Colossians, I Thessalonians. The last seven leaves are still missing. What their contents (save II Thessalonians) was can only be conjectured. Philemon and the Pastorals could not have been compressed into so small a space. Of $\mathfrak{P}^{47}$, containing the Revelation, ten small leaves containing 9:10-17:2 remain. These provide a welcome addition to the relatively slim collection of codices of this writing. All three of these papyri have already been published.[21] In this excellent study the complete text with convenient apparatus is printed together with careful introductions and singularly judicious preliminary discussions of the types of text which they seem to present. That they will have to be considered in all subsequent discussions of the early textual forms is certain.

The first of the vellum manuscripts in uncials to be mentioned is Codex Vaticanus, regularly known by the symbol B. It is universally regarded as

[19] Bell and Skeat, *Fragments of an Unknown Gospel*, 1935.

[20] E. von Dobschütz, *Eberhard Nestle's Einführung in das griechische Neue Testament*, 1923, pp. 85 f.

[21] F. G. Kenyon, *The Chester Beatty Biblical Papyri*, 1933-1936.

written in the fourth century, probably in Alexandria. It originally contained both Old and New Testament, but the last folios containing the end of Hebrews, I and II Timothy, Titus, Philemon, and the Apocalypse (?) have been lost, and the text breaks off at Hebr. 9:14. It is a sumptuous manuscript, nearly square in shape (10½x10 inches), written with three narrow columns to the page. The New Testament section was written by two different scribes. Several correctors have worked on it. One of them (generally dated in the tenth or eleventh century) re-inked it, and left untouched the letters which he wished to change. He also added breathings and accents. Westcott and Hort considered it by far the best witness to the original text, called by them the *Neutral*. Although subsequent critics have been inclined to consider Hort's estimate of its purity a little high, its preëminence is still generally and deservedly conceded. It is, however, to be noted that in the Pauline letters the text is not of precisely the same nature as in the gospels, Acts, and Catholics, but has a distinct *Western* element, if it be proper to speak of a *Western* text outside of the gospels and Acts.[22] Moreover, it is to be remarked that whenever the readings of B are supported by other witnesses, however few, their claim is insistent; on the contrary, its "singular," that is, unique, readings, although rarely to be described as stupid blunders are far less impressive.

Closely associated with B is the four column ℵ (Codex Sinaiticus), now the great show piece of the British Museum. The romantic story of its discovery nearly a century ago by Tischendorf is so generally known that it need not be repeated. He naturally prized it very highly. The essential difference between the text of his famous "eighth edition" and that of Westcott and Hort is due to the fact that ℵ was for him the guide as was B for the British editors. It too is to be dated in the fourth century, perhaps a little later than B, and to be seen as coming from Alexandria. Although a luxurious codex, it is more carelessly written than B and contains many dialectical peculiarities and not a few crude errors. Its text is distinctly mixed, although its base is plainly *Neutral*. Like B its singular readings rarely approve themselves. Several correctors have worked on the manuscript. Of these one group, styled ℵ^{c}, which worked between the fifth and seventh centuries, is by far the most important, and, according to Lake, who published a sumptuous photographic edition of this manuscript in 1911, introduced the majority of the corrections. Unlike B, the whole text of the New Testament is preserved. In the Old Testament it is now not complete. In addition to the canonical books it contains both Barnabas and Hermas. The relationship between B and ℵ has been often debated. Hort's dictum, that the supposition that they have a text in any one book or chapter of the New Testament which is derived from a single near ancestor falls to the ground, is generally allowed today. In addition to the variation of text the fact that the order of the books of the New Testament is different is significant. In B, as has already been suggested, Acts and

[22] See below, p. 493.

the Catholic epistles precede Paul; in ℵ they follow. The guess which has been often hazarded that since B and ℵ are written with three and four columns to the page, respectively, they are two of the fifty manuscripts which Eusebius says he was commissioned to have made for Constantine[23] would not appear to have any basis in fact.

Second only to B and ℵ in interest is D, the bilingual Codex Bezæ. This manuscript is perhaps to be dated from the fifth century, although the older scholars placed it a century later. It is really two manuscripts: the successive left-hand pages are Greek, the right Latin. This latter is not to be regarded as a translation of the companion pages, but as having had its own independent history, although evidencing the same general type of text. The exact relationship between the two has not been thoroughly decided, although it has been the subject of much discussion. Perhaps it is safest to say that each side has influenced the other. The Latin side (referred to by the small letter d) is one of the witnesses for the so-called Old Latin versions (see below), that is, the Latin text current before the official revision made by Jerome at the behest of Pope Damasus, and known today as the Vulgate. D is written on large pages (10x8 inches) in single columns with lines of unequal length. The lines are written colometrically, that is, are "sense-lines," divided with an eye to producing units of thought. This type of writing, often employed by classical authors, is not uncommon in New Testament manuscripts. Unlike B and ℵ, D did not originally have the whole New Testament. In addition to the gospels and Acts it originally contained at least some of the Catholic epistles since on the page immediately preceding Acts stand the closing verses of III John. Approximately sixty-six pages which originally stood after the gospels have been lost. It has been occasionally assumed that these contained the Apocalypse and three Johannine letters, to form a sort of *corpus johanneum*, as the text of those four writings would approximately fill (as the seven Catholic epistles would not) the conjectured missing pages. If the order of the gospels in this manuscript had been that to which we are accustomed, that is, with John just before these other Johannine writings, the argument would perhaps be more impressive. Instead the gospels occur in the so-called *Western* order, that is, Matthew, John, Luke, Mark. D's real claim to interest is not its age, but its type of text. It is distinctly different from that of B and ℵ and is the best example of the type of text which most critics call *Western*. More must be said later of this type of text, the crux of modern discussion; suffice it to say here that on the whole it is a fuller and more discursive text. Most (but by no means all) critics regard it as inferior to that of the other old uncials, but yet as a text which at a very early time achieved an immense popularity. That D was written where Latin was known is obvious from its Latin partner d. The place of origin has generally been assumed to be Gaul, that is, southern France, since it was discovered in the ancient city

[23] Eusebius, *Vita Constantini* iv,35-37.

of Lyons. Ropes inclined to Sicily as its place of origin. The various arguments are summarized by him in his altogether admirable edition of the text of Acts[24] and need not be repeated here.

L (Codex Regius) is another very interesting and important manuscript. It contains the four gospels, with parts of Matthew, Mark, and John missing. Although carelessly written, and not earlier than the eighth century it has a very good text, distinctly like that of B but often forsaking the text of the latter to agree with readings also found in Origen. Hort considered it one of the best two witnesses for the text he styled *Alexandrian*, but which today many critics would prefer to call modified *Neutral*. Of the readings which appear to be grammatical and stylistic betterings of the type of text of which B is the best example L has the largest share. It is also of interest as being one of the few uncials to give the shorter ending of Mark. This stands after Mark 16:8 and is followed by the so-called longer conclusion (Mark 16:9-20). To each conclusion stands a note: "These also are somewhere current" and "And there are these also current." Hort believed that the exemplar of L had only the shorter conclusion. It would appear to me that the scribe did not consider either authoritative.

The discovery of the significance of Θ (the Koridethi gospel codex) has been spoken of by Streeter[25] as "comparable in importance to that of א or the Sinaitic Syriac." While rather later than those already described (save L) it may be mentioned here. It was not until long after its discovery in a remote Caucasus valley that its full text was made available to scholars. Even more recently Lake has shown that with five valuable but puzzling groups of minuscules[26] and to a measure the Georgian version it forms a definite family. These seven witnesses frequently disagree among themselves, but the disagreements are due to the fact that all have been corrected by the ecclesiastical text which became dominant in the fourth century. No two of them have precisely the same corrections. If these readings be removed, their common nature is at once apparent. It is becoming increasingly common to refer to this type of text as *Cæsarean*, following the lead of Canon Streeter. Not improbably this was the type of text which Eusebius used for the fifty manuscripts he had produced for the emperor (see p. 489). The scribe—Dr. Blake of Harvard thinks he was a Georgian—was by no means familiar with Greek. Since the Greek letters are drawn rather than written, there is no criterion available for purposes of dating. It may perhaps be placed in the seventh or eighth century.

W, or as it is often styled the Washington or Freer manuscript from its place in the Freer Collection of the Smithsonian Institution, is of the greatest importance. Its 374 pages contain the four gospels in the so-called *Western*

[24] *The Text of Acts,* Vol. III, pp. lxiii-lxviii in the edition by Jackson and Lake, *The Beginnings of Christianity*. Subsequent references to Ropes in this chapter will be to this volume.

[25] *The Four Gospels,* p. 79.

[26] Fam. 1, fam. 13 (the "Ferrar group"), 28, 565, and 700.

order, as does D. It was written in either the fourth or the fifth century, perhaps in Egypt. Prof. H. A. Sanders, who has edited this manuscript,[27] has shown that it is of by no means uniform text throughout. In fact this is one of its chief values, since it provides samples of the various rival texts even in the same books. In Matthew the text is distinctly *Byzantine* or *Ecclesiastical*. Mark 1:1-5:30 is thoroughly *Western*; while it is not precisely that of D, it is almost identical with the Greek text underlying the African Latin version to be found in e. The rest of Mark is classified as *Cæsarean* by Lake. John and the first seven chapters of Luke are mainly *Neutral*, while the remainder of Luke, like Matthew, is *Byzantine*. Thus it would appear that W is an earlier witness to the *Ecclesiastical* or *Byzantine* text than the writings of Chrysostom who is usually cited as the first to bear witness to the text that was to lay its blight upon nearly all extant copies. Furthermore, it stands as an ally of D, long considered the only Greek witness to the debated *Western* text.

Mention must now be made of A (Codex Alexandrinus) which has been the longest and best known of all the Greek uncials. Like B and ℵ it originally contained both Old and New Testaments. In addition it has I and II Clement and originally carried the Psalms of Solomon. It has usually been dated in the fifth century, but there seems no compelling reason against a somewhat later date. Although it has been known for more than three hundred years as *Alexandrinus* because it had been in Alexandria during the years that Cyril Lucar (who later presented it to Charles I of England) was patriarch, there seems little direct evidence to connect its origin with that city. Modern critics are inclined to the view that it came originally from Constantinople and was taken by Cyril Lucar to Alexandria from Mount Athos. A note in Latin by the hand of Cyril connects it with a Christian woman named Thecla. The note is of interest, but raises more questions than it solves:

> This book of sacred Scripture of the New and Old Testament, as we know from tradition, was written by the hand of Thecla, a noble Egyptian lady, about thirteen hundred years ago, shortly after the Council of Nicea. The name of Thecla at the end of the book was erased, but with the blotting out of Christianity in Egypt by the Mohammedans the books of Christians at the same time were reduced to the same condition. Therefore though the name of Thecla has been blotted out and torn away, memory and recent tradition preserve it. ✠ Cyrillus Patriarcha Constantin.

Like W its text is by no means uniform. In the gospels it is distinctly *Byzantine*, although with a mixture of *Western* readings. Since Matt. 1:1-25:5 is not extant, the discovery of W, which in that gospel has essentially the same text, was peculiarly fortunate. The *Western* element is smaller in Acts and the Pauline letters; in Acts, according to Ropes,[28] "corrections from the An-

[27] *The New Testament MSS. in the Freer Collection.*

[28] *Op. cit.*, p. liv.

tiochian [*i.e., Byzantine*] cannot be affirmed." Its text of Revelation is perhaps the best of all extant manuscripts, even as that of ℵ is here the least trustworthy. It cannot be too often repeated that the student should ever keep in mind that when operating with ancient manuscripts it is most unsafe to consider them all of a piece. To all intents and purposes they are often separate manuscripts. Although A has long been known and, as one of the few old complete Bibles, is usually cited early in the descriptive lists in modern books, its value is distinctly less than that of those already described. In addition to the loss of most of Matthew other shorter lacunæ occur. John 6:50-8:52, II Cor. 4:13-12:7, one leaf from I Clement, and two from II Clement are missing. It is of interest to observe that this old manuscript did not contain the famous *pericope adulteræ*. Although, as has just been mentioned, John 6:50-8:52 is wanting, certainty that this section was not included in the missing verses is achieved by calculating the extent of the space missing. In contradistinction to D, B, and ℵ, which have respectively one, three, and four columns to the page, A has two. The hands of three separate scribes are to be distinguished in the New Testament pages. Aside from those made either by the original scribes or *diorthotes* the corrections of this manuscript are of little significance.

Another uncial which originally contained the whole Bible is C (Codex Ephraemi or, to give it its full title, Codex Ephraemi Syri rescriptus). This manuscript, about the early days of which little is known, fell into evil straits. Most of the Old Testament has perished; of the New only 145 leaves remain. It has been calculated that when complete this section contained 238 leaves. But not only has it suffered mutilation, but, as the title suggests, was subjected to the indignity of being erased and rewritten. This type of manuscript is technically styled a palimpsest. Due to shortage of materials not infrequently the ink of old manuscripts was removed by washing or scraping, and the resulting vellum used again. Occasionally the original ink may have faded to such an extent that mechanical means were not necessary. C is such a manuscript. In the twelfth century the now extant part was used to hold a Greek translation of thirty-eight treatises of St. Ephraem of Syria. Fortunately the original writing was in one column to the page, the superimposed later text in two. Hence by the use of chemical reagents and the abuse of eyesight most of the earlier text has been recovered. Its text, too, is mixed. In the gospels its text is in general agreement with that of B and ℵ although by no means identical with it, containing as it does both *Western* and *Byzantine* readings. Lake calls it "fundamentally *Alexandrian*," but with clear evidence of both *Western* and *Byzantine* influence. Much the same can be said of its text in Acts and the Pauline letters; here, however, the effects of the *Byzantine* revision are less clearly marked.

Only a few of the other uncials need be mentioned, and they but briefly. The first of these is another manuscript styled D (Codex Claromontanus) or

D^{paul} to distinguish it from Codex Bezæ. This sixth-century manuscript, which is also bilingual, contains the Pauline letters, athough it has suffered some minor losses. Due to the fact that its text shows some of the peculiarities exhibited by witnesses (notably D and W^{mark}) of the so-called *Western* text of the gospels and Acts, D^{paul} is also generally styled *Western*. Actually, however, it is far from certain that this "paraphrastic rewriting" embraced more than the gospels and Acts. One of the values of D^{paul} is the so-called "Clermont list," which stands between Philemon and Hebrews and which gives the list of (Old and) New Testament writings in the most surprising order: Matthew, John, Mark, Luke, Romans, I and II Corinthians, Galatians, Ephesians, I and II Timothy, Titus, Colossians, Philemon, I and II Peter, James, I, II, and III John, Jude, Barnabas, Revelation, Acts, Shepherd of Hermas, Acts of Paul, and Revelation of Peter. Before I Peter, Barnabas, and the last three in the list stand dashes. Philippians, I and II Thessalonians, and Hebrews are not listed, but whether from inadvertence or design can only be conjectured. Closely associated with D^{paul} are three other manuscripts. The first of these is E^{paul} (Codex Sangermanensis), a ninth-century copy of D^{paul}, and sharply to be differentiated from the eighth-century gospel manuscript, Codex Basiliensis, also styled E, and the sixth (or seventh) century Acts manuscript, Codex Laudianus, generally styled E^{acts}, which is bilingual and which has a Greek text (itself not *Western* in base) which has been frequently brought into harmony with the corresponding Latin text by the insertion of the Greek translation of the Latin (*Western*) additions. F^{paul} (Codex Augiensis), dated in the ninth century and to be differentiated from the comparatively unimportant F (Codex Boreeli) of the gospels, is closely connected with G^{paul}, although probably not a copy of it as Hort maintained. This latter, G^{paul} (Codex Boernerianus), is a ninth-century Greek copy of the Pauline letters (with the exception of Hebrews) and has a Latin version written interlineally. It originally was a part of the gospel manuscript Δ (Codex Sangallensis). According to Lake[29] D^{paul} and G^{paul} stand in such close relationship as to suggest a close common ancestor which D^{paul} the more faithfully represents.

Brief mention may be made of two other gospel manuscripts Π (Codex Petropolitanus) and K (Codex Cyprius). That some sort of relationship between them existed has long been realized. Mrs. Lake in her doctorial dissertation[30] has made a strong case for her view that these are but two of a large family of manuscripts, the archetype of which is not K (which she redates in the eleventh century) but the ninth century Π.

Four manuscripts which stand together, not only in type of text but in outward appearance, deserve a brief word. These are N (Codex Purpureus

[29] *Op. cit.*, p. 20.

[30] Silva Lake, *Family* Π *and the Codex Alexandrinus* (*Studies and Documents* V), 1936. The student will find this volume a good introduction to the mysteries of text analysis.

Petropolitanus), Σ (Codex Rossanensis), O (Codex Sinopensis, and Φ (Codex Beratinus). All four are gospel codices, N carrying fragments of all four, Φ and Σ having Matthew and Mark almost complete, while O contains now but a fragment of Matthew. They are all sixth-century fragments of *de luxe* editions written on parchment stained a deep purple. The letters of O are in gold, those of the other three are silver, although in both N and Σ the names of Jesus and God are in gold. Σ is further adorned with miniatures in water-colour. All of them had checkered existences; sections of N, for example, were in four different libraries until, at the end of the last century, it was acquired by the Russian Tsar. In general their text is of the same general type, that of the ecclesiastical revision (although Φ, while closely allied, shows a distinct *Western* infiltration), and was not until recently considered of especial interest, although similarities in N and the famous "Ferrar group" (now styled fam. 13) had been noted. More recently Streeter has discovered a genuine relationship between NΣ and fam. Θ, *i.e.,* the Cæsarean text. It is not necessary here to do more than make reference to this important discovery.[31]

It is unnecessary to mention the remaining uncials. While many of them are of interest as well as of importance to the expert, by and large their texts are of the later conventional pattern and mention of them would but confuse the beginner. Full information for the advanced student is readily available in the various volumes and monographs intended for the expert.

Only a small fraction of the known Greek manuscripts are written in uncials. Nor is it safe to discount these as later and hence less important. One ninth-century manuscript containing the gospels has Matthew and Mark in uncials, Luke and John in the minuscule hand. The two parts are respectively referred to as Λ and 566. Another, 579, although of the thirteenth century, has a text in Mark, Luke, and John closely akin to that of B and ℵ, and apparently in this section was copied directly from a sixth-century uncial manuscript. In Matthew, on the contrary, the text is of no especial interest. This is sufficient to illustrate that these manuscripts are not to be weighed like potatoes, but to be examined with the same care accorded to the uncials. Of the more than three thousand which are at least partially known it is impossible to mention more than a mere handful, and unnecessary since the great majority of them have a text more or less completely reflecting the fourth-century *Byzantine* revision. A few, for one reason or another, deserve a special word. 33, known since the days of Eichhorn as the "queen of the cursives," is of the (ninth or) tenth century, and contains the whole New Testament save Revelation. Although influenced to a degree by the *Byzantine* text, it none the less is a close supporter of B and ℵ. Hort considered its text of Acts second only to 81 among the minuscules. This latter codex (formerly styled 61) now containing only Acts is an excellent ally of B, although seven

[31] B. H. Streeter, *The Four Gospels,* pp. 575-578.

centuries later. In contrast to these two stands the sixteenth-century Testament 61 which is of interest chiefly because it is the earliest known Greek codex to contain the text about the "three heavenly witnesses" (I John 5:7,8). It was the discovery of the passage in this manuscript which led Erasmus to yield to the protests of his critics and to include the words in his third edition (1522). Mention has already been made of the groups called respectively fam. 13 and fam. 1 as being related to Θ and several other witnesses of what is now coming to be known as the *Cæsarean* text. Fam. 13, called the "Ferrar group" after the Dublin scholar who observed that 13, 69, 124, and 346 were very like in text, is now believed to have descended from a common uncial archetype. In addition to these four, seven others (543, 788, 826, 828, 983, 1689, and 1209) are to be joined. All save 69 are of the eleventh or twelfth century; this one exception is probably from the fifteenth century. The most-often cited peculiarity of this family is that the *pericope adulteræ* occurs after Luke 21:38. Fam. 1 is also of interest although but two of the family (1 and 1582) are of particular importance. 1 (formerly dated in the tenth, but now in the twelfth century) contains the whole New Testament save Revelation. It was among those used by Erasmus to correct his proofs for the New Testament text. Unfortunately he sent 2, a much inferior twelfth-century gospel codex, to the printers. Had 1 been employed, the resulting text of his edition would have been far better. Associated with 1 is 1^r, a twelfth-century codex of Revelation. It, too, was employed by Erasmus, but while of good text was defective at the end (Rev. 22:16-21 being omitted). To remedy this lack Erasmus himself translated the Latin for these verses into Greek. As a consequence the *Textus Receptus* still contains words not found in any Greek manuscript. Since the *Textus Receptus*[32] was the text employed by the translators of the King James Version, the stronghold of those who still talk about verbal inspiration, this little eddy of history should give pause—unless, of course, Erasmus be somewhat belatedly admitted to the ranks of the peculiarly inspired.

1739, a tenth-century manuscript which now contains the Acts, Catholics, and Pauline epistles (but which originally probably also had the gospels) is of especial importance, not only for its many marginal notes, but also for its text. The archetype of 1739 was compiled in a library where the writings of Origen, as well as copies of the New Testament, were available. For the Pauline letters this exemplar followed an ancient codex containing the text of Origen. In Romans, however, the text employed was not drawn from that codex, but directly from Origen's lost commentary on Romans. This demonstrable connexion of the text of 1739 in Paul with the text of Origen makes this codex perhaps the best witness to the Origenian-*Cæsarean* text of the Pauline epistles in existence. The text underlying the Acts and Catholics is

[32] The phrase *Textus Receptus* is due to the remark by Elzevir in his second edition (1633), *Textum ergo habes nunc ab omnibus receptum.* In no small measure was his optimism justified, since this continued for centuries to be the standard on the Continent just as the essentially similar third edition (1550) of Stephanus was for England.

of a somewhat different character; yet it too is of prime importance. So far as Acts is concerned, there is no trace of *Byzantine* readings; the text is *Neutral* and *Western* in about equal proportions. This is precisely the formula suggested by champions of the *Cæsarean* text.

Occasionally the value of a manuscript is increased by the later corrector. Such a manuscript is 424. This is an eleventh-century copy of all save the gospels. The Pauline section (formerly 67) has been corrected in the margin presumably from a very old manuscript startlingly akin to B and M. These corrections (in Tischendorf they are marked 67**) are of great interest.

Purple minuscules are by no means unknown. Occasionally their text is of interest. Such is 565, a ninth- or tenth-century gospel manuscript written in gold, which Streeter styled "the most important ally of Θ, so far as Mark is concerned." While 16 is not a purple manuscript, it is a highly decorative affair. It is a bilingual (Greek and Latin) gospel codex in which different coloured inks are employed. The narrative sections are in vermilion; the words of Jesus and of the angels, together with the genealogies of Jesus, are in crimson. Blue is the colour used for the quotations from the Old Testament and for the words of those speakers (the disciples, Zacharias, Elisabeth, Mary, Simeon, and John the Baptist) of whom the author approves. The words of the Pharisees, Judas Iscariot, the Scribes, the devil, the centurion, the multitudes, and (perhaps by inadvertence) the shepherds are in black. Of no importance textually, it remains a unique and interesting example of scribal ingenuity. Two other manuscripts of particular interest may be mentioned—2400 and 574. Both have recently been published by University of Chicago scholars. The former is the Rockefeller McCormick New Testament, the latter the Four Gospels of Karahissar. Both are probably late thirteenth-century and were perhaps written by the same hand. Their particular interest lies in the plethora of illustrations—seventy-four in the former, sixty-five in the latter. In the expert hands of Professor H. R. Willoughby they add an important chapter to mediæval iconography.

It is unnecessary to mention any more of the minuscules. Notice should, however, be drawn to the immensely valuable undertaking of the Lakes in publishing a series of volumes containing photographs of dated Greek minuscules.[33] Several volumes have already appeared. These will be of incalculable value in providing criteria for dating the great plethora of manuscripts which are unfortunately not so equipped.

This brief survey of Greek manuscripts may be concluded with a reference to another type of manuscripts, *viz.,* lesson-books or, as they are more commonly called, *lectionaries.* The majority of manuscripts have a continuous text of the book or books they contain. There are, however, a great number which do not, and for a very good reason. One of the chief reasons copies of

[33] K. and S. Lake, *Dated Greek Minuscule Manuscripts,* 1934 ff.

the sacred writings were made was to provide books for public readings in church. At an early date it became common for a particular section to be read on a particular day. Thus the text of the gospels and to a lesser degree that of Acts and the epistles came to be divided into lections. At first these were apparently read from a continuous text. Many manuscripts contain the abbreviations of the words "beginning" and "end" ($\overset{\chi}{\alpha\rho}$ and $\overset{\lambda}{\tau\epsilon}$) indicating the start and close of these lections. Eventually, however, it proved more convenient to have them collected in the proper order in separate manuscripts. These are the lectionaries. As a general rule they faithfully reproduce the text, but with occasional minor alterations. If a section chanced to start with the words, "And he said," this might be changed to the more explicit "And the Lord said"; instead of the simple "After this . . ." frequently is to be seen a brief paraphrase to indicate the connexion. As a general rule these alterations are obvious and easily removed. Occasionally, however, they are deeper seated. The great majority of the lectionaries are of the gospels, and are generally called *Evangelaria*; others of the Acts, either with or without the epistles, are styled *Apostoli* or *Praxapostoli*. As a general rule they fall into three sections giving, respectively, the readings: (1) for the movable year, that is, starting with Easter and falling into four divisions; (2) for the fixed year, starting with September 1 and on the basis of months and days; (3) for special days and celebrations in the local church.[34] These lectionaries were often lavishly illuminated and bound between bejewelled covers. Not infrequently they were equipped with musical signs to guide the one who intoned or sang them. They are very hard to date since they continued to use the uncial hand long after it had given way to the minuscule in continuous texts. Few, if any, are earlier than the eighth century. Occasionally bilingual lectionaries, for example, in Greek and Arabic, are found. It is customary to refer to lectionaries by their own series of Arabic numerals. Gregory[35] lists 1545 of them. It is unnecessary here to refer to any of them individually. Until recently little attention has been paid to them. It is not inconceivable that they might be of considerable value if adequately studied.

Although it was born in Aramaic-speaking Palestine, Christianity came into the Roman world as a Greek-speaking religion; all of its books were written in Greek. When Paul wrote to the Christians in Rome he wrote not in Latin, but in Greek. But all the world did not speak Greek. Gradually even in districts where Greek had earlier been if not the official tongue at least understood by all this knowledge lapsed. In other parts Greek was so imperfectly known that it could not be used as a medium of intercourse. In consequence translation of some of the New Testament writings came

[34] This may be conveniently studied in C. R. Gregory, *Canon and Text of the New Testament*, pp. 384-393.

[35] *Die griechischen Handschriften*, pp. 123-171.

to be made, in some cases long before the conception of a *new* Testament arose. Of these translations, technically called *versions,* thousands of copies exist and bring their own problems to the textual critic. Not all are translations from the Greek. There are many secondary versions, that is, translations of translations. Until the time of Tyndale all English translations were from the Latin. The Armenian was perhaps made from Syriac; the Georgian surely from Armenian. The Arabic comes in part from Greek, in part through Syriac and Coptic. Obviously the textual value of these lies in their witness to the Greek text (or texts) in varying removes behind them. Once that text can be determined the same methods of criticism and analysis must be employed as those already outlined above. But before that stage is reached there are other steps. The same mixture which we saw in Greek manuscripts exists in greater or less degree in the manuscripts of the versions. Again it must not be assumed that all in the same language attests the same version. To cite but one example: In Latin there are thousands of manuscripts which give in varying degrees of purity the text of the Vulgate, that is, Jerome's revision of the Latin manuscripts of his day. But before Jerome there were at least two, perhaps three, distinct types of Latin text whose mutual relationship is still not definitely known. Just as many of the Vulgate manuscripts embody readings of the so-called Old Latin type, so other manuscripts, although basically Old Latin, have been mixed with the Vulgate. In addition it is necessary to determine the quality of the translation. Is it a literal translation? At times the translations are so painfully literal that one can be sure of not only the words but the order of the original which was being rendered. Is it a more or less free paraphrase? Thus the versions, while immensely valuable, at times being based on Greek exemplars older than even our oldest Greek manuscripts, require a high technical knowledge on the part of those who would operate with them successfully. They have been the subject of much study in recent years. The detailed results of these studies is available in the several treatises on the text of the New Testament. We must content ourselves here with a bare mention of the more important of the versions and a few of the manuscripts which carry them.

Of the primary versions the Old Latin is conspicuous. Apparently it did not take its rise in Italy. Here Greek was in common use until the fourth century. Paul wrote to the Romans in Greek. The Roman author of I Clement also employed that medium. The emperor Marcus Aurelius penned his meditations in Greek. The third century Hippolytus wrote his treatises in excellent Greek. Outside Italy in the Roman West Greek was also long employed. Irenæus of Lyons (in Gaul) used it so far as is known in all his voluminous writing. But while in the second and third centuries there was not the pressing need of a Latin version in Italy, Sicily, and at least parts of Gaul and Spain, the situation in the Roman province of Africa, taken from Carthage in the second century B.C., was very different. Here Latin, not Greek, was not only the official language, but, as Souter styles it, "the language of civilisation." It would appear that here, rather than in Rome, the earliest translations of New Testament writings made their appearance. Cyprian (*ob.* 258 A.D.) makes definite and undoubted use of a Latin version. Certain indications in the form of his quotations make clear that this was of long standing and confirm the hints in the writings of Tertullian that while the latter habitually made his own translations there was available a Latin version with which he was familiar and which he occasionally employed. Two fourth- or fifth-century gospel manuscripts k and e,[36] which together contain practically all of the four gospels, have a text in substantial agreement with the New Testament quotations which abound in the writings of Cyprian. Hence these two manuscripts are usually referred to as "African Latin." The Fleury palimpsest h, a sixth-century manuscript containing part of Acts, is also of this general type. Most of the Old Latin manuscripts, however, are of a different type. This is generally styled "European Latin," although some critics incline to see two different types here, "European" and "Italic." Nor is the relationship yet clear between the "African" and "European." Probably the latter is a later translation, which is precisely what we would expect. It was only as the use of Greek lapsed in the West and as Christianity reached the lower strata of society that the need arose. But, when it did arise, was it a new translation or was it a revision of the older African Latin? There is perhaps a slight possibility in favour of the latter. Ropes[37] makes the plausible suggestion that a revision as early as 350 A.D. of the African Latin on the basis of Greek manuscripts of a *non-Western* type (*i.e.*, with a text akin to B א) accounts at least in Acts for the rise of the so-called European Latin. Streeter, on the contrary, sees in the European Latin text of the gospels "a type of text at the furthest remove from that of B." Of the several manuscripts of the European Latin b and a may be mentioned. Like k and e these are fourth- or fifth-century gospels in only partial preservation; b apparently occupies a central position among its fellows since all agree with it more than with one another. Some scholars (notably Burkitt) think that it represents the type of text Jerome used as the basis of his revision. a, which may be the older of the two, has many "African" readings, which may suggest that it stands midway between the text of k and e, on the one hand, and b, on the other. These manuscripts evidence the so-called *Western* text as the type from which they came. In fact, they line up with D and W^{mark} as the

[36] Manuscripts of the Old Latin are regularly referred to by small letters, although most of them have names. k and e are, respectively, Codex Bobiensis and Codex Palatinus. This latter, a purple *de luxe*, is to be sharply differentiated from e^{acts} which is the Latin side of E (Laudianus) as d is of Bezæ.

[37] *Op. cit.*, p. cxxi.

clearest representatives of this type of text, which, in one form or another, was dominant for many years throughout the Christian world.

From one translation, or, as many would prefer to say, from several independent translations, there soon arose a medley of variant readings. As Jerome phrased it, in his day there were almost as many types as there were Latin manuscripts. And Augustine a little later gave caustic expression to the confusion of the text which had now come to be in general use: "Whenever *in earlier days* a Greek manuscript came into any man's hand, provided he fancied he had any skill at all in both languages he did not hesitate to translate it." Toward the end of the fourth century Damasus, then the Roman pontiff (366-384 A.D.) decided to bring order out of chaos. He directed his secretary, Jerome, to revise the existent texts and to produce one which could be used by all. Jerome, apparently reluctantly, complied. By 383 or 384 he had finished the text of the gospels, and in the next year the rest of the New Testament. This was not a new translation, but a revision of the Latin texts on the basis of the Greek manuscripts which appeared to him the best witnesses to the original text.[38] Although the Old Latin appears to rest upon a distinctly *Western* text, the standard by which Jerome corrected them was apparently distinctly akin to that of the Old Uncials, at least for the gospels and Acts. Instead of the so-called *Western* order (Matthew, John, Luke, Mark) of the Old Latin, he arranged the gospels (apparently following the order of the codex or codices which he was using as a guide) in the order of the Great Uncials. His standard for the revision of the epistles is less certain, and for a good reason. He realized the strong opposition that was bound to follow his innovations, and hence made as few alterations of the familiar phraseology as possible. In fact, each successive book (and this applies even to the gospels themselves) shows a lesser degree of alteration. Accordingly, the epistles appear to have been altered but very little. This revision by Jerome is known as the Vulgate. Jerome did not so designate it. The use of the word in this connexion does not antedate the Council of Trent, which determined (see pp. 473 f.) that the books were to be read "in the old Latin Vulgate edition." It is inter-

[38] After completing the revision of the text of the New Testament in Rome he went to Bethlehem and produced a version of the Old Testament. He claimed that this was a new translation from the Septuagint on the basis of the hexaplaric text, *i.e.*, the fifth column of Origen's Hexapla. Whether this was a fresh translation or simply a revision of the Old Latin text to this standard is not certain, for Jerome's statements about his own achievements cannot always be relied upon. At any rate, this work convinced him of the need of a fresh translation from the Hebrew. This he made. This translation, save in the Psalms, is the Old Testament Vulgate. He produced three editions of the Psalms, known respectively as the Roman, Gallican, and Hebrew Psalter. The Roman was made in Rome while he was at work on the New Testament, and like the latter was simply a revision of the Old Latin. This revision never had much vogue. The Gallican was a part of his translation (or revision) of the hexaplaric text. This was gradually adopted and is today the text of the Psalms in the Vulgate. The Hebrew Psalter was part of his translation of the Old Testament from Hebrew. It never succeeded in ousting the more popular Gallican Psalter and has never been used to any great extent.

esting to observe that the text of this "Old Latin Vulgate" had not been exactly determined when the council made its famous decision. A half-century later (1590) Pope Sixtus V made an edition of the Latin text and announced that it was the Vulgate to which the earlier council had referred. But this edition proved unacceptable. Two years later his successor, Clement VIII, caused a new edition to appear, but to avoid embarrassment had the fact that it was a new edition concealed. Hence this edition of 1592 is known as the Sixtine Vulgate and continues to the present day as the official text of the Roman Communion. As has been remarked in another connexion, "In life, as in chess, bishops move obliquely."

Probably in official circles Jerome's revision was at once received. But in many circles conservative souls were lacerated. Augustine, who apparently himself accepted it,[39] was aware of opposition to it and told Jerome of one bishop who was put into an awkward position by his flock, who were outraged at the effrontery of one who would change God's holy word. Every editor and translator has caused similar pain to similar persons. No manuscripts of the Vulgate have come down which preserve the text without alteration, although it is possible to reconstruct it for the gospels and Acts with reasonable confidence. Mixture and confusion between the Old Latin readings and the Vulgate were inevitable. It is comparatively easy to identify Vulgate manuscripts of the gospels, for they generally carry the prefatory letter which Jerome wrote to Damasus as well as the Eusebian Canons[40] which he employed. Many of the Vulgate manuscripts are referred to by abbreviation of their names, as *am.* (Codex Amiatinus), written in England in the eighth century and perhaps the best witness to Jerome's text, and *fuld.* (Codex Fuldensis), written for Victor of Capua in the middle of the sixth century. The gospels of this manuscript contain the text of Jerome put in the form of the *Diatessaron* of Tatian, that is, with the four gospels skilfully interwoven into one continuous narrative. Many other Vulgate manuscripts are referred to by their own Arabic numerals.

The next versions to be referred to are the Syriac. The discoveries of recent years have greatly enriched our knowledge of the history of the text in Syriac-speaking churches of the East. Until recently it was believed that not later than the third century—probably in the second—there had been made a Syriac translation which was in wide use. This translation, called the Peshitto, was of the same textual type as the *Textus Receptus*, and hence

[39] This has been doubted on the basis of a remark by him that among the various translations the "Itala" is to be preferred. This has given rise (1) to the custom of referring to the Old Latin itself as the *Itala*, (2) to the designation as "Itala" of a type of text different from both the "African" and "European" Latin. Probably by it Augustine meant Jerome's revision. This probability is heightened by his word just quoted that "in earlier days" there had been a general tendency for each to make his own translation.

[40] See p. 507, n. 49.

the Peshitto was, to use Sanday's phrase, the "sheet anchor" for those who refused to believe that the *Textus Receptus* was based not on the primitive text, but on the later (fourth century) *Byzantine* or ecclesiastic (or as Hort called it Syrian[41]) revision. Now it is generally admitted that the Peshitto was neither a new translation nor made in the second century, but a revision made at the behest of Rabbula, the bishop of Edessa, in the first part of the fifth century. Prior to his time the Syriac churches used the gospels in the continuous harmonized form of the *Diatessaron* which Tatian had made about 170 A.D., probably first in Greek and then later translated for his compatriots into Syriac. Unfortunately, no copy of this important work exists, although an Arabic translation of it and the Codex Fuldensis mentioned in a preceding page probably preserve its general order. The commentary of Ephraem the Syrian (*ob.* 373) was on the *Diatessaron* and is an aid to the reconstruction of its text. All the quotations of the fourth century Syriac fathers show that Tatian's work was almost universally employed. Although the Syriac church, as such, employed this form of the gospels until the fifth century, it is none the less clear that a version of the separate gospels prior to the Peshitto did exist and that the Peshitto was in part at least a revision of this text. The reason for this assumption was the discovery of two fragments of Syriac gospel manuscripts. One of these was found in 1842 west of Cairo. Its significance was not realized for several years, and it was not until 1858 that it was published. It is now known as the Curetonian Syriac (Syr^{cur}) and contains fragments of all four separate gospels. This was considered by many as a degenerate form of the Peshitto until in 1892 another Syriac fragment of a fourth-century palimpsest (the upper writing was late eighth century) was discovered by two English women at Mt. Sinai. This fragment (Syr^{sin}) was studied by Professor Burkitt and found to be clearly related to the Syr^{cur}, although an older and better witness to what is now called the Old Syriac text. Although many of the problems are still to be solved, it is clear that a Syriac text of the separate gospels did exist well before the time of Rabbula, and that this text had a curious resemblance to that of the African Latin, but that it was by no means widely used. The discovery of the Armenian text of Ephraem's *Commentary on Acts*, which also shows the same relationship to that of the African Latin, further indicated that while Ephraem did not employ this text for the gospels, it was used by him in Acts. It is not impossible that this type of text was made in the third century, perhaps in Antioch, and that while to a degree influenced by the *Diatessaron* did not prevail against it. In Acts, however, since it was without rival, it proved

[41] The use of the word *Syrian* for this revision is unfortunate, for it suggests a connexion with the Syriac church or versions, which of course it did not have and which Hort did not intend to imply. In the English translation of Jülicher's *Introduction*, p. 624, this error is made in the rendering, "a late Syriac text, more and more widely distributed from the year 350 onwards." Here the translator not unnaturally misunderstood "spätsyrischen."

more acceptable. Did it in Acts depend upon a possible Syriac translation of Tatian's? Did Tatian also translate some at least of the Pauline epistles?

Rabbula, bishop of Edessa (411-435), apparently ordered a revision of the Syriac text in accord with available Greek manuscripts. Since apparently one of his purposes was to supplant the *Diatessaron* it appears to me probable that the basis of his revision was the Old Syriac text of the separate gospels, the Acts, and Pauline letters. Particularly in the case of the gospels his revision reflects the type of text called *Byzantine*, which had been made, presumably in Antioch, rather more than a century before, and which had become accredited. Thus his translation was in general not a fresh translation. The word "in general" is wise since apparently now for the first time the three Catholic epistles, I John, I Peter, and James, were rendered into Syriac. The Peshitto became the standard version of the Syriac-speaking church (*i.e.*, the Assyrian) and caused the speedy downfall of the *Diatessaron*, although at first vigorous measures were apparently necessary. The remark of Theodoret, bishop of Cyrrhus for many years (*ca.* 423-458), is here of interest:

> He [Tatian] composed also the gospel called the *Diatessaron* having cut out the genealogies and the rest of the passages which prove that the Lord was born of the seed of David according to the flesh. Not only those who were of his own seed but those who follow the apostolic doctrines used it, not perceiving the wickedness of its composition, but in great sincerity using it on account of its brevity. I found myself more than two hundred copies of it held in high esteem in our churches, and, having collected them, laid them aside and in their stead introduced the gospels of the four evangelists.[42]

Despite these strong-arm measures the *Diatessaron* continued to be known until the Middle Ages, being highly prized, for example, by the Nestorians. Many manuscripts of the Peshitto exist which preserve the text with amazing fidelity; some of them are from the very century in which Rabbula laboured.

In 508 the Peshitto was revised by Polycarp of Hierapolis at the direction of his bishop Philoxenus. Why he made the revision (called the Philoxenian) can only be conjectured. Not only was the text of the Peshitto revised, but the other four Catholic epistles (II Peter, II and III John, and Jude) and Revelation were for the first time rendered into Syriac. Perhaps this was not considered a new version. At any rate, no manuscript of it is known to exist, and only the text of the five additional books has come down to us. A century later (616) this revision was itself revised near Alexandria by Thomas of Harkel, who had been expelled from his bishopric in Syria. Of his work on the gospels he wrote as follows:

> The book of the four holy gospels was translated . . . in the city of Mabog

[42] *Hæret. Fab.* i,20.

(*i.e.*, Hierapolis) in the year of Alexander of Macedon 819 (*i.e.*, 508 A.D.). . . . Afterwards it was collated with much difficulty by me, the poor Thomas, by the help of two (or three) manuscripts in Antonia of the great city of Alexandria in the monastery of the Antonians; . . . it was again written out and collated in the aforesaid place in the year of the same Alexander 927 (*i.e.*, 616 A.D.).[43]

Ropes has characterized this translation (styled the Harclean) of the twenty-seven books as a "painfully exact imitation of Greek idiom and order of words, often in disregard of Syriac modes of expression, and so completely and conscientiously carried through that doubt scarcely ever arises as to the Greek text intended by the translator."[44] In the gospels this revision is based on a distinctly *Byzantine* text; in Acts the readings of the margin—he employed an elaborate system of diacritical marks—are of far greater interest than that of the text and afford one of the best witnesses to the so-called *Western* text of Acts. Unlike the Philoxenian, many manuscripts of the Harclean are extant; one of these containing the gospels is dated in the seventh century, another in the eighth. In the apparatus of Tischendorf the Harclean is referred to as Syr^{p} (*i.e.*, "*posterior*"), the Peshitto as Syr^{sch} (after Schaff, one of its earliest editors).

Of the Egyptian versions, or, as they are usually styled, the Coptic, a brief word may be appended, although the subject bristles with uncertainties. In Alexandria itself versions were of course unnecessary, since Greek had been the official tongue from the days of Alexander the Great. Outside of Alexandria it was another story. As Christianity worked down to the lower strata—and particularly primitive and degraded strata they were—versions became necessary. Two of these versions in different but allied dialects are of significance, the Sahidic and the Bohairic. Of these the Sahidic or, as it was formerly called from the city of Thebes in Upper Egypt, the Thebaic, was apparently the older and may be dated in the early fourth, or perhaps even the late third, century and is generally regarded the earliest Egyptian version. Although the text is distinctly like that of B ℵ,[45] the presence of many *Western* readings has led many scholars (notably Lake) to the assumption that it was based on a mixed text in which both *Western* and *Neutral* were found. Ropes, on the contrary, feels that at least for Acts the basis was a *Western* text almost completely corrected by a manuscript like B. It is of interest that in the gospels Matthew and John are more closely akin to B than are Luke and Mark. Does this suggest that in the original Sahidic version the *Western* order of the gospels occurred and that, as is often the case, the reviser became increasingly less thorough as the task continued? Coptic is written in Greek characters. A recently discovered

[43] J. G. C. Adler, *Novi Testamenti Versiones Syriacæ*, pp. 47 f.

[44] *Op. cit.*, p. clvii.

[45] T, a fifth century bilingual (Greek-Sahidic) set of fragments of Luke and John, is said to have a text "identical with that found in BL" (Streeter).

manuscript in the Sahidic dialect is written in a hand so similar to that of B that it has been assigned to approximately the same date.

The Bohairic or Memphitic was the dialect of Lower Egypt, that is, near Memphis in the Delta. This version is surely later than the Sahidic, perhaps as late as 700, although as Ropes remarks, "a date earlier in the seventh century, not too long after the Mohammedan conquest, is not unlikely." Manuscripts of this version do not antedate the ninth century. On the whole they appear to indicate a text of the type which *Hort* called *Neutral* and with very few readings which may safely be styled *Western*.

Of the other versions little need be said. Few men are competent to express opinions. Regarding the Ethiopic there is no concensus of opinion. Souter[46] classes it as a secondary version, and expresses himself most cautiously as to its value: "According to some, at least, who know the Ethiopic version well, it is valueless for the purposes of New Testament textual criticism." Ropes, on the contrary, with the support of Lake, considers it an independent version made from the Greek and later revised by the aid of the Arabic. Of its value he remarks: "The excellence and usefulness of at least many parts of the Ethiopic text of the Old Testament and the character of its New Testament readings in Matthew i-x, justify the expectation that an investigation of this version in Acts and the other parts of the New Testament would produce interesting and valuable results."[47] All the manuscripts are late.

The last two versions to be named, the Armenian and Georgian, may be mentioned together. Until recently little attention was paid to either, for they appeared to be secondary or tertiary versions. Recent investigations, notably by Dr. Blake of Harvard, one of the few living scholars to know Georgian, have revealed some extraordinary facts. These are crisply summarized by Lake:

The facts which we propose to put forward are these: The Georgian version, probably made in the fifth century, is the best single witness we possess to the type of text which we call Cæsarean, but which is also found in more or less corrupt form in some half-dozen Greek manuscripts. Since it was used by Origen in Cæsarea it was in existence in the third century. The Georgian version, however, is not directly translated from Greek manuscripts, but from Armenian; and the Armenian, which we possess at present in two forms, has been so heavily corrected to the standard of later texts that it would never have been regarded as Cæsarean had it not been for the Georgian version. Until the present the general opinion of Syriac and Armenian scholars has been that the Armenian version was translated from Syriac and not from Greek. But if so, the Armenian version, which

[46] *The Text and Canon of the New Testament*, p. 73.
[47] *Op. cit.*, p. cxlvii.

was Cæsarean in type, as is proved by the Georgian version, must be a translation from a Syriac of the same character, and no such Syriac is now extant.[48]

With this statement of the type of surprise which the textual critic may expect and which illustrates how he may be compelled overnight to revise his tentative conclusions we can conclude this imperfect sketch of the versions. It need hardly be said that this brief description is not intended to equip students to handle them; it has been written simply to reveal some of the problems and to prevent them from feeling entirely lost when they chance to read modern discussions of the text of the New Testament.

We have seen that the critic who would dream of the eventual reconstruction of what is approximately the original text of the various New Testament writings must concern himself with far more than the various Greek manuscripts which have made their appearance through the centuries. At a time certainly as early as any extant Greek manuscript versions were in widespread use, and some of the manuscripts of these versions are, to put it conservatively, far closer in point of time to the formation of the versions themselves than are even the earliest Greek manuscripts to the autographs of the several authors. But we can go a step further. From the earliest days Christian writers quoted, at times extensively, from the writings which we call the New Testament. The books of many of these writers—today we call them the Fathers—are in existence. Why, then, are they not of great value in revealing the texts of the "Bibles" and other revered "Scriptures" which these Fathers knew and used? Obviously they are, and these *patristic citations* constitute a third division of the critic's *apparatus criticus.* But a moment's reflection reveals that the matter is not so simple as might first appear. In the great majority of cases we do not have critical editions of the Fathers. Our texts of them are from manuscripts which are themselves copies. Hence all the inaccuracies to which scribes were prone are introduced, nor can we assume that the same reverence which may well have characterized the attitude of the scribe as he copied sacred writings was felt as the writings of the ancient worthies were reproduced. Again, we must make allowance for the fact that in their copying of this Father or that there would be a distinct tendency to make his Scriptural quotations "accurate," that is, in agreement with the text which the particular scribe knew and reverenced in his Bible. And finally, not infrequently, as we have repeatedly seen, the Fathers quoted from memory, and not infrequently their memories were at least hazy. Not only when their Scripture was in the form of long rolls would it have been both awkward and tedious to have unrolled them to verify each quotation; even when codices were available there were no convenient divisions into chap-

[48] "The text of the Gospels" in *Studies in Early Christianity*, edited by S. J. Case, p. 41.

ters and verses,[49] no indices or concordances at hand to make reference easy.

None the less, the value of the testimony of these quotations is very great. Not only do they throw light on the comparative date of the various types of texts, but on their geographical distribution. As has already been remarked, the fact that Cyprian and to a lesser degree Tertullian quote a type of text distinctly akin to that found in k and e warrant calling that type of Latin version "African." Just as most Greek manuscripts after the fifth century reveal a striking agreement of text which leads textual critics to prize in general only the readings of those manuscripts which differ from the run of the mill, so by the fifth century the Fathers too, show evidence of a widespread and generally accepted text. Hence those after the fifth century are of little value to the critic interested in probing back to the earlier days. Before Chrysostom, who died 407 A.D., all the Fathers, save for some in Alexandria, appear to have used texts which were of the type generally styled *Western* today. The African group already referred to (Tertullian, Cyprian, Novatian), another group of those who while residing in the West stemmed from the East and wrote in Greek (Justin, Marcion, Irenæus, Hippolytus), a group of eastern Fathers who also wrote in Greek (including Eusebius of Cæsarea), others in the East who wrote not in Greek

[49] The division of the various books into modern chapters is probably to be ascribed to Stephen Langton, an archbishop of Canterbury who died in 1228. A little later Hugo of St. Caro made an additional division of these chapters into sections lettered A B C D. In the sixteenth century Robert Stephanus invented the modern division into verses—his son Henri says his father did it *inter equitandum*, "while riding"—and they first appear in his edition of 1551. In the early days occasional divisions were made, among which were the so-called "Vatican sections," which attempted to follow the breaks in the sense. Eusebius of Cæsarea, following an earlier attempt by Ammonius of Alexandria, made it possible, when reading the gospels, to tell which sections of a particular gospel were unique, which to be found in some or all of the other three; and by an ingenious set of tables, called the "Eusebian Canons," enabled the reader to turn to the various parallels. This was accomplished by dividing each gospel into sections of varying length and by numbering them consecutively in the margin. In Matthew there are 355, in Mark 236, in Luke 342, in John 232. Under this number (of course expressed by Greek letters) is another from 1-10. This indicates in which table that particular section is to be found with its parallels, if any. Thus opposite the story of the dove at the baptism of Jesus in Matthew is to be found $\overset{\iota\delta}{\alpha}$, *i.e.*, $\overset{14}{1}$. Turning to canon 1, which contains those sections common to all four gospels, and looking down Matthew's list to 14, we find opposite it in Mark the letter signifying 5, in Luke 13, in John 15. Turning to each of these gospels and looking in their margin to their fifth, thirteenth, and fifteenth sections, respectively, we find the parallel passage. Considerable ingenuity must have been demanded in the divisions of the gospels into these sections. This had to be done not in accord with a logical sense division but with an eye to its absence or presence in the other gospels. As soon as this situation changed in the slightest—it might be in the midst of an incident after only a few words or it might be after two pages—a new section starts. Many manuscripts are equipped with this combination of "Ammonian Sections and Eusebian Canons." In the preface of Lloyd's Oxford edition the Canons are printed together with the letter of Eusebius to Carpianus in which he describes his scheme. Then in the margin of the text the symbols occur. It is almost a pity that this practice is not followed in modern critical Greek texts, for it is extraordinarily convenient for the student, if only to indicate to him whether the other gospels have parallel incidents or not. The reader who is interested in these and other ancient divisions will find them described in Lake's *Text of the New Testament*, pp. 55-61.

but in Syriac, finally even Clement of Alexandria—in the writing of all of these the same general type of text although with many variations is to be found. Few things are more certain than that this type of text was for many years the dominant one in Christendom. Opinions have differed as to its nature and value. Westcott and Hort were convinced that despite its early and wide popularity it did not represent the primitive text. Others have concluded that, since there is no evidence that the type of text which Westcott and Hort considered the best representative of the primitive text—they called it the *Neutral* to indicate its freedom from *Western* and *Syrian* (*Byzantine*) corruptions—existed before the third century, it, not the *Western*, should be considered a late production and that the dominant text, although, of course, it had suffered corruption, was the fairest example of the primitive text. Still others, notably Canon Streeter, consider both of these views wrong. The "Western text" of the critics was not an entity at all. Rather it is a conglomerate of no less than four distinct types of text (two geographically eastern, two western) which had severally grown up in the four great centres, Antioch, Cæsarea, Italy and Gaul, and Carthage. Recently Ropes has made the interesting suggestion that it was a distinct type of text, although the name *Western* is not particularly apposite, and that it represents a deliberate revision of the primitive text made early in the second century when the various Christian writings were combined to form a canon of Scripture. The primitive text—he prefers to call it the text of the Old Uncials—while not in any general use continued to be copied. In Alexandria after the time of Clement it came into its own, being essentially the text of Origen and of Athanasius.

In this volume it is not profitable to go further into this fascinating but perplexing confusion.[50] On one point there is almost universal agreement, *viz.*, that in the early fourth century, probably in Antioch, perhaps by Lucian, a drastic revision was made which speedily supplanted the deeply entrenched *Western* text. Fortunately, however, this ecclesiastical (?) revision did not entirely blot out its earlier rivals, although most of those manuscripts which were copied from exemplars which had been made before the revision came to be more or less mixed in type through conformation with it. It complicated matters immensely for the later critic. None the less, the ancient evidence, although confused and tangled, still remains. The future, very possibly the near future, will see many more pages written into the history of the development of the New Testament text. Fresh discoveries of papyri may have much to tell us. In the interim the student of Christian

[50] For an able summary of the history of modern textual criticism see Lake, *op. cit.*, pp. 62-86. Every student should read the essay at the end of Westcott and Hort's edition of the Greek text, *The New Testament*, pp. 542-583, which gives not only a summary of their own views, but a capital introduction to textual criticism. The student who wishes to go further into the problems of text will find the companion volume indispensable. In addition to the various books already cited in this chapter the list in Lake, *op. cit.*, p. 97, should be consulted.

beginnings who is fortunate enough to be able to use any Greek text at all may rest quite confident that, though some of the conclusions which Westcott and Hort reached may need restatement, the text they produced may be used with gratitude and easy conscience. His fellow student, who, like many early Christians before him, needs a version as a key to unlock these pages from the past, will find a trustworthy one in the *American Revised Version.* He may miss the sonorous and beautiful cadences of the familiar *King James.* It is to be hoped that from the pulpit he will hear that read for many years to come. In a real sense it *is* "six feet above contradiction." In his study, however, he will find its modern descendant a distinctly safer guide. For those who enjoy the so-called "modern translations" there are several good ones at hand. Not infrequently do they throw fresh light and reveal new slants. Whichever of these texts he uses, he may well be grateful to those who have laboured in quarries where the rock is hard.

AFTERWORD

ALTHOUGH the volume has grown to a considerably greater size than I first visaged when I started its composition some years ago, it is still but fragmentary and incomplete. I am well aware that some sections may seem—and for that matter, may be—sadly out of proportion. I have not tried to write it to measure nor to count the words in each chapter. My one purpose has been to try to put within one set of covers the material which it appears to me a student of the New Testament and of the Christian beginnings needs to know. I hope that through it all, on every page, one note may be discerned:

To love it you must know it;
To know it you must love it.

Appendix I

THE HASMONEANS

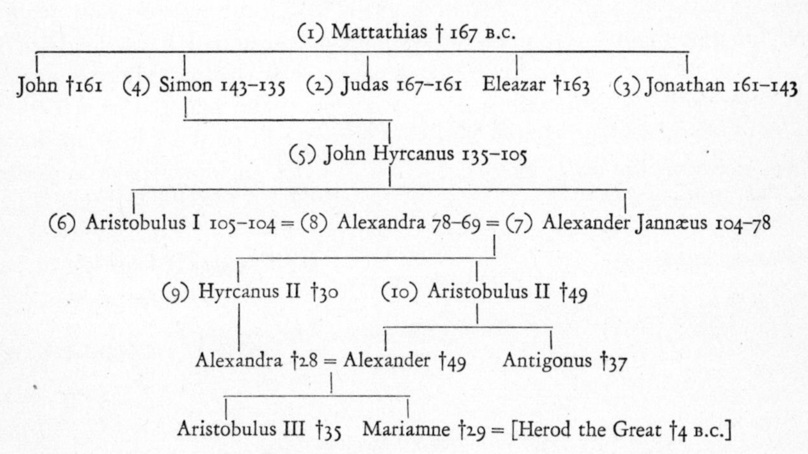

N.B.: The figures in parenthesis indicate the order in which these members came to power; the symbol † signifies "died"; the symbol = signifies "married to."

FOUR PERIODS OF LATER JEWISH HISTORY

I. 538–331. Persian rule and domination, ended by Alexander the Great at Arbela.
II. 331–167. Alexander and his successors.
- (a) 331–198 In the hands of Egypt.
- (b) 198–[142] In the hands of Syria.

III. [167]–63. Independence of Judea under Hasmoneans.
- (a) 167–165 Gaining power.
- (b) 165–142 Religious freedom.
- (c) 142– 63 Religious freedom and political independence.

IV. 63 B.C.–70 A.D. Roman domination.
- (a) 63–40 B.C. Rome vs. Hasmoneans.
- (b) 40 B.C.–44 A.D. Rise and rule of house of Herod (but subject to Rome).
  - (1) 6 A.D.–41 A.D. Judea, Samaria, Idumea (*i.e.*, Roman province of Judea) under Roman procurators.
  - (2) 41–44. All Palestine under Agrippa.
- (c) 44–70. All Palestine under direct Roman rule, ending in destruction of Jerusalem.

Appendix II

THE SELEUCIDÆ

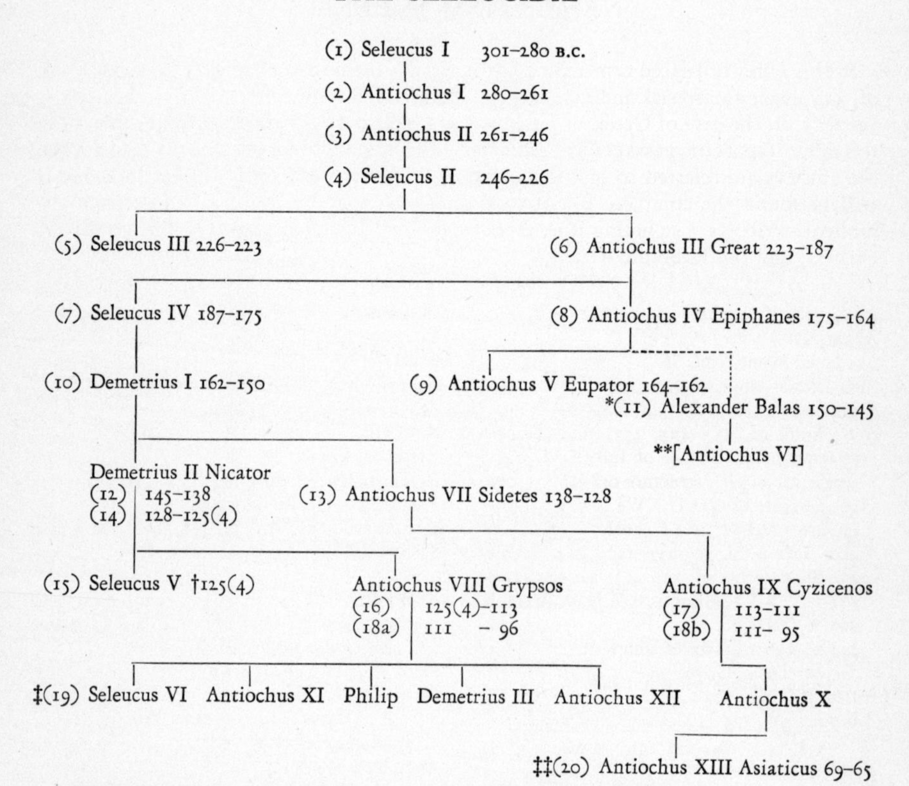

* Claimed to be natural son of Antiochus IV and usurped throne 150–145.

** Sponsored by Trypho and disputed succession with Demetrius II.

‡ In conflict (95–83) among selves and with Antiochus X.

‡‡ Tigranes of Armenia ruled Syria 83–69; Antiochus XIII set up by Lucullus and removed by Pompey when Syria became a Roman province.

N.B.: The figures in parenthesis are for convenience in following the confused succession; the dates, their years of rule.

Index I

NAMES AND SUBJECTS

In this index full-faced type indicates the title or theme of a chapter (*e.g.*, Acts, Book of, **413–425**); an asterisk indicates a principal or important reference (*e.g.*, Agrippa I, 75–77*). In the case of Greek or Latin writers whose works are cited frequently, only the more important passages are indicated in this index, but reference is made when the authors are referred to or commented upon rather than simply cited. In Index II will be found the complete list of such citations, together with all those from the biblical writings (including the Apocrypha and Pseudepigrapha), the Apostolic Fathers, and the Rabbinic writings.

Index II

PASSAGES CITED

An asterisk after a page indicates that the passage is there quoted or explained.

BIBLICAL REFERENCES (OLD TESTAMENT, APOCRYPHA, PSEUDEPIGRAPHA, AND NEW TESTAMENT)

GREEK AND LATIN WRITERS

RABBINIC WRITINGS